To my wife, Anne Marie Baillie

Contents

7   W.V.O. Quine   307

8   Truth and Meaning   356

9   Reference and Essence   394

Preface

This anthology collects some of the most important contributions to contemporary analytic philosophy. Before going any further, I should say a few words about what I mean by "contemporary" and "analytic." Both terms can be given contrastive definitions. So, I mean "contemporary" as opposed to "modern," and thus my selections are taken from the past century or so. Regarding the meaning of "analytic," the first thing to say is that I mean "analytic" as opposed to "continental," though not in any strict geographical sense. First, I do not want this anthology to contribute to the recent (and thankfully lessening) cold war between philosophy in English-speaking countries and elsewhere. But second, and more importantly, many of the most important contributors to analytic philosophy were from Europe, particularly from Austria and Germany. Furthermore, these philosophers, such as Gottlob Frege, the man now commonly regarded as the founder of analytic philosophy, need to be understood against a background of philosophical activity that falls heavily into the continental side of the present schism. As Michael Dummett has recently remarked,

> The sources of analytical philosophy were the writings of philosophers who wrote, principally or exclusively, in the German language; and this would have remained obvious to everyone had it not been for the plague of Nazism which drove so many German-speaking philosophers across the Atlantic. (*Origins of Analytic Philosophy*, Cambridge: Harvard University Press, 1993, p. ix)

The term "analytic" derives from the primary role assigned to the practice of conceptual analysis in the first part of this century. This movement first became known through the rebellion of G.E. Moore and Bertrand Russell against the then dominant idealist tradition. In Russell's case, the development of modern logic (initially by Gottlob Frege, later and independently by himself and A.N. Whitehead) afforded the possibility of stating the content of a sentence in a way that revealed its true logical structure, thereby making its ontological commitments clear. This, he thought, provided a prophylactic against metaphysical excess.

Russell and Moore represent two sides of an ongoing tension in analytic philosophy in the first part of this century. Both are preoccupied with language and see questions of meaning as prior to those of psychology, epistemology, or ontology. Both see the method of conceptual analysis as the cornerstone of correct philosophical practice. However, they disagree over the status of ordinary natural languages. Russell follows Frege in seeing natural languages as fundamentally flawed, being subject to vagueness and ambiguity. He believed that reliable results could be obtained only by devising a logically perfect language in which the implications of any sentence could be deduced by a purely formal procedure. Moore, on the other hand, had no revisionary aims concerning ordinary language and saw it as an adequate tool for achieving philosophical results, providing it is used with care. This attitude was adopted by Ludwig Wittgenstein and the "ordinary language philosophers" of mid-century Oxford, represented in this anthology by Gilbert Ryle, J.L. Austin, and H.P. Grice.

By the middle of the century, it had become apparent that most actual attempts at conceptual analysis were failures. For example, the Positivists could not successfully formulate a reduction of statements about material objects to those concerning sense-data. Nor could their attempts to reduce discourse about mental states to talk about behavioral dispositions succeed. In the light of these failures, the ideal of conceptual analysis itself came under renewed scrutiny. The reductive nature of the enterprise was critiqued by Wittgenstein's insistence that if we actually look at how particular terms are used by people, we find it rare that they can be given strict necessary and sufficient conditions for their application.

The analytic ideal was further damaged by W.V.O. Quine's demonstration that the analytic/synthetic distinction was theoretically untenable. Prior to Quine, the assumption had been that since philosophy consists in conceptual analysis, which was a purely a priori enterprise, philosophy is therefore fundamentally different from the sciences, in both its method and its subject matter. Such a strict division rested on the assumption that a clear distinction could be given between truths solely due to facts about meanings and those resting on the way the world is. The collapse of this latter distinction lead to an undermining of this hard distinction between philosophy and empirical disciplines. Following Quine, the dominant view is that philosophy is, if not the same as, then at least *continuous* with empirical sciences.

There are no necessary and sufficient conditions for being an analytic philosopher. Most present-day analytic philosophers would regard conceptual analysis, of the type practiced by Moore, as occupying a small part of their time at best, and as being just one tool at their disposal. It is probably the best policy to regard analytic philosophy as a "form of life," in the Wittgensteinian sense. Thus, I will use the term "analytic philosophy" to mean philosophy in the tradition of such founders as Frege, Russell, and Wittgenstein, and which continues to constitute the dominant paradigm of philosophy as practiced in the English-speaking world.

This anthology has quite deliberately taken a "big names" approach. I have focused on those philosophers that students must be exposed to in order to grasp the central themes in contemporary analytic philosophy. I have also deliberately limited my subject matter to the areas of philosophy sometimes classed as the "core": that is, philosophy of mind and language, epistemology, metaphysics, and philosophical logic. I have not attempted to cover all areas of analytic philosophy in this century. For example, you will find nothing in aesthetics, ethics, or sociopolitical philosophy. In each of these cases, I have judged that one or two selections (which is all that space could afford) would be misleading and less than useful. Each would require an anthology in itself, and some good ones are available.

Of course, it would be arrogant to claim that these selections comprise *the* essential readings in twentieth-century analytic philosophy. At most, it can comprise *a* set of essential readings. However, I am confident that there will be little controversy over what I have included. There will, of course, be disagreements over what is excluded. Philosophers may have been omitted due to space considerations, or possibly because their work could not be easily encapsulated in a couple of short readings, or because their work didn't fit in with the book's overall narrative.

Finally, I have chosen not to burden readers with large lists of books for further reading. Rather, I have restricted myself to a few books or articles that I know, from first hand experience, are both readable and illuminating.

CHAPTER 1

Gottlob Frege

Introduction to Gottlob Frege

Gottlob Frege was born in Wismar, Germany, in 1848. He studied at the Universities of Jena and Gottingen, where he received his Ph.D. in mathematics. Frege spent his entire academic career at Jena, first as an unsalaried privatdozent, and eventually as Professor of Mathematics. At his death in 1925, his achievements had hardly been noticed by either philosophers or mathematicians. Regarding Frege's first book, the *Begriffsschrift*, published in 1879, Bertrand Russell remarked, "In spite of the epoch-making nature of this work, I was, I believe, the first person who ever read it—more than twenty years after its publication (*Introduction to Mathematical Philosophy*, p. 25). Frege's reputation as the founder of analytic philosophy, and as the greatest logician since Aristotle, has been recognized in only the past three decades. In fact, the present selections of his work were not translated into English until the 1950s.

Frege's philosophical theories are a development of his treatment of problems in the philosophy of mathematics. He held the thesis of *logicism*, namely that the concepts of mathematics could be defined in terms of those of logic, and mathematical truths derived from logical axioms. In order to prove this logicist thesis, he needed to develop a language in which logical properties and relations could be precisely stated. Since he believed that natural languages were inadequate, essentially subject to vagueness and ambiguity, he constructed an artificial language—*Begriffsschrift* (which translates as *Concept Script*)—for this task. This new symbolism was designed to contain only features relevant to logical inference. In the *Begriffsschrift*, Frege constructed a propositional calculus in which all logical laws could be derived

1

from an axiomatic base and, most importantly, devised a predicate calculus based on the quantifiers, allowing a treatment of propositions involving multiple generality. While Frege's own choice of symbolism is no longer used, modern logic as we now know it is unquestionably based on the framework which he first presented in the *Begriffsschrift* and further developed in later works.

Three principles in the introduction to *The Foundations of Arithmetic* comprise a useful summary of Frege's position. They apply beyond the domain of arithmetic and represent the essence of his theory of the relations between minds, language, and reality. It will help to treat each of these principles in turn.

> 1. *Always separate the psychological from the logical, the subjective from the objective.*

This states Frege's opposition to *Psychologism*, the conceiving of logical laws as empirical laws describing mental phenomena. Such a position resulted from a failure to distinguish the *mental act* from its *content* (the *thought* expressed). While empirical causal laws can be formulated concerning relationships between judgments, thoughts are related by logical laws. Frege regarded thoughts as abstract objects existing independently of individual judgments. Abstracta were distinguished both from physical objects existing in space and time, and from ideas in the mind. They were *objective* in the sense of being intersubjective—that is, different thinkers can entertain the same thought—whereas mental processes such as images are essentially subjective and private. Thoughts were also independent of judgments in the sense that one can consider a thought without any commitment regarding its truth-value. When A believes that *p*, and B disagrees, they are disagreeing about *p* —that is, they share the same thought.

In *The Basic Laws of Arithmetic*, Frege argues that Psychologism allows the possibility of creatures governed by totally different laws of logic, who would accept inferences that we would reject, and vice versa. Psychologism bars us from asking the surely legitimate question of whose set of laws are the *correct* ones, since it cannot allow any genuine error or disagreement between us, but only *psychological difference*. As Frege correctly points out, logic has an irreducibly normative relation to our thoughts, whereas a record of psychological difference remains purely on the descriptive level.

Let us turn now to the second principle, the "context principle."

> 2. *Never ask the meaning of a word in isolation, but only in the context of a sentence.*

Here, Frege is pointing to the fact that an assertion is the most basic linguistic act— that of *saying something* —and that this requires a sentence. Also, the habit of examining words individually is what leads to the temptation to look for something, such as an image, that each could stand for. "But we ought always to keep before our eyes a complete proposition. Only in a proposition do the words really have a meaning. It may be that mental images float before us for a while, but these need not correspond to the logical elements in the judgment. It is enough if the proposition taken as a whole has a sense; it is this that confers on its parts also their content" (*The Foundations of Arithmetic*, p. 71). This is perfectly compatible with Frege's other view that a sentence's semantic properties are a function of those of its constituent parts. Frege's main attack here is on Empiricism, with its claim that thoughts were constructed from "ideas," which in turn were derived by abstraction from sense-experience. Such theories faced one overwhelming problem: A thought has a truth-value; mere ideas, words, or concepts do not. How then does their being joined together result in a truth-value?

Let us now turn to the third principle,

3. *Never lose sight of the distinction between concept and object.*

Logicians had assumed since Aristotle that all propositions had a subject-predicate structure. Frege regarded this as a superficial grammatical distinction that didn't represent a statement's real logical structure. As before, he took his lead from math, employing its distinction between *function* and *argument*. Consider the expression "$x^2 + 1$." It is a "functor," that is, a function expression referring to a function. Any numeral replacing the variable x is called the *argument* for that function. The number yielded when we do this is called the *value* of that function for that argument. So the argument 1 gives $1^2 + 1$, namely 2; the argument 4 gives $4^2 + 1$, equal to 17. It is important to note that x doesn't stand for anything, it could be omitted, leaving a space. It is a way of marking a space, of showing that the functor is essentially incomplete, or "unsaturated." It only has a value when "completed" by an argument. Arguments, on the other hand, are themselves complete or saturated, independent of their surrounding functions. They represent objects; the numeral 5 represents the number 5, and so on. The essentially unsaturated nature of functions, and their difference to arguments, solved two problems for Frege. First, the fact that the same function can be saturated with a vast number of different arguments explained how we are capable of understanding and using a seemingly limitless number of sentences. Second, it explained how a truth-value could be produced by the saturating of a function by an argument. This could not be explained by the Empiricist model, in which a thought was considered to be a mere concatenation of ideas.

Frege extended this model to linguistic expressions. Take the expression "the capital of France." We can analyze this in terms of function and argument, taking *the capital of …* as a function, and *France* as the argument, giving Paris as the value. The same function, when given the argument *Portugal*, yields Lisbon as a value. So we can consider *the capital of …* as a function that maps objects onto objects (in this case, countries onto cities). Likewise, "The Queen of England" takes the function *The Queen of …* , which, when saturated with the argument *England*, yields Elizabeth Windsor as a value. I emphasize that Frege's view, in "Function and Concept," is that arguments are objects, and not names of objects, as he had previously stated in the *Begriffsschrift.*

This analysis can be applied to whole indicative sentences. Consider an expression like "$x^2 = 36$." Clearly, the variable x can be replaced by a variety of numbers as possible arguments. When we insert 6, we get the true sentence $6^2 = 36$. When we insert 5, we get the falsehood $5^2 = 36$. Frege takes "True" and "False" to be the values, and the referents, of these sentences. He defines a *concept* as a function which has a truth-value as a value. Frege considered True and False to be abstract objects.

Take a simple indicative sentence like "Wittgenstein wrote the Tractatus." We can take ... *wrote the Tractatus* as a concept which gives the value True when given the argument *Wittgenstein*, but False when given any other argument, such as Frege, Sting, and so forth. Alternately, we can take *Wittgenstein wrote* ... as the concept, and *the Tractatus* as the argument, again yielding the value True. In general, a sentence is true if the concept yields the value True for the object represented by the argument. As in the arithmetical examples, True and False are not taken to be *properties* of sentences, but abstract objects which are the *values* of sentences.

Possibly Frege's greatest contribution to the study of logic and language was his introduction of the *quantifiers* —the universal quantifier, now represented as $\forall x$, and the existential quantifier, $\exists x$. (In the *Begriffsschrift*, Frege employed only the universal quantifier, but this and the existential quantifier are interdefinable.) To explain the use of the quantifiers, we need to distinguish first- and second-level functions/concepts. We have already seen the first-level concepts, which takes objects as arguments, yielding True and False as values. A second-level concept takes *first-level concepts* as arguments, again yielding truth-values.

I will illustrate this using the existential quantifier to analyze statements involving existence. Take "dragons exist." Traditionally, one would take "dragons" as the subject, and "exist" as the predicate. Frege, on the other hand, represents the sentence as being equivalent to the claim that the first-level concept ... *is a dragon has instances*. In other words, it asserts that there is some argument which will yield True when inserted into that function. So ... *has instances* is a second-level concept that takes ... *is a dragon* as an argument.

$(\exists x)Fx$ correlates the concept ... *is an F* with True if and only if some object falls under F

$(\forall x)Fx$ correlates the concept ... *is an F* with True if and only if every object falls under F.

SENSE AND MEANING

I should note that Frege's "Uber Sinn und Bedeutung" had long been translated as "On Sense and Reference." However, in recent years, opinion has been that "Meaning," rather than "Reference," is closer to what Frege intended by "Bedeutung."

The best way to appreciate the problem that led Frege to make this famous distinction is to consider identity statements, such as

1. *The Morning Star is the Morning Star.*

2. *The Morning Star is the Evening Star.*

Frege was insistent that these statements were asserting that identity held between *objects*, not *names* for objects. That is, these statements were about the world, not about linguistic signs themselves. Now these identity statements employ *names*, that is, "The Morning Star" and "The Evening Star." It is now known that these are both names for Venus.

Frege was probably the first philosopher to stress the *compositionality* of language: The meaning of a sentence is a function of the meaning of its constituents and its syntactic structure. Take "Portland is south of Seattle." If you alter the positions of "Portland" and "Seattle" you get a different sentence—one with a different meaning, truth-condition, and truth-value. These same results happen if you replace one word with another, for example "San Francisco" for "Seattle." In the *Begriffsschrift*, Frege had also assumed (like Mill, and virtually everyone else) that a name's sole linguistic contribution to the meaning of a sentence was referential. The combination of a referential theory of names plus compositionality created a problem for Frege, which was highlighted in identity statements.

Clearly important differences exist between 1 and 2, since the latter expresses a posteriori geographical information, whereas the former, being a logical truth, is knowable a priori. Secondly, they clearly express different thoughts, since someone can assent to one and deny the other without falling into contradiction. Similarly, we can say that someone who knows 1, and then learns 2, has learned something new. These two conditions constitute criteria for when X and Y constitute distinct thoughts. In fact, these latter two points can be made equally well without resorting to identity statements. Consider

3. *The Morning Star was hard to locate last Wednesday.*

4. *The Evening Star was hard to locate last Wednesday.*

Frege recognized that these considerations showed that the following statements were incompatible:

(a) The semantic role of names is purely referential.
(b) The reference of a sentence is a function of the references of its parts..

After all, "The Morning Star" and "The Evening Star" are coreferential terms, and all the other words and syntax of the sentences are identical, so why do 1 and 2, and 3 and 4 differ?

Frege's solution was that reference does not exhaust a name's semantic function. This is his famous distinction between *Sinn* and *Bedeutung*. *Sinn* is commonly translated as "sense." *Bedeutung* had long been translated as "reference," but, increasingly, (as with the present translation) as "meaning." In this introduction, I will capitalize this use of "meaning," to distinguish it from the more general, non-theoretical sense of the word.

Without entering into these translational debates, we can get a fair idea of the rudiments of Frege's distinction here. A name's Meaning is *whatever it picks out*. Sense is harder to pin down. We can distinguish three main points:

(a) A sense is a "mode of presentation," that is, a way of conceiving of the thing referred to;
(b) A sense, unlike a mental image, is intersubjectively accessible, and therefore mind-independent;

(c) A term's sense *determines* its Meaning. In other words, if expressions x and y are identical in sense, then they are co-referential. On the other hand, x and y can be coreferential while differing in sense. In current jargon, we might say that Meaning *supervenes* on sense.

(d) Frege adds that a nonreferring expression can still have a sense; "Vulcan" (the supposed tenth planet) or "Santa Claus."

The sense/Meaning distinction is also applied to whole sentences:

(a) The Meaning of a sentence is its truth-value.

(b) The sense of a sentence is the thought it expresses.

So sentences 1, 2, and 3, 4, have the same Meaning but different senses. Their senses differ because they express different thoughts. Their component parts, "The Morning Star" and "The Evening Star" can be shown to differ in sense simply because their substitution yields a different thought.

However, the theory hits a problem when faced with nonextensional contexts, such as those involving propositional attitudes (e.g., S believes that p, S fears that q):

5. *Bob believes that the Morning Star is made of cheese.*

6. *Bob believes that the Evening Star is made of cheese.*

As before, we get the latter sentence from the former by substituting coreferential terms. But by Frege's principles, since a sentence's Meaning is a function of the Meanings of its parts, shouldn't the two sentences be coreferential, and necessarily so? And surely they are not: The truth of 5 does not imply that of 6.

Frege's way out involves his theory of *Indirect Meaning*. Basically, Frege said that in nonextensional contexts, a term's normal sense (i.e., in extensional contexts) becomes its Meaning. Thus, whereas in 1 and 2, "The Morning Star" and "The Evening Star" have different senses yet the same Meaning, in 5 and 6 they have different Meanings. Therefore, his principle of compositionality survives. Or does it? How would the theory of Indirect Meaning cope with an example like this:

7. *Bob believes that the Morning Star is made of cheese, but it is not.*

Prima facie, the Meaning of "the Morning Star" and "it" are the same—in fact, it is hard to understand the sentence if this isn't so—but Frege seems bound to deny it, since "the Morning Star" occurs in an intensional context.

BIBLIOGRAPHY

Works by Frege

Frege's work is gathered in the following books:

The Basic Laws of Arithmetic, trans. Montgomery Furth (Berkeley: University of California Press, 1965).

Collected Papers on Mathematics, Logic and Philosophy, ed. Brian McGuinness, (Oxford: Basil Blackwell, 1984).
Conceptual Notation and Related Articles, trans. T. W. Bynum, (New York: Oxford University Press, 1972).
The Foundations of Arithmetic, trans. J. L. Austin (Oxford: Basil Blackwell, 1953).
Translations from the Philosophical Writings of Gottlob Frege, 3rd Edition, ed. P.T. Geach and Max Black, (Oxford: Basil Blackwell, 1980).

Further Reading

The leading commentator on Frege is undoubtedly Michael Dummett. However, his books are long and his style difficult. Still, anyone with a serious interest in Frege ought to study them, beginning with *Frege: Philosophy of Language* (Cambridge: Harvard University Press, 1973); followed by *The Interpretation of Frege's Philosophy* (Cambridge: Harvard University Press, 1981).

One recent short introduction is Anthony Kenny, *Frege* (New York: Penguin Books, 1995). This book is usefully organized in chronological sequence, rather than by subject matter. Thus, each of Frege's works is given a self-contained section.

Another recent book, which places Frege in the context of nineteenth-century European thought, is Wolfgang Carl, *Frege's Theory of Sense and Reference* (Cambridge: Cambridge University Press, 1994).

Function and Concept

Gottlob Frege

Rather a long time ago* I had the honour of addressing this Society about the symbolic system that I entitled *Begriffsschrift*. To-day I should like to throw light upon the subject from another side, and tell you about some supplementations and new conceptions, whose necessity has occurred to me since then. There can here be no question of setting forth my ideography [*Begriffsschrift*] in its entirety, but only of elucidating some fundamental ideas.

My starting-point is what is called a function in mathematics. The original meaning of this word was not so wide as that which it has since obtained; it will be well to begin by dealing with this first usage, and only then consider the later extensions. I shall for the moment be speaking only of functions of a single argument. The first place where a scientific expression appears with a clear-cut meaning is where it is required for the statement [p. 2] of a law. This case arose, as regards to functions, upon the discovery of higher Analysis. Here for the first time it was a matter of setting forth laws holding for functions in general. So we must go back to the time when higher Analysis was discovered, if we want to know what the word 'function' was

---

An address given to the *Jenaische Gesellschaft für Medicin and Naturwissenschaft*, January 9, 1891.
*On January 10, 1879, and January 27, 1882.

originally taken to mean. The answer that we are likely to get to this question is: 'A function of x was taken to be a mathematical expression containing x, a formula containing the letter x.'

Thus, e.g., the expression

$$2\,x^3 + x$$

would be a function of x, and

$$2.2^3 + 2$$

would be a function of 2. This answer cannot satisfy us, for here no distinction is made between form and content, sign and thing signified; a mistake, admittedly, that is very often met with in mathematical works, even those of celebrated authors. I have already pointed out on a previous occasion* the defects of current formal theories in arithmetic. We there have talk about signs that neither have nor are meant to have any content, but nevertheless properties are ascribed to them which are unintelligible except as belonging to the content of a sign. So also here; [p. 3] a mere expression, the form for a content, cannot be the heart of the matter; only the content itself can be that. Now what is the content of '$2.2^3 + 2$'? What does it mean? The same thing as '18' or '3.6.' What is expressed in the equation '$2.2^3 + 2 = 18$' is that the right-hand complex of signs has the same meaning as the left-hand one, I must here combat the view that, e.g., $2 + 5$ and $3 + 4$ are equal but not the same. This view is grounded in the same confusion of form and content, sign and thing signified. It is as though one wanted to regard the sweet-smelling violet as differing from *Viola odorata* because the names sound different. Difference of sign cannot by itself be a sufficient ground for difference of the thing signified. The only reason why in our case the matter is less obvious is that what the numeral 7 means is not anything perceptible to the senses. There is at present a very widespread tendency not to recognize as an object anything that cannot be perceived by means of the senses; this leads here to numerals' being taken to be numbers, the proper objects of our discussion; and then, I admit, 7 and $2 + 5$ would indeed be different. But such a conception [p. 4] is untenable, for we cannot speak of any arithmetical properties of numbers whatsoever without going back to what the signs stand for. For example, the property belonging to 1, of being the result of multiplying itself by itself, would be a mere myth; for no microscopical or chemical investigation, however far it was carried, could ever detect this property in the possession of the innocent character that we call a figure one. Perhaps there is talk of a definition; but no definition is creative in the sense of being able to endow a thing with properties that it has not already got—apart from the one property of expressing and signifying something in virtue of the defintion.* The characters we

---

* *Die Grundlagen der Arithmetik*, Breslau, 1884; *Sitzungsberichte der Jenaischen Gesellschaft für Medicin und Naturwissenschaft*, 1885, meeting of July 17th.

† Cf. the essays: *Zählen und Messen erkenntnistheoretisch betrachtet*, by H. von Helmholtz, and *Ueber den Zahlbegriff*, by Leopold Kronecker (*Philosophische Aufsätze. Eduard Zeller zu seinen fünfzigjährigen Doctorjubiläum gewidmet*, Leipzig, 1687).

‡ In definition it is always a matter of associating with a sign a sense or a reference. Where sense and reference are missing, we cannot properly speak either of a sign or of a defintion.

call numerals have, on the other hand, physical and chemical properties depending on the writing material. One could imagine the introduction some day of quite new numerals, just as, e.g., the Arabic numerals superseded the Roman. Nobody is seriously going to suppose that in this way we should get quite new numbers, quite new arithmetical objects, with properties still to be investigated. Thus, we must distinguish between numerals and what they stand for; and if so, we shall have to recognize that the expressions '2,' '1 + 1,' '3 − 1,' '6:3' [p. 5] stand for the same thing, for it is quite inconceivable where the difference between them could lie, Perhaps you say: 1 + 1 is a sum, but 6:3 is a quotient. But what is 6:3? The number that when multiplied by 3 gives the result 6. We say '*the* number,' not 'a number'; by using the definite article, we indicate that there is only a single number. Now we have:

$$(1 + 1) + (1 + 1) + (1 + 1) = 6,$$

and thus (1 + 1) is the very number that was designated as (6:3). The different expressions correspond to different conceptions and aspects, but nevertheless always to the same thing. Otherwise the equation $x^2 = 4$ would not just have the roots 2 and −2, but also the root (1 + 1) and countless others, all of them different, even if they resembled one another in a certain respect. By recognizing only two real roots, we are rejecting the view that the sign of equality does not stand for complete coincidence but only for partial agreement. If we adhere to this truth, we see that the expressions:

'$2.1^3 + 1$,'

'$2.2^3 + 2$,'

'$2.4^3 + 4$,'

stand for numbers, viz. 3, 18, 132. So if the function were really the reference of a mathematical expression, it would just be a number; and nothing new would have been gained for arithmetic [by speaking of functions]. Admittedly, people who use the word [p.6] 'function' ordinarily have in mind expressions in which a number is just indicated indefinitely by the letter x, e.g.

'$2.x^3 + x$';

but that makes no difference; for this expression likewise just indicates a number indefinitely, and it makes no essential difference whether I write it down or just write down 'x.'

All the same, it is precisely by the notation that uses 'x' to indicate [a number] indefinitely that we are led to the right conception. People call x the argument, and recognize the same function again in

'$2.1^3 + 1$,'

'$2.4^3 + 4$,'

'$2.5^3 + 5$,'

only with different arguments, viz., 1, 4 and 5. From this we may discern that it is the common element of these expressions that contains the essential peculiarity of a function; i.e. what is present in

'$2.x.^3 + x$'

over and above the letter 'x.' We could write this somewhat as follows:

'$2.($ $)^3 + ($ $).$'

I am concerned to show that the argument does not belong with the function, but goes together with the function to make up a complete whole; for the function by itself must be called incomplete, in need of supplementation, or 'unsaturated.' And in this respect functions differ fundamentally from numbers. Since such is the essence of the function, we can explain why, [p. 7] on the one hand, we recognize the same function in '$2.1^3 + 1$' and '$2.2^3 + 2$,' even though these expressions stand for different numbers, whereas, on the other hand, we do not find one and the same function in '$2.1^3 + 1$' and '$4 - 1$' in spite of their equal numerical values. Moreover, we now see how people are easily led to regard the form of the expression as what is essential to the function. We recognize the function in the expression by imagining the latter as split up, and the possibility of thus splitting it up is suggested by its structure.

The two parts into which the mathematical expression is thus split up, the sign of the argument and the expression of the function, are dissimilar; for the argument is a number, a whole complete in itself, as the function is not. (We may compare this with the division of a line by a point. One is inclined in that case to count the dividing-point along with both segments; but if we want to make a clean division, i.e. so as not to count anything twice over or leave anything out, then we may only count the dividing-point along with one segment. This segment thus becomes fully complete in itself, and may be compared to the argument; whereas the other is lacking in something—viz. the dividing-point, which one may call its endpoint, does not belong to it. Only by completing it with this endpoint, or with a line that has two endpoints, do we get from it something entire.) For instance, if I say 'the function $2.x^3 + x$; x must not [p. 8] be considered as belonging to the function; this letter only serves to indicate the kind of supplementation that is needed; it enables one to recognize the places where the sign for the argument must go in.

We give the name 'the value of a function for an argument' to the result of completing the function with the argument. Thus, e.g., 3 is the value of the function $2.x^3 + x$ for the argument 1, since we have: $2.1^3 + 1 = 3$.

There are functions, such as $2 + x - x$ or $2 + 0.x$, whose value is always the same, whatever the argument; we have $2 = 2 + x - x$ and $2 = 2 + 0.x$. Now if we counted the argument as belonging with the function, we should hold that the number 2 is this function. But this is wrong. Even though here the value of the function is always 2, the function itself must nevertheless be distinguished from 2; for the expression for a function must always show one or more places that are intended to be filled up with the sign of the argument.

The method of analytic geometry supplies us with a means of intuitively representing the values of a function for different arguments. If we regard the argument as the numerical value of an abscissa, and the corresponding value of the function as the numerical value of the ordinate of a point, we obtain a set of points that presents itself to intuition (in ordinary cases) as a curve. Any point on the curve corresponds to an argument together with the associated value of the function.

[p. 9] Thus, e.g.,

$$y = x^2 - 4x$$

yields a parabola; here 'y' indicates the value of the function and the numerical value of the ordinate, and 'x' similarly indicates the argument and the numerical value of the abscissa. If we compare with this the function

$$x\ (x - 4),$$

we find that they have always the same value for the same argument. We have generally:

$$x^2 - 4x = x\ (x - 4).$$

whatever number we take for x. Thus the curve we get from

$$y = x^2 - 4x$$

is the same as the one that arises out of

$$y = x\ (x - 4).$$

I express this as follows: the function $x\ (x - 4)$ has the same range of values as the function $x^3 - 4x$.
If we write

$$x^2 - 4x = x\ (x - 4),$$

we have not put one function equal to the other, but only the values of one equal to those of the other. And if we so understand this equation that it is to hold whatever argument may be substituted for x, then we have thus expressed that an equality holds generally. But we can also say: 'the value-range of the [p. 10] function $x(x - 4)$ is equal to that of the function $x^2 - 4x$, and here we have an equality between ranges of values. The possibility of regarding the equality holding generally between values of functions as a [particular] equality, viz. an equality between ranges of values, is, I think, indemonstrable; it must be taken to be a fundamental law of logic.*
We may further introduce a brief notation for the value-range of a function. To this end I replace the sign of the argument in the expression for the function by a Greek vowel, enclose the whole in brackets, and prefix to it the same Greek letter with a smooth breathing. Accordingly, e.g.,

$$ἐ(ε^2 - 4ε)$$

is the value-range of the function $x^2 - 4x$ and

$$ά(a.(a - 4))$$

is the value-range of the function $x(x - 4)$, so that in

$$'ἐ(ε^2 - 4ε) = ά(a.(a - 4))'$$

---

* In many phases of ordinary mathematical terminology, the word 'function' certainly corresponds to what I have here called the value range of a function. But function, in the sense of the word employed here, is the logically prior [notion].

we have the expression for: the first range of values is the same as the second. A different choice of Greek letters is made on purpose, in order to indicate that there is nothing that obliges us to take the same one.

[p. 11] If we understand

$$`x^2 - 4x = x\,(x = 4)'$$

in the same sense as before, this expresses the same sense, but in a different way. It presents the sense as an equality holding generally; whereas the newly-introduced expression is simply an equation, and its right side, and equally its left side, stands for something complete in itself. In

$$`x^2 - 4x = x(x - 4)'$$

the left side considered in isolation indicates a number only indefinitely, and the same is true of the right side. If we just had '$x^2 - 4x$' we could write instead '$y^2 - 4y$' without altering the sense; for 'y' like 'x' indicates a number only indefinitely. But if we combine the two sides to form an equation, we must choose the same letter for both sides, and we thus express something that is not contained in the left side by itself, nor in the right side, nor in the 'equals' sign; viz. generality. Admittedly what we express is the generality of an equality; but primarily it is a generality.

Just as we indicate a number indefinitely by a letter, in order to express generality, we also need letters to indicate a function indefinitely. To this end people ordinarily use the letters f and F, thus: '$f(x)$,' '$F(x)$,' where 'x' replaces the argument. Here the need of the function for supplementation is expressed by the fact [p. 12] that the letter f or F carries along with it a pair of brackets; the space between these is meant to receive the sign for the argument. Thus

$$\acute{\epsilon}\, F\, (\epsilon)$$

indicates the graph of a function that is left undetermined.

Now how has the reference of the word 'function' been extended by the progress of science? We can distinguish two directions in which this has happened.

In the first place, the field of mathematical operations that serve for constructing functions has been extended. Besides addition, multiplication, exponentiation, and their converses, the various means of transition to the limit have been introduced—to be sure, without people's being always clearly aware that they were thus adopting something essentially new. People have gone further still, and have actually been obliged to resort to ordinary language, because the symbolic language of Analysis failed; e.g. when they were speaking of a function whose value is 1 for rational and 0 for irrational arguments.

Secondly, the field of possible arguments and values for functions has been extended by the admission of complex numbers. In conjunction with this, the sense of the expressions 'sum,' 'product,' etc., had to be defined more widely.

In both directions I go still further. I begin by adding to the signs $+$, $-$, etc., which serve for constructing a functional [p. 13] expression, also signs such as $=$, $>$, $<$, so that I can speak, e.g., of the function $x^2 = 1$, where x takes the place of the argument as before. The first question that arises here is what the values of this function are for different arguments. Now if we replace x successively by $-1, 0, 1, 2$, we get:

$$(-1)^2 = 1,$$
$$0^2 = 1,$$
$$1^2 = 1,$$
$$2^2 = 1.$$

Of these equations the first and third are true, the others false. I now say: the value of our function is a truth-value' and distinguish between the truth-values of what is true and what is false. I call the first, for short, the True; and the second, the False. Consequently, e.g., '$2^2 = 4$' stands for the True as, say, '2^2' stands for 4. and '$2^2 = 1$' stands for the False. Accordingly

'$2^2 = 4$,' '$2 > 1$,' $2^4 = 4^2$,'

stand for the same thing, viz. the True, so that in

$$(2^2 = 4) = (2 > 1)$$

we have a correct equation.

The objection here suggests itself that '$2^2 = 4$' and '$2 > 1$' nevertheless make quite different assertions, express quite different thoughts; but likewise '$2^4 = 4^2$' and '$4.4 = 4^2$' express different thoughts; and yet we can replace '2^4' by 4.4,' since both signs have the same reference. Consequently, '$2^4 = 4^2$' and $4.4 = 4^2$' [p. 14] likewise have the same reference. We see from this that from identity of reference there does not follow identity of the thought [expressed]. If we say 'the Evening Star is a planet with a shorter period of revolution than the Earth,' the thought we express is other than in the sentence 'the Morning Star is a planet with a shorter period of revolution than the Earth'; for somebody who does know that the Morning Star is the Evening Star might regard one as true and the other as false. And yet both sentences must have the same reference; for it is just a matter of interchanging the words 'Evening Star' and 'Morning Star,' which have the same reference, i.e. are proper names of the same heavenly body. We must distinguish between sense and reference. '2^4' and '4^2' certainly have the same reference, i.e. they are proper names of the same number; but they have not the same sense; consequently, '$2^4 = 4^2$' and '$4.4 = 4^2$' have the same reference, but not the same sense (which means, in this case: they do not contain the same thought).*

Thus, just as we write:

'$2^4 = 4.4$'

we may also write with equal justification

'$(2^4 = 4^2) = (4.4 = 4^2)$'

and '$(2^2 = 4) = (2 > 1)$.

---

* I do not fail to see that this way of putting it may at first seem arbitrary and artificial, and that it would be desirable to establish my view by going further into the matter. Cf. my forthcoming essay *Ueber Sinn und Bedeutung* ['Sense and Meaning'] in the *Zeitschrift für Philosophie und phil. Kritrik.*

[p. 15] It might further be asked: What, then, is the point of admitting the signs $=, >, <$, into the field of those that help to build up a functional expression? Nowadays, it seems, more and more supporters are being won by the view that arithmetic is a further development of logic; that a more rigorous establishment of arithmetical laws reduces them to purely logical laws and so such laws alone. I too am of this opinion, and I base upon it the requirement that the symbolic language of arithmetic must be expanded into a logical symbolism. I shall now have to indicate how this is done in our present case.

We saw that the value of our function $x^2 = 1$ is always one of the two truth-values. Now if for a definite argument, e.g. - 1, the value of the function is the True, we can express this as follows: 'the number - 1 has the property that its square is 1'; or, more briefly, '-1 is a square root of 1'; or, '-1 falls under the concept: square root of 1.' If the value of the function $x^2 = 1$' for an argument, e.g. for 2, is the False, we can express this as follows: 2 is not a square root of 1' or '2 does not fall under the concept: square root of 1.' We thus see how closely that which is called a concept in logic is connected with what we call a function. Indeed, we may say at once: a concept is a function whose value is always a truth-value. Again, the value of the function

$$(x + 1)^2 = 2(x + 1)$$

[p. 16} is always a truth-value. We get the True as its value, e.g., for the argument -1, and this can also be expressed thus: -1 is a number less by 1 than a number whose square is equal to its double. This expresses the fact that -1 falls under a concept. Now the functions

$$x^2 = 1 \text{ and } (x + 1)^2 = 2(x + 1)$$

always have the same value for the same argument, viz. the True for the arguments -1 and $+1$, and the False for all other arguments. According to our previous conventions we shall also say that these functions have the same range of values, and express this in symbols as follows:

$$\acute{\epsilon}(\epsilon^2 = 1) = \acute{a}((a + 1)^2 = 2(a + 1)).$$

In logic this is called identity of the extension of the concepts. Hence we can designate as an extension the value-range of a function whose value for every argument is a truth-value.

We shall not stop at equations an inequalities. The linguistic form of equations is a statement. A statement contains (or at least purports to contain) a thought as its sense; and this thought is in general true or false: i.e. it has in general a truth-value, which must be regarded as the reference of the sentence, just as (say) the number 4 is the reference of the expression '2 + 2,' or London of the expression 'the capital of England.'

[p. 17] Statements in general, just like equations or inequalities or expressions in Analysis, can be imagined to be split up into two parts; one complete in itself, and the other in need of supplementation, or 'unsaturated.' Thus, e.g. we split up the sentence

'Caesar conquered Gaul'

into 'Caesar' and 'conquered Gaul.' The second part is 'unsaturated'—it contains an empty place; only when this place is filled up with a proper name, or with an expression that replaces a proper name, does a complete sense appear. Here too I give the name 'function' to what this 'unsaturated' part stands for. In this case the argument is Caesar.

We see that here we have undertaken to extend [the application of the term] in the other direction, viz. as regards what can occur as an argument. Not merely numbers, but objects in general, are now admissible; and here persons must assuredly be counted as objects. The two truth-values have already been introduced as possible values of a function; we must go further and admit objects without restriction as values of functions. To get an example of this, let us start, e.g., with the expression

'the capital of the German Empire.'

This obviously takes the place of a proper name, and stands for an object. If we now split up into the parts

[p. 18] 'the capital of' and 'the German Empire'

where I count the [German] genitive form as going with the first part, then this part is 'unsaturated,' whereas the other is complete in itself. So in accordance with what I said before, I call

'the capital of x'

the expression of a function. If we take the German Empire as the argument, we get Berlin as the value of the function.

When we have thus admitted objects without restriction as arguments and values of functions, the question arises what it is that we are here calling an object. I regard a regular definition as impossible, since we have here something too simple to admit of logical analysis. It is only possible to indicate what is meant. Here I can only say briefly: An object is anything that is not a function, so that an expression for it does not contain any empty place.

A statement contains no empty place, and therefore we must regard what it stands for as an object. But what a statement stands for is a truth-value. Thus the two truth-values are objects.

Earlier on we presented equations between ranges of values, e.g.:

$$\acute{\epsilon}(\epsilon^2 - 4\epsilon) = \acute{a}\,(a(a - 4)).'$$

We can split this up into '$\acute{\epsilon}(\epsilon^2 - 4\epsilon)$' and '$(\ ) = \acute{a}(a(a - 4))$.' This latter part needs supplementation, since on the left of the [p. 19] 'equals' sign it contains an empty place. The first part, '$\acute{\epsilon}(\epsilon^2 - 4\epsilon)$,' is fully complete in itself and thus stands for an object. Value-ranges of functions are objects, whereas functions themselves are not. We gave the name 'value-range' also to $\acute{\epsilon}(\epsilon^2 = 1)$, but we could also have termed it the extension of the concept: square root of 1. Extensions of concepts likewise are objects, although concepts themselves are not.

After thus extending the field of things that may be taken as arguments, we must get more exact specifications as to what the signs already in use stand for. So long as the only objects dealt with in arithmetic are the integers, the letters a and b in '*a* + *b*' indicate only integers; the plus-sign need be defined only between integers. Every extension of the field to which the objects indicated by *a* and *b* belong obliges us to give a new definition of the plus-sign. It seems to be demanded by scientific rigour that we should have provisos against an expression's possibly coming to have no reference; we must see to it that we never perform calculations with empty signs in the belief that we are dealing with objects. People have in the past carried out invalid procedures with divergent infinite series. It is thus necessary to lay down rules from which it follows, e.g., what

$$\text{'}\odot + 1\text{'}$$

stands for, if '$\odot$' is to stand for the Sun. What rules we lay down [p. 20] is a matter of a comparative indifference; but it is essential that we should do so—that '*a* + *b*' should always have a reference, whatever signs for definite objects may be inserted in place of '*a*' and '*b*.' This involves the requirement as regards concepts, that, for any argument, they shall have a truth-value as their value; that it shall be determinate, for any object, whether it falls under the concept or not. In other words; as regards concepts we have a requirement of sharp delimitation; if this were not satisfied it would be impossible to set forth logical laws about them. For any argument *x* for which '*x* + 1' were devoid of reference, the function $x + 1 = 10$ would likewise have no value, and thus no truth-value either, so that the concept:

'what gives the result 10 when increased by 1'

would have no sharp boundaries. The requirement of the sharp delimitation of concepts thus carries along with it this requirement for functions in general that they must have a value for *every* argument.

We have so far considered truth-values only as values of functions, not as arguments. By what I have just said, we must get a value of a function when we take a truth-value as the argument; but as regards the signs already in common use, the only point, in most cases, of a rule to this effect is that there should *be* a rule; it does not much matter what is determined upon. But now we must deal with certain functions that are of importance to us precisely when this argument is a truth-value.

[p. 21] I introduce the following as such a function

$$\text{———} \, x;$$

I lay down the rule that the value of this function shall be the True if the True is taken as argument, and that contrariwise, in all other cases the value of this function is the False—i.e. both when the argument is the False and when it is not a truth-value at all. Accordingly, e.g.

$$\text{———} \, 1 + 3 = 4$$

is the True, whereas both

$$\text{———} \, 1 + 3 = 5$$

and also

$$\text{———} \, 4$$

are the False. Thus this function has as its value the argument itself, when that is a truth-value. I used to call this horizontal stroke the content-stroke (*Inhaltsstrich*)—a name that no longer seems to me appropriate. I now wish to call it simply the horizontal.

If we write down an equation or inequality, e.g. $5 > 4$, we ordinarily wish at the same time to express a judgment; in our example, we want to assert that 5 is greater than 4. According to the view I am here presenting, '$5 > 4$' and '$1 + 3 = 5$' just give us expressions for truth-values, without making any assertion. This separation of the act from the subject-matter of judgment seems to be indispensable; for otherwise we could not express a mere supposition—the putting of a case without a [p. 22] simultaneous judgment as to its arising or not. We thus need a special sign in order to be able to assert something. To this end I make use of a vertical stroke at the left end of the horizontal, so that, e.g., by writing

$$\vdash\!\!\!\!-\!\!\!-\!\!\!-\!\!\!- 2 + 3 = 5$$

we assert that $2 + 3$ equals 5. Thus here we are not just writing down a truth-value, as in

$$2 + 3 = 5,$$

but also at the same time saying that it is the True.*

The next simplest function, we may say, is the one whose value is the False for just those arguments for which the value of $\longrightarrow x$ is the True, and, conversely, is the True for the arguments for which the value of $\longrightarrow x$ is the False. I symbolize it thus:

$$\longrightarrow_{\!\!\top}\! x,$$

and here I call the little vertical stroke the stroke of negation. I conceive of this as a function with the argument $\longrightarrow x$:

$$(\longrightarrow_{\!\!\top}\! x) = (\longrightarrow_{\!\!\top}\! (\longrightarrow x))$$

where I imagine the two horizontal strokes to be fused together. But we also have:

$$(\longrightarrow(\longrightarrow_{\!\!\top}\! x)) = (\longrightarrow_{\!\!\top}\! x),$$

[p. 23] since the value of $\longrightarrow_{\!\!\top}\! x$ is always a truth-value. I thus regard the bits of the stroke in $\longrightarrow_{\!\!\top}\! x$' to the right and to the left of the stroke of negation as horizontals, in the sense of the word that I defined previously. Accordingly, e.g.:

$$\longrightarrow_{\!\!\top}\! 2^2 = 5$$

---

* The assertion sign (*Urheilsstrich*) cannot be used to construct a functional expression; for it does not serve, in conjunction with other signs, to designate an object. '$\longrightarrow 2 + 3 = 5$' does not designate anything; it asserts something.

stands for the True, and we may add the assertion-sign:

$$\vdash_{\top} 2^2 = 5;$$

and in this we assert that $2^2 = 5$ is not the True, or that 2^2 is not 5. But moreover

$$\underline{\quad}_{\top} 2$$

is the True, since $\underline{\qquad}$ 2 is the False:

$$\vdash_{\top} 2$$

i.e. 2 is not the True.

My way of presenting generality can best be seen as in example. Suppose what we have to express is that every object is equal to itself. In

$$x = x$$

we have a function, whose argument is indicated by 'x.' We now have to say that the value of this function is always the True, whatever we take as argument. I now take the sign

$$\underline{\quad}^{a}_{\smile}\!\!\!-f(a)$$

to mean the True when the function $f(x)$ always has the True as its value, whatever the argument may be; in all other cases

[p. 24] $\underline{\quad}^{a}_{\smile}\!\!\!-f(a)$

is to stand for the False. For our function $x = x$ we get the first case. Thus

$$\underline{\quad}^{a}_{\smile}\!\!\!-f(a)$$

is the True; and we write this as follows:

$$\vdash^{a}_{\smile}\!\!\!-a = a$$

The horizontal strokes to the right and to the left of the concavity are to be regarded as horizontals in our sense. Instead of 'a,' any other Gothic letter could be chosen; except those which are to serve as letters for a function, like f and F.

This notation affords the possibility of negating generality, as in

$$\underline{\quad}_{\top}{}^{a}_{\smile}\!\!\!-a^2 = 1.$$

That is to say, $\underline{\quad}^{a}_{\smile}\!\!\!-a^2 = 1$ is the False, since not every argument makes the value of the function $x^2 = 1$ to be the True. (Thus, e.g., we get $2^2 = 1$ for the argument 2, and this is the False.) Now if $\underline{\quad}^{a}_{\smile}\!\!\!- a^2 = 1$ is the False, then $\underline{\quad}_{\top}{}^{a}_{\smile}\!\!\!-a^2 = 1$ is the True, according to the rule that we laid down previously for the stroke of negation. Thus we have

$$\vdash_{\top}{}^{a}_{\smile}\!\!\!-a^2 = 1;$$

i.e. 'not every object is a square root of 1,' or 'there are objects that are not square roots of 1.'

[p. 25] Can we also express: There are square roots of 1? Certainly: we need only take, instead of the function $x^2 = 1$; the function

$$\underset{\top}{}\!\!-\!x^2 = 1.$$

By fusing together the horizontals in

$$-\underset{a}{\cup}\!-\ \underset{\top}{}\!\!-\!a^2 = 1$$

we get

$$-\underset{a}{\cup}\underset{\top}{}\!-\!a^2 = 1.$$

This stands for the False, since not every argument makes the value of the function

$$\underset{\top}{}\!-\!x^2 = 1$$

to be True. E.g.:

$$\underset{\top}{}\!-\!1^2 = 1$$

is the False, for $1^2 = 1$ is the True. Now since

$$-\underset{a}{\cup}\underset{\top}{}\!-\!a^2 = 1$$

is thus the False,

$$\underset{\top}{}\!-\underset{a}{\cup}\underset{\top}{}\!-\!a^2 = 1$$

is the True:

$$\vdash\underset{\top}{}\!-\underset{a}{\cup}\underset{\top}{}\!-\!a^2 = 1;$$

i.e. 'not every argument makes the value of the function

$$\underset{\top}{}\!-\!x^2 = 1$$

to be the True,' or: 'not every argument makes the value of the function $x^2 = 1$ to be the False,' or: 'there is at least one square root of 1.'

At this point there may follow a few examples in symbols and words.

$$\vdash\underset{\top}{}\!-\underset{a}{\cup}\underset{\top}{}\!-\!a \geqq 0,$$

there is at least one positive number;

[p. 26] $\vdash\underset{\top}{}\!-\underset{a}{\cup}\underset{\top}{}\!-\!a < 0,$

there is at least one negative number;

$$\vdash\!\!\!\overset{a}{\smile}\!\!\!- a^3 - 3a^2 + 2a = 0,$$

there is at least one root of the equation

$$x^2 - 3x^2 + 2x + 0.$$

From this we may see how to express existential sentences, which are so important. If we use the functional letter f as an indefinite indication of a concept, then

$$\overset{a}{\smile}\!\!\!-f(a)$$

gives us the form that includes the last examples (if we abstract from the assertion-sign). The expressions

$$\overset{a}{\smile}\!\!\!-a^2 = 1, \qquad \overset{a}{\smile}\!\!\!-a \geqq 0,$$

$$\overset{a}{\smile}\!\!\!-a < 0, \qquad \overset{a}{\smile}\!\!\!-a^2 - 3a^2 + 2a = 0$$

arise from this form in a manner analogous to that in which x^2 gives arise to '1^2,' '2^3,' '3^2.' Now just as in x^2 we have a function whose argument is indicated by 'x,' I also conceive of

$$\overset{a}{\smile}\!\!\!-f(a)$$

as the expression of a function whose argument is indicated by 'f.' Such a function is obviously a fundamentally different one from those we have dealt with so far; for only a function can occur as its argument. Now just as functions are fundamentally different from objects, so also functions whose arguments are and must be functions are fundamentally different from functions whose arguments are objects and cannot be anything else. I call [p. 27] the latter first-level, the former second-level, functions. In the same way, I distinguish between first-level and second-level concepts.* Second-level functions have actually long been used in Analysis; e.g. definite integrals (if we regard the function to be integrated as the argument).

I will now add something about functions with two arguments. We get the expression for a function by splitting up the complex sign for an object into a 'saturated' and an 'unsaturated' part. Thus, we split up this sign for the True,

$$3 > 2,$$

into '3' and '$x > 2$.' We can further split up the 'unsaturated' part '$x > 2$' in the same way, into '2' and

$$x > y,$$

where 'y' enables us to recognize the empty place previously filled up by '2.' In

---

* Cf. my *Grundlagen der Arithmetik,* Breslau, 1884. I there used the term 'second- order' instead of 'second-level.' The ontological proof of God's existence suffers from the fallacy of treating existence as a first-level concept.

$$x > y$$

we have a function with two arguments, one indicated by 'x' and the other by 'y'; and in

$$3 > 2$$

[p. 28] we have the value of this function for the arguments 3 and 2. We have here a function whose value is always a truth-value. We called such functions of one argument concepts; we call such functions of two arguments relations. Thus we have relations also, e.g., in

$$x^2 + y^2 = 9$$

and in

$$x^2 + y^2 > 9,$$

whereas the function

$$x^2 + y^2$$

has numbers as values. We shall therefore not call this a relation.

At this point I may introduce a function not peculiar to arithmetic. The value of the function

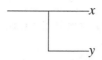

is to be the False if we take the True as the y-argument and at the same time take some object that is not the True as the x-argument; in all other cases the value of this function is to be the True. The lower horizontal stroke, and the two bits that the upper one is split into by the vertical, are to be regarded as horizontals [in one sense]. Consequently, we can always regard as the arguments of our function ———x and ———y, i.e. truth-values.

Among functions of one argument we distinguished first-level and second-level ones. Here, a greater multiplicity is possible. A function of two arguments may be of the same level in relation [p. 29] to them, or of different levels; there are equal-levelled and unequal-levelled functions. Those we have dealt with up to now were equal-levelled. An example of an unequal-levelled function is the differential quotient, if we take the arguments to be the function that is to be differentiated and the argument for which it is differentiated; or the definite integral, so long as we take as arguments the function to be integrated and the upper limit. Equal-levelled functions can again be divided into first-level and second-level ones. An example of a second-level one is

$$F(f(1)),$$

where 'F' and 'f' indicate the arguments.

In regard to second-level functions with one argument, we must make a distinction, according as the role of this argument can be played by a function of one or of two arguments; for a function of one argument is essentially so different from one with two arguments that the one function cannot occur as an argument in the same place as the other. Some second-level functions of one argument require that this should be a function with one argument; others, that it should be a function with two arguments; and these two classes are sharply divided.

$$
\begin{array}{c}
\underset{e}{\,}\quad\underset{d}{\,}\quad\underset{a}{\,}\!\!-d = a \\
\qquad\qquad\;\; F\,(e,\,a) \\
\qquad\qquad\; F\,(e,\,d)
\end{array}
$$

[p. 30] is an example of a second-level function with one argument, which requires that this should be a function of two arguments. The letter F here indicates the argument, and the two places, separated by a comma, within the brackets that follow F bring it to our notice that F represents a function with two arguments.

For functions of two arguments there arises a still greater multiplicity.

If we look back from here over the development of arithmetic, we discern an advance from level to level. At first people did calculations with individual numbers, 1, 3, etc.

$$2 + 3 = 5,\, 2 \cdot 3 = 6$$

are theorems of this sort. Then they went on to more general laws that hold good for all numbers. What corresponds to this in symbolism is the transition to the literal notation.

A theorem of this sort is

$$(a + b)c = a.\,c + b.c$$

At this stage they had got to the point of dealing with individual functions; but were not yet using the word, in its mathematical sense, and had not yet formed the conception of what it now stands for. The next higher level was the recognition of general laws about functions, accompanied by the coinage of the technical term 'function.' What corresponds to this in symbolism is the introduction of letters like f, F, to indicate functions indefinitely. A theorem of this sort is

$$\frac{df(x) \cdot F(x)}{dx} = \frac{F(x).df(x)}{dx} + \frac{f(x).dF(x)}{dx}$$

[p. 31] Now at this point people had particular second-level functions, but lacked the conception of what we have called second-level functions. By forming that, we make the next step forward. One might think that this would go on. But probably this last step is already no so rich in consequences as the earlier ones; for instead of second-level functions one can deal, in further advances, with first-level functions—as shall be shown elsewhere. But this does not banish from the world the difference between first-level and second-level functions; for it is not made arbitrarily, but founded deep in the nature of things.

Again, instead of functions of two arguments we can deal with functions of a single but complex argument; but the distinction between functions of one and of two arguments still holds in all its sharpness.

On Sense and Meaning

Gottlob Frege

[25] Equality[1] gives rise to challenging questions which are not altogether easy to answer. Is it a relation? A relation between objects, or between names or signs of objects? In my *Begriffsschrift*[2] I assumed the latter. The reasons which seem to favour this are the following: $a = a$ and $a = b$ are obviously statements of differing cognitive value; $a = a$ holds *a priori* and, according to Kant, is to be labelled analytic, while statements of the form $a = b$ often contain very valuable extensions of our knowledge and cannot always be established *a priori*. The discovery that the rising sun is not new every morning, but always the same, was one of the most fertile astronomical discoveries. Even today the re-identification of a small planet or a comet is not always a [26] matter of course. Now if we were to regard equality as a relation between that which the names 'a' and 'b' designate, it would seem that $a = b$ could not differ from $a = a$ (i.e. provided $a = b$ is true). A relation would thereby be expressed of a thing to itself, and indeed one in which each thing stands to itself but to no other thing. What we apparently want to state by $a = b$ is that the signs or names 'a' and 'b' designate the same thing, so that those signs themselves would be under discussion; a relation between them would be asserted. But this relation would hold between the names or signs only in so far as they named or designated something. It would be mediated by the connection of each of the two signs with the same designated thing. But this is arbitrary. Nobody can be forbidden to use any arbitrarily producible event

---

"On Sense and Meaning," trans. P.T. Geach, from P.T. Geach and Max Black, eds, *Translations from the Philosophical Writings of Gottlob Frege*, 3rd edition (Oxford: Basil Blackwell, 1980).

[1] I use this word in the sense of identity and understand '$a = b$' to have the sense of 'a is the same as b' or 'a and b coincide'.

[2] [The reference is to Frege's *Begriffsschrift, eine der arithmetischen nachgebildete Formelsprache des reinen Denkens* (Halle, 1879); English translation, *Conceptual Notation* (London, 1972).]

or object as a sign for something. In that case the sentence $a = b$ would no longer refer to the subject matter, but only to its mode of designation; we would express no proper knowledge by its means. But in many cases this is just what we want to do. If the sign 'a' is distinguished from the sign 'b' only as an object (here, by means of its shape), not as a sign (i.e. not by the manner in which it designates something), the cognitive value of $a = a$ becomes essentially equal to that of $a = b$, provided $a = b$ is true. A difference can arise only if the difference between the signs corresponds to a difference in the mode of presentation of the thing designated. Let a, b, c be the lines connecting the vertices of a triangle with the midpoints of the opposite sides. The point of intersection of a and b is then the same as the point of intersection of b and c. So we have different designations for the same point, and these names ('point of intersection of a and b', 'point of intersection of b and c') likewise indicate the mode of presentation; and hence the statement contains actual knowledge.

It is natural, now, to think of there being connected with a sign (name, combination of words, written mark), besides that which the sign designates, which may be called the meaning of the sign, also what I should like to call the *sense* of the sign, wherein the mode of presentation is contained. In our example, accordingly, the [27] meaning of the expressions 'the point of intersection of a and b' and the 'the point of intersection of b and c' would be the same, but not their sense. The meaning of 'evening star' would be the same as that of 'morning star,' but not the sense.

It is clear from the context that by sign and name I have here understood any designation figuring as a proper name, which thus has as its meaning a definite object (this word taken in the widest range), but not a concept or a relation, which shall be discussed further in another article.[3] The designation of a single object can also consist of several words or other signs. For brevity, let every such designation be called a proper name.

The sense of a proper name is grasped by everybody who is sufficiently familiar with the language or totality of designations to which it belongs;[4] but this serves to illuminate only a single aspect of the thing meant, supposing it to have one. Comprehensive knowledge of the thing meant would require us to be able to say immediately whether any given sense attaches to it. To such knowledge we never attain.

The regular connection between a sign, its sense, and what it means is of such a kind that to the sign there corresponds a definite sense and to that in turn a definite thing meant, while to a given thing meant (an object) there does not belong only a single sign. The same sense has different expressions in different languages or even

---

[3] ['On Concept and Object' in Geach and Black, op. cit.]

[4] In the case of an actual proper name such as 'Aristotle' opinions as to the sense may differ. It might, for instance, be taken to be the following: the pupil of Plato and teacher of Alexander the Great. Anybody who does this will attach another sense to the sentence 'Aristotle was born in Stagira' than will a man who takes as the sense of the name: the teacher of Alexander the Great who was born in Stagira. So long as the thing meant remains the same, such variations of sense may be tolerated, although they are to be avoided in the theoretical structure of a demonstrative science and ought not to occur in a perfect language.

in the same language. To be sure, exceptions to this regular behaviour occur. To every expression belonging to a complete totality of signs, there should certainly correspond a definite sense; but natural languages [28] often do not satisfy this condition, and one must be content if the same word has the same sense in the same context. It may perhaps be granted that every grammatically well-formed expression figuring as a proper name always has a sense. But this is not to say that to the sense there also corresponds a thing meant. The words 'the celestial body most distant from the Earth' have a sense, but it is very doubtful if there is also a thing they mean. The expression 'the least rapidly convergent series' has a sense but demonstrably there is nothing it means, since for every given convergent series, another convergent, but less rapidly convergent, series can be found. In grasping a sense, one is not certainly assured of meaning anything.

If words are used in the ordinary way, what one intends to speak of is what they mean. It can also happen, however, that one wishes to talk about the words themselves or their sense. This happens, for instance, when the words of another are quoted. One's own words then first designate words of the other speaker, and only the latter have their usual meaning. We then have signs of signs. In writing, the words are in this case enclosed in quotation marks. Accordingly, a word standing between quotation marks must not be taken as having its ordinary meaning.

In order to speak of the sense of an expression 'A' one may simply use the phrase 'the sense of the expression "A"'. In indirect speech one talks about the sense, e.g., of another person's remarks. It is quite clear that in this way of speaking words do not have their customary meaning but designate what is usually their sense. In order to have a short expression, we will say: In indirect speech, words are used *indirectly* or have their *indirect* meaning. We distinguish accordingly the *customary* from the *indirect* meaning of a word; and its *customary* sense from its *indirect* sense. The indirect meaning of a word is accordingly its customary sense. Such exceptions must always be borne in mind if the mode of connection between sign, sense, and meaning in particular cases is to be correctly understood. [29]

The meaning and sense of a sign are to be distinguished from the associated idea. If what a sign means is an object perceivable by the senses, my idea of it is an internal image,[5] arising from memories of sense impressions which I have had and acts, both internal and external, which I have performed. Such an idea is often imbued with feeling; the clarity of its separate parts varies and oscillates. The same sense is not always connected, even in the same man, with the same idea. The idea is subjective: one man's idea is not that of another. There result, as a matter of course, a variety of differences in the ideas associated with the same sense. A painter, a horseman, and a zoologist will probably connect different ideas with the name 'Bucephalus'.

---

[5] We may include with ideas direct experiences: here, sense-impressions and acts themselves take the place of the traces which they have left in the mind. The distinction is unimportant for our purposes, especially since memories of sense-impressions and acts always go along with such impressions and acts themselves to complete the pepetual image. One may on the other hand understand direct experience as including any object in so far as it is sensibly perceptible or spatial.

This constitutes an essential distinction between the idea and sign's sense, which may be the common property of many people, and so is not a part or a mode of the individual mind. For one can hardly deny that mankind has a common store of thoughts which is transmitted from one generation to another.[6]

In the light of this, one need have no scruples in speaking simply of *the* sense, whereas in the case of an idea one must, strictly speaking, add whom it belongs to and at what time. It might perhaps be said: Just as one man connects this idea, and another that idea, with the same word, so also one man can associate this sense and another that sense. But there still remains a difference in the mode of connection. They are not prevented from grasping the same sense; [30] but they cannot have the same idea. *Si duo idem faciunt, non est idem.* If two persons picture the same thing, each still has his own idea. It is indeed sometimes possible to establish differences in the ideas, or even in the sensations, of different men; but an exact comparison is not possible, because we cannot have both ideas together in the same consciousness.

The meaning of a proper name is the object itself which we designate by using it; the idea which we have in that case is wholly subjective; in between lies the sense, which is indeed no longer subjective like the idea, but is yet not the object itself. The following analogy will perhaps clarify these relationships. Somebody observes the Moon through a telescope. I compare the Moon itself to the meaning; it is the object of the observation, mediated by the real image projected by the object glass in the interior of the telescope, and by the retinal image of the observer. The former I compare to the sense, the latter is like the idea or experience. The optical image in the telescope is indeed one-sided and dependent upon the standpoint of observation; but it is still objective, inasmuch as it can be used by several observers. At any rate it could be arranged for several to use it simultaneously. But each one would have his own retinal image. On account of the diverse shapes of the observers' eyes, even a geometrical congruence could hardly be achieved, and an actual coincidence would be out of the question. This analogy might be developed still further, by assuming A's retinal image made visible to B; or A might also see his own retinal image in a mirror. In this way we might perhaps show how an idea can itself be taken as an object, but as such is not for the observer what it directly is for the person having the idea. But to pursue this would take us too far afield.

We can now recognize three levels of difference between words, expressions, or whole sentences. The difference may concern at most the ideas, or the sense but not the meaning, or, finally, the meaning as well. With respect to [31] the first level, it is to be noted that, on account of the uncertain connection of ideas with words, a difference may hold for one person, which another does not find. The difference between a translation and the original text should properly not overstep the first level. To the possible differences here belong also the colouring and shading which poetic eloquence seeks to give to the sense. Such colouring and shading are not objective, and must be evoked by each hearer or reader according to the hints of the poet or the

---

[6] Hence it is inadvisable to use the word 'idea' to designate something so basically different.

speaker. Without some affinity in human ideas art would certainly be impossible; but it can never be exactly determined how far the intentions of the poet are realized.

In what follows there will be no further discussion of ideas and experiences; they have been mentioned here only to ensure that the idea aroused in the hearer by a word shall not be confused with its sense or its meaning.

To make short and exact expressions possible, let the following phraseology be established:

> A proper name (word, sign, sign combination, expression) *expresses* its sense, *means* or *designates* its meaning. By employing a sign we express its sense and designate its meaning.

Idealists or sceptics will perhaps long since have objected: 'You talk, without further ado, of the Moon as an object; but how do you know that the name "the Moon" has any meaning? How do you know that anything whatsoever has a meaning?' I reply that when we say 'the Moon', we do not intend to speak of our idea of the Moon, nor are we satisfied with the sense alone, but we presuppose a meaning. To assume that in the sentence 'The Moon is smaller than the Earth' the idea of the Moon is in question, would be flatly to misunderstand the sense. If this is what the speaker wanted, he would use the phrase 'my idea of the Moon'. Now we can of course be mistaken in the presupposition, and such mistakes have indeed occurred. But the question whether the presupposition is perhaps always mistaken need [32] not be answered here; in order to justify mention of that which a sign means it is enough, at first, to point our intention in speaking or thinking. (We must then add the reservation: provided such a meaning exists.)

So far we have considered the sense and meaning only of such expressions, words, or signs as we have called proper names. We now inquire concerning the sense and meaning of an entire assertoric sentence. Such a sentence contains a thought.[7] Is this thought, now, to be regarded as its sense or its meaning? Let us assume for the time being that the sentence does mean something. If we now replace one word of the sentence by another having the same meaning, but a different sense, this can have no effect upon the meaning of the sentence. Yet we can see that in such a case the thought changes; since, e.g., the thought in the sentence 'The morning star is a body illuminated by the Sun' differs from that in the sentence 'The evening star is a body illuminated by the Sun'. Anybody who did not know that the evening star is the morning star might hold the one thought to be true, the other false. The thought, accordingly, cannot be what is meant by the sentence, but must rather be considered as its sense. What is the position now with regard to the meaning? Have we a right even to inquire about it? Is it possible that a sentence as a whole has only a sense, but no meaning? At any rate, one might expect that such sentences occur, just as there are parts of sentences having sense but no meaning. And sentences which contain proper names without meaning will be of this kind. The sentence 'Odysseus was set ashore at Ithaca

---

[7] By a thought I understand not the subjective performance of thinking but its objective content, which is capable of being the common property of several thinkers.

while sound asleep' obviously has a sense. But since it is doubtful whether the name 'Odysseus', occurring therein, means anything, it is also doubtful whether the whole sentence does. Yet it is certain, nevertheless, that anyone who seriously took the sentence to be true or false would ascribe to the name 'Odysseus' a meaning, not merely a sense; for it is of what [33] the name means that the predicate is affirmed or denied. Whoever does not admit the name has meaning can neither apply nor withhold the predicate. But in that case it would be superfluous to advance to what the name means; one could be satisfied with the sense, if one wanted to go no further than the thought. If it were a question only of the sense of the sentence, the thought, it would be needless to bother with what is meant by a part of the sentence; only the sense, not the meaning, of the part is relevant to the sense of the whole sentence. The thought remains the same whether 'Odysseus' means something or not. The fact that we concern ourselves at all about what is meant by a part of the sentence indicates that we generally recognize and expect a meaning for the sentence itself. The thought loses value for us as soon as we recognize that the meaning of one of its parts is missing. We are therefore justified in not being satisfied with the sense of a sentence, and in inquiring also as to its meaning. But now why do we want every proper name to have not only a sense, but also a meaning? Why is the thought not enough for us? Because, and to the extent that, we are concerned with its truth-value. This is not always the case. In hearing an epic poem, for instance, apart from the euphony of the language we are interested only in the sense of the sentences and the images and feelings thereby aroused. The question of truth would cause us to abandon aesthetic delight for an attitude of scientific investigation. Hence it is a matter of no concern to us whether the name 'Odysseus', for instance, has meaning, so long as we accept the poem as a work of art.[8] It is the striving for truth that drives us always to advance from the sense to the thing meant.

We have seen that the meaning of a sentence may always be sought, whenever the meaning of its components is involved; and that this is the case when and only when we are inquiring after the truth-value. [34]

We are therefore driven into accepting the *truth-value* of a sentence as constituting what it means. By the truth-value of a sentence I understand the circumstance that it is true or false. There are no further truth-values. For brevity I call the one the True, the other the False. Every assertoric sentence concerned with what its words mean is therefore to be regarded as a proper name, and its meaning, if it has one, is either the True or the False. These two objects are recognized, if only implicitly, by everybody who judges something to be true—and so even by a sceptic. The designation of the truth-values as objects may appear to be an arbitrary fancy or perhaps a mere play upon words, from which no profound consequences could be drawn. What I am calling an object can be more exactly discussed only in connection with concept and relation. I will reserve this for another article.[9] But so much should already be

---

[8] It would be desirable to have a special term for signs intended to have only sense. If we name them say, representations, the words of the actors on the stage would be representations; indeed the actor himself would be a representation.

[9] ['On Concept and Object' in Geach and Black, op. cit.]

clear, that in every judgement,[10] no matter how trivial, the step from the level of thoughts to the level of meaning (the objective) has already been taken.

One might be tempted to regard the relation of the thought to the True not as that of sense to meaning, but rather as that of subject to predicate. One can, indeed, say: 'The thought that 5 is a prime number is true'. But closer examination shows that nothing more has been said than in the simple sentence '5 is a prime number'. The truth claim arises in each case from the form of the assertoric sentence, and when the latter lacks its usual force, e.g., in the mouth of an actor upon the stage, even the sentence 'The thought that 5 is a prime number is true' contains only a thought, and indeed the same thought as the simple '5 is a prime number'. It follows that the relation of the thought to the True may not be compared with that of subject to predicate. [35]

Subject and predicate (understood in the logical sense) are just elements of thought; they stand on the same level for knowledge. By combining subject and predicate, one reaches only a thought, never passes from sense to meaning, never from a thought to its truth-value. One moves at the same level but never advances from one level to the next. A truth-value cannot be a part of a thought, any more than, say, the Sun can, for it is not a sense but an object.

If our supposition that the meaning of a sentence is its truth-value is correct, the latter must remain unchanged when a part of the sentence is replaced by an expression with the same meaning. And this is in fact the case. Leibniz gives the definition: '*Eadem sunt, quae sibi mutuo substitui possunt, salva veritate*'. If we are dealing with sentences for which the meaning of their component parts is at all relevant, then what feature except the truth-value can be found that belongs to such sentences quite generally and remains unchanged by substitutions of the kind just mentioned?

If now the truth-value of a sentence is its meaning, then on the one hand all true sentences have the same meaning and so, on the other hand, do all false sentences. From this we see that in the meaning of the sentence all that is specific is obliterated. We can never be concerned only with the meaning of a sentence; but again the mere thought alone yields no knowledge, but only the thought together with its meaning, i.e. its truth-value. Judgements can be regarded as advances from a thought to a truth-value. Naturally this cannot be a definition. Judgement is something quite peculiar and incomparable. One might also say that judgements are distinctions of parts within truth-values. Such distinction occurs by a return to the thought. To every sense attaching to a truth-value would correspond its own manner of analysis. However, I have here used the word 'part' in a special sense. I have in fact transferred the relation between the parts and the whole of the sentence to its meaning, by calling the meaning of a word part of the meaning of the sentence, if the word itself [36] is a part of the sentence. This way of speaking can certainly be attacked, because the total meaning and one part of it do not suffice to determine the remainder, and because the word 'part' is already used of bodies in another sense. A special term would need to be invented.

---

[10] A judgement, for me is not the mere grasping of a thought, but the admission of its truth.

The supposition that the truth-value of a sentence is what it means shall now be put to further test. We have found that the truth-value of a sentence remains unchanged when an expression is replaced by another with the same meaning: but we have not yet considered the case in which the expression to be replaced is itself a sentence. Now if our view is correct, the truth-value of a sentence containing another as part must remain unchanged when the part is replaced by another sentence having the same truth-value. Exceptions are to be expected when the whole sentence or its part is direct or indirect quotation; for in such cases as we have seen, the words do not have their customary meaning. In direct quotation, a sentence designates another sentence, and in indirect speech a thought.

We are thus led to consider subordinate sentences or clauses. These occur as parts of a sentence complex, which is, from the logical standpoint, likewise a sentence—a main sentence. But here we meet the question whether it is also true of the subordinate sentence that its meaning is a truth-value. Of indirect speech we already know the opposite. Grammarians view subordinate clauses as representatives of parts of sentences and divide them accordingly into noun clauses, adjective clauses, adverbial clauses. This might generate the supposition that the meaning of a subordinate clause was not a truth-value but rather of the same kind as the meaning of a noun or adjective or adverb—in short, of a part of a sentence, whose sense was not a thought but only a part of a thought. Only a more thorough investigation can clarify the issue. In so doing, we shall not follow the grammatical categories strictly, but rather group together what is logically of the same kind. Let us first search for cases in which the sense of the subordinate clause, as we have just supposed, is not an independent thought. [37]

The case of an abstract[11] noun clause, introduced by 'that,' includes the case of indirect meaning, coincident with what is customarily their sense. So here, the subordinate clause has for its meaning a thought, not a truth-value and for its sense not a thought, but the sense of the words 'the thought that (etc.)', which is only a part of the thought in the entire complex sentence. This happens after 'say', 'hear', 'be of the opinion', 'be convinced', 'conclude', and similar words.[12] There is a different, and indeed somewhat complicated, situation after words like 'perceive', 'know', 'fancy', which are to be considered later.

That in the cases of the first kind the meaning of the subordinate clause is in fact the thought can also be recognized by seeing that it is indifferent to the truth of the whole whether the subordinate clause is true or false. Let us compare, for instance, the two sentences 'Copernicus believed that the planetary orbits are circles' and 'Copernicus believed that the apparent motion of the Sun is produced by the real motion of the Earth'. One subordinate clause can be substituted for the other

---

[11] [Frege probably means clauses grammatically replaceable by an abstract noun-phrase; e.g. 'Smith denies *that dragons exist*' = 'Smith denies *the existence of dragons*'; or again, in this context after 'denies', 'that Brown is wise' is replaceable by 'the wisdom of Brown'. (*Tr.*)]

[12] In 'A lied in saying he had seen B', the subordinate clause designates a thought which is said (1) to have been asserted by A (2) while A was convinced of its falsity.

without harm to the truth. The main clause and the subordinate clause together have as their sense only a single thought, and the truth of the whole includes neither the truth nor the untruth of the subordinate clause. In such cases it is not permissible to replace one expression in the subordinate clause by another having the same customary meaning, but only by one having the same indirect meaning, i.e. the same customary sense. Somebody might conclude: The meaning of a sentence is not its truth-value, for in that case it could always be replaced by another sentence of the same truth-value. But this proves too much; one might just as well claim that the meaning of 'morning star' is not Venus, since one may not always say 'Venus' in place of 'morning star'. One has the right to conclude only that the meaning of a sentence is not *always* its truth-value, and that 'morning star' does not [38] always mean the planet Venus, viz. when the word has its indirect meaning. An exception of such a kind occurs in the subordinate clause just considered, which has a thought as its meaning.

If one says 'It seems that … ' one means 'It seems to me that … ' or 'I think that … ' We therefore have the same case again. The situation is similar in the case of expressions such as 'to be pleased', 'to regret', 'to approve', 'to blame', 'to hope', 'to fear'. If, toward the end of the battle of Waterloo, Wellington was glad that the Prussians were coming, the basis for his joy was a conviction. Had he been deceived, he would have been no less pleased so long as his illusion lasted; and before he became so convinced he could not have been pleased that the Prussians were coming—even though in fact they might have been already approaching.

Just as a conviction or a belief is the ground of a feeling, it can, as in inference, also be the ground of a conviction. In the sentence: 'Columbus inferred from the roundness of the Earth that he could reach India by travelling towards the west', we have as the meanings of the parts two thoughts, that the Earth is round, and that Columbus by travelling to the west could reach India. All that is relevant here is that Columbus was convinced of both, and that the one conviction was a ground for the other. Whether the Earth is really round and Columbus could really reach India by travelling west, as he thought, is immaterial to the truth of our sentence; but it is not immaterial whether we replace 'the Earth' by 'the planet which is accompanied by a moon whose diameter is greater than the fourth part of its own'. Here also we have the indirect meaning of the words.

Adverbial final clauses beginning 'in order that' also belong here; for obviously the purpose is a thought; therefore: indirect meaning for the words, subjunctive mood.

A subordinate clause with 'that' after 'command', 'ask', 'forbid', would appear in direct speech as an imperative. Such a sentence has no meaning but only a sense. A command, a request, are indeed not thoughts, but they stand on the same level as thoughts. Hence in subordinate clauses depending upon 'command,' [39] 'ask,' etc., words have their indirect meaning. The meaning of such a clause is therefore not a truth-value but a command, a request, and so forth.

The case is similar for the dependent question in phrases such as 'doubt whether', 'not to know what'. It is easy to see that here also the words are to be taken to have their indirect meaning. Dependent clauses, expression questions and beginning with 'who', 'what', 'where', 'when', 'how', 'by what means', etc., seem at times to approximate very closely to adverbial clauses in which words have their customary meanings. These cases are distinguished linguistically in German by the mood of the verb. With the subjunctive, we have a dependent question and indirect meanings of the words, so that a proper name cannot in general be replaced by another name of the same object.

In the cases so far considered the words of the subordinate clauses had their indirect meaning, and this made it clear that the meaning of the subordinate clause itself was indirect, i.e. not a truth-value but a thought, a command, a request, a question. The subordinate clause could be regarded as a noun, indeed one could say: as a proper name of that thought, that command, etc., which it represented in the context of the sentence structure.

We now come to other subordinate clauses, in which the words do have their customary meaning without however a thought occurring as sense and a truth-value as meaning. How this is possible is best made clear by examples.

Whoever discovered the elliptic form of the planetary orbits died in misery.

If the sense of the subordinate clause were here a thought, it would have to be possible to express it also in a separate sentence. But it does not work, because the grammatical subject 'whoever' has no independent sense and only mediates the relation with the consequent clause 'died in misery.' For this reason the sense of the subordinate clause is not a complete thought, and what it means is Kepler, not a truth-value. One might object that the sense of the whole does contain a thought as part, viz. that there was somebody who first discovered the elliptic form of the planetary orbits; for whoever takes the whole to be true [40] cannot deny this part. This is undoubtedly so; but only because otherwise the dependent clause 'whoever discovered the elliptic form of the planetary orbits' would have nothing to mean. If anything is asserted there is always an obvious presupposition that the simple or compound proper names used have meaning. If therefore one asserts 'Kepler died in misery,' there is a presupposition that the name 'Kepler' designates something; but it does not follow that the sense of the sentence 'Kepler died in misery' contains the thought that the name 'Kepler' designates something. If this were the case the negation would have to run not

Kepler did not die in misery

but

Kepler did not die in misery, or the name 'Kepler' has no reference.

That the name 'Kepler' designates something is just as much a presupposition for the assertion

Kepler died in misery

as for the contrary assertion. Now languages have the fault of containing expressions which fail to designate an object (although their grammatical form seems to qualify them for that purpose) because the truth of some sentence is a prerequisite. Thus it depends on the truth of the sentence:

There was someone who discovered the elliptic form of the planetary orbits

whether the subordinate clause

Whoever discovered the elliptic form of the planetary orbits

really designates an object, or only seems to do so while in fact there is nothing for it to mean. And thus it may appear as if our subordinate clause contained as a part of its sense the thought that there was somebody who discovered the elliptic form of the planetary orbits. If this were right the negation would run:

Either whoever discovered the elliptic form of the planetary orbits did not die in misery or there was nobody who discovered the elliptic form of the planetary orbits. [41]

This arises from an imperfection of language, from which even the symbolic language of mathematical analysis is not altogether free; even there combinations of symbols can occur that seem to mean something but (at least so far) do not mean anything, e.g. divergent infinite series. This can be avoided, e.g., by means of the special stipulation that divergent infinite series shall mean the number 0. A logically perfect language (*Begriffsschrift*) should satisfy the conditions, that every expression grammatically well constructed as a proper name out of signs already introduced shall in fact designate an object, and that no new sign shall be introduced as a proper name without being secured a meaning. The logic books contain warnings against logical mistakes arising from the ambiguity of expressions. I regard as no less pertinent a warning against apparent proper names without any meaning. The history of mathematics supplies errors which have arisen in this way. This lends itself to demagogic abuse as easily as ambiguity—perhaps more easily. 'The will of the people' can serve as an example; for it is easy to establish that there is at any rate no generally accepted meaning for this expression. It is therefore by no means unimportant to eliminate the source of these mistakes, at least in science, once and for all. Then such objections as the one discussed above would become impossible, because it could never depend upon the truth of a thought whether a proper name had meaning.

With the consideration of these noun clauses may be coupled that of types of adjective and adverbial clauses which are logically in close relation to them.

Adjective clauses also serve to construct compound proper names, though, unlike noun clauses, they are not sufficient by themselves for this purpose. These adjective clauses are to be regarded as equivalent to adjectives. Instead of 'the square root of 4 which is smaller than 0', one can also say 'the negative square root of 4'. We have here the case of a compound proper name constructed from the expression for a concept with the help of the singular definite article. This is at any rate permissible if the concept applies to one [42] and only one single object.[13] Expressions for concepts can be so constructed that marks of a concept are given by adjective clauses as, in our example, by the clause 'which is smaller than 0'. It is evident that such an adjective clause cannot have a thought as sense or a truth-value as meaning, any more than the noun clause could. Its sense, which can also in many cases be expressed by a single adjective, is only a part of a thought. Here, as in the case of the noun clause, there is no independent subject and therefore no possibility of reproducing the sense of the subordinate clause in an independent sentence.

Places, instants, stretches of time, logically considered, are objects; hence the linguistic designation of a definite place, a definite instant, or a stretch of time is to be regarded as a proper name. Now adverbial clauses of place and time can be used to construct such a proper name in much the same way as we have seen noun and adjective clauses can. In the same way, expressions for concepts that apply to places, etc., can be constructed. It is to be noted here also that the sense of these subordinate clauses cannot be reproduced in an independent sentence, since an essential component, viz. the determination of place or time, is missing and is just indicated by a relative pronoun or a conjunction.[14]

In conditional clauses, also, there most often [43] recognizably occurs an indefinite indicator, with a correlative indicator in the dependent clause. (We have already seen this occur in noun, adjective, and adverbial clauses.) In so far as each indicator relates to the other, both clauses together form a connected whole, which as a rule expresses only a single thought. In the sentence

> If a number is less than 1 and greater than 0, its square is less than 1 and greater than 0

---

[13] In accordance with what was said above, an expression of the kind in question must actually always be assured of meaning, by means of a special stipulation, e.g. by the convention that it shall count as meaning 0 when the concept applies to no object or to more than one.

[14] In the case of these sentences, various interpretations are easily possible. The sense of the sentence, 'After Schleswig–Holstein was separated from Denmark, Prussia and Austria quarrelled' can also be rendered in the form 'After the separation of Schleswig–Holstein from Denmark, Prussia and Austria quarrelled.' In the version, it is surely sufficiently clear that the sense is not to be taken as having as a part the thought that Schleswig–Holstein was once separated from Denmark, but that this is the necessary presupposition in order for the expression 'after the separation of Schleswig–Holstein from Denmark' to have any meaning at all. To be sure, our sentence can also be interpreted as saying that Schleswig–Holstein was once separated from Denmark. We then have a case which is to be considered later. In order to understand the difference more clearly, let us project ourselves into the mind of a Chinese who, having little knowledge of European history, believes it to be false that Schleswig–Holstein was ever separated from Denmark. He will take our sentence, in the first version, to be neither true nor false but will deny it to have any meaning, on the ground that its subordinate clause lacks a meaning. This clause would only apparently determine a time. If he interpreted our sentence in the second way, however, he would find a thought expressed in it which he would take to be false, beside a part which would be without meaning for him.

the component in question is 'a number' in the antecedent clause and 'its' in the consequent clause. It is by means of this very indefiniteness that the sense acquires the generality expected of a law. It is this which is responsible for the fact that the antecedent clause alone has no complete thought as its sense and in combination with the consequent clause expresses one and only one thought, whose parts are no longer thoughts. It is, in general, incorrect to say that in the hypothetical judgement two judgements are put in reciprocal relationship. If this or something similar is said, the word 'judgement' is used in the same sense as I have connected with the word 'thought,' so that I would use the formulation: 'A hypothetical thought establishes a reciprocal relationship between two thoughts.' This could be true only if no indefinite indicator were present;[15] but in such a case there would also be no generality.

If an instant of time is to be indefinitely indicated in both the antecedent and the consequent clause, this is often achieved merely by using the present tense of the verb, which in such a case however does not indicate the temporal present. This grammatical form is then the indefinite indicator in the main and subordinate clauses. An example of this is: 'When [44] the Sun is in the tropic of Cancer, the longest day in the northern hemisphere occurs'. Here, also, it is impossible to express the sense of the subordinate clause in a full sentence, because this sense is not a complete thought. If we say: 'The Sun is in the tropic of Cancer', this would refer to our present time and thereby change the sense. Neither is the sense of the main clause a thought; only the whole, composed of main and subordinate clauses, has such a sense. It may be added that several common components may be indefinitely indicated in the antecedent and consequent clauses.

It is clear that noun clauses with 'who' or 'what' and adverbial clauses with 'where', 'when', 'wherever', 'whenever' are often to be interpreted as having the sense of antecedent clauses, e.g. 'who touches pitch, defiles himself'.

Adjective clauses can also take the place of conditional clauses. Thus the sense of the sentence previously used can be given in the form 'The square of a number which is less than 1 and greater than 0 is less than 1 and greater than 0'.

The situation is quite different if the common component of the two clauses is designated by a proper name. In the sentence:

Napoleon, who recognized the danger to his right flank, himself led his guards against the enemy position

two thoughts are expressed:

1. Napoleon recognized the danger to his right flank

2. Napoleon himself led his guards against the enemy position.

When and where this happened is to be fixed only by the context, but is nevertheless to be taken as definitely determined thereby. If the entire sentence is uttered as an

---

[15] At times there is no linguistically explicit indicator and one must be read off from the entire context.

assertion, we thereby simultaneously assert both component sentences. If one of the parts is false, the whole is false. Here we have the case that the subordinate clause by itself has a complete thought as sense (if we complete it by indication of place and time). The meaning of the subordinate clause is accordingly a truth-value. We can therefore expect that it may be replaced, without harm to the truth-value of the whole, by a sentence having the [45] same truth-value. This is indeed the case; but it is to be noted that for purely grammatical reasons, its subject must be 'Napoleon', for only then can it be brought into the form of an adjective clause attaching to 'Napoleon'. But if the demand that it be expressed in this form is waived, and the connection shown by 'and', this restriction disappears.

Subsidiary clauses beginning with 'although' also express complete thoughts. This conjunction actually has no sense and does not change the sense of the clause but only illuminates it in a peculiar fashion.[16] We could indeed replace the conces-sive clause without harm to the truth of the whole by another of the same truth-value; but the light in which the clause is placed by the conjunction might then easily appear unsuitable, as if a song with a sad subject were to be sung in a lively fashion.

In the last cases the truth of the whole included the truth of the component clauses. The case is different if an antecedent clause expresses a complete thought by containing, in place of an indefinite indicator, a proper name or something which is to be regarded as equivalent. In the sentence

If the Sun has already risen, the sky is very cloudy

the time is the present, that is to say, definite. And the place is also to be thought of as definite. Here it can be said that a relation between the truth-values of antecedent and consequent clauses has been asserted, viz. that the case does not occur in which the antecedent means the True and the consequent the False. Accordingly, our sentence is true if the Sun has not yet risen, whether the sky is very cloudy or not, and also if the Sun has risen and the sky is very cloudy. Since only truth-values are here in question, each component clause can be replaced by another of the same truth-value without changing the truth-value of the whole. To be sure, the light in which the subject then appears would usually be unsuitable; the thought might easily seem [46] inane; but this has nothing to do with its truth-value. One must always observe that there are overtones of subsidiary thoughts, which are however not explicitly expressed and therefore should not be reckoned in the sense. Hence, also, no account need be taken of their truth-values.[17]

The simplest cases have now been discussed. Let us review what we have learned.

The subordinate clause usually has for its sense not a thought, but only a part of one, and consequently no truth-value is being meant. The reason for this is either

---

[16] Similarly in the case of 'but', 'yet'.

[17] The thought of our sentence might also be expressed thus: 'Either the Sun has not risen yet or the sky is very cloudy'—which shows how this kind of sentence connection is to be understood.

that the words in the subordinate clause have indirect meaning, so that the meaning, not the sense, of the subordinate clause is a thought; or else that, on account of the presence of an indefinite indicator, the subordinate clause is incomplete and expresses a thought only when combined with the main clause. It may happen, however, that the sense of the subsidiary clause is a complete thought, in which case it can be replaced by another of the same truth value without harm to the truth of the whole—provided there are no grammatical obstacles.

An examination of all the subordinate clauses which one may encounter will soon provide some which do not fit well into these categories. The reason, so far as I can see, is that these subordinate clauses have no such simple sense. Almost always, it seems, we connect with the main thoughts expressed by us subsidiary thoughts which, although not expressed, are associated with our words, in accordance with psychological laws, by the hearer. And since the subsidiary thought appears to be connected with our words on its own account, almost like the main thought itself, we want it also to be expressed. The sense of the sentence is thereby enriched, and it may well happen that we have more simple thoughts than clauses. In many cases the sentence must be understood in this way, in others it may be doubtful whether the subsidiary thought belongs to the sense of the sentence or [47] only accompanies it.[18] One might perhaps find that the sentence

> Napoleon, who recognized the danger to his right flank, himself led his guards against the enemy position

expresses not only the two thoughts shown above, but also the thought that the knowledge of the danger was the reason why he led the guards against the enemy position. One may in fact doubt whether this thought is just slightly suggested or really expressed. Let the question be considered whether our sentence is false if Napoleon's decision had already been made before he recognized the danger. If our sentence could be true in spite of this, the subsidiary thought should not be understood as part of the sense. One would probably decide in favour of this. The alternative would make for a quite complicated situation: We should have more simple thoughts than clauses. If the sentence

> Napoleon recognized the danger to his right flank

were now to be replaced by another having the same truth-value, e.g.

> Napoleon was already more than 45 years old

not only would our first thought be changed, but also our third one. Hence the truth-value of the latter might change—viz. if his age was not the reason for the decision to lead the guards against the enemy. This shows why clauses of equal truth-value can-

---

[18] This may be important for the question whether an assertion is a lie, or an oath a perjury.

not always be substituted for one another in such cases. The clause expresses more through its connection with another than it does in isolation.

Let us now consider cases where this regularly happens. In the sentence:

> Bebel fancies that the return of Alsace-Lorraine would appease France's desire for revenge

two thoughts are expressed, which are not however shown by means of antecedent and consequent clauses, viz:

1. Bebel believes that the return of Alsace-Lorraine would appease France's desire for revenge [48]
2. The return of Alsace-Lorraine would not appease France's desire for revenge.

In the expression of the first thought, the words of the subordinate clause have their indirect meaning, while the same words have their customary meaning in the expression of the second thought. This shows that the subordinate clause in our original complex sentence is to be taken twice over, with different meanings: once for a thought, once for a truth-value. Since the truth-value is not the total meaning of the subordinate clause, we cannot simply replace the latter by another of equal truth-value. Similar considerations apply to expressions such as 'know', 'discover', 'it is known that'.

By means of a subordinate causal clause and the associated main clause we express several thoughts, which however do not correspond separately to the original clauses. In the sentence: 'Because ice is less dense than water, it floats on water' we have

(1) Ice is less dense than water;
(2) If anything is less dense than water, it floats on water;
(3) Ice floats on water.

The third thought, however, need not be explicitly introduced, since it is contained in the remaining two. On the other hand, neither the first and third nor the second and third combined would furnish the sense of our sentence. It can now be seen that our subordinate clause

> because ice is less dense than water

expresses our first thought, as well as a part of our second. This is how it comes to pass that our subsidiary clause cannot be simply replaced by another of equal truth-value; for this would alter our second thought and thereby might well alter its truth-value.

The situation is similar in the sentence

If iron were less dense than water, it would float on water. [49]

Here we have the two thoughts that iron is not less dense than water, and that something floats on water if it is less dense than water. The subsidiary clause again expresses one thought and a part of the other.

If we interpret the sentence already considered

> After Schleswig–Holstein was separated from Denmark, Prussia and Austria quarrelled

in such a way that it expresses the thought that Schleswig–Holstein was once separated from Denmark, we have first this thought, and secondly the thought that, at a time more closely determined by the subordinate clause, Prussia and Austria quarrelled. Here also the subordinate clause expresses not only one thought but also a part of another. Therefore it may not in general be replaced by another of the same truth-value.

It is hard to exhaust all the possibilities given by language; but I hope to have brought to light at least the essential reasons why a subordinate clause may not always be replaced by another of equal truth-value without harm to the truth of the whole sentence structure. These reasons arise:

(1) when the subordinate clause does not, have a truth-value as its meaning, inasmuch as it expresses only a part of a thought;
(2) when the subordinate clause does have a truth-value as its meaning but is not restricted to so doing, inasmuch as its sense includes one thought and part of another.

The first case arises:

(a) for words having indirect meaning
(b) if a part of the sentence is only an indefinite indicator instead of a proper name.

In the second case, the subsidiary clause may have to be taken twice over, viz. once in its customary meaning, and the other time in indirect meaning; or the sense of a part of the subordinate clause may likewise be a component of another thought, which, taken together with the thought directly expressed by the subordinate clause, makes up the sense of the whole sentence.

It follows with sufficient probability from the foregoing that the cases where a subordinate clause is not replaceable by another of the same value cannot be brought in disproof of our view [50] that a truth-value is the meaning of a sentence that has a thought as its sense.

Let us return to our starting point.

If we found '$a = a$' and '$a = b$' to have different cognitive values, the explanation is that for the purpose of acquiring knowledge, the sense of the sentence, viz., the thought expressed by it, is no less relevant than its meaning, i.e. its truth-value. If now $a = b$, then indeed what is meant by 'b' is the same as what is meant by 'a', and hence the truth-value of '$a = b$' is the same as that of '$a = a$'. In spite of this, the sense of 'b' may differ from that of 'a', and thereby the thought expressed in '$a = b$' differs from that of '$a = a$'. In that case the two sentences do not have the same cognitive value. If we understand by 'judgement' the advance from the thought to its truth-value, as in the present paper, we can also say that the judgements are different.

CHAPTER 2

Bertrand Russell and Ludwig Wittgenstein: Logical Atomism

Introduction to Bertrand Russell

Bertrand Russell was born in 1872 into a distinguished English family. His grandfather, Lord John Russell, had been prime minister and introduced the Reform Bill in 1832. His parents were atheists ("freethinkers") and appointed their friend John Stuart Mill as Russell's nonreligious godfather. Unfortunately, his parents died when he was young, and he was sent to live with his paternal grandmother. The misery caused by his subjection to her joyless, puritanical Presbyterianism may have sowed the seed of his subsequent loathing of organized religion. Russell went to Cambridge in 1890 to study mathematics, encountering philosophy during his subsequent study for the Moral Sciences Tripos. He was a fellow of Trinity College, Cambridge, from 1895 to 1901, and a lecturer there from 1910 to 1916, until he was fired due to his opposition to World War I. While a student, Russell encountered Alfred North Whitehead, then a Fellow and Lecturer in Mathematics. They were later to collaborate in the massive three-volume *Principia Mathematica*, which endeavored to prove that all concepts and statements of mathematics could be stated purely in the language of logic. Unknown to them, much of this work had already been done by Gottlob Frege. After Whitehead, Russell's most distinguished collaborator was his student Ludwig Wittgenstein. Their research into the foundations of logic led to the metaphysical system known as Logical Atomism.

Most of Russell's significant philosophical work was achieved by the time of World War I. In fact, he spent long years away from academic life, teaching only briefly at the University of Chicago and UCLA from 1936 to 1940. Apart from his philosophical output, enormous in its own right, Russell also did a great deal of popular writing, on every subject from Bolshevism to the Theory of Relativity. This included one philosophical "best seller," *A History of Western Philosophy*. His writings on sex and marriage provoked an outcry from self-appointed guardians of public morals, leading to a notorious court case in which Russell's appointment at the City College of New York was rescinded. A judge was of the opinion that Russell's presence would constitute a grave risk to "public health, safety and morals." But Russell was no stranger to controversy. He had been jailed in 1918 for published remarks, judged to be libelous, about the U.S. Army's alleged intimidation of strikers. He was again imprisoned, at the age of eighty nine, as part of a protest of the Campaign for Nuclear Disarmament, an organization he helped found. He was a political activist all his life, standing unsuccessfully for Parliament on three occasions, on behalf of the National Union of Women's Suffrage Societies in 1907, and for the Labour Party in 1922 and 1923. He received the Nobel Prize for Literature in 1950, as much for his sociopolitical as for his philosophical work. He died in 1970.

During his early days at Cambridge, Russell was influenced by the then dominant Absolute Idealists, as represented there by J. M. E. McTaggart and in Oxford by F. H. Bradley, whose *Appearance and Reality* (1893) marked that movement's highest point. According to this neo-Hegelian theory, the universe constitutes a single indivisible entity, "the Absolute." To consider any part as independent of the whole was to distort that thing's nature, as the only self-subsistent entity is the Absolute itself. Bradley attempted to prove his thesis a priori by arguing that the opposing model of the universe as consisting in a multitude of independent entities, qualities, and relations was self-contradictory.

In support of this allegedly inconsistent model, Russell focused his attack on Bradley's theory of internal relations, which he judged to be the cornerstone of Idealism. According to Bradley, when two things enter into a relation, then this fact enters into the nature of both relata. Thus, if aRb, the relation to b is a factor internal to a's nature. A full grasp of a's nature must involve a grasp of *all* its relations. Thus, we have a monistic model of the universe—as one single entity, whose nature is spiritual. By contrast, Russell's *atomism*, where reality consists of a set of mutually independent entities, rested on a theory of external relations. That is, he viewed relations as irreducible to facts about entities or properties.

Russell didn't jump directly from Idealism into the Logical Atomism which marked his mature philosophy. Around the time of *The Principles of Mathematics*, he briefly adopted a Platonic Realist theory, similar to that of Alexius Meinong, which represented an extremely hard-line version of a referential theory of meaning. Thus, every linguistic expression stands for some thing, with some sort of "being," if not necessarily existence in space and time. "*Being* is that which belongs to every conceivable term, to every possible object of thought—in short to everything that can possibly occur in any proposition, true or false, and to all such propositions themselves. Being belongs to whatever can be counted". . . "Numbers, the Homeric gods, relations, chimeras and four-dimensional spaces all have being, for if they were not entities of a kind, we could make no propositions about them. Thus being is a general attribute of everything, and to mention anything is to show that it is" (para. 427). One of the motivations for his subsequent work was to avoid the cluttered ontology to which a theory led. "Logic must no more admit a unicorn than zoology can; for logic is concerned with the real world just as truly as zoology, though with its more abstract and general features."

I will begin my discussion of Russell's mature work with his Theory of Descriptions, which dates from the publication of "On Denoting" in 1905. While some influential persons (notably Kripke) write as if Frege and Russell had a shared theory on issues of meaning and reference, significant differences exist between them, which can be traced back to (among other things) Russell's empiricist leanings. Russell is not interested in logical analysis purely for its own sake. Rather, his employment of logical techniques is deeply intertwined with his ontological and epistemological concerns. When he translates an ordinary language proposition into a more logically pellucid form, he does so to reveal the proposition's ontological commitments, about which we may be misled by its surface grammar. As we shall see, this analysis commits us only to the existence of things with which we are directly acquainted.

The Theory of Descriptions is designed to solve certain puzzles regarding apparently referring expressions. The first, which inspired Frege's distinction between sense and Meaning, concerned *identity statements*: How do we account for the difference between "A is A" and "A is B"? If A and B are coreferential terms, then, by the referential theory of meaning (which Russell always adhered to), it would seem that the two statements must be equivalent. But clearly they are not. One is a tautology, and the other an empirical discovery; also, one can believe that A is A without believing that A is B.

A second problem concerned *negative existentials*, such as "Satan does not exist." Clearly, this is a meaningful statement; but this fact requires that its component, "Satan," has meaning. However, if the meaning of a referring expression is the thing it denotes, then Satan must, in some sense, exist: Yet that is what the statement explicitly denies! Thus, the statement seems to be self-contradictory.

A closely related problem concerns any statement about a nonexistent entity, for example, "The present king of France is bald." Clearly, this is not true; but neither can we say that it is false, as that would imply that its negation be true—but the set of non-bald things does not include the present king of France. Such a statement would seem to threaten the Law of the Excluded Middle, which states that p and p can't both be false.

Russell's solution is to say that none of the grammatical subject terms in these problematic statements are genuine singular referring terms. Rather, they are *descriptions* and as such require an entirely different analysis to genuinely referring expressions (which he called "names"). They are "incomplete symbols," "propositional functions" (corresponding to Frege's "unsaturated" entities). They are therefore general expressions, concerning properties, not particular things.

Two basic differences exist between Russell and Frege's treatments of these problematic cases. First, Russell, unlike Frege, insists on a distinction between names and descriptions. Second, Russell rejects Frege's introduction of *Sinn*, sticking to a pure referential theory. Let us take the above-mentioned example,

1. *The present king of France is bald.*

and compare Russell and Frege's treatments of it. Frege's view would be that 1 has no reference, since one of its components, the descriptive phrase, lacks a referent; however, he would say that 1 still expresses a thought, since the description has a sense.

Russell was uneasy about the introduction of senses. He seems to have thought that their nature was problematic, posing serious ontological and epistemological problems as to the nature of such senses, and how they are to be encountered by the mind. Occam's Razor was never far from Russell's hand, and so he was reluctant to introduce such an additional class of entities if he could avoid it. Likewise, he had to avoid such dubious entities as Meinong's "subsisting" entities. Again, take the sort of examples that motivated Frege's distinction between sense and Meaning:

2. *The author of* Oliver Twist *is dead.*

3. *The author of* David Copperfield *is dead.*

Frege would say that 2 and 3 expressed different thoughts, and that the descriptions had different senses, but he would insist that both the statements and their embedded descriptions were coreferential. Russell denies this last claim, since the descriptions are not referring expressions at all.

As an entry into Russell's theory, let us look at what he says about *indefinite* descriptions; that is, expressions of the form "an F" which, prima facie, have the potential to pick out more than one individual. Compare these two sentences:

4. *A philosopher is drunk in the Twilight Room.*

5. *Jim Baillie is drunk in the Twilight Room.*

For 4 to be true, all that is required is that some philosopher be inebriated at the designated location. No specific sage is demanded. Anyone will do. Thus, since I would fit the bill, if 5 is true, then 4 is true—but not vice versa. In order for 5 to be true, *I* have to be drunk in that select hostelry. No one else will do. No matter how many other philosophers are present, no matter how merry, it is beside the point.

The truth-conditions of 4 make essential reference to my good self, whereas those of 5 mention no person or object at all, but express a relation between two properties. Precisely, it claims that the property of being a philosopher and the property of being drunk in the Twilight Room have at least one coinstantiation. That is, there's something which satisfies both.

Let us now turn to the more important case of *definite* descriptions. These differ from indefinite descriptions only in being *uniquely* satisfiable. Returning to 1, Russell's analysis would be this:

(a) There is at least one thing which is a present king of France;

(b) There is at most one thing which is a present king of France;

(c) Whatever is a present king of France is bald.

Notice that the analysis says "*a* present king of France," not "*the* present king of France"; that is, it mentions a propositional function. So 1 is really a conjunction of three distinct claims and is false, since conjunct (a) is false.

Now consider these two sentences:

6. *The author of* Waverley *was Scottish.*

7. *Sir Walter Scott was Scottish.*

As with 4 and 5, these have different truth-conditions, and thus say different things. There is no reference to Sir Walter in 6. It merely says that the property of being the author of *Waverley* is uniquely instantiated by something Scottish (or "Scotch" as Russell annoyingly puts it). It would be true if any other Scot wrote that book, for example, Sean Connery or myself. So, as before, the true logical form concerns a relation between properties, with no reference to individuals. Incidentally, Russell's employment of this example has led to some confusion, and accusations of inconsistency, since, as we shall see in a moment, he is committed to denying that "Sir Walter Scott" is a name, but is as much a description as "the author of *Waverley*." The most charitable interpretation is to say that Russell was merely using "Sir Walter Scott" to *stand in for* a name in order to illustrate the distinction between names and descriptions.

Russell then recognized that "Fregean" puzzles regarding coreferential expressions yielding different thoughts could occur in the case of ordinary names. As before, he had to account for this phenomenon without recourse to senses. Take this example:

8. *George Eliot wrote* Middlemarch.

9. *Mary Anne Evans wrote* Middlemarch.

Again, 8 and 9 are cognitively distinct—one could know or believe one without the other. Russell has to explain this while holding to a referential theory of meaning. He took the radical step of claiming that ordinary names were not genuine (i.e., logically proper) names at all: The correct analysis of sentences involving ordinary names would replace them with definite descriptions. Thus, if I say 8, I'm really saying that "the F wrote *Middlemarch*," where "the F" states some definite description satisfied by the author. Some other description would be utilized in 9. So, fully explicated, such sentences are saying something of this form: "There is one and only one F, and whoever is F wrote *Middlemarch*."

Take the following example:

11. *David Hume was an atheist.*

The name would be replaced by a definite description and analyzed as before:

12. *The author of* A Treatise of Human Nature *was an atheist.*

(a) *There is at least one thing which was an author of* A Treatise on Human Nature.

(b) *There is at most one thing which was an author of* A Treatise on Human Nature.

(c) *Whatever is an author of* A Treatise on Human Nature *was an atheist.*

But surely many definite descriptions can correspond to "David Hume." For example, someone who knew of him primarily as a historian might associate the name with the description "the author of *The History of England.*" So which definite description is a name a disguise for? Russell seems to suggest that the reduction of an ordinary name to a definite description occurs not with sentence types but with particular sentence tokens. Thus, when used to assert a particular proposition, the name is equivalent to the description in the user's mind. This, of course, has the consequence that sentence meanings may vary not only between different speakers but also within the same speaker over time.

The only case in which names are not reduced to definite descriptions is that of *logically proper names*, which stand for things we are directly acquainted with. The paradigm cases are demonstratives standing for sense-data. Here, Russell's Empiricism reveals itself, since proper names are a linguistic analogue to the "simple ideas" of classical Empiricism. Russell's idea is that any sentence involving an ordinary name is to be analyzed into sentences involving definite descriptions; the names within these descriptions are to be likewise analyzed (for example, *A Treatise on Human Nature* is a name), and we will eventually hit a basic level at which no further analysis is possible. This is the level of logically proper names, which merely *indicate* particulars but have no descriptive content.

At this point, we should bring in another strand of Russell's theory, his distinction between *knowledge by acquaintance* and *knowledge by description.* This, in turn, rests on a distinction between knowledge of truths (i.e., knowing facts) and knowledge of things. Within the latter category, we can distinguish knowledge by acquaintance—which we acquire by being directly, noninferentially confronted with something—and knowledge by description—when we have information about something, relative to a description. Thus, descriptive knowledge of something involves knowing certain truths about it, as so described.

Russell supports a *Principle of Acquaintance*, which asserts that knowledge by description ultimately rests on knowledge by acquaintance: "Every proposition which we can understand must be composed wholly of constituents with which we are acquainted" ("Knowledge by Acquaintance and Knowledge by Description," 1911, p. 219). Thus, in making any sort of judgment, all components must be ultimately reduced to objects of acquaintance, which are "present to the mind." It is easy to see how this principle accords with his techniques of logical analysis. Basically, logic is a tool of ontological economy, showing that what purported to be referring expressions could be analyzed and reduced, and thereby shown to be mere constructions out of objects of acquaintance. Russell's version of Occam's Razor, his *logical constructionism,* states, "Wherever possible, replace inferred entities by logical constructions." So what can we be acquainted with? Russell suggests several categories. Firstly, unsurprisingly, we have sense-data. Secondly, we have universals, since every thought must include a general concept. To this, he adds the data of memory and of introspection. He vacillates over whether we have acquaintance with one's self as a separate entity, or whether to make the Humean reduction and conceive of it as a construct from one's ideas and impressions.

Inspired by his pupil Wittgenstein, Russell developed his earlier theories of logic, semantics, and epistemology into one integrated metaphysical theory which he called *Logical Atomism*. The project is to use logical analysis to reveal the basic structure of language, and hence of the world. As J. O. Urmson says, "The shortest account of Logical Atomism that can be given is that the world has the structure of Russell's mathematical logic" (p. 6). I will go into greater detail about the nature of this structure when I discuss Wittgenstein's *Tractatus*. For the moment, the basic idea is that the structure of the world is precisely isomorphic with the structure of a logically perfect language (i.e., that of *Principia Mathematica*). Thus, in getting clear on the structure of language, we discover the ultimate structure of the world. In such a language, for each particular there would correspond one and only one name. At the basic sentential level there would be atomic propositions, corresponding to atomic facts. Atomic propositions are constituted from objects of acquaintance. Atomic propositions are of two forms: (1) a particular possessing a property or (2) a relation between particulars. All other propositions are truth-functions of atomic propositions. Logical Atomism holds to a correspondence theory of truth: An atomic proposition is true it corresponds to an actual situation in the world; a complex/molecular proposition's truth is a function of the truth-values of the atomic propositions from which it is made up. Thus "*p* or *q*" is true if at least one of *p* or *q* is true.

We are acquainted with the components of atomic propositions. These include (1) sense-data, (2) universals; (3) thoughts—the contents of acts of memory or introspection. Atomic propositions are foundational, both logically and justificatory. The mark of atomicity is simplicity, that is unanalysibility. Wittgenstein also demanded logical independence of other atomic propositions. Each atomic proposition must include at least one name (i.e., singular referring expression), and at least one "incomplete" general expression, such as a property or relation term.

BIBLIOGRAPHY

Works by Russell
The following is a small sample of Russell's philosophical work:
The Analysis of Matter (London, 1921).
The Analysis of Mind (London, 1927).
Human Knowledge: Its Scope and Limits (London & New York: Routledge, 1994).
An Inquiry into Meaning and Truth (London & New York: Routledge, 1980).
Introduction to Mathematical Philosophy (London & New York: Routledge, 1993).
Mysticism and Logic (London: Allen & Unwin, 1919).
Our Knowledge of the External World (London & New York: Routledge, 1993).
The Philosophy of Logical Atomism (Open Court, 1985)
Principia Mathematica (with Alfred North Whitehead), (Cambridge University Press, 1962).
Principles of Mathematics (New York: W.W. Norton, 1995).
The Problems of Philosophy (Indianapolis: Hackett, 1990).

Further Reading

A good survey of the main Russellian themes is R. M. Sainsbury, *Russell* (London: Routledge, 1979).
     See also Sainsbury's article on Philosophical Logic in *Philosophy: A Guide Through the Subject,*
     (Oxford: 1995), which gives an unorthodox view of Russell's intentions, quite different to mine.
Stephen Neale, *Descriptions,* (Cambridge: MIT Press, 1990), offers a very contemporary and sophis-
     ticated elaboration and defense of a Russellian Theory of Descriptions.
For details on Russell's extraordinary life, see his own *Autobiography of Bertrand Russell*; and Ray
     Monk, *Bertrand Russell: The Spirit of Solitude,* (London: Jonathan Cape, 1996.)
The quote from J.O. Urmson was from his *Philosophical Analysis* (Oxford: Clarendon Press, 1956).

Descriptions

Bertrand Russell

We dealt in the preceding chapter with the words *all* and *some*; in this chapter we shall
consider the word the in the singular, and in the next chapter we shall consider the
word *the* in the plural. It may be thought excessive to devote two chapters to one word,
but to the philosophical mathematician it is a word of very great importance: like
Browning's Grammarian with the enclitic $\delta\epsilon$, I would give the doctrine of this word
if I were "dead from the waist down" and not merely in a prison.

   We have already had occasion to mention "descriptive functions," *i.e.* such
expressions as "the father of *x*" or "the sine of *x*." These are to be defined by first
defining "descriptions."

   A "description" may be of two sorts, definite and indefinite (or ambiguous).
An indefinite description is a phrase of the form "a so-and-so," and a definite description is a phrase of the form "the so-and-so" (in the singular). Let us begin with the
former.

   "Who did you meet?" "I met a man." "That is a very indefinite description."
We are therefore not departing from usage in our terminology. Our question is: What
do I really assert when I assert "I met a man"? Let us assume, for the moment, that
my assertion is true, and that in fact I met Jones. It is clear that what I assert is *not* "I
met Jones." I may say "I met a man, but it was not Jones"; in that case, though I lie, I
do not contradict myself, as I should do if when I say I met a man I really mean that I
met Jones. It is clear also that the person to whom I am speaking can understand what
I say, even if he is a foreigner and has never heard of Jones.

From *Introduction to Mathematical Philosophy,* (London & New York 1953). Reprinted by permission of Routledge.

But we may go further: not only Jones, but no actual man, enters into my statement. This becomes obvious when the statement is false, since then there is no more reason why Jones should be supposed to enter into the proposition than why anyone else should. Indeed the statement would remain significant, though it could not possibly be true, even if there were no man at all. "I met a unicorn" or "I met a sea-serpent" is a perfectly significant assertion, if we know what it would be to be a unicorn or a sea-serpent, *i.e.* what is the definition of these fabulous monsters. Thus it is only what we may call the *concept* that enters into the proposition. In the case of "unicorn," for example, there is only the concept: there is not also, somewhere among the shades, something unreal which may be called "a unicorn." Therefore, since it is significant (though false) to say "I met a unicorn," it is clear that this proposition, rightly analysed, does not contain a constituent "a unicorn," though it does contain the concept "unicorn."

The question of "unreality," which confronts us at this point, is a very important one. Misled by grammar, the great majority of those logicians who have dealt with this question have dealt with it on mistaken lines. They have regarded grammatical form as a surer guide in analysis than, in fact, it is. And they have not known what differences in grammatical form are important. "I met Jones" and "I met a man" would count traditionally as propositions of the same form, but in actual fact they are of quite different forms: the first names an actual person, Jones; while the second involves a propositional function, and becomes, when made explicit: "The function 'I met x and x is human' is sometimes true." (It will be remembered that we adopted the convention of using "sometimes" as not implying more than once.) This proposition is obviously not of the form "I met x," which accounts for the existence of the proposition "I met a unicorn" in spite of the fact that there is no such thing as "a unicorn."

For want of the apparatus of propositional functions, many logicians have been driven to the conclusion that there are unreal objects. It is argued, *e.g.* by Meinong,[1] that we can speak about "the golden mountain," "the round square," and so on; we can make true propositions of which these are the subjects; hence they must have some kind of logical being, since otherwise the propositions in which they occur would be meaningless. In such theories, it seems to me, there is a failure of that feeling for reality which ought to be preserved even in the most abstract studies. Logic, I should maintain, must no more admit a unicorn than zoology can; for logic is concerned with the real world just as truly as zoology, though with its more abstract and general features. To say that unicorns have an existence in heraldry, or in literature, or in imagination, is a most pitiful and paltry evasion. What exists in heraldry is not an animal, made of flesh and blood, moving and breathing of its own initiative. What exists is a picture, or a description in words. Similarly, to maintain that Hamlet, for example, exists in his own world, namely, in the world of Shakespeare's imagination, just as truly as (say) Napoleon existed in the ordinary world, is to say something deliberately confusing, or else confused to a degree which is scarcely credible. There is only one world, the "real" world: Shakespeare's imagination is part of it, and the thoughts that he had in writing Hamlet are real. So are the thoughts that we have in

---

[1] *Untersuchungen zur Gegenstandstheorie und Psychologie*, 1904.

reading the play. But it is of the very essence of fiction that only the thoughts, feelings, etc., in Shakespeare and his readers are real, and that there is not, in addition to them, an objective Hamlet. When you have taken account of all the feelings roused by Napoleon in writers and readers of history, you have not touched the actual man; but in the case of Hamlet you have come to the end of him. If no one thought about Hamlet, there would be nothing left of him; if no one had thought about Napoleon, he would have soon seen to it that some one did. The sense of reality is vital in logic, and whoever juggles with it by pretending that Hamlet has another kind of reality is doing a disservice to thought. A robust sense of reality is very necessary in framing a correct analysis of propositions about unicorns, golden mountains, round squares, and other such pseudo-objects.

In obedience to the feeling of reality, we shall insist that,in the analysis of propositions, nothing "unreal" is to be admitted. But, after all, if there *is* nothing unreal, how, it may be asked, *could* we *admit* anything unreal? The reply is that, in dealing with propositions, we are dealing in the first instance with symbols, and if we attribute significance to groups of symbols which have no significance, we shall fall into the error of admitting unrealities, in the only sense in which this is possible, namely, as objects described. In the proposition "I met a unicorn," the whole four words together make a significant proposition, and the word "unicorn" by itself is significant, in just the same sense as the word "man." But the *two* words "a unicorn" do not form a subordinate group having a meaning of its own. Thus if we falsely attribute meaning to these two words, we find ourselves saddled with "a unicorn," and with the problem how there can be such a thing in a world where there are no unicorns. "A unicorn" is an indefinite description which describes nothing. It is not an indefinite description which describes something unreal. Such a proposition as "*x* is unreal" only has meaning when "*x*" is a description, definite or indefinite; in that case the proposition will be true if "*x*" is a description which describes nothing. But whether the description "*x*" describes something or describes nothing, it is in any case not a constituent of the proposition in which it occurs; like "a unicorn" just now, it is not a subordinate group having a meaning of its own. All this results from the fact that, when "*x*" is a description, "*x* is unreal" or "*x* does not exist" is not nonsense, but is always significant and sometimes true.

We may now proceed to define generally the meaning of propositions which contain ambiguous descriptions. Suppose we wish to make some statement about "a so-and-so," where "so-and-so's" are those objects that have a certain property ϕ, *i.e.* those objects x for which the propositional function ϕx is true. (*E.g.* if we take "a man" as our instance of "a so-and-so," ϕx will be "x is human.") Let us now wish to assert the property ψ of "a so-and-so," *i.e.* we wish to assert that "a so-and-so" has that property which x has when ψx is true. (*E.g.* in the case of "I met a man," ψx will be "I met x.") Now the proposition that "a so-and-so" has the property ψ is *not* a proposition of the form "ψx." If it were, "a so-and-so" would have to be identical with x for a suitable x; and although (in a sense) this may be true in some cases, it is certainly not true in such a case as "a unicorn." It is just this fact, that the statement that a so-and-so has the property ψ is not of the form ψx, which makes it possible for "a so-and-so" to be, in a certain dearly definable sense, "unreal." The definition is as follows:—

The statement that "an object having the property ϕ has the property ψ"

means:

"The joint assertion of ϕx and ψx is not always false."

So far as logic goes, this is the same proposition as might be expressed by "some ϕ's are ψ's"; but rhetorically there is a difference, because in the one case there is a suggestion of singularity, and in the other case of plurality. This, however, is not the important point. The important point is that, when rightly analysed, propositions verbally about "a so-and-so" are found to contain no constituent represented by this phrase. And that is why such propositions can be significant even when there is no such thing as a so-and-so.

The definition of *existence*, as applied to ambiguous descriptions, results from what was said at the end of the preceding chapter. We say that "men exist" or "a man exists" if the propositional function "x is human" is sometimes true; and generally "a so-and-so" exists if "x is so-and-so" is sometimes true. We may put this in other language. The proposition "Socrates is a man" is no doubt *equivalent* to "Socrates is human," but it is not the very same proposition. The *is* of "Socrates is human" expresses the relation of subject and predicate; the *is* of "Socrates is a man" expresses identity. It is a disgrace to the human race that it has chosen to employ the same word "is" for these two entirely different ideas—a disgrace which a symbolic logical language of course remedies. The identity in "Socrates is a man" is identity between an object named (accepting "Socrates" as a name, subject to qualifications explained later) and an object ambiguously described. An object ambiguously described will "exist" when at least one such proposition is true, *i.e.* when there is at least one true proposition of the form "x is a so-and-so," where "x" is a name. It is characteristic of ambiguous (as opposed to definite) descriptions that there may be any number of true propositions of the above form—Socrates is a man, Plato is a man, etc. Thus "a man exists" follows from Socrates, or Plato, or anyone else. With definite descriptions, on the other hand, the corresponding form of proposition, namely, "x is the so-and-so" (where "x" is a name), can only be true for one value of x at most. This brings us to the subject of definite descriptions, which are to be defined in a way analogous to that employed for ambiguous descriptions, but rather more complicated.

We come now to the main subject of the present chapter, namely, the definition of the word *the* (in the singular). One very important point about the definition of "a so-and-so" applies equally to "the so-and-so"; the definition to be sought is a definition of propositions in which this phrase occurs, not a definition of the phrase itself in isolation. In the case of "a so-and-so," this is fairly obvious: no one could suppose that "a man" was a definite object, which could be defined by itself. Socrates is a man, Plato is a man, Aristotle is a man, but we cannot infer that "a man" means the same as "Socrates" means and also the same as "Plato" means and also the same as "Aristotle" means, since these three names have different meanings. Nevertheless, when we have enumerated all the men in the world, there is nothing left of which we can say, "This is a man, and not only so, but it is *the* 'a man,' the quintessential entity that is just an indefinite man without being anybody in particular." It is of course quite clear that whatever there is in the world is definite: if it is a man it is one definite man and not any other. Thus there cannot be such an entity as "a man" to be found in the world, as opposed to specific men. And accordingly it is natural that we do not define "a man" itself, but only the propositions in which it occurs.

In the case of "the so-and-so" this is equally true, though at first sight less obvious. We may demonstrate that this must be the case, by a consideration of the difference between a *name* and a *definite description*. Take the proposition, "Scott is the author of *Waverley*." We have here a name, "Scott," and a description, "the author of *Waverley*," which are asserted to apply to the same person. The distinction between a name and all other symbols may be explained as follows:—

A name is a simple symbol whose meaning is something that can only occur as subject, *i.e.* something of the kind that, in Chapter XIII, we defined as an "individual" or a "particular." And a "simple" symbol is one which has no parts that are symbols. Thus "Scott" is a simple symbol, because, though it has parts (namely, separate letters), these parts are not symbols. On the other hand, "the author of *Waverley*" is not a simple symbol, because the separate words that compose the phrase are parts which are symbols. If, as may be the case, whatever *seems* to be an "individual" is really capable of further analysis, we shall have to content ourselves with what may be called "relative individuals," which will be terms that, throughout the context in question, are never analysed and never occur otherwise than as subjects. And in that case we shall have correspondingly to content ourselves with "relative names." From the standpoint of our present problem, namely, the definition of descriptions, this problem, whether these are absolute names or only relative names, may be ignored, since it concerns different stages in the hierarchy of "types," whereas we have to compare such couples as "Scott" and "the author of *Waverley*," which both apply to the same object, and do not raise the problem of types. We may, therefore, for the moment, treat names as capable of being absolute; nothing that we shall have to say will depend upon this assumption, but the wording may be a little shortened by it.

We have, then, two things to compare: (1) a *name*, which is a simple symbol, directly designating an individual which is its meaning, and having this meaning in its own right, independently of the meanings of all other words; (2) a *description*, which consists of several words, whose meanings are already fixed, and from which results whatever is to be taken as the "meaning" of the description.

A proposition containing a description is not identical with what that proposition becomes when a name is substituted, even if the name names the same object as the description describes. "Scott is the author of *Waverley*" is obviously a different proposition from "Scott is Scott": the first is a fact in literary history, the second a trivial truism. And if we put anyone other than Scott in place of "the author of *Waverley*," our proposition would become false, and would therefore certainly no longer be the same proposition. But, it may be said, our proposition is essentially of the same form as (say) "Scott is Sir Walter," in which two names are said to apply to the same person. The reply is that, if "Scott is Sir Walter" really means "the person named 'Scott' is the person named 'Sir Walter,'" then the names are being used as descriptions: *i.e.* the individual, instead of being named, is being described as the person having that name. This is a way in which names are frequently used in practice, and there will, as a rule, be nothing in the phraseology to show whether they are being used in this way or *as* names. When a name is used directly, merely to indicate what we are speaking about, it is no part of the *fact* asserted, or of the falsehood if our assertion happens to be false: it is merely part of the symbolism by which we express our thought. What we want to express is something which might (for example) be translated into a foreign language; it is something for which the actual words are a vehicle, but of which they are no part. On the other hand, when we make a proposition about "the person called 'Scott,'" the actual name "Scott" enters into what we are asserting, and not merely into the language used in making the assertion. Our proposition will now be a different one if we substitute "the person called 'Sir Walter.'" But so long as we are using names as names, whether we say" Scott" or whether we say "Sir Walter" is as irrelevant to what we are asserting as whether we speak English or French. Thus so long as names are used *as* names, "Scott is Sir Walter" is the same trivial proposition as "Scott is Scott." This completes the proof that "Scott is the author of *Waverley*" is not the same proposition as results from substituting a name for "the author of *Waverley*," no matter what name may be substituted.

When we use a variable, and speak of a propositional function, ϕx say, the process of applying general statements about x to particular cases will consist in substituting a name for the letter "x," assuming that ϕ is a function which has individuals for its arguments. Suppose, for example, that ϕx is "always true"; let it be, say, the "law of identity," $x = x$. Then we may substitute for "x" any name we choose, and we shall obtain a true proposition. Assuming for the moment that "Socrates," "Plato," and "Aristotle" are names (a very rash assumption), we can infer from the law of identity that Socrates is Socrates, Plato is Plato, and Aristotle is Aristotle. But we shall commit a fallacy if we attempt to infer, without further premises, that the author of *Waverley* is the author of *Waverley*. This results from what we have just proved, that, if we substitute a name for "the author of *Waverley*" in a proposition, the proposition we obtain is a different one. That is to say, applying the result to our present case: If "x" is a name, "$x = x$" is not the same proposition as "the author of *Waverley* is the author of *Waverley*," no matter what name "x" may be. Thus from the fact that all propositions of the form "$x = x$" are true we cannot infer, without more ado, that the author of *Waverley* is the author of *Waverley*. In fact, propositions of the form "the so-and-so is the so-and-so" are not always true: it is necessary that the so-and-so should exist (a term which will be explained shortly). It is false that the present King of France is the present King of France, or that the round square is the round square. When we substitute a description for a name, propositional functions which are "always true" may become false, if the description describes nothing. There is no mystery in this as soon as we realise (what was proved in the preceding paragraph) that when we substitute a description the result is not a value of the propositional function in question.

We are now in a position to define propositions in which a definite description occurs. The only thing that distinguishes "the so-and-so" from "a so-and-so" is the implication of uniqueness. We cannot speak of "*the* inhabitant of London," because inhabiting London is an attribute which is not unique. We cannot speak about "the present King of France," because there is none; but we can speak about "the present King of England." Thus propositions about "the so-and-so" always imply the corresponding propositions about "a so-and-so," with the addendum that there is not more than one so-and-so. Such a proposition as "Scott is the author of *Waverley*" could not be true if *Waverley* had never been written, or if several people had written it; and no more could any other proposition resulting from a propositional function x by the substitution of "the author of *Waverley*" for "x." We may say that "the author of *Waverley*" means "the value of x for which 'x wrote *Waverley*' is true." Thus the proposition "the author of *Waverley* was Scotch," for example, involves:

(1) "x wrote *Waverley*" is not always false;

(2) "if x and y wrote *Waverley*, x and y are identical" is always true;

(3) "if x wrote *Waverley*, x was Scotch" is always true.

These three propositions, translated into ordinary language, state:

(1) at least one person wrote *Waverley*;

(2) at most one person wrote *Waverley*;

(3) whoever wrote *Waverley* was Scotch.

All these three are implied by "the author of *Waverley* was Scotch." Conversely, the three together (but no two of them) imply that the author of *Waverley* was Scotch. Hence the three together may be taken as defining what is meant by the proposition "the author of *Waverley* was Scotch."

We may somewhat simplify these three propositions. The first and second together are equivalent to: "There is a term c such that 'x wrote *Waverley*' is true when x is c and is false when x is not c." In other words, "There is a term c such that 'x wrote *Waverley*' is always equivalent to 'x is c.'" (Two propositions are "equivalent" when both are true or both are false.) We have here, to begin with, two functions of x, "x wrote *Waverley*" and "x is c" and we form a function of c by considering the equivalence of these two functions of x for all values of x; we then proceed to assert that the resulting function of c is "sometimes true," *i.e.* that it is true for at least one value of c. (It obviously cannot be true for more than one value of c.) These two conditions together are defined as giving the meaning of "the author of *Waverley* exists."

We may now define "the term satisfying the function ϕx exists." This is the general form of which the above is a particular case. "The author of *Waverley*" is "the term satisfying the function 'x wrote *Waverley*.'" And "the so-and-so" will always involve reference to some propositional function, namely, that which defines the property that makes a thing a so-and-so. Our definition is as follows:—

"The term satisfying the function ϕx exists" means:

"There is a term c such that ϕx is always equivalent to 'x is c.'"

In order to define "the author of *Waverley* was Scotch," we have still to take account of the third of our three propositions, namely, "Whoever wrote *Waverley* was Scotch." This will be satisfied by merely adding that the c in question is to be Scotch. Thus "the author of Waverley was Scotch" is:

"There is a term c such that (1) 'x wrote *Waverley*' is always equivalent to 'x is c,' (2) c is Scotch."

And generally: "the term satisfying ϕx satisfies ψx" is defined as meaning:

"There is a term c such that (1) ϕx is always equivalent to 'x is c,' (2) ψc is true."

This is the definition of propositions in which descriptions occur.

It is possible to have much knowledge concerning a term described, *i.e.* to know many propositions concerning "the so-and-so," without actually knowing what the so-and-so is, *i.e.* without knowing any proposition of the form "x is the so-and-so," where "x" is a name, In a detective story propositions about "the man who did the deed" are accumulated, in the hope that ultimately they will suffice to demonstrate that it was A who did the deed. We may even go so far as to say that, in all such knowledge as can be expressed in words—with the exception of "this" and "that" and a few other words of which the meaning varies on different occasions—no names, in the strict sense, occur, but what seem like names are really descriptions. We may inquire significantly whether Homer existed, which we could not do if "Homer" were a name. The proposition "the so-and-so exists" is significant, whether true or false; but if a is the so-and-so (where "a" is a name), the words "a exists" are meaningless. It is only of descriptions—definite or indefinite—that existence can be significantly asserted; for, if "a" is a name, it *must* name something: what does not name anything is not a name, and therefore, if intended to be a name, is a symbol devoid of meaning, whereas a description, like "the present King of France," does not become incapable of occurring significantly merely on the ground that it describes nothing, the reason being that it is a *complex* symbol, of which the meaning is derived from that of its constituent symbols. And so, when we ask whether Homer existed, we are using the word "Homer" as an abbreviated description: we may replace it by (say) "the author of the *Iliad* and the *Odyssey*." The same considerations apply to almost all uses of what look like proper names.

When descriptions occur in propositions, it is necessary to distinguish what may be called "primary" and "secondary" occurrences. The abstract distinction is as follows. A description has a "primary" occurrence when the proposition in which it occurs results from substituting the description for "x" in some propositional function ϕx; a description has a "secondary" occurrence when the result of substituting the description for x in ϕx gives only *part* of the proposition concerned. An instance will make this clearer. Consider "the present King of France is bald." Here "the present King of France" has a primary occurrence, and the proposition is false. Every proposition in which a description which describes nothing has a primary occurrence is false. But now consider "the present King of France is not bald." This is ambiguous. If we are first to take "x is bald," then substitute "the present King of France" for "x" and then deny the result, the occurrence of "the present King of France" is secondary and our proposition is true; but if we are to take "x is not bald" and substitute "the present King of France" for "x" then "the present King of France" has a primary occurrence and the proposition is false. Confusion of primary and secondary occurrences is a ready source of fallacies where descriptions are concerned.

Descriptions occur in mathematics chiefly in the form of *descriptive functions, i.e.* "the term having the relation R to *y*," or "the R of *y*" as we may say, on the analogy of "the father of *y*" and similar phrases. To say "the father of *y* is rich," for example, is to say that the following propositional function of *c*: "*c* is rich, and '*x* begat *y*' is always equivalent to '*x* is *c*,'" is "sometimes true," *i.e.* is true for at least one value of *c*. It obviously cannot be true for more than one value.

The theory of descriptions, briefly outlined in the present chapter, is of the utmost importance both in logic and in theory of knowledge. But for purposes of mathematics, the more philosophical parts of the theory are not essential, and have therefore been omitted in the above account, which has confined itself to the barest mathematical requisites.

The Philosophy of Logical Atomism

Bertrand Russell

II. PARTICULARS, PREDICATES, AND RELATIONS

I propose to begin today the analysis of facts and propositions, for in a way the chief thesis that I have to maintain is the legitimacy of analysis, because if one goes into what I call Logical Atomism that means that one does believe the world can be analysed into a number of separate things with relations and so forth, and that the sort of arguments that many philosophers use against analysis are not justifiable.

In a philosophy of logical atomism one might suppose that the first thing to do would be to discover the kinds of atoms out of which logical structures are composed. But I do not think that is quite the first thing; it is one of the early things, but not quite the first. There are two other questions that one has to consider, and one of these at least is prior. You have to consider:

1. Are the things that look like logically complex entities really complex?
2. Are they really entities?

The second question we can put off; in fact, I shall not deal with it fully until my last lecture. The first question, whether they are really complex, is one that you have to consider at the start. Neither of these questions is, as it stands, a very precise question. I do not pretend to start with precise questions. I do not think you can start with

From *The Philosophy of Logical Atomism* (Illinois: Open Court, 1985). Reprinted by pemission of Open Court.

anything precise. You have to achieve such precision as you can, as you go along. Each of these two questions, however, is *capable* of a precise meaning, and each is really important.

There is another question which comes still earlier, namely: what shall we take as prima facie examples of logically complex entities? That really is the first question of all to start with. What sort of things shall we regard as prima facie complex?

Of course, all the ordinary objects of daily life are apparently complex entities: such things as tables and chairs, loaves and fishes, persons and principalities and powers—they are all on the face of it complex entities. All the kinds of things to which we habitually give proper names are on the face of them complex entities: Socrates, Piccadilly, Rumania, Twelfth Night or anything you like to think of, to which you give a proper name, they are all apparently complex entities. They seem to be complex systems bound together into some kind of a unity, that sort of a unity that leads to the bestowal of a single appellation. I think it is the contemplation of this sort of apparent unity which has very largely led to the philosophy of monism, and to the suggestion that the universe as a whole is a single complex entity more or less in the sense in which these things are that I have been talking about.

For my part, I do not believe in complex entities of this kind, and it is not such things as these that I am going to take as the prima facie examples of complex entities. My reasons will appear more and more plainly as I go on. I cannot give them all today, but I can more or less explain what I mean in a preliminary way. Suppose, for example, that you were to analyse what appears to be a fact about Piccadilly. Suppose you made any statement about Piccadilly, such as: 'Piccadilly is a pleasant street.' If you analyse a statement of that sort correctly, I believe you will find that the fact corresponding to your statement does not contain any constituent corresponding to the word 'Piccadilly'. The word 'Piccadilly' will form part of many significant propositions, but the facts corresponding to these propositions do not contain any single constituent, whether simple or complex, corresponding to the word 'Piccadilly'. That is to say, if you take language as a guide in your analysis of the fact expressed, you will be led astray in a statement of that sort. The reasons for that I shall give at length in Lecture VI, and partly also in Lecture VII, but I could say in a preliminary way certain things that would make you understand what I mean. 'Piccadilly', on the face of it, is the name for a certain portion of the earth's surface, and I suppose, if you wanted to define it, you would have to define it as a series of classes of material entities, namely those which, at varying times, occupy that portion of the earth's surface. So that you would find that the logical status of Piccadilly is bound up with the logical status of series and classes, and if you are going to hold Piccadilly as real, you must hold that series of classes are real, and whatever sort of metaphysical status you assign to them, you must assign to it. As you know, I believe that series and classes are of the nature of logical fictions: therefore that thesis, if it can be maintained, will dissolve Piccadilly into a fiction. Exactly similar remarks will apply to other instances: Rumania, Twelfth Night, and Socrates. Socrates, perhaps, raises some special questions, because the question what constitutes a person has special difficulties in it. But, for the sake of argument, one might identify Socrates with the series of his experiences. He would be really a series of classes, because one has many experiences simultaneously. Therefore he comes to be very like Piccadilly.

Considerations of that sort seem to take us away from such prima facie complex entities as we started with to others as being more stubborn and more deserving of analytical attention, namely facts. I explained last time what I meant by a fact, namely, that sort of thing that makes a proposition true or false, the sort of thing which is the case when your statement is true and is not the case when your statement is false. Facts are, as I said last time, plainly something you have to take account of if you are going to give a complete account of the world. You cannot do that by merely enumerating the particular things that are in it: you must also mention the relations of these things, and their properties, and so forth, all of which are facts, so that facts certainly belong to an account of the objective world, and facts do seem much more clearly complex and much more not capable of being explained away than things like Socrates and Rumania. However you may explain away the meaning of the word 'Socrates', you will still be left with the truth that the proposition 'Socrates is mortal' expresses a fact. You may not know exactly what Socrates means, but it is quite clear that 'Socrates is mortal' does express a fact. There is clearly some valid meaning in saying that the fact expressed by 'Socrates is mortal' is *complex*. The things in the world have various properties, and stand in various relations to each other. That they have these properties and relations are *facts*, and the things and their qualities or relations are quite clearly in some sense or other components of the facts that have those qualities or relations. The analysis of apparently complex *things* such as we started with can be reduced by various means, to the analysis of facts which are apparently about those things. Therefore it is with the analysis of *facts* that one's consideration of the problem of complexity must begin, not with the analysis of apparently complex things.

The complexity of a fact is evidenced, to begin with, by the circumstance that the proposition which asserts a fact consists of several words, each of which may occur in other contexts. Of course, sometimes you get a proposition expressed by a single word but if it is expressed fully it is bound to contain several words. The proposition 'Socrates is mortal' may be replaced by 'Plato is mortal' or by 'Socrates is human'; in the first case we alter the subject, in the second the predicate. It is clear that all the propositions in which the word 'Socrates' occurs have something in common, and again all the propositions in which the word 'mortal' occurs have something in common, something which they do not have in common with all propositions, but only with those which are about Socrates or mortality. It is clear, I think, that the facts corresponding to propositions in which the word 'Socrates' occurs have something in common corresponding to the common word 'Socrates' which occurs in the propositions, so that you have that sense of complexity to begin with, that in a fact you can get something which it may have in common with other facts, just as you may have 'Socrates is human' and 'Socrates is mortal', both of them facts, and both having to do with Socrates, although Socrates does not constitute the whole of either of these facts. It is quite clear that in that sense there is a possibility of cutting up a fact into component parts, of which one component may be altered without altering the others, and one component may occur in certain other facts though not in all other facts. I want to make it clear, to begin with, that there is a sense in which facts can be analysed. I am not concerned with all the difficulties of any analysis, but only with meeting the prima facie objections of philosophers who think you really cannot analyse at all.

I am trying as far as possible again this time, as I did last time, to start with perfectly plain truisms. My desire and wish is that the things I start with should be so obvious that you wonder why I spend my time stating them. This is what I aim at, because the point of philosophy is to start with something so simple as not to seem worth stating, and to end with something so paradoxical that no one will believe it.

One prima facie mark of complexity in propositions is the fact that they are expressed by several words. I come now to another point, which applies primarily to propositions and thence derivatively to facts. You can understand a proposition when you understand the words of which it is composed even though you never heard the proposition before. That seems a very humble property, but it is a property which marks it as complex and distinguishes it from words whose meaning is simple. When you know the vocabulary, grammar, and syntax of language, you can understand a proposition in that language even though you never saw it before. In reading a newspaper, for example, you become aware of a number of statements which are new to you, and they are intelligible to you immediately, in spite of the fact that they are new, because you understand the words of which they are composed. This characteristic, that you can understand a proposition through the understanding of its component words, is absent from the component words when those words express something simple. Take the word 'red', for example, and suppose as one always has to do—that 'red' stands for a particular shade of colour. You will pardon that assumption, but one never can get on otherwise. You cannot understand the meaning of the word 'red' except through seeing red things. There is no other way in which it can be done. It is no use to learn languages, or to look up dictionaries. None of these things will help you to understand the meaning of the word 'red'. In that way it is quite different from the meaning of a proposition. Of course, you can give a definition of the word 'red', and here it is very important to distinguish between a definition and an analysis. All analysis is only possible in regard to what is complex, and it always depends, in the last analysis, upon direct acquaintance with the objects which are the meanings of certain simple symbols. It is hardly necessary to observe that one does not define a thing but a symbol. (A 'simple' symbol is a symbol whose parts are not symbols.) A simple symbol is quite a different thing from a simple thing. Those objects which it is impossible to symbolize otherwise than by simple symbols may be called 'simple', while those which can be symbolized by a combination of symbols may be called 'complex'. This is, of course, a preliminary definition, and perhaps somewhat circular, but that doesn't much matter at this stage.

I have said that 'red' could not be understood except by seeing red things. You might object to that on the ground that you can define red for example, as 'The colour with the greatest wavelength'. That, you might say, is a definition of 'red' and a person could understand that definition even if he had seen nothing red, provided he understood the physical theory of colour. But that does not really constitute the meaning of the word 'red' in the very slightest. If you take such a proposition as 'This is red' and substitute for it 'This has the colour with the greatest wavelength', you have a different proposition altogether. You can see that at once, because a person who knows nothing of the physical theory of colour can understand the proposition 'This is red', and can know that it is true, but cannot know that 'This has the colour which has the greatest wavelength'. Conversely, you might have a hypothetical person who could not see red, but who understood the physical theory of colour and could apprehend the proposition 'This has the colour with the greatest wavelength', but who would not be able to understand the proposition 'This is red' as understood by the normal uneducated person. Therefore it is clear that if you define 'red' as 'The colour with the greatest wavelength', you are not giving the actual meaning of the word at all; you are simply giving a true description, which is quite a different thing, and the propositions which result are different propositions from those in which the word 'red' occurs. In that sense the word 'red' cannot be defined, though in the sense in which a correct description constitutes a definition it can be defined. In the sense of analysis you cannot define 'red'. That is how it is that dictionaries are able to get on, because a dictionary professes to define all words in the language by means of words in the language, and therefore it is clear that a dictionary must be guilty of a vicious circle somewhere, but it manages it by means of correct descriptions.

I have made it clear, then, in what sense I should say that the word 'red' is a simple symbol and the phrase 'This is red' a complex symbol. The word 'red' can only be understood through acquaintance with the object, whereas the phrase 'Roses are red' can be understood if you know what 'red' is and what 'roses' are, without ever having heard the phrase before. That is a clear mark of what is complex. It is the mark of a complex symbol, and also the mark of the object symbolized by the complex symbol. That is to say, propositions are complex symbols, and the facts they stand for are complex.

The whole question of the meaning of words is very full of complexities and ambiguities in ordinary language. When one person uses a word, he does not mean by it the same thing as another person means by it. I have often heard it said that that is a misfortune. That is a mistake. It would be absolutely fatal if people meant the same things by their words. It would make all intercourse impossible, and language the most hopeless and useless thing imaginable, because the meaning you attach to your words must depend on the nature of the objects you are acquainted with, and since different people are acquainted with different objects, they would not be able to talk to each other unless they attached quite different meanings to their words. We should have to talk only about logic—a not wholly undesirable result. Take, for example, the word 'Piccadilly'. We, who are acquainted with Piccadilly, attach quite a different meaning to that word from any which could be attached to it by a person who had never been in London: and, supposing that you travel in foreign parts and expatiate on Piccadilly, you will convey to your hearers entirely different propositions from those in your mind. They will know Piccadilly as an important street in London; they may know a lot about it, but they will not know just the things one knows when one is walking along it. If you were to insist on language which was unambiguous, you would be unable to tell people at home what you had seen in foreign parts. It would be altogether incredibly inconvenient to have an unambiguous language, and therefore mercifully we have not got one.

Analysis is not the same thing as definition. You can define a term by means of a correct description, but that does not constitute an analysis. It is analysis, not definition, that we are concerned with at the present moment, so I will come back to the question of analysis.

We may lay down the following provisional definitions:

That the components of a proposition are the symbols we must understand in order to understand the proposition;

That the components of the fact which makes a proposition true or false, as the case may be, are the *meanings* of the symbols which we must understand in order to understand the proposition.

That is not absolutely correct, but it will enable you to understand my meaning. One reason why it fails of correctness is that it does not apply to words which, like 'or' and 'not', are parts of propositions without corresponding to any part of the corresponding facts. This is a topic for Lecture III.

I call these definitions *preliminary* because they start from the complexity of the proposition, which they define psychologically, and proceed to the complexity of the fact, whereas it is quite clear that in an orderly, proper procedure it is the complexity of the fact that you would start from. It is also clear that the complexity of the fact cannot be something merely psychological. If in astronomical fact the earth moves round the sun, that is genuinely complex. It is not that you think it complex, it is a sort of genuine objective complexity, and therefore one ought in a proper, orderly procedure to start from the complexity of the world and arrive at the complexity of the proposition. The only reason for going the other way round is that in all abstract matters symbols are easier to grasp. I doubt, however, whether complexity, in that fundamental objective sense in which one starts from complexity of a fact, is definable at all. You cannot analyse what you mean by complexity in that sense. You must just apprehend it—at least so I am inclined to think. There is nothing one could say about it, beyond giving criteria such as I have been giving. Therefore, when you cannot get a real proper analysis of a thing, it is generally best to talk round it without professing that you have given an exact definition.

It might be suggested that complexity is essentially to do with symbols, or that it is essentially psychological. I do not think it would be possible seriously to maintain either of these views, but they are the sort of views that will occur to one, the sort of thing that one would try, to see whether it would work. I do not think they will do at all. When we come to the principles of symbolism which I shall deal with in Lecture VII, I shall try to persuade you that in a logically correct symbolism there will always be a certain fundamental identity of structure between a fact and the symbol for it; and that the complexity of the symbol corresponds very closely with the complexity of the facts symbolized by it. Also, as I said before, it is quite directly evident to inspection that the fact, for example, that two things stand in a certain relation to one another—e.g. that this is to the left of that—is itself objectively complex, and not merely that the apprehension of it is complex. The fact that two things stand in a certain relation to each other, or any statement of that sort, has a complexity all of its own. I shall therefore in future assume that there is an objective complexity in the world, and that it is mirrored by the complexity of propositions.

A moment ago I was speaking about the great advantages that we derive from the logical imperfections of language, from the fact that our words are all ambiguous. I propose now to consider what sort of language a logically perfect language would be. In a logically perfect language the words in a proposition would correspond one by one with the components of the corresponding fact, with the exception of such words as 'or', 'not', 'if', 'then', which have a different function. In a logically perfect language, there will be one word and no more for every simple object, and everything that is not simple will be expressed by a combination of words, by a combination derived, of course, from the words for the simple things that enter in, one word for each simple component. A language of that sort will be completely analytic, and will show at a glance the logical structure of the facts asserted or denied. The language which is set forth in *Principia Mathematica* is intended to be a language of that sort. It is a language which has only syntax and no vocabulary whatsoever. Barring the omission of a vocabulary I maintain that it is quite a nice language. It aims at being the sort of a language that, if you add a vocabulary, would be a logically perfect language. Actual languages are not logically perfect in this sense, and they cannot possibly be, if they are to serve the purposes of daily life. A logically perfect language, if it could be constructed, would not only be intolerably prolix, but, as regards its vocabulary, would be very largely private to one speaker. That is to say, all the names that it would use would be private to that speaker and could not enter into the language of another speaker. It could not use proper names for Socrates or Piccadilly or Rumania for the reasons which I went into earlier in the lecture. Altogether you would find that it would be a very inconvenient language indeed. That is one reason why logic is so very backward as a science, because the needs of logic are so extraordinarily different from the needs of daily life. One wants a language in both, and unfortunately it is logic that has to give way, not daily life. I shall, however, assume that we have constructed a logically perfect language, and that we are going on State occasions to use it, and I will now come back to the question which I intended to start with, namely, the analysis of facts.

The simplest imaginable facts are those which consist in the possession of a quality by some particular thing. Such facts, say, as 'This is white'. They have to be taken in a very sophisticated sense. I do not want you to think about the piece of chalk I am holding, but of what you see when you look at the chalk. If one says, 'This is white' it will do for about as simple a fact as you can get hold of. The next simplest would be those in which you have a relation between two facts, such as: 'This is to the left of that.' Next you come to those where you have a triadic relation between three particulars. (An instance which Royce gives as '*A* gives *B* to *C*.') So you get relations which require as their minimum three terms, those we call triadic relations; and those which require four terms, which we call tetradic, and so on. There you have a whole infinite hierarchy of facts—facts in which you have a thing and a quality, two things and a relation, three things and a relation, four things and a relation, and so on. That whole hierarchy constitutes what I call *atomic* facts, and they are the simplest sort of fact. You can distinguish among them some simpler than others, because the ones containing a quality are simpler than those in which you have, say, a pentadic relation, and so on. The whole lot of them, taken together, are as facts go very simple, and are what I call atomic facts. The propositions expressing them are what I call *atomic propositions*.

In every atomic fact there is one component which is naturally expressed by a verb (or, in the case of quality, it may be expressed by a predicate, by an adjective). This one component is a quality or dyadic or triadic or tetradic … relation. It would be very convenient, for purposes of talking about these matters, to call a quality a 'monadic relation' and I shall do so; it saves a great deal of circumlocution.

In that case, you can say that all atomic propositions assert relations of varying orders. Atomic facts contain, besides the relation, the terms of the relation—one term if it is a monadic relation, two if it is dyadic, and so on. These 'terms' which come into atomic facts I define as 'particulars'.

> Particulars = terms of relations in atomic facts. Df.

That is the definition of particulars, and I want to emphasize it because the definition of a particular is something purely logical. The question whether this or that is a particular, is a question to be decided in terms of that logical definition. In order to understand the definition it is not necessary to know beforehand 'This is a particular' or 'That is a particular'. It remains to be investigated what particulars you can find in the world, if any. The whole question of what particulars you actually find in the real world is a purely empirical one which does not interest the logician as such. The logician as such never gives instances, because it is one of the tests of a logical proposition that you need not know anything whatsoever about the real world in order to understand it.

Passing from atomic facts to atomic propositions, the word expressing a monadic relation or quality is called a 'predicate', and the word expressing a relation of any higher order would generally be a verb, sometimes a single verb, sometimes a whole phrase. At any rate the verb gives the essential nerve, as it were, of the relation. The other words that occur in the atomic propositions, the words that are not the predicate or verb, may be called the subjects of the proposition. There will be one subject in a monadic proposition, two in a dyadic one, and so on. The subjects in a proposition will be the words expressing the terms of the relation which is expressed by the proposition.

The only kind of word that is theoretically capable of standing for a particular is a *proper name*, and the whole matter of proper names is rather curious.

> Proper names = words for particulars. Df.

I have put that down although, as far as a common language goes, it is obviously false. It is true that if you try to think how you are to talk about particulars, you will see that you cannot ever talk about a particular particular except by means of a proper name. You cannot use general words except by way of description. How are you to express in words an atomic proposition? An atomic proposition is one which does mention actual particulars, not merely describe them but actually name them, and you can only name them by means of names. You can see at once for yourself, therefore, that every other part of speech except proper names is obviously quite incapable of standing for a particular. Yet it does seem a little odd if, having made a dot on the blackboard, I call it 'John'. You would be surprised, and yet how are you to know otherwise what it is that I am speaking of. If I say, 'The dot that is on the right-hand side is white' that is a proposition. If I say 'This is white' that is quite a different proposition. 'This' will do very well while we are all here and can see it, but if I wanted to talk about it tomorrow it would be convenient to have christened it and called it 'John'. There is no other way in which you can mention it. You cannot really mention *it* itself except by means of a name.

What pass for names in language, like 'Socrates', 'Plato', and so forth, were originally intended to fulfil this function of standing for particulars, and we do accept, in ordinary daily life, as particulars all sorts of things that really are not so. The names that we commonly use, like 'Socrates', are really abbreviations for descriptions; not only that, but what they describe are not particulars but complicated systems of classes or series. A name, in the narrow logical sense of a word whose meaning is a particular, can only be applied to a particular with which the speaker is acquainted, because you cannot name anything you are not acquainted with. You remember, when Adam named the beasts, they came before him one by one, and he became acquainted with them and named them. We are not acquainted with Socrates, and therefore cannot name him. When we use the word 'Socrates', we are really using a description. Our thought may be rendered by some such phrase as, 'The Master of Plato', or 'The philosopher who drank the hemlock', or 'The person whom logicians assert to be mortal', but we certainly do not use the name as a name in the proper sense of the word.

That makes it very difficult to get any instance of a name at all in the proper strict logical sense of the word. The only words one does use as names in the logical sense are words like 'this' or 'that'. One can use 'this' as a name to stand for a particular with which one is acquainted at the moment. We say 'This is white'. If you agree that 'This is white', meaning the 'this' that you see, you are using 'this' as a proper name. But if you try to apprehend the proposition that I am expressing when I say 'This is white', you cannot do it. If you mean this piece of chalk as a physical object, then you are not using a proper name. It is only when you use 'this' quite strictly, to stand for an actual object of sense, that it is really a proper name. And in that it has a very odd property for a proper name, namely that it seldom means the same thing two moments running and does not mean the same thing to the speaker and to the hearer. It is an *ambiguous* proper name, but it is really a proper name all the same, and it is almost the only thing I can think of that is used properly and logically in the sense that I was talking of for a proper name. The importance of proper names, in the sense of which I am talking, is in the sense of logic, not of daily life. You can see why it is that in the logical language set forth in *Principia Mathematica* there are not any names, because there we are not interested in particular particulars but only in general particulars, if I may be allowed such a phrase.

Particulars have this peculiarity, among the sort of objects that you have to take account of in an inventory of the world, that each of them stands entirely alone and is completely self-subsistent. It has the sort of self-subsistence that used to belong to substance, except that it usually only persists through a very short time, so far as our experience goes. That is to say, each particular that there is in the world does not in any way logically depend upon any other particular. Each one might happen to be the whole universe; it is a merely empirical fact that this is not the case. There is no reason why you should not have a universe consisting of one particular and nothing else. That is a peculiarity of particulars. In the same way, in order to understand a name for a particular, the only thing necessary is to be acquainted with that particular. When you are acquainted with that particular, you have a full, adequate, and complete understanding of the name, and no further information is required. No further information as to the facts that are true of that particular would enable you to have a fuller understanding of the meaning of the name … .

III. ATOMIC AND MOLECULAR PROPOSITIONS

I did not quite finish last time the syllabus that I intended for Lecture II, so I must first do that.

I had been speaking at the end of my last lecture on the subject of the self-subsistence of particulars, how each particular has its being independently of any other and does not depend upon anything else for the logical possibility of its existence. I compared particulars with the old conception of substance, that is to say, they have the quality of self-subsistence that used to belong to substance, but not the quality of persistence through time. A particular, as a rule, is apt to last for a very short time indeed, not an instant but a very short time. In that respect particulars differ from the old substances but in their logical position they do not. There is, as you know, a logical theory which is quite opposed to that view, a logical theory according to which, if you really understood any one thing, you would understand everything. I think that rests upon a certain confusion of ideas. When you have acquaintance with a particular, you understand that particular itself quite fully, independently of the fact that there are a great many propositions about it that you do not know, but propositions concerning the particular are not necessary to be known in order that you may know what the particular itself is. It is rather the other way round. In order to understand a proposition in which the name of a particular occurs, you must already be acquainted with that particular. The acquaintance with the simpler is presupposed in the understanding of the more complex, but the logic that I should wish to combat maintains that in order thoroughly to know any one thing, you must know all its relations and all its qualities, all the propositions in fact in which that thing is mentioned; and you deduce of course from that that the world is an interdependent whole. It is on a basis of that sort that the logic of monism develops. Generally one supports this theory by talking about the 'nature' of a thing, assuming that a thing has something which you call its 'nature' which is generally elaborately confounded and distinguished from the thing, so that you can get a comfortable see-saw which enables you to deduce whichever results suit the moment. The 'nature' of the thing would come to mean all the true propositions in which the thing is mentioned. Of course it is clear that since everything has relations to everything else, you cannot know all the facts of which a thing is a constituent without having some knowledge of everything in the universe. When you realize that what one calls 'knowing a particular' merely means acquaintance with that particular and is presupposed in the understanding of any proposition in which that particular is mentioned, I think you also realize that you cannot take the view that the understanding of the name of the particular presupposes knowledge of all the propositions concerning that particular.

I should like to say about understanding, that that phrase is often used mistakenly. People speak of 'understanding the universe' and so on. But, of course, the only thing you can really understand (in the strict sense of the word) is a symbol, and to understand a symbol is to know what it stands for.

I pass on from particulars to predicates and relations and what we mean by understanding the words that we use for predicates and relations. A very great deal of what I am saying in this course of lectures consists of ideas which I derived from my friend Wittgenstein. But I have had no opportunity of knowing how far his ideas have changed since August 1914, nor whether he is alive or dead, so I cannot make anyone but myself responsible for them.

Understanding a predicate is quite a different thing from understanding a name. By a predicate, as you know, I mean the word that is used to designate a quality such as red, white, square, round, and the understanding of a word like that involves a different kind of act of mind from that which is involved in understanding a name. To understand a name you must be acquainted with the particular of which it is a name, and you must know that it is the name of that particular. You do not, that is to say, have any suggestion of the form of a proposition, whereas in understanding a predicate you do. To understand 'red', for instance, is to understand what is meant by saying that a thing is red. You have to bring in the form of a proposition. You do not have to know, concerning any particular 'this', that 'This is red' but you have to know what is the meaning of saying that anything is red. You have to understand what one would call 'being red'. The importance of that is in connection with the theory of types, which I shall come to later on. It is in the fact that a predicate can never occur except as a predicate. When it seems to occur as a subject, the phrase wants amplifying and explaining, unless, of course, you are talking about the word itself. You must say '"Red" is a predicate', but then you must have 'red' in inverted commas because you are talking about the word 'red'. When you understand 'red' it means that you understand propositions of the form that 'x is red'. So that the understanding of a predicate is something a little more complicated than the understanding of a name, just because of that. Exactly the same applies to relations, and in fact all those things that are not particulars. Take, e.g., 'before' in 'x is before y': you understand 'before' when you understand what that would mean if x and y were given. I do not mean you know whether it is true, but you understand the proposition. Here again the same thing applies. A relation can never occur except as a relation, never as a subject. You will always have to put in hypothetical terms, if not real ones, such as 'If I say that x is before y, I assert a relation between x and y'. It is in this way that you will have to expand such a statement as '"Before" is a relation' in order to get its meaning.

The different sorts of words, in fact, have different sorts of uses and must be kept always to the right use and not to the wrong use, and it is fallacies arising from putting symbols to wrong uses that lead to the contradictions concerned with types.

There is just one more point before I leave the subjects I meant to have dealt with last time, and that is a point which came up in discussion at the conclusion of the last lecture, namely, that if you like you can get a formal reduction of (say) monadic relations to dyadic, or of dyadic to triadic, or of all the relations below a certain order to all above that order, but the converse reduction is not possible. Suppose one takes, for example, 'red'. One says, 'This is red', 'That is red', and so forth. Now, if anyone is of the opinion that there is reason to try to get on without subject-predicate propositions, all that is necessary is to take some standard red thing and have a relation which one might call 'colour-likeness', sameness of colour, which would be a direct relation, not consisting in having a certain colour. You can then define the things which are red, as all the things that have colour-likeness to this standard thing. That is practically the treatment that Berkeley and Hume recommended, except that they did not recognize that they were reducing qualities to relations, but thought they were getting rid of 'abstract ideas' altogether. You can perfectly well do in that way a formal reduction of predicates to relations. There is no objection to that either empirically or logically. If you think it is worth while you can proceed in exactly the same way with dyadic relations, which you can reduce to triadic. Royce used to have a great affection for that process. For some reason he always liked triadic relations better than dyadic ones; he illustrated his preference in his contributions to mathematical logic and the principles of geometry.

All that is possible. I do not myself see any particular point in doing it as soon as you have realized that it is possible. I see no particular reason to suppose that the simplest relations that occur in the world are (say) of order *n*, but there is no *a priori* reason against it. The converse reduction, on the other hand, is quite impossible except in certain special cases where the relation has some special properties. For example, dyadic relations can be reduced to sameness of predicate when they are symmetrical and transitive. Thus, e.g. the relation of colour-likeness will have the property that if *A* has exact colour-likeness with *B* and *B* with *C*, then *A* has exact colour-likeness with *C*; and if *A* has it with *B*, *B* has it with *A*. But the case is otherwise with asymmetrical relations.

Take for example '*A* is greater than *B*'. It is obvious that '*A* is greater than *B*' does not consist in *A* and *B* having a common predicate, for if it did it would require that *B* should also be greater than *A*. It is also obvious that it does not consist merely in their having different predicates, because if *A* has a different predicate from *B*, *B* has a different predicate from *A*, so that in either case, whether of sameness or difference of predicate, you get a symmetrical relation. For instance, if *A* is of a different colour from *B*, *B* is of a different colour from *A*. Therefore when you get symmetrical relations, you have relations which it is formally possible to reduce to either sameness of predicate or difference of predicate, but when you come to asymmetrical relations there is no such possibility. This impossibility of reducing dyadic relations to sameness or difference of predicate is a matter of a good deal of importance in connection with traditional philosophy, because a great deal of traditional philosophy depends upon the assumption that every proposition really is of the subject-predicate form, and that is certainly not the case. That theory dominates a great part of traditional metaphysics and the old idea of substance and a good deal of the theory of the Absolute, so that that sort of logical outlook which had its imagination dominated by the theory that you could always express a proposition in a subject-predicate form has had a very great deal of influence upon traditional metaphysics.

That is the end of what I ought to have said last time, and I come on now to the proper topic of today's lecture, that is *molecular* propositions. I call them molecular propositions because they contain other propositions which you may call their atoms, and by molecular propositions I mean propositions having such words as 'or', 'if', 'and', and so forth. If I say, 'Either today is Tuesday, or we have all made a mistake in being here', that is the sort of proposition that I mean that is molecular. Or if I say, 'If it rains, I shall bring my umbrella', that again is a molecular proposition because it contains the two parts 'It rains' and 'I shall bring my umbrella'. If I say, 'It did rain and I did bring my umbrella', that again is a molecular proposition. Or if I say, 'The supposition of its raining is incompatible with the supposition of my not bringing my umbrella', that again is a molecular proposition. There are various propositions of that sort, which you can complicate *ad infinitum*. They are built up out of propositions related by such words as 'or', 'if', 'and', and so on. You remember that I defined an atomic proposition as one which contains a single verb. Now there are two different lines of complication in proceeding from these to more complex propositions. There is the line that I have just been talking about, where you proceed to molecular propositions, and there is another line which I shall come to in a later lecture, where you have not two related propositions, but one proposition containing two or more verbs. Examples are got from believing, wishing, and so forth. 'I believe Socrates is mortal.' You have there two verbs, 'believe' and 'is'. Or 'I wish I were immortal'. Anything like that where you have a wish or a belief or a doubt involves two verbs. A lot of psychological attitudes involve two verbs, not, as it were, crystallized out, but two verbs within the one unitary proposition. But I am talking today about molecular propositions and you will understand that you can make propositions with 'or' and 'and' and so forth, where the constituent propositions are not atomic, but for the moment we can confine ourselves to the case where the constituent propositions are atomic. When you take an atomic proposition, or one of these propositions like 'believing', when you take any proposition of that sort, there is just one fact which is pointed to by the proposition, pointed to either truly or falsely. The essence of a proposition is that it can correspond in two ways with a fact, in what one may call the true way or the false way. You might illustrate it in a picture like this:

True: $\overrightarrow{\text{Prop. Fact}}$

False: $\text{Fact} \overrightarrow{\text{Prop.}}$

Supposing you have the proposition 'Socrates is mortal', either there would be the fact that Socrates is mortal or there would be the fact that Socrates is not mortal. In the one case it corresponds in a way that makes the proposition true, in the other case in a way that makes the proposition false. That is one way in which a proposition differs from a name.

There are, of course, two propositions corresponding to every fact, one true and one false. There are no false facts, so you cannot get one fact for every proposition but only for every pair of propositions. All that applies to atomic propositions. But when you take such a proposition as '*p* or *q*', 'Socrates is mortal or Socrates is living still', there you will have two different facts involved in the truth or the falsehood of your proposition '*p* or *q*'. There will be the fact that corresponds to *p* and there will be the fact that corresponds to *q*, and both of those facts are relevant in discovering the truth or falsehood of '*p* or *q*'. I do not suppose there is in the world a single disjunctive fact corresponding to '*p* or *q*'. It does not look plausible that in the actual objective world there are facts going about which you could describe as '*p* or *q*', but I would not lay too much stress on what strikes one as plausible: it is not a thing you can rely on altogether. For the present I do not think any difficulties will arise from the supposition that the truth or falsehood of this proposition '*p* or *q*' does not depend upon a single objective fact which is disjunctive but depends on the two facts one of which corresponds to p and the other to q: p will have a fact corresponding to it and q will have a fact corresponding it. That is to say, the truth or falsehood of this proposition 'p or q' depends upon two facts and not upon one, as p does and as q does. Generally speaking, as regards these things that you make up out of two propositions, the whole of what is necessary in order to know their meaning is to know under what circumstances they are true, given the truth or falsehood of p and the truth or falsehood of q. That is perfectly obvious. You have as a schema, for 'p or q', using

'*TT*' for 'p and q both true'

'*TF*' for 'p true and q false', etc.

TT	*TF*	*FT*	*FF*
T	*T*	*T*	*F*

where the bottom line states the truth or the falsehood of 'p or q'. You must not look about the real world for an object which you can call 'or', and say, 'Now, look at this. This is "or".' There is no such thing, and if you try to analyse 'p or q' in that way you will get into trouble. But the meaning of disjunction will be entirely explained by the above schema.

I call these things truth-functions of propositions, when the truth or falsehood of the molecular proposition depends only on the truth or falsehood of the propositions that enter into it. The same applies to 'p and q' and 'if p then q' and 'p is incompatible with q'. When I say 'p is incompatible with q' I simply mean to say that they are not both true. I do not mean any more. Those sorts of things are called truth-functions, and these molecular propositions that we are dealing with today are instances of truth-functions. If p is a proposition, the statement that 'I believe p' does not depend for its truth or falsehood, simply upon the truth or falsehood of p, since I believe some but not all true propositions and some but not all false propositions.

Introduction to Wittgenstein's
Tractatus Logico-Philosophicus

Ludwig Wittgenstein was born in Vienna in 1889, into the family of a wealthy Austrian industrialist. He was one of eight children, three of whom committed suicide. Unlike other boys of his background and ability, he never attended a gymnasium, but was educated at home, before attending a realschule. He entered Manchester University in 1908 as a student of aeronautical engineering, but his interests soon shifted from the practical problems of the mathematics of propeller design to the foundations of mathematics. The turning point was his discovery of Bertrand Russell's *The Principles of Mathematics*. On the recommendation of Gottlob Frege, Wittgenstein transferred to Cambridge to study with Russell in 1912.

Even though Russell was at that time at the height of his powers, as the most accomplished philosophical logician in the English-speaking world, and despite Wittgenstein having had no other exposure to logic or philosophy, the two were soon collaborating as equals. Their research into the foundations of logic eventually led to Wittgenstein's *Tractatus Logico-Philosophicus*, published in 1922. The final drafts were written as a prisoner of war, Wittgenstein having volunteered for the Austrian Army.

Wittgenstein seems to have undergone intense personal experiences during the war. It is a fair guess to say that had the book been written prior to, or without, his war experience, its contents would have consisted purely of philosophical logic. However, the continual nearness of death and suffering exacerbated his already ongoing moral crisis to catalyze a change in the form of his life. Thus, the book's final sections involve a strange synthesis of logic and mysticism (strongly influenced by his study of Schopenhauer, one of the few philosophers he is known to have read) in which each remark is interpretable on two levels, either as a statement of logic or as a spiritual aphorism.

Another formative influence was his reading of Tolstoy's *The Gospels in Brief*. Upon his discharge from the army, Wittgenstein gave away all his considerable wealth and for the rest of his life lived with an ostentatious frugality that only those born into money could achieve or desire. Believing that the *Tractatus* had solved all the problems of philosophy (and seen how little it mattered), and having become sickened of the trials of finding a publisher, Wittgenstein abandoned the full-time practice of philosophy and earned a living as an elementary schoolteacher. In line with his Tolstoyan belief in the nobility of poverty, he chose to work in remote farming communities, where he fit in as well as could be expected. During this time, his only philosophical work was sparked by visits from Frank Ramsey (1903-1930), the Cambridge prodigy charged with translating the *Tractatus*. However, on his return to Vienna, Wittgenstein entered into discussions with the Vienna Circle, who had been greatly inspired by their interpretation of his book.

Wittgenstein returned to Cambridge in 1929, the *Tractatus* having been accepted as a Ph.D. thesis, and was appointed to a fellowship at Trinity College. He later succeeded G. E. Moore as professor of philosophy in 1939, although war broke out before he could commence his duties. Having become a British citizen following the German annexation of Austria in 1938, he contributed to the war effort by working as a hospital porter. He lasted as professor only two years, resigning for good in 1947. Throughout his life, he seems to have loathed academic surroundings. He died in 1951.

Although he published only one short article (immediately disowned) after the *Tractatus*, he produced an enormous amount of work, which his perfectionism forbade him to publish in his lifetime. At present, about twelve volumes of his notebooks and manuscripts have been published, along with several books of students' class notes. In these, we see his gradual undermining of the *Tractatus*, through the brief verificationism of *Philosophical Remarks*, into successive drafts of what would be his most important work, *Philosophical Investigations*.

Before discussing the content of the *Tractatus*, it is appropriate to say something about its unique form. It consists of seven root propositions, numbered 1 through 7, which constitute the book's basic narrative thread. Between each of these whole numbers, there is a tree-structure of elaborations on preceding remarks. For example, proposition 4 is developed in 4.1, 4.2, 4.3, 4.4, and 4.5. Each of these, in turn, have different levels of branches in which particular themes are discussed. Thus, 4.1 begats 4.11, which begats 4.111.

In his preface, Wittgenstein asserts that the "problems of philosophy"—that is, of philosophy as traditionally considered—arise through misunderstanding the logic of our language. He aims to investigate this underlying structure in order to show the limits of what can be legitimately said, to reveal that traditional metaphysics, among other things, lies beyond that limit. As he conceives of it, the job of philosophy is not to *solve* metaphysical questions by providing answers to them, but to *dissolve* them by showing that there is nothing to answer, since they are illusions, pseudo-problems with no real sense.

It is helpful to think of Wittgenstein as asking a *transcendental* question: Given that we can talk and think about things, and state facts, what must be the case for this to be possible? His answer lies in his Picture Theory: We can state facts through language because of a *structural isomorphism* between language and the world. Every language, at its most basic level, must share this common structure. An investigation of the structure of language will thereby reveal the true structure of reality. *Thought* must also share this common structure, since what can be said is coextensive with what can be thought.

The Picture Theory states how propositions relate to *facts*. The other central theme in the *Tractatus* concerns how propositions relate to *each other*. Here, the central concept is truth-functionality. Language consists of propositions, which state facts. At the most basic level, we have elementary propositions, from which all other propositions are constructed by logical connectives. An elementary proposition stands for (is a picture of) an atomic fact. It is true if it corresponds to an actual fact. We can use language to describe the world because of these utterly basic propositions, which directly "map onto" facts in the world and whose truth-value does not depend on other propositions. All other propositions, that is, "molecular" propositions, are truth-functions of these—their truth-value is determined by those of their constituent elementary propositions.

An elementary proposition is a structured set of names. Unlike Russell, Wittgenstein never offers any suggestions on what objects these names would denote. His theory is purely formal, unlike that of Russell's, who attempted to ally his version of Logical Atomism with Empiricism, leading him to take names to include demonstratives which denoted sense-data. Both philosophers agreed that ordinary names do not count as "names" in the strict sense. Wittgenstein never gives any examples of names or of elementary propositions, merely arguing a priori that there must be some, in order for factual discourse to occur. His only demand is that elementary propositions must be logically independent of each other. If two propositions are logically related, then they have a common component, which proves they have a structure which precludes them being elementary. However, this demand is more restrictive than it looks and indeed seems to exclude every imaginable candidate. Take Russell's sense-data. Taken as propositions about the same thing, at the same time, "This is red" and "This is green" are logically related, being contraries. However, this mutual incompatibility cannot be read off the structure of the propositions, since "X is red and X is green" is not a formal contradiction. At the time of writing the *Tractatus,* Wittgenstein seemed remarkably unconcerned about his inability to produce an elementary proposition, and of the problems facing plausible candidates. However, these problems would eventually lead him to reject the conclusions of his early work.

Elementary propositions are pictures of atomic facts. A picture can represent a fact because each "element" in it maps onto some thing or feature in the world. That is, they share a logical, or "pictorial" form, which makes representation possible. It is a purely abstract, formal requirement, not fixed to any particular material realization. Anything can represent a fact, so long as it shares its form. In such a way, one might say that an analogue recording on vinyl and a digital compact disc are both "pictures" of a live musical performance, since every element in the performance is located, in its correct place, on either format. Linguistic representation is just one special case of a general theory of representation.

So an elementary proposition is a structured set of names, not just a collection, since the same collection of names, rearranged, would picture some other fact— "John loves Mary" differs from "Mary loves John." This is the key to the opening lines of the *Tractatus*, where Wittgenstein says that the world is made up of *facts*, not of *things*. The same objects, in different combinations, would constitute different facts which, together, would make up different possible worlds. The actual world is made up of the facts corresponding to the set of true propositions.

So if a proposition pictures an actual fact, then it is true—however, I can understand it without knowing its truth-value. Likewise, its meaning is the same whether it is true or false. In general, a proposition has a sense (i.e., a meaning) because its names stand for things. A proposition does not itself stand for something, as is shown by false propositions being meaningful. It has meaning by depicting a *possible* state of affairs.

I will now turn to Wittgenstein's views on the nature of the propositions of logic. As we have seen, to have a sense is to picture a possible state of affairs. Likewise, to understand a proposition is to know which possible state of affairs it pictures; that is, what would make it true, and what would make it false. The possibility of being true and of being false is a prerequisite of having a sense at all, as is having a meaning which is graspable prior to knowing its truth-value. However, neither is the case for tautologies or contradictions, since these are always true or false respectively, and can be shown a priori to be so. As Wittgenstein says, I learn nothing about the weather if I know that either it is raining or it is not raining. So such a proposition lacks sense, in that it does not represent a possible state of affairs. However, it is not nonsensical in any pejorative way. You can construct a truth-table for a tautology, whereas you cannot for gibberish like "$\&p{\sim}vq$."

Wittgenstein takes his "fundamental thought" (4.0312) to be that the logical constants do not represent: that is, they are not names. This ties in with his claim that in understanding a proposition, you grasp both what it would be for it to be true, and to be false. So, if you understand p, there is no extra element that must be grasped in order to understand ${\sim}p$. Understanding p and ${\sim}p$ involve grasping the same fact. Like all constants, a negation sign is an "operator" on a proposition. Specifically, it "cancels" a proposition; likewise, a second negation cancels the first. ${\sim}{\sim}p$ contains no more elements, and no more information, than p. Thus, nothing *in the world* corresponds to "${\sim}$". A truth-table constitutes a reductive definition of a constant. Thus, "p,q" and "(TTTF)(p, q)" are equivalent.

The thesis that all meaningful discourse is descriptive poses problems not only for logic but also for Wittgenstein's own enterprise itself. By his own admission, he is trying to say something that cannot be said. After all, the propositions of the *Tractatus* do not state facts in the world. Rather, they concern the relationship between language and reality. These propositions are not located within the limits of legitimate discourse, because they concern these limits themselves. As Wittgenstein says, neither the picturing relation itself, nor what makes it possible, can themselves be pictured. For example, take a picture of a house. That it is a picture, and in virtue of what it is a picture, are not themselves represented within the picture. However, as he says in one of his most notoriously enigmatic remarks, although these factors cannot be *said*, they can be *shown*. This means, at least in part, that a correct understanding of the logical structure of a proposition makes everything clear—the logical isomorphism will be openly on show, rather than disguised by surface grammar.

This helps us make sense of the disarming last sections of the book, where Wittgenstein says that its propositions are senseless. He doesn't mean that they are wrong or rubbish, but rather that they are useful, elucidatory nonsense. They have no sense because they are about the limits of language, and the word-world relation, neither of which are within the limits of the sayable. They are useful as tools to stop others from speaking nonsense. Once this lesson is learned, the tools can be discarded. This ties in with Wittgenstein's view of the nature of philosophy as it ought to be practiced. Philosophy, unlike science, doesn't consist in the discovery of facts, but rather in the activity of demarcating the limits of the factual. Philosophy clarifies the nature of propositions, by revealing the logic of our language, and thereby of what can be said. What can be said are pictures of facts; philosophical logic is purely a priori, and there are no a priori facts—so philosophy is unsayable. Much traditional philosophy made the cardinal error of not realizing this fundamental difference between philosophy and the empirical sciences, and either offered empirical claims at a high level of generality, in a way that violated the logic of language, or made superempirical claims that transcended the boundaries of the sayable.

This explains Wittgenstein's saying, in the preface, that while all the problems of philosophy have been solved, his book shows how little has been achieved by their solution. All that really mattered to him, that is, how to live a moral life—was literally unsayable. Wittgenstein could never be said to have believed in the literal truth of Christian dogma. For him, Christianity was a practice, a way of life, which could only be shown by doing it, not talking about it. This mirrors the way in which logical form cannot be a subject for coherent discussion but can only be shown by the formulation and use of a correct symbolism.

BIBLIOGRAPHY

Works by Wittgenstein
The two translations of the *Tractatus* are by
F. P. Ramsey and C. K. Ogden (London: Routledge, 1922).
D. F. Pears and B. F. McGuinness (London: Routledge, 1961).

Further Reading
Good introductions include the following:
G. E. M. Anscombe, *An Introduction to Wittgenstein's Tractatus* (London: Hutchinson, 1959).
David Pears, *The False Prison*, Vol. 1 (Oxford: Clarendon Press, 1987).
Anthony Kenny, *Wittgenstein* (Cambridge: Harvard University Press, 1974).
For a story of Wittgenstein's unusual life, see Ray Monk, *Ludwig Wittgenstein: The Duty of Genius*, (New York: Free Press, 1990).

Tractatus Logico-Philosophicus

Ludwig Wittgenstein
Anthony Kenny, editor

1	The world is everything that is the case.
1.1	The world is the totality of facts, not of things.
1.11	The world is determined by the facts, and by these being *all* the facts.
1.12	For the totality of facts determines both what is the case, and also all that is not the case.
1.13	The facts in logical space are the world.

From *The Wittgenstein Reader*, edited by Anthony Kenny, (Cambridge: Blackwell) 1996. Reprinted by permission of Routledge.

1.2	The world divides into facts.
1.21	Any one can either be the case or not be the case, and everything else remain the same.
2	What is the case, the fact, is the existence of atomic facts.
2.01	An atomic fact is a combination of objects (entities, things).
2.011	It is essential to a thing that it can be a constituent part of an atomic fact.
2.012	In logic nothing is accidental: if a thing *can* occur in an atomic fact the possibility of that atomic fact must already be prejudged in the thing.
2.013	Everything is, as it were, in a space of possible atomic facts. I can think of this space as empty, but not of the thing without the space.
2.014	Objects contain the possibility of all states of affairs.
2.0141	The possibility of its occurrence in atomic facts is the form of the object.
2.02	The object is simple.
2.0201	Every statement about complexes can be analysed into a statement about their constituent parts, and into those propositions which completely describe the complexes.
2.021	Objects form the substance of the world. Therefore they cannot be compound.
2.022	It is clear that however different from the real one an imagined world may be, it must have something—a form—in common with the real world.
2.023	This fixed form consists of the objects.
2.024	Substance is what exists independently of what is the case.
2.025	It is form and content.
2.0251	Space, time and colour (colouredness) are forms of objects.
2.026	Only if there are objects can there be a fixed form of the world.
2.027	The fixed, the existent and the object are one.
2.03	In the atomic fact objects hang one in another, like the links of a chain.
2.031	In the atomic facts the objects are combined in a definite way.
2.032	The way in which objects hang together in the atomic fact is the structure of the atomic fact.
2.033	The form is the possibility of the structure.
2.034	The structure of the fact consists in the structures of the atomic facts.
2.04	The totality of existent atomic facts is the world.
2.05	The totality of existent atomic facts also determines which atomic facts do not exist.
2.06	The existence and non-existence of atomic facts is the reality. (The existence of atomic facts we also call a positive fact, their non-existence a negative fact.)
2.061	Atomic facts are independent of one another.
2.062	From the existence or non-existence of an atomic fact we cannot infer the existence or non-existence of another.
2.063	The total reality is the world.
2.1	We make to ourselves pictures of facts.
2.11	The picture presents the facts in logical space, the existence and non-existence of atomic facts.
2.12	The picture is a model of reality.

2.13   To the objects correspond in the picture the elements of the picture.

2.131   The elements of the picture stand, in the picture, for the objects.

2.14   The picture consists in the fact that its elements are combined with one another in a definite way.

2.141   The picture is a fact.

2.15   That the elements of the picture are combined with one another in a definite way, represents that the things are so combined with one another.

This connexion of the elements of the picture is called its structure, and the possibility of this structure is called the form of representation of the picture.

2.151   The form of representation is the possibility that the things are combined with one another as are the elements of the picture.

2.1511   Thus the picture is linked with reality; it reaches up to it.

2.1512   It is like a scale applied to reality.

2.15121   Only the outermost points of the dividing lines touch the object to be measured.

2.1513   According to this view the representing relation which makes it a picture, also belongs to the picture.

2.1514   The representing relation consists of the co-ordinations of the elements of the picture and the things.

2.1515   These co-ordinations are as it were the feelers of its elements with which the picture touches reality.

2.16   In order to be a picture a fact must have something in common with what it pictures.

2.161   In the picture and pictured there must be something identical in order that the one can be a picture of the other at all.

2.17   What the picture must have in common with reality in order to be able to represent it after its manner—rightly or falsely—is its form of representation.

2.171   The picture can represent every reality whose form it has.

The spatial picture, everything spatial, the coloured, everything coloured, etc.

2.172   The picture, however, cannot represent its form of representation; it shows it forth.

2.173   The picture represents its object from without (its standpoint is its form of representation), therefore the picture represents its object rightly or falsely.

2.174   But the picture cannot place itself outside of its form of representation.

2.18   What every picture, of whatever form, must have in common with reality in order to be able to represent it at all—rightly or falsely—is the logical form, that is, the form of reality.

2.181   If the form of representation is the logical form, then the picture is called a logical picture.

2.182   Every picture is *also* a logical picture. (On the other hand, for example, not every picture is spatial.) blue print / painting / visual

2.19   The logical picture can depict the world.

2.2	The picture has the logical form of representation in common with what it pictures.
2.201	The picture depicts reality by representing a possibility of the existence and non-existence of atomic facts.
2.202	The picture represents a possible state of affairs in logical space.
2.203	The picture contains the possibility of the state of affairs which it represents.
2.21	The picture agrees with reality or not; it is right or wrong, true or false.
2.22	The picture represents what it represents, independently of its truth or falsehood, through the form of representation.
2.221	What the picture represents is its sense.
2.222	In the agreement or disagreement of its sense with reality, its truth or falsity consists.
2.223	In order to discover whether the picture is true or false we must compare it with reality.
2.224	It cannot be discovered from the picture alone whether it is true or false.
2.225	There is no picture which is *a priori* true.
3	The logical picture of the facts is the thought.
3.01	The totality of true thoughts is a picture of the world.
3.02	The thought contains the possibility of the state of affairs which it thinks. What is thinkable is also possible.
3.03	We cannot think anything unlogical, for otherwise we should have to think unlogically.
3.04	An *a priori* true thought would be one whose possibility guaranteed its truth.
3.05	We could know *a priori* that a thought was true only if its truth was to be recognized from the thought itself (without an object of comparison).
3.1	In the proposition the thought is expressed perceptibly through the senses.
3.11	We use the sensibly perceptible sign (sound or written sign, etc.) of the proposition as a projection of the possible state of affairs. The method of projection is the thinking of the sense of the proposition.
3.12	The sign through which we express the thought I call the propositional sign. And the proposition is the propositional sign in its projective relation to the world.
3.13	To the proposition belongs everything which belongs to the projection; but not what is projected. Therefore the possibility of what is projected but not this itself. In the proposition, therefore, its sense is not yet contained, but the possibility of expressing it. ('The content of the proposition' means the content of the significant proposition.) In the proposition the form of its sense is contained, but not its content.
3.14	The propositional sign consists in the fact that its elements, the words, are combined in it in a definite way. The propositional sign is a fact.
3.142	Only facts can express a sense, a class of names cannot.

3.1432   We must not say 'The complex sign "*aRb*" says "*a* stands in relation *R* to *b*"'; but we must say '*That "a"* stands in a certain relation to "*b*" says *that aRb*'.

3.144   States of affairs can be described, but not *named*.

(Names resemble points; propositions resemble arrows, they have sense.)

3.2   In the propositions thoughts can be so expressed that to the objects of the thoughts correspond the elements of the propositional sign.

3.201   These elements I call 'simple signs' and the proposition 'completely analysed'.

3.202   The simple signs employed in propositions are called names.

3.203   The name means the object. The object is its meaning. ('A' is the same sign as 'A'.)

3.21   To the configuration of the simple signs in the propositional sign corresponds the configuration of the objects in the state of affairs.

3.22   In the proposition the name represents the object.

3.221   Objects I can only *name*. Signs represent them. I can only speak *of* them. I cannot *assert them*. A proposition can only say *how* a thing is, not *what* it is.

3.23   The postulate of the possibility of the simple signs is the postulate of the determinateness of the sense.

3.24   A proposition about a complex stands in internal relation to the proposition about its constituent part.

A complex can only be given by its description, and this will either be right or wrong. The proposition in which there is mention of a complex, if this does not exist, becomes not nonsense but sumply false.

That a propositional element signifies a complex can be seen from an indeterminateness in the proposition in which it occurs. We *know* that everything is not yet determined by this proposition. (The notation for generality *contains* a prototype.)

The combination of the symbols of a complex in a simple symbol can be expressed by a definition.

3.25   There is one and only one complete analysis of the proposition.

3.251   The proposition expresses what it expresses in a definite and clearly specifiable way: the proposition is articulate.

3.26   The name cannot be analysed further by any definition. It is a primitive sign.

3.3   Only the proposition has sense; only in the context of a proposition has a name meaning.

3.31   Every part of a proposition which characterizes its sense I call an expression (a symbol).

(The proposition itself is an expression.)

Expressions are everything—essential for the sense of the proposition—that propositions can have in common with one another.

An expression characterises a form and a content.

3.32   The sign is the part of the symbol perceptible by the senses.

3.321   Two different symbols can therefore have the sign (the written sign or the sound sign) in common—they then signify in different ways.

3.322   It can never indicate the common characteristic of two objects that we symbolise them with the same sign but by different *methods of symbolising*. For the sign is arbitrary. We could therefore equally well choose two different signs and where then would be what was common in the symbolisation?

3.323   In the language of everyday life it very often happens that the same word signifies in two different ways—and therefore belongs to two different symbols—or that two words, which signify in different ways, are apparently applied in the same way in the proposition.

Thus the word 'is' appears as the copula, as the sign of equality, and as the expression of existence; 'to exist' as an intransitive verb like 'to go'; 'identical' as an adjective; we speak of *something* but also of the fact of *something* happening.

(In the proposition 'Green is green'—where the first word is a person's name and the last an adjective—these words have not merely different meanings but they are *different symbols*.)

3.324   Thus there easily arise the most fundamental confusions (of which the whole of philosophy is full).

3.325   In order to avoid these errors, we must employ a symbolism which excludes them, by not applying the same sign in different symbols and by not applying signs in the same ways which signify in different ways. A symbolism, that is to say, which obeys the rules of *logical* grammar—of logical syntax.

The logical symbolism of Frege and Russell is such a language which, however, does still not exclude all errors.

3.326   In order to recognise the symbol in the sign we must consider the significant use.

3.327   The sign determines a logical form only together with its logical syntactic application.

3.328   If a sign is *not used* then it is meaningless. That is the meaning of Occam's razor.

(If everything in the symbolism works as though a sign had meaning, then it has meaning.)

3.33   In logical syntax the meaning of a sign ought never to play a role; it must admit of being established without mention being thereby made of the *meaning* of a sign; it ought to presuppose *only* the description of the expressions.

3.34   A proposition possesses essential and accidental features.

Accidental are the features which are due to a particular way of producing the propositional sign. Essential are those which alone enable the proposition to express its sense.

3.341   The essential in a proposition is therefore that which is common to all propositions which can express the same sense.

And in the same way in general the essential in a symbol is that which all symbols which can fulfil the same purpose have in common.

3.342　In our notations there is indeed something arbitrary, but *this* is not arbitrary, namely that *if* we have determined anything arbitrarily, then something else *must* be the case. (This results from the *essence* of the notation.)

3.343　Definitions are rules for the translation of one language into another. Every correct symbolism must be translatable into every other according to such rules. It is *this* which all have in common.

3.344　What signifies in the symbol is what is common to all those symbols by which it can be replaced according to the rules of logical syntax.

3.4　The proposition determines a place in logical space: the existence of this logical place is guaranteed by the existence of the constituent parts alone, by the existence of the significant proposition.

3.41　The propositional sign and the logical co-ordinates: that is the logical place.

3.411　The geometrical and the logical place agree in that each is the possibility of an existence.

3.42　Although a proposition may only determine one place in logical space, the whole logical space must already be given by it.

(Otherwise denial, the logical sum, the logical product, etc. would always introduce new elements—in co-ordination.)

(The logical scaffolding round the picture determines the logical space. The proposition reaches through the whole logical space.)

3.5　The applied, thought, propositional sign is the thought.

4　The thought is the significant proposition.

4.01　The proposition is a picture of reality.

The proposition is a model of the reality as we think it is.

4.011　At the first glance the proposition—say as it stands printed on paper—does not seem to be a picture of the reality of which it treats. But nor does the musical score appear at first sight to be a picture of a musical piece; nor does our phonetic spelling (letters) seem to be a picture of our spoken language. And yet these symbolisms prove to be pictures—even in the ordinary sense of the word—of what they represent.

4.012　It is obvious that we perceive a proposition of the form aRb as a picture. Here the sign is obviously a likeness of the signified.

4.02　This we see from the fact that we understand the sense of the propositional sign, without having had it explained to us.

4.021　The proposition is a picture of reality, for I know the state of affairs presented by it, if I understand the proposition. And I understand the proposition without its sense having been explained to me.

4.022　The proposition *shows* its sense.

The proposition *shows* how things stand, *if* it is true. And it *says*, that they do so stand.

4.023　The proposition determines reality to this extent, that one only needs to say 'Yes' or 'No' to it to make it agree with reality.

Reality must therefore be completely described by the proposition.

A proposition is the description of a fact.

As the description of an object describes it by its external properties so propositions describe reality by its internal properties.

The proposition constructs a world with the help of a logical scaffolding, and therefore one can actually see in the proposition all the logical features possessed by reality *if* it is true. One can *draw conclusions* from a false proposition.

4.024   To understand a proposition means to know what is the case if it is true.

(One can therefore understand it without knowing whether it is true or not.)

One understands it if one understands its constituent parts.

4.025   The translation of one language into another is not a process of translating each proposition of the one into a proposition of the other, but only the constituent parts of propositions are translated.

(And the dictionary does not only translate substantives but also adverbs and conjunctions, etc., and it treats them all alike.)

4.026   The meanings of the simple signs (the words) must be explained to us, if we are to understand them.

But propositions are self-explanatory.

4.027   It is essential to propositions, that they can communicate a *new* sense to us.

4.03   A proposition must communicate a new sense with old words.

The proposition communicates to us a state of affairs, therefore it must be *essentially* connected with the state of affairs.

And the connexion is, in fact, that it is its logical picture.

The proposition only asserts something, in so far as it is a picture.

4.031   In the proposition a state of affairs is, as it were, put together for the sake of experiment.

One can say, instead of, 'This proposition has such and such a sense', 'This proposition represents such and such a state of affairs'.

4.0311   One name stands for one thing, and another for another thing, and they are connected together. And so the whole, like a living picture, presents the atomic fact.

4.0312   The possibility of propositions is based upon the principle of the representation of objects by signs.

My fundamental thought is that the 'logical constants' do not represent. That the *logic* of facts cannot be represented.

4.032   The proposition is a picture of its state of affairs, only in so far as it is logically articulated.

(Even the proposition 'ambulo' is composite, for its stem gives a different sense with another termination, or its termination with another stem.)

4.04   In the proposition there must be exactly as many things distinguishable as there are in the state of affairs, which it represents.

They must both possess the same logical (mathematical) multiplicity (cf. Hertz's *Mechanics*, on Dynamic Models).

4.041	This mathematical multiplicity naturally cannot in its turn be represented. One cannot get outside it in the representation.
4.05	Reality is compared with the proposition.
4.06	Propositions can be true or false only by being pictures of the reality.
4.1	A proposition presents the existence and non-existence of atomic facts.
4.11	The totality of true propositions is the total natural science (or the totality of the natural sciences).
4.111	Philosophy is not one of the natural sciences.
	(The word 'philosophy' must mean something which stands above or below, but not beside the natural sciences.)
4.112	The object of philosophy is the logical clarification of thoughts.
	Philosophy is not a theory but an activity.
	A philosophical work consists essentially of elucidations.
	The result of philosophy is not a number of 'philosophical propositions', but to make propositions clear.
	Philosophy should make clear and delimit sharply the thoughts which otherwise are, as it were, opaque and blurred.
4.113	Philosophy limits the disputable sphere of natural science.
4.114	It should limit the thinkable and thereby the unthinkable.
	It should limit the unthinkable from within through the thinkable.
4.115	It will mean the unspeakable by clearly displaying the speakable.
4.116	Everything that can be thought at all can be thought clearly. Everything that can be said can be said clearly.
4.12	Propositions can represent the whole reality, but they cannot represent what they must have in common with reality in order to be able to represent it—the logical form.
	To be able to represent the logical form, we should have to be able to put ourselves with the propositions outside logic, that is outside the world.
4.121	Propositions cannot represent the logical form: this mirrors itself in the propositions.
	That which mirrors itself in language, language cannot represent.
	That which expresses *itself* in language, *we* cannot express by language.
	The propositions show the logical form of reality.
	They exhibit it.
4.2	The sense of a proposition is its agreement and disagreement with the possibilities of the existence and non-existence of the atomic facts.
4.21	The simplest proposition, the elementary proposition, asserts the existence of an atomic fact.
4.211	It is a sign of an elementary proposition, that no elementary proposition can contradict it.
4.22	The elementary proposition consists of names. It is a connexion, a concatenation of names.
4.23	The name occurs in the proposition only in the context of the elementary proposition.
4.24	The names are the simple symbols, I indicate them by single letters (x,y,z).

The elementary proposition I write as function of the names, in the form 'fx' "$\Phi(x,y)$", etc.

Or I indicate it by the letters p, q, r.

4.25 If the elementary proposition is true, the atomic fact exists; if it is false the atomic fact does not exist.

4.26 The specification of all true elementary propositions describes the world completely. The world is completely described by the specification of all elementary propositions, plus the specification which of them are true and which false.

4.27 With regard to the existence of n atomic facts there are

$$\kappa_n = \sum_{v=0}^{n} \binom{n}{v} \text{ possibilities.}$$

It is possible for all combinations of atomic facts to exist, and the others not to exist.

4.28 To these combinations correspond the same number of possibilities of the truth—and falsehood—of n elementary propositions.

4.3 The truth-possibilities of the elementary propositions mean the possibilities of the existence and nonexistence of the atomic facts.

4.31 The truth-possibilities can be presented by schemata of the following kind ('T' means 'true', 'F' 'false'. The rows of T's and F's under the row of the elementary propositions mean their truth-possibilities in an easily intelligible symbolism).

p	q	r
T	T	T
F	T	T
T	F	T
T	T	F
F	F	T
F	T	F
T	F	F
F	F	F

p	q
T	T
F	T
T	F
F	F

p
T
F

4.4 A proposition is the expression of agreement and disagreement with the truth-possibilities of the elementary propositions.

4.41 The truth-possibilities of the elementary propositions are the conditions of the truth and falsehood of the propositions.

4.411 It seems probable even at first sight that the introduction of the elementary propositions is fundamental for the comprehension of the other kinds of propositions. Indeed the comprehension of the general propositions depends *palpably* on that of the elementary propositions.

4.42   With regard to the agreement and disagreement of a proposition with the truth-possibilities of n elementary propositions there are

$$\sum_{K=0}^{K_n} \binom{K_n}{K} = L_n \text{ possibilities.}$$

4.45   For n elementary propositions there are L possible groups of truth-conditions.

The groups of truth-conditions which belong to the truth-possibilities of a number of elementary propositions can be ordered in a series.

4.46   Among the possible groups of truth-conditions there are two extreme cases.

In the one case the proposition is true for all the truth-possibilities of the elementary propositions. We say that the truth-conditions are *tautological*.

$$x+x=2x$$

In the second case the proposition is false for all the truth-possibilities. The truth-conditions are *self-contradictory*. $x-x=1$

In the first case we call the proposition a tautology, in the second case a contradiction.

4.461   The proposition shows what it says, the tautology and the contradiction that they say nothing.

The tautology has no truth-conditions, for it is unconditionally true; and the contradiction is on no condition true.

Tautology and contradiction are without sense.

(Like the point from which two arrows go out in opposite directions.)

(I know, e.g. nothing about the weather, when I know that it rains or does not rain.)

4.5   Now it appears to be possible to give the most general form of proposition; i.e. to give a description of the propositions of some one sign language, so that every possible sense can be expressed by a symbol, which falls under the description, and so that every symbol which falls under the description can express a sense, if the meanings of the names are chosen accordingly.

It is clear that in the description of the most general form of proposition *only* what is essential to it may be described—otherwise it would not be the most general form.

That there is a general form is proved by the fact that there cannot be a proposition whose form could not have been foreseen (i.e. constructed). The general form of proposition is: Such and such is the case.

4.51   Suppose *all* elementary propositions were given me: then we can simply ask: what propositions I can build out of them. And these are *all* propositions, and *so* they are limited.

4.52   The propositions are everything which follows from the totality of all elementary propositions (of course also from the fact that it is the *totality of them all*). (So, in some sense, one could say, that *all* propositions are generalisations of the elementary propositions.)

4.53   The general propositional form is a variable.

5   Propositions are truth-functions of elementary propositions.
         (An elementary proposition is a truth-function of itself.)

5.01   The elementary propositions are the truth-arguments of propositions.

5.1   The truth-functions can be ordered in series.
         That is the foundation of the theory of probability.

5.101   The truth-functions of every number of elementary propositions can be
         written in a schema of the following kind:

(T T T T) (p, q) Tautology (if p then p, and if q then q) $[p{\supset}p, q{\supset}q]$

(F T T T) (p, q) in words: Not both p and q. $[\sim(p, q)]$

(T F T T) (p, q) ″ ″ If q then p. $[q \supset p]$

(T T F T) (p, q) ″ ″ If p then q. $[p \supset q]$

(T T T F) (p, q) ″ ″ p or q. $[p \vee q]$

(F F T T) (p, q) ″ ″ Not q. $[\sim q]$

(F T F T) (p, q) ″ ″ Not p. $[\sim p]$

(F T T F) (p, q) ″ ″ p or q, but not both. $[p . \sim q: \mathrm{v}: q. \sim p]$

(T F F T) (p, q) ″ ″ If p, then q; and if q, then p. $[p \equiv q]$

(T F T F) (p, q) ″ ″ p

(T T F F) (p, q) ″ ″ q

(F F F T) (p, q) ″ ″ Neither p nor q. $[\sim p . \sim q$ or $p/q]$

(F F T F) (p, q) ″ ″ p and not q. $[p. \sim q]$

(F T F F) (p, q) ″ ″ q and not p. $[q. \sim p]$

(T F F F) (p, q) ″ ″ p and q. $[p. q]$

(F F F F) (p, q) Contradiction (p and not p; and q and not q.)
                        $[p. \sim p. q. \sim q]$

Those truth-possibilities of its truth-arguments, which verify the proposition, I shall call its *truth-grounds*.

5.11   If the truth-grounds which are common to a number of propositions are
         all also truth-grounds of some one proposition, we say that the truth of this
         proposition follows from the truth of those propositions.

5.12   In particular the truth of a proposition p follows from that of a proposition q, if all the truth-grounds of the second are truth-grounds of the first.

5.121   The truth-grounds of q are contained in those of p; p follows from 'q'.

5.122   If p follows from q, the sense of 'p' is contained in that of 'q'.

5.123   If a god creates a world in which certain propositions are true, he creates thereby also a world in which all propositions consequent on them are true. And similarly he could not create a world in which the proposition 'p' is true without creating all its objects.

5.124   A proposition asserts every proposition which follows from it.

5.13   That the truth of one proposition follows from the truth of other propositions, we perceive from the structure of the propositions.

5.133   All inference takes place *a priori*.

5.134   From an elementary proposition no other can be inferred.

5.135   In no way can an inference be made from the existence of one state of affairs to the existence of another entirely different from it.

5.136   There is no causal nexus which justifies such an inference.

5.14   If a proposition follows from another, then the latter says more than the former, the former less than the latter.

5.141   If p follows from q and q from p then they are one and the same proposition.

5.142   A tautology follows from all propositions: it says nothing.

5.143   Contradiction is something shared by propositions, which *no* proposition has in common with another. Tautology is that which is shared by all propositions, which have nothing in common with one another.

Contradiction vanishes so to speak outside, tautology inside all propositions.

Contradiction is the external limit of the propositions, tautology their substanceless centre.

5.15   If T_r is the number of the truth-grounds of the proposition 'r', T_{rs} the number of those truth-grounds of the proposition 's' which are at the same time truth-grounds of 'r', then we call the ratio $T_{rs} : T_r$ the measure of the *probability* which the proposition 'r' gives to the proposition 's'.

5.2   The structures of propositions stand to one another in internal relations.

5.21   We can bring out these internal relations in our manner of expression, by presenting a proposition as the result of an operation which produces it from other propositions (the bases of the operation).

5.22   The operation is the expression of a relation between the structures of its result and its bases.

5.23   The operation is that which must happen to a proposition in order to make another out of it.

5.24   An operation shows itself in a variable; it shows how we can proceed from one form of proposition to another.

It gives expression to the difference between the forms.

(And that which is common to the bases, and the result of an operation, is the bases themselves.)

5.25   The occurrence of an operation does not characterise the sense of a proposition.

For an operation does not assert anything; only its result does, and this depends on the bases of the operation.

(Operation and function must not be confused with one another.)

5.251   A function cannot be its own argument, but the result of an operation can be its own basis.

5.3   All propositions are results of truth-operations on the elementary propositions.

The truth-operation is the way in which a truth-function arises from elementary propositions.

According to the nature of truth-operations, in the same way as out of elementary propositions arise their truth-functions, from truth-functions arises a new one. Every truth-operation creates from truth-functions of elementary propositions another truth-function of elementary propositions, i.e. a pro- position. The result of every truth-operation on the results of truth-operations on elementary propositions is also the result of *one* truth-operation on elementary propositions.

Every proposition is the result of truth-operations on elementary propositions.

5.31   The Schemata No. 4.31 are also significant, if '*p*', '*q*', '*r*', etc. are not elementary propositions.

And it is easy to see that the propositional sign in No. 4.42 expresses one truth-function of elementary propositions even when '*p*' and '*q*' are truth-functions of elementary propositions.

5.32   All truth-functions are results of the successive application of a finite number of truth-operations to elementary propositions.

5.4   Here it becomes clear that there are no such things as 'logical objects' or 'logical constants' (in the sense of Frege and Russell.)

5.41   For all those results of truth-operations on truth-functions are identical, which are one and the same truth-function of elementary propositions.

5.42   That v, ⊃, etc. are not relations in the sense of right and left, etc., is obvious.

The possibility of crosswise definition of the logical 'primitive signs' of Frege and Russell shows by itself that these are not primitive signs and that they signify no relations.

And it is obvious that the '⊃' which we define by means of ~ and 'v' is identical with that by which we define 'v' with the help of ~, and that this 'v' is the same as the first, and so on.

5.43   That from a fact *p* an infinite number of *others* should follow, namely ~~*p*, ~~~~*p* etc., is no less wonderful that the infinite number of propositions of logic (of mathematics) should follow from half a dozen 'primitive propositions'.

But all propositions of logic say the same thing. That is, nothing.

5.46   When we have rightly introduced the logical signs, the sense of all their combinations has been already introduced with them: therefore not only '*pvq*' but also ~(*pv*~*q*), etc., etc. We should then already have introduced the effect of all possible combinations of brackets; and it would then have become clear that the proper general primitive signs are not '*pvq*', (∃*x*). *fx*', etc., but the most general form of their combinations.

5.47   It is clear that everything which can be said *beforehand* about the form of *all* propositions at all can be said *no one occasion*.

For all logical operations are already contained in the elementary proposition. For '*fa*' says the same as '(∃*x*) . *fx* . *x* = *a*'.

Where there is composition, there is argument and function, and where these are, all logical constants already are.

One could say: the one logical constant is that which *all* propositions, according to their nature, have in common with one another.

That however is the general form of proposition.

5.471   The general form of proposition is the essence of proposition.

5.5   Every truth-function is a result of the successive application of the operation ($—$ $—$ $—$ $—$ $—$ $—$ $—$ T) (ξ . . . .) to elementary propositions.

This operation denies all the propositions in the right-hand bracket, and I call it the negation of these propositions.

5.51   If ξ has only one value, then $N(\bar{\xi}) = {\sim}p$ (not p), if it has two values then $N(\xi) = {\sim}p{\sim}q$ (neither p nor q).

5.511   How can the all-embracing logic which mirrors the world use such special catches and manipulations? Only because all these are connected into an infinitely fine network, to the great mirror.

5.512   '${\sim}p$' is true if 'p is false. Therefore in the true proposition '${\sim}p$' 'p' is a false proposition. How then can the stroke '${\sim}$' bring it into agreement with reality?

That which denies in '${\sim}p$' is however not '${\sim}$', but that which all signs of this notation, which deny p, have in common.

Hence the common rule according to which '${\sim}p$', '${\sim}{\sim}{\sim}p$', '${\sim}p, {\sim}p$', etc., etc. (to infinity) are constructed. And this which is common to them all mirrors denial.

5.513   We could say: what is common to all symbols, which assert both p and q, is the proposition '$p.q$'. What is common to all symbols, which assert either p or q, is the proposition 'pvq.'

And similarly we can say: Two propositions are opposed to one another when they have nothing in common with one another; and every proposition has only one negative, because there is only one proposition which lies altogether outside it.

5.52   If the values of ξ are the total values of a function fx for all values of x, then $N(\bar{\xi}) = {\sim}(\exists x) . fx$.

5.521   I separate the concept *all* from the truth-function.

Frege and Russell have introduced generality in connexion with the logical product or the logical sum. Then it would be difficult to understand the propositions '$(\exists x) . fx$' and '$(x). fx$' in which both ideas lie concealed.

5.522   That which is peculiar to the 'symbolism of generality' is firstly, that it refers to a logical prototype, and secondly, that it makes constants prominent.

5.523   The generality symbol occurs as an argument.

5.524   If the objects are given, therewith are *all* objects given. If thee elementary propositions are given, then there with *all* elementary propositions are also given.

5.53   Identity of the object I express by identity of the sign and not by means of a sign of identity. Difference of the objects by difference of the signs.

5.531   I write therefore not '$f(a,b) . a = b$', but '$f(a,a)$ (or '$f(b,b)$). And not '$f(a,b) .{\sim}a = b$'. but '$f(a,b)$.

5.533   The identity sign is therefore not an essential constituent of logical notation.

5.54   In the general propositional form, propositions occur in a proposition only as bases of the truth-operations.

5.541   At first sight it appears as if there were also a different way in which one proposition could occur in another.

Especially in certain propositional forms of psychology, like 'A thinks, that p is the case', or 'A thinks p', etc.

Here it appears superficially as if the proposition p stood to the object A in a kind of relation.

And in modern epistemology (Russell, Moore, etc.) these propositions have been conceived in this way.

5.542   But it is clear that 'A believes that p', 'A thinks p', 'A says p', are of the form ' "p" says p': and here we have no co-ordination of a fact and an object, but a co-ordination of facts by means of a co-ordination of their objects.

5.5421   This shows that there is no such thing as the soul—the subject, etc.—as it is conceived in contemporary superficial psychology.

A composite soul would not be a soul any longer.

5.5422   The correct explanation of the form of the proposition 'A judges p' must show that it is impossible to judge a nonsense. (Russell's theory does not satisfy this condition.)

5.5423   To perceive a complex means to perceive that its constituents are combined in such and such a way.

5.55   We must now answer *a priori* the question as to all possible forms of the elementary propositions.

The elementary proposition consists of names. Since we cannot give the number of names with different meanings, we cannot give the composition of the elementary proposition.

5.551   Our fundamental principle is that every question which can be decided at all by logic can be decided off-hand.

(And if we get into a situation where we need to answer such a problem by looking at the world, this shows that we are on a fundamentally wrong track.)

5.552   The 'experience' which we need to understand logic is not that such and such is the case, but that something *is*; but that is *no* experience.

Logic *precedes* every experience—that something is *so*.

It is before the How, not before the What.

5.6   *The limits of my language* mean the limits of my world.

5.61   Logic fills the world: the limits of the world are also its limits.

We cannot therefore say in logic: This and this there is in the world, that there is not.

For that would apparently presuppose that we exclude certain possibilities, and this cannot be the case since otherwise logic must get outside the limits of the world: that is, if it could consider these limits from the other side also.

What we cannot think, that we cannot think: we cannot therefore *say* what we cannot think.

5.62   This remark provides a key to the question, to what extent solipsism is a truth.

In fact what solipsism *means* is quite correct, only it cannot be *said*, but it shows itself.

That the world is *my* world, shows itself in the fact that the limits of that language (*the* language which I understand) mean the limits of *my* world.

5.621   The world and life are one.

5.63   I am my world. (The microcosm.)

5.631   The thinking, presenting subject; there is no such thing.

If I wrote a book 'The world as I found it', I should also have therein to report on my body and say which members obey my will and which do not, etc. This then would be a method of isolating the subject or rather of showing that in an important sense there is no subject: that is to say, of it alone in this book mention could *not* be made.

5.64   Here we see that solipsism strictly carried out coincides with pure realism. The I in solipsism shrinks to an extensionless point and there remains the reality coordinated with it.

5.641   There is therefore really a sense in which in philosophy we can talk of a non-psychological I.

The I occurs in philosophy through the fact that the 'world is my world'.

The philosophical I is not the man, not the human body or the human soul of which psychology treats, but the metaphysical subject, the limit—not a part of the world.

6   The general form of truth-function is: $[\bar{p}\bar{\xi}N(\bar{\xi})]$.

6.001   This says nothing else than that every proposition is the result of successive applications of the operation N' $(\bar{\xi})$ to the elementary propositions.

6.1   The propositions of logic are tautologies.

6.11   The propositions of logic therefore say nothing. (They are the analytical propositions.)

6.111   Theories which make a proposition of logic appear substantial are always false. One could e.g. believe that the words 'true' and 'false' signify two properties among other properties, and then it would appear as a remarkable fact that every proposition possesses one of these properties. This now by no means appears self-evident, no more so than the proposition 'All roses are either yellow or red' would sound even if it were true. Indeed our proposition now gets quite the character of a proposition of natural science and this is a certain symptom of its being falsely understood.

6.112   The correct explanation of logical propositions must give them a peculiar position among all propositions.

6.113   It is the characteristic mark of logical propositions that one can perceive in the symbol alone that they are true; and this fact contains in itself the whole philosophy of logic. And so also it is one of the most important facts that the truth or falsehood of *non*-logical propositions can *not* be recognised from the propositions alone.

6.12   The fact that the propositions of logic are tautologies *shows* the formal—logical—properties of language, of the world.

That its constituent parts connected together *in this way* give a tautology characterises the logic of its constituent parts.

In order that propositions connected together in a definite way may give a tautology they must have definite properties of structure. That they give a tautology when *so* connected shows therefore that they possess these properties of structure.

6.121 The propositions of logic demonstrate the logical properties of propositions, by combining them into propositions which say nothing.

This method could be called a zero-method. In a logical proposition propositions are brought into equilibrium with one another, and the state of equilibrium then shows how these propositions must be logically constructed.

6.122 Whence it follows that we can get on without logical propositions, for we can recognise in an adequate notation the formal properties of the propositions by mere inspection.

6.13 Logic is not a theory but a reflexion of the world.

Logic is transcendental.

6.2 Mathematics is a logical method.

The propositions of mathematics are equations, and therefore pseudo-propositions.

6.21 Mathematical propositions express no thoughts.

6.211 In life it is never a mathematical proposition which we need, but we use mathematical propositions *only* in order to infer from propositions which do not belong to mathematics to others which equally do not belong to mathematics.

(In philosophy the question 'Why do we really use that word, that proposition?' constantly leads to valuable results.)

6.22 The logic of the world which the propositions of logic show in tautologies, mathematics shows in equations.

6.23 If two expressions are connected by the sign of equality, this means that they can be substituted for one another. But whether this is the case must show itself in the two expressions themselves.

It characterises the logical form of two expressions, that they can be substituted for one another.

6.24 The method by which mathematics arrives at its equations is the method of substitution.

For equations express the substitutability of two expressions, and we proceed from a number of equations to new equations, replacing expressions by others in accordance with the equations.

6.3 Logical research means the investigation of *all regularity*. And outside logic all is accident.

6.31 The so-called law of induction cannot in any case be a logical law, for it is obviously a significant proposition. And therefore it cannot be a law *a priori* either.

6.32 The law of causality is not a law but the form of a law.

6.33 We do not *believe a priori* in a law of conservation, but we *know a priori* the possibility of a logical form.

6.34	All propositions, such as the law of causation, the law of continuity in nature, etc. etc., all these are *a priori* intuitions of possible forms of the propositions of science.
6.36	If there were a law of causality, it might run: 'There are natural laws'. But that can clearly not be said: it shows itself.
6.361	In the terminology of Hertz we might say: only *uniform* connexions are *thinkable*.
6.362	What can be described can happen too, and what is excluded by the law of causality cannot be described.
6.363	The process of induction is the process of assuming the *simplest* law that can be made to harmonize with our experience.
6.3631	This process, however, has no logical foundation but only a psychological one.
	It is clear that there are no grounds for believing that the simplest course of events will really happen.
6.36311	That the sun will rise tomorrow, is an hypothesis; and that means that we do not *know* whether it will rise.
6.37	A necessity for one thing to happen because another has happened does not exist. There is only *logical* necessity.
6.371	At the basis of the whole modern view of the world lies the illusion that the so-called laws of nature are the explanations of natural phenomena.
6.372	So people stop short at natural laws as at something unassailable, as did the ancients at God and Fate.
	And they both are right and wrong. But the ancients were clearer, in so far as they recognised one clear terminus, whereas the modern system makes it appear as though *everything* were explained.
6.373	The world is independent of my will.
6.374	Even if everything we wished were to happen, this would only be, so to speak, a favour of fate, for there is no *logical* connexion between will and world, which would guarantee this, and the assumed physical connexion itself we could not again will.
6.375	As there is only a *logical* necessity, so there is only a *logical* impossibility.
6.3751	For two colours, e.g. to be at one place in the visual field, is impossible, logically impossible, for it is excluded by the logical structure of colour.
	Let us consider how this contradiction presents itself in physics. Somewhat as follows: That a particle cannot at the same time have two velocities, i.e. that at the same time it cannot be in two places, i.e. that particles in different places at the same time cannot be identical.
	(It is clear that the logical product of two elementary propositions can neither be a tautology nor a contradiction. The assertion that a point in the visual field has two different colours at the same time, is a contradiction.)
6.4	All propositions are of equal value.
6.41	The sense of the world must lie outside the world. In the world everything is as it is and happens as it does happen. *In* it there is no value—and if there were, it would be of no value.

If there is a value which is of value, it must lie outside all happening and being-so. For all happening and being-so is accidental.

What makes it non-accidental cannot lie *in* the world, for otherwise this would again be accidental.

It must lie outside the world.

6.42   Hence also there can be no ethical propositions.

Propositions cannot express anything higher.

6.421   It is clear that ethics cannot be expressed.

Ethics is transcendental.

(Ethics and aesthetics are one.)

6.423   Of the will as the subject of the ethical we cannot speak.

And the will as a phenomenon is only of interest to psychology.

6.43   If good or bad willing changes the world, it can only change the limits of the world, not the facts; not the things that can be expressed in language.

In brief, the world must thereby become quite another. It must so to speak wax or wane as a whole.

The world of the happy is quite another than that of the unhappy.

6.431   As in death, too, the world does not change, but ceases.

6.4311   Death is not an event of life. Death is not lived through.

If by eternity is understood not endless temporal duration but timelessness, then he lives eternally who lives in the present.

Our life is endless in the way that our visual field is without limit.

6.4312   The temporal immortality of the human soul, that is to say, its eternal survival after death, is not only in no way guaranteed, but this assumption in the first place will not do for us what we always tried to make it do. Is a riddle solved by the fact that I survive for ever? Is this eternal life not as enigmatic as our present one? The solution of the riddle of life in space and time lies *outside* space and time.

(It is not problems of natural science which have to be solved).

6.432   *How* the world is, is completely indifferent for what is higher. God does not reveal himself *in* the world.

6.4321   The facts all belong only to the task and not to its performance.

6.44   Not *how* the world is, is the mystical, but *that* it is.

6.45   The contemplation of the world *sub specie aeterni* is its contemplation as a limited whole.

The feeling of the world as a limited whole is the mystical feeling.

6.5   For an answer which cannot be expressed the question too cannot be expressed.

The riddle does not exist.

If a question can be put at all, then it *can* also be answered.

6.51   Scepticism is *not* irrefutable, but palpably senseless, if it would doubt where a question cannot be asked.

For doubt can only exist where there is a question: a question only where there is an answer, and this only where something *can* be *said*.

6.52   We feel that even if *all possible* scientific questions be answered, then problems of life have still not been touched at all. Of course there is then no question left, and just this is the answer.

6.521   The solution of the problem of life is seen in the vanishing of this problem.

(Is not this the reason why men to whom after long doubting the sense of life became clear, could not then say wherein this sense consisted?)

6.522   There is indeed the inexpressible. This *shows* itself; it is the mystical.

6.53   The right method of philosophy would be this. To say nothing except what can be said, i.e. the propositions of natural science, i.e. something that has nothing to do with philosophy: and then always, when someone else wished to say something metaphysical, to demonstrate to him that he has given no meaning to certain signs in his propositions. This method would be unsatisfying to the other—he would not have the feeling that we were teaching him philosophy—but it would be the only strictly correct method.

6.54   My propositions are elucidatory in this way: he who understands me finally recognises them as senseless, when he has climbed out through them, on them, over them. (He must so to speak throw away the ladder, after he has climbed up on it.)

He must surmount these propositions; then he sees the world rightly.

7   Whereof one cannot speak, thereof one must be silent.

CHAPTER 3
Logical Positivism

Introduction to Logical Positivism

The Vienna Circle was a group of philosophers, mathematicians, and scientists who gathered under the leadership of Moritz Schlick, and who, inspired by Whitehead and Russell's *Principia Mathematica* and Wittgenstein's *Tractatus*, attempted to forge a scientifically respectable philosophy that would clear away the old metaphysics and put philosophy at last on a firm foundation. They are usually referred to either as Logical Positivists or Logical Empiricists, displaying their historical antecedents in the logic of Frege, Russell and Wittgenstein, the Positivism of Mach, and the Empiricism of Hume. Their members included philosophers Rudolf Carnap, Freidrich Waismann, and Herbert Feigl; the Marxist sociologist and economist Otto Neurath; and mathematicians Hans Hahn and Kurt Godel.

Moritz Schlick was born in Berlin in 1882. He studied physics at the University of Berlin under Max Planck, and received his doctorate there in 1904. His interests always spanned both physics and philosophy. He published one of the first expositions of Einstein's Relativity Theory, *Space and Time in Contemporary Physics*, in 1917, and *General Theory of Knowledge* in 1918. After teaching at the Universities of Rostock and Kiel, he took the chair of Philosophy at the University of Vienna in 1921, where he remained until his murder by an insane student in 1936.

Rudolf Carnap was born in 1891 in Ronsorf, Germany. He studied at the Universities of Jena and Frieburg, and taught primarily at the University of Vienna, the German University in Prague, the University of Chicago, and UCLA. Although relatively ignored in Britain, and disapproved of in Oxford, Carnap's influence on the development of philosophy in USA has been second to none. His earliest philosophical influences were Gottlob Frege, with whom he studied in Jena, and Bertrand Russell. In his autobiography, he describes the revelatory impact of reading Russell's *Our Knowledge of the External World*: "Henceforth the application of the new logical instrument for the purposes of analyzing scientific concepts and of clarifying philosophical concepts has been the essential aim of my philosophical activity" (p. 13).

Carnap's first major work was *Der Logische Aufbau der Welt*, which attempted to analyze ordinary concepts in terms of "a temporal sequence of continually changing forms in the two-dimensional visual field" (p. 16). It was a systematic endeavor at a phenomenal reconstruction of our theory of the world. However, while he formulated his theory in the language of phenomenalism, he stressed his neutrality over the ontological dispute between phenomenalists and realists. He considered the choice of language as a purely methodological issue, determined by pragmatic factors alone. The adoption of a phenomenalist language did not ontologically commit him to a phenomenalist metaphysics. This "principle of tolerance" remained with him throughout his career and resurfaces in "Empiricism, Semantics and Ontology."

The work of the Circle received widespread exposure with the publication of Ayer's *Language, Truth, and Logic* in 1936. Alfred Jules Ayer was born in London in 1910. After school at Eton, he entered Christ Church, Oxford, on a Classics scholarship in 1929. As with many Oxford philosophers of the day, he was first exposed to philosophy while studying Greats. After receiving a First, Christ Church appointed him to a lectureship, enabling him to travel. On the advice of his tutor, Gilbert Ryle, he visited the Vienna Circle in 1932. Ayer was to publish over twenty books (notably *The Foundations of Empirical Knowledge*, 1940, and *The Problem of Knowledge*, 1956) and numerous essays, but his first book remains his best-known work. Ayer was Grote Professor of Mind and Logic, at University College, London, from 1946 to 1959. In those years, he transformed the department from a state of disrepair into the first-rate unit it remains today. He then took the Wykeham Chair in Logic at Oxford, where he sought, with some success, to counteract the influence of J.L. Austin's methods of linguistic analysis. He received a knighthood in 1970. He retired in 1978 and remained a well-known public figure until his death in 1989.

The name "the Vienna Circle" dates from 1929. When Schlick was a visiting professor at Stanford, Carnap, Neurath, and Hahn chose to celebrate his return to Vienna by producing a manifesto titled *Wissenschaftliche Weltauffasug, Der Weiner Kress* ("The Scientific World View: The Vienna Circle"). The name soon stuck. In the next few years, they publicized their views through various conferences and monographs, and by founding their own journal, *Erkenntnis*. One of the most notable features of the work of the Circle, apart from its actual content, was its explicitly collaborative nature, still so rare in philosophy.

Apart from Ayer, visitors to the Circle included Karl Popper and W.V. Quine. However, the most influential contact was with Ludwig Wittgenstein, back in Vienna after his disastrous efforts at elementary schoolteaching. The meetings were not always harmonious, since Wittgenstein's religious, artistic temperament conflicted with Carnap's scientific outlook. Wittgenstein came to an arrangement with Freidrich Waismann, whereby the latter would write a book putting Wittgenstein's then current ideas, in turbulent transition from the *Tractatus*, into an orderly form—a thankless task. Wittgenstein rejected every draft Waismann produced because in the intervening time he had substantially revised his position. Waismann abandoned the book, which was published posthumously (1979).

By the time of Schlick's death, the Circle had began to break up, dispersing notably to the United States and Britain, in the wake of the open hostility of the right-wing Austrian government, soon to be followed by the annexation of Austria by the Nazis in 1938.

The Positivists claimed that philosophy's traditional problems could be revealed by logical analysis to be "pseudo-problems," the expression of which were literally nonsensical. Like Kant, they were extremely conscious of the discrepancy between philosophy and the sciences, in that the sciences seemed to be progressing in leaps and bounds, yet philosophical problems had long been in stalemate. On the one hand, the sciences were accumulating data and constructing better theories; on the other hand, traditional philosophy ("metaphysics") was still struggling with the same set of problems since the Greeks. In fact, the only exception to this philosophical impasse was logic. However, the Positivists' reaction to this situation differed greatly from that of Kant: "Metaphysics collapses not because the solving of its tasks is an enterprise to which the human reason is unequal (as Kant thought) but because there is no such task" (Schlick, "The Turning Point in Philosophy," in Schlick, 1978).

Logical Positivism can be viewed as an updating of classical and nineteenth-century Empiricism via the new logic of Frege, Russell, and Wittgenstein. Recall "Hume's Fork," intended to display all that could possibly be known:

> *Relations of Ideas*: Not facts themselves, but relations between them, discovered a priori;

> *Matters of Fact*: Contingent facts, empirically discoverable.

Hume said that anything knowable fits into one of these mutually exclusive categories. Positivism takes these categories to exhaust the *meaningful,* rather than the knowable. That is, anything that could be legitimately said was either an empirical statement or a tautology. Its truth-value could be checked either by looking for a 'match' with the world or by purely formal considerations. Anything whose truth-value could not be determined was judged to be meaningless. Thus, anything that fitted neither of these categories was not knowable, because there was nothing there to know.

So, while the Positivists are a clear example of the view that philosophy is the handmaiden of the sciences, the work of the philosopher is, in a sense, prior to that of the scientist, while fundamentally distinct from it. Put bluntly, the scientist is concerned with truth, the philosopher with meaning. Before you can tell whether any claim *p* is true, you have to know what *p* means, and, a fortiori, you have to determine that *p* has a meaning at all.

These factors led to what has become known as the *Verification Principle*, or (as Ayer calls it) the *Criterion of Verifiability.* There are several aspects of this, which need to be kept distinct (although Positivists didn't always do so).

1. It is a *criterion of meaningfulness*: That is, to possess meaning at all, the statement expressed by a nonanalytic sentence must be somehow checkable against experience.

2a. *A theory of meaning:* a principle stating what fixes the specific meaning of certain sentences: The meaning is determined by the experiences that would enable you to tell whether its corresponding statement is true or not. This is sometimes cryptically expressed by saying "The meaning of a sentence is its method of verification."

2b. This yields a *theory of understanding*: I understand a sentence if I know how to verify what it states.

Application of the Verification Principle led to many areas of discourse being judged to be meaningless:

1. Traditional metaphysics—claims about the nature of reality, God, and so on. If God, or the nature of reality, are inaccessible, and thereby uncheckable by experience, any statements regarding them are meaningless. Traditional philosophical disputes (e.g., Realism versus Idealism) were also judged meaningless. Since no possible experience could decide between such theses, there is no substantive disagreement here. In other words, they are *pseudo-problems*. Thus, Carnap says that such conflicts are best understood as questions about which *language* to adopt. (Ayer diverges from this position in explicitly favoring Phenomenalism, and so is surely open to the "charge" of constructing a metaphysical theory.)

2. Ethics, religion, aesthetics. At this point, we must be more precise over charges of meaninglessness. Positivists said that these lacked *cognitive* meaning—that is, having no descriptive content. Such utterances were distinguishable from mere gibberish by having *non-cognitive* meaning (i.e., emotive, imperative, etc.) In other words, while they may express various feelings or emotions, or a certain attitude to life, they lack a truth-value. The Positivist view was that a common source of intellectual confusion was mixing up fundamentally different classes of sentences; for example taking there to be cognitive meaning when only emotive meaning was present.

3. Wittgenstein's *Tractatus* made a claim that caused Positivists a great deal of difficulty: He said that philosophical statements about language, or about the relationship between language and reality, were not about facts in the world either, and so were strictly senseless, since they didn't picture a possible fact.

Incidentally, the Positivists are commonly thought to have seriously misinterpreted Wittgenstein, in deriving their verificationism from the *Tractatus*. The truth is less obvious. They were in close communication with Wittgenstein in 1929-34, by which time his views had altered. With the great deal of posthumously published work by Wittgenstein, it is clear that he went through a verificationist phase at that time. It is this, as much as the *Tractatus*, that the Circle responded to, despite the fact that the *Tractatus* provided the initial inspiration for much of its ideas.

One Positivist aim was to provide a clear dividing line between sense and nonsense, which was equivalent to the distinction between science (conceived of as a unified system of empirical inquiry) and nonscience. Positivists tried to do this by constructing a system within which every legitimate claim could be justified. Logical truths were true by definition. This aprioricity extended to mathematical truths, given their logicist assumption that mathematics reduced to logic. Factual claims, on the other hand, were to be validated by derivation from some basic propositions. (These are referred to as "elementary," "observation," or "protocol" statements). There was an ongoing disagreement regarding what this foundation consisted in. In the beginning, influenced by Logical Atomism, they went for reports of sense-data. The pre-Vienna Carnap began from a phenomenological basis in the *Aufbau*, and the members most under Wittgenstein's influence, Schlick and Waismann, took this line: "In order to arrive at the meaning of a sentence or proposition we must go beyond propositions. For we cannot hope to explain the meaning of a proposition merely by presenting another proposition . . . I could always go on asking "But what does this new proposition mean?" You see there would never be any end to this kind of inquiry. The discovery of the meaning of any proposition must ultimately be achieved by some act, some immediate procedure, for instance, as the showing of yellow; it cannot be given in a proposition" (Schlick, "The Future of Philosophy," p. 128, in Schlick, 1978).

The motive behind this is classical foundationalism, with its Cartesian demand for a bedrock of absolute certainty. While statements about material objects are always in need of justification, this is unavailable and unnecessary in the case of sense-data. However, this choice of foundation puts a strain on the Positivists' demand for scientific legitimacy. If all statements can be logically analyzed into those referring to sense-data, then scientific knowledge would have a subjective and private foundation, and would lack the objectivity it prides itself upon. Later, under Neurath's influence, the Positivists traded in certainty for scientific respectability, and took protocol sentences to describe intersubjectively available states of affairs, open to any suitably located observer. I will return to the issue of protocol statements in a moment.

Let us now return to the Verification Principle, and the notion of verifiability. We can distinguish two theses here, between verifiability *in practice* and *in principle*. Certain claims, perhaps about distant planets, may not be actually verifiable right now, due to technological limitations. On the other hand, we have a clear idea of the way in which they could be verified. This distinction is the core of Carnap's ("Testability and Meaning") distinction between confirmability and testability: A proposition is *confirmable* if we know which type of procedure would confirm it; it is *testable* if we can actually perform this procedure.

It was recognized that the demands of confirmability or testability had to be interpreted "*weakly*." That is, that the tests provide grounds for a proposition's *probable* truth, rather than its certain truth. If we took the latter position, too much would be ruled out that Positivists wanted to keep. By a "strong verifiability," initially favored by Schlick and Waismann, a sentence S would be meaningful only where there is an entailment between S and some set of observational statements O. This demand arose from the Atomist claim that all significant sentences be *analyzable* in terms of (i.e., *reducible to*) sets of elementary propositions.

The weak thesis, demanding only that O gives grounds for S's acceptance, seems far more plausible. In fact, any attempts to show any logical entailments between reports of sensations and statements about the world fail.

1. From the fact that it is raining outside, it doesn't follow that anyone sees it, or even that they would see it, if certain specifiable conditions were satisfied. Consider this:

   It is raining outside → (if I were to look out the open window, with my glasses on, in normal light → I would have sense-impressions as of rain).

   The trouble is that no matter how much you add to the antecedent of the parenthesized conditional, it is still logically possible for it to be all satisfied, yet the consequent not occur.

2. Neither does any entailment occur the other way round. Even if you have certain sense-impressions, this by itself doesn't commit you to the existence of any particular object or event in the world. You could, for example, be dreaming or hallucinating.

Strong verifiability also faced a problem with universal statements. Recall that the Positivists regarded science as the paradigm of knowledge. Science, by its very nature, postulates laws, that is, counterfactual-supporting universal statements. But, as is well-known, no finite number of observed cases can entail a statement of universal form. Given that a true universal statement is equivalent to a negative existential, then these too would be meaningless. However, this was not the end of problems for universal statements. Let p be the universal statement "All water boils at 212F." p would not be strongly verifiable. Now consider its negation, ~p: "Some water does not boil at 212F." This *is* verifiable, by Ayer's criterion (in "The Elimination of Metaphysics"), in that it logically follows from a finite, consistent class of observation statements, namely "This is water" and "This does not boil at 212F." So, in such a case, ~p would be verified as true, and thereby meaningful. But in that case, given a classical account of negation, ~~p would be false, and thus meaningful. But ~~p is, by classical logic, equivalent to p.

The adoption of "weak verification" was not without its problems either. This becomes apparent by comparing Ayer's original formulation with the one offered in the preface to the second edition of *Language, Truth, and Logic*. For any statement to be meaningful, he originally required that some "experiential proposition" (i.e., an observational statement) be deducible from it plus some other premises, without being deducible from these other premises alone. By the second edition, he came to see that this didn't work. Take this modus ponens syllogism:

> *If God exists, then Oregon is larger than Rhode Island; God exists; therefore Oregon is larger than Rhode Island.*

Or consider this disjunctive syllogism:

> *Either God is finite or Oregon is larger than Rhode Island; God is not finite, therefore Oregon is larger than Rhode Island.*

Thus, blatantly metaphysical statements ("God exists," "God is not finite") pass Ayer's test. In the introduction to the second edition, he was driven by these results to construct a far more complex criterion:

"I propose to say that a statement is directly verifiable if it is either itself an observation-statement, or is such that in conjunction with one or more observation-statements it entails at least one observation-statement which is not deducible from these other premises alone; and I propose to say that a statement is indirectly verifiable if it satisfies the following conditions: first, that in conjunction with certain other premises it entails one or more directly verifiable statements which are not deducible from these other premises alone; and secondly, that these other premises do not include any statement that is not either analytic, or directly verifiable, or capable of being independently established as indirectly verifiable. And I can now reformulate the principle of verification as requiring of a literally meaningful statement, which is not analytic, that it should be either directly or indirectly verifiable, in the foregoing sense" (p. 13).

However, as Carl Hempel (1950) showed, this could still admit metaphysical claims. Let p stand for "My shirt is blue"; let q stand for "My shirt is red"; let r stand for "The Absolute is infinite."

1 $\sim p$ & r

2 p v $\sim q$

3 $\sim p$ 1 Simp

4 $\sim q$ 2,3 DS

But since both "p v $\sim q$" and "$\sim q$" are observation statements, "$\sim p$ & r" is a meaningful statement, and so talk of the Absolute, or anything else, can occur in meaningful discourse. So nothing is excluded. Alonzo Church, in his review of Ayer's book, also proved that one could prove any statement to be meaningful, so long as there were three mutually independent observation sentences.

    I now return to the question of the nature and status of protocol statements. One of the strangest developments in Positivism was the shift from an empiricist foundationalism to a fallibilist coherentism in which all connection to external reality has been removed. This move, primarily by Carnap and Neurath, is criticized by Schlick in "The Foundation of Knowledge." This shift, of course, brought them perilously close to the Idealists they so despised. Originally, the Positivists advocated an empiricist view similar to Russell's Logical Atomism: (1) They accepted that all knowledge ultimately rests on acquaintance and that all genuinely fact-stating sentences could be analyzed into reports of sense-experience; (2) They favored a correspondence theory in which a statement is true if it corresponds to an extralinguistic fact. They took Russell to have shown the possibility of a perfect language in which all genuinely informative statements could be explicitly expressed in a way that revealed how they could be derived from atomic propositions by logical analysis.

    However, in line with classical objections to the correspondence theory, Neurath convinced Carnap of the unsatisfactoriness of this picture. How can experience verify a proposition, when the two are of such different types? This seemed to be an example of unjustified metaphysics. The inability to clearly account for the relation of correspondence, and for semantic relations between language and facts, led them to become wary of semantics per se. In brief, they denied that a proposition could be verified by being compared with something extralinguistic like a fact, but could only be compared to other propositions, and logically related only to them. Thus emerged a formal, coherentist account of justification, and even of meaning. The meaning of a statement was given purely in terms of its syntactic form and its logical relations to *other propositions*. In turn, the meaning of an individual word is specified by the role it plays in such a set of statements.

Still, they acknowledged that knowledge required some sort of foundation. As before, the tension between the quest for Cartesian certainty and scientific objectivity led to disagreements about the nature and epistemological status of protocol statements. Carnap took protocols to report private experiences but believed that these could be translated into physical language reports. With Carnap and his "Principle of Tolerance," the issue was always a conventional, pragmatic matter of which language to choose. There was nothing intrinsically right or wrong, legitimate or illegitimate about either physicalist or phenomenal languages, and pseudo-problems are created by thinking that there is.

Neurath was less tolerant and demanded that these protocol statements record physical events, reported in physical language; for example "Otto reported at 2:15 p.m. that a temperature reading of 100 degrees was perceived by Otto." By this physicalist perspective, he gave up the claim to certainty. Carnap initially resisted this conclusion, making his protocol statements the epistemically privileged observational base. However, his formal intralinguistic theory can give no justification for such privilege. By cutting them off from the world, he cannot take the old view of comparing them with reality—but purely formal, structural relations are insufficient to fill this gap. Soon, following Neurath, he surrendered their privileged position. At this point, no real empiricism is left.

The reason for this move into syntactic coherentism was the assumption that the correspondence theory was intrinsically inadequate since no philosophically satisfactory accounts of semantic properties like truth could be given. So, "Positivists eager to get on with the analytic task of a 'rational reconstruction' of science faced a dilemma: either to risk metaphysics and nonsense by talking about the ineffable relations between language and reality, or risk divorcing scientific truth from objective fact altogether" (Romanos p. 135). Only when he encountered Tarski's semantic conception of truth was Carnap persuaded of the possibility of a satisfactory correspondence theory, and of the legitimacy of semantics as a scientific discipline.

Let us now return to the Verification Principle. How did it stand up to its own demand? Schlick proposed it as an empirical fact: "nothing but a simple statement of the way in which meaning is actually assigned to propositions." This is clearly false, for example, religious believers often regard themselves as saying something that is literally true, even when they have no idea how to prove their claims. Ayer regarded it as analytic: "not as an empirical hypothesis, but as a definition." Again, taken as lexicographic definition that actually described ordinary usage, it is false to say that people generally regard "meaningful" and "verifiable" as synonymous, or even as coextensive. As a third alternative, Carnap took it to be a revisionary definition, or a *proposal* to restrict the meaningful to the verifiable. The justification for this proposal would be a purely pragmatic matter. But in that case, the Verification Principle would be in the same boat as moral prescriptions and could be granted only non-cognitive meaning.

Another aspect of this is relevant here to the Verification Principle's status. The Positivists didn't *discover* the principle, judge it to be correct, then abide by its decisions. This is shown by their extreme difficulty in getting a satisfactory formulation of what they wanted. It is rather that they *already* had a clear idea of what they wanted a principle to do—admit science and everyday judgments, but exclude religion, metaphysics, and so on. Successive formulations were either too strict, excluding what they wanted to keep, or too loose, admitting virtually everything, metaphysics included. Their attitude to the principle is like that in law: A rule is formulated which looks to give results in accordance with our intuitive and considered judgments on justice; unexpected counter-examples or difficult cases emerge; the law is altered to accommodate them.

Parallel to the problem of the status of the Verification Principle is the more general question of the status of philosophical statements—an issue initially raised in the *Tractatus*. In the beginning, Schlick and Waismann agreed with Wittgenstein that philosophy didn't consist in a set of facts, but in an *activity* of showing what meaning consisted in. That is, philosophy consists in an activity of performing logical analysis on sentences, which can explicitly reveal whether it possesses cognitive meaning, and what it specifically means. But this forces the question of into what category do descriptions of this method themselves fall.

Carnap placed them on the formal, analytic side, saying that such philosophical sentences were not meaningless, but best understood as being about language—more specifically, formal descriptions of the "logical syntax" of a system of words. In *The Logical Syntax of Language*, he distinguished the *object language*—the language under study—from the *metalanguage*—in which the theory of the metalanguage is to be stated. His task was to devise a metalanguage in which to provide a logical analysis of language.

Carnap distinguished three types of sentences:

1. Synthetic empirical sentences, explicitly about states of affairs, for example "the book is green;"

2. Syntactical sentences, explicitly about words, for example "the word 'book' is a thing-word;"

3. Quasi-syntactic sentences like "the book is a thing."

This third type of sentence has a misleading form. It looks like it belongs in the same category as **1**, but it really belongs with **2**. This is because it is expressed in the misleading "material mode," whereas its true logical type is displayed when it is re-expressed in the formal mode, where it is translated into **2**. Quasi-syntactic sentences contain certain "universal words" stating logically basic categories (e.g., *thing, object, property, relation, fact, state, process, space, time, number*) but presented as ordinary predicates.

This distinction allowed Carnap to give a precise diagnosis of the central Positivist thesis that many philosophical problems and disputes are really pseudo-problems caused by being deceived by the surface grammar of ordinary language expressions. The trouble is caused by expressing syntactic claims in the material mode. For example, consider the debate between realists and phenomenalists. On the surface, this looks like a case of contrary factual claims, that is, respectively, that objects are made up of sense-data, and that objects are made up of atoms. However, says Carnap, this is really only a dispute about linguistic conventions, that is about the linguistic status of object-expressions. On the one hand, we have the suggestion that any sentence involving an object-word be equivalent to a set of sentences involving expressions denoting sense-data; secondly, we have the suggestion that sentences involving object-words be taken as equivalent to a set of sentences including expressions in the language of physics. For Carnap, following his Principle of Tolerance, it makes no sense to ask "Which convention is the right one?" since there is no genuine fact of the matter here.

In Carnap's "Empiricism, Semantics and Ontology," the distinction between empirical and syntactical sentences is modified into the distinction between internal and external questions. Within a language that permits us to talk of physical objects, we can ask questions about the ontological status of individuals or types of physical objects, such as "How many students are in this class?" or "Are there any diamonds as big as a soccer ball?" These are *internal* questions, since they can only be meaningfully offered from within the rule-governed practice of "physical object language." The truth-value of such an internal question would be checked empirically.

These questions must be distinguished from *external* questions, concerning the framework itself. Corresponding to the above internal questions would be the external question "Are there material objects?" Corresponding to internal questions about numbers, such as "Is ëfive' an odd number?" or "Is 'five' larger than 'six'?," would be the external question about numbers themselves, such as "Are there numbers?" These external questions are not factual. There is no empirically or formally discoverable fact of the matter that determines their truth-value. Rather, one's answer to an external question reduces to the decision whether or not to adopt the linguistic framework it depicts. That is, it is a matter of choice, to be judged solely by the usefulness of the terminology. So the debate between Realists and Phenomenalists is not a factual debate to be settled by evidence. Rather, the acceptance of a certain framework enables claims about evidence to take place. As always, Carnap advocates tolerance in the adoption of frameworks.

BIBLIOGRAPHY

Further Reading
Two good anthologies of Positivist writings are
A. J. Ayer ed., *Logical Positivism*, (New York: Free Press 1959).
Oswald Hanfling, *Essential Readings in Logical Positivism*, (Oxford: Basil Blackwell, 1981).

Original works include
A. J. Ayer, *Language, Truth, and Logic*, 2nd ed. (New York: Dover, 1946).
Rudolf Carnap, *The Logical Structure of the World* (Berkeley: University of California Press, 1967).
Rudolf Carnap, *The Logical Syntax of Language*, (New York: Harcourt Brace Jovanovich, 1937).

Rudolf Carnap, *Meaning and Necessity* (Chicago: University of Chicago Press, 1956).

Rudolf Carnap, *Philosophy and Logical Syntax* (New York: AMS Press, 1976).

Rudolf Carnap, "Testability and Meaning," *Philosophy of Science*, Vol. 3, no. 4 (1936), and Vol. 4. no. 1, (1937)

Otto Neurath, *Foundations of the Social Sciences* (Chicago: University of Chicago Press, 1944).

Moritz Schlick, *Philosophical Papers*, trans. P. Heath (Dordrecht: D. Reidel, 1978).

Freidrich Waismann, *Philosophical Papers*, ed. B. McGuinness (Dordrecht D. Reidel, 1977).

Friedrich Waismann, *Wittgenstein and the Vienna Circle*, ed. B. McGuinness (Oxford: Basil Blackwell, 1979).

Other works mentioned were

Alonzo Church, "Review of Language, Truth, and Logic," *Journal of Symbolic Logic*, Vol. 14.

Carl Hempel, "The Empiricist Criterion of Meaning," in A. J. Ayer, *Logical Positivism*, (New York: Free Press, 1959).

Commentaries include

Oswald Hanfling, *Logical Positivism*, (New York: Columbia University Press, 1981).

George D. Romanos, *Quine and Analytic Philosophy*, (Cambridge: MIT Press, 1983.)

Paul Schilpp, ed. *The Philosophy of Rudolf Carnap*, Library of Living Philosophers, Vol. 11, (La Salle, Ill.: Open Court, 1963). (This book includes Carnap's "Intellectual Autobiography")

The Elimination of Metaphysics

A. J. Ayer

The traditional disputes of philosophers are, for the most part, as unwarranted as they are unfruitful. The surest way to end them is to establish beyond question what should be the purpose and method of a philosophical enquiry. And this is by no means so difficult a task as the history of philosophy would lead one to suppose. For if there are any questions which science leaves it to philosophy to answer, a straightforward process of elimination must lead to their discovery.

We may begin by criticising the metaphysical thesis that philosophy affords us knowledge of a reality transcending the world of science and common sense. Later on, when we come to define metaphysics and account for its existence, we shall find that it is possible to be a metaphysician without believing in a transcendent reality; for we shall see that many metaphysical utterances are due to the commission of logical errors, rather than to a conscious desire on the part of their authors to go beyond the limits of experience. But it is convenient for us to take the case of those who believe that it is possible to have knowledge of a transcendent reality as a starting-point for

---

* From A. J. Ayer, *Language, Truth, and Logic*, reprinted by permission of Dover Publication.

our discussion. The arguments which we use to refute them will subsequently be found to apply to the whole of metaphysics.

One way of attacking a metaphysician who claimed to have knowledge of a reality which transcended the phenomenal world would be to enquire from what premises his propositions were deduced. Must he not begin, as other men do, with the evidence of his senses? And if so, what valid process of reasoning can possibly lead him to the conception of a transcendent reality? Surely from empirical premises nothing whatsoever concerning the properties, or even the existence, of anything super-empirical can legitimately be inferred. But this objection would be met by a denial on the part of the metaphysician that his assertions were ultimately based on the evidence of his senses. He would say that he was endowed with a faculty of intellectual intuition which enabled him to know facts that could not be known through sense-experience. And even if it could be shown that he was relying on empirical premises, and that his venture into a non-empirical world was therefore logically unjustified, it would not follow that the assertions which he made concerning this non-empirical world could not be true. For the fact that a conclusion does not follow from its putative premise is not sufficient to show that it is false. Consequently one cannot overthrow a system of transcendent metaphysics merely by criticising the way in which it comes into being. What is required is rather a criticism of the nature of the actual statements which comprise it. And this is the line of argument which we shall, in fact, pursue. For we shall maintain that no statement which refers to a "reality" transcending the limits of all possible sense-experience can possibly have any literal significance; from which it must follow that the labours of those who have striven to describe such a reality have all been devoted to the production of nonsense.

It may be suggested that this is a proposition which has already been proved by Kant. But although Kant also condemned transcendent metaphysics, he did so on different grounds. For he said that the human understanding was so constituted that it lost itself in contradictions when it ventured out beyond the limits of possible experience and attempted to deal with things in themselves. And thus he made the impossibility of a transcendent metaphysic not, as we do, a matter of logic, but a matter of fact. He asserted, not that our minds could not conceivably have had the power of penetrating beyond the phenomenal world, but merely that they were in fact devoid of it. And this leads the critic to ask how, if it is possible to know only what lies within the bounds of sense-experience, the author can be justified in asserting that real things do exist beyond, and how he can tell what are the boundaries beyond which the human understanding may not venture, unless he succeeds in passing them himself. As Wittgenstein says, "in order to draw a limit to thinking, we should have to think both sides of this limit,"[1] a truth to which Bradley gives a special twist in maintaining that the man who is ready to prove that metaphysics is impossible is a brother metaphysician with a rival theory of his own.[2]

Whatever force these objections may have against the Kantian doctrine, they have none whatsoever against the thesis that I am about to set forth. It cannot here be

---

[1] *Tractatus Logico-Philosophicus*, Preface.

[2] Bradley, *Appearance and Reality*, 2nd ed., p.1.

said that the author is himself overstepping the barrier he maintains to be impassable. For the fruitlessness of attempting to transcend the limits of possible sense-experience will be deduced, not from a psychological hypothesis concerning the actual constitution of the human mind, but from the rule which determines the literal significance of language. Our charge against the metaphysician is not that he attempts to employ the understanding in a field where it cannot profitably venture, but that he produces sentences which fail to conform to the conditions under which alone a sentence can be literally significant. Nor are we ourselves obliged to talk nonsense in order to show that all sentences of a certain type are necessarily devoid of literal significance. We need only formulate the criterion which enables us to test whether a sentence expresses a genuine proposition about a matter of fact, and then point out that the sentences under consideration fail to satisfy it. And this we shall now proceed to do. We shall first of all formulate the criterion in somewhat vague terms, and then give the explanations which are necessary to render it precise.

The criterion which we use to test the genuineness of apparent statements of fact is the criterion of verifiability. We say that a sentence is factually significant to any given person, if, and only if, he knows how to verify the proposition which it purports to express—that is, if he knows what observations would lead him, under certain conditions, to accept the proposition as being true, or reject it as being false. If, on the other hand, the putative proposition is of such a character that the assumption of its truth, or falsehood, is consistent with any assumption whatsoever concerning the nature of his future experience, then, as far as he is concerned, it is, if not a tautology, a mere pseudo-proposition. The sentence expressing it may be emotionally significant to him; but it is not literally significant. And with regard to questions the procedure is the same. We enquire in every case what observations would lead us to answer the question, one way or the other; and, if none can be discovered, we must conclude that the sentence under consideration does not, as far as we are concerned, express a genuine question, however strongly its grammatical appearance may suggest that it does.

As the adoption of this procedure is an essential factor in the argument of this book, it needs to be examined in detail.

In the first place, it is necessary to draw a distinction between practical verifiability, and verifiability in principle. Plainly we all understand, in many cases believe, propositions which we have not in fact taken steps to verify. Many of these are propositions which we could verify if we took enough trouble. But there remain a number of significant propositions, concerning matters of fact, which we could not verify even if we chose; simply because we lack the practical means of placing ourselves in the situation where the relevant observations could be made. A simple and familiar example of such a proposition is the proposition that there are mountains on the farther side of the moon.[1] No rocket has yet been invented which would enable me to go and look at the farther side of the moon, so that I am unable to decide the matter by actual observation. But I do know what observations would decide it for me, if, as is theoretically conceivable, I were once in a position to make them. And therefore I say that the

---

[1] This example has been used by Professor Schlick to illustrate the same point.

proposition is verifiable in principle, if not in practice, and is accordingly significant. On the other hand, such a metaphysical pseudo-proposition as "the Absolute enters into, but is itself incapable of, evolution and progress,"[1] is not even in principle verifiable. For one cannot conceive of an observation which would enable one to determine whether the Absolute did, or did not, enter into evolution and progress. Of course it is possible that the author of such a remark is using English words in a way in which they are not commonly used by English-speaking people, and that he does, in fact, intend to assert something which could be empirically verified. But until he makes us understand how the proposition that he wishes to express would be verified, he fails to communicate anything to us. And if he admits, as I think the author of the remark in question would have admitted, that his words were not intended to express either a tautology or a proposition which was capable, at least in principle, of being verified, then it follows that he has made an utterance which has no literal significance even for himself.

A further distinction which we must make is the distinction between the "strong" and the "weak" sense of the term "verifiable." A proposition is said to be verifiable, in the strong sense of the term, if, and only if, its truth could be conclusively established in experience. But it is verifiable, in the weak sense, if it is possible for experience to render it probable. In which sense are we using the term when we say that a putative proposition is genuine only if it is verifiable?

It seems to me that if we adopt conclusive verifiability as our criterion of significance, as some positivists have proposed,[2] our argument will prove too much. Consider, for example, the case of general propositions of law—such propositions, namely, as "arsenic is poisonous"; "all men are mortal"; "a body tends to expand when it is heated." It is of the very nature of these propositions that their truth cannot be established with certainty by any finite series of observations. But if it is recognised that such general propositions of law are designed to cover an infinite number of cases, then it must be admitted that they cannot, even in principle, be verified conclusively. And then, if we adopt conclusive verifiability as our criterion of significance, we are logically obliged to treat these general propositions of law in the same fashion as we treat the statements of the metaphysician.

In face of this difficulty, some positivists[3] have adopted the heroic course of saying that these general propositions are indeed pieces of nonsense, albeit an essentially important type of nonsense. But here the introduction of the term "important" is simply an attempt to hedge. It serves only to mark the authors' recognition that their view is somewhat too paradoxical, without in any way removing the paradox. Besides, the difficulty is not confined to the case of general propositions of law, though it is there revealed most plainly. It is hardly less obvious in the case of propositions about the remote past. For it must surely be admitted that, however strong the evidence in favour of historical statements may be, their truth can never become more than highly probable. And to maintain that they also constituted an important, or unimportant,

---

[1] A remark taken at random from *Appearance and Reality*, by F. H. Bradley.

[2] e.g. M. Schlick, "Positivismus und Realismus," *Erkenntnis*, Vol. I, 1930. F. Waismann, "Logische Analyse des Warscheinlichkeitsbegriffs," Erkenntnis, Vol. I, 1930.

[3] e.g. M. Schlick, "Die Kausalität in der gegenwärtigen Physik," *Naturwissenschaft*, Vol. 19, 1931.

type of nonsense would be unplausible, to say the very least. Indeed, it will be our contention that no proposition, other than a tautology, can possibly be anything more than a probable hypothesis. And if this is correct, the principle that a sentence can be factually significant only if it expresses what is conclusively verifiable is self-stultifying as a criterion of significance. For it leads to the conclusion that it is impossible to make a significant statement of fact at all.

Nor can we accept the suggestion that a sentence should be allowed to be factually significant if, and only if, it expresses something which is definitely confutable by experience.[1] Those who adopt this course assume that, although no finite series of observations is ever sufficient to establish the truth of a hypothesis beyond all possibility of doubt, there are crucial cases in which a single observation, or series of observations, can definitely confute it. But, as we shall show later on, this assumption is false. A hypothesis cannot be conclusively confuted any more than it can be conclusively verified. For when we take the occurrence of certain observations as proof that a given hypothesis is false, we presuppose the existence of certain conditions. And though, in any given case, it may be extremely improbable that this assumption is false, it is not logically impossible. We shall see that there need be no self-contradiction in holding that some of the relevant circumstances are other than we have taken them to be, and consequently that the hypothesis has not really broken down. And if it is not the case that any hypothesis can be definitely confuted, we cannot hold that the genuineness of a proposition depends on the possibility of its definite confutation.

Accordingly, we fall back on the weaker sense of verification. We say that the question that must be asked about any putative statement of fact is not, Would any observations make its truth or falsehood logically certain? but simply, Would any observations be relevant to the determination of its truth or falsehood? And it is only if a negative answer is given to this second question that we conclude that the statement under consideration is nonsensical.

To make our position clearer, we may formulate it in another way. Let us call a proposition which records an actual or possible observation an experiential proposition. Then we may say that it is the mark of a genuine factual proposition, not that it should be equivalent to an experiential proposition, or any finite number of experiential propositions, but simply that some experiential propositions can be deduced from it in conjunction with certain other premises without being deducible from those other premises alone.[2]

This criterion seems liberal enough. In contrast to the principle of conclusive verifiability, it clearly does not deny significance to general propositions or to propositions about the past. Let us see what kinds of assertion it rules out.

A good example of the kind of utterance that is condemned by our criterion as being not even false but nonsensical would be the assertion that the world of sense-experience was altogether unreal. It must, of course, be admitted that our senses do sometimes deceive us. We may, as the result of having certain sensations, expect certain other sensations to be obtainable which are, in fact, not obtainable. But, in all

---

[1] This has been proposed by Karl Popper in his *Logik de Forschung*.

[2] This is an over-simplified statement, which is not literally correct. I give what I believe to be the correct formulation in the Introduction, p. 13.

such cases, it is further sense-experience that informs us of the mistakes that arise out of sense-experience. We say that the senses sometimes deceive us, just because the expectations to which our sense-experiences give rise do not always accord with what we subsequently experience. That is, we rely on our senses to substantiate or confute the judgements which are based on our sensations. And therefore the fact that our perceptual judgements are sometimes found to be erroneous has not the slightest tendency to show that the world of sense-experience is unreal. And, indeed, it is plain that no conceivable observation, or series of observations, could have any tendency to show that the world revealed to us by sense-experience was unreal. Consequently, anyone who condemns the sensible world as a world of mere appearance, as opposed to reality, is saying something which, according to our criterion of significance, is literally nonsensical.

An example of a controversy which the application of our criterion obliges us to condemn as fictitious is provided by those who dispute concerning the number of substances that there are in the world. For it is admitted both by monists, who maintain that reality is one substance, and by pluralists, who maintain that reality is many, that it is impossible to imagine any empirical situation which would be relevant to the solution of their dispute. But if we are told that no possible observation could give any probability either to the assertion that reality was one substance or to the assertion that it was many, then we must conclude that neither assertion is significant. We shall see later on[1] that there are genuine logical and empirical questions involved in the dispute between monists and pluralists. But the metaphysical question concerning "substance" is ruled out by our criterion as spurious.

A similar treatment must be accorded to the controversy between realists and idealists, in its metaphysical aspect. A simple illustration, which I have made use of in a similar argument elsewhere,[2] will help to demonstrate this. Let us suppose that a picture is discovered and the suggestion made that it was painted by Goya. There is a definite procedure for dealing with such a question. The experts examine the picture to see in what way it resembles the accredited works of Goya, and to see if it bears any marks which are characteristic of a forgery; they look up contemporary records for evidence of the existence of such a picture, and so on. In the end, they may still disagree, but each one knows what empirical evidence would go to confirm or discredit his opinion. Suppose, now, that these men have studied philosophy, and some of them proceed to maintain that this picture is a set of ideas in the perceiver's mind, or in God's mind, others that it is objectively real. What possible experience could any of them have which would be relevant to the solution of this dispute one way or the other? In the ordinary sense of the term "real," in which it is opposed to "illusory," the reality of the picture is not in doubt. The disputants have satisfied themselves that the picture is real, in this sense, by obtaining a correlated series of sensations of sight and sensations of touch. Is there any similar process by which they could discover whether the picture was real, in the sense in which the term "real" is opposed to "ideal"? Clearly there is none. But, if that is so, the problem is fictitious according to our criterion. This does not mean that the realist-idealist controversy may be dis-

---

[1] In Chapter VIII.

[2] Vide "Demonstration of the Impossibility of Metaphysics," *Mind*, 1934, p.339.

missed without further ado. For it can legitimately be regarded as a dispute concerning the analysis of existential propositions, and so as involving a logical problem which, as we shall see, can be definitively solved.[1] What we have just shown is that the question at issue between idealists and realists becomes fictitious when, as is often the case, it is given a metaphysical interpretation.

There is no need for us to give further examples of the operation of our criterion of significance. For our object is merely to show that philosophy, as a genuine branch of knowledge, must be distinguished from metaphysics. We are not now concerned with the historical question how much of what has traditionally passed for philosophy is actually metaphysical. We shall, however, point out later on that the majority of the "great philosophers" of the past were not essentially metaphysicians, and thus reassure those who would otherwise be prevented from adopting our criterion by considerations of piety.

As to the validity of the verification principle, in the form in which we have stated it, a demonstration will be given in the course of this book. For it will be shown that all propositions which have factual content are empirical hypotheses; and that the function of an empirical hypothesis is to provide a rule for the anticipation of experience.[2] And this means that every empirical hypothesis must be relevant to some actual, or possible, experience, so that a statement which is not relevant to any experience is not an empirical hypothesis, and accordingly has no factual content. But this is precisely what the principle of verifiability asserts.

It should be mentioned here that the fact that the utterances of the metaphysician are nonsensical does not follow simply from the fact that they are devoid of factual content. It follows from that fact, together with the fact that they are not *a priori* propositions. And in assuming that they are not *a priori* propositions, we are once again anticipating the conclusions of a later chapter in this book.[3] For it will be shown there that *a priori* propositions, which have always been attractive to philosophers on account of their certainty, owe this certainty to the fact that they are tautologies. We may accordingly define a metaphysical sentence as a sentence which purports to express a genuine proposition, but does, in fact, express neither a tautology nor an empirical hypothesis. And as tautologies and empirical hypotheses form the entire class of significant propositions, we are justified in concluding that all metaphysical assertions are nonsensical. Our next task is to show how they come to be made.

The use of the term "substance," to which we have already referred, provides us with a good example of the way in which metaphysics mostly comes to be written. It happens to be the case that we cannot, in our language, refer to the sensible properties of a thing without introducing a word or phrase which appears to stand for the thing itself as opposed to anything which may be said about it. And, as a result of this, those who are infected by the primitive superstition that to every name a single real entity must correspond assume that it is necessary to distinguish logically between the thing itself and any, or all, of its sensible properties. And so they employ the term

---

[1] Vide Chapter VIII.

[2] Vide Chapter V.

[3] Chapter IV.

"substance" to refer to the thing itself. But from the fact that we happen to employ a single word to refer to a thing, and make that word the grammatical subject of the sentences in which we refer to the sensible appearances of the thing, it does not by any means follow that the thing itself is a "simple entity," or that it cannot be defined in terms of the totality of its appearances. It is true that in talking of "its" appearances we appear to distinguish the thing from the appearances, but that is simply an accident of linguistic usage. Logical analysis shows that what makes these "appearances" the "appearances of" the same thing is not their relationship to an entity other than themselves, but their relationship to one another. The metaphysician fails to see this because he is misled by a superficial grammatical feature of his language.

A simpler and clearer instance of the way in which a consideration of grammar leads to metaphysics is the case of the metaphysical concept of Being. The origin of our temptation to raise questions about Being, which no conceivable experience would enable us to answer, lies in the fact that, in our language, sentences which express existential propositions and sentences which express attributive propositions may be of the same grammatical form. For instance, the sentences "Martyrs exist" and "Martyrs suffer" both consist of a noun followed by an intransitive verb, and the fact that they have grammatically the same appearance leads one to assume that they are of the same logical type. It is seen that in the proposition "Martyrs suffer," the members of a certain species are credited with a certain attribute, and it is sometimes assumed that the same thing is true of such a proposition as "Martyrs exist." If this were actually the case, it would, indeed, be as legitimate to speculate about the Being of martyrs as it is to speculate about their suffering. But, as Kant pointed out,[1] existence is not an attribute. For, when we ascribe an attribute to a thing, we covertly assert that it exists: so that if existence were itself an attribute, it would follow that all positive existential propositions were tautologies, and all negative existential propositions self-contradictory; and this is not the case.[2] So that those who raise questions about Being which are based on the assumption that existence is an attribute are guilty of following grammar beyond the boundaries of sense.

A similar mistake has been made in connection with such propositions as "Unicorns are fictitious." Here again the fact that there is a superficial grammatical resemblance between the English sentences "Dogs are faithful" and "Unicorns are fictitious," and between the corresponding sentences in other languages, creates the assumption that they are of the same logical type. Dogs must exist in order to have the property of being faithful, and so it is held that unless unicorns in some way existed they could not have the property of being fictitious. But, as it is plainly self-contradictory to say that fictitious objects exist, the device is adopted of saying that they are real in some non-empirical sense—that they have a mode of real being which is different from the mode of being of existent things. But since there is no way of testing whether an object is real in this sense, as there is for testing whether it is real in the ordinary sense, the assertion that fictitious objects have a special non-empirical mode of real being is devoid of all literal significance. It comes to be made as a result of the assumption that being fictitious is an attribute. And this is a fallacy of the same

---

[1] Vide *The Critique of Pure Reason*, "Transcendental Dialectic," Book II, Chapter iii, section 4.

[2] This argument is well stated by John Wisdom, *Interpretation and Analysis*, pp. 62, 63.

order as the fallacy of supposing that existence is an attribute, and it can be exposed in the same way.

In general, the postulation of real non-existent entities results from the superstition, just now referred to, that, to every word or phrase that can be the grammatical subject of a sentence, there must somewhere be a real entity corresponding. For as there is no place in the empirical world for many of these "entities," a special non-empirical world is invoked to house them. To this error must be attributed, not only the utterances of a Heidegger, who bases his metaphysics on the assumption that "Nothing" is a name which is used to denote something peculiarly mysterious,[1] but also the prevalence of such problems as those concerning the reality of propositions and universals whose senselessness, though less obvious, is no less complete.

These few examples afford a sufficient indication of the way in which most metaphysical assertions come to be formulated. They show how easy it is to write sentences which are literally nonsensical without seeing that they are nonsensical. And thus we see that the view that a number of the traditional "problems of philosophy" are metaphysical, and consequently fictitious, does not involve any incredible assumptions about the psychology of philosophers.

Among those who recognize that if philosophy is to be accounted a genuine branch of knowledge it must be defined in such a way as to distinguish it from metaphysics, it is fashionable to speak of the metaphysician as a kind of misplaced poet. As his statements have no literal meaning, they are not subject to any criteria of truth or falsehood: but they may still serve to express, or arouse, emotion, and thus be subject to ethical or aesthetic standards. And it is suggested that they may have considerable value, as means of moral inspiration, or even as works of art. In this way, an attempt is made to compensate the metaphysician for his extrusion from philosophy.[2]

I am afraid that this compensation is hardly in accordance with his deserts. The view that the metaphysician is to be reckoned among the poets appears to rest on the assumption that both talk nonsense. But this assumption is false. In the vast majority of cases the sentences which are produced by poets do have literal meaning. The difference between the man who uses language scientifically and the man who uses it emotively is not that the one produces sentences which are incapable of arousing emotion, and the other sentences which have no sense, but that the one is primarily concerned with the expression of true propositions, the other with the creation of a work of art. Thus, if a work of science contains true and important propositions, its value as a work of science will hardly be diminished by the fact that they are inelegantly expressed. And similarly, a work of art is not necessarily the worse for the fact that all the propositions comprising it are literally false. But to say that many literary works are largely composed of falsehoods, is not to say that they are composed of pseudo-propositions. It is, in fact, very rare for a literary artist to produce sentences which have no literal meaning. And where this does occur, the sentences are carefully chosen for their rhythm and balance. If the author writes non-

---

[1] Vide *Was ist Metaphysik*, by Heidegger: criticised by Rudolf Carnap in his "Überwindung der Metaphysik durch logische Analyse der Sprache," *Erkenntnis*, Vol. II, 1932.

[2] For a discussion of this point, see also C. A. Mace, "Representation and Expression," *Analysis* Vol. I, No. 3; and "Metaphysics and Emotive Language," *Analysis*, Vol. II, Nos. 1 and 2.

sense, it is because he considers it most suitable for bringing about the effects for which his writing is designed.

The metaphysician, on the other hand, does not intend to write nonsense. He lapses into it through being deceived by grammar, or through committing errors of reasoning, such as that which leads to the view that the sensible world is unreal. But it is not the mark of a poet simply to make mistakes of this sort. There are some, indeed, who would see in the fact that the metaphysician's utterances are senseless a reason against the view that they have aesthetic value. And, without going so far as this, we may safely say that it does not constitute a reason for it.

It is true, however, that although the greater part of metaphysics is merely the embodiment of humdrum errors, there remain a number of metaphysical passages which are the work of genuine mystical feeling; and they may more plausibly be held to have moral or aesthetic value. But, as far as we are concerned, the distinction between the kind of metaphysics that is produced by a philosopher who has been duped by grammar, and the kind that is produced by a mystic who is trying to express the inexpressible, is of no great importance: what is important to us is to realize that even the utterances of the metaphysician who is attempting to expound a vision are literally senseless; so that henceforth we may pursue our philosophical researches with as little regard for them as for the more inglorious kind of metaphysics which comes from a failure to understand the workings of our language.

The Foundation of Knowledge

Moritz Schlick

All important attempts at establishing a theory of knowledge grow out of the problem concerning the certainty of human knowledge. And this problem in turn originates in the wish for absolute certainty.

The insight that the statements of daily life and science can at best be only probable, that even the most general results of science, which all experiences confirm, can have only the character of hypotheses, has again and again stimulated philosophers since Descartes, and indeed, though less obviously, since ancient times, to search for an unshakeable, indubitable, foundation, a firm basis on which the uncertain structure of our knowledge could rest. The uncertainty of the structure was generally attributed to the fact that it was impossible, perhaps in principle, to construct a firmer one by the power of human thought. But this did not inhibit the search for the bedrock, which exists prior to all construction and does not itself vacillate.

From A.J. Ayer (Ed) *Logical Positivism*, (New York:Free Press) 1959. Reprinted by permission of David Rynin.

This search is a praiseworthy, healthy effort, and it is prevalant even among "relativist" and "sceptics, who would rather not acknowledge it." It appears in different forms and leads to odd differences of opinion. The problem of "protocol statements," their structure and function, is the latest form in which the philosophy or rather the decisive empiricism of our day clothes the problem of the ultimate ground of knowledge.

What was originally meant by "protocol statements," as the name indicates, are those statements which express the *facts* with absolute simplicity, without any moulding, alteration or addition, in whose elaboration every science consists, and which precede all knowing, every judgment regarding the world. It makes no sense to speak of uncertain facts. Only assertions, only our knowledge can be uncertain. If we succeed therefore in expressing the raw facts in "protocol statements," without any contamination, these appear to be the absolutely indubitable starting points of all knowledge. They are, to be sure, again abandoned the moment one goes over to statements which are actually of use in life or science (such a transition appears to be that from "singular" to "universal" statements), but they constitute nevertheless the firm basis to which all our cognitions owe whatever validity they may possess.

Moreover, it makes no difference whether or not these so-called protocol statements have ever actually been made, that is, actually uttered, written down or even only explicitly "thought"; it is required only that one know what statements form the basis for the notations which are actually made, and that these statements be at all times reconstructible. If for example an investigator makes a note, "Under such and such conditions the pointer stands at 10.5," he knows that this means "two black lines coincide," and that the words "under such and such conditions" (which we here imagine to be specified) are likewise to be resolved into definite protocol statements which, if he wished, he could in principle formulate exactly, although perhaps with difficulty.

It is clear, and is so far as I know disputed by no one, that knowledge in life and science in *some* sense *begins* with confirmation of facts, and that the "protocol statements" in which this occurs stand in the same sense at the *beginning* of science. What is this sense? Is "beginning" to be understood in the temporal or logical sense?

Here we already find much confusion and oscillation. If I said above that it is not important whether the decisive statements have been actually made or uttered, this means evidently that they need not stand at the beginning *temporally*, but can be arrived at later just as well if need be. The necessity for formulating them would arise when one wished to make clear to oneself the meaning of the statement that one had actually written down. Is the reference to protocol statements then to be understood in the *logical* sense? In that event they would be distinguished by definite logical properties, by their structure, their position in the system of science, and one would be confronted with the task of actually specifying these properties. In fact, this is the form in which, for example, Carnap used explicitly to put the question of protocol statements, while later[1] declaring it to be a question which is to be settled by an arbitrary decision.

---

[1] See Carnap, "Uber Protokollsätze," *Erkenntnis*, Vol. III, pp. 216 ff.

On the other hand, we find many expositions which seem to presuppose that by "protocol statements" only those assertions are to be understood that also temporally precede the other assertions of science. And is this not correct? One must bear in mind that it is a matter of the ultimate basis of knowledge of *reality*, and that it is not sufficient for this to treat statements as, so to speak, "ideal constructions" (as one used to say in Platonic fashion), but rather that one must concern oneself with real occurrences, with events that take place in time, in which the making of judgments consists, hence with psychic acts of "thought," or physical acts of "speaking" or "writing." Since psychic acts of judgment seem suitable for establishing inter-subjectively valid knowledge only when translated into verbal or written expressions (that is, into a physical system of symbols) "protocol statements" come to be regarded as certain spoken, written or printed sentences, i.e., certain symbol-complexes of sounds or printer's ink, which when translated from the common abbreviations into full-fledged speech, would mean something like: "Mr. N. N. at such and such a time observed so and so at such and such a place." (This view was adopted particularly by O. Neurath).[2] As a matter of fact, when we retrace the path by which we actually arrive at all our knowledge, we doubtless always come up against this same source: printed sentences in books, words out of the mouth of a teacher, our own observations (in the latter case we are ourselves N. N.).

On this view protocol statements would be real happenings in the world and would temporally precede the other real processes in which the "construction of science," or indeed the production of an individual's knowledge consists.

I do not know to what extent the distinction made here between the logical and temporal priority of protocol statements corresponds to differences in the views actually held by certain authors—but that is not important. For we are not concerned to determined who expressed the correct view, but what the correct view *is*. And for this our distinction between the two points of view will serve well enough.

As a matter of fact, these two views are compatible. For the statements that register simple data of observation and stand temporally at the beginning could at the same time be those that by virtue of their structure would have to constitute the logical starting-point of science.

II

The question which will first interest us is this: What progress is achieved by formulating the problem of the ultimate basis of knowledge in terms of protocol statements? The answer to this question will itself pave the way to a solution of the problem.

I think it a great improvement in method to try to aim at the basis of knowledge by looking not for the primary *facts* but for the primary *sentences*. But I also think that this advantage was not made the most of, perhaps because of a failure to realize that what was at issue, fundamentally, was just the old problem of the basis. I

---

[2] Neurath, "Protokollsätze," *Erkenntnis*, Vol. III, pp. 104 ff.

believe, in fact, that the position to which the consideration of protocol statements has led is not tenable. It results in a peculiar relativism, which appears to be a necessary consequence of the view that protocol statements are empirical facts upon which the edifice of science is subsequently built.

That is to say: when protocol statements are conceived in this manner, then directly one raises the question of the certainty with which one may assert their truth, one must grant that they are exposed to all possible doubts.

There appears in a book a sentence which says, for example, that N. N. used such and such an instrument to make such and such an observation. One may under certain circumstances have the greatest confidence in this sentence. Nevertheless, it and the observation it records, can never be considered *absolutely* certain. For the possibilities of error are innumerable. N. N. can inadvertently or intentionally have described something that does not accurately represent the observed fact; in writing it down or printing it, an error may have crept in. Indeed the assumption that the symbols of a book retain their form even for an instant and do not "of themselves" change into new sentences is an empirical hypothesis, which as such can never be strictly verified. For every verification would rest on assumptions of the same sort and on the presupposition that our memory does not deceive us at least during a brief interval, and so on.

This means, of course—and some of our authors have pointed this out almost with a note of triumph—that protocol statements, so conceived, have in principle exactly the same character as all the other statements of science: they are hypotheses, nothing but hypotheses. They are anything but incontrovertible, and one can use them in the construction of the system of science only so long as they are supported by, or at least not contradicted by, other hypotheses. We therefore always reserve the right to make protocol statements subject to correction, and such corrections, quite often indeed, do occur when we eliminate certain protocol statements and declare that they must have been the result of some error.

Even in the case of statements which we ourselves have put forward we do not in principle exclude the possibility of error. We grant that our mind at the moment the judgment was made may have been wholly confused, and that an experience which we now say we had two minutes ago may upon later examination be found to have been an hallucination, or even one that never took place at all.

Thus it is clear that on this view of protocol statements they do not provide one who is in search of a firm basis of knowledge with anything of the sort. On the contrary, the actual result is that one ends by abandoning the original distinction between protocol and other statements as meaningless. Thus we come to understand how people come to think[1] that any statements of science can be selected at will and called "protocol statements," and that it is simply a question of convenience which are chosen.

But can we admit this? Are there really only reasons of convenience? It is not rather a matter of where the particular statements come from, what is their origin, their

---

[1] K. Popper as quoted by Carnap, *op. cit., Erkenntnis*, Vol. III, p. 223.

history? In general, what is meant here by convenience? What is the end that one pursues in making and selecting statements?

The end can be no other than that of science itself, namely, that of affording a *true* description of the facts. For us it is self-evident that the problem of the basis of knowledge is nothing other than the question of the criterion of truth. Surely the reason for bringing in the term "protocol statement" in the first place was that it should serve to mark out certain statements by the truth of which the truth of all other statements comes to be measured, as by a measuring rod. But according to the viewpoint just described this measuring rod would have shown itself to be as relative as, say, all the measuring rods of physics. And it is this view with its consequences that has been commended as the banishing of the last remnant of "absolutism" from philosophy.[1]

But what then remains at all as a criterion of truth? Since the proposal is not that all scientific assertions must accord with certain definite protocol statements, but rather that all statements shall accord with one another, with the result that every single one is considered as, in principle, corrigible, truth can consist only in a *mutual agreement of statements*.

III

This view, which has been expressly formulated and represented in this context, for example, by Neurath, is well known from the history of recent philosophy. In England it is usually called the "coherence theory of truth," and contrasted with the older "correspondence theory." It is to be observed that the expression "theory" is quite inappropriate. For observations on the nature of truth have a quite different character from scientific theories, which always consist of a system of hypotheses.

The contrast between the two views is generally expressed as follows: according to the traditional one, the truth of a statement consists in its agreement with the facts, while according to the other, the coherence theory, it consists in its agreement with the system of other statements.

I shall not in general pursue the question here whether the latter view can not also be interpreted in a way that draws attention to something quite correct (namely, to the fact that in a quite definite sense we cannot "go beyond language" as Wittgenstein puts it). I have here rather to show that, on the interpretation required in the present context, it is quite untenable.

If the truth of a statement is to consist in its coherence or agreement with the other statements, one must be clear as to what one understands by "agreement," and *which* statements are meant by "other."

The first point can be settled easily. Since it cannot be meant that the statement to be tested asserts the same thing as the others, it remains only that they must be compatible with it, that is, that no contradictions exist between them. Truth would consist simply in absence of contradiction. But on the question whether truth can be identified simply with the absence of contradiction, there ought to be no further dis-

---

[1] Carnap, *op. cit.*, p. 228.

cussion. It should long since have been generally acknowledged that only in the case of statements of a tautological nature are truth (if one will apply this term at all) and absence of contradiction to be equated, as for instance with the statements of pure geometry. But with such statements every connection with reality is purposely dissolved; they are only formulas within a determinate calculus; it makes no sense in the case of the statements of *pure* geometry to ask whether they agree with the facts of the world: they need only be compatible with the axioms arbitrarily laid down at the beginning (in addition, it is usually also required that they follow from them) in order to be called true or correct. We have before us precisely what was earlier called *formal* truth and distinguished from *material* truth.

The latter is the truth of synthetic statements, assertions of matters of fact, and if one wishes to describe them by help of the concept of absence of contradiction, of agreement with other statements, one can do so only if one says that they may not contradict *very special* statements, namely just those that express "facts of immediate observation." The criterion of truth cannot be compatibility with any statements whatever, but agreement is required with certain exceptional statements which are not chosen arbitrarily at all. In other words, the criterion of absence of contradiction does not by itself suffice for material truth. It is, rather, entirely a matter of compatibility with very special peculiar statements. And for this compatibility there is no reason not to use—indeed I consider there is every justification for using—the good old expression "agreement with reality."

The astounding error of the "coherence theory" can be explained only by the fact that its defenders and expositors were thinking only of such statements as actually occur in science, and took them as their only examples. Under these conditions the relation of noncontradiction was in fact sufficient, but only because these statements are of a very special character. They have, that is, in a certain sense (to be explained presently) their "origin" in observation statements, they derive, as one may confidently say in the traditional way of speaking, "from experience."

If one is to take coherence seriously as a general criterion of truth, then one must consider arbitrary fairy stories to be as true as a historical report, or as statements in a textbook of chemistry, provided the story is constructed in such a way that no contradiction ever arises. I can depict by help of fantasy a grotesque world full of bizarre adventures: the coherence philosopher must believe in the truth of my account provided only I take care of the mutual compatibility of my statements, and also take the precaution of avoiding any collision with the usual description of the world, by placing the scene of my story on a distant star, where no observation is possible. Indeed, strictly speaking, I don't even require this precaution; I can just as well demand that the others have to adapt themselves to my description; and not the other way round. They cannot then object that, say, this happening runs counter to the observations, for according to the coherence theory there is no question of observations, but only of the compatibility of statements.

Since no one dreams of holding the statements of a story book true and those of a text of physics false, the coherence view fails utterly. Something more, that is, must be added to coherence, namely, a principle in terms of which the compatibility is to be established, and this would alone then be the actual criterion.

If I am given a set of statements, among which are found some that contradict each other, I can establish consistency in a number of ways, by, for example, on one occasion selecting certain statements and abandoning or altering them and on another occasion doing the same with the other statements that contradict the first.

Thus the coherence theory is shown to be logically impossible; it fails altogether to give an unambiguous criterion of truth, for by means of it I can arrive at any number of consistent systems of statements which are incompatible with one another.

The only way to avoid this absurdity is not to allow any statements whatever to be abandoned or altered, but rather to specify those that are to be maintained, to which the remainder have to be accommodated.

IV

The coherence theory is thus disposed of, and we have in the meantime arrived at the second point of our critical considerations, namely, at the question whether *all* statements are corrigible, or whether there are also those that cannot be shaken. These latter would of course constitute the "basis" of all knowledge which we have been seeking, without so far being able to take any step towards it.

By what mark, then, are we to distinguish these statements which themselves remain unaltered, while all others must be brought into agreement with them? We shall in what follows call them not "protocol statements," but "basic statements" for it is quite dubious whether they occur at all among the protocols of science.

The most obvious recourse would doubtless be to find the rule for which we are searching in some kind of economy principle, namely, to say: we are to choose those as basic statements whose retention requires a *minimum* of alteration in the whole system of statements in order to rid it of all contradictions.

It is worth noticing that such an economy principle would not enable us to pick out certain statements as being basic once and for all, for it might happen that with the progress of science the basic statements that served as such up to a given moment would be again degraded, if it appeared more economical to abandon them in favor of newly found statements which from that time on—until further notice—would play the basic role. This would, of course, no longer be the pure coherence viewpoint, but one based on economy; "relativity," however, would characterize it also.

There seems to me no question but that the representatives of the view we have been criticizing did in fact take the economy principle as their guiding light, whether explicitly or implicitly; I have therefore already assumed above that on the relativity view there are purposive grounds which determine the selection of protocol statements, and I asked: Can we admit this?

I now answer this question in the negative. It is in fact not economic purposiveness but quite other characteristics which distinguish the genuine basic statements.

The procedure for choosing these statements would be called economic if it consisted say in conforming to the opinions (or "protocol statements") of the majority of investigators. Now it is of course the case that we do not doubt the existence of a fact, for example a fact of geography or history, or even of a natural law, when we find that in the relevant contexts its existence is very frequently reported. It does not occur to us in those cases to wish to investigate the matter ourselves. We acquiesce in what is universally acknowledged. But this is explained by the fact that we have precise knowledge of the manner in which such factual statements tend to be made, and that this manner wins our confidence; it is not that it agrees with the view of the majority. Quite the contrary, it could only arrive at universal acceptance because everyone feels the same confidence. Whether and to what extent we hold a statement to be corrigible or annulable depends solely on its *origin*, and (apart from very special cases) not at all upon whether maintaining it requires the correction of very many other statements and perhaps a reorganization of the whole system of knowledge.

Before one can apply the principle of economy one must know to *which* statements it is to be applied. And if the principle were the *only* decisive rule the answer could only be: to *all* that are asserted with any claim to validity or have ever been so asserted. Indeed, the phrase "with any claim to validity" should be omitted, for how should we distinguish such statements from those which were asserted quite arbitrarily, as jokes or with intent to deceive? This distinction cannot even be formulated without taking into consideration *the derivation* of the statements. So we find ourselves once more referred to the question of their origin. Without having classified statements according to their origin, any application of the economy principle of agreement would be quite absurd. But once one has examined the statements with respect to their origin it becomes immediately obvious that one has thereby already ordered them in terms of their validity, and that there is no place left for the application of the principle of economy (apart from certain very special cases in still unfinished areas of science). We can see also that the establishment of this order points the way to the basis of which we are in search.

V

Here of course the greatest care is necessary. For we are treading on the path which has been followed from ancient times by all those who have ever embarked upon the journey towards the ultimate grounds of truth. And always they have failed to reach the goal. In the ordering of statements according to their origin which I undertake for the purpose of judging their certainty, I start by assigning a special place to those that I make *myself*. And here a secondary position is occupied by those that lie in the past, for we believe that their certainty can be impaired by "errors of memory"—and indeed in general the more so the farther back in time they lie. On the other hand, the statements which stand at the top, free from all doubt, are those that express facts of one's own "perception," or whatever you like to call it. But in spite of the fact that statements of this sort seem so simple and clear, philosophers have found themselves in a hopeless labyrinth the moment they actually attempted to use them as the foundation of all knowledge. Some puzzling sections of this labyrinth are for example those formulations and deductions that have occupied the center of so many philosophical disputes under the heading "evidence of inner perception," "solipsism," "solipsism of the present moment," "self-conscious certainty," etc. The Cartesian *cogito ergo sum* is the best-known of the destinations to which this path has led—a terminating point to which indeed Augustine had already pushed through. And concerning *cogito ergo sum* our eyes have today been sufficiently opened: we know that it is a mere pseudo-statement, which does not become genuine by being expressed in the form "*cogitatio est*"—"the contents of consciousness exist."[1] Such a statement, which does not express anything itself, cannot in any sense serve as the basis of anything.

It is not itself a cognition, and none rests upon it. It cannot lend certainty to any cognition.

There exists therefore the greatest danger that in following the path recommended one will arrive at empty verbiage instead of the basis one seeks. The critical theory of protocol statements originated indeed in the wish to avoid this danger. But the way out proposed by it is unsatisfactory. Its *essential* deficiency lies in ignoring the different rank of statements, which expresses itself most clearly in the fact that for the system of science which one takes to be the "right" one, one's *own* statements in the end play the only decisive role.

It would be theoretically conceivable that my own observations in no way substantiate the assertions made about the world by other men. It might be that all the books that I read, all the teachers that I hear are in perfect agreement among themselves, that they never contradict one another, but that they are simply incompatible with a large part of my own observation statements. (Certain difficulties would in this case accompany the problem of learning the language and its use in communication, but they can be removed by means of certain assumptions concerning the place in which the contradictions are to appear.) According to the view we have been criticizing I would in such a case simply have to sacrifice my own "protocol statements," for they would be opposed by the overwhelming mass of other statements which would be in mutual agreement themselves, and it would be impossible to expect that these should be corrected in accordance with my own limited fragmentary experience.

But what would actually happen in such a case? Well, under no circumstances would I abandon my own observation statements. On the contrary, I find that I can accept only a system of knowledge into which they fit unmutilated. And I can always construct such a system. I need only view the others as dreaming fools, in whose madness lies a remarkable method, or—to express it more objectively—I would say that the others live in a different world from mine, which has just so much in common with mine as to make it possible to achieve understanding by means of the same language. In any case no matter what world picture I construct, I would test its truth always in terms of my own experience. I would never permit anyone to take this support from me: my own observation statements would always be the ultimate criterion. I should, so to speak, exclaim "What I see, I see!"

VI

In the light of these preliminary critical remarks, it is clear where we have to look for the solution of these confusing difficulties: we must use the Cartesian road in so far as it is good and passable, but then be careful to avoid falling into the *cogito ergo sum*

------
[1] Cf. "Positivismnus und Realiamus," *Erkenntnis*, Vol. III, p. 20.

and related nonsense. We effect this by making clear to ourselves the role which really belongs to the statements expressing "the immediately observed."

What actually lies behind one's saying that they are "absolutely certain"? And in what sense may one describe them as the ultimate ground of all knowledge?

Let us consider the second question first. If we imagine that I at once recorded every observation—and it is in principle indifferent whether this is done on paper or in memory—and then began from that point the construction of science, I should have before me genuine "protocol statements" which stood temporally at the beginning of knowledge. From them would gradually arise the rest of the statements of science, by means of the process called "induction," which consists in nothing else than that I am stimulated or induced by the protocol statements to establish tentative generalizations (hypotheses), from which those first statements, but also an endless number of others, follow logically. If now these others express *the same* as is expressed by later observation statements that are obtained under quite definite conditions which are exactly specifiable beforehand, then the hypotheses are considered to be confirmed so long as no observation statements appear that stand in contradiction to the statements derived from the hypotheses and thus to the hypotheses themselves. So long as this does not occur we believe ourselves to have hit correctly upon a law of nature. Induction is thus nothing but methodically conducted guessing, a psychological, biological process whose conduct has certainly nothing to do with "logic."

In this way the actual procedure of science is described schematically. It is evident what role is played in it by the statements concerning what is "immediately perceived." They are not identical with those written down or memorized, with what can correctly be called "protocol statements," but they are the *occasions* of their formation. The protocol statements observed in a book or memory are, as we acknowledged long ago, so far as their validity goes, doubtless to be compared to hypotheses. For, when we have such a statement before us, it is a mere assumption that it is true, that it agrees with the observation statements that give rise to it. (Indeed it may have been occasioned by no observation statements, but derived from some game or other.) What I call an observation statement cannot be identical with a genuine protocol statement, if only because in a certain sense it cannot be written down at all—a point which we shall presently discuss.

Thus in the schema of the building up of knowledge that I have described, the part played by observation statements is first that of standing temporally at the beginning of the whole process, stimulating it and setting it going. How much of their content enters into knowledge remains in principle at first undetermined. One can thus with some justice see in the observation statements the ultimate origin of all knowledge. But should they be described as the basis, as the ultimate certain ground? This can hardly be maintained, for this "origin" stands in a too questionable relation to the edifice of knowledge. But in addition we have conceived of the true process as schematically simplified. In reality what is actually expressed in protocols stands in a less close connection with the observed, and in general one ought not to assume that any pure observation statements ever slip in between the observation and the "protocol."

But now a second function appears to belong to these statements about the immediately perceived, these "confirmations"* as we may also call them, namely, the corroboration of hypotheses, their *verification*.

Science makes prophecies that are tested by "experience." Its essential function consists in making predictions. It says, for example: "If at such and such a time you look through a telescope adjusted in such and such a manner you will see a point of light (a star) in coincidence with a black mark (cross wires)." Let us assume that in following out these instructions the predicted experience actually occurs. This means that we make an anticipated confirmation, we pronounce an expected judgment of observation, we obtain thereby a feeling of *fulfillment*, a quite characteristic satisfaction: we are *satisfied*. One is fully justified in saying that the confirmation or observation statements have fulfilled their true mission as soon as we obtain this peculiar satisfaction.

And it is obtained in the very moment in which the confirmation takes place, in which the observation statement is made. This is of the utmost importance. For thus the function of the statements about the immediately experienced itself lies in the immediate present. Indeed we saw that they have so to speak no duration, that the moment they are gone one has at one's disposal in their place inscriptions, or memory traces, that can play only the role of hypotheses and thereby lack ultimate certainty. One cannot build any logically tenable structure upon the confirmations, for they are gone the moment one begins to construct. If they stand at the beginning of the process of cognition they are logically of no use. Quite otherwise however if they stand at the end; they bring verification (or also falsification) to completion, and in the moment of their occurrence they have already fulfilled their duty. Logically nothing more depends on them, no conclusions are drawn from them. They constitute an absolute end.

Of course, psychologically and biologically a new process of cognition begins with the satisfaction they create: the hypotheses whose verification ends in them are considered to be upheld, and the formulation of more general hypotheses is sought, the guessing and search for universal laws goes on. The observation statements constitute the origin and stimuli for these events that follow in time, in the sense described earlier.

It seems to me that by means of these considerations a new and clear light is cast upon the problem of the ultimate basis of knowledge, and we see clearly how the

---

* The term used by the author is "Konstatierung" which he sometimes equates with "observation statement" i.e., "Beobachtungssatz," and generally tends to quote, in a manner indicating his awareness that it is a somewhat unusual usage and perhaps a not altogether adequate technical term. Wilfred Sellars in a recently published essay ("Empiricism and the Philosophy of Mind," *Minnesota Studies in the Philosophy of Science*, Volume I, University of Minnesota Press, 1956) uses the term "report" in referring to what seems to be the kind of statement Schlick is discussing. I do not adopt this term, despite some undoubted advantages it has over "confirmation," because of the close connection that "Konstatierung" has with confirmation or verification, a connection so close that Schlick uses the same term unquoted to refer to confirmation. Furthermore, as the test shows, confirmations are never false, as Schlick understands them; but this is certainly not a characteristic of reports, as the term "report" is used in everyday or even scientific language. (Translator's

construction of the system of knowledge takes place and what role the "confirmations" play in it.

Cognition is originally a means in the service of life. In order to find his way about in his environment and to adjust his actions to events, man must be able to foresee these events to a certain extent. For this he makes use of universal statements, cognitions, and he can make use of them only in so far as what has been predicted actually occurs. Now in science this character of cognition remains wholly unaltered; the only difference is that it no longer serves the purposes of life, is not sought because of its utility. With the confirmation of prediction the scientific goal is achieved: the joy in cognition is the joy of verification, the triumphant feeling of having guessed correctly. And it is this that the observation statements bring about. In them science as it were achieves its goal: it is for their sake that it exists. The question hidden behind the problem of the absolutely certain basis of knowledge is, as it were, that of the legitimacy of this satisfaction with which verification fills us. Have our predictions actually come true? In every single case of verification or falsification a "confirmation" answers unambiguously with a yes or a no, with joy of fulfilment or disappointment. The confirmations are final.

Finality is a very fitting word to characterize the function of observation statements. They are an absolute end. In them the task of cognition at this point is fulfilled. That a new task begins with the pleasure in which they culminate, and with the hypotheses that they leave behind does not concern them. Science does not rest upon them but leads to them, and they indicate that it has led correctly. They are really the absolute fixed points; it gives us joy to reach them, even if we cannot stand upon them.

VII

In what does this fixity consist? This brings us to the question we postponed earlier: in what sense can one speak of observation statements as being "absolutely certain"?

I should like to throw light on this by first saying something about a quite different kind of statement, namely about *analytic* statements. I will then compare these to the "confirmations." In the case of analytic statements it is well known that the question of their validity constitutes no problem. They hold *a priori*; one cannot and should not try to look to experience for proof of their correctness for they say nothing whatever about objects of experience. For this reason only "formal truth" pertains to them, i.e., they are not "true" because they correctly express some fact. What makes them true is just their being correctly constructed, i.e. their standing in agreement with our arbitrarily established definitions.

However, certain philosophical writers have thought themselves obliged to ask: Yes, but how do I know in an individual case whether a statement really stands in agreement with the definitions, whether it is really analytic and therefore holds without question? Must I not carry in my head these definitions, the meaning of all the words that are used when I speak or hear or read the statement even if it endures only for a second? But can I be sure that my psychological capacities suffice for this? Is it not possible, for example, that at the end of the statement I should have forgotten or incorrectly remembered the beginning? Must I not thus agree that for psychological reasons I can never be sure of the validity of an analytic judgment also?

To this there is the following answer: the possibility of a failure of the psychic mechanism must of course always be granted, but the consequences that follow from it are not correctly described in the sceptical questions just raised.

It can be that owing to a weakness of memory, and a thousand other causes, we do not understand a statement, or understand it erroneously (i.e. differently from the way it was intended)—but what does this signify? Well, so long as I have not understood a sentence it is not a statement at all for me, but a mere series of words, of sounds or written signs. In this case there is no problem, for only of a statement, not of an uncomprehended series of words, can one ask whether it is analytic or synthetic. But if I have misinterpreted a series of words, but nevertheless interpreted it as a statement, then I know of just *this* statement whether it is analytic or synthetic and therefore valid *a priori* or not. One may not suppose that I could comprehend a statement as such and still be in doubt concerning its analytic character. For if it is analytic I have understood it only when I have understood it as analytic. To understand means nothing else, that is, than to be clear about the rules governing the use of the words in question; but it is precisely these rules of usage that make statements analytic. If I do not know whether a complex of words constitutes an analytic statement or not, this simply means that at that moment I lack the rules of usage: that therefore I have simply not understood the statement. Thus the case is that either I have understood nothing at all, and then nothing more is to be said, or I know whether the statement *which* I understand is synthetic or analytic (which of course does not presuppose that these words hover before me, that I am even acquainted with them). In the case of an analytic statement I know at one and the same time that it is valid, that formal truth belongs to it.

The above doubt concerning the validity of analytic statements was therefore out of order. I may indeed doubt whether I have correctly grasped the meaning of some complex of signs, in fact whether I shall ever understand the meaning of any sequence of words. But I cannot raise the question whether I can ascertain the correctness of an analytic statement. For to understand its meaning and to note its *a priori* validity are in an analytic statement *one and the same* process. In contrast, a synthetic assertion is characterized by the fact that I do not in the least know whether it is true or false if I have only ascertained its meaning. Its truth is determined only by comparison with experience. The process of grasping the meaning is here quite distinct from the process of verification.

There is but one exception to this. And we thus return to our "confirmations." These, that is, are always of the form "Here now so and so," for example "Here two black points coincide," or "Here yellow borders on blue," or also "Here now pain," etc. What is common to all these assertions is that *demonstrative* terms occur in them which have the sense of a present gesture, i.e. their rules of usage provide that in making the statements in which they occur some experience is had, the attention is directed upon something observed. What is referred to by such words as "here," "now," "this here," cannot be communicated by means of general definitions in words, but only by means of them together with pointings or gestures. "This here" has meaning only in connection with a gesture. In order therefore to understand the meaning of such an observation statement one must simultaneously execute the gesture, one must somehow point to reality.

In other words: I can understand the meaning of a "confirmation" only by, and when, comparing it with the facts, thus carrying out that process which is necessary for the verification of all synthetic statements. While in the case of all other synthetic statements determining the meaning is separate from, distinguishable from, determining the truth, in the case of observation statements they coincide, just as in the case of analytic statements. However different therefore "confirmations" are from analytic statements, they have in common that the occasion of understanding them is at the same time that of verifying them: I grasp their meaning at the same time as I grasp their truth. In the case of a confirmation it makes as little sense to ask whether I might be deceived regarding its truth as in the case of a tautology. Both are absolutely valid. However, while the analytic, tautological, statement is empty of content, the observation statement supplies us with the satisfaction of genuine knowledge of reality.

It has become clear, we may hope, that here everything depends on the characteristic of immediacy which is peculiar to observation statements and to which they owe their value and disvalue; the value of absolute validity, and the disvalue of uselessness as an abiding foundation.

A misunderstanding of this nature is responsible for most of the unhappy problems of protocol statements with which our enquiry began. If I make the confirmation "Here now blue," this is *not* the same as the protocol statement "M. S. perceived blue on the nth of April 1934 at such and such a time and such and such a place." The latter statement is a hypothesis and as such always characterized by uncertainty. The latter statement is equivalent to "M. S. made ... (here time and place are to be given) the confirmation 'here now blue.'" And that this assertion is not identical with the confirmation occurring in it is clear. In protocol statements there is *always* mention of perceptions (or they are to be added in thought—the identity of the perceiving observer is important for a scientific protocol), while they are never mentioned in confirmations. A genuine confirmation cannot be written down, for as soon as I inscribe the demonstratives "here," "now," they lose their meaning. Neither can they be replaced by an indication of time and place, for as soon as one attempts to do this, the result, as we saw, is that one unavoidably substitutes for the observation statement a protocol statement which as such has a wholly different nature.

VIII

I believe that the problem of the basis of knowledge is now clarified.

If science is taken to be a system of statements in which one's interest as a logician is confined to their logical connections, the question of its basis, which would then be a "logical" question, can be answered quite arbitrarily. For one is free to define the basis as one wishes. In an abstract system of statements there is no priority and no posteriority. For instance, the most general statements of science, thus those that are normally selected as axioms, could be regarded as its ultimate foundation; but this name could just as well be reserved for the most particular statements, which would then more or less actually correspond to the protocols written down. Or any other choice would be possible. But all the statements of science are collectively and individually *hypotheses* the moment one considers them from the point of view of their truth value, their validity.

If attention is directed upon the relation of science to reality the system of its statements is seen to be that which it really is, namely, a means of finding one's way among the facts; of arriving at the joy of confirmation, the feeling of finality. The problem of the "basis" changes then automatically into that of the unshakeable point of contact between knowledge and reality. We have come to know these absolutely fixed points of contact, the confirmations, in their individuality: they are the only synthetic statements that are not *hypotheses*. They do not in any way lie at the base of science; but like a flame, cognition, as it were, licks out to them, reaching each but for a moment and then at once consuming it. And newly fed and strengthened, it flames onward to the next.

These moments of fulfilment and combustion are what is essential. All the light of knowledge comes from them. And it is for the source of this light the philosopher is really inquiring when he seeks the ultimate basis of all knowledge.

Empiricism, Semantics, and Ontology

Rudolf Carnap

1. THE PROBLEM OF ABSTRACT ENTITIES

Empiricists are in general rather suspicious with respect to any kind of abstract entities like properties, classes, relations, numbers, propositions, etc. They usually feel much more in sympathy with nominalists than with realists (in the medieval sense). As far as possible they try to avoid any reference to abstract entities and to restrict themselves to what is sometimes called a nominalistic language, i.e., one not containing such references. However, within certain scientific contexts it seems hardly possible to avoid them. In the case of mathematics, some empiricists try to find a way out by treating the whole of mathematics as a mere calculus, a formal system for which no interpretation is given or can be given. Accordingly, the mathematician is said to speak not about numbers, functions, and infinite classes, but merely about meaningless symbols and formulas manipulated according to given formal rules. In physics it is more difficult to shun the suspected entities, because the language of physics serves for the communication of reports and predictions and hence cannot be taken, as a mere calculus. A physicist who is suspicious of abstract entities may perhaps try to declare

Reprinted from *Meaning and Necessity*, enlarged edition (Chicago: University of Chicago Press, 1956), pp. 205–221, by permission of the publisher. Copyright 1956 by University of Chicago Press.

a certain part of the language of physics as uninterpreted and uninterpretable, that part which refers to real numbers as space-time coordinates or as values of physical magnitudes, to functions, limits, etc. More probably he will just speak about all these things like anybody else but with an uneasy conscience, like a man who in his everyday life does with qualms many things which are not in accord with the high moral principles he professes on Sundays. Recently the problem of abstract entities has arisen again in connection with semantics, the theory of meaning and truth. Some semanticists say that certain expressions designate certain entities, and among these designated entities they include not only concrete material things but also abstract entities, e.g., properties as designated by predicates and propositions as designated by sentences.[1] Others object strongly to this procedure as violating the basic principles of empiricism and leading back to a metaphysical ontology of the Platonic kind.

It is the purpose of this article to clarify this controversial issue. The nature and implications of the acceptance of a language referring to abstract entities will first be discussed in general; it will be shown that using such a language does not imply embracing a Platonic ontology but is perfectly compatible with empiricism and strictly scientific thinking. Then the special question of the role of abstract entities in semantics will be discussed. It is hoped that the clarification of the issue will be useful to those who would like to accept abstract entities in their work in mathematics, physics, semantics, or any other field; it may help them to overcome nominalistic scruples.

2. LINGUISTIC FRAMEWORKS

Are there properties, classes, numbers, propositions? In order to understand more clearly the nature of these and related problems, it is above all necessary to recognize a fundamental distinction between two kinds of questions concerning the existence or reality of entities. If someone wishes to speak in his language about a new kind of entities, he has to introduce a system of new ways of speaking, subject to new rules; we shall call this procedure the construction of a linguistic *framework* for the new entities in question. And now we must distinguish two kinds of questions of existence: first, questions of the existence of certain entities of the new kind *within the framework*; we call them *internal questions*; and second, questions concerning the existence or reality *of the system of entities as a whole*, called *external questions*. Internal questions and possible answers to them are formulated with the help of the new forms of expressions. The answers may be found either by purely logical methods or by empirical methods, depending upon whether the framework is a logical or a factual one. An external question is of a problematic character which is in need of closer examination.

The World of Things. Let us consider as an example the simplest kind of entities dealt with in the everyday language: the spatio-temporally ordered system of observable things and events. Once we have accepted the *thing* language with its framework for things, we can raise and answer internal questions, e.g., "Is there a white piece of paper on my desk?", "Did King Arthur actually live?", "Are unicorns and centaurs real or merely imaginary?", and the like. These questions are to be answered by empirical investigations. Results of observations are evaluated according to certain rules as confirming or disconfirming evidence for possible answers. (This evaluation is usually carried out, of course, as a matter of habit rather than a deliberate, rational procedure. But it is possible, in a rational reconstruction, to lay down explicit rules for the evaluation. This is one of the main tasks of a pure, as distinguished from a psychological, epistemology.) The concept of reality occurring in these internal questions is an empirical, scientific, nonmetaphysical concept. To recognize something as a real thing or event means to succeed in incorporating it into the system of things at a particular space-time position so that it fits together with the other things recognized as real, according to the rules of the framework.

From these questions we must distinguish the external question of the reality of the thing world itself. In contrast to the former questions, this question is raised neither by the man in the street nor by scientists, but only by philosophers. Realists give an affirmative answer, subjective idealists a negative one, and the controversy goes on for centuries without ever being solved. And it cannot be solved because it is framed in a wrong way. To be real in the scientific sense means to be an element of the system; hence this concept cannot be meaningfully applied to the system itself. Those who raise the question of the reality of the thing world itself have perhaps in mind not a theoretical question as their formulation seems to suggest, but rather a *practical* question, a matter of a practical decision concerning the structure of our language. We have to make the choice whether or not to accept and use the forms of expression in the framework in question.

In the case of this particular example, there is usually no deliberate choice because we all have accepted the thing language early in our lives as a matter of course. Nevertheless, we may regard it as a matter of decision in this sense: we are free to choose to continue using the thing language or not; in the latter case we could restrict ourselves to a language of sense-data and other "phenomenal" entities, or construct an alternative to the customary thing language with another structure, or, finally, we could refrain from speaking. If someone decides to accept the thing language there is no objection against saying that he has accepted the world of things. But this must not be interpreted as if it meant his acceptance of a *belief* in the reality of the thing world; there is no such belief or assertion or assumption, because it is not a theoretical question. To accept the thing world means nothing more than to accept a certain form of language, in other words, to accept rules for forming statements and for testing, accepting, or rejecting them. The acceptance of the thing language leads, on the basis of observations made, also to the acceptance, belief, and assertion of certain statements. But the thesis of the reality of the thing world cannot be among these statements, because it cannot be formulated in the thing language or, it seems, in any other theoretical language.

The decision of accepting the thing language, although itself not of a cognitive nature, will nevertheless usually be influenced by theoretical knowledge, just like any other deliberate decision concerning the acceptance of linguistic or other rules. The purposes for which the language is intended to be used, for instance, the purpose of communicating factual knowledge, will determine which factors are relevant for the decision. The efficiency, fruitfulness, and simplicity of the use of the thing language may be among the decisive factors. And the questions concerning these qualities are indeed of a theoretical nature. But these questions cannot be identified with the question of realism. They are not yes-no questions but questions of degree. The thing language in the customary form works indeed with a high degree of efficiency for most purposes of everyday life. This is a matter of fact, based upon the content of our experiences. However, it would be wrong to describe this situation by saying: "The fact of the efficiency of the thing language is confirming evidence for the reality of the thing world"; we should rather say instead: "This fact makes it advisable to accept the thing language".

The System of Numbers.   As an example of a system which is of a logical rather than a factual nature let us take the system of natural numbers. The framework for this system is constructed by introducing into the language new expressions with suitable rules; (1) numerals like "five" and sentence forms like "there are five books on the table"; (2) the general term "number" for the new entities, and sentence forms like "five is a number"; (3) expressions for properties of numbers (e.g., "odd", "prime"), relations (e.g., "greater than"), and functions (e.g., "plus"), and sentence forms like "two plus three is five"; (4) numerical variables ("m", "n", etc.) and quantifiers for universal sentences ("for every n, ...") and existential sentences ("there is an n such that ...") with the customary deductive rules.

Here again there are internal questions, e.g., "Is there a prime number greater than a hundred?" Here, however, the answers are found, not by empirical investigation based on observations, but by logical analysis based on the rules for the new expressions. Therefore the answers are here analytic, i.e., logically true.

What is now the nature of the philosophical question concerning the existence or reality of numbers? To begin with, there is the internal question which, together with the affirmative answer, can be formulated in the new terms, say, by "There are numbers" or, more explicitly, "There is an n such that n is a number". This statement follows from the analytic statement "five is an number" and is therefore itself analytic. Moreover, it is rather trivial (in contradistinction to a statement like "There is a prime number greater than a million", which is likewise analytic but far from trivial), because it does not say more than that the new system is not empty; but this is immediately seen from the rule which states that words like "five" are substitutable for the new variables. Therefore nobody who meant the question "Are there numbers?" in the internal sense would either assert or even seriously consider a negative answer. This makes it plausible to assume that those philosophers who treat the question of the existence of numbers as a serious philosophical problem and offer lengthy arguments on either side do not have in mind the internal question. And, indeed, if we were to ask them: "Do you mean the question as to whether the framework of numbers, *if* we were to accept it, would be found to be empty or not?", they would probably reply: "Not at all; we mean a question *prior* to the acceptance of the new framework". They might try to explain what they mean by saying that it is a question of the ontological status of numbers; the question whether or not numbers have a certain metaphysical characteristic called reality (but a kind of ideal reality, different from the material reality of the thing world) or subsistence or status of "independent entities." Unfortunately, these philosophers have so far not given a formulation of their question in terms of the common scientific language. Therefore our judgment must be that they have not succeeded in giving to the external question and to the possible answers any cognitive content.

Unless and until they supply a clear cognitive interpretation, we are justified in our suspicion that their question is a pseudo-question, that is, one disguised in the form of a theoretical question while in fact it is nontheoretical; in the present case it is the practical problem whether or not to incorporate into the language the new linguistic forms which constitute the framework of numbers.

The System of Propositions.   New variables, "p", "q", etc., are introduced with a rule to the effect that any (declarative) sentence may be substituted for a variable of this kind; this includes, in addition to the sentences of the original thing language, also all general sentences with variables of any kind which may have been introduced into the language. Further, the general term "proposition"; is introduced. "p is a proposition" may be defined by "p or not p" (or by any other sentence form yielding only analytic sentences). Therefore, every sentence of the form " ... is a proposition" (where any sentence may stand in the place of the dots) is analytic. This holds, for example, for the sentence:

(*a*) "Chicago is large is a proposition".

(We disregard here the fact that the rules of English grammar require not a sentence but a that-clause as the subject of another sentence; accordingly, instead of (*a*) we should have to say "That Chicago is large is a proposition".) Predicates may be admitted whose argument expressions are sentences; these predicates may be either extensional (e.g., the customary truth-functional connectives) or not (e.g., modal predicates like "possible", "necessary", etc.). With the help of the new variables, general sentences may be formed, e.g.,

(*b*) "For every p, either p or not-p".

(*c*) "There is a p such that p is not necessary and not-p is not necessary."

(*d*) "There is a p such that p is a proposition".

(*c*) and (*d*) are internal assertions of existence. The statement "There are propositions" may be meant in the sense of (*d*); in this case it is analytic (since it follows from (*a*) and even trivial. If, however, the statement is meant in an external sense, then it is noncognitive.

It is important to notice that the system of rules for the linguistic expressions of the propositional framework (of which only a few rules have here been briefly indicated) is sufficient for the introduction of the framework. Any further explanations as to the nature of the propositions (i.e., the elements of the system indicated, the values of the variables "p", "q", etc.) are theoretically unnecessary because, if correct, they follow from the rules. For example, are propositions mental events (as in Russell's theory)? A look at the rules shows us that they are not, because otherwise existential statements would be of the form: "If the mental state of the person in question fulfills such and such conditions, then there is a p such that ...". The fact that no references to mental conditions occur in existential statements (like (*c*), (*d*), etc.) shows that propositions are not mental entities. Further, a statement of the existence of linguistic entities (e.g., expressions, classes of expressions, etc.) must contain a reference to a language. The fact that no such reference occurs in the existential statements here, shows that propositions are not linguistic entities. The fact that in these statements no reference to a subject (an observer or knower) occurs (nothing like: "There is a p which is necessary for Mr. X"), shows that the propositions (and their properties, like necessity, etc.) are not subjective. Although characterizations of these or similar kinds are, strictly speaking, unnecessary, they may nevertheless be practically useful. If they are given, they should be understood, not as ingredient parts of the system, but merely as marginal notes with the purpose of supplying to the reader helpful hints or convenient pictorial associations which may make his learning of the use of the expressions easier than the bare system of the rules would do. Such a characterization is analogous to an extrasystematic explanation which a physicist sometimes gives to the beginner. He might, for example, tell him to imagine the atoms of a gas as small balls rushing around with great speed, or the electromagnetic field and its oscillations as quasi-elastic tensions and vibrations in an ether. In fact, however, all that can accurately be said about atoms or the field is implicitly contained in the physical laws of the theories in question.[2]

The System of Thing Properties.   The thing language contains words like "red", "hard", "stone", "house", etc., which are used for describing what things are like. Now we may introduce new variables, say "f", "g", etc., for which those words are substitutable and furthermore the general term "property". New rules are laid down which admit sentences like "Red is a property", "Red is a color", "These two pieces of paper have at least one color in common" (i.e., "There is an f such that f is a color, and ..."). The last sentence is an internal assertion. It is often empirical, factual nature. However, the external statement, the philosophical statement of the reality of properties—a special case of the thesis of the reality of universals—is devoid of cognitive content.

The Systems of Integers and Rational Numbers.   Into a language containing the framework of natural numbers we may introduce first the (positive and negative) integers as relations among natural numbers and then the rational numbers as relations among integers. This involves introducing new types of variables, expressions substitutable for them, and the general terms "integer" and "rational number".

The System of Real Numbers.   On the basis of the rational numbers, the real numbers may be introduced as classes of a special kind (segments) of rational numbers (according to the method developed by Dedekind and Frege). Here again a new type of variables is introduced, expressions substitutable for them (e.g., "$\sqrt{2}$") and the general term "real number".

The Spatio-Temporal Coordinate System for Physics.   The new entities are the space-time points. Each is an ordered quadruple of four real numbers, called its coordinates, consisting of three spatial and one temporal coordinates. The physical state of a spatio-temporal point or region is described either with the help of qualitative predicates (e.g., "hot") or by ascribing numbers as values of a physical magnitude (e.g., mass, temperature, and the like). The step from the system of things (which does not contain space-time points but only extended objects with spatial and temporal relations between them) to the physical coordinate system is again a matter of decision. Our choice of certain features, although itself not theoretical, is suggested by theoretical knowledge, either logical or factual. For example, the choice of real numbers rather than rational numbers or integers as coordinates is not much influenced by the facts of experience but mainly due to considerations of mathematical simplicity. The restriction to rational coordinates would not be in conflict with any experimental knowledge we have, because the result of any measurement is a rational number. However, it would prevent the use of ordinary geometry (which says, e.g., that the diagonal of a square with the side 1 has the irrational value $\sqrt{2}$) and thus lead to great complications. On the other hand, the decision to use three rather than two or four spatial coordinates is strongly suggested, but still not forced upon us, by the result of common observations. If certain events allegedly observed in spiritualistic séances, e.g., a ball moving out of a sealed box, were confirmed beyond any reasonable doubt, it might seem advisable to use four spatial coordinates. Internal questions are here, in general, empirical questions to be answered by empirical investigations. On the other hand, the external questions of the reality of physical space and physical time are pseudo-questions. A question like "Are there (really) space-time points?" is ambiguous. It may be meant as an internal question; then the affirmative answer is, of course, analytic and trivial. Or it may be meant in the external sense: "Shall we introduce such and such forms into our language?"; in this case it is not a theoretical but a practical question, a matter of decision rather than assertion, and hence the proposed formulation would be misleading. Or finally, it may be meant in the following sense: "Are our experiences such that the use of the linguistic forms in question will be expedient and fruitful?" This is a theoretical question of a factual, empirical nature. But it concerns a matter of degree; therefore a formulation in the form "real or not?" would be inadequate.

3. WHAT DOES ACCEPTANCE OF A KIND OF ENTITIES MEAN?

Let us now summarize the essential characteristics of situations involving the introduction of a new kind of entities, characteristics which are common to the various examples outlined above.

The acceptance of a new kind of entities is represented in the language by the introduction of a framework of new forms of expressions to be used according to a new set of rules. There may be new names for particular entities of the kind in question; but some such names may already occur in the language before the introduction of the new framework. (Thus, for example, the thing language contains certainly words of the type of "blue" and "house" before the framework of properties is introduced; and it may contain words like "ten" in sentences of the form "I have ten fingers" before the framework of numbers is introduced.) The latter fact shows that the occurrence of constants of the type in question—regarded as names of entities of the new kind after the new framework is introduced—is not a sure sign of the acceptance of the new kind of entities. Therefore the introduction of such constants is not to be regarded as an essential step in the introduction of the framework. The two essential steps are rather the following. First, the introduction of a general term, a predicate of higher level, for the new kind of entities, permitting us to say of any particular entity that it belongs to this kind (e.g., "Red is a *property*", "Five is a *number*"). Second, the introduction of variables of the new type. The new entities are values of these variables; the constants (and the closed compound expressions, if any) are substitutable for the variables.[3] With the help of the variables, general sentences concerning the new entities can be formulated.

After the new forms are introduced into the language, it is possible to formulate with their help internal questions and possible answers to them. A question of this kind may be either empirical or logical; accordingly a true answer is either factually true or analytic.

From the internal questions we must clearly distinguish external questions, i.e., philosophical questions concerning the existence or reality of the total system of the new entities. Many philosophers regard a question of this kind as an ontological question which must be raised and answered *before* the introduction of the new language forms. The latter introduction, they believe, is legitimate only if it can be justified by an ontological insight supplying an affirmative answer to the question of reality. In contrast to this view, we take the position that the introduction of the new ways of speaking does not need any theoretical justification because it does not imply any assertion of reality. We may still speak (and have done so) of "the acceptance of the new entities" since this form of speech is customary; but one must keep in mind that this phrase does not mean for us anything more than acceptance of the new framework, i.e., of the new linguistic forms. Above all, it must not be interpreted as referring to an assumption, belief, or assertion of "the reality of the entities". There is no such assertion. An alleged statement of the reality of the system of entities is a pseudo-statement without cognitive content. To be sure, we have to face at this point an important question; but it is a practical, not a theoretical question; it is the question of whether or not to accept the new linguistic forms. The acceptance cannot be judged as being either true or false beause it is not an assertion. It can only be judged as being more or less expedient, fruitful, conducive to the aim for which the language is intended. Judgments of this kind supply the motivation for the decision of accepting or rejecting the kind of entities.[4]

Thus it is clear that the acceptance of a linguistic framework must not be regarded as implying a metaphysical doctrine concerning the reality of the entities in question. It seems to me due to neglect of this important distinction that some contemporary nominalists label the admission of variables of abstract types as "Platonism."[5] This is, to say the least, an extremely misleading terminology. It leads to the absurd consequence, that the position of everybody who accepts the language of physics with its real number variables (as a language of communication, not merely as a calculus) would be called Platonistic, even if he is a strict empiricist who rejects Platonic metaphysics.

A brief historical remark may here be inserted. The non-cognitive character of the questions which we have called here external questions was recognized and emphasized already by the Vienna Circle under the leadership of Moritz Schlick, the group from which the movement of logical empiricism originated. Influenced by ideas of Ludwig Wittgenstein, the Circle rejected both the thesis of the reality of the external world and the thesis of its irreality as pseudo-statements;[6] the same was the case for both the thesis of the reality of universals (abstract entities, in our present terminology) and the nominalistic thesis that they are not real and that their alleged names are not names of anything but merely *flatus vocis*. (It is obvious that the apparent negation of a pseudo-statement must also be a pseudo-statement.) It is therefore not correct to classify the members of the Vienna Circle as nominalists, as is sometimes done. However, if we look at the basic anti-metaphysical and proscientific attitude of most nominalists (and the same holds for many materialists and realists in the modern sense), disregarding their occasional pseudo-theoretical formulations, then it is, of course, true to say that the Vienna Circle was much closer to those philosophers than to their opponents.

4. ABSTRACT ENTITIES IN SEMANTICS

The problem of the legitimacy and the status of abstract entities has recently again led to controversial discussions in connection with semantics. In a semantical meaning analysis certain expressions in a language are often said to designate (or name or denote or signify or refer to) certain extralinguistic entities.[7] As long as physical things or events (e.g., Chicago or Caesar's death) are taken as designata (entities designated), no serious doubts arise. But strong objections have been raised, especially by some empiricists, against abstract entities as designata, e.g., against semantical statements of the following kind:

(1) "The word 'red' designates a property of things";
(2) "The word 'color' designates a property of properties of things";
(3) "The word 'five' designates a number";
(4) "The word 'odd' designates a property of numbers";
(5) "The sentence 'Chicago is large' designates a proposition".

Those who criticize these statements do not, of course, reject the use of the expressions in question, like "red" or "five"; nor would they deny that these expressions are meaningful. But to be meaningful, they would say, is not the same as having a meaning in the sense of an entity designated. They reject the belief, which they regard as implicitly presupposed by those semantical statements, that to each expression of the types in question (adjectives like "red", numerals like "five", etc.) there is a particular real entity to which the expression stands in the relation of designation. This belief is rejected as incompatible with the basic principles of empiricism or of scientific thinking. Derogatory labels like "Platonic realism", "hypostatization", or "'Fido'-Fido principle" are attached to it. The latter is the name given by Gilbert Ryle (in his review of my *Meaning and Necessity* [*Philosophy*, 24(1949), 69–76]) to the criticized belief, which, in his view, arises by a naïve inference of analogy: just as there is an entity well known to me, viz. my dog Fido, which is designated by the name "Fido", thus there must be for every meaningful expression a particular entity to which it stands in the relation of designation or naming, i.e., the relation exemplified by "Fido"-Fido. The belief criticized is thus a case of hypostatization, i.e., of treating as names expressions which are not names. While "Fido" is a name, expressions like "red", "five", etc., are said not to be names, not to designate anything.

Our previous discussion concerning the acceptance of frameworks enables us now to clarify the situation with respect to abstract entities as designata. Let us take as an example the statement:

(*a*) "'Five' designates a number".

The formulation of this statement presupposes that our language L contains the forms of expressions which we have called the framework of numbers, in particular, numerical variables and the general term "number." If L contains these forms, the following is an analytic statement in L:

(*b*) "Five is a number".

Further, to make the statement (*a*) possible, L must contain an expression like "designates" or "is a name of" for the semantical relation of designation. If suitable rules for this term are laid down, the following is likewise analytic

(*c*) "'Five' designates five".

(Generally speaking, any expression of the form "' ... ' designates ... " is an analytic statement provided the term " ... " is a constant in an accepted framework. If the latter condition is not fulfilled, the expression is not a statement.) Since (*a*) follows from (*c*) and (*b*), (*a*) is likewise analytic.

Thus it is clear that *if* someone accepts the framework of numbers, then he must acknowledge (*c*) and (*b*) and hence (*a*) as true statements. Generally speaking, if someone accepts a framework for a certain kind of entities, then he is bound to admit the entities as possible designata. Thus the question of the admissibility of entities of a certain type or of abstract entities in general as designata is reduced to the question of the acceptability of the linguistic framework for those entities. Both the nominalistic critics, who refuse the status of designators or names to expressions like "red", "five", etc., because they deny the existence of abstract entities and the skeptics, who express doubts concerning the existence and demand evidence for it, treat the question of existence as a theoretical question. They do, of course, not mean the internal question; the affirmative answer to *this* question is analytic and trivial and too obvious for doubt or denial as we have seen. Their doubts refer rather to the system of entities itself; hence they mean the external question. They believe that only after making sure that there really is a system of entities of the kind in question are we justified in accepting the framework by incorporating the linguistic forms into our language. However, we have seen that the external question is not a theoretical question but rather the practical question whether or not to accept those linguistic forms. This acceptance is not in need of a theoretical justification (except with respect to expediency and fruitfulness), because it does not imply a belief or assertion. Ryle says that the "Fido"-Fido principle is "a grotesque theory". Grotesque or not, Ryle is wrong in calling it a theory. It is rather the practical decision to accept certain frameworks. Maybe Ryle is historically right with respect to those whom he mentions as previous representatives of the principle, viz., John Stuart Mill, Frege, and Russell. If these philosophers regarded the acceptance of a system of entities as a theory, an assertion, they were victims of the same old, metaphysical confusion. But it is certainly wrong to regard *my* semantical method as involving a belief in the reality of abstract entities, since I reject a thesis of this kind as a metaphysical pseudo-statement.

The critics of the use of abstract entities in semantics overlook the fundamental difference between the acceptance of a system of entities and an internal assertion, e.g., an assertion that there are elephants or electrons or prime numbers greater than a million. Whoever makes an internal assertion is certainly obliged to justify it by providing evidence, empirical evidence in the case of electrons, logical proof in the case of the prime numbers. The demand for a theoretical justification, correct in the case of internal assertions, is sometimes wrongly applied to the acceptance of a system of entities. Thus, for example, Ernest Nagel (in his review of my *Meaning and Necessity* [*Journal of Philosophy*, 45 (1948), 467–472]) asks for "evidence relevant for affirming with warrant that there are such entities as infinitesimals or propositions". He characterizes the evidence required in these cases—in distinction to the empirical evidence in the case of electrons—as "in the broad sense logical and dialectical." Beyond this no hint is given as to what might be regarded as relevant evidence. Some nominalists regard the acceptance of abstract entities as a kind of superstition or myth, populating the world with fictitious or at least dubious entities, analogous to the belief in centaurs or demons. This shows again the confusion mentioned, because a superstition or myth is a false (or dubious) internal statement.

Let us take as example the natural numbers as cardinal numbers, i.e., in contexts like "Here are three books". The linguistic forms of the framework of numbers, including variables and the general term "number", are generally used in our common language of communication; and it is easy to formulate explicit rules for their use. Thus the logical characteristics of this framework are sufficiently clear (while many internal questions, i.e., arithmetical questions, are, of course, still open). In spite of this, the controversy concerning the external question of the ontological reality of the system of numbers continues. Suppose that one philosopher says: "I believe that there are numbers as real entities. This gives me the right to use the linguistic forms of the numerical framework and to make semantical statements about numbers as designata of numerals". His nominalistic opponent replies: "You are wrong; there are no numbers. The numerals may still be used as meaningful expressions. But they are not names, there are no entities designated by them. Therefore the word "number" and numerical variables must not be used (unless a way were found to introduce them as merely abbreviating devices, a way of translating them into the nominalistic thing language)." I cannot think of any possible evidence that would be regarded as relevant by both philosophers, and therefore, if actually found, would decide the controversy or at least make one of the opposite theses more probable than the other. (To construe the numbers as classes or properties of the second level, according to the Frege-Russell method, does, of course, not solve the controversy, because the first philosopher would affirm and the second deny the existence of the system of classes or properties of the second level.) Therefore I feel compelled to regard the external question as a pseudo-question, until both parties to the controversy offer a common interpretation of the question as a cognitive question; this would involve an indication of possible evidence regarded as relevant by both sides.

There is a particular kind of misinterpretation of the acceptance of abstract entities in various fields of science and in semantics, that needs to be cleared up. Certain early British empiricists (e.g., Berkeley and Hume) denied the existence of abstract entities on the ground that immediate experience presents us only with particulars, not with universals, e.g., with this red patch, but not with Redness or Color-in-General; with this scalene triangle, but not with Scalene Triangularity or Triangularity-in-General. Only entities belonging to a type of which examples were to be found within immediate experience could be accepted as ultimate constituents of reality. Thus, according to this way of thinking, the existence of abstract entities could be asserted only if one could show either that some abstract entities fall within the given, or that abstract entities can be defined in terms of the types of entity which are given. Since these empiricists found no abstract entities within the realm of sense-data, they either denied their existence, or else made a futile attempt to define universals in terms of particulars. Some contemporary philosophers, especially English philosophers following Bertrand Russell, think in basically similar terms. They emphasize a distinction between the data (that which is immediately given in consciousness, e.g., sense-data, immediately past experiences, etc.) and the constructs based on the data. Existence or reality is ascribed only to the data; the constructs are not real entities; the corresponding linguistic expressions are merely ways of speech not actually designating anything (reminiscent of the nominalists' *flatus vocis*). We shall not criticize here this general conception. (As far as it is principle of accepting certain entities and not accepting others, leaving aside any ontological, phenomenalistic, and nominalistic pseudo-statements, there cannot be any theoretical objection to it.) But if this conception leads to the view that other philosophers or scientists who accept abstract entities thereby assert or imply their occurrence as immediate data, then such a view must be rejected as a misinterpretation. References to space-time points, the electromagnetic field, or electrons in physics, to real or complex numbers and their functions in mathematics, to the excitatory potential or unconscious complexes in psychology, to an inflationary trend in economics, and the like, do not imply the assertion that entities of these kinds occur as immediate data. And the same holds for references to abstract entities as designata in semantics. Some of the criticisms by English philosophers against such references give the impression that, probably due to the misinterpretation just indicated, they accuse the semanticist not so much of bad metaphysics (as some nominalists would do) but of bad psychology. The fact that they regard a semantical method involving abstract entities not merely as doubtful and perhaps wrong, but as manifestly absurd, preposterous, and grotesque, and that they show a deep horror and indignation against this method, is perhaps to be explained by a misinterpretation of the kind described. In fact, of course, the semanticist does not in the least assert or imply that the abstract entities to which he refers can be experienced as immediately given either by sensation or by a kind of rational intuition. An assertion of this kind would indeed be very dubious psychology. The psychological question as to which kinds of entities do and which do not occur as immediate data is entirely irrelevant for semantics, just as it is for physics, mathematics, economics, etc., with respect to the examples mentioned above.[8]

5. CONCLUSION

For those who want to develop or use semantical methods, the decisive question is not the alleged ontological question of the existence of abstract entities but rather the question whether the use of abstract linguistic forms or, in technical terms, the use of variables beyond those for things (or phenomenal data), is expedient and fruitful for the purposes for which semantical analyses are made, viz., the analysis, interpretation, clarification, or construction of languages of communication, especially languages of science. This question is here neither decided nor even discussed. It is not a question simply of yes or no, but a matter of degree. Among those philosophers who have carried out semantical analyses and thought about suitable tools for this work, beginning with Plato and Aristotle and, in a more technical way on the basis of modern logic, with C. S. Peirce and Frege, a great majority accepted abstract entities. This does, of course, not prove the case. After all, semantics in the technical sense is still in the initial phases of its development, and we must be prepared for possible fundamental changes in methods. Let us therefore admit that the nominalistic critics may possibly be right. But if so, they will have to offer better arguments than they have so far. Appeal to ontological insight will not carry much weight. The critics will have to show that it is possible to construct a semantical method which avoids all references to abstract entities and achieves by simpler means essentially the same results as the other methods.

The acceptance or rejection of abstract linguistic forms, just as the acceptance or rejection of any other linguistic forms in any branch of science will finally be decided by their efficiency as instruments, the ratio of the results achieved to the amount and complexity of the efforts required. To decree dogmatic prohibitions of certain linguistic forms instead of testing them by their success or failure in practical use, is worse than futile it is positively harmful because it may obstruct scientific progress. The history of science shows examples of such prohibitions based on prejudices deriving from religious, mythological, metaphysical, or other irrational sources, which slowed up the developments for shorter or longer periods of time. Let us learn from the lessons of history. Let us grant to those who work in any special field of investigation the freedom to use any form of expression which seems useful to them; the work in the field will sooner or later lead to the elimination of those forms which have no useful function. *Let us be cautious in making assertions and critical in examining them, but tolerant in permitting linguistic forms.*

NOTES

1.   The terms "sentence" and "statement" are here used synonymously for declarative (indicative, propositional) sentences.

2.   In my book *Meaning and Necessity* (Chicago, 1947) I have developed a semantical method which takes propositions as entities designated by sentences (more specifically, as intensions

of sentences). In order to facilitate the understanding of the systematic development, I added some informal, extrasystematic explanations concerning the nature of propositions. I said that the term "proposition" "is used neither for a linguistic expression nor for a subjective, mental occurrence, but rather for something objective that may or may not be exemplified in nature. ... We apply the term 'proposition' to any entities of a certain logical type, namely, those that may be expressed by (declarative) sentences in a language" (p. 27). After some more detailed discussions concerning the relation between propositions and facts, and the nature of false propositions, I added: "It has been the purpose of the preceding remarks to facilitate the understanding of our conception of propositions. If, however, a reader should find these explanations more puzzling than clarifying, or even unacceptable, he may disregard them" (p. 31) (that is, disregard these extrasystematic explanations, not the whole theory of the propositions as intensions of sentences, as one reviewer understood). In spite of this warning, it seems that some of those readers who were puzzled by the explanations, did not disregard them but thought that by raising objections against them they could refute the theory. This is analogous to the procedure of some laymen who by (correctly) criticizing the ether picture or other visualizations of physical theories, thought they had refuted those theories. Perhaps the discussions in the present paper will help in clarifying the role of the system of linguistic rules for the introduction of a framework for entities on the one hand, and that of extrasystematic explanations concerning the nature of the entities on the other.

3.   W. V. Quine was the first to recognize the importance of the introduction of variables as indicating the acceptance of entities. "The ontology to which one's use of language commits him comprises simply the objects that he treats as falling ... within the range of values of his variables" "Notes on Existence and Necessity," *Journal of Philosophy*, 40 (1943), 118. Compare Quine, "Designation and Existence," *Journal of Philosophy*, 36 (1939), 701–709, and "On Universals," *Journal of Symbolic Logic*, 12 (1947), 74–84.

4.   For a closely related point of view on these questions see the detailed discussions in Herbert Feigl, "Existential Hypotheses," *Philosophy of Science*, 17 (1950), 35–62.

5.   Paul Bernays, "Sur le platonisme dans les mathématiques," *L'Enseignement math.*, 34 (1935), 52–69. W. V. Quine, see previous footnote and a recent paper ["On What There Is," *Review of the Metaphysics*, 2 (1948), 21–38.] Quine does not acknowledge the distinction which I emphasize above, because according to his general conception there are no sharp boundary lines between logical and factual truth, between questions of meaning and questions of fact, between the acceptance of a language structure and the acceptance of an assertion formulated in the language. This conception, which seems to deviate considerably from customary ways of thinking, will be explained in his article [Semantics]. When Quine in the article [What] classifies my logicistic conception of mathematics (derived from Frege and Russell) as "platonic realism" (p. 33), this is meant (according to a personal communication from him) not as ascribing to me agreement with Plato's metaphysical doctrine of universals, but merely as referring to the fact that I accept a language of mathematics containing variables of higher levels. With respect to the basic attitude to take in choosing a language form (an "ontology" in Quine's terminology, which seems to me misleading), there appears now to be agreement between us: "the obvious counsel is tolerance and an experimental spirit" ([What], p. 38).

6.   See Carnap, *Scheinprobleme in der Philosophie; das Fremdpsychische und der Realismusstreit*, Berlin, 1928. Moritz Schlick. *Positivismus and Realismus*, reprinted in *Gesammelte Aufsätze*, Wien, 1938.

7.   See [1]; *Meaning and Necessity* (Chicago, 1947). The distinction I have drawn in the latter book between the method of the name-relation and the method of intension and extension is not essential for our present discussion. The term "designation" is used in the present article in a neutral way; it may be understood as referring to the name-relation or to the intension-relation or to the extension-relation or to any similar relations used in other semantical methods.

8.   Wilfrid Sellars ("Acquaintance and Description Again." in *Journal of Philos.*, 46 (1949), 496–504; see pp. 502 f.) analyzes clearly the roots of the mistake "of taking the designation relation of semantic theory to be a reconstruction of *being present to an experience*".

CHAPTER 4

Ludwig Wittgenstein: Rules and Private Language

Introduction to Wittgenstein's *Philosophical Investigations*

Philosophical Investigations was the culmination of ideas which Wittgenstein had been developing since the mid-1930s. It is a relatively late work, and as close to a final draft as he could achieve. Since it was the first of his writings to be posthumously released, what was most conspicuous was the radical difference in content and approach from that of the *Tractatus*. With the gradual publication of his notebooks, and numerous transcriptions of his lectures between 1929 and 1947, we now have a less partial view which reveals the gradual move from Logical Atomism to Wittgenstein's mature work.

Perhaps the most obvious place to begin describing the differences between the two books is at the beginning of *Philosophical Investigations*, where Wittgenstein attacks the Tractarian doctrine that language functions only to state facts. He now says that language comprises a large variety of different, interconnecting "language-games" that cannot be reduced to a single one:

> But how many kinds of sentence are there? Say assertion, question and command?—There are countless kinds: countless different kinds of use of what we call "symbols," "words," "sentences." And this multiplicity is not something fixed, given once and for all; but new types of language, new language-games, as we may say, come into existence, and others

become obsolete and get forgotten. … Here the term "language-game" is meant to bring into prominence the fact that the speaking of language is part of an activity, or of a form of life … It is interesting to compare the multiplicity of the tools in language and of the ways they are used, the multiplicity of kinds of word and sentence, with what logicians have said about the structure of language. (Including the author of the *Tractatus Logico-Philosophicus*)" (#23).

In the *Tractatus,* Wittgenstein said that the limits of the meaningful were already dictated, prior to use, by the nature of reality, that is, by facts in the world. In the *Investigations,* the meaning of a word or sentence is governed only by the self-regulating practices of linguistic communities. That is, language is not accountable to anything beyond itself. It cannot be reformed or replaced by virtue of any external authority, whether it be logic, the nature of reality, or any essential nature of language. He likewise held in the *Tractatus* that the sense of a term, and thereby the rule for its use, had to be totally determinate, excluding all vagueness or ambiguity. His later position is that while this may be so in some special (e.g., technical) contexts, such a stricture is seldom necessary or desirable.

Wittgenstein always held to the view that philosophy was fundamentally different from the sciences, in that it discovers no new facts but merely clarifies facts already available to us. He only changed his mind on how philosophy ought to perform its task. The *Tractatus* said that the method was logical analysis, revealing the true form of the fact in which its isomorphism with reality was made clear; in the *Investigations*, it was to be done by detailed description of the ways in which words actually operated, and thereby indicating when these rules were violated. Unlike the *Tractatus*, the *Investigations* never offers a general theory of language. Rather, it is explicitly antitheoretical, seeing the impulse to generalize as a prime source of philosophical confusion. In *The Blue Book*, he criticizes this "craving for generality" and a "contempt for the particular case," that is, of failing to appreciate the diversity of ways in which words can be used, and of falsely assimilating the use of some words to that of others. Two common errors are (1) to treat all words as if they were names, denoting objects; and (2) to treat "grammatical" sentences, explicating the logic of a particular concept, as if they were making empirical claims. Wittgenstein thinks that if we restrict ourselves to accurate descriptions of particular usages, paying attention to differences, then we will stand a good chance of avoiding philosophical error. He sometimes speaks of philosophy as a "therapeutic" practice: In the way that a therapist might uncover deep hidden traumas, a careful examination of grammar will unravel deeply entrenched hidden errors that cause the "mental cramp" symptomatic of philosophical perplexity. Once the false picture is dismantled, the problems disappear.

RULE-FOLLOWING AND UNDERSTANDING

Over the past fifteen years, these sections (roughly from #138 to #242) have received more attention than any other area in Wittgenstein's work. By common consent, the impetus has been the publication of Saul Kripke's *Wittgenstein on Rules and Private Language.* I will briefly describe Kripke's controversial interpretation later. For the moment consider this summary of Wittgenstein's position by Colin McGinn: "Understanding is not an *inner* process of supplying an *interpretation* of a sign which *justifies* one in reacting with a sign in a certain way; it is, rather, an *ability* to engage in a *practice* or *custom* of *using* a sign *over time* in accordance with one's *natural propensities*" (p. 42). I will now elaborate on these points.

Wittgenstein denies that to "mean something" by a word (or any sign) is to experience some mental event, some state of mind like an awareness of some image. Of course, he's not denying that such phenomena occur—merely that they are neither necessary nor sufficient for meaning or understanding. He is opposing a long tradition, most obviously represented by the empiricists, whereby meaning and understanding were thought of as akin to experiential states such as sensations. Wittgenstein stresses their differences: First, we can think of a sensation lasting for a particular period, or as starting or stopping at a certain time. Second, we can conceive of a sensation, for instance, a pain, as having a certain degree of intensity, which can vary over time. Neither of these factors make sense as applied to understanding a word, or meaning something by it. One further difference is this: My understanding of the meaning of a word does not cease to exist when I am not actively contemplating it, since it can be "called into action" whenever needed. If cognitive capacities are to have a model at all, it should be practical skills and abilities.

Like Gilbert Ryle, who was greatly influenced by his later work, Wittgenstein opposes taking thinking to consist in some process of "interpretation," by reference to some internal "rule" that exists prior to linguistic activity. He points out that the usage of words can be correct or incorrect. However, the mere presence of some image or idea in the mind could not anchor this normativity. That is, contra empiricism, word meaning cannot derive from idea-meaning; one cannot check that a word is being used correctly by consulting some image that functions as an exemplar for linguistic usage, that is, that one's situation "matches" this internal prototype. Wittgenstein is also attacking a conception of rules that is implicit in the *Tractatus*, where the structure of language constitutes a set of algorithms which, if followed, would guarantee meaningful talk or thought. These rules, and the meanings they produced, were considered to be independent of any individual or social practice. Recall that one of the central claims of the *Tractatus* was that language pictured the world, and that a proposition was true if it corresponded to a fact in the world. This implies that whether a proposition is true, and thereby whether a particular usage of a term is correct, is dictated by the way the world is, independent of our mind or practice.

However, no image is intrinsically meaningful. It is a sign like any other, and therefore must be interpreted. But how is this to be done? Clearly, resort to some other, second-order images will set us off on an infinite regress, since they will in turn require interpretation. Similar considerations would apply to the idea that one inwardly consults some linguistic formula, to apply in concrete situations. As before, such a rule will itself need to be interpreted. Thus, "any interpretation still hangs in the air along with what it interprets."

In these difficult passages, Wittgenstein is attacking the deeply entrenched assumption that understanding takes place "in the mind," privately and prior to actual public usage, in a way that somehow normatively grounds that usage. He illustrates the absurdity of such a position by taking the example of the simple mathematical sequence "0, 2, 4, 6. ... " Any competent person would immediately "see" how to continue the series. This will be done with extreme rapidity and ease, as if "automatically," without having to consciously deliberate over, or actively "choose" the next number. We say that such a person understands, or grasps, the rule "+2." Of this there is no doubt. But it is not so obvious to say what this understanding consists in. As G.E. Moore would say, its *truth* is undeniable, but its *analysis* is problematic.

Given that we can seemingly automatically give the next number for any stage of the sequence, one can be easily misled into thinking that there is some "queer" mental state in which the complete series is already "in the mind" prior to the concrete context of verbalization; and some equally "queer" mental act by which we can scan this series "like tracks laid out before the mind." In other words, we can be fooled into thinking that what causes, and explains, our practice of correctly producing the number *n* + 2, for any member *n*, is that the entire numerical series is *already there* in your mind, prior to, and independent of, the manifestation of this knowledge. But this can't be how it is: Not only is the series infinite, but, as we have seen, it would merely be another sign, needing interpretation itself. The same point can be made in terms of predicates, such as "red." Clearly, this concept has potentially unlimited application. Likewise, anyone who understands this concept can correctly apply it in any number of standard cases. But we cannot explain this practice in terms of some mental state or act in which all possible applications of "red" are contained.

So what *does* determine correct usage? What makes a certain development of a sequence the "right" way? Suppose that you follow the rule "+2" up to a certain point. This achievement, by itself, doesn't uniquely determine what the next sequent should be. It is no use saying "the rule '+2' determines it." That would be to beg the question in favor of a certain interpretation of that rule—but a rule is a sign like any other and is not self-interpreting. Some have taken Wittgenstein as claiming that what determines that 1004, rather than 1005, follows 1002 in the sequence obeying "+2" is merely a shared public practice, that is, the groundless fact that this is how we do it.

Before going on, I will make a few remarks about Saul Kripke's work on these areas. It is wise to follow Kripke's advice on the ideas he presents: "The present paper should be thought of as expounding neither 'Wittgenstein's' argument nor 'Kripke's': rather Wittgenstein's argument as it struck Kripke, as it presented a problem for him" (p. 5). While few are convinced that Kripke has accurately represented Wittgenstein's intentions, all are agreed that his work is of the highest quality in its own right, and raises some of the deepest problems at the heart of many contemporary debates.

Kripke presents considerations leading to skepticism about meaning. That is, he considers all plausible candidates that could determine the meaning of words, in such a way as to ground the normativity of meaning, and concludes that all fail the grade. He considers these candidates: mental states, actual usage, and dispositions to usage. These all fail because they *underdetermine* the meaning of the sign. His point is that actual or dispositional usage of terms must be finite, yet concepts have potentially unlimited application, so there will always be more that one interpretation of that sign which is compatible with all we can do. Kripke takes the sign "+," and looks in vain for facts that would establish that someone had been using this sign to stand for the function of addition rather than "quaddition," a function whose values have, so far, completely paralleled those of addition, but which diverge some time in the future. His second point is this: Facts about one's mental states, or about actual or dispositional usage of terms, can only cover how we do use, or *would* use this term. But this only covers the descriptive aspect of use—it doesn't tell you whether you *should* have done so. But meaning is essentially normative. For a word to have a definite meaning, there must be a fact of the matter over whether any particular use of it is correct or not. So, in the absence of any fact that could ground this normativity, Kripke denies that there is a fact of the matter about what one's words mean or whether they mean anything at all. He calls this conclusion his "sceptical paradox," in line with Wittgenstein's #201.

He then goes on to propose the "sceptical solution" to the paradox. He takes as his model Hume's account of causation, which reconstructs our justification of ascriptions of causation, even though there are no facts out there in the world corresponding to causal power. Hume's solution goes like this: Causation is not warranted on the observation of a single correlation between two events; rather, once a "constant conjunction" of certain event-types has been noted, we are led to expect the latter when presented with the former. This internal associative connection, this "custom and habit," is falsely projected onto the world itself. Kripke argues that just as we can't talk of causation in an isolated one-off case, nor can we talk of a single individual meaning anything by his words, but only as a member of a linguistic community. One uses a term correctly if it accords with the common practice. So this move involves giving up the idea that meaning must be grounded in facts about the speaker, and replacing it with "assertibility conditions," comprising of communal practice, itself not grounded in any prior facts.

THE PRIVATE LANGUAGE ARGUMENT

The Private Language Argument was long considered to start at #243 and continue to #315. More contemporary readings take it to be integrally connected with earlier remarks on rule-following and understanding. As Kripke correctly notes, the conclusion of the Private Language Argument is explicitly stated in #202.

Traditional philosophy, whether empiricist, rationalist, realist, idealist, and the like, had all assumed (or at least adhered to doctrines which logically committed them to the claim) that thinking took place in a "private language," in which words acquired their meaning by being associated with experiences. That is, these experiences (often thought to be images) were taken to supply the "rule" that determined the meaning and the correct use of the term. It would follow that each person has his or her own private language, learned by an essentially private process of *internal ostensive definition* in which an appropriate mental "exemplar" is created, to be later employed to ground the correct usage of terms.

As was long recognized, such a picture inevitably led to skepticism and linguistic solipsism: Each person's language is essentially unintelligible to others, since only oneself has access to the mental states which confer meaning on one's terms. Thus, mutual understanding would be impossible: In order for X to understand Y's language,

X would have to employ Y's mental states. Nor can X even say that Y's terms have a meaning similar to that of his own, or that Y has experiences similar to his own. To be warranted in saying that two things are similar, one needs access to both.

The Private Language Argument makes use of Wittgenstein's earlier conclusions about the practice of ostensive definition (#27-#35). Clearly we can indicate what a word means by pointing to something. However, one will succeed in communicating the meaning only if one's audience places the act in a wider context. For example, if I already know that somebody is trying to indicate a color word to me (i.e., if I understand the grammar of color words), then somebody pointing and saying, "*This* is sepia," will help me to understand "sepia" (#30). However, the mere act of pointing, by itself, is not enough. Suppose that our learner were a *tabula rasa*, lacking all cultural or linguistic background. Suppose that I were to point to a table and say, "*This* is a table." I can, with equal justification, be interpreted as pointing not only to a table, but to wood, furniture, brownness, quadrupeds, and so on. Just knowing that the particular pointed to is called "table" doesn't tell me what a table is. In other words, a single act of ostensive definition cannot reveal a concept's principle of individuation. It does not reveal *in virtue of what* this thing is a table, nor *what else* counts as a table. But unless you know all this, and thereby apply the concept in its general usage, you have not grasped the concept. Take chess (#31): Unless I already know a fair amount about the game, then merely knowing that an indicated piece is "the king" isn't much help, since it doesn't tell you the piece's use—its role in the game, what it can do, what counts as correct usage, and the like. In sum, Wittgenstein argues that ostensive definition cannot be the basis of language learning, since it can work only when considerable background is already in place. He will argue that a private language, based on *internal* ostensive definition, is thereby impossible.

Wittgenstein defines a "private language" as *a language whose terms refer to the subject's sensations, not to intersubjectively accessible objects*. Wittgenstein explicitly contrasts the imagined private language user with a soliloquist, whose language is, as a matter of contingent fact, known only to himself but remains sharable in principle. As with all of Wittgenstein's work, the Private Language Argument is subject to heated debate regarding interpretation. Some influential commentators suggest that he is saying that one can only have a language as a member of a linguistic community. Others say that all that is required is that one's usage be independently checkable by reference to some independent standard—which needn't require other people.

In #258, Wittgenstein says that the traditional skeptical worry that no one could understand what anyone else meant is a red herring—the real problem is that *I could not understand my own private language*. Such a purported language is a sham, since it can contain no genuine rules for governing correct usage. Suppose that the private language user notes the occurrence of a certain sensation, and calls it "S." That is, "S" is defined by a private ostensive definition: He focuses on the sensation, invents the sign, and sets up an association between them. Wittgenstein replies that this is a mere "idle ceremony," incapable of conferring meaning on "S." I cannot "point" to a sensation as I can point to a table. Physical objects are separable from me and exist independent of me whereas my sensations do not. A genuine definition establishes a term's meaning by laying down a rule for its future use, but just concentrating on a sensation and saying "S" cannot do this. The crucial point is this: Nothing a private language user can do can ensure that all usage of "S" is consistent. It is not that I can't be sure that I've remembered the meaning of "S" correctly. This would be to assume that its meaning had already been fixed, and that I may have got it wrong. The problem is the more fundamental one that no genuine criterion of "correctness" has ever been established. Suppose I object "But it sure seems like an "S"!" Wittgenstein replies that something can only seem like an "S" if the meaning of "S" has been antecedently established, and this has not taken place here. Rather (#202, #258) we have a case in which whatever *seems* to be right *is* right - but unless we can make a genuine distinction between appearance and reality, between the "seems" and the "is," then there can be no "right."

In #265, Wittgenstein pursues this point by imagining someone who tries to justify his calling a sensation "S" by appeal to a *mental table* in which memory-samples of various types of sensations are correlated with signs or words. The idea is that to check whether I am now using "S" correctly, I would access the appropriate memory-sample corresponding to "S," and check that my present sensation matched it. But, as Wittgenstein says, such a procedure is a sham, as there is no genuine check on the usage of "S." All this supposed checking the table can be is "remembering what "S" means"—which is what it was meant to establish.

The situation is different when we check our usage against some external criterion. Suppose I say that my shirt is indigo. I can check whether I'm right by consulting a color chart (i.e., of the kind found in a paint store), looking for a match with my shirt. So the chart supplies a rule which I can employ to check my usage of "indigo." This procedure can work because the table is external and independent of what's inside my head. A table that exists only in my memory is not independent of my usage of "S," and thus cannot really check it. Now consider this case: Suppose that I cannot remember when a particular flight arrives; suppose that I've left my timetable at home but have memorized its information; I can thus consult a mental image of that timetable, derived from memory—and I can either do it correctly or incorrectly. Success is possible only because I can apply an external check via the physical timetable, whose contents are independent of my memory of them. If my memory matches what is in that timetable, I remember correctly. Checking a mental table alone is, as Wittgenstein says, like buying a second copy of the same newspaper to check if what the first one says is true. It follows that a private language is unlearnable, and therefore impossible.

In #270, Wittgenstein contrasts the case of someone who correlates "S" with some *public* phenomena. For example, he may notice that a certain type of sensation is always accompanied by a rise in blood pressure. He would then be able to tell whether his blood pressure was rising by merely noting the occurrence of the sensation. In such a case, "S" has a genuine use, namely "the sensation that indicates that my blood pressure is rising." But "S" is thereby not part of a private language. The purported "private object" itself plays no genuine part on the practice. Wittgenstein makes this point with a famous analogy, #293: Suppose that everyone has a box with something in it, which everyone calls a "beetle"; nobody can see into anyone else's box, so each person knows what "beetle" indicates purely from his or her own case.

If "beetle" had a genuine use in their shared language, the objects in the boxes become irrelevant, playing no role in communication.

As an adjunct to the Private Language Argument, Wittgenstein makes some other remarks on the notion of privacy, as attached to sensations, in #246–#257. We can distinguish two separate aspects of privacy:

(1) The existence, and nature of my sensations cannot be communicated, nor known by anyone apart from myself;
(2) My sensations are nontransferable—only I can have mine.

Claim (1) is a conjunction of two separate claims. Take the example of pain:

(1a) No one else can know whether I'm in pain
(1b) I can know whether I'm in pain.

Consider (1a) first. Wittgenstein says that it can be interpreted in two ways. First, taken on a literal, common-sense level, it is just plain false; for example, if I have been shot, and am writhing around groaning. He adds that there are cases in which pretense isn't a live option (e.g., babies or animals). The idea here is that "pretending" is a sophisticated game, derivative on a grasp of the non-learned correlation between pain and pain behavior in standard conditions. Second, if you mean "know" in the sense of "without any conceivable doubt," Wittgenstein avoids the skeptical admission of this, with its corollary assumption that this presents a problem. Rather, he remarks that the claim is senseless when taken in this way: It only makes sense to say that you know something when the possibility of doubt or error exists. This is the very reason why (1b) is senseless. It doesn't state an empirical claim—rather, it is a "grammatical proposition" illustrating this factor about the concept of pain.

Similar remarks apply to (b)—it isn't a factual claim that only I can have my pain, since this factor is constitutive of the notion of pain. However, privacy, in the sense of (1), is not implied, since my coughs or belches are equally nontransferable but all too publicly accessible.

In #244, Wittgenstein suggests his positive view, that a sensation-word like "pain" has not primarily a descriptive use (i.e., to describe some inner state) but an expressive function. That is, it is a learned replacement for innate pain-behavior. These natural correlations between pain and behavior supply the context enabling one to grasp the grammar of "pain." Wittgenstein's position is more subtle than a hard-line behaviorism. He is not identifying nor reducing pain to pain-behavior. On the other hand, he opposes the skeptical position that pain and pain-behavior are only contingently related, while acknowledging that pretense or concealment can occur. His point is that one could not grasp the concept of "pain" purely from one's own case, by private ostensive definition. Behavioral criteria, general by their nature, are required. We learn the concept by becoming familiar with general truths about standard correlations between pain and typical causes, and typical responses. Once we understand all this, then we can acknowledge the existence of nonstandard cases in which the usual links do not occur. But these don't cast everything into doubt, since grasp of their possibility depends on the standard cases, in the same way that counterfeit money is parasitic on genuine.

So pain-behavior supplies "criteria" for ascriptions of pain. That is, the fact that certain behavior generally occur in response to physical injury is not a necessary connection; nor is it a mere contingent connection that supplies empirical evidence for the presence of pain; rather, it is what we might call a *constitutive assumption* for use of "pain." That is, anyone who didn't understand that certain sensations and certain behavior are reliably correlated with certain types of injury, could not be said to grasp the concept of pain.

BIBLIOGRAPHY

Works by Wittgenstein

The Blue and Brown Books (Oxford: Basil Blackwell, 1969).

On Certainty, ed. G. E. M. Anscombe and G. H. von Wright (Oxford: Basil Blackwell, 1969).

Philosophical Grammar, ed. Rush Rhees, trans. Anthony Kenny (Oxford: Basil Blackwell, 1974).

Philosophical Investigations, trans. G. E. M. Anscombe (New York: Macmillan, 1973).

Philosophical Remarks, ed. Rush Rhees (Oxford: Basil Blackwell, 1975).

Remarks on the Foundations of Mathematics, ed. G. H. von Wright, R. Rhees, and G. E. M. Anscombe; trans. G. E. M. Anscombe, (Oxford: Basil Blackwell 1978).

Remarks on the Philosophy of Psychology, ed. G. H. von Wright and Heikki Nyman (Oxford: Basil Blackwell, 1980).

Zettel, ed. G. E. M. Anscombe and G. H. von Wright; trans. G. E. M. Anscombe, (Oxford: Basil Blackwell, 1967).

Further Reading

Robert Fogelin, *Wittgenstein*, 2nd ed., (London: Routledge, 1987).

P. M. S. Hacker, *Insight and Illusion* (rev. ed.) (Oxford: Clarendon Press, 1986).

Saul Kripke, *Wittgenstein on Rules and Private Language* (Oxford: Basil Blackwell, 1982).

Colin McGinn, *Wittgenstein on Meaning* (Oxford: Basil Blackwell, 1984). (This includes detailed discussions of Kripke.)

David Pears, *The False Prison*, Vol. Two (Oxford: Clarendon Press, 1988).

For a recent survey on following a rule, see Paul Boghossian, "The Rule-Following Considerations," *Mind,* Vol. 98, 1989.

The best biography of Wittgenstein is by Ray Monk, *Wittgenstein: The Duty of Genius*, (New York: Free Press, 1990).

Selections from *Philosophical Investigations*

Ludwig Wittgenstein

138. But can't the meaning of a word that I understand fit the sense of a sentence that I understand? Or the meaning of one word fit the meaning of another?—Of course, if the meaning is the *use* we make of the word, it makes no sense to speak of such 'fitting.' But we *understand* the meaning of a word when we hear or say it; we grasp it in a flash, and what we grasp in this way is surely something different from the 'use' which is extended in time!

139. When someone says the word "cube" to me, for example, I know what it means. But can the whole *use* of the word come before my mind, when I *understand* it in this way?

Well, but on the other hand isn't the meaning of the word also determined by this use? And can these ways of determining meaning conflict? Can what we grasp *in a flash* accord with a use, fit or fail to fit it? And how can what is present to us in an instant, what comes before our mind in an instant, fit a *use*?

What really comes before our mind when we *understand* a word?—Isn't it something like a picture? Can't it *be* a picture?

Well, suppose that a picture does come before your mind when you hear the word "cube", say the drawing of a cube. In what sense can this picture fit or fail to fit a use of the word "cube"?—Perhaps you say: "It's quite simple;—if that picture occurs to me and I point to a triangular prism for instance, and say it is a cube, then this use of the word doesn't fit the picture."—But doesn't it fit? I have purposely so chosen the example that it is quite easy to imagine a *method of projection* according to which the picture does fit after all.

From *Philosophical Investigations*, trans. G.E.M. Anscombe (Oxford: Blackwell, 1953). Reprinted by permission of Macmillan.

Must I *know* whether I understand a word? Don't I also sometimes imagine myself to understand a word (as I may imagine I understand a kind of calculation) and then realize that I did not understand it? ("I thought I knew what 'relative' and 'absolute' motion meant, but I see that I don't know.")

(a) "I believe the right word in this case is. ... " Doesn't this shew that the meaning of a word is a something that comes before our mind, and which is, as it were, the exact picture we want to use here? Suppose I were choosing between the words "imposing", "dignified", "proud", "venerable"; isn't it as though I were choosing between drawings in a portfolio?—No: the fact that one speaks of the *appropriate word* does not *shew* the existence of a something that etc. One is inclined, rather, to speak of this picture-like something just because one can find a word appropriate; because one often chooses between words as between similar but not identical pictures; because pictures are often used instead of words, or to illustrate words; and so on.

(b) I see a picture; it represents an old man walking up a steep path leaning on a stick.—How? Might it not have looked just the same if he had been sliding downhill in that position? Perhaps a Martian would describe the picture so. I do not need to explain why *we* do not describe it so.

The picture of the cube did indeed *suggest* a certain use to us, but it was possible for me to use it differently.

140.   Then what sort of mistake did I make; was it what we should like to express by saying: I should have thought the picture forced a particular use on me? How could I think that? What *did* I think? Is there such a thing as a picture, or something like a picture, that forces a particular application on us; so that my mistake lay in confusing one picture with another?—For we might also be inclined to express ourselves like this: we are at most under a psychological, not a logical, compulsion. And now it looks quite as if we knew of two kinds of case.

What was the effect of my argument? It called our attention to (reminded us of) the fact that there are other processes, besides the one we originally thought of, which we should sometimes be prepared to call "applying the picture of a cube". So our 'belief that the picture forced a particular application upon us' consisted in the fact that only the one case and no other occurred to us. "There is another solution as well" means: there is something else that I am also prepared to call a "solution"; to which I am prepared to apply such-and-such a picture, such-and-such an analogy, and so on.

What is essential is to see that the same thing can come before our minds when we hear the word and the application still be different. Has it the *same* meaning both times? I think we shall say not.

141.   Suppose, however, that not merely the picture of the cube, but also the method of projection comes before our mind?—How am I to imagine this?—Perhaps I see before me a schema shewing the method of projection: say a picture of two cubes connected by lines of projection.—But does this really get me any further? Can't I now imagine different applications of this schema too?—Well, yes, but then can't an *application come before my mind*?—It can: only we need to get clearer about our application of *this* expression. Suppose I explain various methods of projection to someone so that he may go on to apply them; let us ask ourselves when we should say that *the* method that I intend comes before his mind.

Now clearly we accept two different kinds of criteria for this: on the one hand the picture (of whatever kind) that at some time or other comes before his mind; on the other, the application which—in the course of time—he makes of what he imagines. (And can't it be clearly seen here that it is absolutely inessential for the picture to exist in his imagination rather than as a drawing or model in front of him; or again as something that he himself constructs as a model?)

Can there be a collision between picture and application? There can, inasmuch as the picture makes us expect a different use, because people in general apply *this* picture like *this*.

I want to say: we have here a *normal* case, and abnormal cases.

142.   It is only in normal cases that the use of a word is clearly prescribed; we know, are in no doubt, what to say in this or that case. The more abnormal the case,

---

What we have to mention in order to explain the significance, I mean the importance, of a concept, are often extremely general facts of nature: such facts as are hardly ever mentioned because of their great generality.

the more doubtful it becomes what we are to say. And if things were quite different from what they actually are—if there were for instance no characteristic expression of pain, of fear, of joy; if rule became exception and exception rule; or if both became phenomena of roughly equal frequency—this would make our normal language-games lose their point.—The procedure of putting a lump of cheese on a balance and fixing the price by the turn of the scale would lose its point if it frequently happened for such lumps to suddenly grow or shrink for no obvious reason. This remark will become clearer when we discuss such things as the relation of expression to feeling, and similar topics.

143.   Let us now examine the following kind of language-game: when A gives an order B has to write down series of signs according to a certain formation rule.

The first of these series is meant to be that of the natural numbers in decimal notation.—How does he get to understand this notation?—First of all series of numbers will be written down for him and he will be required to copy them. (Do not balk at the expression "series of numbers"; it is not being used wrongly here.) And here already there is a normal and an abnormal learner's reaction.—At first perhaps we guide his hand in writing out the series 0 to 9; but then the *possibility of getting him to understand* will depend on his going on to write it down independently.—And here we can imagine, e.g., that he does copy the figures independently, but not in the right order: he writes sometimes one sometimes another at random. And then communications stops at *that* point.—Or again, he makes '*mistakes*' in the order.—The difference between this and the first case will of course be one of frequency.—Or he makes a *systematic* mistake; for example, he copies every other number, or he copies the series 0, 1, 2, 3, 4, 5, ... like this: 1, 0, 3, 2, 5, 4, ... Here we shall almost be tempted to say that he has understood *wrong*.

Notice, however, that there is no sharp distinction between a random mistake and a systematic one. That is, between what you are inclined to call "random" and what "systematic".

Perhaps it is possible to wean him from the systematic mistake (as from a bad habit). Or perhaps one accepts his way of copying and tries to teach him ours as an offshoot, a variant of his.—And here too our pupil's capacity to learn may come to an end.

144.   What do I mean when I say "the pupil's capacity to learn *may* come to an end here"? Do I say this from my own experience? Of course not. (Even if I have had such experience.) Then what am I doing with that proposition? Well, I should like you to say: "Yes, it's true, you can imagine that too, that might happen too!"—But was I trying to draw someone's attention to the fact that he is capable of imagining that?—I wanted to put that picture before him, and his *acceptance* of the picture consists in his now being inclined to regard a given case differently: that is, to compare it with *this* rather than *that* set of pictures. I have changed his *way of looking at things*. (Indian mathematicians: "Look at this.")

145.   Suppose the pupil now writes the series o to 9 to our satisfaction.— And this will only be the case when he is often successful, not if he does it right once in a hundred attempts. Now I continue the series and draw his attention to the recurrence of the first series in the units; and then to its recurrence in the tens. (Which only means that I use particular emphases, underline figures, write them one under another in such-and-such ways, and similar things.)—And now at some point he continues the series independently—or he does not.—But why do you say that? *so* much is obvious!—Of course; I only wished to say: the effect of any further *explanation* depends on his *reaction*.

Now, however, let us suppose that after some efforts on the teacher's part he continues the series correctly, that is, as we do it. So now we can say he has mastered the system.—But how far need he continue the series for us to have the right to say that? Clearly you cannot state a limit here.

146.   Suppose I now ask: "Has he understood the system when he continues the series to the hundredth place?" Or—if I should not speak of 'understanding' in connection with our primitive language-game: Has he got the system, if he continues the series correctly so far?—Perhaps you will say here: to have got the system (or, again, to understand it) can't consist in continuing the series up to *this* or *that* number: *that* is only applying one's understanding. The understanding itself is a state which is the *source* of the correct use.

What is one really thinking of here? Isn't one thinking of the derivation of a series from its algebraic formula? Or at least of something analogous?—But this is where we were before. The point is, we can think of more than *one* application of an algebraic formula; and every type of application can in turn be formulated algebraically; but naturally this does not get us any further.—The application is still a criterion of understanding.

147.   "But how can it be? When *I* say I understand the rule of a series, I am surely not saying so because I have *found out* that up to now I have applied the algebraic formula in such-and-such a way! In my own case it all events I surely know that I mean such-and-such a series; it doesn't matter how far I have actually developed it."—

Your idea, then, is that you know the application of the rule of the series quite apart from remembering actual applications to particular numbers. And you will perhaps say: "Of course! For the series is infinite and the bit of it that I can have developed finite."

148.   But what does this knowledge consist in? Let me ask: *When* do you know that application? Always? day and night? or only when you are actually think-

---

(a) "Understanding a word": a state. But a *mental* state?—Depression, excitement, pain, are called mental states. Carry out a grammatical investigation as follows: we say
   "He was depressed the whole day".
   "He was in great excitement the whole day".
   "He has been in continuous pain since yesterday".—We also say "Since yesterday I have understood this word". "Continuously", though?—To be sure, one can speak of an interruption of understanding. But in what cases? Compare: "When did your pains get less?" and "When did you stop understanding that word?"
(b) "Suppose it were asked: "*When* do you know how to play chess? All the time? or just while you are making a move? And the *whole* of chess during each move?—How queer that knowing how to play chess should take such a short time, and a game so much longer!

ing of the rule? do you know it, that is, in the same way as you know the alphabet and the multiplication table? Or is what you call "knowledge" a state of consciousness or a process—say a thought of something, or the like?

149.   If one says that knowing the ABC is a state of the mind one is thinking of a state of a mental apparatus (perhaps of the brain) by means of which we explain the *manifestations* of that knowledge. Such a state is called a disposition. But there are objections to speaking of a state of the mind here, inasmuch as there ought to be two different criteria for such a state: a knowledge of the construction of the apparatus, quite apart from what it does. (Nothing would be more confusing here than to use the words "conscious" and "unconscious" for the contrast between states of consciousness and dispositions. For this pair of terms covers up a grammatical difference.)

150.   The grammar of the word "knows" is evidently closely related to that of "can", "is able to". But also closely related to that of "understands". ('Mastery' of a technique.)

151.   But there is also *this* use of the word "to know": we say "Now I know!"—and similarly "Now I can do it!" and "Now I understand!"

Let us imagine the following example: A writes series of numbers down; B watches him and tries to find a law for the sequence of numbers. If he succeeds he exclaims: "Now I can go on!"—So this capacity, this understanding, is something that makes its appearance in a moment. So let us try and see what it is that makes its appearance here.—A has written down the numbers 1, 5, 11, 19, 29; at this point B says he knows how to go on. What happened here? Various things may have happened; for example, while A was slowly putting one number after another, B was occupied with trying various algebraic formulae on the numbers which had been written down. After A had written the number 19 B tried the formula $a_n = n^2 + n - 1$; and the next number confirmed his hypothesis.

Or again, B does not think of formulae. He watches A writing his numbers down with a certain feeling of tension, and all sorts of vague thoughts go through his head. Finally be asks himself: "What is the series of differences?" He finds the series 4, 6, 8, 10 and says: Now I can go on.

Or he watches and says "Yes, I know *that* series"—and continues it, just as he would have done if A had written down the series 1, 3, 5, 7, 9.—Or he says nothing at all and simply continues the series. Perhaps he had what may be called the sensation "that's easy!". (Such a sensation is, for example, that of a light quick intake of breath, as when one is slightly startled.)

152.   But are the processes which I have described here *understanding*.

"B understands the principle of the series" surely doesn't mean simply: the formula "$a_n = \ldots$" occurs to B. For it is perfectly imaginable that the formula should occur to him and that he should nevertheless not understand. "He understands" must have more in it than: the formula occurs to him. And equally, more than any of those more or less characteristic *accompaniments* or manifestations of understanding.

153.   We are trying to get hold of the mental process of understanding which seems to be hidden behind those coarser and therefore more readily visible accompaniments. But we do not succeed; or, rather, it does not get as far as a real attempt. For even supposing I had found something that happened in all those cases of understanding,—why should *it* be the understanding? And how can the process of understanding have been hidden, when I said "Now I understand" *because* I understood?! And if I say it is hidden—then how do I know what I have to look for? I am in a muddle.

154.   But wait—if "Now I understand the principle" does not mean the same as "The formula .... occurs to me" (or "I say the formula", "I write it down", etc.)—does it follow from this that I employ the sentence "Now I understand ...." or "Now I can go on" as a description of a process occurring behind or side by side with that of saying the formula?

If there has to be anything 'behind the utterance of the formula' it is *particular circumstances*, which justify me in saying I can go on—when the formula occurs to me.

Try not to think of understanding as a 'mental process' at all.—For *that* is the expression which confuses you. But ask yourself: in what sort of case, in what kind of circumstances, do we say, "Now I know how to go on," when, that is, the formula *has* occurred to me?—

In the sense in which there are processes (including mental processes) which are characteristic of understanding, understanding is not a mental process.

(A pain's growing more and less; the hearing of a tune or a sentence: these are mental processes.) ...

185.   Let us return to our example (143). Now—judged by the usual criteria—the pupil has mastered the series of natural numbers. Next we teach him to write down other series of cardinal numbers and get him to the point of writing down series of the form

o, n, 2n, 3n, etc.

at an order of the form "+n"; so at the order "+1" he writes down the series of natural numbers.—Let us suppose we have done exercises and given him tests up to 1000.

Now we get the pupil to continue a series (say +2) beyond 1000—and he writes 1000, 1004, 1008, 1012.

We say to him: "Look what you've done!"—He doesn't understand. We say: "You were meant to add *two*: look how you began the series!"—He answers: "Yes, isn't it right? I thought that was how I was *meant* to do it."—Or suppose he pointed to the series and said: "But I went on in the same way."—It would now be no use to say: "But can't you see...?"—and repeat the old examples and explanations.—In such a case we might say, perhaps: It comes natural to this person to understand our order with our explanations as *we* should understand the order: "Add 2 up to 1000, 4 up to 2000, 6 up to 3000 and so on."

Such a case would present similarities with one in which a person naturally reacted to the gesture of pointing with the hand by looking in the direction of the line from finger-tip to wrist, not from wrist to finger-tip.

186.   "What you are saying, then, comes to this: a new insight—intuition—is needed at every step to carry out the order '+n' correctly."—To carry it out correctly! How is it decided what is the right step to take at any particular stage?—"The right step is the one that accords with the order—as it was *meant*."—So when you gave the order +2 you meant that he was to write 1002 after 1000—and did you also mean that he should write 1868 after 1866, sand 100036 after 100034, and so on—an infinite number of such propositions?—"No: what I meant was, that he should write the next but one number after *every* number that he wrote; and from this all those propositions follow in turn."—But that is just what is in question: what, at any stage, does follow from that sentence. Or, again, what, at any stage we are to call "being in accord" with that sentence (and with the *mean*-ing you then put into the sentence—whatever may have consisted in). It would almost be more correct to say, not that an intuition was needed at every stage, but that a new decision was needed at every stage.

187.   "But I already knew, at the time when I gave the order, that he ought to write 1002 after 1000."—Certainly; and you can also say you *meant* it then; only you should not let yourself be misled by the grammar of the words "know" and "mean". For you don't want to say that you thought of the step from 1000 to 1002 at that time—and even if you did think of this step, still you did not think of other ones. When you said "I already knew at the time. ... " that meant something like: "If I had then been asked what number should be written after 1000, I should have replied '1002'." And that I don't doubt. This assumption is rather of the same kind as: "If he had fallen into the water then, I should have jumped in after him".—Now, what was wrong with your idea?

188.   Here I should first of all like to say: your idea was that that act of mean-ing the order had in its own way already traversed all those steps: that when you meant it your mind as it were flew ahead and took all the steps before you physically arrived at this or that one.

Thus you were inclined to use such expressions as: "The steps are *really* already taken, even before I take them in writing or orally or in thought." And it seemed as if they were in some *unique* way predetermined, anticipated—as only the act of meaning can anticipate reality.

189.   "But *are* the steps then *not* determined by the algebraic formula?"—The question contains a mistake.

We use the expression: "The steps are determined by the formula ... ". *How* is it used?—We may perhaps refer to the fact that people are brought by their educa-tion (training) so to use the formula $y = x^2$, that they all work out the same value for y when they substitute the same number for x. Or we may say: "These people are so trained that they all take the same step at the same point when they receive the order 'add 3'." We might express this by saying: for these people the order "add 3" com-pletely determines every step from one number to the next. (In contrast with other people who do not know what they are to do on receiving this order, or who react to it with perfect certainty, but each one in a different way.)

On the other hand we can contrast different kinds of formula, and the differ-ent kinds of use (different kinds of training) appropriate to them. Then we *call* for-mulae of a particular kind (with the appropriate methods of use) "formulae which determine a number y for a given value of x", and formulae of another kind, ones which "do not determine the number y for a given value of x". ($y = x^2$ would be of the first kind, $y \neq x^2$ of the second.) The proposition "The formula ... determines a number y" will then be a statement about the form of the formula—and now we must distinguish such a proposition as "The formula which I have written down determines y", or "Here is a formula which determines y", from one of the following kind: "The formula $y = x^2$ determines the number y for a given value of x". The question "Is the formula written down there one that determines y?" will then mean the same as "Is what is there a formula of this kind or that?"—but it is not clear off-hand what we are to make of the question "Is $y = x^2$ a formula which determines y for a given value of x?" One might address this question to a pupil in order to test whether he understands the use of the word "to determine"; or it might be a mathematical problem to prove in a particular system that x has only one square.

190.   It may now be said: "The way the formula is meant determines which steps are to be taken". What is the criterion for the way the formula is meant? It is, for example, the kind of way we always use it, the way we are taught to use it.

We say, for instance, to someone who uses a sign unknown to us: "If by '$x!2$' you mean x^2, then you get *this* value for y, if you mean $2x$, *that* one."—Now ask yourself: how does one *mean* the one thing or the other by "$x!2$"?

That will be how meaning it can determine the steps in advance.

191. "It is as if we could grasp the whole use of the word in a flash." Like *what* e.g.?—Can't the use—in a certain sense—be grasped in a flash? And in *what* sense can it not?—The point is, that it is as if we could 'grasp it in a flash' in yet another and much more direct sense than that.—But have you a model for this? No. It is just that this expression suggests itself to us. As the result of the crossing of different pictures. ...

195.   "But I don't mean that what I do now (in grasping a sense) determines the future use *causally* and as a matter of experience, but that in a *queer* way, the use itself is in some sense present."—But of course it is, 'in *some* sense'! Really the only thing wrong with what you say is the expression "in a queer way". The rest is all right; and the sentence only seems queer when one imagines a different language-game for it from the one in which we actually use it. (Someone once told me that as a child he had been surprised that a tailor could 'sew a dress'—he thought this meant that a dress was produced by sewing alone, by sewing one thread on to another.)

196.   In our failure to understand the use of a word we take it as the expression of a queer *process*. (As we think of time as a queer medium, of the mind as a queer kind of being.)

197.   "It's as if we could grasp the whole use of a word in a flash."—And that is just what we say we do. That is to say: we sometimes describe what we do in these words. But there is nothing astonishing, nothing queer, about what happens. It becomes queer when we are led to think that the future development must in some way already be present in the act of grasping the use and yet isn't present.—For we say that there isn't any doubt that we understand the word, and on the other hand its meaning lies in its use. There is no doubt that I now want to play chess, but chess is the game it is in virtue of all its rules (and so on). Don't I know, then, which game I want to play until I *have* played it? or are all the rules contained in my act of intending? Is it experience that tells me that this sort of game is the usual consequence of such an act of intending? so is it impossible for me to be certain what I am intending to do? And if that is nonsense—what kind of super-strong connexion, on exists between the act of intending and the thing intended?—Where is the connexion effected between the sense of the expression "Let's play a game of chess" and all the rules of the game?—Well, in the list of rules of the game, in the teaching of it, in the day-to-day practice of playing.

198. "But how can a rule shew me what I have to do at *this* point? Whatever I do is, on some interpretation, in accord with the rule."—That is not what we ought to say, but rather: any interpretation still hangs in the air along with what it interprets, and cannot give it any support. Interpretations by themselves do not determine meaning.

"Then can whatever I do be brought into accord with the rule?"—Let me ask this: what has the expression of a rule—say a sign-post—got to do with my actions? What sort of connexion is there here? Well, perhaps this one: I have been trained to react to this sign in a particular way, and now I do so react to it.

But that is only to give a causal connexion; to tell how it has come about that we now go by the sign-post; not what this going-by-the-sign really consists in. On the contrary; I have further indicated that a person goes by a sign-post only in so far as there exists a regular use of sign-posts, a custom.

199. Is what we call "obeying a rule" something that it would be possible for only *one* man to do, and to do only *once* in his life?—This is of course a note on the grammar of the expression "to obey a rule".

It is not possible that there should have been only one occasion on which someone obeyed a rule. It is not possible that there should have been only one occasion on which a report was made, an order given or understood; and so on.—To obey a rule, to make a report, to give an order, to play a game of chess, are *customs* (uses , institutions).

To understand a sentence means to understand a language. To understand a language means to be master of a technique.

200. It is, of course, imaginable that two people belonging to a tribe unacquainted with games should sit at a chess-board and go through the moves of a game of chess; and even with all the appropriate mental accompaniments. And if *we* were to see it we should say they were playing chess. But now imagine a game of chess translated according to certain rules into a series of actions which we do not ordinarily associate with a *game*—say into yells and stamping of feet. And now suppose those two people to yell and stamp instead of playing the form of chess that we are used to; and this in such a way that their procedure is translatable by suitable rules into a game of chess. Should we still be inclined to say they were playing a game? What right would one have to say so?

201. This was our paradox: no course of action could be determined by a rule, because every course of action can be made out to accord with the rule. The answer was: if everything can be made out to accord with the rule, then it can also be made out to conflict with it. And so there would be neither accord nor conflict here.

It can be seen that there is a misunderstanding here from the mere fact that in the course of our argument we give one interpretation after another; as if each one contented us at least for a moment, until we thought of yet another standing behind it. What this shews is that there is a way of grasping a rule which is *not* an *interpretation*, but which is exhibited in what we call "obeying the rule" and "going against it" in actual cases.

Hence there is an inclination to say: every action according to the rule is an interpretation. But we ought to restrict the term "interpretation" to the substitution of one expression of the rule for another.

202.   And hence also 'obeying a rule' is a practice. And to *think* one is obeying a rule is not to obey a rule. Hence it is not possible to obey a rule 'privately': otherwise thinking one was obeying a rule would be the same thing as obeying it. ...

217.   "How am I able to obey a rule?"—if this is not a question about causes, then it is about the justification for my following the rule in the way I do.

If I have exhausted the justifications I have reached bedrock, and my spade is turned. Then I am inclined to say: "This is simply what I do."

(Remember that we sometimes demand definitions for the sake not of their content, but of their form. Our requirement is an architectural one; the definition a kind of ornamental coping that supports nothing.)

218.   Whence comes the idea that the beginning of a series is a visible section of rails invisibly laid to infinity? Well, we might imagine rails instead of a rule. And infinitely long rails correspond to the unlimited application of a rule.

219.   "All the steps are really already taken" means: I no longer have any choice. The rule, once stamped with a particular meaning, traces the lines along which it is to be followed through the whole of space.—But if something of this sort really were the case, how would it help?

No; my description only made sense if it was to be understood symbolically.—I should have said: *This is how it strikes me*.

When I obey a rule, I do not choose.

I obey the rule *blindly*. ...

243.   A human being can encourage himself, give himself orders, obey, blame and punish himself; he can ask himself a question and answer it. We could even imagine human beings who spoke only in monologue; who accompanied their activities by talking to themselves.—An explorer who watched them and listened to their talk might succeed in translating their language into ours. (This would enable him to predict these people's actions correctly, for he also hears them making resolutions and decisions.)

But could we also imagine a language in which a person could write down or give vocal expression to his inner experiences—his feelings, moods, and the rest—for his private use?—Well, can't we do so in our ordinary language?—But that is not what I mean. The individual words of this language are to refer to what can only be known to the person speaking; to his immediate private sensations. So another person cannot understand the language.

244.   How do words *refer* to sensations?—There doesn't seem to be any problem here; don't we talk about sensations every day, and give them names? But how is the connexion between the name and the thing named set up? This question is the same as: how does a human being learn the meaning of the names of sensations?—of the word "pain" for example. Here is one possibility: words are connected with the primitive, the natural, expressions of the sensation and used in their place. A child has hurt himself and he cries; and then adults talk to him and teach him exclamations and, later, sentences. They teach the child new pain-behaviour.

"So you are saying that the word 'pain' really means crying?"—On the contrary: the verbal expression of pain replaces crying and does not describe it.

245.   For how can I go so far as to try to use language to get between pain and its expression?

246. In what sense are my sensations *private*?—Well, only I can know whether I am really in pain; another person can only surmise it.—In one way this is wrong, and in another nonsense. If we are using the word "to know" as it is normally used (and how else are we to use it?), then other people very often know when I am in pain.—Yes, but all the same not with the certainty with which I know it myself!— It can't be said of me at all (except perhaps as a joke) that I *know* I am in pain. What is it supposed to mean—except perhaps that I *am* in pain?

Other people cannot be said to learn of my sensations *only* from my behaviour—for I cannot be said to learn of them. I *have* them.

The truth is: it makes sense to say about other people that they doubt whether I am in pain; but not to say it about myself.

247. "Only you can know if you had that intention." One might tell someone this when one was explaining the meaning of the word "intention" to him. For then it means: *that* is how we use it.

(And here "know" means that the expression of uncertainty is senseless.)

248. The proposition "Sensations are private" is comparable to: "One plays patience by oneself."

249. Are we perhaps over-hasty in our assumption that the smile of an unweaned infant is not a pretence?—And on what experience is our assumption based?

(Lying is a language-game that needs to be learned like any other one.)

250. Why can't a dog simulate pain? Is he too honest? Could one teach a dog to simulate pain? Perhaps it is possible to teach him to howl on particular occasions as if he were in pain, even when he is not. But the surroundings which are necessary for this behaviour to be real simulation are missing.

251. What does it mean when we say: "I can't imagine the opposite of this" or "What would it be like, if it were otherwise?"—For example, when someone has said that my images are private, or that only I myself can know whether I am feeling pain, and similar things.

Of course, here "I can't imagine the opposite" doesn't mean: my powers of imagination are unequal to the task. These words are a defence against something whose form makes it look like an empirical proposition, but which is really a grammatical one.

But why do we say: "I can't imagine the opposite"? Why not: "I can't imagine the thing itself"?

Example: "Every rod has a length." That means something like: we call something (or *this*) "the length of a rod"—but nothing "the length of a sphere." Now can I imagine 'every rod having a length'? Well, I simply imagine a rod. Only this picture, in connexion with this proposition, has a quite different role from one used in connexion with the proposition "This table has the same length as the one over there". For here I understand what it means to have a picture of the opposite (not need it be a mental picture).

But the picture attaching to the grammatical proposition could only shew, say, what is called "the length of a rod". And what should the opposite picture be?

((Remark about the negation of an a priori proposition.))

252. "This body has extension." To this we might reply: "Nonsense!"—but are inclined to reply "Of course!"—Why is this?

253.   "Another person can't have my pains."—Which are *my* pains? What counts as a criterion of identity here? Consider what makes it possible in the case of physical objects to speak of "two exactly the same," for example, to say "This chair is not the one you saw here yesterday, but is exactly the same as it".

In so far as it makes *sense* to say that my pain is the same as his, it is also possible for us both to have the same pain. (And it would also be imaginable for two people to feel pain in the same—not just the corresponding—place. That might be the case with Siamese twins, for instance.)

I have seen a person in a discussion on this subject strike himself on the breast and say: "But surely another person can't have THIS pain!"—The answer to this is that one does not define a criterion of identity by emphatic stressing of the word "this". Rather, what the emphasis does is to suggest the case in which we are conversant with such a criterion of identity, but have to be reminded of it.

254.   The substitution of "identical" for "the same" (for instance) is another typical expedient in philosophy. As if we were talking about shades of meaning and all that were in question were to find words to hit on the correct nuance. That is in question in philosophy only where we have to give a psychologically exact account of the temptation to use a particular kind of expression. What we 'are tempted to say' in such a case is, of course, not philosophy; but it is its raw material. Thus, for example, what a mathematician is inclined to say about the objectivity and reality of mathematical facts, is not a philosophy of mathematics, but something for philosophical *treatment*.

255.   The philosopher's treatment of a question is like the treatment of an illness.

256.   Now, what about the language which describes my inner experiences and which only I myself can understand? *How* do I use words to stand for my sensations?—As we ordinarily do? Then are my words for sensations tied up with my natural expressions of sensation? In that case my language is not a 'private' one. Someone else might understand it as well as I.—But suppose I didn't have any natural expression for the sensation, but only had the sensation? And now I simply *associate* names with sensations and use these names in descriptions.—

257.   "What would it be like if human beings showed no outward signs of pain (did not groan, grimace, etc.)? Then it would be impossible to teach a child the use of the word 'tooth-ache'."—Well, let's assume the child is a genius and itself invents a name for the sensation!—But then, of course, he couldn't make himself understood when he used the word.—So does he understand the name, without being able to explain its meaning to anyone?—But what does it mean to say that he has 'named his pain'?—How has he done this naming of pain?! And whatever he did, what was its purpose?—When one says "He gave a name to his sensation" one forgets that a great deal of stage-setting in the language is presupposed if the mere act of naming is to make sense. And when we speak of someone's having given a name to pain, what is presupposed is the existence of the grammar of the word "pain"; it shews the post where the new word is stationed.

258.   Let us imagine the following case. I want to keep a diary about the recurrence of a certain sensation. To this end I associate it with the sign "S" and write this sign in a calendar for every day on which I have the sensation.—I will remark first of all that a definition of the sign cannot be formulated.—But still I can give myself a kind of ostensive definition.—How? Can I point to the sensation? Not in the ordinary sense. But I speak, or write the sign down, and at the same time I concentrate my attention on the sensation—and so, as it were, point to it inwardly.—But what is this ceremony for? for that is all it seems to be! A definition surely serves to establish the meaning of a sign.—Well, that is done precisely by the concentrating of my attention; for in this way I impress on myself the connexion between the sign and the sensation.—But "I impress it on myself" can only mean: this process brings it about that I remember the connexion *right* in the future. But in the present case I have no criterion of correctness. One would like to say: whatever is going to seem right to me is right. And that only means that here we can't talk about 'right'.

259.   Are the rules of the private language *impressions* of rules?—The balance on which impressions are weighed is not the *impression* of a balance.

260.   "Well, I *believe* that this is the sensation S again."—Perhaps you *believe* that you believe it!

Then did the man who made the entry in the calendar make a note of *nothing whatever*?—Don't consider it a matter of course that a person is making a note of something when he makes a mark—say in a calendar. For a note has a function, and this "S" so far has none.

(One can talk to oneself.—If a person speaks when no one else is present, does that mean he is speaking to himself?)

261.   What reason have we for calling "S" the sign for a *sensation*? For "sensation" is a word of our common language, not of one intelligible to me alone. So the use of this word stands in need of a justification which everybody understands.—And it would not help either to say that it need not be a *sensation*; that when he writes "S", he has something—and that is all that can be said. "Has" and "something" also belong to our common language.—So in the end when one is doing philosophy one gets to the point where one would like just to emit an inarticulate sound.—But such a sound is an expression only as it occurs in a particular language-game, which should now be described.

262.   It might be said: if you have given yourself a private definition of a word, then you must inwardly *undertake* to use the word in such-and-such a way. And how do you undertake that? Is it to be assumed that you invent the technique of using the word; or that you found it ready-made?

263.   "But I can (inwardly) undertake to call THIS 'pain' in the future."—"But is it certain that you have undertaken it? Are you sure that it was enough for this purpose to concentrate your attention on your feeling?"—A queer question.—

264.   "Once you know *what* the word stands for, you understand it, you know its whole use."

265.   Let us imagine a table (something like a dictionary) that exists only in our imagination. A dictionary can be used to justify the translation of a word X by a word Y. But are we also to call it a justification if such a table is to be looked up only in the imagination?—"Well, yes; then it is a subjective justification."—But justification consists in appealing to something independent.—"But surely I can appeal from one memory to another. For example, I don't know if I have remembered the time of departure of a train right and to check it I call to mind how a page of the time-table looked. Isn't it the same here?"—No; for this process has got to produce a memory which is actually *correct*. If the mental image of the time-table could not itself be *tested* for correctness, how could it confirm the correctness of the first memory? (As if someone were to buy several copies of the morning paper to assure himself that what it said was true.)

Looking up a table in the imagination is no more looking up a table than the image of the result of an imagined experiment is the result of an experiment.

266.   I can look at the clock to see what time it is: but I can also look at the dial of a clock in order to *guess* what time it is; or for the same purpose move the hand of a clock till its position strikes me as right. So the look of a clock may serve to determine the time in more than one way. (Looking at the clock in imagination.)

267.   Suppose I wanted to justify the choice of dimensions for a bridge which I imagine to be building, by making loading tests on the material of the bridge in my imagination. This would, of course, be to imagine what is called justifying the choice of dimensions for a bridge. But should we also call it justifying an imagined choice of dimensions?

268.   Why can't my right hand give my left hand money?—My right hand can put it into my left hand. My right hand can write a deed of gift and my left hand a receipt.—But the further practical consequences would not be those of a gift. When the left hand has taken the money from the right, etc., we shall ask: "Well, and what of it?" And the same could be asked if a person had given himself a private definition of a word; I mean, if he has said the word to himself and at the same time has directed his attention to a sensation.

269.   Let us remember that there are certain criteria in a man's behaviour for the fact that he does not understand a word: that it means nothing to him, that he can do nothing with it. And criteria for his 'thinking he understands', attaching some meaning to the word, but not the right one. And, lastly, criteria for his understanding the word right. In the second case one might speak of a subjective understanding. And sounds which no one else understands but which I '*appear to understand*' might be called a "private language".

270.   Let us now imagine a use for the entry of the sign "S" in my diary. I discover that whenever I have a particular sensation a manometer shews that my blood-pressure rises. So I shall be able to say that my blood-pressure is rising without using any apparatus. This is a useful result. And now it seems quite indifferent whether I have recognized the sensation *right* or not. Let us suppose I regularly identify it wrong, it does not matter in the least. And that alone shews that the hypothesis that I make a mistake is mere show. (We as it were turned a knob which looked as if it could be used to turn on some part of the machine; but it was a mere ornament, not connected with the mechanism at all.)

And what is our reason for calling "S" the name of a sensation here? Perhaps the kind of way this sign is employed in this language-game.—And why a "particular sensation," that is, the same one every time? Well, aren't we supposing that we write "S" every time?

271.   "Imagine a person whose memory could not retain *what* the word 'pain' meant—so that he constantly called different things by that name—but nevertheless used the word in a way fitting in with the usual symptoms and presuppositions of pain"—in short he uses it as we all do. Here I should like to say: a wheel that can be turned though nothing else moves with it, is not part of the mechanism.

272. The essential thing about private experience is really not that each person possesses his own exemplar, but that nobody knows whether other people also have *this* or something else. The assumption would thus be possible—though unverifiable—that one section of mankind had one sensation of red and another section another.

273. What am I to say about the word "red"?—that it means something 'confronting us all' and that everyone should really have another word, besides this one, to mean his *own* sensation of red? Or is it like this: the word "red" means something known to everyone; and in addition, for each person, it means something known only to him? (Or perhaps rather: it *refers* to something known only to him.)

274. Of course, saying that the word "red" "refers to" instead of "means" something private does not help us in the least to grasp its function; but it is the more psychologically apt expression for a particular experience in doing philosophy. It is as if when I uttered the word I cast a sidelong glance at the private sensation, as it were in order to say to myself: I know all right what I mean by it.

275. Look at the blue of the sky and say to yourself "How blue the sky is!"—When you do it spontaneously—without philosophical intentions—the idea never crosses your mind that this impression of colour belongs only to *you*. And you have no hesitation in exclaiming that to someone else. And if you point at anything as you say the words you point at the sky. I am saying: you have not the feeling of pointing-into-yourself, which often accompanies 'naming the sensation' when one is thinking about 'private language'. Nor do you think that really you ought not to point to the colour with your hand, but with your attention. (Consider what it means "to point to something with the attention".)

276. But don't we at least *mean* something quite definite when we look at a colour and name our colour-impression? It is as if we detached the colour-*impression* from the object, like a membrane. (This ought to arouse our suspicions.)

277. But how is it even possible for us to be tempted to think that we use a word to *mean* at one time the colour known to everyone—and at another the 'visual impression' which *I* am getting *now*? How can there be so much as a temptation here?—I don't turn the same kind of attention on the colour in the two cases. When I mean the colour impression that (as I should like to say) belongs to me alone I immerse myself in the colour—rather like when I 'cannot get my fill of a colour'. Hence it is easier to produce this experience when one is looking at a bright colour, or at an impressive colour-scheme.

278. "I know how the colour green looks to *me*"—surely that makes sense!—Certainly: what use of the proposition are you thinking of?

279. Imagine someone saying: "But I know how tall I am!" and laying his hand on top of his head to prove it.

280. Someone paints a picture in order to shew how he imagines a theatre scene. And now I say: "This picture has a double function: it informs others, as pictures or words inform—but for the one who gives the information it is a representation (or piece of information?) of another kind: for him it is the picture of his image, as it can't be for anyone else. To him his private impression of the picture means what he has imagined, in a sense in which the picture cannot mean this to others."—And what right have I to speak in this second case of a representation or piece of information—if these words were rightly used in the *first* case?

281.   "But doesn't what you say come to this: that there is no pain, for example, without *pain-behaviour*?"—It comes to this: only of a living human being and what resembles (behaves like) a living human being can one say: it has sensations; it sees; is blind; hears; is deaf; is conscious or unconscious.

282.   "But in a fairy tale the pot too can see and hear!" (Certainly; but it *can* also talk.)

"But the fairy tale only invents what is not the case: it does not talk *nonsense*."— It is not as simple as that. Is it false or nonsensical to say that a pot talks? Have we a clear picture of the circumstances in which we should say of a pot that it talked? (Even a nonsense-poem is not nonsense in the same way as the babbling of a child.)

We do indeed say of an inanimate thing that it is in pain: when playing with dolls for example. But this use of the concept of pain is a secondary one. Imagine a case in which people ascribed pain *only* to inanimate things; pitied *only* dolls! (When children play at trains their game is connected with their knowledge of trains. It would nevertheless be possible for the children of a tribe unacquainted with trains to learn this game from others, and to play it without knowing that it was copied from anything. One might say that the game did not make the same *sense* to them as to us.)

283.   What gives us *so much as the idea* that living beings, things, can feel?

Is it that my education has led me to it by drawing my attention to feelings in myself, and now I transfer the idea to objects outside myself? That I recognize that there is something there (in me) which I can call "pain" without getting into conflict with the way other people use this word?—I do not transfer my idea to stones, plants, etc.

Couldn't I imagine having frightful pains and turning to stone while they lasted? Well, how do I know, if I shut my eyes, whether I have not turned into a stone? And if that has happened, in what sense will *the stone* have the pains? In what sense will they be ascribable to the stone? And why need the pain have a bearer at all here?!

And can one say of the stone that it has a soul and *that* is what has the pain? What has a soul or pain, to do with a stone?

Only of what behaves like a human being can one say that it *has* pains.

For one has to say it of a body, or, if you like of a soul which some body *has*. And how can a body *have* a soul?

284.   Look at a stone and imagine it having sensations.—One says to oneself: How could one so much as get the idea of ascribing a *sensation* to a *thing*? One might as well ascribe it to a number!—And now look at a wriggling fly and at once these difficulties vanish and pain seems able to get a foothold here, where before everything was, so to speak, too smooth for it.

And so, too, a corpse seems to us quite inaccessible to pain.—Our attitude to what is alive and to what is dead, is not the same. All our reactions are different.—If anyone says: "That cannot simply come from the fact that a living thing moves about in such-and-such a way and a dead one not", then I want to intimate to him that this is a case of the transition 'from quantity to quality'.

285.   Think of the recognition of *facial expressions*. Or of the description of facial expressions—which does not consist in giving the measurements of the face! Think, too, how one can imitate a man's face without seeing one's own in a mirror.

286.   But isn't it absurd to say of a *body* that it has pain?—And why does one feel an absurdity in that? In what sense is it true that my hand does not feel pain, but I in my hand?

What sort of issue is: Is it the *body* that feels pain?—How is it to be decided? What makes it plausible to say that it is *not* the body?—Well, something like this: if someone has a pain in his hand, then the hand does not say so (unless it writes it) and one does not comfort the hand, but the sufferer: one looks into his face.

287.   How am I filled with pity *for this man*? How does it come out what the object of my pity is? (Pity, one may say, is a form of conviction that someone else is in pain.)

288.   I turn to stone and my pain goes on.—Suppose I were in error and it was no longer *pain*?—But I can't be in error here; it means nothing to doubt whether I am in pain!—That means: if anyone said "I do not know if what I have got is a pain or something else", we should think something like, he does not know what the English word "pain" means; and we should explain it to him.—How? Perhaps by means of gestures, or by pricking him with a pin and saying: "See, that's what pain is!" This explanation, like any other, he might understand right, wrong, or not at all. And he will shew which he does by his use of the word, in this as in other cases.

If he now said, for example: "Oh, I know what 'pain' means; what I don't know is whether *this*, that I have now, is pain"—we should merely shake our heads and be forced to regard his words as a queer reaction which we have no idea what to do with. (It would be rather as if we heard someone say seriously: "I distinctly remember that some time before I was born I believed. ... ")

That expression of doubt has no place in the language-game; but if we cut out human behaviour, which is the expression of sensation, it looks as if I might *legitimately* begin to doubt afresh. My temptation to say that one might take a sensation for something other than what it is arises from this: if I assume the abrogation of the normal language-game with the expression of a sensation, I need a criterion of identity for the sensation; and then the possibility of error also exists.

289.   "When I say 'I am in pain' I am at any rate justified *before myself*."—What does that mean? Does it mean: "If someone else could know what I am calling 'pain', he would admit that I was using the word correctly"?

To use a word without a justification does not mean to use it without right.

290.   What I do is not, of course, to identify my sensation by criteria: but to repeat an expression. But this is not the *end* of the language-game: it is the beginning.

But isn't the beginning the sensation—which I describe?—Perhaps this word "describe" tricks us here. I say "I describe my state of mind" and "I describe my room". You need to call to mind the differences between the language-games.

291.   What we call "*descriptions*" are instruments for particular uses. Think of a machine-drawing, a cross-section, an elevation with measurements, which an engineer has before him. Thinking of a description as a word-picture of the facts has something misleading about it: one tends to think only of such pictures as hang on our walls: which seem simply to portray how a thing looks, what it is like. (These pictures are as it were idle.)

292. Don't always think that you read off what you say from the facts; that you portray these in words according to rules. For even so you would have to apply the rule in the particular case without guidance.

293.   If I say of myself that it is only from my own case that I know what the word "pain" means—must I not say the same of other people too? And how can I generalize the *one* case so irresponsibly?

Now someone tells me that *he* knows what pain is only from his own case!— Suppose everyone had a box with something in it: we call it a "beetle". No one can look into anyone else's box, and everyone says he knows what a beetle is only by looking at *his* beetle.—Here it would be quite possible for everyone to have something different in his box. One might even imagine such a thing constantly changing.—But suppose the word "beetle" had a use in these people's language?—If so it would not be used as the name of a thing. The thing in the box has no place in the language-game at all; not even as a *something*: for the box might even be empty.—No, one can 'divide through' by the thing in the box; it cancels out, whatever it is.

That is to say: if we construe the grammar of the expression of sensation on the model of 'object and designation' the object drops out of consideration as irrelevant.

294.   If you say he sees a private picture before him, which he is describing, you have still made an assumption about what he has before him. And that means that you can describe it or do describe it more closely. If you admit that you haven't any notion what kind of thing it might be that he has before him—then what leads you into saying, in spite of that, that he has something before him? Isn't it as if I were to say of someone: "He *has* something. But I don't know whether it is money, or debts, or an empty till."

295.   "I know ... only from my *own* case"—what kind of proposition is this meant to be at all? An experiential one? No.—A grammatical one?

Suppose everyone does say about himself that he knows what pain is only from his own pain.—Not that people really say that, or are even prepared to say it. But *if* everybody said it—it might be a kind of exclamation. And even if it gives no information, still it is a picture, and why should we not want to call up such a picture? Imagine an allegorical painting take the place of those words.

When we look into ourselves as we do philosophy, we often get to see just such a picture. A full-blown pictorial representation of our grammar. Not facts; but as it were illustrated turns of speech.

296.   "Yes, but there is *something* there all the same accompanying my cry of pain. And it is on account of that that I utter it. And this something is what is important—and frightful."—Only whom are we informing of this? And on what occasion?

297.   Of course, if water boils in a pot, steam comes out of the pot and also pictured steam comes out of the pictured pot. But what if one insisted on saying that there must also be something boiling in the picture of the pot?

298.   The very fact that we should so much like to say: "*This* is the important thing"—while we point privately to the sensation—is enough to shew how much we are inclined to say something which gives no information.

299.   Being unable—when we surrender ourselves to philosophical thought—to help saying such-and-such; being irresistibly inclined to say it—does not mean being forced into an *assumption*, or having an immediate perception or knowledge of a state of affairs.

300.   It is—we should like to say—not merely the picture of the behaviour that plays a part in the language-game with the words "he is in pain", but also the picture of the pain. Or, not merely the paradigm of the behaviour, but also that of the pain.—It is a misunderstanding to say "The picture of pain enters into the language-game with the word 'pain'." The image of pain is not a picture and *this* image is not replaceable in the language-game by anything that we should call a picture.—The image of pain certainly enters into the language game in a sense; only not as a picture.

301.   An image is not a picture, but a picture can correspond to it.

302.   If one has to imagine someone else's paid on the model of one's own, this is none too easy a thing to do: for I have to imagine pain which I *do not feel* on the model of the pain which I *do feel*. That is, what I have to do is not simply to make a transition in imagination from one place of pain to another. As, from pain in the hand to pain in the arm. For I am not to imagine that I feel pain in some region of his body. (Which would also be possible.)

Pain-behaviour can point to a painful place—but the subject of pain is the person who gives it expression.

303.   "I can only *believe* that someone else is in pain, but I *know* it if I am."— Yes: one can make the decision to say "I believe he is in pain" instead of "He is in pain". But that is all.—What looks like an explanation here, or like a statement about a mental process, is in truth an exchange of one expression for another which, while we are doing philosophy, seems the more appropriate one.

Just try—in a real case—to doubt someone else's fear or pain.

304.   "But you will surely admit that there is a difference between pain-behaviour accompanied by pain and pain-behaviour without any pain?"—Admit it? What greater difference could there be?—"And yet you again and again reach the conclusion that the sensation itself is a *nothing*."—Not at all. It is not a *something*, but not a *nothing* either! The conclusion was only that a nothing would serve just as well as a something about which nothing could be said. We have only rejected the grammar which tries to force itself on us here.

The paradox disappears only if we make a radical break with the idea that language always functions in one way, always serves the same purpose: to convey thoughts—which may be about houses, pains, good and evil, or anything else you please.

305.   "But you surely cannot deny that, for example, in remembering, an inner process takes place."—What gives the impression that we want to deny anything? When one says "Still, an inner process does take place here"—one wants to go on: "After all, you *see* it." And it is this inner process that one means by the word "remembering".—The impression that we wanted to deny something arises from our setting our faces against the picture of the 'inner process'. What we deny is that the picture of the inner process gives us the correct idea of the use of the word "to remember". We say that this picture with its ramifications stands in the way of out seeing the use of the word as it is.

306. Why should I deny that there is a mental process? But "There has just taken place in me the mental process of remembering … " means nothing more than: "I have just remembered … ". To deny the mental process would mean to deny the remembering; to deny that anyone ever remembers anything.

307. "Are you not really a behaviourist in disguise? Aren't you at bottom really saying that everything except human behaviour is a fiction?"—If I do speak of a fiction, then it is of a *grammatical* fiction.

308. How does the philosophical problem about mental processes and states and about behaviourism arise?—The first step is the one that altogether escapes notice. We talk of processes and states and leave their nature undecided. Sometime perhaps we shall know more about them—we think. But that is just what commits us to a particular way of looking at the matter. For we have a definite concept of what it means to learn to know a process better. (The decisive movement in the conjuring trick has been made, and it was the very one that we thought quite innocent.)—And now the analogy which was to make us understand our thoughts falls to pieces. So we have to deny the yet uncomprehended process in the yet unexplored medium. And now it looks as if we had denied mental processes. And naturally we don't want to deny them.

309. What is your aim in philosophy?—To shew the fly the way out of the fly-bottle.

310. I tell someone I am in pain. His attitude to me will then be that of belief; disbelief; suspicion; and so on.

Let us assume he says: "It's not so bad."—Doesn't that prove that he believes in something behind the outward expression of pain?—His attitude is a proof of his attitude. Imagine not merely the words "I am in pain" but also the answer "It's not so bad" replaced by instinctive noises and gestures.

311. "What difference could be greater?"—In the case of pain I believe that I can give myself a private exhibition of the difference. But I can give anyone an exhibition of the difference between a broken and an unbroken tooth.—But for the private exhibition you don't have to give yourself actual pain; it is enough to *imagine* it—for instance, you screw up your face a bit. And do you know that what you are giving yourself this exhibition of is pain and not, for example, a facial expression? And how do you know what you are to give yourself an exhibition of before you do it? This *private* exhibition is an illusion.

312. But again, *aren't* the cases of the tooth and the pain similar? For the visual sensation in the one corresponds to the sensation of pain in the other. I can exhibit the visual sensation to myself as little or as well as the sensation of pain.

Let us imagine the following: The surfaces of the things around us (stones, plants, etc.) have patches and regions which produce pain in our skin when we touch them. (Perhaps through the chemical composition of these surfaces. But we need not know that.) In this case we should speak of pain-patches on the leaf of a particular plant just as at present we speak of red patches. I am supposing that it is useful to us to notice these patches and their shapes; that we can infer important properties of the objects from them.

313.   I can exhibit pain, as I exhibit red, and as I exhibit straight and crooked and trees and stones.—*That* is what we *call* "exhibiting".

314.   It shews a fundamental misunderstanding, if I am inclined to study the headache I have now in order to get clear about the philosophical problem of sensation.

315.   Could someone understand the word "pain", who had *never* felt pain?—Is experience to teach me whether this is so or not?—And if we say "A man could not imagine pain without having sometime felt it"—how do we know? How can it be decided whether it is true?

CHAPTER 5

Ordinary Language Philosophy

Introduction to G. E. Moore

George Edward Moore was born near London in 1873 and died in Cambridge in 1958. He entered Trinity College, Cambridge in 1892, and was a Fellow there from 1898 to 1904. He began his undergraduate career in Classics but was persuaded by his friend Bertrand Russell to switch to Philosophy. He taught in Cambridge, first as a lecturer and then as Professor, until his retirement. He was professor of philosophy at Cambridge from 1925 until his retirement in 1939, after which he was a visiting professor in several American universities. He was editor of *Mind* from 1921 until 1947.

Moore is probably best known today for his first book, *Principia Ethica*, which launched twentieth-century meta-ethics with the provocative claim that all previous ethical theories had committed the "naturalistic fallacy" of trying to define the Good in naturalistic terms. The most noticeable feature of this book was its self-consciously linguistic orientation. Rather than start by inquiring into the nature of goodness, and the like, Moore investigates the term "good", and its relations (if any) to natural, non-normative concepts. Moore's thesis rested on the "open question argument": Take any account of good that is proposed, for example the Utilitarian identification of "good" with "the greatest happiness for the greatest number." We can still coherently ask whether this Utilitarian ideal is itself good. In fact, "Whatever definition be offered, it may always be asked, with significance, of the complex so defined, whether it is itself good" (p. 15). This is supposed to prove that it is not identical with goodness. From this, Moore derives the conclusion that goodness is a simple unanalyzable non-naturalistic property. However, Moore does not distinguish the question of whether the term "goodness" is *synonymous* with "the greatest happiness of the greatest number" from the issue of whether these two are *co-extensive*. Lack of synonymy does not prove lack of co-extensivity. For example, we would say that gold is the element with atomic number 79. Not only are the terms co-extensive, but they are necessarily coextensive. However, one can clearly entertain the thought "Does gold have the atomic number 79?" One could similarly claim that the identification of goodness with some naturalistic property could be empirically discoverable.

Moore is also famous for instigating the revolt from the neo-Hegelian Idealism then dominant at Cambridge under his teacher, J. M. E. McTaggart, and at Oxford, in the work of F. H. Bradley. Bertrand Russell explicitly credited Moore with his own break with this doctrine. In contrast to Russell's acknowledgment of Moore's lead, he himself was remarkably self-effacing. In his "Intellectual Autobiography" (in Schilpp), Moore famously remarks that "I do not think that the world or the sciences would ever have suggested to me any philosophical problems. What has suggested philosophical problems to me is things which other philosophers have said about the world or the sciences" (p. 14).

The third thing for which Moore is now known is as a defender of "common sense." To illustrate this, I will now turn to "Proof of an External World." Moore begins with a quote from Kant, to the effect that it is a scandal that philosophers have failed to overcome skeptical arguments regarding the existence of "things outside of us." Moore interprets this phrase as referring to things which can be "met with in space" and which are "external to our minds." That is, which are intersubjectively accessible, and the existence of which does not entail that anyone is actually experiencing them. Moore announces that he has such a proof: Holding up one hand, he utters "Here is one hand"; holding up the other hand, he adds "And here is another."

At this point, consternation is likely to break out in any audience even slightly acquainted with philosophy. Suppose that such a sentence had been uttered by a freshman in Philosophy 101. One would smile sympathetically at the student and introduce her to, for example, Descartes' challenge to prove that she is not now dreaming. The student would hopefully then appreciate the skeptical point that if she is dreaming, then no hands are being held up, and that if she does not know that she is not dreaming, then could not the entire physical world be one big illusion?

But the hand-holder, the utterer of our "proof," was no naive freshman. He was Professor of Philosophy at Cambridge University and had long been regarded as one of the greatest living philosophers. Hence the consternation, and the common suspicion that there must be more to Moore's remark than meets the eye. One philosopher to take this line was Norman Malcolm (1942). Given, says Malcolm, that Moore's claim to know that he has two hands merely begs the question against the skeptic, we need to interpret his strategy differently. Malcolm suggests that Moore is employing a Paradigm Case argument against the skeptic. Malcolm starts by saying that since no possible evidence could assuage the skeptic's doubt, skepticism is not an empirical thesis. He interprets Moore as making a semantic ascent and interpreting the skeptic not as primarily saying that we can never have knowledge about the external world, but that "The phrase 'know for certain' is not properly applied to material-thing statements" (p. 354). Moore is then said to refute the skeptic not by appeal to common-sense belief but by a similar linguistic maneuver, drawing on paradigm cases of the correct usage of these epistemic concepts. Such cases will involve objects nearby, of which we have an unobstructed view, in standard lighting conditions—that is, cases like "Here is one hand." In other words, Malcolm's Moore is saying that the grammar (in Wittgenstein's sense of the term) of "knows" and "with certainty" are constituted by such examples, and that therefore we know a priori that the denial of the existence of material objects, or of our knowledge of them, cannot be coherently asserted.

In his "Reply to Malcolm," Moore emphatically rejects this interpretation of his intentions. He is explicit that he is not talking about the usage of words, but is doing exactly what it looks like he is doing—refuting the skeptic by giving clear examples of material objects. Moore seems to regard his "proof" as similar to standard procedures of proof found in everyday life; that is, that of looking for and finding evidence. For example, if someone denies that a page contains three misprints, you study the text closely, find the offending items, and then point them out to the doubter: "Look, here's one misprint, ... here's another, ... and here's a third." The difference between these two examples, for Moore, is only one of degree of generality of the concepts involved. He does not see this as a difference in kind, of the sort that would prevent a similar strategy working against the skeptic in either case.

Moore makes three demands of a successful proof, all of which he believes to be satisfied in this case. Firstly, his premises are different to his conclusion; secondly, he knows his premises to be true; and thirdly, his argument is valid. His opponents have focused mainly on denying the second condition. As we have seen, Moore is accused of merely begging the question against the skeptic. That is, surely he can only use the example of his hands to prove the existence of material objects, and hence of the external world, if he has already shown skeptical arguments to be mistaken or groundless.

Thomas Baldwin (1990) argues that Moore is employing an "argument from differential certainty," of a kind that he used against Hume in *Some Main Problems of Philosophy*. Consider how this strategy would work against Descartes' dreaming doubt. The skeptic would argue the following: *If I don't know that I'm not dreaming, then I don't know that I am seeing a hand; I don't know that I'm not dreaming; therefore I don't know that I am seeing a hand.* Moore would grant the first premise of this *modus ponens* and apply a *modus tollens* to it: *Since I do know that I am seeing a hand, it follows that I know I'm not dreaming.* Now it might appear that we have a stalemate, yet Moore denies this. Adjudicating between the two contrary positions is, he says, a matter of deciding which argument's premises are the more certain. Given that both arguments share the first premise, the dispute comes down to whether a report like "here is a hand" is on stronger ground than the skeptical doubt. Moore maintains that it is. Any concrete particular case will always be more certain than some abstract general thesis, because a generalization can only be made from an induction from particular cases. Therefore, one ought not to accept the skeptic's argument.

It is important to note that Moore is not just saying that he, Moore, is more certain of his particular sense-based report—but that *so is the skeptic*. He is merely reminding the skeptic of that fact. This theme is developed in the earlier paper "A Defense of Common Sense," where he responds to philosophers who deny the existence of material bodies, and so forth, that they really do believe that these things exist, as any study of their speech and behavior will easily reveal. Moore was insistent that the difference between him and skeptics or idealists was not that he, but not they, accepted common-sense beliefs. Rather, the difference was that they, but not he, held other beliefs (philosophical theories) incompatible with common sense.

If this interpretation of Moore is correct, it does not require Moore to claim absolute certainty for common-sense beliefs about the external world, but merely that they are more certain than some premises on which philosophical theses to the contrary are based. Let us grant for the moment that this is what Moore is trying to do. Does it succeed? I have two doubts. Firstly, it seems false that the skeptical position is gathered by an induction from individual cases. Rather, it comes from one consideration which applies to any, or all, cases within a domain. For example, skepticism emerges from empiricism not by an accumulation of data of the form

1. If I directly experience sense-data corresponding to an idea of my hat, but experience my hat only indirectly, then how do I know that anything exists beyond my sense-impression and idea of the hat;

2. as above, substitute "coat" for "hat";

3. and the like, ad infinitum.

Rather, they take one factor: If you are directly acquainted only with sense-impressions and ideas, how are you justified in believing in anything beyond this? Each specific example, as above, is then derived from this consideration. Moore got it the wrong way round.

Second, if by "certainty," Moore is referring to a mere *feeling* of certainty, he needs some argument to show why we ought to rely on it. He would surely need some argument to show why the mere presence of a feeling can give grounds for knowledge. Descartes appreciated that the feeling itself cannot bear that weight and enlisted a nondeceiving God as backup. This is a move that the common-sensical Moore is unwilling to make.

So there remains serious doubt as to whether Moore has satisfactorily dealt with the skeptic. Barry Stroud (1984) offers another diagnosis of Moore's strategy, by distinguishing "internal" and "external" reactions to epistemic inquiries. An internal response takes one's accepted stock of beliefs for granted and gives an affirmative response to our inquiry if it follows from, or generally accords with, this set of background assumptions. So, from this perspective, Moore has proved that here are two hands, because the belief in mind-independent objects is as deeply entrenched in our belief system as a belief can be, and hands are standard examples of such material objects. By contrast, the "external" standpoint involves standing back from our belief-system, calling it all into question, such that we cannot rely on it to infer the presence of the hands easily. For Stroud, while the skeptic is clearly operating from an "external" viewpoint, Moore is sticking solely to an internal stance. Whether he is thereby failing to see the crux of the skeptical challenge or is making the consciously radical move of questioning the legitimacy of the external strategy, is the issue that has to be decided if we are to determine the success, or the philosophical importance of Moore's "proof." One person's denial of philosophy can be another's transformation of it.

In assessing Stroud's interpretation, we need to distinguish two questions: (1) Is this what Moore is trying to do? (2) Even if it isn't, is such a strategy legitimate? On the first question, evidence is sparse—certainly nothing in Moore's work makes explicit reference to any distinction like Stroud's. As to the second, one might question the accuracy of Stroud's depiction of the skeptic regarding the external viewpoint. One might argue that a standard skeptical move is to remain within one's belief-system, in fact taking some beliefs we hold true and deriving the skeptical conclusion from within.

During the last couple of years of his life, Ludwig Wittgenstein was the guest of his former student, Norman Malcolm, and the two enjoyed many debates over the significance of Moore's proof. Wittgenstein's writings on this subject were among his very last, and were posthumously published as *On Certainty*. Wittgenstein's thesis can be seen as a development of his remarks in the *Philosophical Investigations* on the grammar of sensation words (see sections 244-254). Wittgenstein accuses Moore of misusing expressions like "I know that. ... " in his famous examples from "Proof of an External World" and "A Defense of Common Sense." Such cases, like "here is one hand" or "I know that my body has existed for some time" are unlike cases such as "I know that there's a six-pack in the fridge" or "I know that I live in Portland, Oregon," in that I can legitimately claim to *know* only the latter cases. This is an unusual twist on Moore's examples. Moore offered them as cases where I could unquestionably be said to know something. On the contrary, Wittgenstein says that the grammar of "knows" (i.e., the conditions of its correct application) dictates that one can only be said to know something when doubt is conceivable. In the same way that I could not be mistaken about whether or not I was in pain, and thus can't be said to know it, nor can I be said to know that I am holding up one hand—how could I possibly get this wrong? (See my Introduction to Wittgenstein's *Philosophical Investigations* for more details.)

Moore's statements, including his "proof" belong to what Wittgenstein calls a "world picture"—a set of statements forming a basic framework from within which our claims of knowledge, doubt, justification, and so forth, take place. Components of a world picture differ from a classical foundation (e.g., empiricists' sense-datum reports, or Descartes' "Cogito") in that they are not self-justifying—because the concept of justification cannot be meaningfully applied to them: "I did not get my picture of the world by satisfying myself of its correctness; nor do I have it because I am satisfied of its correctness. No, it is the inherited background against which I distinguish between true and false" (#94). So it cannot be either questioned or justified—it is not verified as being in accord with reality, for it constitutes the reality against which all checking takes place.

No statement is intrinsically or eternally part of a world-picture—so its status is relative to a particular "form of life," that is, a linguistic community. What is part of a world picture in one society may be a mere empirical fact or falsehood in another. This is amusingly illustrated by both Moore and Wittgenstein giving the example of no one having been to the moon. For Moore, this is an epitome of certain knowledge; for Wittgenstein, part of a world picture; for us, history.

So for Wittgenstein, "I know that *p*" makes sense only if one can be possibly mistaken about *p*. If someone actually denied any "Moorean" example, you would not use reason (e.g., confronting the person with evidence, etc.) to change his or her mind. The person would be either mad and in need of medication, or operating from within another world picture, in which case you would literally be talking different languages, so no agreement or disagreement could occur.

Wittgenstein concedes that while a sentence might generally function within a community as part of the world picture, and it would thus be inappropriate to be said to be known, still in some exceptional cases such an assertion may be true and justified. He would allow cases such as where someone has a hand severed in an accident and then has it microsurgically reattached. One might then demonstrate in amazement, "I have two hands!"

However, one might argue that this concession is enough to exempt Moore from Wittgenstein's attack. Recall the context of Moore's papers. Both are responses to a community, or form of life, in which these statements had all been doubted. That is, either they had been explicitly questioned, or many members held philosophical views which entailed that they were false. It is against this background that Moore affirms their truth.

BIBLIOGRAPHY

Works by Moore

Philosophical Papers (London: Allen & Unwin, 1959). This contains both "A Proof of the External World" and "A Defense of Common Sense."
Philosophical Studies (London: Routledge 1922).
Principia Ethica (Cambridge: Cambridge University Press, 1903).
Some Main Problems of Philosophy (London: Allen & Unwin, 1953). This consists of his Cambridge lectures from around 1912.

Further Reading

Thomas Baldwin, *G. E. Moore* (London: Routledge 1990). A good survey, drawing upon many unpublished documents.
P. A. Schilpp, *The Philosophy of G. E. Moore*, Library of Living Philosophers, Vol. IV (La Salle, Ill.: Open Court, 1942). This contains numerous papers, including Malcolm's "Moore and Ordinary Language," plus Moore's autobiography and his replies to the papers.
Barry Stroud, *The Significance of Philosophical Skepticism* (Oxford: Clarendon Press, 1984) See Chapter 3.
Ludwig Wittgenstein, *On Certainty* (Oxford: Basil Blackwell, 1969).

Proof of an External World

G. E. Moore

In the preface to the second edition of Kant's *Critique of Pure Reason* some words occur, which, in Professor Kemp Smith's translation, are rendered as follows:

> It still remains a scandal to philosophy ... that the existence of things outside of us ... must be accepted merely on *faith*, and that, if anyone thinks good to doubt their existence, we are unable to counter his doubts by any satisfactory proof.[1]

It seems clear from these words that Kant thought it a matter of some importance to give a proof of 'the existence of things outside of us' or perhaps rather (for it seems to me possible that the force of the German words is better rendered in this way) of 'the existence of *the* things outside of us'; for had he not thought it important that a proof should be given, he would scarcely have called it a 'scandal' that no proof had been given. And it seems clear also that he thought that the giving of such a proof was a task which fell properly within the province of philosophy; for, if it did not, the fact that no proof had been given could not possibly be a scandal to *philosophy*.

Now, even if Kant was mistaken in both of these two opinions, there seems to me to be no doubt whatever that it is a matter of some importance and also a matter which falls properly within the province of philosophy, to discuss the question what sort of proof, if any, can be given of 'the existence of things outside of us.' And to discuss this question was my object when I began to write the present lecture. But I may say at once that, as you will find, I have only, at most, succeeded in saying a very small part of what ought to be said about it.

The words 'it ... remains a scandal to philosophy ... that we are unable ... ' would, taken strictly, imply that, at the moment at which he wrote them, Kant himself was unable to produce a satisfactory proof of the point in question. But I think it is unquestionable that Kant himself did not think that he personally was at the time unable to produce such a proof. On the contrary, in the immediately preceding sentence, he has declared that he has, in the second edition of his *Critique*, to which he is now writing the Preface, given a 'rigorous proof' of this very thing; and has added that he believes this proof of his to be 'the only possible proof.' It is true that in this preceding sentence he does not describe the proof which he has given as a proof of 'the objective reality of outer intuition.' But the context leaves no doubt that he is using these two phrases, 'the objective reality of outer intuition' and 'the existence of things (*or* 'the things') outside of us,' in such a way that whatever is a proof of the first is also necessarily a proof of the second. We must, therefore, suppose that when he speaks as if *we* are unable to give a satisfactory proof, he does not mean to say that

From G.E. Moore, *Philosophical Papers*, Allen & Unwin, 1959, Reprinted by permission of Macmillan Publishing Company.

he himself, as well as others, is *at the moment* unable; but rather that, until he discovered the proof which he has given, both he himself and everybody else *were* unable. Of course, if he is right in thinking that he has given a satisfactory proof, the state of things which he describes came to an end as soon as his proof was published. As soon as that happened, any one who read it was able to give a satisfactory proof by simply repeating that which Kant had given, and the 'scandal' to philosophy had been removed once for all.

If, therefore, it were certain that the proof of the point in question given by Kant in the second edition, is a satisfactory proof, it would be certain that at least one satisfactory proof can be given; and all that would remain of the question which I said I proposed to discuss, would be, firstly, the question as to what *sort* of a proof this of Kant's is, and secondly the question whether (contrary to Kant's own opinion) there may not perhaps be other proofs, of the same or of a different sort, which are also satisfactory. But I think it is by no means certain that Kant's proof is satisfactory. I think it is by no means certain that he did succeed in removing once for all the state of affairs which he considered to be a scandal to philosophy. And I think, therefore, that the question whether it is possible to give *any* satisfactory proof of the point in question still deserves discussion.

But what is the point in question? I think it must be owned that the expression 'things outside of us' is rather an odd expression, and an expression the meaning of which is certainly not perfectly clear. It would have sounded less odd if, instead of 'things outside of us' I had said 'external things,' and perhaps also the meaning of this expression would have seemed to be clearer; and I think we make the meaning of 'external things' clearer still, if we explain that this phrase has been regularly used by philosophers as short for 'things external to *our minds*.' The fact is that there has been a long philosophical tradition, in accordance with which the three expressions 'external things,' 'things external to *us*,' and 'things external to *our minds*' have been used as equivalent to one another and have, each of them, been used as if they needed no explanation. The origin of this usage I do not know. It occurs already in Descartes; and since he uses the expressions as if they needed no explanation, they had presumably been used with the same meaning before. Of the three, it seems to me that the expression 'external to *our minds*' is the clearest, since it at least makes clear that what is meant is not 'external to *our bodies*'; whereas both the other expressions might be taken to mean this: and indeed there has been a good deal of confusion, even among philosophers, as to the relation of the two conceptions 'external things' and 'things external to *our bodies*'. But even the expression 'things external to our minds' seems to me to be far from perfectly clear; and if I am to make really clear what I mean by 'proof of the existence of things outside of us', I cannot do it by merely saying that by 'outside of us' I mean 'external to our minds'.

There is a passage (*K.d.r.V.*, A 373) in which Kant himself says that the expression 'outside of us' 'carries with it an unavoidable ambiguity'. He says that 'sometimes it means something which exists *as a thing in itself* distinct from us, and sometimes something which merely belongs to external *appearance*'; he calls things which are 'outside of us' in the first of these two senses 'objects which might be called external in the transcendental sense', and things which are so in the second '*empirically external* objects'; and he says finally that, in order to remove all uncertainty as to the latter conception, he will distinguish empirically external objects from objects which might be called 'external' in the transcendental sense,'by calling them outright things which are *to be met with in space*'.

I think that this last phrase of Kant's, 'things which are to be met with in space', does indicate fairly clearly what sort of things it is with regard to which I wish to inquire what sort of proof, if any, can be given that there are any things of that sort. My body, the bodies of other men, the bodies of animals, plants of all sorts; stones, mountains, the sun, the moon, stars and planets, houses and other buildings, manu-factured articles of all sorts—chairs, tables, pieces of paper, etc., are all of them 'things which are to be met with in space'. In short of all things of the sort that philosophers have been used to call 'physical objects', 'material things', or 'bodies' obviously come under this head. But the phrase 'things that are to be met with in space' can be natu-rally understood as applying also in cases where the names 'physical object', 'materi-al thing', or 'body' can hardly be applied. For instance, shadows are sometimes to be met with in space, although they could hardly be properly called 'physical objects', 'material things', or 'bodies'; and although in one usage of the term 'thing', it would not be proper to call a shadow a 'thing', yet the phrase 'things which are to be met with in space' can be naturally understood as synonymous with 'whatever can be met with in space', and this is an expression which can quite properly be understood to include shadows. I wish the phrase 'things which are to be met with in space' to be understood in this wide sense; so that if a proof can be found that there ever have been as many as two different shadows it will follow at once that there have been at least two 'things which were to be met with in space', and this proof will be as good a proof of the point in question, as would be a proof that there have been at least two 'physi-cal objects' of no matter what sort.

The phrase 'things which are to be met with in space' can, therefore, be natu-rally understood as having a very wide meaning—a meaning even wider than that of 'physical object' or 'body', wide as is the meaning of these latter expressions. But wide as is its meaning, it is not, in one respect, so wide as that of another phrase which Kant uses as if it were equivalent to this one; and a comparison between the two will, I think, serve to make still clearer what sort of things it is with regard to which I wish to ask what proof, if any, can be given that there are such things.

The other phrase which Kant uses as if it were equivalent to 'things which are to be met with in space' is used by him in the sentence immediately preceding that previously quoted in which he declares that the expression 'things outside of us' 'car-ries with it an unavoidable ambiguity' (A 373). In this preceding sentence he says that an 'empirical object' 'is called *external*, if it is presented (*vorgestellt*) *in space*'. He treats, therefore, the phrase 'presented in space' as if it were equivalent to 'to be met with in space'. But it is easy to find examples of 'things,' of which it can hardly be denied that they are 'presented in space,' but of which it could, quite naturally, be emphatically denied that they are 'to be met with in space.' Consider, for instance, the following description of one set of circumstances under which what some psy-chologists have called a 'negative after-image' and others a 'negative after-sensation' can be obtained. 'If, after looking steadfastly at a white patch on a black ground, the eye be turned to a white ground a grey patch is seen for some little time.' (Foster's *Text-book of Physiology*, iv. iii. 3, p. 1266; quoted in Stout's *Manual of Psychology*,

3rd edition, p. 280.) Upon reading these words recently, I took the trouble to cut out of a piece of white paper a four-pointed star, to place it on a black ground, to 'look steadfastly' at it, and then to turn my eyes to a white sheet of paper: and I did find that I saw a grey patch for some little time—I not only saw a grey patch, but I saw it *on* the white ground, and also this grey patch was of roughly the same shape as the white four-pointed star at which, I had 'looked steadfastly' just before—it also was a four-pointed star. I repeated this simple experiment successfully several times. Now each of those grey four-pointed stars, one of which I saw in each experiment, was what is called an 'after-image' or 'after-sensation'; and can anybody deny that each of these after-images can be quite properly said to have been presented in space? I saw each of them on a real white background, and, if so, each of them was 'presented' on a real white background. But though they were 'presented in space' everybody, I think, would feel that it was gravely misleading to say that they were 'to be met with in space.' The white star at which I 'looked steadfastly,' the black ground on which I saw it, and the white ground on which I saw the after-images, were, of course, 'to be met with in space': they were, in fact, 'physical objects' or surfaces of physical objects. But one important difference between them, on the one hand, and the grey after-images, on the other, can be quite naturally expressed by saying that the latter were *not* 'to be met with in space.' And one reason why this is so is, I think, plain. To say that so and so was at a given time 'to be met with in space' naturally suggests that there are conditions such that *any one* who fulfilled them might, conceivably, have 'perceived' the 'thing' in question—might have seen it, if it was a visible object, have felt it, if it was a tangible one, have heard it, if it was a sound, have smelt it, if it was a smell. When I say that the white four-pointed paper star, at which I looked steadfastly, was a 'physical object' and was 'to be met with in space,' I am implying that *any one*, who had been in the room at the time, and who had normal eyesight and a normal sense of touch, might have seen and felt it. But, in the case of those grey after-images which I saw, it is not conceivable that any one besides myself should have seen any one of them. It is, of course, quite conceivable that other people, if they had been in the room with me at the time, and had carried out the same experiment which I carried out, would have seen grey after-images *very like* one of those which I saw: there is no absurdity in supposing even that they might have seen after-images *exactly* like one of those which I saw. But there is an absurdity in supposing that any one of the after-images which I saw could also have been seen by any one else: in supposing that two different people can ever see the *very same* after-image. One reason, then, why we should say that none of those grey after-images which I saw was 'to be met with in space,' although each of them was certainly 'presented in space' to me, is simply that none of them could conceivably have been seen by any one else. It is natural so to understand the phrase 'to be met with in space', that is to say of anything which a man perceived that it was to be met with in space is to say that it might have been perceived by *others* as well as by the man in question.

Negative after-images of the kind described are, therefore, one example of 'things' which, though they must be allowed to be 'presented in space', are nevertheless *not* 'to be met with in space', and are *not* 'external to our minds' in the sense with which we shall be concerned. And two other important examples may be given.

The first is this. It is well known that people sometimes see things double, an occurrence which has also been described by psychologists by saying that they have a 'double image', or two 'images', of some object at which they are looking. In such cases it would certainly be quite natural to say that each of the two 'images' is 'presented in space': they are seen, one in one place, and the other in another, in just the same sense in which each of those grey after-images which I saw was seen at a particular place on the white background at which I was looking. But it would be utterly unnatural to say that, when I have a double image, each of the two images is 'to be met with in space'. On the contrary it is quite certain that *both* of them are not 'to be met with in space'. If both were, it would follow that somebody else might see the *very same* two images which I see; and, though there is no absurdity in supposing that another person might see a pair of images exactly similar to a pair which I see, there is an absurdity in supposing that any one else might see the *same identical pair*. In every case, then, in which any one sees anything double, we have an example of at least one 'thing' which, though 'presented in space' is certainly not 'to be met with in space'.

And the second important example is this. Bodily pains can, in general, be quite properly said to be 'presented in space'. When I have a toothache, I feel it *in* a particular region of my jaw or *in* a particular tooth; when I make a cut on my finger smart by putting iodine on it, I feel the pain in a particular place in my finger; and a man whose leg has been amputated may feel a pain *in* a place where his foot might have been if he had not lost it. It is certainly perfectly natural to understand the phrase 'presented in space' in such a way that if, in the sense illustrated, a pain is felt *in* a particular place, that pain is 'presented in space'. And yet of pains it would be quite unnatural to say that they are 'to be met with in space', for the same reason as in the case of after-images or double images. It is quite conceivable that another person should feel a pain exactly like one which I feel, but there is an absurdity in supposing that he could feel *numerically the same* pain which I feel. And pains are in fact a typical example of the sort of 'things' of which philosophers say that they are *not* 'external' to our minds, but 'within' them. Of any pain which *I* feel they would say that it is necessarily *not* external to my mind but *in* it.

And finally it is, I think, worth while to mention one other class of 'things', which are certainly not 'external' objects and certainly not 'to be met with in space', in the sense with which I am concerned, but which yet some philosophers would be inclined to say are 'presented in space', though they are not 'presented in space' in quite the same sense in which pains, double images, and negative after-images of the sort I described are so. If you look at an electric light and then close your eyes, it sometimes happens that you see, for some little time, against the dark background which you usually see when your eyes are shut, a bright path similar in shape to the light at which you have just been looking. Such a bright patch, if you see one, is another example of what some psychologists have called 'after-images' and others 'after-sensations'; but, unlike the negative after-images of which I spoke before, it is seen when your eyes are shut. Of such an after-image, seen with closed eyes, some philosophers might be inclined to say that this image too was 'presented in space', although it is certainly not 'to be met with in space'. They would be inclined to say that it is 'presented in space', because it certainly is presented as at some little distance from the person who is seeing it: and how can a thing be presented as at some little distance from me, without being 'presented in space'? Yet there is an important difference between such after-images, seen with closed eyes, and after-images of the sort I previously described—a difference which might lead other philosophers to deny that these after-images, seen with closed eyes, are 'presented in space' at all. It is a difference which can be expressed by saying that when your eyes are shut, you are not seeing any part of *physical* space at all—of the space which is referred to when we talk of 'things which are to be met with in *space*'. An after-image seen with closed eyes certainly is presented in *a* space, but it may be questioned whether it is proper to say that it is presented in *space*.

It is clear, then, I think, that by no means everything which can naturally be said to be 'presented in space' can also be naturally said to be 'a thing which is to be met with in space'. Some of the 'things,' which are presented in space, are very emphatically *not* to be met with in space: or, to use another phrase, which may be used to convey the same notion, they are emphatically *not* 'physical realities' at all. The conception 'presented in space' is therefore, in one respect, much wider than the conception 'to be met with in space': many 'things' fall under the first conception which do not fall under the second—many after-images, one at least of the pair of 'images' seen whenever any one sees double, and most bodily pains, are 'presented in space', though none of them are to be met with in space. From the fact that a 'thing' is presented in space, it by no means follows that it is to be met with in space. But just as the first conception is, in one respect, wider than the second, so, in another, the second is wider than the first. For there are many 'things' to be met with in space, of which it is not true that they are presented in space. From the fact that a 'thing' is to be met with in space, it by no means follows that it is presented in space. I have taken 'to be met with in space' to imply, as I think it naturally may, that a 'thing' *might* be perceived; but from the fact that a thing *might* be perceived, it does not follow that it *is* perceived; and if it is not actually perceived, then it will not be presented in space. It is characteristic of the sorts of 'things', including shadows, which I have described as 'to be met with in space', that there is no absurdity in supposing with regard to any one of them which *is*, at a given time, perceived, both (1) that it might have existed at another time, without being perceived; (2) that it might have existed at another time, without being perceived at that other time; and (3) that during the whole period of its existence, it need not have been perceived at any time at all. There is, therefore, no absurdity in supposing that many things, which were at one time to be met with in space, never were 'presented' at any time at all, and that many things which *are* to be met with in space now, are not now 'presented' and also never were and never will be. To use a Kantian phrase, the conception of 'things which are to be met with in space' embraces not only objects of actual experience, but also objects of *possible* experience; and from the fact that a thing is or was an object of *possible* experience, it by no means follows that it either was or is or will be 'presented' at all.

I hope that what I have now said may have served to make clear enough what sorts of 'things' I was originally referring to as 'things outside us' or 'things external to our minds'. I said that I thought that Kant's phrase 'things that are to be met with in space' indicated fairly clearly the sorts of 'things' in question; and I have tried to make the range clearer still, by pointing out that this phrase only serves the purpose, if (*a*) you understand it in a sense, in which many 'things', e.g. after-images, double images, bodily pains, which might be said to be 'presented in space', are nevertheless *not* to be reckoned as 'things that are to be met with in space', and (*b*) you realize clearly that there is no contradiction in supposing that there have been and are 'to be met with in space' things which never have been, are not now, and never will be perceived, nor in supposing that among those of them which have at some time been perceived many existed at times at which they were not being perceived. I think it will now be clear to every one that, since I do not reckon as 'external things' after-images, double images, and bodily pains, I also should not reckon as 'external things', any of the 'images' which we often 'see with the mind's eye' when we are awake, nor any of those which we see when we are asleep and dreaming; and also that I was so using the expression 'external' that from the fact that a man was at a given time having a visual hallucination, it will follow that he was seeing at that time something which was *not* 'external' to his mind, and from the fact that he was at a given time having an auditory hallucination, it will follow that he was at the time hearing a sound which was *not* 'external' to his mind. But I certainly have not made my use of these phrases, 'external to our minds' and 'to be met with in space', so clear that in the case of every kind of 'thing' which might be suggested, you would be able to tell at once whether I should or should not reckon it as 'external to our minds' and 'to be met with in space'. For instance, I have said nothing which makes it quite clear whether a reflection which I see in a looking-glass is or is not to be regarded as 'a thing that is to be met with in space' and 'external to our minds', nor have I said anything which makes it quite clear whether the sky is or is not to be so regarded. In the case of the sky, everyone, I think, would feel that it was quite inappropriate to talk of it as 'a thing that is to be met with in space'; and most people, I think, would feel a strong reluctance to affirm, without qualification, that reflections which people see in looking-glasses are 'to be met with in space'. And yet neither the sky nor reflections seen in mirrors are in the same position as bodily pains or after-images in the respect which I have emphasized as a reason for saying of these latter that they are *not* to be met with in space—namely that there is an absurdity in supposing that *the very same* pain which I feel could be felt by some one else or that *the very same* after-image which I see could be seen by some one else. In the case of reflections in mirrors we should quite naturally, in certain circumstances, use language which implies that another person may see the same reflection which we see. We might quite naturally say to a friend: 'Do you see that reddish reflection in the water there? I can't make out what it's a reflection of', just as we might say, pointing to a distant hill-side: 'Do you see that white speck on the hill over there? I can't make out what it is.' And in the case of the sky, it is quite obviously *not* absurd to say that other people see it as well as I.

It must, therefore, be admitted that I have not made my use of the phrase 'things to be met with in space', nor therefore that of 'external to our minds', which the former was used to explain, so clear that in the case of every kind of 'thing' which may be mentioned, there will be no doubt whatever as to whether things of that kind are or are not 'to be met with in space' or 'external to our minds'. But this lack of a clear-cut definition of the expression 'things that are to be met with in space', does not, so far as I can see, matter for my present purpose. For my present purpose it is, I think, sufficient if I make clear, in the case of many kinds of things, that I am so using the phrase 'things that are to be met with in space', that, in the case of each of these kinds, from the proposition that there are things of that kind it *follows* that there are things to be met with in space. And I have, in fact, given a list (though by no means an exhaustive one) of kinds of things which are related to my use of the expression 'things that are to be met with in space' in this way. I mentioned among others the bodies of men and of animals, plants, stars, houses, chairs, and shadows; and I want now to emphasize that I am so using 'things to be met with in space' that, in the case of each of these kinds of 'things', from the proposition that there are 'things' of that kind it *follows* that there are things to be met with in space: e.g. from the proposition that there are plants or that plants exist it *follows* that there are things to be met with in space, from the proposition that shadows exist, it *follows* that there are things to be met with in space, and so on, in the case of all kinds of 'things' which I mentioned in my first list. That this should be clear is sufficient for my purpose, because, if it is clear, then it will also be clear that, as I implied before, if you have proved that two plants exist, or that a plant and a dog exist, or that a dog and a shadow exist, &c., &c., you will *ipso facto* have proved that there are things to be met with in space: you will not require *also* to give a separate proof that from the proposition that there are plants it *does* follow that there are things to be met with in space.

Now with regard to the expression 'things that are to be met with in space' I think it will readily be believed that I may be using it in a sense such that no proof is required that from 'plants exist' there follows 'there are things to be met with in space'; but with regard to the phrase 'things external to our minds' I think the case is different. People may be inclined to say: 'I can see quite clearly that from the proposition "At least two dogs exist at the present moment" there *follows* the proposition "At least two things are to be met with in space at the present moment", so that if you can prove that there are two dogs in existence at the present moment you will *ipso facto* have proved that two things at least are to be met with in space at the present moment. I can see that you do not also require a separate proof that from "Two dogs exist" "Two things are to be met with in space' *does* follow; it is quite obvious that there couldn't be a dog which wasn't to be met with in space. But it is not by any means so clear to me that if you can prove that there are two dogs or two shadows, you will *ipso facto* have proved that there are two things *external to our minds*. Isn't it possible that a dog, though it certainly must be "to be met with in space", might *not* be an external object—an object external to our minds? Isn't a separate proof required that anything that is to be met with in space must be external to our minds? Of course, if you are using "external" as a mere synonym for "to be met with in space", no proof will be required that dogs are external objects: in that case, if you can prove that two dogs exist, you will *ipso facto* have proved that there are some external things. But I find it difficult to believe that you, or anybody else, do really use "external" as a mere synonym for "to be met with in space"; and if you don't, isn't some proof required that whatever is to be met with in space must be external to our minds?'

Now Kant, as we saw, asserts that the phrases 'outside of us' or 'external' are in fact used in two very different senses; and with regard to one of these two senses, that which he calls the 'transcendental' sense, and which he tries to explain by saying that it is a sense in which 'external' means 'existing *as a thing in itself* distinct from us', it is notorious that he himself held that things which are to be met with in space are *not* 'external' in that sense. There is, therefore, according to him, *a* sense of 'external', a sense in which the word has been commonly used by philosophers—such that, if 'external' be used in that sense, then from the proposition 'Two dogs exist' it will *not* follow that there are some external things. What this supposed sense is I do not think that Kant himself ever succeeded in explaining clearly; nor do I know of any reason for supposing that philosophers ever have used 'external' in a sense, such that in *that* sense things that are to be met with in space are *not* external. But how about the other sense, in which, according to Kant, the word 'external' has been commonly used—that which he calls 'empirically external'? How is this conception related to the conception 'to be met with in space'? It may be noticed that in the passages which I quoted (A 373), Kant himself does not tell us at all clearly what he takes to be the proper answer to this question. He only makes the rather odd statement that, in order to remove all uncertainty as to the conception 'empirically external', he will distinguish objects to which it applies from those which might be called 'external' in the transcendental sense, by 'calling them outright things which are *to be met with in space*'. These odd words certainly suggest, as one possible interpretation of them, that in Kant's opinion the conception 'empirically external' is *identical* with the conception 'to be met with in space'—that he does think that 'external', when used in this second sense, is a mere synonym for 'to be met with in space'. But, if this is his meaning, I do find it very difficult to believe that he is right. Have philosophers, in fact, ever used 'external' as a mere synonym for 'to be met with in space'? Does he himself do so?

I do not think they have, nor that he does himself; and, in order to explain how they have used it, and how the two conceptions 'external to our minds' and 'to be met with in space' are related to one another, I think it is important expressly to call attention to a fact which hitherto I have only referred to incidentally: namely the fact that those who talk of certain things as 'external to' our minds, do, in general, as we should naturally expect, talk of other 'things', with which they wish to contrast the first, as 'in' our minds. It has, of course, been often pointed out that when 'in' is thus used, followed by 'my mind', 'your mind', 'his mind', &c., 'in' is being used metaphorically. And there are some metaphorical uses of 'in', followed by such expressions, which occur in common speech, and which we all understand quite well. For instance, we all understand such expressions as 'I had you in mind, when I made that arrangement' or 'I had you in mind, when I said that there are some people who can't bear to touch a spider'. In these cases 'I was thinking of you' can be used to mean the same as 'I had you in mind'. But it is quite certain that this particular metaphorical use of 'in' is not the one in which philosophers are using it when they contrast what is 'in' my mind with what is 'external' to it. On the contrary, in their use of 'external', you will be external to my mind even at a moment when I have you in mind. If we want to discover what this peculiar metaphorical use of '*in* my mind' is, which is such that nothing, which is, in the sense we are now concerned with, 'external' to my mind, can ever be 'in' it, we need, I think, to consider instances of the sort of 'things' which they would say are 'in' my mind in this special sense. I have already mentioned three such instances, which are, I think, sufficient for my present purpose: any bodily pain which I feel, any after-image which I see with my eyes shut, and any image which I 'see' when I am asleep and dreaming, are typical examples of the sort of 'thing' of which philosophers have spoken as '*in* my mind'. And there is no doubt, I think, that when they have spoken of such things as my body, a sheet of paper, a star—in short 'physical objects' generally—as 'external', they have meant to emphasize some important difference which they feel to exist between such things as these and such 'things' as a pain, an after-image seen with closed eyes, and a dream-image. But *what* difference? What difference do they feel to exist between a bodily pain which I feel or an after-image which I see with closed eyes, on the one hand, and my body itself, on the other—what difference which leads them to say that whereas the bodily pain and the after-image are 'in' my mind, my body itself is *not* 'in' my mind—not even when I am feeling it and seeing it or thinking of it? I have already said that one difference which there is between the two, is that my body is to be met with in space, whereas the bodily pain and the after-image are not. But I think it would be quite wrong to say that this is *the* difference which has led philosophers to speak of the two latter as 'in' my mind, and of my body as *not* 'in' my mind.

The question what the difference is which has led them to speak in this way, is not, I think, at all an easy question to answer; but I am going to try to give, in brief outline, what I *think* is a right answer.

It should, I think, be noted, first of all, that the use of the word 'mind', which is being adopted when it is said that any bodily pains which I feel are 'in my mind', is one which is not quite in accordance with any usage common in ordinary speech, although we are very familiar with it in philosophy. Nobody, I think, would say that bodily pains which I feel are 'in my mind', unless he was also prepared to say that it is *with* my mind that I feel bodily pains; and to say this latter is, I think, not quite in accordance with common non-philosophic usage. It is natural enough to say that it is with my mind that I remember, and think, and imagine, and feel *mental* pains—e.g. disappointment, but not, I think, quite so natural to say that it is with my mind that I feel *bodily* pains, e.g. a severe headache; and perhaps even less natural to say that it is with my mind that I see and hear and smell and taste. There is, however, a well-established usage according to which seeing, hearing, smelling, tasting, and having a bodily pain are just as much *mental* occurrences or processes as are remembering, or thinking, or imagining. This usage was, I think, adopted by philosophers, because they saw a real resemblance between such statements as 'I saw a cat', 'I heard a clap of thunder', 'I smelt a strong smell of onions', 'My finger smarted horribly', on the one hand, and such statements as 'I remembered having seen him', 'I was thinking out a plan of action', 'I pictured the scene to myself', 'I felt bitterly disappointed', on the other—a resemblance which puts all these statements in one class together, as contrasted with other statements in which 'I' or 'my' is used, such as, e.g., 'I was less than four feet high', 'I was lying on my back', 'My hair was very long'. What is the resemblance in question? It is a resemblance which might be expressed by saying that all the first eight statements are the sort of statements which furnish data for psychology, while the three latter are not. It is also a resemblance which may be expressed, in a way now common among philosophers, by saying that in the case of all the first eight statements, if we make the statement more specific by adding a date, we get a statement such that, if it is true, then it *follows* that I was 'having an experience' at the date in question, whereas this does not hold for the three last statements. For instance, if it is true that I saw a cat between 12 noon and 5 minutes past, to-day, it *follows* that I was 'having some experience' between 12 noon and 5 minutes past, to-day; whereas from the proposition that I was less than four feet high in December 1877, it does not *follow* that I had any experiences in December 1877. But this philosophic use of 'having an experience' is one which itself needs explanation, since it is not identical with any use of the expression that is established in common speech. An explanation, however, which is, I think, adequate for the purpose, can be given by saying that a philosopher, who was following this usage, would say that I was at a given time 'having an experience' if and only if either (1) I was conscious at the time or (2) I was dreaming at the time or (3) something else was true of me at the time, which resembled what is true of me when I am conscious and when I am dreaming, in a certain very obvious respect in which what is true of me when I am dreaming resembles what is true of me when I am conscious, and in which what would be true of me, if at any time, for instance, I had a vision, would resemble both. This explanation is, of course, in some degree vague; but I think it is clear enough for our purpose. It amounts to saying that, in this philosophic usage of 'having an experience', it would be said of me that I was, at a given time, having *no* experience, if I was at the time neither conscious nor dreaming nor having a vision nor *anything else of the sort*; and, of course, this is vague in so far as it has not been specified what else would be *of the sort*: this is left to be gathered from the instances given. But I think this is sufficient: often at night when I am asleep, I am neither conscious nor dreaming nor having a vision nor *anything else of the sort*—that is to say, I am having no experiences. If this explanation of this philosophic usage of 'having an experience' is clear enough, then I think that what has been meant by saying that any pain which I feel or any after-image which I see with my eyes closed is '*in* my mind', can be explained by saying that what is meant is neither more nor less than that there would be a contradiction in supposing *that very same pain* or *that very same after-image* to have existed at a time at which I was having no experience; or, in other words, that from the proposition, with regard to any time, that *that* pain or *that* after-image existed at that time, it *follows* that I was having some experience at the time in question. And if so, then we can say that the felt difference between bodily pains which I feel and after-images which I see, on the one hand, and my body on the other, which has led philosophers to say that any such pain or after-image is '*in* my mind', whereas my body *never* is but is always 'outside of' or 'external to' my mind, is just this, that whereas there is a contradiction in supposing a pain which I feel or an after-image which I see to exist at a time when I am having no experience, there is no contradiction in supposing my body to exist at a time when I am having no experience; and we can even say, I think, that just this and nothing more is what they have meant by these puzzling and misleading phrases 'in my mind' and 'external to my mind'.

But now, if to say of anything, e.g. my body, that it is external to *my* mind, merely means that from a proposition to the effect that it existed at a specified time, there in no case follows the further proposition that *I* was having an experience at the time in question, then to say of anything that it is external to *our* minds, will mean similarly that from a proposition to the effect that it existed at a specified time, it in no case follows that any of *us* were having experiences at the time in question. And if by *our* minds be meant, as is, I think, usually meant, the minds of human beings living on the earth, then it will follow that any pains which animals may feel, any after-images they may see, any experiences they may have, though not external to *their* minds, yet are external to *ours*. And this at once makes plain how different is the conception 'external to our minds' from the conception 'to be met with in space'; for, of course, pains which animals feel or after-images which they see are no more to be met with in space than are pains which *we* feel or after-images which *we* see. From the proposition that there are external objects—objects that are not in any of *our* minds, it does *not* follow that there are things to be met with in space; and hence 'external to our minds' is not a mere synonym for 'to be met with in space'; that is to say, 'external to our minds' and 'to be met with in space' are two different conceptions. And the true relation between these conceptions seems to me to be this. We have already seen that there are ever so many kinds of 'things', such that, in the case of each of these kinds, from the proposition that there is at least one thing of that kind there *follows* the proposition that there is at least one thing to be met with in space: e.g. this follows from 'There is at least one star', from 'There is at least one human body', from 'There is at least one shadow', &c. And I think we can say that of every kind of thing of which this is true, it is also true that from the proposition that there is at least one 'thing' of that kind there *follows* the proposition that there is at least one thing external to our minds: e.g. from 'There is at least one star' there follows not only 'There is at least one thing to be met with in space' but also 'There is at least one external thing', and similarly in all other cases. My reason for saying this is as follows. Consider any kind of thing, such that anything of that kind, if there is anything of it, must be 'to be met with in space': e.g. consider the kind 'soap-bubble'. If I say of anything which I am perceiving, 'That is a soap-bubble', I am, it seems to me, certainly implying that there would be no contradiction in asserting that it existed before I perceived it and that it will continue to exist, even if I cease to perceive it. This seems to me to be part of what is meant by saying that it is a real soap-bubble, as distinguished, for instance, from an hallucination of a soap-bubble. Of course, it by no means follows, that if it really is a soap-bubble, it did in fact exist before I perceived it or will continue to exist after I cease to perceive it: soap-bubbles are an example of a kind of 'physical object' and 'thing to be met with in space', in the case of which it is notorious that particular specimens of the kind often do exist only so long as they are perceived by a particular person. But a thing which I perceive would not be a soap-bubble unless its existence at any given time were *logically independent* of my perception of it at that time; unless that is to say, from the proposition, with regard to a particular time, that it existed at that time, it *never* follows that I perceived it at that time. But, if it is true that it would not be a soap-bubble, unless it *could* have existed at any given time without being perceived by me at that time, it is certainly also true that it would not be a soap-bubble, unless it *could* have existed at any given time, without its being true that I was having any experience of any kind at the time in question: it would not be a soap-bubble, unless, whatever time you take, from the proposition that it existed at that time it does *not* follow that I was having any experience at that time. That is to say, from the proposition with regard to anything which I am perceiving that it is a soap-bubble, there *follows* the proposition that it is external to *my* mind. But if, when I say that anything which I perceive is a soap-bubble, I am implying that it is external to *my* mind, I am, I think, certainly also implying that it is also external to all other minds:

I am implying that it is not a thing of a sort such that things of that sort *can* only exist at a time when somebody is having an experience. I think, therefore, that from any proposition of the form 'There's a soap-bubble!' there does really *follow* the proposition 'There's an external object!' 'There's an object external to *all* our minds!' And, if this is true of the kind 'soap-bubble', it is certainly also true of any other kind (including the kind 'unicorn') which is such that, if there are any things of that kind, it follows that there are *some* things to be met with in space.

I think, therefore, that in the case of all kinds of 'things', which are such that if there is a pair of things, both of which are of one of these kinds, or a pair of things one of which is of one of them and one of them of another, then it will follow at once that there are some things to be met with in space, it is true also that if I can prove that there are a pair of things, one of which is of one of these kinds and another of another, or a pair both of which are of one of them, then I shall have proved *ipso facto* that there are at least two 'things outside of us'. That is to say, if I can prove that there exist now both a sheet of paper and a human hand, I shall have proved that there are now 'things outside of us'; if I can prove that there exist now both a shoe and sock, I shall have proved that there are now 'things outside of us'; &c.; and similarly I shall have proved it, if I can prove that there exist now two sheets of paper, or two human hands, or two shoes, or two socks, &c. Obviously, then, there are thousands of different things such that, if, at any time, I can prove any one of them, I shall have proved the existence of things outside of us. Cannot I prove any of these things?

It seems to me that, so far from its being true, as Kant declares to be his opinion, that there is only one possible proof of the existence of things outside of us, namely the one which he has given, I can now give a large number of different proofs, each of which is a perfectly rigorous proof; and that at many other times I have been in a position to give many others. I can prove now, for instance, that two human hands exist. How? By holding up my two hands, and saying, as I make a certain gesture with the right hand, 'Here is one hand', and adding, as I make a certain gesture with the left, 'and here is another'. And if, by doing this, I have proved *ipso facto* the existence of external things, you will all see that I can also do it now in numbers of other ways: there is no need to multiply examples.

But did I prove just now that two human hands were then in existence? I do want to insist that I did; that the proof which I gave was a perfectly rigorous one; and that it is perhaps impossible to give a better or more rigorous proof of anything whatever. Of course, it would not have been a proof unless three conditions were satisfied; namely (1) unless the premiss which I adduced as proof of the conclusion was different from the conclusion I adduced it to prove; (2) unless the premiss which I adduced was something which I *knew* to be the case, and not merely something which I believed but which was by no means certain, or something which, though in fact true, I did not know to be so; and (3) unless the conclusion did really follow from the premiss. But all these three conditions were in fact satisfied by my proof. (1) The premiss which I adduced in proof was quite certainly different from the conclusion, for the conclusion was merely 'Two human hands exist at this moment'; but the premiss was something far more specific than this—something which I expressed by showing you my hands, making certain gestures, and saying the words 'Here is one hand, and here is another'. It is quite obvious that the two were different, because it is quite obvious that the conclusion might have been true, even if the premiss had been false. In asserting the premiss I was asserting much more than I was asserting in asserting the conclusion. (2) I certainly did at the moment *know* that which I expressed by the combination of certain gestures with saying the words 'There is one hand and here is another'. I *knew* that there was one hand in the place indicated by combining a certain gesture with my first utterance of 'here' and that there was another in the different place indicated by combining a certain gesture with my second utterance of 'here'. How absurd it would be to suggest that I did not know it, but only believed it, and that perhaps it was not the case! You might as well suggest that I do not know that I am now standing up and talking—that perhaps after all I'm not, and that it's not quite certain that I am! And finally (3) it is quite certain that the conclusion did follow from the premiss. This is as certain, as it is that if there is one hand here and another here *now*, then it follows that there are two hands in existence *now*.

My proof, then, of the existence of things outside of us did satisfy three of the conditions necessary for a rigorous proof. Are there any other conditions necessary for a rigorous proof, such that perhaps it did not satisfy one of them? Perhaps there may be; I do not know; but I do want to emphasize that, so far as I can see, we all of us do constantly take proofs of this sort as absolutely conclusive proofs of certain conclusions—as finally settling certain questions, as to which we were previously in doubt. Suppose, for instance, it were a question whether there were as many as three misprints on a certain page in a certain book. A says there are, B is inclined to doubt it. How could A prove that he is right? Surely he *could* prove it by taking the book, turning to the page, and pointing to three separate places on it, saying 'There's one misprint here, another here, and another here': surely that is a method by which it *might* be proved! Of course, A would not have proved, by doing this, that there were at least three misprints on the page in question, unless it was certain that there was a misprint in each of the places to which he pointed. But to say that he *might* prove it in this way, is to say that it *might* be certain that there was. And if such a thing as that could ever be certain, then assuredly it was certain just now that there was one hand in one of the two places I indicated and another in the other.

I did, then, just now, give a proof that there were *then* external objects; and obviously, if I did, I could *then* have given many other proofs of the same sort that there were external objects *then*, and could now give many proofs of the same sort that there are external objects *now*.

But if what I am asked to do is to prove that external objects have existed *in the past*, then I can give many different proofs of this also, but proofs which are in important respects of a different *sort* from those just given. And I want to emphasize that, when Kant says it is a scandal not to be able to give a proof of the existence of external objects, a proof of their existence in the past would certainly *help* to remove the scandal of which he is speaking. He says that, if it occurs to any one to question their existence, we ought to be able to confront him with a satisfactory proof. But by a person who questions their existence, he certainly means not merely a person who questions whether any exist at the moment of speaking, but a person who questions whether any have *ever* existed; and a proof that some have existed in the past would certainly therefore be relevant to *part* of what such a person is questioning. How then can I prove that there have been external objects in the past? Here is one proof. I can say: 'I held up two hands above this desk not very long ago; therefore two hands exist-ed not very long ago; therefore at least two external objects have existed at some time in the past, Q.E.D.' This is a perfectly good proof, provided I *know* what is asserted in the premiss. But I *do* know that I held up two hands above this desk not very long ago. As a matter of fact, in this case you all know it too. There's no doubt whatever that I did. Therefore I have given a perfectly conclusive proof that external objects have existed in the past; and you will all see at once that, if this is a conclusive proof, I could have given many others of the same sort, and could now give many others. But it is also quite obvious that this sort of proof differs in important respects from the sort of proof I gave just now that there were two hands existing *then*.

I have, then, given two conclusive proofs of the existence of external objects. The first was a proof that two human hands existed at the time when I gave the proof; the second was a proof that two human hands had existed at a time previous to that at which I gave the proof. These proofs were of a different sort in important respects. And I pointed out that I could have given, then, many other conclusive proofs of both sorts. It is also obvious that I could give many others of both sorts now. So that, if these are the sort of proof that is wanted, nothing is easier than to prove the existence of external objects.

But now I am perfectly well aware that, in spite of all that I have said, many philosophers will still feel that I have not given any satisfactory proof of the point in question. And I want briefly, in conclusion, to say something as to why this dissatis-faction with my proofs should be felt.

One reason why, is, I think, this. Some people understand 'proof of an exter-nal world' as including a proof of things which I haven't attempted to prove and haven't proved. It is not quite easy to say *what* it is that they want proved—*what* it is that is such that unless they got a proof of it, they would not say that they had a proof of the existence of external things; but I can make an approach to explaining what they want by saying that if I had proved the propositions which I used as *premisses* in my two proofs, then they would perhaps admit that I had proved the existence of exter-nal things, but, in the absence of such a proof (which, of course, I have neither given, nor attempted to give), they will say that I have not given what they mean by a proof of the existence of external things. In other words they want a proof of what I assert *now* when I hold up my hands and say 'Here's one hand and here's another'; and, in the other case, they want a proof of what I assert *now* when I say 'I did hold up two hands above this desk just now'. Of course what they really want is not merely a proof of these two propositions, but something like a general statement as to how *any* propo-sitions of this sort may be proved. This, of course, I haven't given; and I do not believe it can be given: if this is what is meant by proof of the existence of external things, I do not believe that any proof of the existence of external things is possible. Of course, in some cases what might be called a proof of propositions which seem like these can be got. If one of you suspected that one of my hands was artificial he might be said to get a proof of my proposition 'Here's one hand, and here's another', by coming up and examining the suspected hand close up, perhaps touching and pressing it, and so establishing that it really was a human hand. But I do not believe that any proof is possible in nearly all cases. How am I to prove now that 'Here's one hand, and here's another'? I do not believe I can do it. In order to do it, I should need to prove for one thing, as Descartes pointed out, that I am not now dreaming. But how can I prove that I am not? I have, no doubt, conclusive reasons for asserting that I am not now dreaming; I have conclusive evidence that I am awake: but that is a very different thing from being able to prove it. I could not tell you what all my evidence is; and I should require to do this at least, in order to give you a proof.

But another reason, why some people would feel dissatisfied with my proofs is, I think, not merely that they want a proof of something which I haven't proved, but that they think that, if I cannot give such extra proofs, then the proofs that I have given are not conclusive proofs at all. And this, I think, is a definite mistake. They would say: 'If you cannot prove your premiss that here is one hand and here is another, then you do not know it. But you yourself have admitted that, if you did not know it, then your proof was not conclusive. Therefore your proof was not, as you say it was, a conclusive proof.' This view that, if I cannot prove such things as these, I do not know them, is, I think, the view that Kant was expressing in the sentence which I quoted at the beginning of this lecture, when he implies that so long as we have no proof of the existence of external things, their existence must be accepted merely on *faith*. He means to say, I think, that if I cannot prove that there is a hand here, I must accept it merely as a matter of faith—I cannot know it. Such a view, though it has been very common among philosophers, can, I think, be shown to be wrong—though shown only by the use of premisses which are not known to be true, unless we do know of the existence of external things. I can know things, which I cannot prove; and among things which I certainly did know, even if (as I think) I could not prove them, were the premisses of my two proofs. I should say, therefore, that those, if any, who are dissatisfied with these proofs merely on the ground that I did not know their premisses, have no good reason for their dissatisfaction.

NOTE

1. B xxxix, note: Kemp Smith, p. 34. The German words are 'so bleibt es immer ein Skandal der Philosophie ..., das Dasein der Dinge ausser uns ... bloss auf *Glauben* annehmen zu müssen, und wenn es jemand einfällt es zu bezweifeln, ihm keinen genugtuenden Beweis entgegenstellen zu können'.

Introduction to Gilbert Ryle

Gilbert Ryle was born in Brighton, England, in 1900, and went to Oxford as a Classics scholar. He achieved remarkable academic success, gaining Firsts not only in both parts of Literae Humaniores (Classical Honour Moderations and Greats), consisting of Latin and Greek, Ancient History, plus Philosophy; but also in the then newly established PPE (Politics, Philosophy, and Economics), or "Modern Greats," as it was then called. He was immediately appointed lecturer in Philosophy at Christ Church, Oxford, in 1924. He remained at Oxford all his working life, holding the Waynflete Chair in Metaphysical Philosophy from 1945 until retiring in 1968. He was editor of *Mind* for over twenty years, succeeding G. E. Moore in 1947.

It was in these postwar years that Ryle exercised an influence on British philosophy that remains to this day. This was achieved not merely by his publications or his teaching but also by his establishment of the postgraduate B.Phil. degree at Oxford. The postwar expansion in higher education left a shortage of suitably trained teachers. The B.Phil., consisting of several exams plus a thesis, was intended to give a detailed grounding in several areas of the subject, giving people the background needed to teach. Up until the war, most British philosophers had no degree beyond the undergraduate level, a First in Greats being considered sufficient proof of one's abilities. The B.Phil. was an immediate and lasting success, and established Oxford as the primary center for philosophy in Britain, such that to this day, the majority of teaching positions there are held by Oxford graduates. Whether this domination has been good for British philosophy is a moot point.

Ryle always had extremely wide-ranging philosophical interests and regularly went beyond the rather rigid and narrow Oxford curriculum of the day. Early in his teaching career, he achieved notoriety by teaching a course titled "Logical Objectivism: Bolzano, Brentano, Husserl and Meinong." He also wrote a review of *Being and Time* that showed that he did not see Heidegger as the comical figure the Positivists portrayed him as.

Ryle's earliest publications were primarily in philosophical logic, although he would never have thought of himself as a logician, per se. He never displayed any aptitude for, nor interest in, advanced formal techniques but, rather, applied informal methods to reveal the true logical form of sentences. Ryle's technique ties in with his view of the nature of philosophy itself. The first expression of his view was in "Systematically Misleading Expressions" (1932) but is shown at its most refined in his inaugural lecture, "Philosophical Arguments" (1945).

Ryle was in large agreement with the Positivist claim that philosophy is distinguished not by any specific subject matter, nor by the investigation of "philosophical facts," but by a particular practice. He agreed that philosophical statements were not synthetic claims about the world. However, neither are philosophical propositions analytic, constructed out of synonymous expressions. Rather, they are second-order statements: elucidatory analyses of statements, revealing their true logical form. Very often a philosophical statement will comprise an explicit comparison between apparent and real logical form. The philosophical puzzles caused by this surface form are thereby dissolved.

In seeing philosophy as a purely a priori, conceptual activity, Ryle agrees with the Positivists and Wittgenstein that philosophy is fundamentally different to the sciences. More than this, he was disarmingly honest about his lack of knowledge in the sciences, in a way that would now seem shockingly naive. Thus, when interviewed about the a priori methodology of his masterpiece, *The Concept of Mind*, Ryle denied that his admitted ignorance of psychology or neuroscience had hindered him in writing about the mind. Thus, while in agreement with Wittgenstein that philosophy doesn't *discover* any facts but merely rearranges and explicates those already known, Ryle seems to think that all the facts we really need to know to undertake philosophical analysis are known to the common man.

As I mentioned, Ryle uses logic to indicate when surface grammar is misleading. He does this by taking a statement as it is ordinarily conceived and investigating its logical implications and presuppositions, showing that it will lead to undesirable consequences, such as paradox or contradiction. Each proposition has certain "logical powers": That is, it enters into a certain network of logical relations with other propositions. Propositions with very similar logical powers have the same logical form. A corollary claim can be made about the logical powers of concepts, since a concept, for Ryle, is an abstraction from a set of propositions. Thus, the logical power of a concept is the set of propositions it belongs to.

At this point, we should mention one of Ryle's most famous expressions, now common philosophical parlance, namely 'category mistake.' To make a category mistake is to miscategorize a concept. As the Positivists were well aware, the taxonomy of ordinary grammar was not sufficient to place all natural language expressions in their appropriate type. Very different expressions, with very different logical properties, could be placed in the same grammatical category. "Concepts and propositions carry with them no signal to indicate the logical types to which they belong" (p. 200). This has to be revealed by logical analysis.

Ryle's primary method for exposing a category mistake is to employ *reductio ad absurdum*. For example, take these two statements: "Bob weighs 160 pounds," and "The average man weighs 150 pounds." On the surface, these look to be structurally identical. This might make us think that the grammatical subject terms, "Bob" and "The average man" are of the same "type" or "category"—having the same logical powers—and hence able to function in analogous ways within similar sets of sentences. Ryle shows the difference between them by taking the apparent similarity at face value, and exposing the implications of such a practice. For example, consider "Bob owes me $5." The sentence obtained by substituting subject terms, "The average man owes me $5," is peculiar to say the least. Another test that "The average man" isn't a genuine referring expression is the Russellian move of re-expressing the proposition, eliminating mention of the expression, while retaining the sense of the original sentence.

Once this "negative" stage has been accomplished, and the roots of the error have been identified, the positive task becomes that of identifying the correct logical form of the statement, and the logical "powers" of the concepts involved. This procedure became known as "mapping the logical geography of the concepts." However, this cannot be done directly, but again by a process of elimination, via exposure of absurdity. Once this has been achieved for any given concept, the task then becomes to show how it relates to other concepts.

It could be said that *reductio* has a role in Ryle's philosophy that is analogous to that of the critical experiment to scientific hypotheses, according to Popper—namely that of rooting out impostors. That which resists absurdity is cautiously retained. However, the prospect of future absurdity can never be discounted, since the logical powers of any given proposition are unlimited. That is, it has logical relations to an indefinite number of other propositions, and nobody can attend to all of them. Most of us are generally concerned with that small section of logical power relating to every-day use.

Ryle's most famous work, *The Concept of Mind*, was published in 1949. It is a detailed application of his techniques to the philosophy of mind, and to the category mistakes at the heart of Cartesian Dualism—a theory so fundamentally mistaken that it "continues to distort the continental geography of the subject" (p. 8). In this mas-terpiece, this "sustained piece of analytical hatchet-work" (Autobiographical Sketch, p. 12), Ryle maps the logical geography of a variety of mental concepts, such as will, emotion, intelligence, imagination, and self-knowledge. However, the core of the book is in two major claims. Firstly, that most mental acts are cases of "knowing how" rather than "knowing that." That is, they should be considered as practical abilities rather than as items of propositional knowledge. The second major thesis of the book concerns the category mistake of seeing mental states as internal occurrent states, tem-porally prior to and logically distinct from action, and which cause and regulate action. On the contrary, Ryle takes mental states to be dispositions of persons; that is, ten-dencies to respond in certain ways in certain contexts. Thus, in ascribing a mental state you commit yourself to a generalization of the form S $\rightarrow$ R (where "S" is any environmental stimulus, and "R" a behavioral response, or disposition to so act) such that we can predict that R will follow S.

It is a matter of some controversy as to whether Ryle intended this as merely a conceptual analysis of "disposition," or also as a substantive account of their nature and function in human behavior. If the latter (as seems more plausible—after all, the theory he was attacking, Cartesian Dualism, was not primarily a theory about words), then it is open to serious criticism. In particular, it cannot explain action. Any hypo-thetical generalization S $\rightarrow$ R can't explain why R happened; that is, why did S cause *R* rather than *T*? Why did *S*, rather than *Z*, cause R? This requires reference to some occurrent, internal properties. It is the same with the supposedly analogous analysis of "solubility": "X is soluble" $=_{df}$ If X is placed in unsaturated water, X will dissolve. But suppose one asks *why* X dissolved? It is not enough to say "Because it's the sort of thing which dissolves when placed in unsaturated water, and it was so placed." We want to know why X dissolves (e.g., what makes X dissolve, and Y not). To answer this, one must resort to the micro-structural properties of the physical-chemical type to which X belongs. In a similar way, it may be argued, explanations of behavior must, at the bottom, refer to physical states, the real bearers of the causal powers that Descartes wrongly ascribed to the immaterial mind.

Some of the central themes of *The Concept of Mind* are prefigured in "Know-ing How and Knowing That." Ryle opposes the idea that intelligence consists primar-ily in "acts of thinking, namely, the operations of considering propositions"—that is, in particular private mental acts consisting in the contemplation of information, whether they be particular facts or principles/rules. He rejects the idea that all the real intellectual work is done internally, prior to the action, and where the action is a mere effect of the "thinking."

In what follows, I will abbreviate "knowing how" and "knowing that" as "KH" and "KT," respectively. Ryle sees intelligence as a form of KH, not KT. Secondly, he argues that KH is prior to KT—that is, all cases of KT are dependent on KH. Taking intelligence as KT is one instance of the category mistake (or "type mistake" as he calls it here) at the heart of Cartesianism. To be intelligent is just to act intelligently: "There is no gap between intelligence and practice corresponding to the familiar gap between theory and practice." Ryle isn't just saying that successful action is the best evidence of intelligence—it *is* intelligence.

He attempts to refute the claim that intelligence is KT by arguing that such an assumption leads to a regress. Suppose that acting intelligently in circumstances C required knowledge that p (e.g., knowledge of certain facts or rules). But facts and rules can be considered well or badly (i.e., intelligently or not). Rules have to be implemented—and what is to determine this? Suppose the "intellectualist" hypothesizes another, second-order set of facts or rules, to regulate the use of the first ones. But these are just more facts or rules which, as before, can be applied either well or badly. How is this to be done? By some other, third-order facts? By adhering to the view that intelligence is KT, we are off on a regress of propositional knowledge.

A second regress is also generated: The "intellectualist" view is committed to a sharp distinction between theory and practice. Recall that all the real work is done internally, prior to action; the action is a contingent corollary. But for action to result, some other faculty must be postulated, to act as the interface between them. This faculty, thinks Ryle, must be such as to cooperate with two such radically different faculties responsible for theory and practice. So it must contain, in itself, such a division. But what, then, would connect its two parts to each other? Would some other interface be required?

For Ryle, the problem is overcome by taking intelligence to consist in a practice of successful performance. The difference in "doing X intelligently" and "doing X stupidly" does not consist in the existence of separate components (e.g., X + I as opposed to X + S). It is to display a disposition to perform X well regularly, in a variety of different contexts, to which one exhibits sensitivity. To support his thesis, Ryle argues that one can know all the facts, yet still do X badly. For example, you can have memorized hundreds of chess games, yet still play poorly, because you didn't apply this knowledge correctly (e.g., you didn't see that *this* point in *this* game was a case where this strategy was to apply). The intellectualist might reply, "This just shows you didn't really know the information—if you had and had attended to it, you would have done the right thing." Ryle is on stronger ground, since no accumulation of information is self-applying. This relates to the notorious "frame problem" in Artificial Intelligence. It isn't enough to *have* information—one must *see its relevance*. Recall, it is not enough to have more information about information (e.g., "this is a situation of type S—move M applies here.") This information itself needs to be recognized and applied.

Suppose that the intellectualist came back and said, "I admit that we're not consciously, explicitly engaging in rule-following, nor in consideration of facts. But we are doing so unconsciously—we're just not aware of it." Ryle replies that facts are facts, rules are rules, whether implicitly or explicitly considered. The same problems apply to such implicit information.

Ryle acknowledges that KT is useful in regulating practice when one is *learning* how to do something. But even then, he insists that KT is merely an aid to the training, not the training itself, which consists in practice. When one has mastered the skill, it is not because one has somehow internalized a rule, which one then unconsciously applies in new cases. Such a rule is a mere emergent distillation of tried and tested successful practices. While intelligent behavior can be accurately described in terms of rules, this is merely a case of "fitting a rule," not of actually "conforming to" a rule (to use Quine's distinction). That is, the rule is a subsequent abstraction from the particular pattern of practice, not something prior to it, causing or regulating it. We don't explain successful practice via the rule.

BIBLIOGRAPHY

Works by Ryle
Ryle's most important articles are assembled in two volumes of his *Collected Papers* (New York: Barnes and Noble, 1971). "Systematically Misleading Expressions," "Philosophical Arguments," and the present selection are all in Volume II.
His most important books are
The Concept of Mind (London: Hutchinson, 1949).
Dilemmas (Cambridge: Cambridge University Press, 1954).

Further Reading
William Lyons, *Gilbert Ryle* (Sussex: Harvester Press, 1980), is a good survey.
O. Wood and G. Pitcher (eds.), *Ryle: Critical Essays* (New York: Doubleday, 1970.)
The interview I mentioned is by Bryan Magee, in his *Modern British Philosophy* (New York: St. Martin's Press, 1971).

Knowing How and Knowing That

Gilbert Ryle

Preamble
In this paper, I try to exhibit part of the logical behaviour of the several concepts of intelligence, as these occur when we characterise either practical or theoretical activities as clever, wise, prudent, skilful, etc.

    The prevailing doctrine (deriving perhaps from Plato's account of the tripartite soul) holds: (1) that Intelligence is a special faculty, the exercises of which are those specific internal acts which are called acts of thinking, namely, the operations of considering propositions; (2) that practical activities merit their titles 'intelligent', 'clever', and the rest only because they are accompanied by some such internal acts of considering propositions (and particularly 'regulative' propositions). That is to say,

Reprinted from "Proceedings of the Aristotelian Society," vol. XLVI, 1946, by permission of the editor.

doing things is never itself an exercise of intelligence, but is, at best, a process introduced and somehow steered by some ulterior act of theorising. (It is also assumed that
theorising is not a sort of doing, as if 'internal doing' contained some contradiction.)

To explain how thinking affects the course of practice, one or more go-
between faculties are postulated which are, by definition, incapable of considering
regulative propositions, yet are, by definition, competent correctly to execute them.

In opposition to this doctrine, I try to show that intelligence is directly exercised as well in some practical performances as in some theoretical performances and
that an intelligent performance need incorporate no 'shadow-act' of contemplating
regulative propositions.

Hence there is no gap between intelligence and practice corresponding to the
familiar gap between theory and practice. There is no need, therefore, to postulate any
Janus-headed go-between faculty, which shall be both amenable to theory and influential over practice.

That thinking-operations can themselves be stupidly or intelligently performed is a notorious truth which by itself upsets the assumed equation of 'exercising
intelligence' with 'thinking'. Else 'stupid thinking' would be a self-contradictory
expression and 'intelligent thinking' would be a tautology. It also helps to upset the
assumed type-difference between thinking and doing, since only subjects belonging
to the same type can share predicates. But thinking and doing do share lots of predicates, such as 'clever', 'stupid', 'careful', 'strenuous', 'attentive', etc.

To bring out these points I rely largely on variations of one argument. I argue
that the prevailing doctrine leads to vicious regresses, and these in two directions.
(1) If the intelligence exhibited in any act, practical or theoretical, is to be credited to
the occurrence of some ulterior act of intelligently considering regulative propositions, no intelligent act, practical or theoretical, could ever begin. If no one possessed
any money, no one could get any money on loan. This is the turn of the argument that
I chiefly use. (2) If a deed, to be intelligent, has to be guided by the consideration of
a regulative proposition, the gap between that consideration and the practical application of the regulation has to be bridged by some go-between process which cannot by
the pre-supposed definition itself be an exercise of intelligence and cannot, by definition, be the resultant deed. This go-between application-process has somehow to marry
observance of a contemplated maxim with the enforcement of behaviour. So it has to
unite in itself the allegedly incompatible properties of being kith to theory and kin to
practice, else it could not be the applying of the one in the other. For, unlike theory, it
must be able to influence action, and, unlike impulses, it must be amenable to regulative propositions. Consistency requires, therefore, that this schizophrenic broker must
again be subdivided into one bit which contemplates but does not execute, one which
executes but does not contemplate and a third which reconciles these irreconcilables.
And so on for ever.

(Some philosophers postulate a special class of acts, known as 'volitions', to
perform this desperate task. Others postulate some special impulses which can both
motivate action and lend docile ears to regulative propositions.) In fact, of course,
whatever 'applying' may be, it *is* a proper exercise of intelligence and it is *not* a process
of considering propositions.

Regresses of this pattern show, I suggest, not only that the prevailing doctrine is mistaken in equating exercises of intelligence with acts of theorising, but also what sort of a mistake it is. It is that radical sort of mistake which can be labelled a 'type-mistake'. I shall here content myself with stating summarily what this mistake is. I do not develop this logicians' moral in the remainder of this paper.

Adverbs expressing intelligence-concepts (such as 'shrewdly', 'wittily', 'methodically', 'scrupulously', etc.) have hitherto been construed in the wrong logical type or category, namely, as signalising the occurrence of special internal acts of that proprietary brand which we call 'thought' or 'theory'.

But in fact they signalise not that a performance incorporates extra acts, whether of this brand or of any other brand, but that the performance itself possesses a certain style, method or *modus operandi*. Intelligently to do something (whether internally or externally) is not to do two things, one 'in our heads' and the other perhaps in the outside world; it is to do one thing in a certain manner. It is somewhat like dancing gracefully, which differs from St. Vitus' dance, not by its incorporation of any extra motions (internal or external) but by the way in which the motions are executed. There need be no more moves in a job efficiently performed than in one inefficiently performed, though it is patent that they are performed in very different ways. Nor need a tidy room contain an extra article of furniture to be the *real* nominee of the adjective 'tidy'.

Phrases such as 'technical skill', 'scrupulous conduct' and even 'practical reason' denote capacities to execute not tandem operations but single operations with special procedures.

This is why ordinary language does not provide specific verbs corresponding to our specific intelligence-adverbs and adjectives.

(This is not quite true of the adverb 'voluntarily', since here philosophers have coined the specific verb 'to will'. But this verb has no ingenuous employment. If it was ever employed, it would be a proper question to ask, 'When we will, do we always, sometimes or ever will voluntarily?' Attempts to answer this question would quickly get the verb relegated to its proper place, on the shelf tenanted by 'phlogiston'.)

To put it in Aristotelian terms, intelligence-concepts belong to the category not of ποιεῖν or of πάσχειν but of πῶζ. This is why we, like Aristotle, squirm when we hear intelligence-criteria addressed as 'Values' or 'The Good'. For these locutions and associated courtesies suggest that they are superior but occult substances, which is an even worse type-mistake than treating them as superior but occult activities or occurrences.

Philosophers have not done justice to the distinction which is quite familiar to all of us between knowing that something is the case and knowing how to do things. In their theories of knowledge they concentrate on the discovery of truths or facts, and they either ignore the discovery of ways and methods of doing things or else they try to reduce it to the discovery of facts. They assume that intelligence equates with the contemplation of propositions and is exhausted in this contemplation.

I want to turn the tables and to prove that knowledge-how cannot be defined in terms of knowledge-that and further, that knowledge-how is a concept logically prior to the concept of knowledge-that. I hope to show that a number of notorious cruces and paradoxes remain insoluble if knowing-that is taken as the ideal model of all operations of intelligence. They are resolved if we see that a man's intelligence or stupidity is as directly exhibited in some of his doings as it is in some of his thinking.

Consider, first, our use of the various intelligence-predicates, namely, 'wise', 'logical', 'sensible', 'prudent', 'cunning', 'skilful', 'scrupulous', 'tasteful', 'witty', etc., with their converses 'unwise', 'illogical', 'silly', 'stupid', 'dull', 'unscrupulous', 'without taste', 'humourless', etc. What facts or what sorts of facts are known to the sensible which are not known to the silly? For example, what truths does the clever chess-player know which would be news to his stupid opponent? Obviously there is no truth or set of truths of which we could say, 'If only the stupid player had been informed of them, he would be a clever player,' or 'When once he had been apprised of these truths he would play well.' We can imagine a clever player generously imparting to his stupid opponent so many rules, tactical maxims, 'wrinkles', etc. that he could think of no more to tell him; his opponent might accept and memorise all of them, and be able and ready to recite them correctly on demand. Yet he might still play chess stupidly, that is, be unable intelligently to apply the maxims, etc.

The intellectualist (as I shall call him) might defend his case by objecting that the stupid player did not 'really' or 'fully' know these truths. He had them by heart; but this was perhaps just a set of verbal habits, like the schoolboy's rote-knowledge of the multiplication table. If he seriously and attentively considered these truths he would then be or become a clever player. Or, to modify the suggestion to avert an obvious rejoinder, if he seriously and attentively considered these truths not just while in bed or while in church but while playing chess, and especially if he considered the maxim relevant to a tactical predicament at the moment when he was involved in that predicament, then he would make the intelligent move. But, unfortunately, if he was stupid (*a*) he would be unlikely to tell himself the appropriate maxim at the moment when it was needed and (*b*) even if by luck this maxim did occur to him at the moment when it was needed, he might be too stupid to follow it. For he might not see that it was the appropriate maxim or if he did, he might not see how to apply it. In other words it requires intelligence not only to discover truths, but also to apply them, and knowing how to apply truths cannot, without setting up an infinite process, be reduced to knowledge of some extra bridge-truths. The application of maxims, etc., is certainly not any mere contemplation of them. Equally certainly it can be intelligently or stupidly done. (This is the point where Aristotle's attempted solution of Socrates' puzzle broke down. 'How can the back-slider know moral and prudential maxims and still fail to behave properly?' This is only a special case of the general problem. 'How can a man be as well-informed as you please and still be a fool?' 'Why is a fool not necessarily an ignoramus?')

To switch over to a different example. A pupil fails to follow an argument. He understands the premises and he understands the conclusion. But he fails to see that the conclusion follows from the premises. The teacher thinks him rather dull but tries to help. So he tells him that there is an ulterior proposition which he has not considered, namely, that *if these premises are true, the conclusion is true*. The pupil understands this and dutifully recites it alongside the premises, and still fails to see that the conclusion follows from the premises even when accompanied by the assertion that these premises entail this conclusion. So a second hypothetical proposition is added to his store; namely, that the conclusion is true if the premises are true as well as the first hypothetical proposition that if the premises are true the conclusion is true. And still the pupil fails to see. And so on for ever. He accepts rules in theory but this does not *force* him to apply them in practice. He considers reasons, but he fails to reason. (This is Lewis Carroll's puzzle in 'What the Tortoise said to Achilles'. I have met no successful attempt to solve it.)

What has gone wrong? Just this, that knowing how to reason was assumed to be analysable into the knowledge or supposal of some propositions, namely, (1) the special premises, (2) the conclusion, plus (3) some extra propositions about the implication of the conclusion by the premises, etc., etc., *ad infinitum*.

'Well but surely the intelligent reasoner *is* knowing rules of inference whenever he reasons intelligently.' Yes, of course he is, but knowing such a rule is not a case of knowing an extra fact or truth; it is knowing how to move from acknowledging some facts to acknowledging others. Knowing a rule of inference is not possessing a bit of extra information but being able to perform an intelligent operation. Knowing a role is knowing how. It is realised in performances which conform to the rule, not in theoretical citations of it.

It is, of course, true that when people can reason intelligently, logicians can then extract the nerve of a range of similar inferences and exhibit this nerve in a logicians' formula. And they can teach it in lessons to novices who first learn the formula by heart and later find out how to detect the presence of a common nerve in a variety of formally similar but materially different arguments. But arguing intelligently did not before Aristotle and does not after Aristotle require the separate acknowledgment of the truth or 'validity' of the formula. 'God hath not ... left it to Aristotle to make (men) rational.' Principles of inference are not extra premises and knowing these principles exhibits itself not in the recitation of formulae but in the execution of valid inferences and in the avoidance, detection and correction of fallacies, etc. The dull reasoner is not ignorant; he is inefficient. A silly pupil may know by heart a great number of logicians' formulae without being good at arguing. The sharp pupil may argue well who has never heard of formal logic.

There is a not unfashionable shuffle which tries to circumvent these considerations by saying that the intelligent reasoner who has not been taught logic knows the logicians' formulae 'implicitly' but not 'explicitly'; or that the ordinary virtuous person has 'implicit' but not 'explicit' knowledge of the rules of right conduct; the skilful but untheoretical chess-player 'implicitly' acknowledges a lot of strategic and tactical maxims, though he never formulates them and might not recognise them if they were imparted to him by some Clausewitz of the game. This shuffle assumes that knowledge-how must be reducible to knowledge-that, while conceding that no operations of acknowledging-that need be actually found occurring. It fails to explain how, even if such acknowledgements did occur, their maker might still be a fool in his performance.

All this intellectualist legend must be rejected, not merely because it tells psychological myths but because the myths are not of the right type to account for the facts which they are invented to explain. However many strata of knowledge-that are postulated, the same crux always recurs that a fool might have all that knowledge without knowing how to perform, and a sensible or cunning person might know how to perform who had not been introduced to those postulated facts; that is, there still remains the same gulf, as wide as ever, between having the postulated knowledge of those facts and knowing how to use or apply it; between acknowledging principles in thought and intelligently applying them in action.

I must now try to speak more positively about what it is like to know-how. (*a*) When a person knows how to do things of a certain sort (e.g., make good jokes, conduct battles or behave at funerals), his knowledge is actualised or exercised in what he does. It is not exercised (save *per accidens*) in the propounding of propositions or in saying 'Yes' to those propounded by others. His intelligence is exhibited by deeds, not by internal or external dicta. A good experimentalist exercises his skill not in reciting maxims of technology but in making experiments. It is a ruinous but popular mistake to suppose that intelligence operates only in the production and manipulation of propositions, i.e., that only in ratiocinating are we rational. (*b*) When a person knows how to do things of a certain sort (e.g., cook omelettes, design dresses or persuade juries), his performance is in some way governed by principles, rules, canons, standards or criteria. (For most purposes it does not matter which we say.) It is always possible in principle, if not in practice, to explain why he tends to succeed, that is, to state the reasons for his actions. It is tautology to say that there is a method in his cleverness. But his observance of rules, principles, etc. must, if it is there at all, be realised in his performance of his tasks. It need not (though it can) be also advertised in an extra performance of paying some internal or external lip-service to those rules or principles. He *must* work judiciously; he *may* also propound judgments. For propounding judgments is just another special activity, which can itself be judiciously or injudiciously performed. Judging (or propositional thinking) is one (but only one) way of exercising judiciousness or betraying silliness; it has its own rules, principles and criteria, but again the intelligent application of these does not pre-require yet another lower stratum of judgments on how to think correctly.

In short the propositional acknowledgement of rules, reasons or principles is not the parent of the intelligent application of them; it is a step-child of that application.

In some ways the observance of rules and the using of criteria resemble the employment of spectacles. We look through them but not at them. And as a person who looks much at his spectacles betrays that he has difficulties in looking through them, so people who appeal much to principles show that they do not know how to act.

There is a point to be expounded here. I have been arguing in effect that ratiocination is not the general condition of rational behaviour but only one species of it. Yet the traditional associations of the word 'rational' are such that it is commonly assumed that behaviour can only be rational if the overt actions taken are escorted by internal operations of considering and acknowledging the reasons for taking them, i.e., if we preach to ourselves before we practise. 'How else [it would be urged] could principles, rules, reasons, criteria, etc. govern performances, unless the agent thought of them while or before acting?' People equate rational behaviour with premeditated or reasoned behaviour, i.e., behaviour in which the agent internally persuades himself by arguments to do what he does. Among the premisses of these postulated internal arguments will be the formulae expressing the principles, rules, criteria or reasons which govern the resultant intelligent actions. This whole story now seems to me false in fact and refutable in logic. We do not find in fact that we persuade ourselves by arguments to make or appreciate jokes. What sorts of arguments should we use? Yet it certainly requires intelligence or rationality to make and see jokes. But worse than this, when we do, as often happens, go through the process of persuading ourselves to do things, this process is itself one which can be intelligently or stupidly executed. So, if the assumption were correct, it would be necessary for us to start one stage further back and to persuade ourselves with second-order arguments to employ first-order persuasions of a cogent and not of a silly type. And so on *ad infinitum*. The assumption, that is, credits the rationality of any given performance to the rational execution of some anterior performance, which would in its turn require exactly the same treatment. So no rational performance could ever be begun. Aristotle's Practical Syllogism fails to explain intelligent conduct, since its explanation is circular. For the postulated syllogising would itself need to be intelligently conducted.

What has happened once again is that intellectuals have tried to explain prudence, say, or skill by reference to a piece of acknowledging-that, leaving unexplained the fact that this internal operation would itself have to be cannily executed. They have tried to explain, e.g., practical flair by reference to an intellectual process which, unfortunately for their theory, again requires flair.

We should, before leaving this side of the matter, notice one variant of the doctrine that knowing-how is reducible to a set of knowings-that. It could be argued that as knowing-how always involves the knowing of a rule (in some broad sense of 'rule'), this could be equated with the knowing not of *any* sort of truth, but of the truth of a general hypothetical of the pattern 'whenever so and so, then such and such'. For much, though not all, intelligent behaviour does consist in taking the steps likely to lead to desired results. The knowledge involved might therefore be knowing that when actions of a certain sort are taken in certain situations, results of a certain sort tend to occur.

The answer to this is twofold: (1) a man might accept any set of such hypothetical propositions and still not know how to cook or drive a car. He might even know them well enough to be a good teacher and still be stupid in his own performances. Conversely a girl might be a clever cook who had never considered any such general hypothetical propositions. If she had the knack or flair, she could do without news of the inductive generalisation.

(2) The suggested general hypotheticals are inductive generalisations. But making sound, as distinct from rash inductions is itself an intelligent performance. Knowing how to make inductions cannot await news of this higher-order induction, that when people assemble certain quantities of evidence in certain ways and produce conclusions of certain sorts, those conclusions tend to be true. Else induction could never begin; nor could the suggested higher-order induction have any data.

There is another difficulty. Sometimes we do go through the internal operation of persuading ourselves to do things, just as we often go through the external operation of persuading other people to do things. Let us suppose that the persuasion is cogent, i.e., that the recipient is convinced by it. What happens then? Does he necessarily do what he has been persuaded to do? Does he necessarily practise what he preaches? Notoriously not. I frequently persuade myself to smoke less, filling and lighting my pipe at the very moment when I am saying 'yes' to the conclusion of the argument. Like Medea, I listen and am convinced, but I do not obey. You say, 'Ah, but you weren't "really" or "effectively" convinced. You said "yes" in some theoretical or academic way, but you were not wise enough to say "yes" in the practical way of putting your pipe back in your pocket.' Certainly. This proves that unwisdom in conduct cannot be defined in terms of the omission of any ratiocinations and consequently that wisdom in conduct cannot be defined solely in terms of the performance of any ratiocinations. The intelligent application in practice of principles, reasons, standards, etc. is not a legatee of the consideration of them in theory; it can and normally does occur without any such consideration. Indeed we could not consider principles of method in theory unless we or others already intelligently applied them in practice. Acknowledging the maxims of a practice presupposes knowing how to perform it. Rules, like birds, must live before they can be stuffed.

(c) We certainly can, in respect of many practices, like fishing, cooking and reasoning, extract principles from their applications by people who know how to fish, cook and reason. Hence Izaak Walton, Mrs Beeton and Aristotle. But when we try to express these principles we find that they cannot easily be put in the indicative mood. They fall automatically into the imperative mood. Hence comes the awkwardness for the intellectualist theories of stating what are the truths or facts which we acknowledge when we acknowledge a rule or maxim. We cannot call an imperative a truth or falsehood. The Moral Law refuses to behave like a fact. You cannot affirm or deny Mrs Beeton's recipes. So, in the hope of having it both ways, they tend to speak guardedly of the 'validity' rather than the 'truth' of such regulative propositions, an idiom which itself betrays qualms about the reduction of knowing-how to knowing-that.

What is the use of such formulae if the acknowledgement of them is not a condition of knowing how to act but a derivative product of theorising about the nerves of such knowledge? The answer is simple. They are useful pedagogically, namely, in lessons to those who are still learning how to act. They belong to manuals for novices. They are not quasi-premisses in the postulated self-persuasions of those who know how to act; for no such self-persuasions occur. They are imperative because they are disciplinary, because they are in the idiom of the mentor. They are banisters for toddlers, i.e., they belong to the methodology and not to the methods of intelligent practices. What logicians have long half-realised about the *venue* and functions of their rule-formulae has yet to be learned by moral philosophers about their imperatives and ought-statements. When they have learned this they will cease to ask such questions as whether conscience is an intuitive or discursive faculty. For knowing how to behave is not a sort of knowing-that, so it is neither an intuitive nor a discursive sort of knowing-that. The question itself is as nonsensical as would be the corresponding question about the sense of humour or the ability to infer. Other bogus ethico-epistemological questions also vanish, like the question whether imperatives or ought-statements are synthetic or analytic, *a priori* or *a posteriori* truths. How should we deal with such questions if posed about Mrs Beeton's recipes?

Another ethical muddle is also cleared up. Philosophers sometimes say that conscience issues imperatives or dictates. Now 'conscience' is an old-fashioned faculty-word, but if the assertion means that the conscientious man exercises his consciousness by issuing propositions or prescriptions, then this is false. Knowing how to behave is exhibited by correct behaviour, just as knowing how to cook is exhibited by palatable dishes. True, the conscientious man may be asked to instruct other agents how to behave, and then he will, if he knows how, publish maxims or specific prescriptions exemplifying maxims. But a man might know how to behave without knowing how to give good advice.

Sometimes a man might give good advice who did not know how to behave. Knowing how to advise about behaviour is not the same thing as knowing how to behave. It requires at least three extra techniques: ability to abstract, ability to express and ability to impress. In another class of cases, a generally conscientious man might, in certain interference-conditions, not know how to behave, but be puzzled and worried about his line of action. He might then remind himself of maxims or prescriptions, i.e., he might resume, for the moment, the adolescent's task of learning how to behave. He would be issuing imperatives or ought-propositions to himself, but he would be doing so just because he did not know how to behave. He would be patching up a gap in his knowledge-how. And he might be bad at self-counsel without being a bad man. He might have a correct 'hunch' that his self-suasions were invalid, though he could detect no fallacy in them. There would be a circle in the attempted description of conscience as a faculty which issues imperatives; for an imperative is a formula which gives a description or partial definition of what is known when some one knows how to behave. You couldn't define a good chef as one who cites Mrs Beeton's recipes, for these recipes describe how good chefs cook, and anyhow the excellence of a chef is not in his citing but in his cooking. Similarly skill at arguing is not a readiness to quote Aristotle but the ability to argue validly, and it is just this ability some of the principles applied in which were extracted by Aristotle. Moral imperatives and ought-statements have no place in the lives of saints or complete sinners. For saints are not still learning how to behave and complete sinners have not yet begun to learn. So neither experiences scruples. Neither considers maxims.

Logical rules, tactical maxims and technical canons are in the same way helpful only to the half-trained. When a person knows how to do things of a certain sort, we call him 'acute', 'shrewd', 'scrupulous', 'ingenious', 'discerning', 'inventive', 'an expert cook', 'a good general', or 'a good examiner', etc. In doing so we are describing a part of his character, or crediting him with a certain dispositional excellence. Correspondingly when we describe some particular action as clever, witty or wise, we are imputing to the agent the appropriate dispositional excellence. The way in which rules, standards, techniques, criteria, etc. govern his particular performances is one with the way in which his dispositional excellences are actualised in those performances. It is second nature in him to behave thus and the rules etc. are the living nerves of that second nature. To be acute and consistent in reasoning is certainly to apply rules of inference to the propositions considered. But the reasoner does not have both to consider propositions and to cast sidelong glances at a formula; he just considers the propositions efficiently. The rules are the rails of his thinking, not extra termini of it. The good chess-player observes rules and tactical principles, but he does not think of them; he just plays according to them. We observe rules of grammar, style and etiquette in the same way. Socrates was puzzled why the knowledge which constitutes human excellence cannot be imparted. We can now reply. Learning-how differs from learning-that. We can be instructed in truths, we can only be disciplined in methods. Appropriate exercises (corrected by criticisms and inspired by examples and precepts) can inculcate second natures. But knowledge-how cannot be built up by accumulation of pieces of knowledge-that.

An explanatory word is necessary here. 'Discipline' covers two widely disparate processes, namely, habituation and education, or drill and training. A circus seal can be drilled or 'conditioned' into the performance of complicated tricks, much as the recruit is drilled to march and slope arms. Drill results in the production of automatisms, i.e. performances which can be done perfectly without exercising intelligence. This is habituation, the formation of blind habits. But education or training produces not blind habits but intelligent powers. In inculcating a skill I am not training a pupil to do something blindly but to do something intelligently. Drill dispenses with intelligence, training enlarges it. (It is a pity that Aristotle's sensible account of the formation of wise characters has been vitiated by the translator's rendering of ἐθισμός as 'habituation'. Aristotle was talking about how people learn to behave wisely, not how they are drilled into acting mechanically.) When the recruit reaches the stage of learning to shoot and read maps, he is not drilled but taught. He is taught to perform in the right way, i.e., to shoot and to use maps with 'his head'. Unlike the seal he becomes a judge of his own performance—he learns what mistakes are and how to avoid or correct them. He learns how to teach himself and so to better his instructions. He acquires not a habit but a skill (though naturally skills contain habits). (Neglect of this distinction between conditioning and training is what vitiates Hume's account of Induction.) The fact that mathematics, philosophy, tactics, scientific method and literary style cannot be imparted but only inculcated reveals that these too are not bodies of information but branches of knowledge-how. They are not sciences but (in the old sense) disciplines. The experts in them cannot tell us what they know, they can only show what they know by operating with cleverness, skill, elegance or taste. The advance of knowledge does not consist only in the accumulation of discovered truths, but also and chiefly in the cumulative mastery of methods.

One last point. I have, I hope, proved that knowing-how is not reducible to any sandwich of knowing-that, and that our intelligence-predicates are definable in terms of knowing-how. I now want to prove that knowing-that presupposes knowing-how.

(1) To know a truth, I must have discovered or established it. But discovering and establishing are intelligent operations, requiring rules of method, checks, tests, criteria, etc. A scientist or an historian is primarily a man who knows how to decide certain sorts of questions. Only secondarily is he a man who has discovered a lot of facts, i.e., has achieved successes in his application of these rules etc. (though of course he only learns how to discover through exercises in discovery; he does not begin by perfecting his method and only later go on to have successes in applying it). A scientist, that is, is primarily a knower-how and only secondarily a knower-that. He couldn't discover any particular truths unless he knew how to discover. He could know how to discover, without making this or that particular discovery.

(2) But when I have found out something, even then irrespective of the intelligence exercised in finding it out, I can't be said to have knowledge of the fact unless I can intelligently exploit it. I mean this. I might once have satisfied myself of something, say the distance between Oxford and Henley; and I might have enshrined this

in a list of road distances, such that I could on demand reel off the whole list, as I can reel off the multiplication table. So in this sense I have not forgotten what I once found out. But if, when told that Nettlebed is so far out from Henley, I cannot tell you how far Nettlebed is from Oxford, or if, when shown a local map, I can see that Oxford to Banbury is about as far as Oxford to Henley but still cannot tell you how far Oxford is from Banbury or criticise false estimates given by others, you would say that I don't know the distance any longer, i.e., that I have forgotten it or that I have stowed it away in a corner where it is not available.

Effective possession of a piece of knowledge-that involves knowing how to use that knowledge, when required, for the solution of other theoretical or practical problems. There is a distinction between the museum-possession and the workshop-possession of knowledge. A silly person can be stocked with information, yet never know how to answer particular questions.

The uneducated public erroneously equates education with the imparting of knowing-that. Philosophers have not hitherto made it very clear what its error is. I hope I have provided part of the correction.

Introduction to H. P. Grice

H.P. Grice was born in Birmingham, England, in 1913. The "H" standing for "Herbert", he chose to go by his middle name, Paul. After studying at Corpus Christi and Merton Colleges, he remained in Oxford until 1967 as a Fellow and Tutor at St. John's College. He then emigrated to the United States, where he taught at the University of California, Berkeley, until his retirement in 1979. Among his many honors, Grice was elected to the British Academy in 1966, and delivered several prestigious sets of lectures, including the William James Lectures at Harvard, and the John Locke Lectures at Oxford. He died in 1988.

At a time in which academics usually internalize the pressure to "publish or perish," H. P. Grice was a rarity in his extreme reluctance to release his work into print. One unfortunate result of this reticence is that recognition of how various aspects of his work fit together has been delayed. With the exception of a few articles, all enormously influential, most of his published work is posthumous. His major piece of work, the William James Lectures for 1967, was only published in its entirety in 1989. At the time of this writing, there remains a vast amount of still unpublished work, including several book-length pieces. We can only hope that they will be made available in the future.

Grice begins his discussion of meaning by distinguishing *natural* and *nonnatural* meaning. The former includes such cases as "dark clouds mean rain," and where "mean" is roughly equivalent to "is a reliable indicator of." He introduces this natural meaning primarily to get it out of the way, and distinguish it from the article's main concern, nonnatural meaning (meaning$_{NN}$). Within meaning$_{NN}$, we must distinguish

1. What came to be called *utterer's meaning*: sentences of the form *"By uttering x, U meant that p"*;
2. *Sentence meaning*: what sentence x literally means.

Within 2, we can apply the token/type distinction, and distinguish

(a) What x meant on this occasion of use;
(b) The general meaning of sentence x.

At this point I should make some terminological notes regarding Grice's expression of (1). In the original article "Meaning," he uses the letter A to represent the speaker. However, in later, more detailed developments of his theory, the speaker is represented by U (utterer), and A represents the audience. In what follows, I will use the latter convention. Second, Grice is employing a deliberately wide, artificial sense of "utterance," standing for any complete communicative act, which need not be verbal or written but could include gestures, drawings, and the like.

Grice argues that the most basic form of meaning$_{NN}$ is utterer's meaning, and that token sentence-meaning (*"x means that p"*) is equivalent to or elliptical for *"By uttering x, U means that p."* He proposes to analyze sentence-type meaning in terms of this prior form: *'x means$_{NN}$ that so-and-so'* might as a first shot be equated with some statement or disjunction of statements about what 'people' (vague) intend (with qualifications about 'recognition') to effect by x." In other words, the meaning of that sentence is the content that it is standardly or conventionally employed to communicate, by virtue of the mechanism to be discussed below.

As to utterer's meaning, Grice proposes to analyze this primary semantic concept in terms of the *psychological* concepts of intention, belief, and recognition. The analysis will implicitly include desire (and other propositional attitudes). The 1957 formulation is "*'A meant something by x'* is (roughly) equivalent to 'A intended the utterance of x to produce some effect in an audience by means of the recognition of this intention'; and we may add that to ask what A meant is to ask for a specification of the intended effect."

In Grice's 1969 formulation, published in (1989), this has been tightened up into the following:

"By uttering x, U meant something" is true if U uttered x intending

1. To produce some response r in some audience A;

2. A to recognize that U intends 1;

3. A's recognition that U intends 2 to function as a reason for 1.

So, for example, if U utters an indicative sentence, r is some belief, whose content is semantically related to that of x. Thus, if U says "it is raining," A's intended belief is that it is raining. If U utters a command, then r is some behavioral response. For example, if U says "shut the door," r is A's shutting the door. If x is a question, then r is an appropriate answer. Let us examine this analysis in more detail.

As an analysis, it is intended to state necessary and sufficient conditions for an utterance to be an example of meaning$_{NN}$. Second, it is a piece of a priori conceptual analysis; that is, not attempting to discover a scientific relationship between kinds, but to describe the relations between our concepts. Third, it is a reductive analysis: All other cases of meaning$_{NN}$ are to be derived from utterer's meaning, and this, in turn, is to be explicated in terms of psychological concepts.

The central concept in the analysis is that of a higher-order communicative intention. As we shall see, this means that cases of utterer's meaning take place between (at least two) *persons*. That is, both participants must be able to have mental states and to ascribe them to others. Also, they must be able to act from reasons, rather than from brute causality.

After the publication of "Meaning," various *counter examples* to Grice's analysis were offered, which he attempted to deal with in his William James Lectures and elsewhere. I will give a sample of the debate.

1. Surely there are many cases where we would hold that U means that x, but deny that U intends that A believe that x. One type of case would be where U assumes that A *already knows* that x, for example, where a student is answering a teacher. Another sort of case would be where U assumes that A is so set in her ways that she can never be made to believe that x; for example, where x concerns Darwinism and A is an evangelist on U's doorstep. (For further cases, see Avramides [1989], p. 60.)

Grice attempted to deal with these sorts of cases by amending clause (1) to

(1′) *A to think that U thinks that x*

where this is either an end in itself, or done as a means to communicate that x. However, this move cannot deal with other sorts of counter-examples, such as "reminding," where U is trying to jog A's memory regarding x. In response, Grice suggests (1) be altered to

(1″) *A actively to believe that x.*

However, I agree with Stephen Neale (1992) that the sheer diversity of speech acts makes it unlikely that any one of these suggestions will fit all possible cases, and that therefore a disjunctive analysis is required.

2. Various writers, notably P. F. Strawson (1964) and Stephen Schiffer (1972) have constructed counter-examples to show that Grice's three conditions are not jointly sufficient to demarcate utterer's meaning. What is common to these cases is that U's intentions are not completely explicit. I have constructed an example that fits Strawson's structure:

> Suppose that my good friend Bob and I are both believers in the supernatural, and that Bob plans to buy a house which I believe to be haunted. I make an audiotape of appropriately spooky noises, and conceal it in the house, and do this in such a way that Bob can see me doing it. However, while I know that Bob can see me, he's not aware that I know he sees me. Due to our friendship, Bob knows that his welfare is my concern, and that I wouldn't want him to believe that the house was haunted unless it actually was. So Bob

realizes, from my action, that I want him to believe that the house is haunted, and thereby comes to believe that it is haunted. His recognition of my intention is his reason for believing the house to be haunted.

This case clearly satisfies Grice's requirements. However, Strawson would say, surely my "utterance" of concealing the tape doesn't *mean*$_{NN}$ that the house is haunted. The trouble, he would say, is that I intend Bob not to know that I am aware that he is watching me. That is, there is an element of deceit which rules out communication. Strawson would demand that Grice add a fourth condition here, namely that I intend that Bob recognize my intention to get him to recognize my (basic) intention to get him to think that the house was haunted.

However, Schiffer showed that a similar counter-example can be made against this four-part criterion, again exploiting an element of deceit on the part of U. The door is obviously open for an infinite regress of higher-order intentions. So the Gricean would appear to have a dilemma: On the one hand, for any analysis, there would appear to be a set of counter-examples available; on the other hand, the cost of dealing with the counter-examples is to ascribe such a complex structure of higher-order intentions to both U and A that their attribution becomes less and less psychologically plausible. That is, it is not whether we do have such intentions, either explicitly or tacitly; rather the question is whether we are capable of having them. Grice (1982) attempts to avoid the regress by pooling all higher-level intentions into one clause, eliminating the deceit at the heart of the problems:

(4′) *U does not intend A to be deceived about U's intentions.*

3. Various commentators have expressed doubt over the necessity of Grice's condition (3). In his examples (e.g., of Herod presenting Salome with the severed head of John the Baptist), Grice remarked that while conditions (1) and (2) are satisfied (i.e., Herod wanted Salome to believe that John was dead, and for her to recognize his intention), still the "utterance" did not *mean*$_{NN}$ that St. John was dead. As Neale remarks, many of us do not follow Grice's intuition on this case. So why does Grice rule out meaning$_{NN}$ here? It seems that he feels that the presence of some *naturally* meaningful data interferes with meaning$_{NN}$ by making the recognition of the utterer's intention causally superfluous. For example, the fact that the saint's head is separated from his torso makes it blatantly obvious that he is dead—no taking of the "intentional stance" (to employ Dennett's terminology) to Herod is required. My view is that Grice adds (3) to stress the rational, normative nature of communication and ascription of meaning$_{NN}$. The trouble with the above example is that the transmission of the belief, from U to A, can take place purely in the realm of brute causality, and not of reasons.

As well as his work on meaning, Grice's most influential contribution to philosophy of language was his distinction between an utterance's semantic and pragmatic implications. While the theory sketched in "Meaning" can be fairly seen as a case of analyzing an utterance's meaning in terms of how it is used, Grice's wider project, in the context of which his developing work on utterer's meaning should be understood, resists an *identification* of meaning with use.

In "Logic and Conversation" (in 1989), Grice gives this famous example to illustrate the distinction between semantic and pragmatic implications: Suppose my student X is applying for a job in philosophy, and he has asked me to write a letter of reference for him to Professor A. My letter is restricted to saying that X has an excellent command of English, and attended my class regularly. Now A will undoubtedly take it that I am suggesting that X's philosophical abilities are wanting—but, equally clearly, my words do not literally mean that. What I *say* is about his English and attendance, but what I *mean* goes beyond this. Grice would say that I have employed a form of pragmatic implication called "conversational implicature." A is justified in drawing the inference that I mean to impart to him that X is a weak candidate, since he is justified in making a (tacit) assumption that I am observing (tacit) conventions of communication (collectively called "The Cooperative Principle"), where U ought to express to A all and only what he believes to be true and relevant to the matter in hand. So, since A knows that I am in a position to make an informed judgment on X's philosophical ability, he takes its conspicuous absence, and my focus on irrelevancies, as a sign that all is not well. Only by such a process of reasoning can A make sense of my utterance.

Grice used his distinction between semantic and pragmatic features as a check on the assimilation of meaning and use by "ordinary language" philosophers. For example, Strawson (1952) had argued that the disjunction symbol "v" was semantically different from the English term "or," because the semantic role of "v" can be specified purely truth-functionally. For example, from p I can infer that "$p \lor q$." By contrast, suppose I know that p is the case, yet offer "p or q" in response to an inquiry. For example, you ask me where a colleague is, and I reply, "either in her office or out to lunch." You will take it that I don't know which it is, and therefore would be aggrieved if you discover that I knew she was in her office. It follows, argues Strawson, that since the rules governing the correct usage of "v" and "or" differ, they have different meanings. Grice replies that the semantic properties of "or" are equivalent to those of "v," but that "or" also has certain non-semantic, pragmatic implicatures, governed by the Cooperative Principle. In this case, I have broken the principle since I didn't give you all the relevant information in response to your inquiry.

BIBLIOGRAPHY

Works by Grice

Most of Grice's most famous work has been published as *Studies in the Way of Words* (Cambridge: Harvard University Press, 1989). This includes the William James Lectures, plus several other papers, including "Meaning."

At the moment, Grice's only other book is *The Conception of Value* (Oxford: Clarendon Press, 1991). Most of this material was originally delivered as the Carus Lectures for 1983.

Further Reading

The best short survey of Grice's work in the philosophy of language is Stephen Neale, "Paul Grice and the Philosophy of Language," in *Linguistics and Philosophy,* Vol. 15, 1992.

Some full-length works extending Grice's program are

Anita Avramides, *Meaning and Mind* (Cambridge: MIT Press, 1989).

Brian Loar, *Mind and Meaning* (Cambridge: Cambridge University Press, 1981).

Stephen Schiffer, *Meaning* (Oxford: Clarendon Press, 1972).

A pessimistic appraisal of the Gricean project can be found in Schiffer's *Remnants of Meaning* (Cambridge: MIT Press, 1987).

Richard Grandy and Richard Warner, eds., *Philosophical Grounds of Rationality: Intentions, Categories, Ends* (Oxford: Clarendon Press, 1986), is a set of papers in honor of Grice, with his replies, including an autobiographical sketch. (Notice that the initials of the title form the acronym PGRICE. Is that cute or what?

The Strawson works mentioned above are "Intention and Convention in Speech Acts," *Philosophical Review*, Vol. 73, 1964; and *Introduction to Logical Theory* (London: Methuen, 1952).

One influential development of the Gricean analysis of sentence meaning in terms of communicative conventions is by David Lewis, in *Convention* (Cambridge: Harvard University Press), and "Languages and Language," in *Philosophical Papers: Volume 1* (Oxford: Oxford University Press, 1983).

Meaning

H. P. Grice

Consider the following sentences:

"Those spots mean (meant) measles."

"Those spots didn't mean anything to me, but to the doctor they meant measles."

"The recent budget means that we shall have a hard year."

(1) I cannot say, "Those spots meant measles, but he hadn't got measles," and I cannot say, "The recent budget means that we shall have a hard year, but we shan't have." That is to say, in cases like the above, *x meant that p* and *x means that p* entail *p*.

(2) I cannot argue from "Those spots mean (meant) measles" to any conclusion about "what is (was) meant by those spots"; for example, I am not entitled to say, "What was meant by those spots was that he had measles." Equally I cannot draw from the statement about the recent budget the conclusion "What is meant by the recent budget is that we shall have a hard year."

H. P. Grice: "Meaning," *Philosophical Review*, vol. 66, 1957.

(3) I cannot argue from "Those spots meant measles" to any conclusion to the effect that somebody or other meant by those spots so-and-so. *Mutatis mutandis*, the same is true of the sentence about the recent budget.

(4) For none of the above examples can a restatement be found in which the verb "mean" is followed by a sentence or phrase in quotation marks. Thus "Those spots meant measles" cannot be reformulated as "Those spots meant 'measles'" or as "Those spots meant 'he has measles.'"

(5) On the other hand, for all these examples an approximate restatement can be found beginning with the phrase "The fact that ..."; for example, "The fact that he had those spots meant that he had measles" and "The fact that the recent budget was as it was means that we shall have a hard year."

Now contrast the specimen sentences with the following:

"Those three rings on the bell (of the bus) mean that the bus is full."

"That remark, 'Smith couldn't get on without his trouble and strife,' meant that Smith found his wife indispensable."

(1) I can use the first of these and go on to say, "But it isn't in fact full—the conductor has made a mistake"; and I can use the second and go on, "But in fact Smith deserted her seven years ago." That is to say, here *x means that p* and *x meant that p* do not entail *p*.

(2) I can argue from the first to some statement about "what is (was) meant" by the rings on the bell and from the second to some statement about "what is (was) meant" by the quoted remark.

(3) I can argue from the first sentence to the conclusion that somebody (namely the conductor) meant, or at any rate should have meant, by the rings that the bus is full, and I can argue analogously for the second sentence.

(4) The first sentence can be restated in a form in which the verb "mean" is followed by a phrase in quotation marks, that is, "Those three rings on the bell mean 'the bus is full.'" So also can the second sentence.

(5) Such a sentence as "The fact that the bell has been rung three times means that the bus is full" is not a restatement of the meaning of the first sentence. Both may be true, but they do not have, even approximately, the same meaning.

When the expressions "means," "means something," "means that" are used in the kind of way in which they are used in the first set of sentences, I shall speak of the sense, or senses, in which they are used, as the *natural* sense, or senses, of the expressions in question. When the expressions are used in the kind of way in which they are used in the second set of sentences, I shall speak of the sense, or senses, in which they are used, as the *nonnatural* sense, or senses, of the expressions in question. I shall use the abbreviation "means$_{NN}$" to distinguish the nonnatural sense or senses.

I propose, for convenience, also to include under the head of natural senses of "mean" such senses of "mean" as may be exemplified in sentences of the pattern "*A* means (meant) *to do* so-and-so (by *x*)," where *A* is a human agent. By contrast, as the previous examples show, I include under the head of nonnatural senses of "mean" any senses of "mean" found in sentences of the patterns "*A* means (meant) something by x" or "A means (meant) by x that … " (This is overrigid; but it will serve as an indication.)

I do not want to maintain that *all* our uses of "mean" fall easily, obviously, and tidily into one of the two groups I have distinguished; but I think that in most cases we should be at least fairly strongly inclined to assimilate a use of "mean" to one group rather than to the other. The question which now arises is this: "What more can be said about the distinction between the cases where we should say that the word is applied in a natural sense and the cases where we should say that the word is applied in a nonnatural sense?" Asking this question will not of course prohibit us from trying to give an explanation of "meaning$_{NN}$" in terms of one or another natural sense of "mean."

This question about the distinction between natural and nonnatural meaning is, I think, what people are getting at when they display an interest in a distinction between "natural" and "conventional" signs. But I think my formulation is better. For some things which can mean$_{NN}$ something are not signs (e.g. words are not), and some are not conventional in any ordinary sense (e.g. certain gestures); while some things which mean naturally are not signs of what they mean (cf. the recent budget example).

I want first to consider briefly, and reject, what I might term a causal type of answer to the question, "What is meaning$_{NN}$?" We might try to say, for instance, more or less with C. L. Stevenson,[1] that for x to mean$_{NN}$ something, x must have (roughly) a tendency to produce in an audience some attitude (cognitive or otherwise) and a tendency, in the case of a speaker, to *be* produced *by* that attitude, these tendencies being dependent on "an elaborate process of conditioning attending the use of the sign in communication."[2] This clearly will not do.

(1) Let us consider a case where an utterance, if it qualifies at all as meaning$_{NN}$ something, will be of a descriptive or informative kind and the relevant attitude, therefore, will be a cognitive one, for example, a belief. (I use "utterance" as a neutral word to apply to any candidate for meaning$_{NN}$; it has a convenient act-object ambiguity.) It is no doubt the case that many people have a tendency to put on a tailcoat when they think they are about to go to a dance, and it is no doubt also the case that many people, on seeing someone put on a tailcoat, would conclude that the person in question was about to go to a dance. Does this satisfy us that putting on a tailcoat means$_{NN}$ that one is about to go to a dance (or indeed means$_{NN}$ anything at all)? Obviously not. It is no help to refer to the qualifying phrase "dependent on an elaborate process of conditioning." For if all this means is that the response to the sight of a tailcoat being put on is in some way learned or acquired, it will not exclude the present case from being one of meaning$_{NN}$. But if we have to take seriously the second part of the qualifying phrase ("attending the use of the sign in communication"), then the account of meaning$_{NN}$ is obviously circular. We might just as well say, "X has meaning$_{NN}$ if it is used in communication," which, though true, is not helpful.

(2) If this is not enough, there is a difficulty—really the same difficulty, I think—which Stevenson recognizes: how we are to avoid saying, for example, that

---

[1] *Ethics and Language* (New Haven, 1944), ch. 3.

[2] Ibid., p. 57.

"Jones is tall" is part of what is meant by "Jones is an athlete," since to tell someone that Jones is an athlete would tend to make him believe that Jones is tall. Stevenson here resorts to invoking linguistic rules, namely, a permissive rule of language that "athletes may be nontall." This amounts to saying that we are not prohibited by rule from speaking of "nontall athletes." But why are we not prohibited? Not because it is not bad grammar, or is not impolite, and so on, but presumably because it is not meaningless (or, if this is too strong, does not in any way violate the rules of meaning for the expressions concerned). But this seems to involve us in another circle. Moreover, one wants to ask why, if it is legitimate to appeal here to rules to distinguish what is meant from what is suggested, this appeal was not made earlier, in the case of groans, for example, to deal with which Stevenson originally introduced the qualifying phrase about dependence on conditioning.

A further deficiency in a causal theory of the type just expounded seems to be that, even if we accept it as it stands, we are furnished with an analysis only of statements about the *standard* meaning, or the meaning in general, of a "sign." No provision is made for dealing with statements about what a particular speaker or writer means by a sign on a particular occasion (which may well diverge from the standard meaning of the sign); nor is it obvious how the theory could be adapted to make such provision. One might even go further in criticism and maintain that the causal theory ignores the fact that the meaning (in general) of a sign needs to be explained in terms of what users of the sign do (or should) mean by it on particular occasions; and so the latter notion, which is unexplained by the causal theory, is in fact the fundamental one. I am sympathetic to this more radical criticism, though I am aware that the point is controversial.

I do not propose to consider any further theories of the "causal-tendency" type. I suspect no such theory could avoid difficulties analogous to those I have outlined without utterly losing its claim to rank as a theory of this type.

I will now try a different and, I hope, more promising line. If we can elucidate the meaning of

"x meant$_{NN}$ something (on a particular occasion)" and

"x meant$_{NN}$ that so-and-so (on a particular occasion)"

and of

"A meant$_{NN}$ something by x (on a particular occasion)" and

"A meant$_{NN}$ by x that so-and-so (on a particular occasion),"

this might reasonably be expected to help us with

"x means$_{NN}$ (timeless) something (that so-and-so)"

"A means$_{NN}$ (timeless) by x something (that so-and-so),"

and with the explication of "means the same as," "understands," "entails," and so on. Let us for the moment pretend that we have to deal only with utterances which might be informative or descriptive.

A first shot would be to suggest that "*x* meant_{NN} something" would be true if *x* was intended by its utterer to induce a belief in some "audience" and that to say what the belief was would be to say what *x* meant_{NN}. This will not do. I might leave *B*'s handkerchief near the scene of a murder in order to induce the detective to believe that *B* was the murderer; but we should not want to say that the handkerchief (or my leaving it there) meant_{NN} anything or that I had meant_{NN} by leaving it that *B* was the murderer. Clearly we must at least add that, for *x* to have meant_{NN} anything, not merely must it have been "uttered" with the intention of inducing a certain belief but also the utterer must have intended an "audience" to recognize the intention behind the utterance.

This, though perhaps better, is not good enough. Consider the following cases:

(1) Herod presents Salome with the head of St. John the Baptist on a charger.

(2) Feeling faint, a child lets its mother see how pale it is (hoping that she may draw her own conclusions and help).

(3) I leave the china my daughter has broken lying around for my wife to see.

Here we seem to have cases which satisfy the conditions so far given for meaning_{NN}. For example, Herod intended to make Salome believe that St. John the Baptist was dead and no doubt also intended Salome to recognize that he intended her to believe that St. John the Baptist was dead. Similarly for the other cases. Yet I certainly do not think that we should want to say that we have here cases of meaning_{NN}.

What we want to find is the difference between, for example, "deliberately and openly letting someone know" and "telling" and between "getting someone to think" and "telling."

The way out is perhaps as follows. Compare the following two cases:

(1) I show Mr. *X* a photograph of Mr. *Y* displaying undue familiarity to Mrs. *X*.

(2) I draw a picture of Mr. *Y* behaving in this manner and show it to Mr. *X*.

I find that I want to deny that in (1) the photograph (or my showing it to Mr. *X*) meant_{NN} anything at all; while I want to assert that in (2) the picture (or my drawing and showing it) meant_{NN} something (that Mr. *Y* had been unduly familiar), or at least that I had meant_{NN} by it that Mr. *Y* had been unduly familiar. What is the difference between the two cases? Surely that in case (1) Mr. *X*'s recognition of my intention to make him believe that there is something between Mr. *Y* and Mrs. *X* is (more or less) irrelevant to the production of this effect by the photograph. Mr. *X* would be led by the photograph at least to suspect Mrs. *X* even if, instead of showing it to him, I had left it in his room by accident; and I (the photograph shower) would not be unaware of this. But it will make a difference to the effect of my picture on Mr. *X* whether or not he takes me to be intending to inform him (make him believe something) about Mrs. *X*, and not to be just doodling or trying to produce a work of art.

But now we seem to be landed in a further difficulty if we accept this account. For consider now, say, frowning. If I frown spontaneously, in the ordinary course of events, someone looking at me may well treat the frown as a natural sign of displeasure. But if I frown deliberately (to convey my displeasure), an onlooker may be expected, provided he recognizes my intention, *still* to conclude that I am displeased. Ought we not then to say, since it could not be expected to make any difference to the onlooker's reaction whether he regards my frown as spontaneous or as intended to be informative, that my frown (deliberate) does *not* mean$_{NN}$ anything? I think this difficulty can be met; for though in general a deliberate frown may have the same effect (with respect to inducing belief in my displeasure) as a spontaneous frown, it can be expected to have the same effect only *provided* the audience takes it as intended to convey displeasure. That is, if we take away the recognition of intention, leaving the other circumstances (including the recognition of the frown as deliberate), the belief-producing tendency of the frown must be regarded as being impaired or destroyed.

Perhaps we may sum up what is necessary for *A* to mean something by *x* as follows. *A* must intend to induce by *x* a belief in an audience, and he must also intend his utterance to be recognized as so intended. But these intentions are not independent; the recognition is intended by *A* to play its part in inducing the belief, and if it does not do so something will have gone wrong with the fulfillment of *A*'s intentions. Moreover, *A*'s intending that the recognition should play this part implies, I think, that he assumes that there is some chance that it will in fact play this part, that he does not regard it as a foregone conclusion that the belief will be induced in the audience whether or not the intention behind the utterance is recognized. Shortly, perhaps, we may say that "*A* meant$_{NN}$ something by *x*" is roughly equivalent to "*A* uttered *x* with the intention of inducing a belief by means of the recognition of this intention." (This seems to involve a reflexive paradox, but it does not really do so.)

Now perhaps it is time to drop the pretense that we have to deal only with "informative" cases. Let us start with some examples of imperatives or quasi-imperatives. I have a very avaricious man in my room, and I want him to go; so I throw a pound note out of the window. Is there here any utterance with a meaning$_{NN}$? No, because in behaving as I did, I did not intend his recognition of my purpose to be in any way effective in getting him to go. This is parallel to the photograph case. If, on the other hand, I had pointed to the door or given him a little push, then my behavior might well be held to constitute a meaningful$_{NN}$ utterance, just because the recognition of my intention would be intended by me to be effective in speeding his departure. Another pair of cases would be (1) a policeman who stops a car by standing in its way and (2) a policeman who stops a car by waving.

Or, to turn briefly to another type of case, if, as an examiner, I fail a man, I may well cause him distress or indignation or humiliation; and if I am vindictive, I may intend this effect and even intend him to recognize my intention. But I should not be inclined to say that my failing him meant$_{NN}$ anything. On the other hand, if I cut someone in the street, I do feel inclined to assimilate this to the cases of meaning$_{NN}$, and this inclination seems to me dependent on the fact that I could not reasonably expect him to be distressed (indignant, humiliated) unless he recognized my intention to affect him in this way. If my college stopped my salary altogether, I should accuse them of ruining me; if they cut it by one pound, I might accuse them of insulting me; with some larger cuts I might not know quite what to say.

Perhaps then we may make the following generalizations.

(1) "*A* meant$_{NN}$ something by *x*" is (roughly) equivalent to "*A* intended the utterance of *x* to produce some effect in an audience by means of the recognition of this intention"; and we may add that to ask what *A* meant is to ask for a specification of the intended effect (though, of course, it may not always be possible to get a straight answer involving a "that" clause, for example, "a belief that … ").

(2) "*x* meant something" is (roughly) equivalent to "Somebody meant$_{NN}$ something by *x*." Here again there will be cases where this will not quite work. I feel inclined to say that (as regards traffic lights) the change to red meant$_{NN}$ that the traffic was to stop; but it would be very unnatural to say, "Somebody (e.g. the Corporation) meant$_{NN}$ by the red-light change that the traffic was to stop." Nevertheless, there seems to be *some* sort of reference to somebody's intentions.

(3) "*x* means$_{NN}$ (timeless) that so-and-so" might as a first shot be equated with some statement or disjunction of statements about what "people" (vague) intend (with qualifications about "recognition") to effect by *x*. I shall have a word to say about this.

Will any kind of intended effect do, or may there be cases where an effect is intended (with the required qualifications) and yet we should not want to talk of meaning$_{NN}$? Suppose I discovered some person so constituted that, when I told him that whenever I grunted in a special way I wanted him to blush or to incur some physical malady, thereafter whenever he recognized the grunt (and with it my intention), he did blush or incur the malady. Should we then want to say that the grunt meant$_{NN}$ something? I do not think so. This points to the fact that for *x* to have meaning$_{NN}$, the intended effect must be something which in some sense is within the control of the audience, or that in some sense of "reason" the recognition of the intention behind *x* is for the audience a reason and not merely a cause. It might look as if there is a sort of pun here ("reason for believing" and "reason for doing"), but I do not think this is serious. For though no doubt from one point of view questions about reasons for believing are questions about evidence and so quite different from questions about reasons for doing, nevertheless to recognize an utterer's intention in uttering *x* (descriptive utterance), to have a reason for believing that so-and-so, is at least quite like "having a motive for" accepting so-and-so. Decisions "that" seem to involve decisions "to" (and this is why we can "refuse to believe" and also be "compelled to believe"). (The "cutting" case needs slightly different treatment, for one cannot in any straightforward sense "decide" to be offended; but one can refuse to be offended.) It looks, then, as if the intended effect must be something within the control of the audience, or at least the *sort* of thing which is within its control.

One point before passing to an objection or two. I think it follows that from what I have said about the connection between meaning$_{NN}$ and recognition of intention that (insofar as I am right) only what I may call the primary intention of an utterer is relevant to the meaning$_{NN}$ of an utterance. For if I utter *x*, intending (with the aid of the recognition of this intention) to induce an effect *E*, and intend this effect *E* to lead to a further effect *F*, then insofar as the occurrence of *F* is thought to be dependent solely on *E*, I cannot regard *F* as in the least dependent on recognition of my intention to induce *E*. That is, if (say) I intend to get a man to do something by giving him some information, it cannot be regarded as relevant to the meaning$_{NN}$ of my utterance to describe what I intend him to do.

Now some question may be raised about my use, fairly free, of such words as "intention" and "recognition." I must disclaim any intention of peopling all our talking life with armies of complicated psychological occurrences. I do not hope to solve any philosophical puzzles about intending, but I do want briefly to argue that no special difficulties are raised by my use of the word "intention" in connection with meaning. First, there will be cases where an utterance is accompanied or preceded by a conscious "plan," or explicit formulation of intention (e.g. I declare how I am going to use *x*, or ask myself how to "get something across"). The presence of such an explicit "plan" obviously counts fairly heavily in favor of the utterer's intention (meaning) being as "planned"; though it is not, I think, conclusive; for example, a speaker who has declared an intention to use a familiar expression in an unfamiliar way may slip into the familiar use. Similarly in nonlinguistic cases: if we are asking about an agent's intention, a previous expression counts heavily; nevertheless, a man might plan to throw a letter in the dustbin and yet take it to the post; when lifting his hand, he might "come to" and say *either* "I didn't intend to do this at all" *or* "I suppose I must have been intending to put it in."

Explicitly formulated linguistic (or quasilinguistic) intentions are no doubt comparatively rare. In their absence we would seem to rely on very much the same kinds of criteria as we do in the case of nonlinguistic intentions where there is a general usage. An utterer is held to intend to convey what is normally conveyed (or normally intended to be conveyed), and we require a good reason for accepting that a particular use diverges from the general usage (e.g. he never knew or had forgotten the general usage). Similarly in nonlinguistic cases: we are presumed to intend the normal consequences of our actions.

Again, in cases where there is doubt, say, about which of two or more things an utterer intends to convey, we tend to refer to the context (linguistic or otherwise) of the utterance and ask which of the alternatives would be relevant to other things he is saying or doing, or which intention in a particular situation would fit in with some purpose he obviously has (e.g. a man who calls for a "pump" at a fire would not want a bicycle pump). Nonlinguistic parallels are obvious: context is a criterion in settling the question of why a man who has just put a cigarette in his mouth has put his hand in his pocket; relevance to an obvious end is a criterion in settling why a man is running away from a bull.

In certain linguistic cases we ask the utterer afterward about his intention, and in a few of these cases (the very difficult ones, such as a philosopher being asked to explain the meaning of an unclear passage in one of his works), the answer is not based on what he remembers but is more like a decision, a decision about how what he said is to be taken. I cannot find a nonlinguistic parallel here; but the case is so special as not to seem to contribute a vital difference.

All this is very obvious; but surely to show that the criteria for judging linguistic intentions are very like the criteria for judging nonlinguistic intentions is to show that linguistic intentions are very like nonlinguistic intentions.

Introduction to J. L. Austin

John Langshaw Austin was born in Lancaster, England, in 1911 and (apart from visiting professorships) spent his academic career at Oxford University. Having gone to Balliol College on a Classics scholarship, he received his first exposure to philosophy while studying Greats. He was made a Fellow of All Souls in 1933 and taught at Magdalen, where he was appointed fellow and tutor in 1935. He served in intelligence during the war with such success that he emerged as a lieutenant colonel, with an O.B.E., Croix de Guerre, and as an Officer of the Legion of Merit. He returned to Oxford, where he was appointed White's Professor of Ethics in 1952, a position he held until his death from cancer in 1960.

Given that Austin published little in his lifetime, and given that his influence and reputation have declined considerably in the last couple of decades, it is instructive to recall that Austin once had a stature in British philosophy second only to Wittgenstein, dominating the Oxford scene to the extent that Wittgenstein had done in Cambridge. However, while Wittgenstein is now regarded as a major innovator, on par with Russell, Austin is often considered a figure of primarily historical interest, whose philosophical method constitutes a temporary aberration in the subject.

One exception to the above is in philosophy of language, where his theory of speech acts is acknowledged to be of lasting importance. Austin distinguished (1) the *locutionary* act, of making a meaningful utterance; (2) the *illocutionary* act, what is done by the locutionary act; and (3) the *perlocutionary* act, the effect of your act on an audience. Thus, a student might say to me, "I promise to return your book tomorrow" (locutionary); thereby making a promise (illocutionary); and causing me to believe her (perlocutionary).

When people attack "Oxford philosophy," Austin usually takes most of the heat. He is frequently named as the chief culprit in taking philosophy away from the "big questions," and reducing it to a game of petty linguistic hairsplitting, of the sort that only a classical scholar could play: and all this in the name of ordinary language. Cynics would say that the language of a bunch of upper-middle-class ex-public-school-boys with Firsts in Greats is as far from the language of the mythical "plain man" as the most technical formulations of Russell, Carnap, and company could hope to aspire to.

I choose my words carefully here. The amount of *ad hominem* attacks on "Oxford philosophy" is remarkable for a discipline that prides itself on rational argument. This hostility has its roots in the British class system, as Paul Grice identifies:

> It is possible that some of the animosity directed against so-called "ordinary language philosophy" may have come from people who saw this "movement" as a sinister attempt on the part of a decaying intellectual establishment whose home lay within the ancient walls of Oxford and Cambridge (walls of stone, not of red brick) and whose upbringing was founded on a classical education, to preserve control of philosophy by gearing philosophical practice to the deployment of a proficiency specially accessible to the establishment, namely a highly developed sensitivity to the richness of linguistic usage" (Grandy and Warner, p. 51).

It is common to attribute Austin's dominance as much to his powerful personality as to his philosophical ability. The following quote, from Sir Geoffrey Warnock, one of his closest associates, is typical:

> ... he did succeed in haunting most of the philosophers in England, and to his colleagues it seemed that his terrifying intelligence was never at rest. Many of them used to wake up in the night with a vision of the stringy, wiry Austin standing over their pillow like a bird of prey. Their daylight hours were no better. They would write some philosophical sentences and then read them over as Austin might, in an expressionless, frigid voice, and their blood would run cold. Some of them were so intimidated by the mere fact of his existence that they weren't able to publish a single article during his lifetime (Mehta, p. 56).

However, in sharp contrast, his students are unanimous in remembering his kindness and supportiveness (see George Pitcher, in Berlin [1973]). As an outsider, it seems safest to see him as a natural leader, one of those people to whom everyone instinctively defers.

In considering Austin's methodology, it is worth recalling that a recurring theme in philosophy, at least since Kant, is an embarrassment at the seeming lack of progress in the solving of philosophical problems. Each successive explanation of this alleged impasse is more down-to-earth than the previous ones. For Kant, the mind is constitutionally unequal to the task of metaphysics, as traditionally conceived; for the Positivist, metaphysical claims were meaningless—they couldn't be known because there was nothing there to know; Ryle, Wittgenstein, and Carnap (in various ways) thought that philosophical perplexity was caused by misunderstanding the logic of our language, and by thereby committing category mistakes. For Austin, the lack of progress in philosophy was mostly down to sloppiness and laziness. Like Descartes, he believed that the main source of intellectual error is to prematurely assent to claims which one has failed to check sufficiently thoroughly.

Thus, as we shall soon see, Austin is insistent that the "Argument from Illusion" is a pseudo-problem. He means this not in the way the Positivists did (i.e., as in lacking cognitive meaning or in failing to make any perceivable difference to our experience.) He saw the Argument as being itself an illusion caused by sloppy thinking. That is, there is a degree of contrivance about it, caused by unreflective emphasis on a small set of well-worn examples, and insufficient attention paid to the complexity and variety of actual usage of key concepts. Warnock (1990) lists many of the culprits that Austin identified:

" ... carelessness; haste; a persistent tendency to invent and rely on ill-defined and slippery technical terms; over-simplification; reckless and premature generalization; and, perhaps above all, a predilection for ambitious either-or dichotomies" (p. 7).

"Ordinary language philosophy" is often presented as a straw man, an anemic parody of the actual practice of Austin and his colleagues. Nobody ever said that ordinary usage was sacrosanct; nor that it be the ultimate arbiter of philosophical dispute; nor that philosophers ought to devote their attention exclusively to it. Rather, in the best tradition of British philosophy, (people like Hume, Mill, Russell, and, indeed, his worthy opponent Ayer), Austin attempts to write in clear, plain prose and to avoid armoring it with technicalities. Where he differs from these writers is in a hypersensitivity to all the nuances of ordinary language, and in an explicit belief that any concept that has a well-established use therein will stand a good chance of making a useful distinction, since it arose out of a genuine practice, in contrast to neologisms of technical philosophy. So Austin sets himself explicitly against Russell's well-known taunt that ordinary language merely embodies a Stone Age metaphysics. So for Austin it makes sense, when investigating a philosophical problem, to make sure that you are clear on the common usages of the important concepts involved, before you go on to more specialized usages. These two famous quotes from "A Plea for Excuses" make all this clear:

> First, words are our tools, and, as a minimum, we should use clean tools: we should know what we mean and what we do not, and we must forearm ourselves against the traps that language sets us. Secondly, words are not (except in their own little corner) facts or things: we need therefore to prize them off the world, to hold them apart from and against it, so that we can realize their inadequacies and arbitrariness, and can re-look at the world without blinkers. Thirdly, and more hopefully, our common stock of words embodies all the distinctions men have found worth drawing, and the connexions they have found worth marking, in the lifetimes of many generations: these surely are likely to be more numerous, more sound, since they have stood up to the long test of the survival of the fittest, and more subtle, at least in all ordinary and reasonably practical matters, than any that you or I are likely to think up in our arm-chairs of an afternoon—the most favoured alternative method (*Philosophical Papers*, pp. 181–182).
>
> Certainly ordinary language has no claim to be the last word, if there is such a thing. It embodies, indeed, something better than the metaphysics of the Stone Age, namely, as was said, the inherited experience and acumen of many generations of men. . . . [But] certainly ordinary language is *not* the last word: in principle it can everywhere be supplemented and improved upon and superceded. Only remember, it *is* the *first* word." (Ibid., p. 185)

I give these quotes with some trepidation, since their high profile has inadvertently led to a distorted view of Austin's work. By all accounts, Austin was profoundly distrustful of big general statements about philosophy. It is therefore ironic that his name occurs now mostly in the context of the most general, meta-philosophical discussion. However, as the texts reveal, he offered no "philosophy." That is, he never proceeds from a theoretical standpoint from which all the big questions can be answered (e.g., Empiricism); nor do his various views combine into a complex whole. Rather, his views tend to be (1) *reactive*—that is, attacking a theory or, to be more precise, a particular author's expression of a theory. They are also (2) *miniaturist*—for example, *Sense and Sensibilia* never develops an overall response to Argument from Illusion, nor to the philosophical theories that it is enlisted to support. Rather, he spends considerable time on seemingly small points, such as the enumeration of subtly different usages of key concepts, for example, "looks," "seems" and "appears" (in Section IV). As Warnock (1969) accurately observes, this shows his difference from Wittgenstein and Ryle: While they were concerned with *big* category mistakes, Austin was the master at making extremely fine and subtle distinctions. The only constant in his work is not its philosophical content but his method—his painstaking attention to detail. He is particularly good at indicating cases in which dissimilar items have been grouped together. For example, as the Argument from Illusion runs together illusions and delusions (and all the different types of situations in which either can occur); likewise his differentiation of uses of "looks,"'"seems" and "appears,"'or his acute observations on the functions of "real" (Section VII).

Sense and Sensibilia, is, of course, a pun on his almost-namesake Jane Austen's *Sense and Sensibility*. The book was published posthumously, edited by Geoffrey Warnock from lectures Austin had given at Oxford since 1946, and at Berkeley in 1958. Thus, the final form of expression is often Warnock's, and, as he acknowledges, perhaps Austin would have toned down the sarcasm had he lived to determine its finished form. The main aim of *Sense and Sensibilia* is to mount a critique of the "sense-datum theory" promoted in Ayer's *Foundations of Empirical Knowledge*, including its employment of the Argument from Illusion. This venerable argument goes like this:

Suppose that you believe in a world of material objects. Still, you must grant that things can look different to the way they really are. Thus, a circular plate, when seen from some angles, can look elliptical; you can misidentify objects in bad light, and so forth. Take the former case, where I see something that looks elliptical, but that I believe is round. What, then, am I actually seeing? Not the plate, since it isn't elliptical. Rather, I am having a *sense-datum*, from which (along with various beliefs about how things can look under nonstandard circumstances) I infer that this plate is round. However, this process, by which I directly perceive sense-data, on the basis of which I infer the existence of physical objects, is common to both veridical and erroneous perceptions. It would be absurd to create an ontological split between such cases. Thus, contrary to common belief, noone ever directly perceived physical objects.

This presentation is totally standard, and has been repeated in hundreds of books and thousands of lectures. However, Austin sees it as containing many confusions and unjustified assumptions, causes of philosophical error. The Argument presents us with various sets of dualisms: We have the "plain man," the pre-philosophical *naif*, who believes that he typically perceived a particular ontological class of entities, namely "material objects"; in contrast, "the philosopher" denies this: To him, we actually perceive, or are directly aware of, another ontologically distinct class of things—sense-data—from which we either construct (Phenomenalism) or infer (Indirect Realism) the existence of an external world of material objects; the philosopher then draws a corresponding epistemological difference—knowledge of the former is incorrigible, whereas that of the latter is fallible.

Austin responds that these "bogus dichotomies" oversimplify and distort the way things really are. Take the distinction between what the plain man and the philosopher believe. Austin rejects the claim that people generally believe that they directly perceive a particular sort of thing, a material object. First, he goes beyond the cliched examples (sticks in water, etc.) and emphasizes the heterogeneity of the commonplace world: In what sense are rainbows, shadows, clouds, the same sort of thing—a material object? Obviously, one might reply that they all fall under the laws of physics. Austin wouldn't deny this, but that's not his point. He would reply that this shows that "material object," no less than "sense-data," is a technical term. It occurs only at a high level of abstraction—either as a foil for "sense-data" or as a fundamental category of physical science. In neither case does it have a clear use in everyday discourse. Turning now to the other, opposed category, sense-data, it is by no means clear that this is a well-defined concept. I take it that Austin means that we await principled answers to questions like the following: How do you count sense-data? That is, when is one sense-datum, rather than two, present? How do you classify sense-data? That is, when are *x* and *y* the same kind of sense-data? and so on.

He continues, in Section X, to argue that it is misleading to set up a strict either–or distinction between sentences expressing incorrigible judgments about sense-data, and fallible claims about material objects. Austin says that *statements,* not sentences, are either incorrigible or not, and this is heavily dependent on who says it, where, and when. To see what he means, take these two cases:

1. *Someone who is unsure of color-words, who utters, "I am having a sensation of magenta"*;

2. *A farmer looks into a field, and says, "That beast is a Jersey cow."*

Austin would say that 2 is on firmer epistemological ground, despite the fact that it makes a claim about the physical world, yet 1 refers only to sense-data.

While Austin has nothing against technical terms in principle, he demands at least the standards of clarity that are available (to a well-trained mind) in ordinary language. In particular, he urges vigilance regarding cases in which a technical term may try to pass as a commonplace and philosophically neutral term, for example "material object," or the dichotomy between what is "directly" or "indirectly" perceived.

Austin regarded philosophy as an activity, something that one primarily *did,* rather than wrote about. His principle activities were teaching and group discussion. As with the Positivists, scrupulous attention was given to "the facts." However, for Austin, these did not primarily consist of scientific data, but facts about the ordinary uses of words. Famously (or infamously) when undertaking a philosophical analysis of a certain subject, he would list the important concepts, then get his dictionary and record all the nontechnical uses of the terms. This, of course, was never intended to be the last word, but the first word. However, there is some truth in the charge that Austin never (or very rarely) got beyond the first word, nor showed much interest in doing so. This criticism is often allied with the accusation that he would tear everyone else's arguments to bits, with painstaking attention to detail, but never offer anything constructive in its place. As his friend Sir Isaiah Berlin once exclaimed, "You are like a greyhound that refuses to race but bites the other greyhounds to prevent their racing either" (see Ayer [1977], p. 160).

One is always left with the suspicion that Austin's impact on the problems of epistemology and mind does not cut that deep. His responses to Ayer strike me as primarily "editorial." That is, he goes over the prose with a fine tooth-comb, exposing inadequacies of expression, sloppiness of argument, and the like. While he is mostly correct in what he says, the feeling remains that Ayer (or someone else) can go back, reformulate his position more carefully, and the "problems of philosophy" are back, not dissolved, but renewed.

On the other hand, perhaps Austin would be content with this. He was adamant that philosophy should be a cooperative activity. Whereas the Positivists are praised for adopting collectivist working practices (and thereby behaving like good scientists), in Austin's case it is dismissed as a mere eccentricity. However, as Warnock plausibly comments, Austin's war experiences proved to him that large problems can often be solved by being broken down into a set of smaller, more manageable problems, each delegated to groups of specially trained personnel. He was of the opinion that such a project would be well worth trying in philosophy. It seemed common sense to him that if a thesis could be assented to by a diverse set of serious and informed persons, then it stood a strong chance of being correct. This project, of course, never got off the ground. Still, it does give us another way of reading what Austin was trying to do in these lectures. Perhaps he was just utilizing his unique skills to make his own contribution to the wider cooperative project of philosophy. Recall that he had no principled objection to Phenomenalism (or any other "ism" for that matter), but only to what he thought to be inadequate presentations of it. Thus, while it is true that Austin never offers a detailed philosophical theory of perception to replace that of Ayer, and ignores all psychological and physiological details, this would be a criticism only if he meant to produce a grand theory. He did not—that would involve the work of many specialists, most of whom were not he.

So how should we view Austin? I believe that the most favorable way is this: He never said that his was the only way to do philosophy. Given the unclarity that he thought to be typically at the root of philosophical problems, he believed that it would be premature, and therefore unwise, to claim to know in advance how they are to be solved. So, the more ways, the better. Austin has given us another way to do philosophy. He has expanded the philosophers' palette. His methods might solve some problems or contribute to doing so.

BIBLIOGRAPHY

Works by Austin

Austin's work is collected in three volumes, all published posthumously by Oxford University Press: *Philosophical Papers*, 1970; *Sense and Sensibilia*, 1962; and *How to Do Things with Words*, 1962 (on his theory of speech acts).

Further Reading

The only full-length study of Austin is Geoffrey Warnock, *J. L Austin* (London: Routledge, 1990).

K. T. Fann, ed. *A Symposium of John Austin* (London: Routledge, 1969); and Isaiah Berlin, ed., *J. L. Austin* (Oxford: Clarendon Press, 1973), both combine philosophical papers with personal reminiscences of Austin.

Sense and Sensibilia is a response to A.J. Ayer, *The Foundations of Empirical Knowledge*, (New York: St. Martin's Press, 1955). For Ayer's reply to Austin, see "Has Austin Refuted the Sense-Datum Theory?"*Synthese*, Vol. XVII, 1967.

The Grice quote is from his contribution to Richard E. Grandy and Richard Warner, *Philosophical Grounds of Rationality* (Oxford: Clarendon Press, 1986).

Other books mentioned were

A.J. Ayer, *Part of My Life* (Oxford: Oxford University Press, 1977).

Ved Mehta, *Fly and the Fly-Bottle* (New York: Penguin, 1965).

Geoffrey Warnock, *English Philosophy Since 1900* (Oxford: Oxford University Press, 1969).

Selections from *Sense and Sensibilia*

J. L. Austin

II

Let us have a look, then, at the very beginning of Ayer's *Foundations*—the bottom, one might perhaps call it, of the garden path. In these paragraphs[1] we already seem to see the plain man, here under the implausible aspect of Ayer himself, dribbling briskly into position in front of his own goal, and squaring up to encompass his own destruction.

> It does not normally occur to us that there is any need for us to justify our belief in the existence of material things. At the present moment, for example, I have no doubt whatsoever that I really am perceiving the familiar objects, the chairs and table, the pictures and books and flowers with which my room is furnished; and I am therefore satisfied that they exist. I recognize indeed that people are sometimes deceived by their senses, but this does not lead me to suspect that my own sense-perceptions cannot in general be trusted, or even that they may be deceiving me now. And this is not, I believe, an exceptional attitude. I believe that, in practice, most people agree with John Locke that 'the certainty of things existing *in rerum natura*, when we have the testimony of our senses for it, is not only as great as our frame can attain to, but as our condition needs'.
>
> When, however, one turns to the writings of those philosophers who have recently concerned themselves with the subject of perception, one may begin to wonder whether this matter is quite so simple. It is true that they do, in general, allow that our belief in the existence of material things is well founded; some of them, indeed, would say that there were occasions on which we knew for certain the truth of such propositions as 'this is a cigarette' or 'this is a pen'. But even so they are not, for the most part, prepared to admit that such objects as pens or cigarettes are ever directly perceived. What, in their opinion, we directly perceive is always an object of a different kind from these; one to which it is now customary to give the name of 'sense-datum'.

Now in this passage some sort of contrast is drawn between what we (or the ordinary man) believe (or believes), and what philosophers, at least 'for the most part', believe or are 'prepared to admit'. We must look at both sides of this contrast, and with particular care at what is assumed in, and implied by, what is actually said. The ordinary man's side, then, first.

1. It is clearly implied, first of all, that the ordinary man believes that he perceives material things. Now this, at least if it is taken to mean that he would *say* that

---

Reprinted from *Sense and Sensibilia*, (Oxford: Oxford University Press, 1962). Reprinted by permission of Oxford University Press.

[1] A. J. Ayer, *Foundations of Empirical Knowledge* (London: Macmillan, 1940).

he perceives material things, is surely wrong straight off; for 'material thing' is not an expression which the ordinary man would use—nor, probably, is 'perceive'. Presumably, though, the expression 'material thing' is here put forward, not as what the ordinary man would *say*, but as designating in a general way the *class* of things of which the ordinary man both believes and from time to time says that he perceives particular instances. But then we have to ask, of course, what this class comprises. We are given, as examples, 'familiar objects'—chairs, tables, pictures, books, flowers, pens, cigarettes; the expression 'material thing' is not here (or anywhere else in Ayer's text) further defined.[1] But *does* the ordinary man believe that what he perceives is (always) something like furniture, or like these other 'familiar objects'—moderate-sized specimens of dry goods? We may think, for instance, of people, people's voices, rivers, mountains, flames, rainbows, shadows, pictures on the screen at the cinema, pictures in books or hung on walls, vapours, gases—all of which people say that they see or (in some cases) hear or smell, i.e. 'perceive'. Are these all 'material things'? If not, exactly which are not, and exactly why? No answer is vouchsafed. The trouble is that the expression 'material thing' is functioning *already*, from the very beginning, simply as a foil for 'sense-datum'; it is not here given, and is never given, any other role to play, and apart from this consideration it would surely never have occurred to anybody to try to represent as some single *kind of things* the things which the ordinary man says that he 'perceives'.

2. Further, it seems to be also implied (*a*) that when the ordinary man believes that he is not perceiving material things, he believes he is being deceived by his senses; and (*b*) that when he believes he is being deceived by his senses, he believes that he is not perceiving material things. But both of these are wrong. An ordinary man who saw, for example, a rainbow would not, if persuaded that a rainbow is not a material thing, at once conclude that his senses were deceiving him; nor, when for instance he knows that the ship at sea on a clear day is much farther away than it looks, does he conclude that he is not seeing a material thing (still less that he *is* seeing an immaterial ship). That is to say, there is no more a simple contrast between what the ordinary man believes when all is well (that he is 'perceiving material things') and when something is amiss (that his 'senses are deceiving him' and he is *not* 'perceiving material things') than there is between what he believes that he perceives ('material things') and what philosophers for their part are prepared to admit, whatever that may be. The ground is already being prepared for *two* bogus dichotomies.

3. Next, is it not rather delicately hinted in this passage that the plain man is really a bit naive?[2] It 'does not normally occur' to him that his belief in 'the existence of material things' needs justifying—but perhaps it *ought* to occur to him. He has 'no doubt whatsoever' that he really perceives chairs and tables—but perhaps he ought to have a doubt or two and not be so easily 'satisfied'. That people are sometimes

---

[1] Compare Price's list on p. 1 of *Perception*—'chairs and tables, cats and rocks'—though he complicates matters by adding 'water' and 'the earth'. See also p. 280, on 'physical objects', 'visuo-tactual solids'.

[2] H. H. Price, *Perception* (London: Methuen, 1932), p. 26, says that he *is* naive, though it is not, it seems, certain that he is actually a Naive Realist.

deceived by their senses 'does not lead him to suspect' that all may not be well—but perhaps a more reflective person *would* be led to suspect. Though ostensibly the plain man's position is here just being described, a little quiet undermining is already being effected by these turns of phrase.

4. But, perhaps more importantly, it is also implied, even taken for granted, that there is *room* for doubt and suspicion, whether or not the plain man feels any. The quotation from Locke, with which most people are said to agree, in fact contains a strong *suggestio falsi*. It suggests that when, for instance, I look at a chair a few yards in front of me in broad daylight, my view is that I have (*only*) as much certainty as I need and can get that there is a chair and that I see it. But in fact the plain man would regard doubt in such a case, not as far-fetched or over-refined or somehow unpractical, but as plain *nonsense*; he would say, quite correctly, 'Well, if that's not seeing a real chair then *I don't know what is.*' Moreover, though the plain man's alleged belief that his 'sense-perceptions' can 'in general' or 'now' be trusted is implicitly contrasted with the philosophers' view, it turns out that the philosophers' view is not just that his sense-perceptions *can't* be trusted 'now', or 'in general', or as often as he thinks; for apparently philosophers 'for the most part' really maintain that what the plain man believes to be the case is really *never* the case—'what, in their opinion, we directly perceive is *always* an object of a different kind'. The philosopher is not really going to argue that things go wrong more often than the unwary plain man supposes, but that in some sense or some way he is wrong all the time. So it is misleading to hint, not only that there is always room for doubt, but that the philosophers' dissent from the plain man is just a matter of degree; it is really not *that* kind of disagreement at all.

5. Consider next what is said here about deception. We recognize, it is said, that 'people are sometimes deceived by their senses', though we think that, in general, our 'sense-perceptions' can 'be trusted'.

Now first, though the phrase 'deceived by our senses' is a common metaphor, it *is* a metaphor; and this is worth noting, for in what follows the same metaphor is frequently taken up by the expression 'veridical' and taken very seriously. In fact, of course, our senses are dumb—though Descartes and others speak of 'the testimony of the senses', our senses do not *tell* us anything, true or false. The case is made much worse here by the unexplained introduction of a quite new creation, our 'sense-perceptions'. These entities, which of course don't really figure at all in the plain man's language or among his beliefs, are brought in with the implication that whenever we 'perceive' there is an *intermediate* entity *always* present and *informing* us about something else—the question is, can we or can't we trust what it says? Is it 'veridical'? But of course to state the case in this way is simply to soften up the plain man's alleged views for the subsequent treatment; it is preparing the way for, by practically attributing to *him*, the so-called philosophers' view.

Next, it is important to remember that talk of deception only *makes sense* against a background of general non-deception. (You can't fool all of the people all of the time.) It must be possible to *recognize* a case of deception by checking the odd case against more normal ones. If I say, 'Our petrol-gauge sometimes deceives us', I am understood: though usually what it indicates squares with what we have in the tank, sometimes it doesn't—it sometimes points to two gallons when the tank turns out to be nearly empty. But suppose I say, 'Our crystal ball sometimes deceives us': this is puzzling, because really we haven't the least idea what the 'normal' case—not being deceived by our crystal ball—would actually be.

The cases, again, in which a plain man might say he was 'deceived by his senses' are not at all common. In particular, he would *not* say this when confronted with ordinary cases of perspective, with ordinary mirror-images, or with dreams; in fact, when he dreams, looks down the long straight road, or at his face in the mirror, he is not, or at least is hardly ever, *deceived* at all. This is worth remembering in view of another strong *suggestio falsi*—namely, that when the philosopher cites as cases of 'illusion' all these and many other very common phenomena, he is either simply mentioning cases which the plain man already concedes as cases of 'deception by the senses', or at any rate is only extending a bit what he would readily concede. In fact this is very far indeed from being the case.

And even so—even though the plain man certainly does not accept anything like so *many* cases as cases of being 'deceived by his senses' as philosophers seem to—it would certainly be quite wrong to suggest that he regards all the cases he *does* accept as being of just the same kind. The battle is, in fact, half lost already if this suggestion is tolerated. Sometimes the plain man would prefer to say that his senses were deceived rather than that he was deceived by his senses—the quickness of the hand deceives the eye, &c. But there is actually a great multiplicity of cases here, at least at the edges of which it is no doubt uncertain (and it would be typically scholastic to try to decide) just which are and which are not cases where the metaphor of being 'deceived by the senses' would naturally be employed. But surely even the plainest of men would want to distinguish (*a*) cases where the *sense-organ* is deranged or abnormal or in some way or other not functioning properly; (*b*) cases where the *medium*—or more generally, the conditions—of perception are in some way abnormal or off-colour; and (*c*) cases where a wrong inference is made or a wrong construction is put on things, e.g. on some sound that he hears. (Of course these cases do not exclude each other.) And then again there are the quite common cases of misreadings, mishearings, Freudian over-sights, &c., which don't seem to belong properly under any of these headings. That is to say, once again there is no neat and simple dichotomy between things going right and things going wrong; things may go wrong, as we really all know quite well, in lots of *different* ways—which don't have to be, and must not be assumed to be, classifiable in any general fashion.

Finally, to repeat here a point we've already mentioned, of course the plain man does *not* suppose that all the cases in which he is 'deceived by his senses' are alike in the particular respect that, in those cases, he is not 'perceiving material things', or *is* perceiving something not real or not material. Looking at the Müller-Lyer diagram (in which, of two lines of equal length, one looks longer than the other), or at a distant village on a very clear day across a valley, is a very different kettle of fish from seeing a ghost or from having D.T.s and seeing pink rats. And when the plain man sees on the stage the Headless Woman, what he sees (and this *is* what he sees, whether he knows it or not) is not something 'unreal' or 'immaterial', but a woman against a dark background with her head in a black bag. If the trick is well done, he doesn't (because it's deliberately made very difficult for him) properly size up what he sees, or see *what* it is; but to say this is far from concluding that he sees something *else*.

In conclusion, then, there is less than no reason to swallow the suggestions *either* that what the plain man believes that he perceives most of the time constitutes a *kind* of things (*sc.* 'material objects'), *or* that he can be said to recognize any other single *kind* of cases in which he is 'deceived'.[1] Now let us consider what it is that is said about philosophers.

Philosophers, it is said, 'are not, for the most part, prepared to admit that such objects as pens or cigarettes are ever directly perceived'. Now of course what brings us up short here is the word 'directly'—a great favourite among philosophers, but actually one of the less conspicuous snakes in the linguistic grass. We have here, in fact, a typical case of a word, which already has a very special use, being gradually stretched, without caution or definition or any limit, until it becomes, first perhaps obscurely metaphorical, but ultimately meaningless. One can't abuse ordinary language without paying for it.[2]

1. First of all, it is essential to realize that here the notion of perceiving *indirectly* wears the trousers 'directly' takes whatever sense it has from the contrast with its opposite:[3] while 'indirectly' itself (*a*) has a use only in special cases, and also (*b*) has *different* uses in different cases—though that doesn't mean, of course, that there is not a good reason why we should use the same word. We might, for example, contrast the man who saw the procession directly with the man who saw it *through a periscope*; or we might contrast the place from which you can watch the door directly with the place from which you can see it only *in the mirror. Perhaps* we might contrast seeing you directly with seeing, say, your shadow on the blind; and *perhaps* we might contrast hearing the music directly with hearing it relayed outside the concert-hall. However, these last two cases suggest two further points.

2. The first of these points is that the notion of not perceiving 'directly' seems most at home where, as with the periscope and the mirror, it retains its link with the notion of a kink in *direction*. It seems that we must not be looking *straight at* the object in question. For this reason seeing your shadow on the blind is a doubtful case; and seeing you, for instance, through binoculars or spectacles is certainly not a case of seeing you *indirectly* at all. For such cases as these last we have quite distinct contrasts and different expressions—'with the naked eye' as opposed to 'with a telescope', 'with unaided vision' as opposed to 'with glasses on'. (These expressions, in fact, are much more firmly established in ordinary use than 'directly' is.)

3. And the other point is that, partly no doubt for the above reason, the notion of indirect perception is not naturally at home with senses other than sight. With the

---

[1] I am not denying that cases in which things go wrong *could* be lumped together under some single name. A single name might in itself be innocent enough, provided its use was not taken to imply either (*a*) that the cases were all alike, or (*b*) that they were all in certain ways alike. What matters is that the facts should not be pre-judged and (therefore) neglected.

[2] Especially if one abuses it without realizing what one is doing. Consider the trouble caused by unwitting stretching of the word 'sign', so as to yield—apparently—the conclusion that, when the cheese *is* in front of our noses, we see *signs* of cheese.

[3] Compare, in this respect, 'real', 'proper', 'free', and plenty of others. 'It's real'—what exactly are you saying it isn't? 'I wish we had a proper stair-carpet'—what are you complaining of in the one you've got? (That it's *improper*?) 'Is he free?'—well, what have you in mind that he might be instead? In prison? Tied up in prison? Committed to a prior engagement?

other senses there is nothing quite analogous with the 'line of vision'. The most natural sense of 'hearing indirectly', of course, is that of being *told* something by an intermediary—a quite different matter. But do I hear a shout indirectly, when I hear the echo? If I touch you with a barge-pole, do I touch you indirectly? Or if you offer me a pig in a poke, might I feel the pig indirectly—*through* the poke? And what smelling indirectly might be I have simply no idea. For this reason alone there seems to be something badly wrong with the question, 'Do we perceive things directly or not?', where perceiving is evidently intended to cover the employment of *any* of the senses.

4. But it is, of course, for other reasons too extremely doubtful how far the notion of perceiving indirectly could or should be extended. Does it, or should it, cover the telephone, for instance? Or television? Or radar? Have we moved too far in these cases from the original metaphor? They at any rate satisfy what seems to be a necessary condition—namely, concurrent existence and concomitant variation as between what is perceived in the straightforward way (the sounds in the receiver, the picture and the blips on the screen) and the candidate for what we might be prepared to describe as being perceived indirectly. And this condition fairly clearly rules out as cases of indirect perception seeing photographs (which statically record scenes from the past) and seeing films (which, though not static, are not seen contemporaneously with the events thus recorded). Certainly, there *is* a line to be drawn somewhere. It is certain, for instance, that we should not be prepared to speak of indirect perception in *every* case in which we see something from which the existence (or occurrence) of something else can be inferred; we should *not* say we see the guns indirectly, if we see in the distance only the flashes of guns.

5. Rather differently, if we are to be seriously inclined to speak of something as being perceived indirectly, it seems that it has to be the kind of thing which we (sometimes at least) just perceive, or could perceive, or which—like the backs of our own heads—others could perceive. For otherwise we don't want to say that we perceive the thing *at all*, even indirectly. No doubt there are complications here (raised, perhaps, by the electron microscope, for example, about which I know little or nothing). But it seems clear that, in general, we should want to distinguish between seeing indirectly, e.g. in a mirror, what we might have just *seen*, and seeing signs (or effects), e.g. in a Wilson cloud-chamber, of something not itself perceptible at all. It would at least not come naturally to speak of the latter as a case of perceiving something indirectly.

6. And one final point. For reasons not very obscure, we always prefer in practice what might be called the *cash-value* expression to the 'indirect' metaphor. If I were to report that I see enemy ships indirectly, I should merely provoke the question what exactly I mean. 'I mean that I can see these blips on the radar screen'— 'Well, why didn't you say so then?' (Compare 'I can see an unreal duck.'—'What on earth do you mean? It's a decoy duck'—'Ah, I see. Why didn't you say so at once ?') That is, there is seldom if ever any particular point in actually saying 'indirectly' (or 'unreal'); the expression can cover too many rather different cases to be *just* what is wanted in any particular case.

Thus, it is quite plain that the philosophers' use of 'directly perceive', whatever it may be, is not the ordinary, or any familiar, use; for in *that* use it is not only false but simply absurd to say that such objects as pens or cigarettes are never perceived directly. But we are given no explanation or definition of this new use[1]—on the contrary, it is glibly trotted out as if we were all quite familiar with it already. It is clear, too, that the philosophers' use, whatever it may be, offends against several of the canons just mentioned above—no restrictions whatever seem to be envisaged to any special circumstances or to any of the senses in particular, and moreover it seems that what we are to be said to perceive indirectly is *never*—is not the kind of thing which ever *could* be—perceived directly.

All this lends poignancy to the question Ayer himself asks, a few lines below the passage we have been considering: 'Why may we not say that we are directly aware of material things?' The answer, he says, is provided 'by what is known as the argument from illusion'; and this is what we must next consider. Just possibly the answer may help us to understand the question.

III

The primary purpose of the argument from illusion is to induce people to accept 'sense-data' as the proper and correct answer to the question what they perceive on certain *abnormal, exceptional* occasions; but in fact it is usually followed up with another bit of argument intended to establish that they *always* perceive sense-data. Well, what is the argument?

In Ayer's statement[2] it runs as follows. It is 'based on the fact that material things may present different appearances to different observers, or to the same observer in different conditions, and that the character of these appearances is to some extent causally determined by the state of the conditions and the observer'. As illustrations of this alleged fact Ayer proceeds to cite perspective ('a coin which looks circular from one point of view may look elliptical from another'); refraction ('a stick which normally appears straight looks bent when it is seen in water'); changes in colour-vision produced by drugs ('such as mescal'); mirror-images; double vision; hallucination; apparent variations in tastes; variations in felt warmth ('according as the hand that is feeling it is itself hot or cold'); variations in felt bulk ('a coin seems larger when it is placed on the tongue than when it is held in the palm of the hand'); and the oft-cited fact that 'people who have had limbs amputated may still continue to feel pain in them'.

He then selects three of these instances for detailed treatment. First, refraction—the stick which normally 'appears straight' but 'looks bent' when seen in water. He makes the 'assumptions' (*a*) that the stick does not *really change its shape* when it is placed in water, and (*b*) that it *cannot be* both crooked and straight.[3] He then concludes ('it follows') that 'at least one of the *visual appearances* of the stick is *delusive*'. Nevertheless, even when 'what we see is not the *real quality* of a *material*

---

[1] Ayer takes note of this, rather belatedly, on pp. 60–61.

[2] Ayer, op. cit., pp. 3–5.

[3] It is not only strange, but also important, that Ayer calls these 'assumptions'. Later on he is going to take seriously the notion of denying at least one of them, which he could hardly do if he had recognized them here as the plain and incontestable facts that they are.

thing, it is supposed that we are still seeing something'—and this something is to be called a 'sense-datum'. A sense-datum is to be 'the object of which we are *directly* aware, in perception, if it is not *part* of any *material thing*'. (The italics are mine throughout this and the next two paragraphs.)

Next, mirages. A man who sees a mirage, he says, is 'not perceiving any material thing; for the oasis which he thinks he is perceiving *does not exist*'. But 'his *experience* is not an experience of nothing'; thus 'it is said that he is experiencing sense-data, which are similar in character to what he would be experiencing if he were seeing a real oasis, but are delusive in the sense that *the material thing which they appear to present* is not *really there*'.

Lastly, reflections. When I look at myself in a mirror 'my body *appears to be* some distance behind the glass'; but it cannot actually be in two places at once; thus, my perceptions in this case 'cannot all be *veridical*'. But I do see *something*; and if 'there really is no such material thing as my body in the place where it appears to be, what is it that I am seeing?' Answer—a sense-datum. Ayer adds that 'the same conclusion may be reached by taking any other of my examples'.

Now I want to call attention, first of all, to the name of this argument—the 'argument from *illusion*', and to the fact that it is produced as establishing the conclusion that some at least of our 'perceptions' are *delusive*. For in this there are two clear implications—(*a*) that all the cases cited in the argument are cases of *illusions*; and (*b*) that *illusion* and *delusion* are the same thing. But both of these implications, of course, are quite wrong; and it is by no means unimportant to point this out, for, as we shall see, the argument trades on confusion at just this point.

What, then, would be some genuine examples of illusion? (The fact is that hardly any of the cases cited by Ayer is, at any rate without stretching things, a case of illusion at all.) Well, first, there are some quite clear cases of *optical* illusion—for instance the case we mentioned earlier in which, of two lines of equal length, one is made to look longer than the other. Then again there are illusions produced by professional 'illusionists', conjurors—for instance the Headless Woman on the stage, who is made to look headless, or the ventriloquist's dummy which is made to appear to be talking. Rather different—not (usually) produced on purpose—is the case where wheels rotating rapidly enough in one direction may look as if they were rotating quite slowly in the opposite direction. Delusions, on the other hand, are something altogether different from this. Typical cases would be delusions of persecution, delusions of grandeur. These are primarily a matter of grossly disordered beliefs (and so, probably, behaviour) and may well have nothing in particular to do with perception.[1] But I think we might also say that the patient who sees pink rats has (suffers from) delusions—particularly, no doubt, if, as would probably be the case, he is not clearly aware that his pink rats aren't real rats.[2]

The most important differences here are that the term 'an illusion' (in a perceptual context) does not suggest that something totally unreal is *conjured up*—on

---

[1] The latter point holds, of course, for *some* uses of 'illusion' too; there are the illusions which some people (are said to) lose as they grow older and wiser.

[2] Cp. the white rabbit in the play called *Harvey*.

the contrary, there just is the arrangement of lines and arrows on the page, the woman on the stage with her head in a black bag, the rotating wheels; whereas the term 'delusion' *does* suggest something totally unreal, not really there at all. (The convictions of the man who has delusions of persecution can be *completely* without foundation.) For this reason delusions are a much more serious matter—something is really wrong, and what's more, wrong *with* the person who has them. But when I see an optical illusion, however well it comes off, there is nothing wrong with me personally, the illusion is not a little (or a large) peculiarity or idiosyncrasy of my own; it is quite public, anyone can see it, and in many cases standard procedures can be laid down for producing it. Furthermore, if we are not actually to be taken in, we need to be *on our guard*; but it is no use to tell the sufferer from delusions to be on his guard. He needs to be cured.

Why is it that we tend—if we do—to confuse illusions with delusions? Well, partly, no doubt the terms are often used loosely. But there is also the point that people may have, without making this explicit, different views or theories about the facts of some cases. Take the case of seeing a ghost, for example. It is not generally known, or agreed, what seeing ghosts *is*. Some people think of seeing ghosts as a case of something being conjured up, perhaps by the disordered nervous system of the victim; so in their view seeing ghosts is a case of delusion. But other people have the idea that what is called seeing ghosts is a case of being taken in by shadows, perhaps, or reflections, or a trick of the light—that is, they assimilate the case in their minds to illusion. In this way, seeing ghosts, for example, may come to be labelled sometimes as 'delusion', sometimes as 'illusion'; and it may not be noticed that it makes a difference which label we use. Rather, similarly, there seem to be different doctrines in the field as to what mirages are. Some seem to take a mirage to be a vision conjured up by the crazed brain of the thirsty and exhausted traveller (delusion), while in other accounts it is a case of atmospheric refraction, whereby something below the horizon is made to appear above it (illusion). (Ayer, you may remember, takes the delusion view, although he cites it along with the rest as a case of illusion. He says not that the oasis appears to be where it is not, but roundly that 'it does not exist'.)

The way in which the 'argument from illusion' positively trades on not distinguishing illusions from delusions is, I think, this. So long as it is being suggested that the cases paraded for our attention are cases of *illusion*, there is the implication (from the ordinary use of the word) that there really is something there that we perceive. But then, when these cases begin to be quietly called delusive, there comes in the very different suggestion of something being conjured up, something unreal or at any rate 'immaterial'. These two implications taken together may then subtly insinuate that in the cases cited there really is something that we are perceiving, but that this is an immaterial something; and this insinuation, even if not conclusive by itself, is certainly well calculated to edge us a little closer towards just the position where the sense-datum theorist wants to have us.

So much, then—though certainly there could be a good deal more—about the differences between illusions and delusions and the reasons for not obscuring them. Now let us look briefly at some of the other cases Ayer lists. Reflections, for instance. No doubt you *can* produce illusions with mirrors, suitably disposed. But is just *any* case of seeing something in a mirror an illusion, as he implies? Quite obviously not. For seeing things in mirrors is a perfectly *normal* occurrence, completely familiar, and there is usually no question of anyone being taken in. No doubt, if you're an infant or an aborigine and have never come across a mirror before, you may be pretty baffled, and even visibly perturbed, when you do. But is that a reason why the rest of us should speak of illusion here? And just the same goes for the phenomena of perspective—again, one *can* play tricks with perspective, but in the ordinary case there is no question of illusion. That a round coin should 'look elliptical' (in one sense) from some points of view is exactly what we expect and what we normally find; indeed, we should be badly put out if we ever found this not to be so. Refraction again—the stick that looks bent in water—is far too familiar a case to be properly called a case of illusion. We may perhaps be prepared to agree that the stick looks bent; but then we can see that it's partly submerged in water, so that is exactly how we should expect it to look.

It is important to realize here how familiarity, so to speak, takes the edge off illusion. Is the cinema a case of illusion? Well, just possibly the first man who ever saw moving pictures may have felt inclined to say that here was a case of illusion. But in fact it's pretty unlikely that even he, even momentarily, was actually taken in; and by now the whole thing is so ordinary a part of our lives that it never occurs to us even to raise the question. One might as well ask whether producing a photograph is producing an illusion—which would plainly be just silly.

Then we must not overlook, in all this talk about illusions and delusions, that there are plenty of more or less unusual cases, not yet mentioned, which certainly aren't either. Suppose that a proof-reader makes a mistake—he fails to notice that what ought to be 'causal' is printed as 'casual'; does he have a delusion? Or is there an illusion before him? Neither, of course; he simply *misreads*. Seeing after-images, too, though not a particularly frequent occurrence and not just an ordinary case of see-ing, is neither seeing illusions nor having delusions. And what about dreams? Does the dreamer see illusions? Does he have delusions? Neither; dreams are *dreams*.

Let us turn for a moment to what Price has to say about illusions. He pro-duces,[1] by way of saying 'what the term "illusion" means', the following 'provision-al definition': 'An illusory sense-datum of sight or touch is a sense-datum which is such that we tend to take it to be part of the surface of a material object, but if we take it so we are wrong.' It is by no means clear, of course, what this dictum itself means; but still, it seems fairly clear that the definition doesn't actually fit all the cases of illusion. Consider the two lines again. Is there anything here which we tend to take, wrongly, to be part of the surface of a material object? It doesn't seem so. We just see the two lines, we don't think or even tend to think that we see anything else, we aren't even raising the question whether anything is or isn't 'part of the surface' of—what, anyway? the lines? the page?—the trouble is just that one line looks longer than the other, though it isn't. Nor surely, in the case of the Headless Woman, is it a question whether anything is or isn't part of her surface; the trouble is just that she looks as if she had no head.

---

[1] *Perception*, p. 27.

It is noteworthy, of course, that, before he even begins to consider the 'argument from illusion', Price has already incorporated in this 'definition' the idea that in such cases there is something to be seen *in addition to* the ordinary things—which is part of what the argument is commonly used, and not uncommonly taken, to *prove*. But this idea surely has no place in an attempt to say what 'illusion' *means*. It comes in again, improperly I think, in his account of perspective (which incidentally he also cites as a species of illusion)—'a distant hillside which is full of protuberances, and slopes upwards at quite a gentle angle, will appear flat and vertical. ... This means that the sense-datum, the colour-expanse which we sense, actually *is* flat and vertical.' But why should we accept this account of the matter? Why should we say that there is *anything* we see which *is* flat and vertical, though not 'part of the surface' of any material object? To speak thus is to assimilate all such cases to cases of delusion, where there *is* something not 'part of any material thing.' But we have already discussed the undesirability of this assimilation.

Next, let us have a look at the account Ayer himself gives of some at least of the cases he cites. (In fairness we must remember here that Ayer has a number of quite substantial reservations of his own about the merits and efficacy of the argument from illusion, so that it is not easy to tell just how seriously he intends his exposition of it to be taken; but this is a point we shall come back to.)

First, then, the familiar case of the stick in water. Of this case Ayer says (*a*) that since the stick looks bent but is straight, 'at least one of the visual appearances of the stick is *delusive*'; and (*b*) that 'what we see [directly anyway] is not the real quality of [a few lines later, not part of] a material thing'. Well now: does the stick 'look bent' to begin with? I think we can agree that it does, we have no better way of describing it. But of course it does *not* look *exactly* like a bent stick, a bent stick out of water— at most, it may be said to look rather like a bent stick partly immersed *in* water. After all, we can't help seeing the water the stick is partly immersed in. So exactly what in this case is supposed to be *delusive*? What is wrong, what is even faintly surprising, in the idea of a stick's being straight but looking bent sometimes? Does anyone suppose that if something is straight, then it jolly well has to *look* straight at all times and in all circumstances? Obviously no one seriously supposes this. So what mess are we supposed to get into here, what is the difficulty? For of course it has to be suggested that there *is* a difficulty—a difficulty, furthermore, which calls for a pretty radical solution, the introduction of sense-data. But what is the problem we are invited to solve in this way?

Well, we are told, in this case you are seeing *something*; and what is this something 'if it is not part of any material thing'? But this question is, really, completely mad. The straight part of the stick, the bit not under water, is presumably part of a material thing; don't we see that? And what about the bit *under* water?—we can see that too. We can see, come to that, the water itself. In fact what we see is *a stick partly immersed in water*; and it is particularly extraordinary that this should appear to be called in question—that a question should be raised about *what* we are seeing—since this, after all, is simply the description of the situation with which we started. It was, that is to say, agreed at the start that we were looking at a stick, a 'material thing', part of which was under water. If, to take a rather different case, a church were cunningly camouflaged so that it looked like a barn, how could any serious question be raised about what we see when we look at it? We see, of course, *a church* that now *looks like a barn*. We do *not* see an immaterial barn, an immaterial church, or an immaterial anything else. And what in this case could seriously tempt us to say that we do?

Notice, incidentally, that in Ayer's description of the stick-in-water case, which is supposed to be prior to the drawing of any philosophical conclusions, there has already crept in the unheralded but important expression 'visual appearances'—it is, of course, ultimately to be suggested that all we *ever* get when we see is a appearance (whatever that may be).

Consider next the case of my reflection in a mirror. My body, Ayer says, 'appears to be some distance behind the glass'; but as it's in front, it can't really be behind the glass. So what am I seeing? A sense-datum. What about this? Well, once again, although there is no objection to saying that my body 'appears to be some distance behind the glass', in saying this we must remember what sort of situation we are dealing with. It does not 'appear to be' there in a way which might tempt me (though it might tempt a baby or a savage) to go round the back and look for it, and be astonished when this enterprise proved a failure. (To say that A is *in* B doesn't always mean that if you open B you will find A, just as to say that A is *on* B doesn't always mean that you could pick it off—consider 'I saw my face in the mirror', 'There's a pain in my toe', 'I heard him on the radio', 'I saw the image on the screen', &c. Seeing something in a mirror is not like seeing a bun in a shop-window.) But does it follow that, since my body is not actually located behind the mirror, I am not seeing a material thing? Plainly not. For one thing, I can see the mirror (nearly always anyway). I can see my own body 'indirectly', *sc.* in the mirror. I can also see the reflection of my own body or, as some would say, a mirror-image. And a mirror-image (if we choose this answer) is not a 'sense-datum'; it can be photographed, seen by any number of people, and so on. (Of course there is no question here of either illusion or delusion.) And if the question is pressed, what actually *is* some distance, five feet say, behind the mirror, the answer is, not a sense-datum, but some region of the adjoining room.

The mirage case—at least if we take the view, as Ayer does, that the oasis the traveller thinks he can see 'does not exist'—is significantly more amenable to the treatment it is given. For here we are supposing the man to be genuinely deluded, he is *not* 'seeing a material thing'.[1] We don't actually have to say, however, even here that he is 'experiencing sense-data'; for though, as Ayer says above, 'it is convenient to give a name' to what he is experiencing, the fact is that it already has a name—a *mirage*. Again, we should be wise not to accept too readily the statement that what he is experiencing is '*similar in character* to what he would be experiencing if he were seeing a real oasis'. For is it at all likely, really, to be very similar? And, looking ahead, if we were to concede this point we should find the concession being used against us at a later stage—namely, at the stage where we shall be invited to agree that we see sense-data always, in normal cases too. ...

---

[1] Not even 'indirectly', no such thing is 'presented'. Doesn't this seem to make the case, though more amenable, a good deal less useful to the philosopher? It's hard to see how normal cases could be said to be *very like* this.

X

... This idea that there is a certain kind, or form, of sentence which as such is incorrigible and evidence-providing seems to be prevalent enough to deserve more detailed refutation. Let's consider incorrigibility first of all. The argument begins, it appears, from the observation that there are sentences which can be identified as intrinsically more adventurous than others, in uttering which we stick our necks out further. If for instance I say 'That's Sirius', I am wrong if, though it is a star, that star is not Sirius; whereas, if I had said only 'That's a star', its not being Sirius would leave me unshaken. Again, if I had said only, 'That looks like a star', I could have faced with comparative equanimity the revelation that it isn't a star. And so on. Reflections of this kind apparently give rise to the idea that there is or could be a kind of sentence in the utterance of which I take no chances *at all*, my commitment is absolutely minimal; so that in principle *nothing* could show that I had made a mistake, and my remark would be 'incorrigible'.

But in fact this ideal goal is completely unattainable. There isn't, there couldn't be, any kind of sentence which as such is incapable, once uttered, of being subsequently amended or retracted. Ayer himself, though he is prepared to say that sense-datum sentences are incorrigible, takes notice of one way in which they couldn't be; it is, as he admits, always possible in principle that, however non-committal a speaker intends to be, he may produce the *wrong word*, and subsequently be brought to admit this. But Ayer tries, as it were, to laugh this off as a quite trivial qualification; he evidently thinks that he is conceding here only the possibility of slips of the tongue, purely 'verbal' slips (or of course of lying). But this is not so. There are more ways than these of bringing out the wrong word. I may say 'Magenta' wrongly either by a mere slip, having meant to say 'Vermilion'; or because I don't know quite what 'magenta' means, what shade of colour is called *magenta*; or again, because I was unable to, or perhaps just didn't, really notice or attend to or properly size up the colour before me. Thus, there is always the possibility, not only that I may be brought to admit that 'magenta' wasn't the right word to pick on for the colour before me, but *also* that I may be brought to see, or perhaps remember, that the colour before me just wasn't *magenta*. And this holds for the case in which I say, 'It seems, to me personally, here and now, as if I were seeing something magenta', just as much as for the case in which I say, 'That is magenta.' The first formula may be more cautious, but it isn't *incorrigible*.[1]

---

[1] Ayer doesn't exactly *overlook* the possibility of misdescribing through inattention, failure to notice or to discriminate; in the case of sense-data he tries to *rule it out*. But this attempt is partly a failure, and partly unintelligible. To stipulate that a sense-datum has whatever qualities it appears to have is insufficient for the purpose, since it is *not* impossible to err even in saying only what qualities something appears to have—one may, for instance, not attend to its appearance carefully enough. But to stipulate that a sense-datum just is whatever the speaker takes it to be—so that if he *says* something different it must be a different sense-datum—amounts to making non-mendacious sense-datum statements true by *fiat*; and if so, how could sense-data be, as they are also meant to be, non-linguistic entities *of* which we are aware, *to* which we refer, that against which the factual truth of all empirical statements is ultimately to be tested?

Yes, but, it may be said, even if such cautious formulae are not *intrinsically* incorrigible, surely there will be plenty of cases in which what we say by their utterance will *in fact* be incorrigible—cases in which, that is to say, nothing whatever could actually be produced as a cogent ground for retracting them. Well, yes, no doubt this is true. But then exactly the same thing is true of utterances in which quite different forms of words are employed. For if, when I make some statement, it is true that nothing whatever could in fact be produced as a cogent ground for retracting it, this can only be because I am in, have got myself into, the very best possible position for making that statement—I have, and am entitled to have, *complete* confidence in it when I make it. But whether this is so or not is not a matter of what *kind of sentence* I use in making my statement, but of what *the circumstances* are in which I make it. If I carefully scrutinize some patch of colour in my visual field, take careful note of it, know English well, and pay scrupulous attention to just what I'm saying, I may say, 'It seems to me now as if I were seeing something pink'; and nothing whatever could be produced as showing that I had made a mistake. But equally, if I watch for some time an animal a few feet in front of me, in a good light, if I prod it perhaps, sniff, and take note of the noises it makes, I may say, 'That's a pig'; and this too will be 'incorrigible', nothing could be produced that would show that I had made a mistake. Once one drops the idea that there is a special *kind of sentence* which is *as such* incorrigible, one might as well admit (what is plainly true anyway) that *many* kinds of sentences may be uttered in making statements which are *in fact* incorrigible—in the sense that, when they are made, the circumstances are such that they are quite certainly, definitely, and un-retractably *true*.

Consider next the point about evidence—the idea that there is, again, some special kind of sentences whose function it is to formulate the evidence on which other kinds are based. There are at least two things wrong with this.

First, it is not the case, as this doctrine implies, that whenever a 'material-object' statement is made, the speaker must have or could produce evidence for it. This may sound plausible enough; but it involves a gross misuse of the notion of 'evidence'. The situation in which I would properly be said to have *evidence* for the statement that some animal is a pig is that, for example, in which the beast itself is not actually on view, but I can see plenty of pig-like marks on the ground outside its retreat. If I find a few buckets of pig-food, that's a bit more evidence, and the noises and the smell may provide better evidence still. But if the animal then emerges and stands there plainly in view, there is no longer any question of collecting evidence; its coming into view doesn't provide me with more *evidence* that it's a pig, I can now just *see* that it is, the question is settled. And of course I might, in different circumstances, have just seen this in the first place, and not had to bother with collecting evidence at all. [1] Again, if I actually see one man shoot another, I may *give* evidence, as an eye-witness, to those less favourably placed; but I don't *have* evidence for my own statement that the shooting took place, I actually *saw* it. Once again, then, we find that you

---

[1] I have, it will be said, the 'evidence of my own eyes'. But the point of this trope is exactly that it does *not* illustrate the ordinary use of 'evidence'—that I *don't* have evidence in the ordinary sense.

have to take into account, not just the words used, but the situation in which they are used; one who says 'It's a pig' will sometimes have evidence for saying so, sometimes not; one can't say that the *sentence* 'It's a pig', as such, is of a kind for which evidence is essentially required.

But secondly, as the case we've considered has already shown, it is not the case that the formulation of evidence is the function of any special sort of sentence. The evidence, if there is any, for a 'material-object' statement will usually be formulated in statements of just the same kind; but in general, *any* kind of statement could state evidence for *any* other kind, if the circumstances were appropriate. It is not true in general, for instance, that general statements are 'based on' singular statements and not vice versa; my belief that *this* animal will eat turnips may be based on the belief that most pigs eat turnips; though certainly, in different circumstances, I might have supported the claim that most pigs eat turnips by saying that this pig eats them at any rate. Similarly, and more relevantly perhaps to the topic of perception, it is not true in general that statements of how things are are 'based on' statements of how things appear, look, or seem and not vice versa. I may say, for instance, 'That pillar is bulgy' on the ground that it looks bulgy; but equally I might say, in different circumstances, 'That pillar looks bulgy'—on the ground that I've just built it, and I *built* it bulgy.

We are now in a position to deal quite briefly with the idea that 'material-object' statements are *as such* not conclusively verifiable. This is just as wrong as the idea that sense-datum statements are as such incorrigible (it is not just 'misleading', as Ayer is prepared to allow that it might be). Ayer's doctrine is that 'the notion of certainty does not apply to propositions *of this kind*'.[1] And his ground for saying this is that, in order to verify a proposition of this kind conclusively, we should have to perform the self-contradictory feat of completing 'an infinite series of verifications'; however many tests we may carry out with favourable results, we can never complete all the possible tests, for these are infinite in number; but nothing *less* than all the possible tests would be *enough*.

Now why does Ayer (and not he alone) put forward this very extraordinary doctrine? It is, of course, not true in general that statements about 'material things', as such, *need* to be 'verified'. If, for instance, someone remarks in casual conversation, 'As a matter of fact I live in Oxford', the other party to the conversation may, if he finds it worth doing, verify this assertion; but the *speaker*, of course, has no need to do this—he knows it to be true (or, if he is lying, false). Strictly speaking, indeed, it is not just that he has no *need* to verify his statement; the case is rather that, since he already knows it to be true, nothing whatever that he might do could *count* as his 'verifying' it. Nor need it be true that he is in this position by virtue of having verified his assertion at some previous stage; for of how many people really, who know quite well where they live, could it be said that they have at any time *verified* that they live there? When could they be supposed to have done this? In what way? And why? What we have here, in fact, is an erroneous doctrine which is a kind of mirror-image

---

[1] He is, incidentally, also wrong, as many others have been, in holding that the 'notion of certainty' *does* apply to 'the *a priori* propositions of logic and mathematics' as such. Many propositions in logic and mathematics are not certain at all; and if many are, that is not just because they *are* propositions in logic and mathematics, but because, say, they have been particularly firmly established.

of the erroneous doctrine about evidence we discussed just now; the idea that statements about 'material things' *as such* need to be verified is just as wrong as, and wrong in just the same way as, the idea that statements about 'material things' *as such* must be based on evidence. And both ideas go astray, at bottom, through the pervasive error of neglecting *the circumstances in which* things are said—of supposing that *the words alone* can be discussed, in a quite general way.

But even if we agree to confine ourselves to situations in which statements can be, and do need to be, verified, the case still looks desperate. Why on earth should one think that such verification can't ever be conclusive? If, for instance, you tell me there's a telephone in the next room, and (feeling mistrustful) I decide to verify this, how could it be thought *impossible* for me to do this conclusively? I go into the next room, and certainly there's something there that looks exactly like a telephone. But is it a case perhaps of *trompe l'oeil* painting? I can soon settle that. Is it just a dummy perhaps, not really connected up and with no proper works? Well, I can take it to pieces a bit and find out, or actually use it for ringing somebody up—and perhaps get them to ring me up too, just to make sure. And of course, if I do all these things, I *do* make sure; what more could possibly be required? This object has already stood up to amply enough tests to establish that it really is a telephone; and it isn't just that, for everyday or practical or ordinary purposes, enough is *as good* as a telephone; what meets all these tests just *is* a telephone, no doubt about it.

However, as is only to be expected, Ayer has a reason for taking this extraordinary view. He holds, as a point of general doctrine, that, though in his view statements about 'material things' are never strictly equivalent to statements about sense-data, yet 'to say anything about a material thing is to say something, but not the same thing about classes of sense-data'; or, as he sometimes puts it, a statement about a 'material thing' *entails* 'some set of statements or other about sense-data'. But—and this is his difficulty—there is no *definite* and *finite* set of statements about sense-data entailed by any statement about a 'material thing'. Thus, however assiduously I check up on the sense-datum statements entailed by a statement about a 'material thing', I can never exclude the possibility that there are *other* sense-datum statements, which it also entails, but which, if checked, would turn out to be untrue. But of course, if a statement may be found to entail a false statement, then it itself may thereby be found to be false; and this is a possibility which, according to the doctrine, cannot in principle be finally eliminated. And since, again according to the doctrine, verification just consists in thus checking sense-datum statements, it follows that verification can *never* be conclusive.[1]

Of the many objectionable elements in this doctrine, in some ways the strangest is the use made of the notion of entailment. What does the sentence, 'That is a pig', *entail*? Well, perhaps there is somewhere, recorded by some zoological authority, a statement of the necessary and sufficient conditions for belonging to the species *pig*. And so perhaps, if we use the word 'pig' strictly in that sense, to say of an animal that it's a pig will entail that it satisfies those conditions, whatever they may

---

[1] Material things are put together like jig-saw puzzles; but since the number of pieces in a puzzle is not finite, we can never know that any puzzle is perfect, there may be pieces missing or pieces that won't fit.

be. But clearly it isn't this sort of entailment that Ayer has in mind; nor, for that matter, is it particularly relevant to the use that non-experts make of the word 'pig'.[1] But what other kind of entailment is there? We have a pretty rough idea what pigs look like, what they smell and sound like, and how they normally behave; and no doubt, if something didn't look at all right for a pig, behave as pigs do, or make pig-like noises and smells, we'd say that it wasn't a pig. But are there—do there *have* to be—*statements* of the form, 'It looks … ', 'It sounds …', 'It smells …', of which we could say straight off that 'That is a pig' entails them? Plainly not. We learn the word 'pig', as we learn the vast majority of words for ordinary things, ostensively—by being told, in the presence of the animal, '*That* is a pig'; and thus, though certainly we learn what sort of thing it is to which the word 'pig' can and can't be properly applied, we don't go through any kind of intermediate stage of relating the word 'pig' to a lot of *statements* about the way things look, or sound, or smell. The word is just not introduced into our vocabulary in this way. Thus, though of course we come to have certain expectations as to what will and won't be the case when a pig is in the offing, it is wholly artificial to represent these expectations in the guise of *statements entailed by* 'That is a pig.' And for just this reason it is, at best, wholly artificial to speak as if *verifying* that some animal is a pig consists in checking up on the statements entailed by 'That is a pig.' If we do think of verification in this way, certainly difficulties abound; we don't know quite where to begin, how to go on, or where to stop. But what this shows is, not that 'That is a pig' is very difficult to verify or incapable of being conclusively verified, but that this is an impossible travesty of verification. If the procedure of verification were rightly described in this way, then indeed we couldn't say just what would constitute conclusive verification that some animal was a pig. But this doesn't show that there is actually any difficulty at all, usually, in verifying that an animal is a pig, if we have occasion to do so; it shows only that what verification *is* has been completely misrepresented.[2]

We may add to this the rather different but related point that, though certainly we have more or less definite views as to what objects of particular kinds will and won't do, and of how they will and won't re-act in one situation or another, it would again be grossly artificial to represent these in the guise of definite entailments. There are vast numbers of things which I take it for granted that a telephone won't do, and doubtless an infinite number of things which it never enters my head to consider the possibility that it might do; but surely it would be perfectly absurd to say that 'This is a telephone' *entails* the whole galaxy of statements to the effect that it doesn't and won't do these things, and to conclude that I haven't *really* established that anything

---

[1] Anyway, the official definition won't cover *everything*—freaks, for instance. If I'm shown a five-legged pig at a fair, I can't get my money back on the plea that being a pig entails having only four legs.

[2] Another way of showing that 'entailment' is out of place in such contexts: Suppose that tits, all the tits we've ever come across, are bearded, so that we are happy to say 'Tits are bearded.' Does this *entail* that what isn't bearded isn't a tit? Not really. For if beardless specimens are discovered in some newly explored territory, well, of course we weren't talking about *them* when we said that tits were bearded; we now have to think again, and recognize perhaps this new species of glabrous tits. Similarly, what we say nowadays about tits just doesn't refer *at all* to the prehistoric eo-tit, or to remote future tits, defeathered perhaps through some change of atmosphere.

is a telephone until, *per impossibile*, I have confirmed the whole infinite class of these supposed entailments. Does 'This is a telephone' *entail* 'You couldn't eat it'? Must I try to eat it, and fail, in the course of making sure that it's a telephone?[1]

The conclusions we have reached so far, then, can be summed up as follows:

1. There is no *kind* or *class* of sentences ('propositions') of which it can be said that *as such*
   (a) they are incorrigible;
   (b) they provide the evidence for other sentences; and
   (c) they must be checked in order that other sentences may be verified.
2. It is not true of sentences about 'material things' that *as such*
   (a) they must be supported by or based on evidence;
   (b) they stand in need of verification; and
   (c) they cannot be conclusively verified.

Sentences in fact—as distinct from *statements made in particular circumstances*—cannot be divided up at *all* on these principles, into two groups or any other number of groups. And this means that the general doctrine about knowledge which I sketched at the beginning of this section, which is the real bugbear underlying doctrines of the kind we have been discussing, is *radically* and *in principle* misconceived. For even if we were to make the very risky and gratuitous assumption that what some particular person knows at some particular place and time could systematically be sorted out into an arrangement of foundations and super-structure, it would be a mistake in principle to suppose that the same thing could be done for knowledge *in general*. And this is because there *could* be no *general* answer to the questions what is evidence for what, what is certain, what is doubtful, what needs or does not need evidence, can or can't be verified. If the Theory of Knowledge consists in finding grounds for such an answer, there is no such thing.

---

[1] Philosophers, I think, have taken too little notice of the fact that most words in ordinary use are defined ostensively. For example, it has often been thought to be a puzzle why A *can't* be B, if being A doesn't *entail* being not-B. But it is often just that 'A' and 'B' are brought in as ostensively defined as, words for *different things*. Why can't a Jack of Hearts be a Queen of Spades? Perhaps we need a new term, 'ostensively analytic'.

CHAPTER 6

Wilfrid Sellars: Empiricism and the Philosophy of Mind

Introduction to Wilfrid Sellars

Wilfrid Sellars was born in 1912 in Ann Arbor, where his father, Roy Wood Sellars, taught Philosophy at the University of Michigan. He was educated in Paris, Munich, Michigan, Oxford, and Harvard. His teaching career was spent at the Universities of Iowa, Minnesota, Yale, and Pittsburgh. Sellars possesses the logical rigor and respect for science that matches that of the Positivists, an awareness of the nuances of ordinary language that one associates with his contemporaries at Oxford, a grasp of the history of philosophy more typically found in continental schools, and a breadth of scope usually found prior to this century. He was also an extremely systematic philosopher, his work knitting together to form an integrated vision. Sellars was in many ways ahead of his time, and several of his main ideas are now at the forefront of philosophical research. These include the idea that folk psychology is a theory; functionalism; and conceptual role semantics.

The main theme of the present article is an attack on "the Given." This attack is not restricted to empiricist sense-datum theory, but to any system which posits a foundational body of self-justifying and noninferred knowledge. However, Sellars' attack on sense-data serves as a model for this general attack on "the Given." Sellars denies that one can have knowledge of sense-contents that can function as an epistemic base for knowledge of physical objects. Merely having a sense-content is not sufficient to yield knowledge: While it may be a necessary condition for perceptual knowledge, it is not itself a case of knowledge. In fact, it does not belong in the epistemic realm at all (i.e., as a knowing or a believing, etc.) since it belongs not in the cognitive realm but only in the causal realm. Thus, in Sellars' famous phrase, mere possession of a sense-content does not locate one in the "logical space of reasons." One enters this space in making judgments over intersubjective objects or processes, and which can be evaluated and justified.

Here, Sellars is reaffirming the Kantian position that the possibility of knowledge requires sensory data to be placed under concepts. As we shall see, it requires the data to be interpreted linguistically. Like Kant, he identifies the empiricist error of failing to distinguish sensing and thinking, and of conceiving of thinking in terms of the model of sensing. Hence, Sellars attacks the Empiricist assumption that one acquires concepts by mere ostension, or by abstraction from experience. This puts the cart before the horse, since it assumes that we are "teaching it [i.e., the child] to discriminate elements within a logical space of particulars, universals, facts, etc., of which it is already undiscriminatingly aware, and associate these discriminated elements with verbal symbols." But this is the wrong way round—"… instead of coming to have a concept of something because we have noticed that sort of thing, to have the ability to notice a sort of thing is already to have the concept of that sort of thing, and cannot account for it."

Perceiving is a complex activity. It involves a sensory aspect (which Sellars confusingly calls the "descriptive core") and a cognitive "propositional" aspect. Thus, to see a black cat involves conceiving it *as* a black cat. The difference between seeing a black cat and merely thinking of one involves the presence of the descriptive core, caused by certain visual stimuli impinging on the sense-organs, originating in a black cat.

In Section III, "The Logic of 'Looks,'" Sellars attacks the epistemic primacy of sense-data, by examining the way in which reports of how things "look" function in language. He aims to show that "looks"-talk is parasitic on "is"-talk, that is, about the way things are. He imagines a man called John who encountered physical objects under only standard conditions. In other words, his perceptual equipment is well-functioning, and he perceives things under only standard lighting conditions, and so forth. Since he has learned color-words under only these conditions, John would have no need of anything more than "is"-talk; for example "This is red." The need for "looks"-talk emerges only with nonstandard lighting conditions, for example, electric light. So (as we would say) a tie that looks green under electric light might look blue in natural light. Given that John believes that ties don't change their properties according to location, he needs a way of accounting for the anomaly. He is reluctant to say "It is green," when next confronted with a such a tie indoors. So he hedges by saying, "It is *as though* I were seeing a green necktie." He may also say, "It is blue"—but this would be not an observational *report*, but an *inference*. Only in time, after being confronted with cases like this can he noninferentially report that the tie *is* blue, although it *looks* green.

In Section IV, "Explaining Looks," he asks us to consider the following expressions:

1. x *looks* green to S.

2. x *merely looks* green to S.

3. S *sees that x is green.*

The propositional content of these three report-descriptions is the same, namely "x is green." They all report that a physical object x has the property of being green. The difference concerns how much that report is *endorsed*. Statement 3 reports that x is green, and fully endorses the claim; 1 holds the endorsement back, and 2 denies it. Talk of how things look or seem is conceptually dependent on straightforwardly descriptive judgments about how things are. I can report that x *looks* green only if I can report that x *is* green. Although my report that x is green is noninferred, in the sense that I don't infer it from other premises, it is false to say that it is totally self-justifying.

As we have seen, Sellars opposes the Empiricist tradition that ostensive definition is a paradigm of language-learning, since the mere occurrence of a sense-content cannot yield knowledge. A preconceptual sensing of red may be a necessary condition of knowledge of red, but does not itself constitute knowledge. The basic epistemic unit of perceptual knowledge is "seeing that x is red," and this requires grasp of the relevant concepts. Like Wittgenstein, Sellars holds that ostensive definition doesn't consist in a foundational atomistic procedure of fixing word-object connections. Rather, how one learns a word, and what its meaning consists in, is determined by its place in a wider linguistic context. This theme is developed in Section VII, "The Logic of 'Means.'"

To know that x is green requires a capacity to follow the rules for "color-talk." This includes such factors as being able to identify an object's color by looking at it; knowing what counts as normal conditions for making that report; knowing that making such a report under such conditions is, prima facie, very strong evidence for the truth of the report, and so on. It also requires grasp of other color-words, and th e knowledge that these are mutually exclusive categories (i.e., if x is all-red at time t, then it can't be all-green at t). Thus, while justification is holistic and coherentist, we can still say that some knowledge is noninferential, in that it is not derived from some other, *more basic* knowledge.

Sellars opposes the Empiricist theory that word meaning, and semantic judgments of the form " … means—", should be construed as relations between words and things, properties, and the like. Rather than "red' means red," a more constructive paradigm would be "'red' means 'rouge,'"—that is, an intralinguistic relation, whereby we classify unknown words in terms of those already understood. In the above context, "means" means "plays the same role in English as 'rouge' does in French."

I will extend these points and introduce some more, via the most famous part of the article, the fictional account of the primordial philosopher/psychologist Jones. Sellars is explicit that the story is fictional. He is certainly not saying that these events actually occurred. Rather, the "story is offered as a myth, albeit a plausible myth, and is employed to destroy another myth, that of the Given."

The story commences in the distant past, in a "Rylean" community: that is, where people conceive of "thinking" totally behavioristically. So they use "a language of which the fundamental descriptive vocabulary speaks of public properties of public objects located in Space and enduring through Time." Thus, what they call thinking is, in its primary sense, *saying*. In other words, to "think that p" is to say "p," or in a derivative sense, to have a "short-term, proximate propensity to say 'p.'" The question becomes: "What resources would have to be added to the Rylean language of these talking animals in order that they might come to recognize each other and themselves as animals that *think, observe,* and have *feelings* and *sensations,* as we use these terms?" And secondly, what good reason would they have for extending their language in these ways?

Let us suppose that their language has developed to the point at which it admits *metalinguistic* thinking-utterances—applying the semantic categories of meaning, reference, and truth to their verbal acts. Assume also that their talk of the physical world employs a primitive distinction between observational and theoretical terms. That is, they have the practice of inferring unobservable entities in order to explain the behavior of observable entities. All this, says Sellars, is enough to set the conditions for the introduction of psychological vocabulary.

Jones enters at this point. Jones' curiosity is raised concerning people's propensities to speak (i.e., think). He notices that these inclinations needn't result in speech. He also notes that a series of such unactualized propensities can occur, where one is replaced by another, all in the absence of any overt speech or behavior. Thus, one can have a propensity to speak about sex, then about food, then about drink, without explicitly saying or doing anything. Most importantly, they can still behave intelligibly in such cases. How is this possible? Jones theorizes that they must be subject to some unobserved inner processes. In other words, he abductively *explains* the phenomena via these theoretical entities.

Recall that Jones already possesses an observation/theory distinction. He employs this to postulate these inner processes, which he calls "thoughts." The picture he paints of these thoughts is derived from the example of overt verbalizations. In other words, saying "p" is the *model* for thinking that p. This is an instance of a general principle regarding the introduction of theoretical entities, whereby we conceive of a newly introduced theoretical entity by modeling it on entities already understood. If x is the model for y, we analogically ascribe x's properties to y. So thought is understood as "inner speech."

One other element of Sellars' picture of theory construction is relevant here. When a theoretical term is introduced into a language, its corresponding entity or process appears only as a conclusion from premises concerning observational factors. Thus, for example, one infers the existence of thoughts from the fact that people act intelligibly in the absence of overt verbalization. Once this practice is established, and the new term linguistically "grounded," then otherwise competent language users can be trained to apply it noninferentially. Thus, Jones trains his comrades to recognize their own thoughts—but only after they have been taught how to infer the presence of thoughts (in themselves and others) on the basis of behavioral evidence.

Jones then turns his attention to sense-impressions. They are introduced in the same way—first taken as theoretical entities, postulated to explain the occurrence of thoughts correlated to perceptions. One notable subset of such thoughts would be false perceptual judgments. So, on the one hand, we have perceptual input, and on the other, we have thoughts about the immediate environment. Impressions are hypothesized as the interface between them. The thoughts are caused by nonconceptual inner processes. So what are these impressions? Sellars is insistent that they are "*states* of the perceived subject, *not a class of* particulars." That is, they are states *of* subjects, not things *in* subjects, logically separable from them. (However, he suggests that science will discover particulars that are counterparts to these impressions.) As before, Jones employs a model for these states. This time (despite his caveat), impressions are modeled on the primary and secondary properties of ordinary physical objects. Thus, properties of color, shape, and the like, are analogically extended from their base domain in physical objects, to sense-impressions. Thus, Jones can assert "I had a sense-impression of a red triangle," where this would be an inference, and the impression hypothesized in order to correlate thoughts about x in the presence of x. The causal link would be the presence of an impression of x, where this impression's properties are in some way analogous to those of the external x. As before, Jones first teaches others to infer the presence of impressions, and then to self-ascribe them by introspection.

Notice how this picture totally overturns the Empiricist assumption that knowledge of sense-impressions was a foundation for knowledge of the external world. Sellars reverses this picture, insisting that reports of impressions are derivative on reports about the world.

Finally, Jones makes his big mistake, which was inherited by sense-datum theorists: He "construes as *data* the particulars and arrays of particulars which he has come to be able to observe, and believes them to be antecedent object of knowledge which have somehow been in the framework from the beginning. It is in the very act of *taking* that he speaks of the *given*." Enter Sellars, to unravel the error.

BIBLIOGRAPHY

Works by Sellars
Essays in Philosophy and its History, (Atascadero, CA: Ridgeview, 1975).
The Metaphysics of Epistemology: Lectures by Wilfrid Sellars, (Atascadero, CA: Ridgeview, 1989).
Naturalism and Ontology, (Atascadero, CA: Ridgeview, 1980).
Philosophical Perspectives, Volume 1. *History of Philosophy*; Volume 2. *Metaphysics and Epistemology*, (Atascadero, CA: Ridgeview, 1977).
Science and Metaphysics: Variations on Kantian Themes, (London: Routledge 1967).
Science, Perception and Reality, (London: Routledge, 1963). (Contains the present essay, and the influential "Philosophy and the Scientific Image of Man.")

Further Reading
C.F. Delaney, Michael J. Loux, Gary Gutting, W. David Solomon, *The Synoptic Vision* (University of Notre Dame Press, 1977), is a very useful summary of Sellars' thought, from which I borrowed in preparing this introduction.
Hector-Neri Castanedam, ed., *Action, Knowledge and Reality: Studies in Honor of Wilfrid Sellars* (Indianapolis: Bobbs-Merrill, 1975).
J.C. Pitt, Ed., *The Philosophy of Wilfrid Sellars: Queries and Extensions* (Dordrecht: Reidel 1978).

Empiricism and the Philosophy of Mind

Wilfrid Sellars

I. AN AMBIGUITY IN SENSE-DATUM THEORIES

I presume that no philosopher who has attacked the philosophical idea of givenness or, to use the Hegelian term, immediacy, has intended to deny that there is a difference between *inferring* that something is the case and, for example, *seeing* it to be the case. If the term 'given' referred merely to what is observed as being observed, or, perhaps, to a proper subset of the things we are said to determine by observation, the existence of 'data' would be as noncontroversial as the existence of philosophical perplexities. But, of course, this just is not so. The phrase 'the given' as a piece of professional—epistemological—shoptalk carries a substantial theoretical commitment, and one can deny that there are 'data' or that anything is, in this sense, 'given' without flying in the face of reason.

Many things have been said to be 'given': sense contents, material objects, universals, propositions, real connections, first principles, even givenness itself. And there is, indeed, a certain way of construing the situations which philosophers analyse in these terms which can be said to be the framework of givenness. This framework has been a common feature of most of the major systems of philosophy, including, to use a Kantian turn of phrase, both 'dogmatic rationalism' and 'sceptical empiricism'. It has, indeed, been so pervasive that few, if any, philosophers have been altogether free of it; certainly not Kant, and, I would argue, not even Hegel, that great foe of 'immediacy'. Often what is attacked under its name are only specific varieties of 'given'. Intuited first principles and synthetic necessary connections were the first to come under attack. And many who today attack 'the whole idea of givenness'—and they are an increasing number—are really only attacking sense data. For they transfer to other items, say physical objects or relations of appearing, the characteristic features of the 'given'. If, however, I begin my argument with an attack on sense-datum theories, it is only as a first step in a general critique of the entire framework of givenness.

2. Sense-datum theories characteristically distinguish between an *act* of awareness and, for example, the colour patch which is its *object*. The act is usually called *sensing*. Classical exponents of the theory have often characterized these acts as 'phenomenologically simple' and 'not further analysable'. But other sense-datum theorists—some of them with an equal claim to be considered 'classical exponents'—have held that sensing is analysable. And if, some philosophers seem to have thought

Wilfrid Sellars, "Empiricism and the Philosophy of Mind," *Science, Perception, and Reality* (London: Routledge, 1963).

that if sensing is analysable, then it cannot be an *act*, this has by no means been the general opinion. There are, indeed, deeper roots for the doubt that sensing (if there is such a thing) is an act, roots which can be traced to one of two lines of thought tangled together in classical sense-datum theory. For the moment, however, I shall simply assume that however complex (or simple) the fact that x is sensed may be, it has the form, whatever exactly it may be, by virtue of which for x to be sensed is for it to be the object of an act.

Being a sense datum, or sensum, is a relational property of the item that is sensed. To refer to an item which is sensed in a way which does not entail that it *is* sensed, it is necessary to use some other locution. *Sensibile* has the disadvantage that it implies that sensed items could exist without being sensed, and this is a matter of controversy among sense-datum theorists. *Sense content* is, perhaps, as neutral a term as any.

There appear to be varieties of sensing, referred to by some as *visual sensing, tactual sensing*, etc., and by others as *directly seeing, directly hearing*, etc. But it is not clear whether these are species of sensing in any full-blooded sense, or whether 'x is visually sensed' amounts to no more than 'x is a colour patch which is sensed', 'x is directly heard' than 'x is a sound which is sensed', and so on. In the latter case, being a *visual sensing* or a *direct hearing* would be a relational property of an act of sensing, just as being a sense datum is a relational property of a sense content.

3. Now if we bear in mind that the point of the epistemological category of the given is, presumably, to explicate the idea that empirical knowledge rests on a 'foundation' of non-inferential knowledge of matter of fact, we may well experience a feeling of surprise on noting that according to sense-datum theorists, it is *particulars* that are sensed. For what is *known*, even in non-inferential knowledge, is *facts* rather than particulars, items of the form *something's being thus-and-so* or *something's standing in a certain relation to something else*. It would seem, then, that the sensing of sense contents *cannot* constitute knowledge, inferential *or* non-inferential; and if so, we may well ask, what light does the concept of a sense datum throw on the 'foundations of empirical knowledge'? The sense-datum theorist, it would seem, must choose between saying:

(*a*) It is *particulars* which are sensed. Sensing is not knowing. The existence of sense data does not *logically* imply the existence of knowledge, or

(*b*) Sensing *is* a form of knowing. It is *facts* rather than *particulars* which are sensed.

On alternative (*a*) the fact that a sense content was sensed would be a *non-epistemic* fact about the sense content. Yet it would be hasty to conclude that this alternative precludes *any* logical connection between the sensing of sense contents and the possession of non-inferential knowledge. For even if the sensing of sense contents did not logically imply the existence of non-inferential knowledge, the converse might well be true. Thus, the non-inferential knowledge of particular matter of fact might logically imply the existence of sense data (for example, *seeing that a certain physical object is red* might logically imply *sensing a red sense content*) even though the sensing of a red sense content were not itself a cognitive fact and did not imply the possession of non-inferential knowledge.

On the second alternative, (*b*), the sensing of sense contents would logically imply the existence of non-inferential knowledge for the simple reason that it would *be* this knowledge. But, once again, it would be facts rather than particulars which are sensed.

4. Now it might seem that when confronted by this choice, the sense-datum theorist seeks to have his cake and eat it. For he characteristically insists *both* that sensing is a knowing *and* that it is particulars which are sensed. Yet his position is by no means as hopeless as this formulation suggests. For the 'having' and the 'eating' can be combined without logical nonsense provided that he uses the word *know* and, correspondingly, the word *given* in two senses. He must say something like the following:

> The non-inferential knowing on which our world picture rests is the knowing that certain items, e.g. red sense contents, are of a certain character, e.g. red. When such a fact is non-inferentially known about a sense content, I will say that the sense content is sensed as *being*, e.g. *red*. I will then say that a sense content is *sensed* (full stop) if it is *sensed as being* of a certain character, e.g. red. Finally, I will say of a sense content that it is *known* if it is sensed (full stop), to emphasize that sensing is a *cognitive* or *epistemic* fact.

Notice that, given these stipulations, it is logically necessary that if a sense content be *sensed*, it be *sensed as being of a certain character*, and that if it be *sensed as being of a certain character*, the *fact that it is of this character* be *non-inferentially known*. Notice also that the being sensed of a sense content would be *knowledge* only in a stipulated sense of *know*. To say of a *sense content*—a colour patch, for example—that it was 'known' would be to say that *some fact about it* was non-inferentially known, e.g. that it was red. This *stipulated* use of *know* would, however, receive aid and comfort from the fact that there is, in ordinary usage, a sense of *know* in which it is followed by a noun or descriptive phrase which refers to a particular, thus

Do you know John?

Do you know the President?

Because these questions are equivalent to 'Are you acquainted with John?' and 'Are you acquainted with the President?' the phrase 'knowledge by acquaintance' recommends itself as a useful metaphor for this stipulated sense of *know* and, like other useful metaphors, has congealed into a technical term.

5. We have seen that the fact that a sense content is a *datum* (if, indeed, there are such facts) will logically imply that someone has non-inferential knowledge *only* if to say that a sense content is given is contextually defined in terms of non-inferential knowledge of a fact about this sense content. If this is not clearly realized or held in mind, sense-datum theorists may come to think of the givenness of sense contents as the *basic* or *primitive* concept of the sense-datum framework, and thus sever the logical connection between sense-data and non-inferential knowledge to which the classical form of the theory is committed. This brings us face to face with the fact that in spite of the above considerations, many if not most sense-datum theorists *have* thought of the givenness of sense contents as the basic notion of the sense-datum

framework. What, then, of the logical connection in the direction *sensing sense contents → having non-inferential knowledge*? Clearly it is severed by those who think of sensing as a unique and unanalysable act. Those, on the other hand, who conceive of sensing as an *analysable* fact, while they have prima facie severed this connection (by taking the sensing of sense contents to be the basic concept of the sense-datum framework), will nevertheless, in a sense, have maintained it, if the result they get by analysing *x is a red sense datum* turns out to be the same as the result they get when they analyse *x is non-inferentially known to be red*. The entailment which was thrown out the front door would have sneaked in by the back.

It is interesting to note, in this connection, that those who, in the classical period of sense-datum theories, say from Moore's 'Refutation of Idealism' until about 1938, analysed or sketched an analysis of sensing, did so in *non-epistemic* terms. Typically it was held that for a sense content to be sensed is for it to be an element in a certain kind of relational array of sense contents, where the relations which constitute the array are such relations as spatiotemporal juxtaposition (or overlapping), constant conjunction, mnemic causation—even real connection and belonging to a self. There is, however, one class of terms which is conspicuous by its absence, namely *cognitive* terms. For these, like the 'sensing' which was under analysis, were taken to belong to a higher level of complexity.

Now the idea that epistemic facts can be analysed without remainder—even 'in principle'—into non-epistemic facts, whether phenomenal or behavioural, public or private, with no matter how lavish a sprinkling of subjunctives and hypotheticals is, I believe, a radical mistake—a mistake of a piece with the so-called 'naturalistic fallacy' in ethics. I shall not, however, press this point for the moment, though it will be a central theme in a later stage of my argument. What I do want to stress is that whether classical sense-datum philosophers have conceived of the givenness of sense contents as analysable in non-epistemic terms, or as constituted by acts which are somehow both irreducible *and* knowings, they have without exception taken them to be fundamental in another sense.

6. For they have taken givenness to be a fact which presupposes no learning, no forming of associations, no setting up of stimulus-response connections. In short, they have tended to equate *sensing sense contents* with *being conscious*, as a person who has been hit on the head is *not* conscious, whereas a new-born babe, alive and kicking, *is* conscious. They would admit, of course, that the ability to know that a *person*, namely oneself, is *now*, at a certain time, feeling a pain, *is* acquired and does presuppose a (complicated) process of concept formation. But, they would insist, to suppose that the simple ability to *feel a pain* or *see a colour*, in short, to sense sense contents, is *acquired* and involves a process of concept formation, would be very odd indeed.

But if a sense-datum philosopher takes the ability to sense sense contents to be unacquired, he is clearly precluded from offering an analysis of *x senses a sense content* which presupposes acquired abilities. It follows that he could analyse *x senses red sense content s* as *x non-inferentially knows that s is red* only if he is prepared to admit that the ability to have such non-inferential knowledge as that, for example, a red sense content is red, is itself unacquired. And this brings us face to face with the fact that most empirically minded philosophers are strongly inclined to think that all classificatory consciousness, all knowledge *that something is thus-and-so*, or, in logicians' jargon, all subsumption of particulars under universals, involves learning, concept formation, even the use of symbols. It is clear from the above analysis, therefore, that *classical* sense-datum theories—I emphasize the adjective, for there are other, 'heterodox', sense-datum theories to be taken into account—are confronted by an inconsistent triad made up of the following three propositions:

A. *X senses red sense content s* entails *x non-inferentially knows that s is red.*

B. The ability to sense sense contents is unacquired.

C. The ability to know facts of the form *x is ϕ* is acquired. A and B together entail not-C; B and C entail not-A; A and C entail not-B.

Once the classical sense-datum theorist faces up to the fact that A, B, and C do form an inconsistent triad, which of them will he choose to abandon?

(1) He can abandon A, in which case the sensing of sense contents becomes a noncognitive fact—a noncognitive fact, to be sure which may be a necessary condition, even a *logically* necessary condition, of non-inferential knowledge, but a fact, nevertheless, which cannot *constitute* this knowledge.

(2) He can abandon B, in which case he must pay the price of cutting off the concept of a sense datum from its connection with our ordinary talk about sensations, feelings, after-images, tickles and itches, etc., which are usually thought by sense-datum theorists to be its common sense counterparts.

(3) But to abandon C is to do violence to the predominantly nominalistic proclivities of the empiricist tradition.

7. It certainly begins to look as though the classical concept of a sense datum were a mongrel resulting from a crossbreeding of two ideas:

(1) The idea that there are certain inner episodes—e.g. sensations of red or of C# which can occur to human beings (and brutes) without any prior process of learning or concept formation; and without which it would *in some sense* be impossible to see, for example, that the facing surface of a physical object is red and triangular, or *hear* that a certain physical sound is C#.

(2) The idea that there are certain inner episodes which are the non-inferential knowings that certain items are, for example, red or C#; and that these episodes are the necessary conditions of empirical knowledge as providing the evidence for all other empirical propositions.

And I think that once we are on the lookout for them, it is quite easy to see how these two ideas came to be blended together in traditional epistemology. The *first* idea clearly arises in the attempt to explain the facts of sense perception in scientific style. How does it happen that people can have the experience which they describe by saying, 'It is as though I were seeing a red and triangular physical object', when either there is no physical object there at all, or, if there is, it is neither red nor triangular? The explanation, roughly, posits that in every case in which a person has an experience of this kind, whether veridical or not, he has what is called a 'sensation' or 'impression' 'of a red triangle'. The core idea is that the proximate cause of such a sensation is *only for the most part* brought about by the presence in the neighbourhood of the perceiver of a red and triangular physical object; and that while a baby, say, can have the 'sensation of a red triangle' without either *seeing* or *seeming to see that the facing side of a physical object is red and triangular*, there usually *looks*, to adults, *to be* a physical object with a red and triangular facing surface, when they are caused to have a 'sensation of a red triangle'; while *without* such a sensation, no such experience can be had.

I shall have a great deal more to say about this kind of 'explanation' of perceptual situations in the course of my argument. What I want to emphasize for the moment, however, is that, as far as the above formulation goes, there is no reason to suppose that having the sensation of a red triangle is a *cognitive* or *epistemic* fact. There is, of course, a temptation to assimilate 'having a sensation of a red triangle' to 'thinking of a celestial city' and to attribute to the former the epistemic character, the 'intentionality' of the latter. But this temptation *could* be resisted, and it *could* be held that having a sensation of a red triangle is a fact *sui generis*, neither epistemic nor physical, having its own logical grammar. Unfortunately, the idea that there are such things as sensations of red triangles—in itself, as we shall see, quite legitimate, though not without its puzzles—seems to fit the requirements of another, and less fortunate, line of thought so well that it has almost invariably been distorted to give the latter a reinforcement without which it would long ago have collapsed. This unfortunate, but familiar, line of thought runs as follows:

> The seeing that the facing surface of a physical object is red and triangular is a *veridical* member of a class of experiences—let us call them 'ostensible seeings'—some of the members of which are non-veridical; and there is no inspectible hallmark which guarantees that *any* such experience is veridical. To suppose that the non-inferential knowledge on which our world picture rests consists of such ostensible seeings, hearings, etc., as *happen* to be veridical is to place empirical knowledge on too precarious a footing—indeed, to open the door to scepticism by making a mockery of the word *knowledge* in the phrase 'empirical knowledge'.
>
> Now it is, of course, possible to delimit subclasses of ostensible seeings, hearings, etc., which are progressively less precarious, i.e. more reliable, by specifying the circumstances in which they occur, and the vigilance of the perceiver. But the possibility that any given ostensible seeing, hearing, etc., is non-veridical can never be entirely eliminated. Therefore, given that the foundation of empirical *knowledge* cannot consist of the veridical members of a class not all the members of which are veridical, and from which the non-veridical members cannot be weeded out by 'inspection', this foundation cannot consist of such items as *seeing that the facing surface of a physical object is red and triangular*.

Thus baldly put, scarcely anyone would accept this conclusion. Rather they would take the contrapositive of the argument, and reason that *since* the foundation of empirical knowledge *is* the non-inferential knowledge of such facts, it *does* consist of members of a class which contains non-veridical members. But before it is thus baldly put, it gets tangled up with the first line of thought. The idea springs to mind that *sensations of red triangles* have exactly the virtues which *ostensible seeings of red triangular physical surfaces* lack. To begin with, the grammatical similarity of 'sensation of a red triangle' to 'thought of a celestial city' is interpreted to mean, or, better, gives rise to the presupposition, that *sensations* belong in the same general pigeonhole as *thoughts*—in short, are cognitive facts. *Then*, it is noticed that sensations are *ex hypothesi* far more intimately related to mental processes than external physical objects. It would seem easier to 'get at' a red and triangular physical surface. But, above all, it is the fact that it *does not make sense* to speak of unveridical sensations which strikes these philosophers, though for it to strike them as it does, they must overlook the fact that if it makes sense to speak of an experience as *veridical* it must correspondingly make sense to speak of it as *unveridical*. Let me emphasize that not *all* sense-datum theorists—even of the classical type—have been guilty of *all* these confusions; nor are these *all* the confusions of which sense-datum theorists have been guilty. I shall have more to say on this topic later. But the confusions I have mentioned are central to the tradition, and will serve my present purpose. For the upshot of blending all these ingredients together is the idea that a sensation of a red triangle is the very paradigm of empirical knowledge. And I think that it can readily be seen that this idea leads straight to the orthodox type of sense-datum theory and accounts for the perplexities which arise when one tries to think it through.

II. ANOTHER LANGUAGE?

8. I shall now examine briefly a heterodox suggestion by, for example, Ayer[1] to the effect that discourse about sense data is, so to speak, another language, a language contrived by the epistemologist, for situations which the plain man describes by means of such locutions as 'Now the book looks green to me' and 'There seems to be a red and triangular object over there'. The core of this suggestion is the idea that the vocabulary of sense data embodies no increase in the content of descriptive discourse, as over and against the plain man's language of physical objects in Space and Time, and the properties they have and appear to have. For it holds that sentences of the form

$$X \text{ presents } S \text{ with a } \phi \text{ sense datum}$$

are simply *stipulated* to have the same force as sentences of the form

$$X \text{ looks } \phi \text{ to } S.$$

Thus 'The tomato presents S with a bulgy red sense-datum' would be the contrived counterpart of 'The tomato looks red and bulgy to S' and would mean exactly what the latter means for the simple reason that it was stipulated to do so.

As an aid to explicating this suggestion, I am going to make use of a certain picture. I am going to start with the idea of a *code*, and I am going to enrich this notion

---

[1]Ayer, A. J., *Foundations of Empirical Knowledge*, London: Macmillan, 1940, and 'The Terminology of Sense Data' in *Philosophical Essays*, pp. 66–104, London: Macmillan, 1954. (Also in *Mind*, 54, 1945, pp. 289–312.)

until the codes I am talking about are no longer *mere* codes. Whether one wants to call these 'enriched codes' codes at all is a matter which I shall not attempt to decide.

Now a *code*, in the sense in which I shall use the term, is a system of symbols each of which represents a complete sentence. Thus, as we initially view the situation, there are two characteristic features of a code: (1) Each code symbol is a unit; the parts of a code symbol are not themselves code symbols. (2) Such logical relations as obtain among code symbols are completely parasitical; they derive entirely from logical relations among the sentences they represent. Indeed, to speak about logical relations among code symbols is a way of talking which is introduced in terms of the logical relations among the sentences they represent. Thus, if 'O' stands for 'Everybody on board is sick' and 'Δ' for 'Somebody on board is sick', then 'Δ' would follow from 'O' in the sense that the sentence represented by 'Δ' follows from the sentence represented by 'O'.

Let me begin to modify this austere conception of a code. There is no reason why a code symbol might not have parts which, without becoming full-fledged symbols on their own, do play a role in the system. Thus they might play the role of *mnemonic devices* serving to put us in mind of features of the sentences represented by the symbols of which they are parts. For example, the code symbol for 'Someone on board is sick' might contain the letter S to remind us of the word 'sick', and, perhaps, the reversed letter E to remind those of us who have a background in logic of the word 'someone'. Thus, the flag for 'Someone on board is sick' might be '∃S'. Now the suggestion at which I am obviously driving is that someone might introduce so-called sense-datum sentences as code symbols or 'flags', and introduce the vocables and printables they contain to serve the role of reminding us of certain features of the sentences in ordinary perceptual discourse which the flags as wholes represent. In particular, the role of the vocable or printable 'sense datum' would be that of indicating that the symbolized sentence contains the context ' ... looks ... ', the vocable or printable 'red' that the correlated sentence contains the context ' ... looks red ... ', and so on.

9. Now to take this conception of sense-datum 'sentences' seriously is, of course, to take seriously the idea that there are no independent logical relations between sense-datum 'sentences'. It *looks* as though there were such independent logical relations, for these 'sentences' look like *sentences*, and they have as proper parts vocables or printables which function *in ordinary usage* as *logical words*. Certainly if sense-datum talk is a code, it is a code which is easily mistaken for a language proper. Let me illustrate. At first sight it certainly seems that

    A. The tomato presents S with a red sense datum

entails both

    B. There are red sense data

and

    C. The tomato presents S with a sense datum which has some specific shade of red.

This, however, on the kind of view I am considering, would be a mistake. (B) would follow—even in the inverted commas sense of 'follows' appropriate to code symbols—from (A) only because (B) is the flag for (β), 'Something looks red to somebody', which *does* follow from (α) 'The tomato looks red to Jones' which is represented in the code by (A). And (C) would 'follow' from (A), in spite of appearances, only if (C) were the flag for a *sentence* which *follows* from (α).

I shall have more to say about this example in a moment. The point to be stressed now is that to carry out this view consistently one must deny to such vocables and printables as 'quality', 'is', 'red', 'colour', 'crimson', 'determinable', 'determinate', 'all', 'some', 'exists', etc. etc., *as they occur in sense-datum talk*, the full-blooded status of their counterparts in ordinary usage. They are rather *clues* which serve to remind us which sense-datum 'flag' it would be proper to fly along with which other sense-datum 'flags'. Thus, the vocables which make up the two 'flags'

> (D) All sense data are red

and

> (E) Some sense data are not red

remind us of the genuine logical incompatibility between, for example,

> (F) All elephants are grey

and

> (G) Some elephants are not grey,

and serve, therefore, as a clue to the impropriety of flying these two 'flags' together. For the sentences they symbolize are, presumably,

> (δ) Everything looks red to everybody

and

> (ε) There is a colour other than red which something looks to somebody to have,

and these *are* incompatible.

But one would have to be cautious in using these clues. Thus, from the fact that it is proper to infer

> (H) Some elephants have a determinate shade of pink

from

> (I) Some elephants are pink

it would clearly be a mistake to infer that the right to fly

(K) Some sense data are pink

carries with it the right to fly

(L) Some sense data have a determinate shade of pink.

9. But if sense-datum sentences are really sense-datum 'sentences'—i.e. code flags—it follows, of course, that sense-datum talk neither *clarifies* nor *explains* facts of the form *x looks φ to S* or *x is φ*. That it would appear to do so would be because it would take an almost superhuman effort to keep from taking the vocables and printables which occur in the code (and let me now add to our earlier list the vocable 'directly known') to be *words* which, if homonyms of words in ordinary usage, have their ordinary sense, and which, if invented, have a meaning specified by their relation to the others. One would be constantly tempted, that is, to treat sense-datum flags as though they were sentences in a *theory*, and sense-datum talk as a *language* which gets its use by co-ordinating sense-datum sentences with sentences in ordinary perception talk, *as molecule talk gets its use by co-ordinating sentences about populations of molecules with talk about the pressure of gases on the walls of their containers.* After all,

> x looks red to S $\cdot \equiv \cdot$ there is a class of red sense data which belong to x, and are sensed by S

has at least a superficial resemblance to

> g exerts pressure on w $\cdot \equiv \cdot$ there is a class of molecules which make up g, and which are bouncing off w,

a resemblance which becomes even more striking once it is granted that the former is not an *analysis* of *x looks red to S* in terms of sense data.

There is, therefore, reason to believe that it is the fact that both codes and theories are contrived systems which are under the control of the language with which they are co-ordinated, which has given aid and comfort to the idea that sense-datum talk is 'another language' for ordinary discourse about perception. Yet although the logical relations between sentences in a theoretical language are, in an important sense, under the control of logical relations between sentences in the observation language, nevertheless, within the framework of this control, the theoretical language has an *autonomy* which contradicts the very idea of a code. If this essential difference between theories and codes is overlooked, one may be tempted to try to eat his cake and have it. By thinking of sense-datum talk as *merely another language*, one draws on the fact that codes have no surplus value. By thinking of sense-datum talk as *illuminating* the 'language of appearing', one draws on the fact that theoretical languages, though *contrived*, and depending for their meaningfulness on a co-ordination with the language of observation, have an explanatory function. Unfortunately, these two characteristics are incompatible; for it is just because theories have 'surplus value' that they can provide explanations.

No one, of course, who thinks—as, for example, does Ayer—of the existence of sense data as entailing the existence of 'direct knowledge', would wish to say that sense *data* are theoretical entities. It could scarcely be a theoretical fact that I am directly knowing that a certain sense content is red. On the other hand, the idea that sense *contents* are theoretical entities is not *obviously* absurd—so absurd as to preclude the above interpretation of the plausibility of the 'another-language' approach. For even those who introduce the expression 'sense content' by means of the context ' ... is directly known to be ... ' may fail to keep this fact in mind when putting this expression to use—for example, by developing the idea that physical objects and persons alike are patterns of sense contents. In such a specific context, it is possible to forget that sense *contents*, thus introduced, are essentially sense *data* and not merely items which exemplify sense qualities. Indeed, one may even lapse into thinking of the *sensing* of sense contents, the givenness of sense *data*, as *non-epistemic* facts.

I think it fair to say that those who offer the 'another-language' interpretation of sense data find the illumination it provides to consist primarily in the fact that in the language of sense data, physical objects are patterns of sense contents, so that, viewed in this framework, there is no 'iron curtain' between the knowing mind and the physical world. It is to elaborating plausible (if schematic) translations of physical-object statements into statements about sense contents, rather than to spelling out the force of such sentences as 'Sense content *s* is directly known to be red', that the greater part of their philosophical ingenuity has been directed.

However this may be, one thing can be said with confidence. If the language of sense data *were* merely a code, a notational device, then the cash value of any philosophical clarification it might provide must lie in its ability to illuminate logical relations *within* ordinary discourse about physical objects and our perception of them. Thus, the fact (if it were a fact) that a code can be constructed for ordinary perception talk which 'speaks' of a 'relation of identity' between the components ('sense data') of 'minds' and of 'things', would presumably have as its cash value the insight that ordinary discourse about physical objects and perceivers could (in principle) be constructed from sentences of the form, 'There looks to be a physical object with a red and triangular facing surface over there' (the counterpart in ordinary language of the basic expressions of the code). In more traditional terms, the clarification would consist in making manifest the fact that persons and things are alike logical constructions out of *lookings* or *appearings* (*not* appearances!). But any claim to this effect soon runs into insuperable difficulties which become apparent once the role of 'looks' or 'appears' is understood. And it is to an examination of this role that I now turn.

III. THE LOGIC OF 'LOOKS'

10. Before turning aside to examine the suggestion that the language of sense data is 'another language' for the situations described by the so-called 'language of appearing', I had concluded that classical sense-datum theories, when pressed, reveal themselves to be the result of a mismating of two ideas: (1) The idea that there are certain 'inner episodes', e.g. the sensation of a red triangle or of a C# sound, which occur to human beings and brutes without any prior process of learning or concept formation,

and without which it would—in *some* sense—be impossible to see, for example, that the facing surface of a physical object is red and triangular, or *hear* that a certain physical sound is C#; (2) The idea that there are certain 'inner episodes' which are the non-inferential knowings that, for example, a certain item is red and triangular, or, in the case of sounds, C#, which inner episodes are the necessary conditions of empirical knowledge as providing the evidence for all other empirical propositions. If this diagnosis is correct, a reasonable next step would be to examine these two ideas and determine how that which survives criticism in each is properly to be combined with the other. Clearly we would have to come to grips with the idea of *inner episodes*, for this is common to both.

Many who attack the idea of the given seem to have thought that the central mistake embedded in this idea is exactly the idea that there are inner episodes, whether thoughts or so-called 'immediate experiences', to which each of us has privileged access. I shall argue that this is just not so, and that the Myth of the Given can be dispelled without resorting to the crude verificationisms or operationalisms characteristic of the more dogmatic forms of recent empiricism. Then there are those who, while they do not reject the idea of inner episodes, find the Myth of the Given to consist in the idea that knowledge of these episodes furnishes *premises* on which empirical knowledge rests as on a foundation. But while this idea has, indeed, been the most widespread form of the Myth, it is far from constituting its essence. Everything hinges on *why* these philosophers reject it. If, for example, it is on the ground that the learning of a language is a *public* process which proceeds in a domain of *public* objects and is governed by *public* sanctions, so that *private* episodes—with the exception of a mysterious nod in their direction—must needs escape the net of rational discourse, then, while these philosophers are immune to the form of the myth which has flowered in sense-datum theories, they have no defence against the myth in the form of the givenness of such facts as that *physical object x looks red to person S at time t*, or that *there looks to person S at time t to be a red physical object over there*. It will be useful to pursue the Myth in this direction for a while before more general issues are raised.

11. Philosophers have found it easy to suppose that such a sentence as 'The tomato looks red to Jones' says that a certain triadic relation, *looking* or *appearing*, obtains among a physical object, a person, and a quality,[1] 'A looks ϕ to S' is assimilated to 'x gives y to z'—or, better, since giving is, strictly speaking, an action rather than a relation—to 'x is between y and z', and taken to be a case of the general form 'R(x,y,z)'. Having supposed this, they turn without further ado to the question, 'Is this relation analysable?' Sense-datum theorists have, on the whole, answered 'Yes', and claimed that facts of the form *x looks red to X* are to be analysed in terms of sense data. Some of them, without necessarily rejecting this claim, have argued that facts of this kind are, at the very least, to be *explained* in terms of sense data. Thus, when Broad[2] writes 'If, in fact, nothing elliptical is before my mind, it is very hard to under-

---

[1] A useful discussion of views of this type is to be found in Roderick Chisholm's 'The Theory of Appearing', in Max Black (ed.), *Philosphical Analysis*, pp. 102–18. Ithaca: Cornell Univ. Pr., 1950 and in H. H. Price's *Perception*. London: Methuen, 1932.

[2] Broad, C. D., *Scientific Thought*, London: Kegan Paul, 1923.

stand why the penny should seem *elliptical* rather than of any other shape (p. 240),'
he is appealing to sense data as a means of *explaining* facts of this form. The difference, of course, is that whereas if *x looks φ to S* is correctly *analysed* in terms of sense
data, then no one could believe that x looks *φ* to S without believing that S has sense
data, the same need not be true if *x looks φ to S* is explained in terms of sense data,
for, in the case of some types of explanation, at least, one can believe a fact without
believing its explanation.

On the other hand, those philosophers who reject sense-datum theories in
favour of so-called theories of appearing have characteristically held that facts of the
form *x looks φ to S* are ultimate and irreducible, and that sense data are needed neither for their analysis nor for their explanation. If asked, 'Doesn't the statement "x
looks red to S" have as part of its meaning the idea that s stands in some relation to
something that *is* red?' their answer is in the negative, and, I believe, rightly so.

12. I shall begin my examination of 'X looks red to S at t' with the simple but
fundamental point that the sense of 'red' in which things *look* red is, on the face of it,
the same as that in which things *are* red. When one glimpses an object and decides
that it looks red (to *me, now*, from here) and wonders whether it really *is* red, one is
surely wondering whether the colour—red—which it looks to have is the one it really
does have. This point can be obscured by such verbal manipulations as hyphenating
the words 'looks' and 'red' and claiming that it is the insoluble unity 'looks-red' and
not just 'looks' which is the relation. In so far as this dodge is based on insight, it is
insight into the fact that *looks* is not a relation between a person, a thing, and a quality. Unfortunately, as we shall see, the reason for this fact is one which gives no comfort at all to the idea that it is *looks-red* rather than *looks* which is the relation.

I have, in effect, been claiming that *being red* is logically prior, is a logically
simpler notion, than *looking red*; the function 'x is red' to 'x looks red to y'. In short,
that it just won't do to say that *x is red* is analysable in terms of *x looks red to y*. But
what, then, are we to make of the necessary truth—and it is, of course, a necessary
truth—that

$$\text{x } \textit{is} \text{ red } \cdot \equiv \cdot \text{ x would } \textit{look} \text{ red to standard observers in standard conditions?}$$

There is certainly some sense to the idea that this is at least the schema for a definition of *physical redness* in terms of *looking red*. One begins to see the plausibility
of the gambit that *looking-red* is an insoluble unity, for the minute one gives 'red'
(on the right-hand side) an independent status, it becomes what it obviously is, namely 'red' as a predicate of physical objects, and the supposed definition becomes an
obvious circle.

13. The way out of this troubling situation has two parts. The *second* is to
show how 'x *is* red' can be necessarily equivalent to 'x would *look* red to standard
observers in standard situations' without this being a definition of 'x is red' in terms
of 'x looks red'. But the *first*, and logically prior, step is to show that 'x looks red to
S' does not assert either an unanalysable triadic relation to obtain between x, red, and
S, or an unanalysable dyadic relation to obtain between x and S. Not, however, because
it asserts an *analysable* relation to obtain, but because *looks* is not a relation at all. Or,
to put the matter in a familiar way, one can say that *looks* is a relation if he likes, for

the sentences in which this word appears show some grammatical analogies to sentences built around words which we should not hesitate to classify as relation words; but once one has become aware of certain other features which make them very unlike ordinary relation sentences, he will be less inclined to view his task as that of *finding the answer* to the question 'Is looks a relation?'

14. To bring out the essential features of the use of 'looks', I shall engage in a little historical fiction. A young man, whom I shall call John, works in a necktie shop. He has learned the use of colour words in the usual way, with this exception: I shall suppose that he has never looked at an object in other than standard conditions. As he examines his stock every evening before closing up shop, he says, 'This is red', 'That is green', 'This is purple', etc., and such of his linguistic peers as happen to be present nod their heads approvingly.

Let us suppose, now, that at this point in the story, electric lighting is invented. His friends and neighbours rapidly adopt this new means of illumination, and wrestle with the problems it presents. John, however, is the last to succumb. Just after it has been installed in his shop, one of his neighbours, Jim, comes in to buy a necktie.

'Here is a handsome green one,' says John.

'But it *isn't* green,' says Jim, and takes John outside.

'Well,' says John, 'it was green in there, but now it is blue.'

'No,' says Jim, 'you know that neckties don't change their colour merely as a result of being taken from place to place.'

'But perhaps electricity changes their colour and they change back again in daylight?'

'That would be a queer kind of change, wouldn't it?' says Jim.

'I suppose so,' says bewildered John. 'But we saw that it was green *in there*.'

'No, we didn't see that it was green in there, because it wasn't green, and you can't see what isn't so!'

'Well, this is a pretty pickle,' says John. *'I just don't know what to say.'*

The next time John picks up this tie in his shop and someone asks what colour it is, his first impulse is to say 'It is green'. He suppresses this impulse, and, remembering what happened before, comes out with 'It is blue'. He does not *see* that it is blue, nor would he say that he sees it to be blue. What does he see? Let us ask him.

'I don't know *what* to say. If I didn't know that the tie is blue—and the alternative to granting this is odd indeed—I would swear that I was seeing a green tie and seeing that it is green. It is *as though* I were seeing the necktie to be green.'

If we bear in mind that such sentences as 'This is green' have both a *fact-stating* and a *reporting* use, we can put the point I have just been making by saying that once John learns to stifle the *report* 'This necktie is green' when looking at it in the shop, there is no other *report* about colour and the necktie which he knows how to make. To be sure, he now says 'This necktie is blue'. But he is not making a *reporting* use of this sentence. He uses it as the conclusion of an inference.[1]

---

[1] (Added 1963) When John has mastered looks talk he will be able to say not only 'The tie looks green' but 'The tie looks to be blue', where the latter has the sense of ' ... looks as blue ties look in these circumstances'. The distinction between 'looks ϕ' and 'looks to be ϕ' corresponds to Chisholm's distinction between non-comparative and comparative 'appears'—statements.

15. We return to the shop after an interval, and we find that when John is asked, 'What is the colour of this necktie?' he makes such statements as, 'It looks green, but take it outside and see.' It occurs to us that perhaps in learning to say 'This tie *looks* green' when in the shop, he has learned to make a new kind of report. Thus, it might seem as though his linguistic peers have helped him to notice a new kind of *objective* fact, one which, though a relational fact involving a perceiver, is as logically independent of the beliefs, the conceptual framework of the perceiver, as the fact that the necktie is blue; but a *minimal* fact, one which it is safer to report because one is less likely to be mistaken. Such a minimal fact would be the fact that the necktie looks green to John on a certain occasion, and it would be properly reported by using the sentence, 'This necktie *looks* green.' It is this type of account, of course, which I have already rejected.

But what is the alternative? If, that is, we are not going to adopt the sense-datum analysis. Let me begin by noting that there certainly seems to be something to the idea that the sentence 'This looks green to me now' has a reporting role. Indeed, it would seem to be essentially a report. But if so, *what* does it report, if not a minimal objective fact, and if what it reports is not to be analysed in terms of sense data?

16. Let me next call attention to the fact that the experience of having something look green to one at a certain time is, in so far as it is an experience, obviously very much like that of seeing something to be green, in so far as the latter is an experience. But the latter, of course, is not *just* an experience. And this is the heart of the matter. For to say that a certain experience is a *seeing that* something is the case, is to do more than describe the experience. It is to characterize it as, so to speak, making an assertion or claim, and—which is the point I wish to stress—to *endorse* that claim. As a matter of fact, as we shall see, it is much more easy to see that the statement 'Jones sees that the tree is green' ascribes a propositional claim to Jones's experience and endorses it, than to specify how the statement *describes* Jones's experience.

I realize that by speaking of experiences as containing propositional claims, I may seem to be knocking at closed doors. I ask the reader to bear with me, however, as the justification of this way of talking is one of my major aims. If I am permitted to issue this verbal currency now, I hope to put it on the gold standard before concluding the argument.

16. It is clear that the experience of seeing that something is green is not *merely* the occurrence of the propositional claim 'this is green'—not even if we add, as we must, that this claim is, so to speak, evoked or wrung from the perceiver by the object perceived. Here Nature—to turn Kant's simile (which he uses in another context) on its head—puts us to the question. The something more is clearly what philosophers have in mind when they speak of 'visual impressions' or 'immediate visual experiences'. What exactly is the logical status of these 'impressions' or 'immediate experiences' is a problem which will be with us for the remainder of this argument. For the moment it is the propositional claim which concerns us.

I pointed out above that when we use the word 'see' as in 'S sees that the tree is green' we are not only ascribing a claim to the experience, but endorsing it. It is this endorsement which Ryle has in mind when he refers to *seeing that something is thus and so* as an *achievement*, and to 'sees' as an *achievement word*. I prefer to call it a 'so it is' or 'just so' word, for the root idea is that of *truth*. To characterize S's experience as a *seeing* is, in a suitably broad sense—which I shall be concerned to explicate—to apply the semantical concept of truth to that experience.

Now the suggestion I wish to make is, in its simplest terms, that the statement 'X looks green to Jones' differs from 'Jones sees that x is green' in that whereas the latter both ascribes a propositional claim to Jones's experience *and endorses it*, the former ascribes the claim but does not endorse it. This is the essential difference between the two, for it is clear that two experiences may be identical *as experiences*, and yet one be properly referred to as a *seeing that* something is green, and the other *merely* as a case of something's *looking* green. Of course, if I say 'X *merely looks* green to S' I am not only failing to endorse the claim, I am rejecting it.

Thus, when I say 'X looks green to me now' I am *reporting* the fact that my experience is, so to speak, intrinsically, *as an experience*, indistinguishable from a veridical one of seeing that x is green. Involved in the report is the ascription to my experience of the claim 'x is green'; and the fact that I make this report rather than the simple report 'X is green' indicates that certain considerations have operated to raise, so to speak in a higher court, the question 'to endorse or not to endorse'. I may have reason to think that x may not after all be green.

If I make at one time the report 'X looks green'—which is not only a report, but the withholding of an endorsement—I may later, when the original reasons for withholding endorsement have been rebutted, endorse the original claim by saying, 'I saw that it was green, though at the time I was only sure that it looked green.' Notice that I will only say 'I see that x is green' (as opposed to 'X is green') when the question 'to endorse or not to endorse' has come up. 'I see that x is green' belongs, so to speak, on the same level as 'X looks green' and 'X merely *looks* green'.

17. There are many interesting and subtle questions about the dialectics of 'looks talk', into which I do not have the space to enter. Fortunately, the above distinctions suffice for our present purposes. Let us suppose, then, that to say that 'X looks green to S at t' is, in effect, to say that S has that kind of experience which, if one were prepared to endorse the propositional claim it involves, one would characterize as *seeing x to be green at t*. Thus, when our friend John learns to use the sentence 'This necktie looks green to me' he learns a way of reporting an experience of the kind which, as far as any categories I have yet permitted him to have are concerned, he can only characterize by saying that as an experience it does not differ from seeing something to be green, and that evidence for the proposition 'This necktie is green' is *ipso facto* evidence for the proposition that the experience in question is *seeing that the necktie is green*.

Now one of the chief merits of this account is that it permits a parallel treatment of 'qualitative' and 'existential' seeming or looking. Thus, when I say 'The tree looks bent' I am endorsing that part of the claim involved in my experience which concerns the existence of the tree, but withholding endorsement from the rest. On the other hand, when I say 'There looks to be a bent tree over there' I am refusing to endorse any but the most general aspect of the claim, namely, that there is an 'over there' as opposed to a 'here'. Another merit of the account is that it explains how a necktie, for example, can look red to S at t without looking scarlet or crimson or any other determinate shade of red. In short, it explains how things can have a *merely generic* look, a fact which would be puzzling indeed if looking red were a *natural* as opposed to *epistemic* fact about objects. The core of the explanation, of course, is that the propositional claim involved in such an experience may be, for example, either the more determinable claim 'This is red' or the more determinate claim 'This is crimson'. The complete story is more complicated, and requires some account of the role in these experiences of the 'impressions' or 'immediate experiences' the logical status of which remains to be determined. But even in the absence of these additional details, we can note the resemblance between the fact that x can look red to S, without it being true of some specific shade of red that x looks to S to have that shade, and the fact that S can believe that Cleopatra's Needle is tall, without its being true of some determinate number of feet that S believes it to be that number of feet tall.

18. The point I wish to stress at this time, however, is that the concept of *looking green*, the ability to recognize that something *looks green*, presupposes the concept of *being green*, and that the latter concept involves the ability to tell what colours objects have by looking at them—which, in turn, involves knowing in what circumstances to place an object if one wishes to ascertain its colour by looking at it. Let me develop this latter point. As our friend John becomes more and more sophisticated about his own and other people's visual experiences, he learns under what conditions it is as though one were seeing a necktie to be of one colour when in fact it is of another. Suppose someone asks him, 'Why does this tie look green to me?' John may very well reply, 'Because it is blue, and blue objects look green in this kind of light.' And if someone asks this question when looking at the necktie in plain daylight, John may very well reply, 'Because the tie *is* green'—to which he may add, 'We are in plain daylight, *and in daylight things look what they are.*' We thus see that

x is red · ≡ · x looks red to standard observers in standard conditions

is a necessary truth *not* because the right-hand side is the definition of 'x is red', but because 'standard conditions' means conditions in which things look what they are. And, of course, *which* conditions are standard for a given mode of perception is, at the common sense level, specified by a list of conditions which exhibit the vagueness and open texture characteristic of ordinary discourse.[1]

19. I have arrived at a stage in my argument which is, at least prima facie, out of step with the basic presuppositions of logical atomism. Thus, as long as *looking green* is taken to be the notion to which *being green* is reducible, it could be claimed with considerable plausibility that fundamental concepts pertaining to observable fact have that logical independence of one another which is characteristic of the empiricist tradition. But now, at first sight, the situation is *quite* disquieting. For if the ability to recognize that x looks green presupposes the concept of *being green*, and if this in turn involves knowing in what circumstances to view an object to ascertain its colour, then, since one can scarcely determine what the circumstances are without

---

[1] (Added 1963) Standard circumstances are, indeed, the circumstances in which things look as they are. But the non-trivial character of the above formula emerges when we replace 'standard circumstances' by the mention of a specific kind of circumstance (e.g. daylight) and add that daylight is the standard circumstance of perception, i.e. the condition in which colour words have their primary perceptual use.

noticing that certain objects have certain perceptible characteristics—including colours—it would seem that one could not form the concept of *being green*, and, by parity of reasoning, of the other colours, unless he already had them.

Now, it just won't do to reply that to have the concept of green, to know what it is for something to be green, it is sufficient to respond, when one is *in point of fact* in standard conditions, to green objects with the vocable 'This is green'. Not only must the conditions be of a sort that is appropriate for determining the colour of an object by looking, the subject must *know* that conditions of this sort *are* appropriate. And while this does not imply that one must have concepts before one has them, it does imply that one can have the concept of green only by having a whole battery of concepts of which it is one element. It implies that while the process of acquiring the concept of green may—indeed does—involve a long history of acquiring *piecemeal* habits of response to various objects in various circumstances, there is an important sense in which one has *no* concept pertaining to the observable properties of physical objects in Space and Time unless one has them all—and, indeed, as we shall see, a great deal more besides.[1]

20. Now, I think it is clear what a logical atomist, supposing that he found any merit at all in the above argument, would say. He would say that I am overlooking the fact that the logical space of physical objects in Space and Time rests on the logical space of sense contents, and he would argue that it is concepts pertaining to sense contents which have the logical independence of one another which is characteristic of traditional empiricism. 'After all,' he would point out, 'concepts pertaining to theoretical entities—molecules, for example—have the mutual dependence you have, perhaps rightly, ascribed to concepts pertaining to *physical* fact. But,' he would continue, 'theoretical concepts have empirical content because they rest on—are co-ordinated with—a more fundamental logical space. Until you have disposed, therefore, of the idea that there is a more fundamental logical space than that of physical objects in Space and Time, or shown that it too is fraught with coherence, your incipient *Meditations Hegeliènnes* are premature.'

And we can imagine a sense-datum theorist to interject the following complaint: 'You have begun to write as though you had shown not only that *physical redness* is not to be analysed in terms of *looking red*—which I will grant—but also that physical redness is not to be analysed at all, and, in particular, not to be analysed in terms of the redness of red sense contents. Again, you have begun to write as though you had shown not only that observing that x *looks* red is not more basic than observing that x *is* red, but also that there is *no* form of visual noticing more basic than seeing that x is red, such as the sensing of a red sense content. I grant', he continues, 'that the tendency of sense-datum theorists has been to claim that the *redness* of physical objects is to be analysed in terms of *looking red*, and *then* to claim that *looking red* is itself to be analysed in terms of *red sense contents*, and that you may have undercut

---

[1] (Added 1963) The argument can admit a distinction in principle between a rudimentary concept of 'green' which could be learned without learning the logical space of looks talk, and a richer concept of 'green' in which 'is green' can be challenged by 'merely looks green'. The essential point is that even to have the more rudimentary concept presupposes having a battery of other concepts.

this line of analysis. But what is to prevent the sense-datum theorist from taking the line that the properties of physical objects are *directly* analysable into the qualities and phenomenal relations of sense contents?'

Very well. But once again we must ask, How does the sense-datum theorist come by the framework of sense contents? and, How is he going to convince us that there are such things? For even if *looking red* does not enter into the analysis of physical redness, it is by asking us to reflect on the experience of having something look red to us that he hopes to make this framework convincing. And it therefore becomes relevant to note that my analysis of *x looks red to S at t* has not, at least as far as I have pushed it to date, revealed any such items as sense contents. And it may be relevant to suggest that once we see clearly that physical redness is not to be given a dispositional analysis in terms of *looking red*, the idea that it is to be given *any* kind of dispositional analysis loses a large measure of its plausibility. In any event, the next move must be to press further the above account of qualitative and existential looking.

IV. EXPLAINING LOOKS

21. I have already noted that sense-datum theorists are impressed by the question, 'How can a physical object look red to S, unless something in that situation *is* red and S is taking account of it? If S is not experiencing something red, how does it happen that the physical object looks *red*, rather than green or streaky?' There is, I propose to show, *something* to this line of thought, though the story turns out to be a complicated one. And if, in the course of telling the story, I shall be led to make statements which resemble *some* of the things sense-datum theorists have said, this story will amount to a sense-datum theory only in a sense which robs this phrase of an entire dimension of its traditional epistemological force, a dimension which is characteristic of even such heterodox forms of sense-datum theory as the 'another language' approach.

Let me begin by formulating the question: 'Is the fact that an object looks to S to be red and triangular, or that there looks to S to be a red and triangular object over there, to be explained in terms of the idea that Jones has a sensation—or impression, or immediate experience—of a red triangle?' One point can be made right away, namely that if these expressions are so understood that, say, the immediate experience of a red triangle implies the existence of something—not a physical object—which is red and triangular, and if the redness which this item has is the same as the redness which the physical object *looks* to have, then the suggestion runs up against the objection that the redness physical objects *look* to have is the same as the redness physical objects actually *do* have, so that items which *ex hypothesi* are not physical objects, and which radically, even categorically, differ from physical objects, would have the same redness as physical objects. And while this is, perhaps, not entirely out of the question, it certainly provides food for thought. Yet when it is claimed that 'obviously' physical objects cannot *look* red to one unless one is experiencing something that *is* red, is it not presumed that the redness which the *something* has is the redness which the physical object *looks to have*?

Now there are those who would say that the question, 'Is the fact that an object looks red and triangular to S to be explained—as opposed to notationally reformulated—in terms of the idea that S has an impression of a red triangle?' simply does not arise, on the ground that there are perfectly sound explanations of qualitative and existential lookings which make no reference to 'immediate experiences' or other dubious entities. Thus, it is pointed out, it is perfectly proper to answer the question, 'Why does this object look red?' by saying, 'Because it is an orange object looked at in such and such circumstances.' The explanation is, in principle, a good one, and is typical of the answers we make to such questions in everyday life. But because these explanations are good, it by no means follows that explanations of other kinds might not be equally good, and, perhaps, more searching.

22. On the face of it there are at least two ways in which additional but equally legitimate explanations *might* be forthcoming for such a fact as that *x looks red*. The first of these is suggested by a simple analogy. Might it not be the case that just as there are two kinds of good explanation of the fact that this balloon has expanded, (*a*) in terms of the Boyle–Charles laws which relate to empirical concepts of volume, pressure, and temperature pertaining to gases, and (*b*) in terms of the kinetic theory of gases; so there are two ways of explaining the fact that this object looks red to S: (*a*) in terms of empirical generalizations relating the colours of objects, the circumstances in which they are seen, and the colours they look to have, and (*b*) in terms of a theory of perception in which 'immediate' experiences' play a role analogous to that of the molecules of the kinetic theory.

Now there is such an air of paradox to the idea that 'immediate experiences' are *mere* theoretical entities—entities, that is, which are postulated, along with certain fundamental principles concerning them, to explain uniformities pertaining to sense perception, as molecules, along with the principles of molecular motion, are postulated to explain the experimentally determined regularities pertaining to gases— that I am going to lay it aside until a more propitious context of thought may make it seem relevant. Certainly, those who have thought that qualitative and existential lookings are to be explained in terms of 'immediate experiences' thought of the latter as the most untheoretical of entities, indeed, as *the* observables *par excellence*.

Let us therefore turn to a second way in which, at least prima facie, there might be an additional, but equally legitimate explanation of existential and qualitative lookings. According to this second account, when we consider items of this kind, we *find* that they contain as components items which are properly referred to as, for example, 'the immediate experience of a red triangle'. Let us begin our exploration of this suggestion by taking another look at our account of existential and qualitative lookings. It will be remembered that our account of qualitative looking ran, in rough and ready terms, as follows:

> 'x looks red to S' has the sense of 'S has an experience which involves in a unique way the idea *that x is red* and involves it in such a way that if this idea were true,[1] the experience would correctly be characterized as a seeing that x is red'.

---

[1] (Added 1963) ... and if S knew that the circumstances were normal.

Thus, our account implies that the three situations

(*a*) Seeing that x, over there, is red

(*b*) Its looking to one that x, over there, is red

(*c*) Its looking to one as though there were a red object over there

differ primarily in that (*a*) is so formulated as to involve an endorsement of the idea that x, over there, is red, whereas in (*b*) this idea is only partially endorsed, and in (*c*) not at all. Let us refer to the idea *that x, over there, is red* as the *common propositional content* of these three situations. (This is, of course, not strictly correct, since the propositional content of (*c*) is *existential*, rather than about a presupposedly designated object x, but it will serve my purpose. Furthermore, the common propositional content of these three experiences is much more complex and determinate than is indicated by the sentence we use to describe our experience to others, and which I am using to represent it. Nevertheless it is clear that, subject to the first of these qualifications, the propositional content of these three experiences *could* be identical.)

The propositional content of these three experiences is, of course, but a part of that to which we are logically committed by characterizing them as situations of these three kinds. Of the remainder, as we have seen, part is a matter of the extent to which this propositional content is endorsed. It is the residue with which we are now concerned. Let us call this residue the *descriptive content*. I can then point out that it is implied by my account that not only the *propositional content* but also the *descriptive content* of these three experiences may be identical. I shall suppose this to be the case, though that there must be some factual difference in the *total* situations is obvious.

Now, and this is the decisive point, in characterizing these three experiences, as respectively, a *seeing that x, over there, is red, its looking to one as though x, over there, were red*, and *its looking to one as though there were a red object over there*, we do not specify this common *descriptive* content save *indirectly*, by implying that *if the common propositional content were true,*[1] then all these three situations would be cases of *seeing* that x, over there, is red. Both existential and qualitative lookings are experiences that would be *seeings* if their propositional contents were true.

Thus, the very nature of 'looks talk' is such as to raise questions to which it gives no answer: What is the *intrinsic* character of the common descriptive content of these three experiences? and, How are they able to have it in spite of the fact that whereas in the case of (*a*) the perceiver must be in the presence of a red object over there, in (*b*) the object over there need not be red, while in (*c*) there need be no object over there at all?

23. Now it is clear that if we were required to give a more direct characterization of the common descriptive content of these experiences, we would begin by trying to do so in terms of the quality *red*. Yet, as I have already pointed out, we can scarcely say that this descriptive content is itself something red unless we can pry the term 'red' loose from its prima-facie tie with the category of physical objects. And

---

[1] (Added 1963) ... *and if the subject knew that the circumstances were normal.*

there is a line of thought which has been one of the standard gambits of perceptual epistemology and which seems to promise exactly this. If successful, it would convince us that *redness*—in the most basic sense of this term—is a characteristic of items of the sort we have been calling sense contents. It runs as follows:

> While it would, indeed, be a howler to say that we do not see chairs, tables, etc., but only their facing surfaces, nevertheless, although we see a table, say, and although the table has a back as well as a front, we do not see the back of the table as we see its front. Again, although we see the table, and although the table has an 'inside', we do not see the inside of the table as we see its facing outside. Seeing an object entails seeing its facing surface. If we are seeing that an object is red, this entails seeing that its facing surface is red. A red surface is a two-dimensional red expanse—two-dimensional in that though it may be *bulgy*, and in *this* sense three-dimensional, it has no *thickness*. As far as the analysis of perceptual consciousness is concerned, a red physical object is one that has a red expanse as its surface.
>
> Now a red expanse is not a physical object, nor does the existence of a red expanse entail the existence of a physical object to which it belongs. (Indeed, there are 'wild' expanses which do not belong to any physical object.) The 'descriptive content'—as you put it—which is common to the three experiences (*a*), (*b*) and (*c*) above, is exactly this sort of thing, a bulgy red expanse.

Spelled out thus baldly, the fallacy is, or should be, obvious; it is a simple equivocation on the phrase 'having a red surface'. We start out by thinking of the familiar fact that a physical object may be of one colour 'on the surface' and of another colour 'inside'. We may express this by saying that, for example, the 'surface' of the object is red, but its 'inside' green. But in saying this we are *not* saying that there is a 'surface' in the sense of a bulgy two-dimensional particular, a red 'expanse' which is a component particular in a complex particular which also includes green particulars. The notion of two-dimensional bulgy (or flat) particulars is a product of philosophical (and mathematical) sophistication which can be *related to* our ordinary conceptual framework, but does not belong in an *analysis* of it. I think that in its place it has an important contribution to make. (See below, Section 61 (5).) But this place is in the logical space of an ideal *scientific* picture of the world and not in the logical space of ordinary discourse. It has nothing to do with the logical grammar of our ordinary colour words. It is just a mistake to suppose that as the word 'red' is actually used, it is ever surfaces in the sense of two-dimensional particulars which are red. The only particular involved when a physical object is 'red on the outside, but green inside' is the physical object itself, located in a certain region of Space and enduring over a stretch of Time. The fundamental grammar of the attribute *red* is *physical object x is red at place p and at time t*. Certainly, when we say of an object that it is red, we commit ourselves to no more than that it is red 'at the surface'. And sometimes it is red at the surface by having what we would not hesitate to call a 'part' which is red through and through—thus, a red table which is red by virtue of a layer of red paint. But the red paint is not itself red by virtue of a component—a 'surface' or 'expanse'; a particular with no thickness—which is red. There may, let me repeat, turn out to be some place in the total philosophical picture for the statement that there 'really are' such particulars, and that they are elements in perceptual experience. But this place is not to be found by an analysis of ordinary perceptual discourse, any more than Minkowski four-dimensional Space-Time worms are an *analysis* of what we mean when we speak of physical objects in Space and Time.

V. IMPRESSIONS AND IDEAS: A LOGICAL POINT

24. Let me return to beating the neighbouring bushes. Notice that the common descriptive component of the three experiences I am considering is itself often referred to (by philosophers, at least) as an *experience*—as, for example, an *immediate experience*. Here caution is necessary. The notorious 'ing-ed' ambiguity of 'experience' must be kept in mind. For although *seeing that x, over there, is red* is an *experiencing*—indeed, a paradigm case of experiencing—it does not follow that the descriptive content of this experiencing is itself an experienc*ing*. Furthermore, because the fact that *x, over there, looks red to Jones* would be a *seeing*, on Jones's part, *that x, over there, is red*, if its propositional content were true, and because if it *were* a seeing, it *would be* an experiencing, we must beware of concluding that the fact that *x, over there, looks red to Jones* is itself an *experiencing*. Certainly, the fact that something looks red to me can itself be *experienced*. But it is not itself an experiencing.

All this is not to say that the common descriptive core may not turn out to be an experienc*ing*,[1] though the chances that this is so appear less with each step in my argument. On the other hand, I can say that it is a component in states of affairs which are experienc*ed*, and it does not seem unreasonable to say that it is itself experienc*ed*. But what kind of experience (in the sense of experienc*ed*) *is* it? If my argument to date is sound, I cannot say that it is a *red* experience that is, a red experienced item. I could, of course, introduce a new use of 'red' according to which to say of an 'immediate experience' that it was red, would be the stipulated equivalent of characterizing it as that which could be the common descriptive component of a *seeing* that something is red, and the corresponding qualitative and existential *lookings*. This would give us a *predicate* by which to describe and report the experience, but we should, of course, be only verbally better off than if we could only refer to this kind of experience as *the kind which* could be the common descriptive component of a *seeing* and a qualitative or existential *looking*. And this makes it clear that one way of putting what we are after is by saying that we want to have a *name* for this kind of experience which is truly a *name*, and not just shorthand for a definite description. Does ordinary usage have a *name* for this kind of experience?

I shall return to this quest in a moment. In the meantime it is important to clear the way of a traditional obstacle to understanding the status of such things as *sensations of red triangles*. Thus, suppose I were to say that while the experience I am examining is not a red experience, it is an experience *of red*. I could expect the immediate challenge: 'Is "sensation of a red triangle" any better off than "red and triangular experience"? Does not the existence of a sensation of a red triangle entail the existence of a red and triangular item, and hence, *always on the assumption that red*

---

[1] (Added 1963) The term 'experiencing' in the question 'Is the common descriptive component an experiencing?' is used in an epistemic sense. In the non-epistemic sense of an 'undergoing', the common descriptive component is, of course, an experiencing.

is a property of physical objects, of a red and triangular physical object? Must you not, therefore, abandon this assumption, and return to the framework of sense contents which you have so far refused to do?'

One way out of dilemma would be to assimilate 'Jones has a sensation of a red triangle' to 'Jones believes in a divine Huntress'. For the truth of the latter does not, of course, entail the existence of a divine Huntress. Now, I think that most contemporary philosophers are clear that it is possible to attribute to the context

... sensation of ...

the *logical* property of being such that 'There is a sensation of a red triangle' does not entail 'There is a red triangle' without assimilating the context ' ... sensation of ... ' to the context ' ... believes in ... ' in any closer way. For while mentalistic verbs characteristically provide nonextensional contexts (when they are not 'achievement' or 'endorsing' words), not all nonextensional contexts are mentalistic. Thus, as far as the purely *logical* point is concerned, there is no reason why 'Jones has a sensation of a red triangle' should be assimilated to 'Jones believes in a divine Huntress' rather than to 'It is possible that the moon is made of green cheese' or to any of the other non-extensional contexts familiar to logicians. Indeed there is no reason why it should be assimilated to any of these. ' ... sensation of ... ' or ' ... impression of ... ' could be a context which, though sharing with these others the logical property of nonextensionality, was otherwise in a class by itself.

25. Yet there is no doubt but that *historically* the contexts '... sensation of ...' and ' ... impression of ... ' *were* assimilated to such mentalistic contexts as ' ... believes ... ', ' ... desires ... ', ' ... chooses ... ', in short, to contexts which are either themselves 'propositional attitudes' or involve propositional attitudes in their analysis. This assimilation took the form of classifying sensations with *ideas* or *thoughts*. Thus Descartes uses the word 'thought' to cover not only *judgements, inferences, desires, volitions*, and (occurrent) *ideas of abstract qualities*, but also *sensations, feelings*, and *images*. Locke, in the same spirit, uses the term 'idea' with similar scope. The apparatus of Conceptualism, which had its genesis in the controversy over universals, was given a correspondingly wide application. Just as objects and situations were said to have 'objective being' in our *thoughts*, when we think of them, or judge them to obtain—as contrasted with the 'subjective' or 'formal being' which they have in the world—so, when we have a sensation of a red triangle, the red triangle was supposed to have 'objective being' in our sensation.

In elaborating, for a moment, this conceptualistic interpretation of sensation, let me refer to that which has 'objective being' in a *thought* or *idea* as its *content* or *immanent* object. Then I can say that the fundamental difference between occurrent *abstract ideas* and *sensations*, for both Locke and Descartes, lay in the *specificity* and, above all, the *complexity* of the content of the latter. (Indeed, both Descartes and Locke assimilated the contrast between the simple and the complex in ideas to that between the generic and the specific.) Descartes thinks of sensations as confused thoughts of their external cause; Spinoza of sensations and images as confused thoughts of bodily states, and still more confused thoughts of the external causes of these bodily states. And it is interesting to note that the conceptualistic thesis that abstract entities have only *esse intentionale* (their *esse* is *concipi*) is extended by Descartes and, with less awareness of what he is doing, Locke, to include the thesis that colours, sounds, etc., exist 'only in the mind' (their *esse* is *percipi*) and by Berkeley to cover all perceptible qualities.

Now, I think we would all agree, today, that this assimilation of sensations to thoughts is a mistake. It is sufficient to note that if 'sensation of a red triangle' had the sense of 'episode of the kind which is the common descriptive component of those experiences which *would be* cases of seeing that the facing surface of a physical object is red and triangular if an object *were* presenting a red and triangular facing surface' then it would have the nonextensionality, the noticing of which led to this mistaken assimilation. But while we have indeed escaped from this blind alley, it is small consolation. For we are no further along in the search for a 'direct' or 'intrinsic' characterization of 'immediate experience'.

VI. IMPRESSIONS AND IDEAS: AN HISTORICAL POINT

26. There are those who will say that although I have spoken of exploring blind alleys, it is really I who am blind. For, they will say, if that which we wish to characterize intrinsically is an *experience*, then there *can* be no puzzle about knowing *what kind* of experience it is, though there may be a problem about how this knowledge is to be communicated to others. And, indeed, it is tempting to suppose that if we *should* happen, at a certain stage of our intellectual development, to be able to classify an experience *only* as *of the kind which* could be common to a *seeing* and corresponding qualitative and existential *lookings*, all we would have to do to acquire a 'direct designation' for this kind of experience would be to pitch in, 'examine' it, locate the kind which it exemplifies and which satisfies the above description, name it—say 'ϕ'— and, in full possession of the concept of ϕ, classify such experiences, from now on, as ϕ experiences.

At this point, it is clear, the concept—or, as I have put it, the myth—of the given is being invoked to explain the possibility of a direct account of immediate experience. The myth insists that what I have been treating as one problem really subdivides into two, one of which is really no problem at all, while the other may have no solution. These problems are, respectively

(1) How do we become aware of an immediate experience as of one sort, and of a simultaneous immediate experience as of another sort?
(2) How can I know that the labels I attach to the sorts to which my immediate experiences belong, are attached by you to the same sorts? May not the sort I call 'red' be the sort you call 'green'—and so on systematically throughout the spectrum?

We shall find that the second question, to be a philosophical perplexity, presupposes a certain answer to the first question—indeed the answer given by the myth. And it is to this first question that I now turn. Actually there are various forms taken by the myth of the given in this connection, depending on other philosophical commitments. But they all have in common the idea that the awareness of certain *sorts*— and by 'sorts' I have in mind, in the first instance, determinate sense repeatables—is a primordial, non-problematic feature of 'immediate experience'. In the context of conceptualism, as we have seen, this idea took the form of treating sensations as though they were absolutely specific, and infinitely complicated, *thoughts*. And it is essential to an understanding of the empiricist tradition to realize that whereas the contemporary problem of universals primarily concerns the status of repeatable *determinate* features of particular situations, and the contemporary problem of abstract ideas is at least as much the problem of what it is to be aware of determinate repeatables as of what it is to be aware of determinable repeatables, Locke, Berkeley and, for that matter, Hume saw the problem of abstract ideas as the problem of what it is to be aware of *determinable* repeatables.[1] Thus, an examination of Locke's *Essay* makes it clear that he is thinking of a sensation of white as the sort of thing that can become an abstract idea (occurrent) of White—a thought of White 'in the Understanding'—merely by virtue of being separated from the context of other sensations (and images) which accompany it on a particular occasion. In other words, for Locke an abstract (occurrent) idea of the determinate repeatable Whiteness is nothing more than an isolated *image of white*, which, in turn, differs from a *sensation of white* only (to use a modern turn of phrase) by being 'centrally aroused'.

In short, for Locke, the problem of how we come to be aware of *determinate* sense repeatables is no problem at all. Merely by virtue of having sensations and images we have this awareness. *His* problem of abstract ideas is the problem of how we come to be able to think of generic properties. And, as is clear from the *Essay*, he approaches *this* problem in terms of what might be called an 'adjunctive theory of specification', that is, the view that (if we represent the idea of a determinable as *the idea of being A*) the idea of a determinate form of A can be represented as *the idea of being A and B*. It is, of course, notorious that this won't account for the relation of *the idea of being red* to *the idea of being crimson*. By thinking of *conjunction* as the fundamental logical relation involved in building up complex ideas from simple ones, and as the principle of the difference between determinable and determinate ideas, Locke precluded himself from giving even a plausible account of the relation between ideas of determinables and ideas of determinates. It is interesting to speculate what turn his thought might have taken had he admitted *disjunctive* as well as *conjunctive* complex ideas, *the idea of being A or B* alongside *the idea of being A and B*.

27. But my purpose here is not to develop a commentary on the shortcomings of Locke's treatment of abstract ideas, but to emphasize that something which is a problem for us was not a problem for him. And it is therefore important to note that the same is true of Berkeley. His problem was not, as it is often construed, 'How do we go from the awareness of *particulars* to ideas of *repeatables*?' but rather, 'Granted that in immediate experience we are aware of absolutely *specific* sense qualities, how do we come to be conscious of genera pertaining to them, and in what does this consciousness consist?' (This is not the only dimension of 'abstraction' that concerned him, but it is the one that is central to our purpose.) And, contrary to the usual interpretation, the essential difference between his account and Locke's consists in the fact

---

[1] For a systematic elaboration and defence of the following interpretation of Locke, Berkeley, and Hume, the reader should consult 'Berkeley's Critique of Abstract Ideas', a Ph.D. thesis by John Linnell, submitted to the Graduate Faculty of the University of Minnesota, June, 1954.

that whereas Locke was on the whole[1] committed to the view that there can be an idea which is *of* the genus without being *of* any of its species, Berkeley insists that we can have an idea *of* a genus only by having an idea *of* the genus *as*, to borrow a useful Scotist term, *'contracted' into one of its species.*

Roughly, Berkeley's contention is that if *being A* entails *being B*, then there can be no such thing as an idea which is *of A* without being *of B*. He infers that since *being triangular* entails *having some determinately triangular shape*, there cannot be an idea which is *of triangle* without being *of some determinately triangular shape*. We can be aware of generic triangularity only by having an idea which is of triangularity as 'contracted' into one of the specific forms of triangularity. Any of the latter will do; they are all 'of the same sort'.

28. Now, a careful study of the *Treatise* makes it clear that Hume is in the same boat as Berkeley and Locke, sharing with them the presupposition that we have an unacquired ability to be aware of determinate repeatables. It is often said that whereas he begins the *Treatise* by characterizing 'ideas' in terms which do not distinguish between *images* and *thoughts*, he corrects this deficiency in Book I, Part I, Section vii. What these students of Hume tend to overlook is that what Hume does in this later section is give an account *not* of what it is to think of *repeatables* whether determinable or determinate, but of what it is to think of *determinables*, thus of colour as contrasted with particular shades of colour. And his account of the consciousness of determinables takes for granted that we have a primordial ability to take account of *determinate* repeatables. Thus, his later account is simply built on, and in no sense a revision of, the account of ideas with which he opens the *Treatise*.

How, then, does he differ from Berkeley and Locke? The latter two had supposed that there must be such a thing as an *occurrent* thought of a determinable, however much they differed in their account of such thoughts. Hume, on the other hand, assuming that there are occurrent thoughts of *determinate* repeatables, *denies* that there are occurrent thoughts of *determinables*. I shall spare the reader the familiar details of Hume's attempt to give a constructive account of our consciousness of determinables, nor shall I criticize it. For my point is that however much Locke, Berkeley, and Hume differ on the problem of abstract ideas, they all take for granted that the

---

[1] I say that Locke was 'on the whole' committed to the view that there can be an idea which is *of* the genus without being *of* any of its species, because while he saw that it could not be *of* any one of the species to the exclusion of the others, and saw no way of avoiding this except by making it *of none* of the species, he was greatly puzzled by this, for he saw that in some sense the idea *of the genus* must be *of all the species*. We have already noted that if he had admitted disjunction as a principle of compounding ideas, he could have said that the idea *of the genus* is the idea *of the disjunction of all its species*, that the idea of *being triangular* is the idea of *being scalene or isosceles*. As it was, he thought that to be of all the species it would have to be the idea of *being scalene and isosceles*, which is, of course, the idea of an impossibility.

It is interesting to note that if Berkeley had faced up to the implications of the criterion we shall find him to have adopted, this disjunctive conception of the generic idea is the one he would have been led to adopt. For since *being G*—where 'G' stands for a generic character—entails being S_1 or S_2 or S_3 ... or S_n—where 'S_1' stands for a specific character falling under G—Berkeley should have taken as the unit of ideas concerning triangles, the idea of the genus Triangle as differentiated into the set of specific forms of triangularity. But, needless, to say, if Berkeley *had* taken this step, he could not have thought of a sensation of crimson as a determinate *thought*.

human mind has an innate ability to be aware of certain determinate sorts—*indeed, that we are aware of them simply by virtue of having sensations and images.*

29. Now, it takes but a small twist of Hume's position to get a radically different view. For suppose that instead of characterizing the initial elements of experience as impressions *of*, e.g. *red*, Hume had characterized them as *red particulars* (and I would be the last to deny that not only Hume, but perhaps Berkeley and Locke as well, often treat impressions or ideas *of red* as though they were *red particulars*) then Hume's view, expanded to take into account determinates as well as determinables, would become the view that all consciousness of sorts or repeatables rests on an association of *words* (e.g. 'red') with classes of resembling particulars.

It clearly makes all the difference in the world how this association is conceived. For if the formation of the association involves not only the occurrence of resembling particulars, but also the occurrence of the awareness *that they are resembling particulars*, then the givenness of determinate kinds or repeatables, say crimson, is merely being replaced by the givenness of *facts* of the form *x resembles y*, and we are back with an unacquired ability to be aware of repeatables, in this case the repeatable *resemblance*. Even more obviously, if the formation of the association involves not only the occurrence of red particulars, but the awareness *that they are red*, then the conceptualistic form of the myth has merely been replaced by a realistic version, as in the classical sense-datum theory.

If, however, the association is not mediated by the awareness of facts either of the form *x resembles y*, or of the form *x is ϕ*, then we have a view of the general type which I will call *psychological nominalism*, according to which *all* awareness of *sorts, resemblances, facts*, etc., in short, all awareness of abstract entities—indeed, all awareness even of particulars—is a linguistic affair. According to it, not even the awareness of such sorts, resemblances, and facts as pertain to so-called immediate experience is presupposed by the process of acquiring the use of a language.

Two remarks are immediately relevant: (1) Although the form of psychological nominalism which one gets by modifying Hume's view along the above lines has the essential merit that it avoids the mistake of supposing that there are pure episodes of being aware of sensory repeatables or sensory facts, and is committed to the view that any event which can be referred to in these terms must be, to use Ryle's expression, a mongrel categorical-hypothetical, in particular, a verbal episode *as being the manifestation of associative connections of the word-object and word-word types*, it nevertheless is impossibly crude and inadequate as an account of the simplest concept. (2) Once sensations and images have been purged of epistemic aboutness, the primary reason for supposing that the fundamental associative tie between language and the world must be between words and 'immediate experiences' has disappeared, and the way is clear to recognizing that basic word–world associations hold, for example, between 'red' and red *physical objects*, rather than between 'red' and a supposed class of private red particulars.

The second remark, it should be emphasized, does not imply that private sensations or impressions may not be essential to the formation of these associative connections. For one can certainly admit that the tie between 'red' and red physical objects—which tie makes it possible for 'red' to mean the quality red—is *causally* mediated by sensations of red without being committed to the mistaken idea that it is 'really' sensations of red, rather than red physical objects, which are the primary denotation of the word 'red'.

VII. THE LOGIC OF 'MEANS'

30. There is a source of the Myth of the Given to which even philosophers who are suspicious of the whole idea of *inner episodes* can fall prey. This is the fact that when we picture a child—or a carrier of slabs—learning his *first* language, *we*, of course, locate the language learner in a structured logical space in which *we* are at home. Thus, we conceive of him as a person (or, at least, a potential person) in a world of physical objects, coloured, producing sounds, existing in Space and Time. But though it is *we* who are familiar with this logical space, we run the danger, if we are not careful, of picturing the language learner as having *ab initio* some degree of awareness— 'pre-analytic', limited and fragmentary though it may be—of this same logical space. We picture his state as though it were rather like our own when placed in a strange forest on a dark night. In other words, unless we are careful, we can easily take for granted that the process of teaching a child to use a language is that of teaching it to discriminate elements within a logical space of particulars, universals, facts, etc., of which it is already undiscriminatingly aware, and to associate these discriminated elements with verbal symbols. And this mistake is in principle the same whether the logical space of which the child is supposed to have this undiscriminating awareness is conceived by *us* to be that of physical objects or of private sense contents.

The real test of a theory of language lies not in its account of what has been called (by H. H. Price) 'thinking in absence', but in its account of 'thinking in presence'—that is to say, its account of those occasions on which the fundamental connection of language with non-linguistic fact is exhibited. And many theories which look like psychological nominalism when one views their account of thinking in absence, turn out to be quite 'Augustinian' when the scalpel is turned to their account of thinking in presence.

31. Now, the friendly use I have been making of the phrase 'psychological nominalism' may suggest that I am about to *equate* concepts with words, and thinking, in so far as it is episodic, with verbal episodes. I must now hasten to say that I shall do nothing of the sort, or, at least, that if I *do* do *something* of the sort, the view I shall shortly be developing is only in a relatively Pickwickian sense an equation of thinking with the use of language. I wish to emphasize, therefore, that as I am using the term, the primary connotation of 'psychological nominalism' is the denial that there is any awareness of logical space prior to, or independent of, the acquisition of a language.

However, although I shall later be distinguishing between *thoughts* and their verbal *expression*, there is a point of fundamental importance which is best made before more subtle distinctions are drawn. To begin with, it is perfectly clear that the word 'red' would not be a *predicate* if it did not have the logical syntax characteristic of predicates. Nor would it be the predicate it is, unless, in certain frames of mind, at least, we tended to respond to red objects in standard circumstances with something having the force of 'This is red'. And once we have abandoned the idea that learning to use the word 'red' involves antecedent episodes of the *awareness of redness*—not to be confused, of course, with *sensations of red*—there is a temptation to suppose that the word 'red' means the quality *red* by virtue of these two facts: briefly, the fact that it has the *syntax* of a predicate, and the fact that it is a *response* (in certain circumstances) to red objects.

But this account of the meaningfulness of 'red', which Price has correctly stigmatized as the 'thermometer view', would have little plausibility if it were not reinforced by another line of thought which takes its point of departure from the superficial resemblance of

(In German) '*rot*' means *red*

to such relational statements as

Cowley adjoins Oxford.

For once one assimilates the form

' ... ' means— — —

to the form

x R y

and thus takes it for granted that meaning is a relation between a word and a nonverbal entity, it is tempting to suppose that the relation in question is that of association.

The truth of the matter, of course, is that statements of the form '" ... " means— — —' are *not* relational statements, and that while it is indeed the case that the word '*rot*' could not mean the quality *red* unless it were associated with red things, it would be misleading to say that the semantical statement '"*Rot*" means *red*' says of '*rot*' that it associated with red things. For this would suggest that the semantical statement is, so to speak, definitional shorthand for a longer statement about the associative connections of '*rot*', which is not the case. The rubric '" ... " means— — —' is a linguistic device for conveying the information that a *mentioned* word, in this case '*rot*', plays the same role in a certain linguistic economy, in this case the linguistic economy of German-speaking peoples, as does the word 'red', which is not *mentioned* but *used*—used in a unique way; *exhibited*, so to speak—and which occurs 'on the right-hand side' of the semantical statement.

We see, therefore, how the two statements

'*Und*' means *and*

and

'*Rot*' means *red*

can tell us quite different things about '*und*' and '*rot*', for the first conveys the information that '*und*' plays the purely formal role of a certain logical connective, the second that '*rot*' plays in German the role of the observation word 'red'—in spite of the fact that *means* has the same sense in each statement, and without having to say that the first says of '*und*' that it stands in 'the meaning relation' to Conjunction, or the second that '*rot*' stands in 'the meaning relation' to Redness.[1]

These considerations make it clear that nothing whatever can be inferred about the complexity of the role played by the word 'red' or about the exact way in which the word 'red' is related to red things, from the truth of the semantical statement '"red" means the quality *red*'. And no consideration arising from the 'Fido'-Fido aspect of the grammar of 'means' precludes one from claiming that the role of the word 'red' by virtue of which it can correctly be said to have the meaning it does is a complicated one indeed, and that one cannot understand the meaning of the word 'red'—'know what redness is'—unless one has a great deal of knowledge which classical empiricism would have held to have a purely contingent relationship with the possession of fundamental empirical concepts.

VIII. DOES EMPIRICAL KNOWLEDGE HAVE A FOUNDATION?

32. One of the forms taken by the Myth of the Given is the idea that there is, indeed *must be*, a structure of particular matter of fact such that (*a*) each fact can not only be non-inferentially known to be the case, but presupposes no other knowledge either of particular matter of fact, or of general truths; and (*b*) such that the noninferential knowledge of facts belonging to this structure constitutes the ultimate court of appeals for all factual claims—particular and general—about the world. It is important to note that I characterized the knowledge of fact belonging to this stratum as not only noninferential, but as presupposing no knowledge of other matter of fact, whether particular or general. It might be thought that this is a redundancy, that knowledge (not belief or conviction, but knowledge) which logically presupposes knowledge of other facts *must* be inferential. This, however, as I hope to show, is itself an episode in the Myth.

Now, the idea of such a privileged stratum of fact is a familiar one, though not without its difficulties. Knowledge pertaining to this level is *noninferential*, yet it is, after all, *knowledge*. It is *ultimate*, yet it has *authority*. The attempt to make a consistent picture of these two requirements has traditionally taken the following form:

> Statements pertaining to this level, in order to 'express knowledge' must not only be made, but, so to speak, must be worthy of being made, *credible*, that is, in the sense of worthy of credence. Furthermore, and this is a crucial point, they must be made in a way which *involves* this credibility. For where there is no connection between the making of a statement and its authority, the assertion may express *conviction*, but it can scarcely be said to express knowledge.
>
> The authority—the credibility—of statements pertaining to this level cannot exhaustively consist in the fact that they are supported by *other* statements, for in that case all *knowledge* pertaining to this level would have to be inferential, which not only contradicts the hypothesis, but flies in the face of good sense. The conclusion seems inevitable

---

[1] For an analysis of the problem of abstract entities built on this interpretation of semantical statements, see my 'Empiricism and Abstract Entities' in Paul A. Schlipp (ed.), *The Philosophy of Rudolph Carnap*. Wilmette (Ill.), 1963; also 'Abstract Entities', *The Review of Metaphysics*, June, 1963.

that if some statements pertaining to this level are to express *noninferential* knowledge, they must have a credibility which is not a matter of being supported by other statements. Now there does seem to be a class of statements which fill at least part of this bill, namely such statements as would be said to *report observations*, thus, 'This is red.' These statements, candidly made, have authority. Yet they are not expressions of inference. How, then, is this authority to be understood?

Clearly, the argument continues, it springs from the fact that they are made in just the circumstances in which they are made, as is indicated by the fact that they characteristically, though not necessarily or without exception, involve those so-called token-reflexive expressions which, in addition to the tenses of verbs, serve to connect the circumstances in which a statement is made with its sense. (At this point it will be helpful to begin putting the line of thought I am developing in terms of the *fact-stating* and *observation-reporting* roles of certain sentences.) Roughly, two verbal performances which are tokens of a non-token-reflexive sentence can occur in widely different circumstances and yet make the same statement; whereas two tokens of a token-reflexive sentence can make the same statement only if they are uttered in the same circumstances (according to a relevant criterion of sameness). And two tokens of a sentence, whether it contains a token-reflexive expression—over and above a tensed verb—or not, can make the same *report* only if, made in all candour, they express the *presence*—in *some* sense of 'presence'—of the state of affairs that is being reported; if, that is, they stand in that relation to the state of affairs, whatever the relation may be, by virtue of which they can be said to formulate observations of it.

It would appear, then, that there are two ways in which a sentence token can have credibility: (1) The authority may accrue to it, so to speak, from above, that is, as being a token of a sentence type *all* the token of which, in a certain use, have credibility, e.g. '2 + 2 = 4'. In this case, let us say that token credibility is inherited from type authority. (2) The credibility may accrue to it from the fact that it came to exist in a certain way in a certain set of circumstances, e.g. 'This is red.' Here token credibility is not derived from type credibility.

Now, the credibility of *some* sentence types appears to be *intrinsic*—at least in the limited sense that it is *not* derived from other sentences, type or token. This is, or seems to be, the case with certain sentences used to make analytic statements. The credibility of *some* sentence types accrues to them by virtue of their logical relations to other sentence types, thus by virtue of the fact that they are logical consequences of more basic sentences. It would seem obvious, however, that the credibility of empirical sentence types cannot be traced without remainder to the credibility of other sentence types. And since no empirical sentence type appears to have *intrinsic* credibility, this means that credibility must accrue to *some* empirical sentence types by virtue of their logical relations to certain sentence tokens, and, indeed, to sentence tokens the authority of which is not derived, in its turn, from the authority of sentence types.

The picture we get is that of their being two *ultimate* modes of credibility: (1) The intrinsic credibility of analytic sentences, which accrues to tokens as being tokens of such a type; (2) the credibility of such tokens as 'express observations', a credibility which flows from tokens to types.

33. Let us explore this picture, which is common to all traditional empiricisms, a bit further. How is the authority of such sentence tokens as 'express observational knowledge' to be understood? It has been tempting to suppose that in spite of the obvious differences which exist between 'observation reports' and 'analytic state-

ments', there is an essential similarity between the ways in which they come by their authority. Thus, it has been claimed, not without plausibility, that whereas *ordinary* empirical statements can be *correctly* made without being *true*, observation reports resemble analytic statements in that being correctly made is a sufficient as well as necessary condition of their truth. And it has been inferred from this—somewhat hastily, I believe—that 'correctly making' the report 'This is green' is a matter of 'following the rules for the use of "this", "is", and "green".'

Three comments are immediately necessary:

(1) First a brief remark about the term 'report'. In ordinary usage a report is a report made *by* someone *to* someone. To make a report is to *do* something. In the literature of epistemology, however, the word 'report' or '*Konstatierung*' has acquired a technical use in which a sentence token can play a reporting role (*a*) without being an *overt* verbal performance, and (*b*) without having the character of being 'by someone to someone'—even oneself. There is, of course, such a thing as 'talking to oneself'—*in foro interno*—but, as I shall be emphasizing in the closing stages of my argument, it is important not to suppose that all 'covert' verbal episodes are of this kind.

(2) My second comment is that while *we* shall not assume that because 'reports' *in the ordinary sense* are actions, 'reports' in the sense of *Konstatierungen* are also actions, the line of thought we are considering treats them as such. In other words, it interprets the correctness of *Konstatierungen* as analogous to the rightness of actions. Let me emphasize, however, that not all *ought* is *ought to do*, nor all correctness the correctness of *actions*.

(3) My third comment is that if the expression 'following a rule' is taken seriously, and is not weakened beyond all recognition into the bare notion of exhibiting a uniformity—in which case the lightning-thunder sequence would 'follow a rule'—then it is the knowledge or belief that the circumstances are of a certain kind, and not the mere fact that they *are* of this kind, which contributes to bringing about the action.

34. In the light of these remarks it is clear that *if* observation reports are construed as *actions, if* their correctness is interpreted as the correctness of an *action*, and *if* the authority of an observation report is construed as the fact that making it is 'following a rule' in the proper sense of this phrase, *then* we are face to face with givenness in its most straightforward form. For these stipulations commit one to the idea that the authority of *Konstatierungen* rests on nonverbal episodes of awareness— awareness *that* something is the case, e.g. *that this is green*—which nonverbal episodes have an intrinsic authority (they are, so to speak, 'self-authenticating') which the *verbal* performances (the *Konstatierungen*) properly performed 'express'. One is committed to a stratum of authoritative nonverbal episodes ('awarenesses'), the authority of which accrues to a superstructure of *verbal actions*, provided that the expressions occurring in these actions are properly *used*. These self-authenticating episodes would constitute the tortoise on which stands the elephant on which rests the edifice of empirical knowledge. The essence of the view is the same whether these intrinsically authoritative episodes are such items as the awareness that a certain sense content is green or such items as the awareness that a certain physical object looks to oneself to be green.

35. But what is the alternative? We might begin by trying something like the following: An overt or covert token of 'This is green' in the presence of a green item is a *Konstatierung* and expresses observational knowledge if and only if it is a manifestation of a tendency to produce overt or covert tokens of 'This is green'—given a certain set—if and only if a green object is being looked at in standard conditions. Clearly on this interpretation the occurrence of such tokens of 'This is green' would be 'following a rule' only in the sense that they are instances of a uniformity, a uniformity differing from the lightning–thunder case in that it is an acquired causal characteristic of the language user. Clearly the above suggestion, which corresponds to the 'thermometer view' criticized by Professor Price, and which we have already rejected, won't do as it stands. Let us see, however, if it cannot be revised to fit the criteria I have been using for 'expressing observational knowledge'.

The first hurdle to be jumped concerns the *authority* which, as I have emphasized, a sentence token must have in order that it may be said to express knowledge. Clearly, on this account the only thing that can remotely be supposed to constitute such authority is the fact that one can infer the presence of a green object from the fact that someone makes this report. As we have already noticed, the correctness of a report does not have to be construed as the rightness of an *action*. A report can be correct as being an instance of a general mode of behaviour which, in a given linguistic community, it is reasonable to sanction and support.

The second hurdle is, however, the decisive one. For we have seen that to be the expression of knowledge, a report must not only *have* authority, this authority must *in some sense* be recognized by the person whose report it is. And this is a steep hurdle indeed. For if the authority of the report 'This is green' lies in the fact that the existence of green items appropriately related to the perceiver can be inferred from the occurrence of such reports, it follows that only a person who is able to draw this inference, and therefore who has not only the concept *green*, but also the concept of uttering 'This is green'—indeed, the concept of certain conditions of perception, those which would correctly be called 'standard conditions'—could be in a position to token 'This is green' in recognition of its authority. In other words, for a *Konstatierung* 'This is green' to 'express observational knowledge', not only must it be a *symptom* or *sign* of the presence of a green object in standard conditions, but the perceiver must know that tokens of 'This is green' *are* symptoms of the presence of green objects in conditions which are standard for visual perception.

36. Now it might be thought that there is something obviously absurd in the idea that before a token uttered by, say, Jones could be the expression of observational knowledge, Jones would have to know that overt verbal episodes of this kind are reliable indicators of the existence, suitably related to the speaker, of green objects. I do not think that it is. Indeed, I think that something very like it is true. The point I wish to make now, however, is that if it *is* true, then it follows, as a matter of simple logic, that one could not have observational knowledge of *any* fact unless one knew many *other* things as well. And let me emphasize that the point is not taken care of by distinguishing between *knowing how* and *knowing that*, and admitting that observational knowledge requires a lot of 'know how'. For the point is specifically that observational knowledge of any particular fact, e.g. that this is green, presupposes that one knows general facts of the form *X is a reliable symptom of Y*. And to admit

this requires an abandonment of the traditional empiricist idea that observational knowledge 'stands on its own feet'. Indeed, the suggestion would be anathema to traditional empiricists for the obvious reason that by making observational knowledge *presuppose* knowledge of general facts of the form *X is a reliable symptom of Y*, it runs counter to the idea that we come to know general facts of this form only *after* we have come to know by observation a number of particular facts which support the hypothesis that X is a symptom of Y.

And it might be thought that there is an obvious regress in the view we are examining. Does it not tell us that observational knowledge at time t presupposes knowledge of the form *X is a reliable symptom of Y*, which presupposes *prior* observational knowledge, which presupposes *other* knowledge of the form *X is a reliable symptom of Y*, which presupposes still other, and *prior*, observational knowledge, and so on? This charge, however, rests on too simple, indeed a radically mistaken, conception of what one is saying of Jones when one says that he *knows* that-p. It is not just that the objection supposes that knowing is an *episode*; for clearly there are episodes which we can correctly characterize as knowings, in particular, *observings*. The essential point is that in characterizing an episode or a state as that of *knowing*, we are not giving an empirical description of that episode or state; we are placing it in the logical space of reasons, of justifying and being able to justify what one says.

37. Thus, all that the view I am defending requires is that no tokening by S *now* of 'This is green' is to count as 'expressing observational knowledge' unless it is also correct to say of S that he *now* knows the appropriate fact of the form *X is a reliable symptom of Y*, namely that (and again I oversimplify) utterances of 'This is green' are reliable indicators of the presence of green objects in standard conditions of perception. And while the correctness of this statement about Jones requires that Jones could *now* cite prior particular facts as evidence for the idea that these utterances *are* reliable indicators, it requires only that it is correct to say that Jones *now* knows, thus remembers,[1] that these particular facts *did* obtain. It does not require that it be correct to say that at the time these facts did obtain he *then knew* them to obtain. And the regress disappears.

Thus, while Jones's ability to give inductive reasons *today* is built on a long history of acquiring and manifesting verbal habits in perceptual situations, and, in particular, the occurrence of verbal episodes, e.g. 'This is green', which is superficially like those which are later properly said to express observational knowledge, it does not require that any episode in this prior time be characterizeable as expressing knowledge. (At this point, the reader should reread Section 19 above.)

38. The idea that observation 'strictly and properly so-called' is constituted by certain self-authenticating nonverbal episodes, the authority of which is transmitted to verbal and quasi-verbal performances when these performances are made 'in conformity with the semantical rules of the language', is, of course, the heart of the Myth of the Given. For the *given*, in epistemological tradition, is what is *taken* by these self-authenticating episodes. These 'takings' are, so to speak, the unmoved

---

[1] (Added 1963) My thought was that one can have direct (non-inferential) knowledge of a past fact which one did not or even (as in the case envisaged) *could* not conceptualize at the time it was present.

movers of empirical knowledge, the 'knowings in presence' which are presupposed by all other knowledge, both the knowledge of general truths and the knowledge 'in absence' of other particular matters of fact. Such is the framework in which traditional empiricism makes its characteristic claim that the perceptually given is the foundation of empirical knowledge.

Let me make it clear, however, that if I reject this framework, it is not because I should deny that observings are *inner* episodes, nor that *strictly speaking* they are *nonverbal* episodes. It will be my contention, however, that the sense in which they are nonverbal—which is also the sense in which thought episodes are nonverbal—is one which gives no aid or comfort to epistemological givenness. In the concluding sections of this paper I shall attempt to explicate the logic of inner episodes, and show that we can distinguish between observations and thoughts, on the one hand, and their verbal expression on the other, without making the mistakes of traditional dualism. I shall also attempt to explicate the logical status of *impressions* or *immediate experiences*, and thus bring to a successful conclusion the quest with which my argument began.

One final remark before I begin this task. If I reject the framework of traditional empiricism, it is not because I want to say that empirical knowledge has *no* foundation. For to put it this way is to suggest that it is really 'empirical knowledge so-called', and to put it in a box with rumours and hoaxes. There is clearly *some* point to the picture of human knowledge as resting on a level of propositions—observation reports—which do not rest on other propositions in the same way as other propositions rest on them. On the other hand, I do wish to insist that the metaphor of 'foundation' is misleading in that it keeps us from seeing that if there is a logical dimension in which other empirical propositions rest on observation reports, there is another logical dimension in which the latter rest on the former.

Above all, the picture is misleading because of its static character. One seems forced to choose between the picture of an elephant which rests on a tortoise (What supports the tortoise?) and the picture of a great Hegelian serpent of knowledge with its tail in its mouth (Where does it begin?). Neither will do. For empirical knowledge, like its sophisticated extension, science, is rational, not because it has a *foundation* but because it is a self-correcting enterprise which can put *any* claim in jeopardy, though not *all* at once.

IX. SCIENCE AND ORDINARY USAGE

39. There are many strange and exotic specimens in the gardens of philosophy: Epistemology, Ontology, Cosmology, to name but a few. And clearly there is much good sense—not only rhyme but reason—to these labels. It is not my purpose, however, to animadvert on the botanizing of philosophies and things philosophical, other than to call attention to a recent addition to the list of philosophical flora and fauna, the Philosophy of Science. Nor shall I attempt to locate this new speciality in a classificatory system. The point I wish to make, however, can be introduced by calling to mind the fact that classificatory schemes, however theoretical their purpose, have practical consequences: nominal causes, so to speak, have real effects. As long as

there was no such subject as 'philosophy of science', all students of philosophy felt obligated to keep at least one eye part of the time on both the methodological and the substantive aspects of the scientific enterprise. And if the result was often a confusion of the task of philosophy with the task of science, and almost equally often a projection of the framework of the latest scientific speculations into the common sense picture of the world (witness the almost unquestioned assumption, today, that the common sense world of physical objects in Space and Time must be *analysable* into spatially and temporally, or even spatiotemporally, related *events*), at least it had the merit of ensuring that reflection on the nature and implications of scientific discourse was an integral and vital part of philosophical thinking generally. But now that philosophy of science has nominal as well as real existence, there has arisen the temptation to leave it to the specialists, and to confuse the sound idea that philosophy is not science with the mistaken idea that philosophy is independent of science.

40. As long as discourse was viewed as a map, subdivided into a side-by-side of sub-maps, each representing a sub-region in a side-by-side of regions making up the total subject-matter of discourse, and as long as the task of the philosopher was conceived to be the piecemeal one of analysis in the sense of *definition*—the task, so to speak, of 'making little ones out of big ones'—one could view with equanimity the existence of philosophical specialists—specialists in formal and mathematical logic, in perception, in moral philosophy, etc. For if discourse were as represented above, where would be the harm of each man fencing himself off in his own garden? In spite, however, of the persistence of the slogan 'philosophy is analysis', we now realize that the atomistic conception of philosophy is a snare and a delusion. For 'analysis' no longer connotes the definition of terms, but rather the clarification of the logical structure—in the broadest sense—of discourse, and discourse no longer appears as one plane parallel to another, but as a tangle of intersecting dimensions whose relations with one another and with extra-linguistic fact conform to no single or simple pattern. No longer can the philosopher interested in perception say, 'Let him who is interested in prescriptive discourse analyse its concepts and leave me in peace.' Most if not all philosophically interesting concepts are caught up in more than one dimension of discourse, and while the atomism of early analysis has a healthy successor in the contemporary stress on journeyman tactics, the grand strategy of the philosophical enterprise is once again directed towards that articulated and integrated vision of man-in-the-universe—or, shall I say, discourse-about-man-in-all-discourse—which has traditionally been its goal.

But the moral I wish specifically to draw is that no longer can one smugly say, 'Let the person who is interested in scientific discourse analyse scientific discourse and let the person who is interested in ordinary discourse analyse ordinary discourse.' Let me not be misunderstood. I am not saying that in order to discern the logic—the polydimensional logic—of ordinary discourse, it is necessary to make use of the results or the methods of the sciences. Nor even that, within limits, such a division of labour is not a sound corollary of the journeyman's approach. My point is rather that what we call the scientific enterprise is the flowering of a dimension of discourse which already exists in what historians call the 'prescientific stage', and that failure to understand this type of discourse 'writ large'—in science—may lead, indeed, has often led to a failure to appreciate its role in 'ordinary usage', and, as a result, to a failure to understand the full logic of even the most fundamental, the 'simplest' empirical terms.

41. Another point of equal importance. The procedures of philosophical analysis as such may make no use of the methods or results of the sciences. But familiarity with the trend of scientific thought is essential to the *appraisal* of the framework categories of the common sense picture of the world. For if the line of thought embodied in the preceding paragraphs is sound, if, that is to say, scientific discourse is but a continuation of a dimension of discourse which has been present in human discourse from the very beginning, then one would expect there to be a sense in which the scientific picture of the world *replaces* the common sense picture; a sense in which the scientific account of 'what there is' *supersedes* the descriptive ontology of everyday life.

42. Here one must be cautious. For there is a right way and a wrong way to make this point. Many years ago it used to be confidently said that science has shown, for example, that physical objects are not really coloured. Later it was pointed out that if this is interpreted as the claim that the sentence 'Physical objects have colours' expresses an empirical proposition which, though widely believed by common sense, has been shown by science to be false, then, of course, this claim is absurd. The idea that physical objects are not coloured can make sense only as the (misleading) expression of one aspect of a philosophical critique of the very framework of physical objects located in Space and enduring through Time. In short, 'Physical objects are not really coloured' makes sense only as a clumsy expression of the idea that there are no such things as the coloured physical objects of the common sense world, where this is interpreted, not as an empirical proposition—like 'There are no nonhuman featherless bipeds'—*within* the common sense frame, but as the expression of a rejection (in *some* sense) of this very framework itself, in favour of another built around different, if not unrelated, categories. This rejection need not, of course, be a *practical* rejection. It need not, that is, carry with it a proposal to brain-wash existing populations and train them to speak differently. And, of course, as long as the existing framework is used, it will be *incorrect* to say—otherwise than to make a philosophical point *about the framework*—that no object is really coloured, or is located in Space, or endures through Time. But, *speaking as a philosopher*, I am quite prepared to say that the common sense world of physical objects in Space and Time is unreal—that is, that there are no such things. Or, to put it less paradoxically, that in the dimension of describing and explaining the world, science is the measure of all things, of what is that it is, and of what is not that it is not.

43. There is a widespread impression that reflection on how we learn the language in which, in everyday life, we describe the world, leads to the conclusion that the categories of the common sense picture of the world have, so to speak, an unchallengeable authenticity. There are, of course, different conceptions of just what this fundamental categorial framework is. For some it is sense contents and phenomenal relations between them; for others physical objects, persons, and processes in Space and Time. But whatever their points of difference, the philosophers I have in mind are united in the conviction that what is called the 'ostensive tie' between our fundamental descriptive vocabulary and the world rules out of court as utterly absurd any notion that there are no such things as this framework talks about.

An integral part of this conviction is what I shall call (in an extended sense) the *positivistic conception of science*, the idea that the framework of theoretical objects (molecules, electro-magnetic fields, etc.) and their relationships is, to to speak, an *auxiliary* framework. In its most explicit form, it is the idea that theoretical objects and propositions concerning them are 'calculational devices', the value and status of which consist in their systematizing and heuristic role with respect to confirmable generalizations formulated in the framework of terms which enjoy a direct ostensive link with the world. One is tempted to put this by saying that according to these philosophers, the objects of ostensively linked discourse behave *as if* and *only as if* they were bound up with or consisted of scientific entities. But, of course, these philosophers would hasten to point out (and rightly so) that

X behaves as if it consisted of Y's

makes sense only by contrast with

X behaves as it does because it *does* consist of Y's

whereas their contention is exactly that where the Y's are *scientific* objects, no such contrast makes sense.

The point I am making is that as long as one thinks that there is a framework, whether of physical objects or of sense contents, the absolute authenticity of which is guaranteed by the fact that the learning of this framework involves an 'ostensive step', so long one will be tempted to think of the authority of theoretical discourse as entirely derivative, that of a calculational auxiliary, an effective heuristic device. It is one of my prime purposes, in the following sections, to convince the reader that this interpretation of the status of the scientific picture of the world rests on two mistakes: (1) a misunderstanding (which I have already exposed) of the ostensive element in the learning and use of a language—the Myth of the Given; (2) a reification of the *methodological* distinction between theoretical and non-theoretical discourse into a *substantive* distinction between theoretical and non-theoretical existence.

44. One way of summing up what I have been saying above is by saying that there is a widespread impression abroad, aided and abetted by a naïve interpretation of concept formation, that philosophers of science deal with a mode of discourse which is, so to speak, a peninsular offshoot from the mainland of ordinary discourse. The study of scientific discourse is conceived to be a worthy employment for those who have the background and motivation to keep track of it, but an employment which is fundamentally a hobby divorced from the perplexities of the mainland. But, of course, this summing up won't quite do. For all philosophers would agree that no philosophy would be complete unless it resolved the perplexities which arise when one attempts to think through the relationship of the framework of modern science to ordinary discourse. My point, however, is not that anyone would reject the idea that this is a proper task for philosophy, but that, by approaching the language in which the plain man describes and explains empirical fact with the presuppositions of *givenness*, they are led to a 'resolution' of these perplexities along the lines of what I have called the positivistic or peninsular conception of scientific discourse—a 'resolution' which, I believe, is not only superficial, but positively mistaken.

X. PRIVATE EPISODES: THE PROBLEM

45. Let us now return, after a long absence, to the problem of how the similarity among the experiences of *seeing that an object over there is red, its looking to one that an object over there is red* (when in point of fact it is *not* red) and *its looking to one as though there were a red object over there* (when in fact there is *nothing* over there at all) is to be understood. Part of this similarity, we saw, consists in the fact that they all involve the idea—the proposition, if you please—that the object over there is red. But over and above this there is, of course, the aspect which many philosophers have attempted to clarify by the notion of *impressions* or *immediate experience.*

It was pointed out in Sections 21 ff. above that there are prima facie two ways in which facts of the form *x merely looks red* might be explained, in addition to the kind of explanation which is based on empirical generalizations relating the colour of objects, the circumstances in which they are seen, and the colours they look to have. These two ways are (*a*) the introduction of impressions or immediate experiences as theoretical entities; and (*b*) the *discovery*, on scrutinizing these situations, that they contain impressions or immediate experiences as components. I called attention to the paradoxical character of the first of these alternatives, and refused, at that time, to take it seriously. But in the meantime the second alternative, involving as it does the Myth of the Given, has turned out to be no more satisfactory.

For, in the first place, how are these impressions to be described, if not by using such words as 'red' and 'triangular'. Yet, if my argument, to date, is sound, physical objects alone can be literally red and triangular. Thus, in the cases I am considering there is nothing to be red and triangular. It would seem to follow that 'impression of a red triangle' could mean nothing more than 'impression of *the sort which* is common to those experiences in which we either see that something is red and triangular, or something merely looks red and triangular or there merely looks to be a red and triangular object over there'. And if we can never characterize 'impressions' intrinsically, but only by what is logically a definite description, i.e. as *the kind of entity which* is common to such situations, then we would scarcely seem to be any better off than if we maintained that talk about 'impressions' is a notational convenience, a code, for the language in which we speak of how things look and what there looks to be.

And this line of thought is reinforced by the consideration that once we give up the idea that we begin our sojourn in this world with any—even a vague, fragmentary, and undiscriminating—awareness of the logical space of particulars, kinds, facts, and resemblances, and recognize that even such 'simple' concepts as those of colours are the fruit of a long process of publicly reinforced responses to public objects (including verbal performances) in public situations, we may well be puzzled as to how even if there are such things as impressions or sensations, we could come to know that there are, and to know what sort of thing they are. *For we now recognize that instead of coming to have a concept of something because we have noticed that sort of thing, to have the ability to notice a sort of thing is already to have the concept of that sort of thing, and cannot account for it.*

Indeed, once we think this line of reasoning through, we are struck by the fact that if it is sound, we are faced not only with the question, 'How could we come to have the idea of an "impression" or "sensation"?' but by the question, 'How could we come to have the idea of something's looking red to us, or', to get to the crux of the matter, 'of seeing that something is red?' In short, we are brought face to face with the general problem of understanding how there can be *inner episodes*—episodes, that is, which somehow combine *privacy*, in that each of us has privileged access to his own, with *intersubjectivity*, in that each of us can, in principle, know about the other's. We might try to put this more linguistically as the problem of how there can be a sentence (e.g. 'S has a toothache') of which it is *logically* true that whereas *anybody* can use it to state a fact, only *one* person, namely S himself, can use it to make a report. But while this is a useful formulation, it does not do justice to the supposedly *episodic* character of the items in question. And that this is the heart of the puzzle is shown by the fact that many philosophers who would not deny that there are short-term hypothetical and mongrel hypothetical–categorical facts about behaviour which others can ascribe to us on behavioural evidence, but which only *we* can *report*, have found it to be logical nonsense to speak of non-behavioural *episodes* of which this is true. Thus, it has been claimed by Ryle[1] that the very idea that there are such episodes is a category mistake, while others have argued that though there are such episodes, they cannot be characterized in intersubjective discourse, learned as it is in a context of public objects and in the 'academy' of one's linguistic peers. It is my purpose to argue that both these contentions are quite mistaken, and that not only are inner episodes *not* category mistakes, they are quite 'effable' in intersubjective discourse. And it is my purpose to show, positively, *how* this can be the case. I am particularly concerned to make this point in connection with such inner episodes as sensations and feelings, in short, with what has—unfortunately, I think—been called 'immediate experience'. For such an account is necessary to round off this examination of the Myth of the Given. But before I can come to grips with these topics, the way must be prepared by a discussion of inner episodes of quite another kind, namely *thoughts*.

XI. THOUGHTS: THE CLASSICAL VIEW

46. Recent empiricism has been of two minds about the status of *thoughts*. On the one hand, it has resonated to the idea that in so far as there are *episodes* which are thoughts, they are *verbal* or *linguistic* episodes. Clearly, however, even if candid overt verbal behaviours by people who had learned a language *were* thoughts, there are not nearly enough of them to account for all the cases in which it would be argued that a person was thinking. Nor can we plausibly suppose that the remainder is accounted for by those inner episodes which are often very clumsily lumped together under the heading 'verbal imagery'.

   On the other hand, they have been tempted to suppose that the *episodes* which are referred to by verbs pertaining to thinking include all forms of 'intelligent behaviour', verbal as well as nonverbal, and that the 'thought episodes' which are supposed to be manifested by these behaviours are not really episodes at all, but rather hypothetical and mongrel hypothetical–categorical facts about these and still other behaviours. This, however, runs into the difficulty that whenever we try to

---

[1] Ryle, Gilbert, *The Concept of Mind*. London: Hutchinson's University Library, 1949.

explain what we mean by calling a piece of *nonhabitual* behaviour intelligent, we seem to find it necessary to do so in terms of *thinking*. The uncomfortable feeling will not be downed that the dispositional account of thoughts in terms of intelligent behaviour is covertly circular.

47. Now the classical tradition claimed that there is a family of episodes, neither overt verbal behaviour nor verbal imagery, which are *thoughts*, and that both overt verbal behaviour and verbal imagery owe their meaningfulness to the fact that they stand to these *thoughts* in the unique relation of 'expressing' them. These episodes are introspectable. Indeed, it was usually believed that they could not occur without being known to occur. But this can be traced to a number of confusions, perhaps the most important of which was the idea that *thoughts* belong in the same general category as sensations, images, tickles, itches, etc. This mis-assimilation of thoughts to sensations and feelings was equally, as we saw in Sections 26ff. above, a mis-assimilation of sensations and feelings to thoughts, and a falsification of both. The assumption that if there are thought episodes, they must be immediate experiences is common both to those who propounded the classical view and to those who reject it, saying that they 'find no such experiences'. If we purge the classical tradition of these confusions, it becomes the idea that to each of us belongs a stream of episodes, not themselves immediate experiences, to which we have privileged, but by no means either invariable or infallible, access. These episodes can occur without being 'expressed' by overt verbal behaviour, though verbal behaviour is—in an important sense—their natural fruition. Again, we can 'hear ourselves think', but the verbal imagery which enables us to do this is no more the thinking itself than is the overt verbal behaviour by which it is expressed and communicated to others. It is a mistake to suppose that we must be having verbal imagery—indeed, any imagery—when we 'know what we are thinking'—in short, to suppose that 'privileged access' must be construed on a perceptual or quasi-perceptual model.

Now, it is my purpose to defend such a revised classical analysis of our common sense conception of thoughts, and in the course of doing so I shall develop distinctions which will later contribute to a resolution, in principle, of the puzzle of *immediate experience*. But before I continue, let me hasten to add that it will turn out that the view I am about to expound could, with equal appropriateness, be represented as a modified form of the view that thoughts are *linguistic* episodes.

XII. OUR RYLEAN ANCESTORS

48. But, the reader may well ask, in what sense can these episodes be 'inner' if they are not immediate experiences? and in what sense can they be 'linguistic' if they are neither overt linguistic performances, nor verbal imagery '*in foro interno*'? I am going to answer these and the other questions I have been raising by making a myth of my own, or, to give it an air of up-to-date respectability, by writing a piece of science fiction—anthropological science fiction. Imagine a stage in prehistory in which humans are limited to what I shall call a Rylean language, a language of which the fundamental descriptive vocabulary speaks of public properties of public objects located in Space and enduring through Time. Let me hasten to add that it is also Rylean in that although its basic resources are limited (how limited I shall be discussing in a

moment), its total expressive power is very great. For it makes subtle use not only of the elementary logical operations of conjunction, disjunction, negation, and quantification, but especially of the subjunctive conditional. Furthermore, I shall suppose it to be characterized by the presence of the looser logical relations typical of ordinary discourse which are referred to by philosophers under the headings 'vagueness' and 'open texture'.

I am beginning my myth *in medias res* with humans who have already mastered a Rylean language, because the philosophical situation it is designed to clarify is one in which we are not puzzled by how people acquire a language for referring to public properties of public objects, but are very puzzled indeed about how we learn to speak of inner episodes and immediate experiences.

There are, I suppose, still some philosophers who are inclined to think that by allowing these mythical ancestors of ours the use *ad libitum* of subjunctive conditionals, we have, in effect, enabled them to say anything that *we* can say when we speak of *thoughts, experiences* (seeing, hearing, etc.), and *immediate experiences*. I doubt that there are many. In any case, the story I am telling is designed to show exactly *how* the idea that an intersubjective language *must* be Rylean rest on too simple a picture of the relation of intersubjective discourse to public objects.

49. The questions I am, in effect, raising are, 'What resources would have to be added to the Rylean language of these talking animals in order that they might come to recognize each other and themselves as animals that *think, observe*, and have *feelings* and *sensations*, as we use these terms?' and, 'How could the addition of these resources be construed as reasonable?' In the first place, the language would have to be enriched with the fundamental resources of semantical discourse—that is to say, the resources necessary for making such characteristically semantical statements as '"*Rot*" means red', and '"*Der Mond ist rund*" is true if and only if the moon is round.' It is sometimes said, e.g. by Carnap,[1] that these resources can be constructed out of the vocabulary of formal logic, and that they would therefore already be contained, in principal, in our Rylean language. I have criticized this idea in another place[2] and shall not discuss it here. In any event, a decision on this point is not essential to the argument.

Let it be granted, then, that these mythical ancestors of ours are able to characterize each other's verbal behaviour in semantical terms; that, in other words, they not only can talk about each other's predictions as causes and effects, and as indicators (with greater or less reliability) of other verbal and nonverbal states of affairs, but can also say of these verbal productions that they *mean* thus and so, that they say *that* such and such, that they are true, false, etc. And let me emphasize, as was pointed out in Section 31 above, that to make a semantical statement about a verbal event is not a shorthand way of talking about its causes and effects, although there is a sense of 'imply' in which semantical statements about verbal productions do *imply* information about the causes and effects of these productions. Thus, when I say '"*Es regnet*" means it is raining', my statement 'implies' that the causes and effects of utter-

---

[1] Carnap, Rudolph, *Introduction to Semantics*. Chicago: University of Chicago Press, 1942.

[2] See Chapter 6, p. 200 ff.; also 'Empiricism and Abstract Entities' in Paul A. Schilpp (ed.) *The Philosophy of Rudolph Carnap*. Wilmette (Ill.), 1963.

ances of 'Es regnet' beyond the Rhine parallel the causes and effects of utterances of 'It is raining' by myself and other members of the English-speaking community. And if it did not imply this, it could not perform its role. But this is not to say that semantical statements are definitional shorthand for statements about the causes and effects of verbal performances.

50. With the resources of semantical discourse, the language of our fictional ancestors has acquired a dimension which gives considerably more plausibility to the claim that they are in a position to talk about *thoughts* just as we are. For characteristic of thoughts is their *intentionality, reference,* or *aboutness,* and it is clear that semantical talk about the meaning or reference of verbal expressions has the same structure as mentalistic discourse concerning what thoughts are about. It is therefore all the more tempting to suppose that the intentionality of *thoughts* can be traced to the application of semantical categories to overt verbal performances, and to suggest a modified Rylean account according to which talk about so-called 'thoughts' is shorthand for hypothetical and mongrel categorical–hypothetical statements about overt verbal and nonverbal behaviour, *and* that talk about the *intentionality* of these 'episodes' is correspondingly reducible to semantical talk about the verbal components.

What is the alternative? Classically it has been the idea that not only are there overt verbal episodes which can be characterized in semantical terms, but, *over and above these,* there are certain inner episodes which are properly characterized by the traditional vocabulary of *intentionality.* And, of course, the classical scheme includes the idea that semantical discourse about overt verbal performances is to be analysed in terms of talk about the intentionality of the mental episodes which are 'expressed' by these overt performances. My immediate problem is to see if I can reconcile the classical idea of thoughts as inner episodes which are neither overt behaviour nor verbal imagery and which are properly referred to in terms of the vocabulary of intentionality, with the idea that the categories of intentionality are, at bottom, semantical categories pertaining to overt verbal performances.[1]

XIII. THEORIES AND MODELS

51. But what might these episodes be? And, in terms of our science fiction, how might our ancestors have come to recognize their existence? The answer to these questions is surprisingly straightforward, once the logical space of our discussion is enlarged to include a distinction, central to the philosophy of science, between the language of *theory* and the language of *observation.* Although this distinction is a familiar one, I shall take a few paragraphs to highlight those aspects of the distinction which are of greatest relevance to our problem.

Informally, to construct a theory is, in its most developed or sophisticated form, to postulate a domain of entities which behave in certain ways set down by the fundamental principles of the theory, and to correlate—perhaps, in a certain sense to

---

[1] An earlier attempt of mine along these lines is to be found in 'Mind, Meaning and Behaviour' in *Philosophical Studies*, 3, pp. 83–94 (1952), and 'A Semantical Solution of the Mind–Body Problem' in *Methodos*, 5, pp. 45–84 (1953).

identify—complexes of these theoretical entities with certain non-theoretical objects or situations; that is to say, with objects or situations which are either matters of observable fact or, in principle at least, describable in observational terms. This 'correlation' or 'identification' of theoretical with observational states of affairs is a tentative one 'until further notice', and amounts, so to speak, to erecting temporary bridges which permit the passage from sentences in observational discourse to sentences in the theory, and vice versa. Thus, for example, in the kinetic theory of gases, empirical statements of the form 'Gas g at such and such a place and time has such and such a volume, pressure, and temperature' are correlated with theoretical statements specifying certain statistical measures of populations of molecules. These temporary bridges are so set up that inductively established laws pertaining to gases, formulated in the language of observable fact, are correlated with derived propositions or theorems in the language of the theory, and that no proposition in the theory is correlated with a falsified empirical generalization. Thus, a good theory (at least of the type we are considering) 'explains' established empirical laws by deriving theoretical counterparts of these laws from a small set of postulates relating to unobserved entities.

These remarks, of course, barely scratch the surface of the problem of the status of theories in scientific discourse. And no sooner have I made them, than I must hasten to qualify them—almost beyond recognition. For while this by now classical account of the nature of theories (one of the earlier formulations of which is due to Norman Campbell,[1] and which is to be bound more recently in the writings of Carnap,[2] Reichenbach,[3] Hempel,[4] and Braithwaite[5]) does throw light on the logical status of theories, it emphasizes certain features at the expense of others. By speaking of the construction of a theory as the elaboration of a postulate system which is tentatively correlated with observational discourse, it gives a highly artificial and unrealistic picture of what scientists have actually done in the process of constructing theories. I do not wish to deny that logically sophisticated scientists today *might* and perhaps, on occasion, *do* proceed in true logistical style. I do, however, wish to emphasize two points:

(1) The first is that the fundamental assumptions of a theory are usually developed not by constructing uninterpreted calculi which might correlate in the desired manner with observational discourse, but rather by attempting to find a *model*, i.e. to describe a domain of familiar objects behaving in familiar ways such that we can see how the phenomena to be explained would arise if they consisted of this sort of thing.

---

[1] Campbell, Norman, *Physics: The Elements*. Cambridge: Cambridge University Press, 1920.

[2] Carnap, Rudolph, 'The Interpretation of Physics' in H. Feigl and M. Brodbeck (eds.), *Readings in the Philosophy of Science*, pp. 309–18. New York: Appleton-Century-Crofts, 1953. This selection consists of pp. 59–69 of his *Foundations of Logic and Mathematics*. Chicago: University of Chicago Press, 1939.

[3] Reichenbach, H., *Philosophie der Raum-Zeit-Lehre*. Berlin: de Gruyter, 1928, and *Experience and Prediction*. Chicago: University of Chicago Press, 1938.

[4] Hempel, C. G., *Fundamentals of Concept Formation in Empirical Science*. Chicago: University of Chicago Press, 1952.

[5] Braithwaite, R. B., *Scientific Explanation*. Cambridge: Cambridge University Press, 1920.

The essential thing about a model is that it is accompanied, so to speak, by a commentary which *qualifies* or *limits*—but not precisely nor in all respects—the analogy between the familiar objects and the entities which are being introduced by the theory. It is the descriptions of the fundamental ways in which the objects in the model domain, thus qualified, behave, which, transferred to the theoretical entities, correspond to the postulates of the logistical picture of theory construction.

(2) But even more important for our purposes is the fact that the logistical picture of theory construction obscures the most important thing of all, namely that the process of devising 'theoretical' explanations of observable phenomena did not spring full-blown from the head of modern science. In particular, it obscures the fact that not all common sense inductive inferences are of the form

All observed A's have been B, *therefore* (*probably*) all A's are B,

or its statistical counterparts, and leads one mistakenly to suppose that so-called 'hypothetic-deductive' explanation is limited to the sophisticated stages of science. The truth of the matter, as I shall shortly be illustrating, is that science is continuous with common sense, and the ways in which the scientist seeks to explain empirical phenomena are refinements of the ways in which plain men, however crudely and schematically, have attempted to understand their environment and their fellow men since the dawn of intelligence. It is this point which I wish to stress at the present time, for I am going to argue that the distinction between theoretical and observational discourse is involved in the logic of concepts pertaining to inner episodes. I say 'involved in' for it would be paradoxical and, indeed, incorrect, to say that these concepts *are* theoretical concepts.

52. Now I think it fair to say that some light has already been thrown on the expression 'inner episodes'; for while it would indeed be a category mistake to suppose that the inflammability of a piece of wood is, so to speak, a hidden burning which becomes overt or manifest when the wood is placed on the fire, not all the unobservable episodes we suppose to go on in the world are the offspring of category mistakes. Clearly it is by no means an illegitimate use of 'in'—though it is a use which has its own logical grammar—to say, for example, that 'in' the air around us there are innumerable molecules which, in spite of the observable stodginess of the air, are participating in a veritable turmoil of episodes. Clearly, the sense in which these episodes are 'in' the air is to be explicated in terms of the sense in which the air 'is' a population of molecules, and this, in turn, in terms of the logic of the relation between theoretical and observational discourse.

I shall have more to say on this topic in a moment. In the meantime, let us return to our mythical ancestors. It will not surprise my readers to learn that the second stage in the enrichment of their Rylean language is the addition of theoretical discourse. Thus we may suppose these language-using animals to elaborate, without methodological sophistication, crude, sketchy, and vague theories to explain why things which are similar in their observable properties differ in their causal properties, and things which are similar in their causal properties differ in their observable properties.

XIV. METHODOLOGICAL VERSUS PHILOSOPHICAL BEHAVIOURISM

53. But we are approaching the time for the central episode in our myth. I want you to suppose that in this Neo-Rylean culture there now appears a genius—let us call him Jones—who is an unsung forerunner of the movement in psychology, once revolutionary, now commonplace, known as Behaviourism. Let me emphasize that what I have in mind is Behaviourism as a methodological thesis, which I shall be concerned to formulate. For the central and guiding theme in the historical complex known by this term has been a certain conception, or family of conceptions, of how to go about building a science of psychology.

Philosophers have sometimes supposed that Behaviourists are, as such, committed to the idea that our ordinary mentalistic concepts are *analysable* in terms of overt behaviour. But although behaviourism has often been characterized by a certain metaphysical bias, it is not a thesis about the *analysis* of *existing* psychological concepts, but one which concerns the construction of new concepts. As a methodological thesis, it involves no commitment whatever concerning the logical analysis of common sense mentalistic discourse, nor does it involve a denial that each of us has a privileged access to our state of mind, nor that these states of mind can properly be described in terms of such common sense concepts as believing, wondering, doubting, intending, wishing, inferring, etc. If we permit ourselves to speak of this privileged access to our states of mind as 'introspection', avoiding the implication that there is a 'means' whereby we 'see' what is going on 'inside', as we see external circumstances by the eye, then we can say that Behaviourism, as I shall use the term, does not deny that there is such a thing as introspection, nor that it is, on some topics, at least, quite reliable. The essential point about 'introspection' from the standpoint of Behaviourism is that *we introspect in terms of common sense mentalistic concepts*. And while the Behaviourist admits, as anyone must, that much knowledge is embodied in common sense mentalistic discourse, and that still more can be gained in the future by formulating and testing hypotheses in terms of them, and while he admits that it is perfectly legitimate to call such a psychology 'scientific', he proposes, for his own part, to make no more than a heuristic use of mentalistic discourse, and to construct his concepts 'from scratch' in the course of developing his own scientific account of the observable behaviour of human organisms.

54. But while it is quite clear that scientific Behaviourism is *not* the thesis that common sense psychological concepts are *analysable* into concepts pertaining to overt behaviour—a thesis which has been maintained by some philosophers and which may be called 'analytical' or 'philosophical' Behaviourism—it is often thought that Behaviourism is committed to the idea that the concepts of a behaviouristic psychology must be so analysable, or, to put things right side up, that properly introduced behaviouristic concepts must be built by explicit definition—in the broadest sense—from a basic vocabulary pertaining to overt behaviour. The Behaviourist would thus be saying, 'Whether or not the mentalistic concepts of everyday life are definable in terms of overt behaviour, I shall ensure that this is true of the concepts that I shall employ.' And it must be confessed that many behaviouristically oriented psychologists have believed themselves committed to this austere programme of concept formation.

Now I think it reasonable to say that, *thus conceived*, the behaviouristic programme would be unduly restrictive. Certainly, nothing in the nature of sound scientific procedure requires this self-denial. Physics, the methodological sophistication of which has so impressed—indeed, overly impressed—the other sciences, does not lay down a corresponding restriction on its concepts, nor has chemistry been built in terms of concepts explicitly definable in terms of the observable properties and behaviour of chemical substances. The point I am making should now be clear. The behaviouristic requirement that all concepts should be *introduced* in terms of a basic vocabulary pertaining to overt behaviour is compatible with the idea that some behaviouristic concepts are to be introduced as *theoretical* concepts.

55. It is essential to note that the theoretical terms of a behaviouristic psychology are not only *not* defined in terms of overt behaviour, they are also *not* defined in terms of nerves, synapses, neural impulses, etc. etc. A behaviouristic theory of behaviour is not, as such, a physiological explanation of behaviour. The ability of a framework of theoretical concepts and propositions successfully to explain behavioural phenomena is logically independent of the identification of these theoretical concepts with concepts of neurophysiology. What *is* true—and this is a logical point— is that each special science dealing with some aspect of the human organism operates within the frame of a certain regulative ideal, the ideal of a coherent system in which the achievements of each have an intelligible place. Thus, it is part of the Behaviourist's business to keep an eye on the total picture of the human organism which is beginning to emerge. And if the tendency to premature identification is held in check, there may be considerable heuristic value in speculative attempts at integration; though, until recently, at least, neurophysiological speculations in behaviour theory have not been particularly fruitful. And while it is, I suppose, noncontroversial that when the total scientific picture of man and his behaviour is in, it will involve *some* identification of concepts in behaviour theory with concepts pertaining to the functioning of anatomical structures, it should not be assumed that behaviour theory is committed *ab initio* to a physiological identification of *all* its concepts—that its concepts are, so to speak, physiological from the start.

We have, in effect, been distinguishing between two dimensions of the logic (or 'methodologic') of theoretical terms: (*a*) their role in explaining the selected phenomena of which the theory is the theory; (*b*) their role as candidates for integration in what we have called the 'total picture'. These roles are equally part of the logic, and hence the 'meaning', of theoretical terms. Thus, at any one time the terms in a theory will carry with them as part of their logical force that which it is reasonable to envisage—whether schematically or determinately—as the manner of their integration. However, for the purposes of my argument, it will be useful to refer to these two roles as though it were a matter of a distinction between what I shall call *pure theoretical concepts*, and hypotheses concerning the relation of these concepts to concepts in other specialities. What we *can* say is that the less a scientist is in a position to conjecture about the way in which a certain theory can be expected to integrate with other specialities, the more the concepts of his theory approximate to the status of pure theoretical concepts. To illustrate: we can imagine that Chemistry developed a sophisticated and successful theory to explain chemical phenomena before either electrical or magnetic phenomena were noticed; and that chemists developed as pure theoretical concepts, certain concepts which it later became reasonable to identify with concepts belonging to the framework of electro-magnetic theory.

XV. THE LOGIC OF PRIVATE EPISODES: THOUGHTS

56. With these all too sketchy remarks on Methodological Behaviourism under our belts, let us return once again to our fictional ancestors. We are now in a position to characterize the original Rylean language in which they described themselves and their fellows as not only a *behaviouristic* language, but a behaviouristic language which is restricted to the *non-theoretical* vocabulary of a behaviouristic psychology. Suppose, now, that in the attempt to account for the fact that his fellow men behave intelligently not only when their conduct is threaded on a string of overt verbal episodes—that is to say, as *we* would put it, when they 'think out loud'—but also when no detectable verbal output is present, Jones develops a *theory* according to which overt utterances are but the culmination of a process which begins with certain inner episodes. *And let us suppose that his model for these episodes* which initiate the events which culminate in overt verbal behaviour *is that of overt verbal behaviour itself. In other words, using the language of the model, the theory is to the effect that overt verbal behaviour is the culmination of a process which begins with 'inner speech'.*

It is essential to bear in mind that what Jones means by 'inner speech' is not to be confused with *verbal imagery*. As a matter of fact, Jones, like his fellows, does not as yet even have the concept of an image.

It is easy to see the general lines a Jonesean theory will take. According to it the true cause of intelligent nonhabitual behaviour is 'inner speech'. Thus, even when a hungry person overtly says, 'Here is an edible object', and proceeds to eat it, the true—theoretical—cause of his eating, given his hunger, is not the overt utterance, but the 'inner utterance of this sentence'.

57. The first thing to note about the Jonesean theory is that, as built on the model of speech episodes, *it carries over to these inner episodes the applicability of semantical categories.* Thus, just as Jones has, like his fellows, been speaking of overt utterances as *meaning* this or that, or being *about* this or that, so he now speaks of these inner episodes as *meaning* this or that, or being *about* this or that.

The second point to remember is that although Jones's theory involves a *model*, it is not identical with it. Like all theories formulated in terms of a model, it also includes a *commentary* on the model; a commentary which places more or less sharply drawn restrictions on the analogy between the theoretical entities and the entities of the model. Thus, while his theory talks of 'inner speech', the commentary hastens to add that, of course, the episodes in question are not the wagging of a hidden tongue, nor are any sounds produced by this 'inner speech'.

58. The general drift of my story should now be clear. I shall therefore proceed to make the essential points quite briefly:

(1) What we must suppose Jones to have developed is the germ of a theory which permits many different developments. We must not pin it down to any of the more sophisticated forms it takes in the hands of classical philosophers. Thus, the theory need not be given a Socratic or Cartesian form, according to which this 'inner

speech' is a function of a separate substance; though primitive peoples may have had good reason to suppose that humans consist of two separate things.

(2) Let us suppose Jones to have called these discursive entities *thoughts*. We can admit at once that the framework of thoughts he has introduced is a framework of 'unobserved', 'nonempirical', 'inner' episodes. For we can point out immediately that in these respects they are no worse off than the particles and episodes of physical theory. For these episodes are 'in' language-using animals as molecular impacts are 'in' gases, not as 'ghosts' are in 'machines'. They are 'nonempirical' in the simple sense that they are *theoretical*—not definable in observational terms. Nor does the fact that they are, *as introduced*, unobserved entities imply that Jones could not have good reason for supposing them to exist. Their 'purity' is not a *metaphysical* purity, but, so to speak, a *methodological* purity. As we have seen, the fact that they are not introduced as physiological entities does not preclude the possibility that at a later methodological stage they may, so to speak, 'turn out' to be such. Thus, there are many who would say that it is already reasonable to suppose that these *thoughts* are to be 'identified' with complex events in the cerebral cortex functioning along the lines of a calculating machine. Jones, of course, has no such idea.

(3) Although the theory postulates that overt discourse is the culmination of a process which begins with 'inner discourse', this should not be taken to mean that overt discourse stands to 'inner discourse' *as voluntary movements stand to intentions and motives*. True, overt linguistic events *can* be produced as means to ends. But serious errors creep into the interpretation of both language and thought if one interprets the idea that overt linguistic episodes *express* thoughts, on the model of the use of an instrument. Thus, it should be noted that Jones's theory, as I have sketched it, is perfectly compatible with the idea that the ability to have thoughts is acquired in the process of acquiring overt speech and that only after overt speech is well established, can 'inner speech' occur without its overt culmination.

(4) Although the occurrence of overt speech episodes which are characterizable in semantical terms is explained by the theory in terms of *thoughts* which are *also* characterized in semantical terms, this does not mean that the idea that overt speech 'has meaning' is being *analysed* in terms of the intentionality of thoughts. It must not be forgotten that *the semantical characterization of overt verbal episodes is the primary use of semantical terms, and that overt linguistic events as semantically characterized are the model for the inner episodes introduced by the theory.*

(5) One final point before we come to the denouement of the first episode in the saga of Jones. It cannot be emphasized too much that although these theoretical discursive episodes or *thoughts* are introduced as *inner* episodes—which is merely to repeat that they are introduced as *theoretical* episodes—they are *not* introduced as *immediate experiences*. Let me remind the reader that Jones, like his Neo-Rylean contemporaries, does not as yet have this concept. And even when he, and they, acquire it, by a process which will be the second episode in my myth, it will only be the philosophers among them who will suppose that the inner epidoses introduced for one theoretical purpose—thoughts—must be a subset of immediate experiences, inner episodes introduced for another theoretical purpose.

59. Here, then, is the denouement. I have suggested a number of times that although it would be most misleading to say that concepts pertaining to thinking are

theoretical concepts, yet their status might be illuminated by means of the contrast between theoretical and non-theoretical discourse. We are now in a position to see exactly why this is so. For once our fictitious ancestor, Jones, has developed the theory that overt verbal behaviour is the expression of thoughts, and taught his compatriots to make use of the theory in interpreting each other's behaviour, it is but a short step to the use of this language in self-description. Thus, when Tom, watching Dick, has behavioural evidence which warrants the use of the sentence (in the language of the theory) 'Dick is thinking "p"' (or 'Dick is thinkingl that p'), Dick, using the same behavioural evidence, can say, in the language of the theory, 'I am thinking "p"' (or 'I am thinking that p'). And it now turns out—need it have?—that Dick can be trained to give reasonably reliable self-descriptions, using the language of the theory, without having to observe his overt behaviour. Jones brings this about, roughly, by applauding utterances by Dick of 'I am thinking that p' when the behavioural evidence strongly supports the theoretical statement 'Dick is thinking that p'; and by frowning on utterances of 'I am thinking that p', when the evidence does not support this theoretical statement. Our ancestors begin to speak of the privileged access each of us has to his own thoughts. *What began as a language with a purely theoretical use has gained a reporting role.*

As I see it, this story helps us understand that concepts pertaining to such inner episodes as thoughts are primarily and essentially *inter-subjective*, as inter-subjective as the concept of a positron, and that the reporting role of these concepts—the fact that each of us has a privileged access to his thoughts—constitutes a dimension of the use of these concepts which is *built on* and *presupposes* this inter-subjective status. My myth has shown that the fact that language is essentially an *inter-subjective* achievement, and is learned in inter-subjective contexts—a fact rightly stressed in modern psychologies of language, thus by B. F. Skinner[1] and by certain philosophers, e.g. Carnap,[2] Wittgenstein[3]—is compatible with the 'privacy' of 'inner episodes'. It also makes clear that this privacy is not an 'absolute privacy'. For if it recognizes that these concepts have a reporting use in which one is not drawing inferences from behavioural evidence, it nevertheless insists that the fact that overt behaviour *is* evidence for these episodes *is built into the very logic of these concepts*, just as the fact that the observable behaviour of gases is evidence for molecular episodes is built into the very logic of molecule talk.

XVI. THE LOGIC OF PRIVATE EPISODES: IMPRESSIONS

60. We are now ready for the problem of the status of concepts pertaining to immediate experience. The first step is to remind ourselves that among the inner episodes which belong to the framework of *thoughts* will be perceptions, that is to say, *seeing that the table is brown, hearing that the piano is out of tune*, etc. Until Jones intro-

---

[1] Skinner, B. F., 'The Operational Analysis of Psychological Terms' in Volume LII of the *Psychological Review*, pp. 270–7 (1945). Reprinted in H. Feigl and Brodbeck (eds.), *Readings in the Philosophy of Science*, pp. 585–94. New York: Appleton-Century-Crofts, 1953.

[2] Carnap, Rudolph, *Psychologie in Physicalischer Sprache' Erkentniss*, 3, pp. 107–42 (1933).

[3] Wittgenstein, Ludwig, *Philosophical Investigations*. London: Macmillan, 1953.

duced this framework, the only concepts our fictitious ancestors had of perceptual *episodes* were those of overt verbal *reports*, made, for example, in the context of looking at an object in standard conditions. *Seeing that something is the case* is an inner episode in the Jonesean theory which has as its model *reporting on looking that something is the case*. It will be remembered from an earlier section that just as when I say that Dick *reported* that the table is green, I commit myself to the truth of what he reported, so to say of Dick that he *saw* that the table is green is, in part, to ascribe to Dick the idea '*this* table is green' and to endorse this idea. The reader might refer back to Sections 16ff. for an elaboration of this point.

With the enrichment of the originally Rylean framework to include inner perceptual episodes, I have established contact with my original formulation of the problem of inner experience (Sections 22ff.). For I can readily reconstruct in this framework my earlier account of the *language of appearing*, both *qualitative* and *existential*. Let us turn, therefore, to the final chapter of our historical novel. By now our ancestors speak a quite un-Rylean language. But it still contains no reference to such things as impressions, sensations, or feelings—in short, to the items which philosophers lump together under the heading 'immediate experiences'. It will be remembered that we had reached a point at which, as far as we could see, the phrase 'impression of a red triangle' could only mean something like 'that state of a perceiver—over and above the idea that there is a red and triangular physical object over there—which is common to those situations in which

    (*a*) he sees that the object over there is red and triangular;
    (*b*) the object over there looks to him to be red and triangular;
    (*c*) there looks to him to be a red triangular physical object over there'.

Our problem was that, on the one hand, it seemed absurd to say that impressions, for example, are theoretical entities, while, on the other, the interpretation of impressions as theoretical entities seemed to provide the only hope of accounting for the positive content and explanatory power that the idea that there are such entities appears to have, and of enabling us to understand how we could have arrived at this idea. The account I have just been giving of *thoughts* suggests how this apparent dilemma can be resolved.

For we continue the myth by supposing that Jones develops, in crude and sketchy form, of course, a theory of sense perception. Jones's theory does not have to be either well articulated or precise in order to be the first effective step in the development of a mode of discourse which today, in the case of some sense-modalities at least, is extraordinarily subtle and complex. We need, therefore, attribute to this mythical theory only those minimal features which enable it to throw light on the logic of our ordinary language about immediate experiences. From this standpoint it is sufficient to suppose that the hero of my myth postulates a class of inner—theoretical—episodes which he calls, say, *impressions*, and which are the end results of the impingement of physical objects and processes on various parts of the body, and, in particular, to follow up the specific form in which I have posed our problem, the eye.

61. A number of points can be made right away:

(1) The entities introduced by the theory are *states* of the perceiving subject, *not a class of particulars*. It cannot be emphasized too strongly that the particulars of the common sense world are such things as books, pages, turnips, dogs, persons, noises, flashes, etc., and the Space and Time—Kant's *Undinge*—in which they come to be. What is likely to make us suppose that *impressions* are introduced as particulars is that, as in the case of thoughts, this ur-theory is formulated in terms of a *model*. This time the model is the idea of a domain of 'inner replicas' which, when brought about in standard conditions, share the perceptible characteristics of their physical source. It is important to see that the model is the occurrence 'in' perceivers of *replicas*, not of *perceivings of replicas*. Thus, the model for an impression of a red triangle is a *red and triangular replica*, not a *seeing of a red and triangular replica*. The latter alternative would have the merit of recognizing that impressions are not particulars. But, by misunderstanding the role of models in the formulation of a theory, it mistakenly assumes that if the entities of the model are particulars, the theoretical entities which are introduced by means of the model must themselves be particulars—thus overlooking the role of the commentary. And by taking the model to be *seeing a red and triangular replica*, it smuggles into the language of impressions the logic of the language of thoughts. For seeing is a *cognitive* episode which involves the framework of thoughts, and to take it as the model is to give aid and comfort to the assimilation of impressions to thoughts, and thoughts to impressions which, as I have already pointed out, is responsible for many of the confusions of the classical account of both thoughts and impressions.

(2) The fact that *impressions* are theoretical entities enables us to understand how they can be *intrinsically* characterized—that is to say, characterized by something more than a *definite description*, such as 'entity of *the kind which* has as its standard cause looking at a red and triangular physical object in such and such circumstances' or 'entity of *the kind which* is common to the situations in which there looks to be a red and triangular object'. For although the predicates of a theory owe their meaningfulness to the fact that they are logically related to predicates which apply to the observable phenomena which the theory explains, the predicates of a theory are not shorthand for definite descriptions of properties in terms of these observation predicates. When the kinetic theory of gases speaks of molecules as having *mass*, the term 'mass' is not the abbreviation of a definite description of the form 'the property which … '. Thus, 'impression of a red triangle' does not simply mean 'impression such as is caused by red and triangular physical objects in standard conditions', though it is true—*logically* true—of impressions of red triangles that they are of that sort which *is* caused by red and triangular objects in standard conditions.

(3) If the theory of impressions were developed in true logistical style, we could say that the intrinsic properties of impressions are 'implicitly defined' by the postulates of the theory, as we can say that the intrinsic properties of sub-atomic particles are 'implicitly defined' by the fundamental principles of sub-atomic theory. For this would be just another way of saying that one knows the meaning of a theoretical term when one knows (*a*) how it is related to other theoretical terms, and (*b*) how the theoretical system as a whole is tied to the observation language. But, as I have pointed out, our ur-behaviourist does not formulate his theory in textbook style. He formulates it in terms of a model.

Now the model entities are entities which *do* have intrinsic properties. They are, for example, red and triangular wafers. It might therefore seem that the theory specifies the intrinsic characteristics of impressions to be the familiar perceptible qualities of physical objects and processes. If this were so, of course, the theory would be ultimately incoherent, for it would attribute to impressions—which are clearly not physical objects—characteristics which, if our argument to date is sound, only physical objects can have. Fortunately, this line of thought overlooks what we have called the commentary on the model, which qualifies, restricts, and interprets the analogy between the familiar entities of the model and the theoretical entities which are being introduced. Thus, it would be a mistake to suppose that since the *model* for the impression of a red triangle is a red and triangular wafer, the impression itself is a red and triangular wafer. What can be said is that the impression of a red triangle is *analogous*, to an extent which is by no means neatly and tidily specified, to a red and triangular wafer. The *essential* feature of the analogy is that visual impressions stand to one another in a system of ways of resembling and differing which is structurally similar to the ways in which the colours and shapes of visible objects resemble and differ.

(4) It might be concluded from this last point that the concept of the impression of a red triangle is a 'purely formal' concept, the concept of a 'logical form' which can acquire a 'content' only by means of 'ostensive definition'. One can see why a philosopher might want to say this, and why he might conclude that in so far as concepts pertaining to immediate experiences are *intersubjective*, they are 'purely structural', the 'content' of immediate experience being incommunicable. Yet this line of thought is but another expression of the Myth of the Given. For the theoretical concept of the impression of a red triangle would be no more and no less 'without content' than *any* theoretical concept. And while, like these, it must belong to a framework which is logically connected with the language of observable fact, the logical relation between a theoretical language and the language of observable fact has nothing to do with the epistemological fiction of an 'ostensive definition'.

(5) The impressions of Jones's theory are, as was pointed out above, states of the perceiver, rather than particulars. If we remind ourselves that these states are not introduced as physiological states (see Section 55), a number of interesting questions arise which tie in with the reflections on the status of the scientific picture of the world (Sections 39–44 above) but which, unfortunately, there is space only to adumbrate. Thus, some philosophers have thought it obvious that we can expect that in the development of science it will become reasonable to identify *all* the concepts of behaviour theory with definable terms in neurophysiological theory, and these, in turn, with definable terms in theoretical physics. It is important to realize that the second step of this prediction, at least, is either a *truism* or a *mistake*. It is a truism if it involves a tacit redefinition of 'physical theory' to mean 'theory adequate to account for the observable behaviour of any object (including animals and persons) which has physical properties'. While if 'physical theory' is taken in its ordinary sense of 'theory adequate to explain the observable behaviour of physical objects' it is, I believe, mistaken.

To ask how *impressions* fit together with *electro-magnetic fields*, for example, is to ask a mistaken question. It is to mix the framework of *molar* behaviour theory with the framework of the *micro*-theory of physical objects. The proper question is, rather, 'What would correspond in a *micro*-theory of sentient organisms to *molar* concepts pertaining to impressions?' And it is, I believe, in an answer to this question that one would come upon the *particulars* which sense-datum theorists profess to find (by analysis) in the common sense universe of discourse (cf. Section 23). Furthermore, I believe that in characterizing these particulars, the micro-behaviourist would be led to say something like the following: 'It is such particulars which (from the standpoint of the theory) are being responded to by the organism when it looks to a *person* as though there were a red and triangular physical object over there.' It would, of course, be incorrect to say that, in the ordinary sense, such a particular is red or triangular. What *could* be said,[1] however, is that whereas in the common sense picture physical objects are red and triangular but the impression 'of' a red triangle is neither red nor triangular, in the framework of this micro-theory, the theoretical counterparts of sentient organisms are Space–Time worms characterized by two kinds of variables: (*a*) variables which also characterize the theoretical counterparts of *merely* material objects; (*b*) variables peculiar to sentient things; and that these latter variables are the counterparts in this new framework of the perceptible qualities of the physical objects of the common sense framework. It is statements such as these which would be the cash value of the idea that 'physical objects aren't really coloured; colours exist only in the perceiver', and that 'to see that the facing surface of a physical object is red and triangular is to *mistake* a red and triangular sense content for a physical object with a red and triangular facing side'. Both these ideas clearly treat what is really a speculative philosophical critique (see Section 41) of the common sense framework of physical objects and the perception of physical objects in the light of an envisaged ideal scientific framework, as though it were a matter of distinctions which can be drawn *within* the common sense framework itself.

62. This brings me to the final chapter of my story. Let us suppose that as his final service to mankind before he vanishes without a trace, Jones teaches his theory of perception to his fellows. As before in the case of *thoughts*, they begin by using the language of impressions to draw theoretical conclusions from appropriate premises. (Notice that the evidence for theoretical statements in the language of impressions will include such introspectible inner episodes as *its looking to one as though there were a red and triangular physical object over there*, as well as overt behaviour.) Finally he succeeds in training them to make a *reporting* use of this language. He trains them, that is, to say 'I have the impression of a red triangle' when, and only when, according to the theory, they are indeed having the impression of a red triangle.

Once again the myth helps us to understand that concepts pertaining to certain inner episodes—in this case *impressions*—can be primarily and essentially *inter-subjective*, without being resolvable into overt behavioural symptoms, and that the reporting role of these concepts, their role in introspection, the fact that each of us has a privileged access to his impressions, constitutes a dimension of these concepts which is *built on* and *presupposes* their role in inter-subjective discourse. It also makes clear why the 'privacy' of these episodes is not the 'absolute privacy' of the traditional puz-

---

[1] For a discussion of some logical points pertaining to this framework the reader should consult the essay, 'The Concept of Emergence', by Paul E. Meehl and Wilfrid Sellars, on pp. 239–52 of Volume I of the *Minnesota Studies in the Philosophy of Science*, edited by Herbert Feigl and Michael Scriven and published by the University of Minnesota Press (Minneapolis: 1956).

zles. For, as in the case of thoughts, the fact that overt behaviour is evidence for these episodes is built into the very logic of these concepts as the fact that the observable behaviour of gases is evidence for molecular episodes is built into the very logic of molecule talk.

Notice that what our 'ancestors' have acquired under the guidance of Jones is not 'just another language'—a 'notational convenience' or 'code'—which merely enables them to say what they can already say in the language of qualitative and existential looking. They have acquired another language, indeed, but it is one which, though it rests on a framework of discourse about public objects in Space and Time, has an autonomous logical structure, and contains an *explanation of*, not just a *code for*, such facts as that *there looks to me to be a red and triangular physical object over there*. And notice that while our 'ancestors' came to notice impressions, and the language of impressions embodies a 'discovery' that there are such things, the language of impressions was no more tailored to fit *antecedent* noticings of these entities than the language of molecules was tailored to fit antecedent noticings of molecules.

And the spirit of Jones is not yet dead. For it is the particulars of the micro-theory discussed in Section 61 (5) which are the solid core of the sense contents and sense fields of the sense-datum theorist. Envisaging the general lines of that framework, even sketching some of its regions, he has taught himself to play with it (in his study) as a report language. Unfortunately he mislocates the truth of these conceptions, and, with a modesty forgivable in any but a philosopher, confuses his own creative enrichment of the framework of empirical knowledge, with an analysis of knowledge as it was. He construes as *data* the particulars and arrays of particulars which he has come to be able to observe, and believes them to be antecedent objects of knowledge which have somehow been in the framework from the beginning. It is in the very act of *taking* that he speaks of the *given*.

63. I have used a myth to kill a myth—the Myth of the Given. But is my myth really a myth? Or does the reader not recognize Jones as Man himself in the middle of his journey from the grunts and groans of the cave to the subtle and polydimensional discourse of the drawing room, the laboratory, and the study, the language of Henry and William James, of Einstein and of the philosophers who, in their efforts to break out of discourse to an *arché* beyond discourse, have provided the most curious dimension of all.

CHAPTER 7

W.V.O. Quine

Introduction to W.V.O. Quine
"Two Dogmas of Empiricism"

Willard Van Orman Quine was born in Akron, Ohio, in 1908. After majoring in mathematics at Oberlin College, he took a doctorate in philosophy at Harvard. His thesis, "The Logic of Sequences: A Generalization of *Principia Mathematica*," was supervised by A.N. Whitehead. Having received a Traveling Fellowship, Quine visited Vienna, where he attended meetings of the Vienna Circle. He went on to Prague for discussions with Carnap, and with Tarski in Warsaw. Quine described his weeks in Prague and Warsaw as "intellectually the most rewarding months I have known." Apart from various visiting professorships, Quine has spent his academic career at Harvard, from where he retired in 1978. He is the author of nineteen books (so far) and literally hundreds of articles in logic and philosophy. He is commonly regarded as the greatest living philosopher in the English-speaking world.

The two "dogmas" under fire are (1) *the analytic/synthetic distinction*—that is, that there is a clear and theoretically viable distinction between sentences whose truth is purely a matter of the meanings of their constituent words, and those whose truth is determined by facts in the world; and (2) *reductionism*—that every cognitively significant statement is derivable from a set of experiential reports. Quine's aim is not to refute Empiricism (he has always considered himself an Empiricist) but to follow its principles through more thoroughly, to produce an Empiricism without dogmas. Most of the paper centers on his attack on the first "dogma." Quine's method is to prove that no noncircular account of analyticity can be found. He will conclude from this that analyticity, and its cognate circle of terms such as "synonymy" and even "meaning" itself are theoretically unsound.

After running through different characterizations of analyticity and the analytic/synthetic distinction through the ages, he considers the standard Positivist criterion that "a statement is analytic when it is true by virtue of meanings and independent of fact." He comments that this alone cannot distinguish logical truths from analytic truths in general. Still, it might seem obvious that we can characterize an analytic truth as one derivable from a logical truth *by substitution of synonyms*. For example, we get "All bachelors are unmarried" from "All unmarried men are unmarried" by replacing "unmarried men" with the synonym "bachelors." But this means that an account of analyticity requires an explication of synonymy. This is what Quine endeavors to provide.

His first attempt is via the notion of *definition*. This proves to be no help, since definitions turn out to be either stipulations or reports of preexisting synonyms. That is, the practice of definition presupposes a grasp of synonymy, so it can't explicate it. He then tries the notion of *substitution*: Two terms x and y are synonyms if one can replace the other without altering the truth-value of the embedding sentence. However, this alone cannot distinguish synonyms from nonsynonymous co-extensive terms, like "creature with heart" and "creature with kidneys." Such a distinction would require the intensional operator "necessarily." However, says Quine, an account of this operator will rely on the concept of analyticity that it is being asked to clarify.

Quine then comments that these problems with analyticity are not due to the inherent flaws of natural languages, since these difficulties also occur for any artificial language. One can certainly devise a Carnapian semantical rule specifying all the analytic statements in a language L_0. Thus, we can say that "S is analytic in L_0 iff. ... " However, this is "analytic in L_0," not "analytic" *per se*. More importantly, it doesn't tell you in virtue of what something is analytic. Mere stipulation has no explanatory power.

As a last try, Quine considers whether synonymy, and thereby analyticity, might be elucidated via the Positivists' Verificationist theory of meaning. For example, couldn't one say that two statements *p* and *q* are synonymous if they are confirmed by the same evidence? But this, says Quine, would be to assume the second dogma, reductionism. This is the view that each statement is verifiable individually, by its own set of confirming data. By contrast, Quine famously asserts that "our statements about the external world face the tribunal of sense-experience not individually but only as a corporate body." This is known as the *Quine-Duhem thesis* (after Pierre Duhem, 1861–1916), or *confirmation holism*. One aspect of this thesis is that no statement is immune from revision. No matter how many observations we make which are, prima facie, confirmations of a claim *p*, we are not logically bound to admit *p*. When we confirm *p* from experience, we implicitly take it that many other statements *q, r, s* are also true. Experience confirms *p* only in conjunction with some wider set of claims. I can reject *p* in the face of observations O_1–O_n by rejecting some other statement from *q* to *z*. Whether and how I do so is ultimately a pragmatic matter. What matters is preserving the coherency, simplicity, and efficacy of the belief-system as a whole. This very point can be applied to the question of an analytic/synthetic distinction itself. Quine would say that whether or not we admit such a distinction is to be justified not by discovering some fact of the matter regarding it, but on whether the distinction earns its keep. Quine concludes that it does not. Sure, one could presumably keep it by making a host of compensatory adjustments to beliefs and/or meanings, but, if Quine is right, it is not worth the effort.

When Quine said that no statement was immune to revision, he applied this thesis to *all* statements, including logical and analytical truths, commonly assumed to be necessarily true, and therefore unrevisable under any conditions. To Quine, as with J.S. Mill, empiricism cannot justify such claims to necessity. Statements that we call "necessary truths" are merely those for which we can imagine no circumstances that would lead us to reject them. But this shows only that they are deeply entrenched beliefs. Thus, they are not different in *kind* from any other beliefs, but simply in their degree of entrenchment.

Quine uses his thesis of confirmation holism to derive a correlated thesis regarding semantics. While not explicitly stated, the following argument is commonly attributed to him:

1. *Verificationism*— A statement's meaning is its method of verification

2. *Quine-Duhem thesis*—Statements are confirmed by experiences holistically, that is, relative to assumptions about other statements; therefore

3. *Semantic holism*—every statement in a language determines the meaning of every other.

However, it is misleading to ascribe a "holistic theory of meaning" to Quine. Rather, his position is that the above considerations make the notion of "meaning" theoretically suspect. This would follow from his negative results regarding analyticity and synonymy: If no clear sense of "meaning the same as" can be found, then "meaning" itself remains in need of specification. As he said in another context, "no entity without identity." Furthermore, since intentional states (e.g., beliefs and desires) are type-individuated by their content, Quine is now considered to have fathered eliminativism over the mind (i.e., regarding folk psychology) as well as in semantics.

One of the most influential responses to Quine was from the Oxford school of "ordinary language philosophy," with Paul Grice and Peter Strawson's "In Defense of a Dogma." They accord with Quine's rejection of reductionism, but argue that this does not justify abandoning the analytic/synthetic distinction.

Grice and Strawson (G&S) spend a lot of time clarifying precisely what Quine's rejection of the analytic/synthetic distinction amounts to. They distinguish several possible theses:

(a) No such distinction exists.

(b) The distinction is vague or inadequately specified.

(c) The distinction is inaccurately specified and cannot fulfill the function it is assumed to have.

G&S point out that (b) and (c) require the falsity of (a). Quine could be comfortable with all this, since thesis (c) is closest to his aim. G&S argue not only that theses (a) and (b) are false but also that the distinction is well-understood and thereby legiti- mate, which is provable by the fact that it is applied uniformly both in common lan- guage and in philosophy. Grice later came to doubt the power of this response since "the fact that a certain concept or distinction is frequently deployed by a population of speakers and thinkers offers no guarantee that the concept or distinction in ques- tion can survive rigorous theoretical scrutiny." (Grandy and Warner, p. 55).

Quine stated that no formal distinction between analytic and synthetic sen- tences can be given. G&S read him, plausibly, as thereby demanding that necessary and sufficient conditions of applicability be given in terms which do not themselves require defining in terms of analyticity. G&S remark that this is a pretty stringent demand and doubt whether any expression could pass it. Instead, they offer a clear but "less formal" explication of the distinction, by means of paradigm cases. They begin with the notion of "logical impossibility." While Quine never explicitly consid- ers this case, G&S are correct that it is in the "family" of "analytic," given its interde- finability with "necessity." So they offer a clear example of the distinction between logical and natural/causal impossibility. Consider these two statements:

1. *My three-year-old understands Russell's Theory of Types.*

2. *My three-year-old is an adult.*

One would be extremely skeptical of 1, but could conceive of evidence that would confirm it; that is, being confronted with the infant prodigy in question. However, we do not understand 2, so long as the words have their standard literal meanings. It makes sense only as a dramatic way of saying that the child is wise beyond her years—that is, as if she were an adult. We can explicate the distinction exemplified in these two sentences via the distinction between "not *believing* something" and "not *understand- ing* something."

G&S say that this informally drawn distinction is compatible with Quine's claim that no statement is immune from revision, since we can distinguish two ways in which one could hold onto it: by altering one's beliefs or by changing the mean- ings of the words. The latter would be required for 2. Likewise, certain claims could be *rejected* only if the meaning of some component were to change. It is debatable how much damage this does to Quine's main point. Perhaps he could agree to all this but insist that these two ways of keeping or dropping a sentence are on a par. That is, the fact that a sentence can be dropped only by changing its meaning doesn't thereby confer on it some epistemological privilege. There is always a choice, justified pri- marily on pragmatic grounds, whether to adjust one's belief-system in response to an unwelcome observation by changing a belief or changing a meaning.

One other noteworthy point in this article: G&S point out that accepting the Quine-Duhem thesis doesn't rule out a noncircular account of synonymy. Suppose that we grant Quine that any statement p can only be confirmed by experiences O_1–O_n when p is considered in conjunction with a set of other statements q to z. You could still say that *p* and *q* are synonymous if they are confirmed by the same experiences, *when considered in conjunction with the same set of other statements.* Quine would no doubt reply that this set would have to be large, comprising most (if not all) of the language.

BIBLIOGRAPHY

Works by Quine
Quine's main philosophical (rather than strictly logical) works include the following:
From a Logical Point of View (Cambridge: Harvard University Press, 1961). (Includes "On What There Is" and "Two Dogmas of Empiricism.")
From Stimulus to Science (Cambridge: Harvard University Press, 1996).
Ontological Relativity and Other Essays (New York: Columbia University Press, 1969).
The Pursuit of Truth, rev. ed. (Cambridge: Harvard University Press, 1992).
The Roots of Reference (La Salle, Ill: Open Court, 1973).
Theories and Things (Cambridge: Harvard University Press, 1981).
Ways of Paradox and Other Essays, rev. ed. (Cambridge: Harvard University Press 1976).
Word and Object (Cambridge: MIT Press, 1960).
His autobiography is *The Time of My Life* (Cambridge: MIT Press, 1985).

Further Readings
Two excellent surveys are
Roger Gibson, *The Philosophy of W.V. Quine* (University of South Florida Press, 1982).
Christopher Hookway, *Quine* (Stanford, Calif.: Stanford University Press, 1988).
Also highly recommended is George D. Romanos, *Quine and Analytic Philosophy* (Cambridge: MIT Press, 1983), which gives a detailed analysis of Quine's apprenticeship and subsequent rebellion from his greatest mentor, Rudolf Carnap.
Grice and Strawson's "In Defense of a Dogma" originally appeared in *The Philosophical Review*, Vol. 65, 1956, and is reprinted in Grice's *Studies in the Way of Words* (Cambridge: Harvard University Press, 1989).
The other quote from Grice is from "Reply to Richards," in *Philosophical Grounds of Rationality*. eds., Richard E Grandy and Richard Warner (Oxford: Clarendon Press, 1986).

Two Dogmas of Empiricism

W.V.O. Quine

Modern empiricism has been conditioned in large part by two dogmas. One is a belief in some fundamental cleavage between truths which are *analytic*, or grounded in meanings independently of matters of fact, and truths which are *synthetic*, or grounded in fact. The other dogma is *reductionism*: the belief that each meaningful statement is equivalent to some logical construct upon terms which refer to immediate experience. Both dogmas, I shall argue, are ill-founded. One effect of abandoning them is, as we shall see, a blurring of the supposed boundary between speculative metaphysics and natural science. Another effect is a shift toward pragmatism.

1. BACKGROUND FOR ANALYTICITY

Kant's cleavage between analytic and synthetic truths was foreshadowed in Hume's distinction between relations of ideas and matters of fact, and in Leibniz's distinction between truths of reason and truths of fact. Leibniz spoke of the truths of reason as true in all possible worlds. Picturesqueness aside, this is to say that the truths of reason are those which could not possibly be false. In the same vein we hear analytic statements defined as statements whose denials are self-contradictory. But this definition has small explanatory value; for the notion of self-contradictoriness, in the quite broad sense needed for this definition of analyticity, stands in exactly the same need of clarification as does the notion of analyticity itself. The two notions are the two sides of a single dubious coin.

Kant conceived of an analytic statement as one that attributes to its subject no more than is already conceptually contained in the subject. This formulation has two shortcomings: it limits itself to statements of subject-predicate form, and it appeals to a notion of containment which is left at a metaphorical level. But Kant's intent, evident more from the use he makes of the notion of analyticity than from his definition of it, can be restated thus: a statement is analytic when it is true by virtue of meanings and independently of fact. Pursuing this line, let us examine the concept of *meaning* which is presupposed.

Meaning, let us remember, is not to be identified with naming.[1] Frege's example of 'Evening Star' and 'Morning Star', and Russell's of 'Scott' and 'the author of *Waverley*', illustrate that terms can name the same thing but differ in meaning. The distinction between meaning and naming is no less important at the level of abstract terms. The terms '9' and 'the number of the planets' name one and the same abstract

---

W.V.O. Quine; "Two Dogmas of Empiricism," from his *From a Logical Point of View* (Cambridge, MA: Harvard University Press, 1953).

[1] W.V.O. Quine, *From a Logical Point of View*, p. 9.

entity but presumably must be regarded as unlike in meaning; for astronomical observation was needed, and not mere reflection on meanings, to determine the sameness of the entity in question.

The above examples consist of singular terms, concrete and abstract. With general terms, or predicates, the situation is somewhat different but parallel. Whereas a singular term purports to name an entity, abstract or concrete, a general term does not; but a general term is *true of* an entity, or of each of many, or of none.[2] The class of all entities of which a general term is true is called the *extension* of the term. Now paralleling the contrast between the meaning of a singular term and the entity named, we must distinguish equally between the meaning of a general term and its extension. The general terms 'creature with a heart' and 'creature with kidneys', for example, are perhaps alike in extension but unlike in meaning.

Confusion of meaning with extension, in the case of general terms, is less common than confusion of meaning with naming in the case of singular terms. It is indeed a commonplace in philosophy to oppose intension (or meaning) to extension, or, in a variant vocabulary, connotation to denotation.

The Aristotelian notion of essence was the forerunner, no doubt, of the modern notion of intension or meaning. For Aristotle it was essential in men to be rational, accidental to be two-legged. But there is an important difference between this attitude and the doctrine of meaning. From the latter point of view it may indeed be conceded (if only for the sake of argument) that rationality is involved in the meaning of the word 'man' while two-leggedness is not; but two-leggedness may at the same time be viewed as involved in the meaning of 'biped' while rationality is not. Thus from the point of view of the doctrine of meaning it makes no sense to say of the actual individual, who is at once a man and a biped, that his rationality is essential and his two-leggedness accidental or vice versa. Things had essences, for Aristotle, but only linguistic forms have meanings. Meaning is what essence becomes when it is divorced from the object of reference and wedded to the word.

For the theory of meaning a conspicuous question is the nature of its objects: what sort of things are meanings? A felt need for meant entities may derive from an earlier failure to appreciate that meaning and reference are distinct. Once the theory of meaning is sharply separated from the theory of reference, it is a short step to recognizing as the primary business of the theory of meaning simply the synonymy of linguistic forms and the analyticity of statements; meanings themselves, as obscure intermediary entities, may well be abandoned.[3]

The problem of analyticity then confronts us anew. Statements which are analytic by general philosophical acclaim are not, indeed, far to seek. They fall into two classes. Those of the first class, which may be called *logically true*, are typified by:

(1) No unmarried man is married.

The relevant feature of this example is that it not merely is true as it stands, but remains true under any and all reinterpretations of 'man' and 'married'. If we suppose a prior

---

[2] See Quine, op. cit., p. 10, and pp. 107–115.

[3] See Quine, op. cit., pp. 11f, and below, pp. 48f.

inventory of *logical* particles, comprising 'no', 'un-', 'not', 'if', 'then', 'and', etc., then in general a logical truth is a statement which is true and remains true under all reinterpretations of its components other than the logical particles.

But there is also a second class of analytic statements, typified by:

(2) No bachelor is married.

The characteristic of such a statement is that it can be turned into a logical truth by putting synonyms for synonyms; thus (2) can be turned into (1) by putting 'unmarried man' for its synonym 'bachelor'. We still lack a proper characterization of this second class of analytic statements, and therewith of analyticity generally, inasmuch as we have had in the above description to lean on a notion of "synonymy" which is no less in need of clarification than analyticity itself.

In recent years Carnap has tended to explain analyticity by appeal to what he calls state-descriptions.[4] A state-description is any exhaustive assignment of truth values to the atomic, or noncompound, statements of the language. All other statements of the language are, Carnap assumes, built up of their component clauses by means of the familiar logical devices, in such a way that the truth value of any complex statement is fixed for each state-description by specifiable logical laws. A statement is then explained as analytic when it comes out true under every state description. This account is an adaptation of Leibniz's "true in all possible worlds." But note that this version of analyticity serves its purpose only if the atomic statements of the language are, unlike 'John is a bachelor' and 'John is married', mutually independent. Otherwise there would be a state-description which assigned truth to 'John is a bachelor' and to 'John is married', and consequently 'No bachelors are married' would turn out synthetic rather than analytic under the proposed criterion. Thus the criterion of analyticity in terms of state-descriptions serves only for languages devoid of extra-logical synonym-pairs, such as 'bachelor' and 'unmarried man'—synonym-pairs of the type which give rise to the "second class" of analytic statements. The criterion in terms of state-descriptions is a reconstruction at best of logical truth, not of analyticity.

I do not mean to suggest that Carnap is under any illusions on this point. His simplified model language with its state-descriptions is aimed primarily not at the general problem of analyticity but at another purpose, the clarification of probability and induction. Our problem, however, is analyticity; and here the major difficulty lies not in the first class of analytic statements, the logical truths, but rather in the second class, which depends on the notion of synonymy.

2. DEFINITION

There are those who find it soothing to say that the analytic statements of the second class reduce to those of the first class, the logical truths, by *definition*; 'bachelor', for example, is *defined* as 'unmarried man'. But how do we find that 'bachelor' is defined as 'unmarried man'? Who defined it thus, and when? Are we to appeal to the nearest

---

[4] Rudolf Carnap, *Meaning and Necessity* (Chicago: University of Chicago Press, 1947), pp. 9ff; *Logical Foundations of Probability*, (Chicago: University of Chicago Press, 1950) pp. 70ff.

dictionary, and accept the lexicographer's formulation as law? Clearly this would be to put the cart before the horse. The lexicographer is an empirical scientist, whose business is the recording of antecedent facts; and if he glosses 'bachelor' as 'unmarried man' it is because of his belief that there is a relation of synonymy between those forms, implicit in general or preferred usage prior to his own work. The notion of synonymy presupposed here has still to be clarified, presumably in terms relating to linguistic behavior. Certainly the "definition" which is the lexicographer's report of an observed synonymy cannot be taken as the ground of the synonymy.

Definition is not, indeed, an activity exclusively of philologists. Philosophers and scientists frequently have occasion to "define" a recondite term by paraphrasing it into terms of a more familiar vocabulary. But ordinarily such a definition, like the philologist's, is pure lexicography, affirming a relation of synonymy antecedent to the exposition in hand.

Just what it means to affirm synonymy, just what the interconnections may be which are necessary and sufficient in order that two linguistic forms be properly describable as synonymous, is far from clear; but, whatever these interconnections may be, ordinarily they are grounded in usage. Definitions reporting selected instances of synonymy come then as reports upon usage.

There is also, however, a variant type of definitional activity which does not limit itself to the reporting of preëxisting synonymies. I have in mind what Carnap calls *explication*—an activity to which philosophers are given, and scientists also in their more philosophical moments. In explication the purpose is not merely to paraphrase the definiendum into an outright synonym, but actually to improve upon the definiendum by refining or supplementing its meaning. But even explication, though not merely reporting a preëxisting synonymy between definiendum and definiens, does rest nevertheless on *other* preexisting synonymies. The matter may be viewed as follows. Any word worth explicating has some contexts which, as wholes, are clear and precise enough to be useful; and the purpose of explication is to preserve the usage of these favored contexts while sharpening the usage of other contexts. In order that a given definition be suitable for purposes of explication, therefore, what is required is not that the definiendum in its antecedent usage be synonymous with the definiens, but just that each of these favored contexts of the definiendum, taken as a whole in its antecedent usage, be synonymous with the corresponding context of the definiens.

Two alternative definientia may be equally appropriate for the purposes of a given task of explication and yet not be synonymous with each other; for they may serve interchangeably within the favored contexts but diverge elsewhere. By cleaving to one of these definientia rather than the other, a definition of explicative kind generates, by fiat, a relation of synonymy between definiendum and definiens which did not hold before. But such a definition still owes its explicative function, as seen, to preexisting synonymies.

There does, however, remain still an extreme sort of definition which does not hark back to prior synonymies at all: namely, the explicitly conventional introduction of novel notations for purposes of sheer abbreviation. Here the definiendum becomes synonymous with the definiens simply because it has been created expressly for the purpose of being synonymous with the definiens. Here we have a really transparent case of synonymy created by definition; would that all species of synonymy were as intelligible. For the rest, definition rests on synonymy rather than explaining it.

The word 'definition' has come to have a dangerously reassuring sound, owing no doubt to its frequent occurrence in logical and mathematical writings. We shall do well to digress now into a brief appraisal of the role of definition in formal work.

In logical and mathematical systems either of two mutually antagonistic types of economy may be striven for, and each has its peculiar practical utility. On the one hand we may seek economy of practical expression—ease and brevity in the statement of multifarious relations. This sort of economy calls usually for distinctive concise notations for a wealth of concepts. Second, however, and oppositely, we may seek economy in grammar and vocabulary; we may try to find a minimum of basic concepts such that, once a distinctive notation has been appropriated to each of them, it becomes possible to express any desired further concept by mere combination and iteration of our basic notations. This second sort of economy is impractical in one way, since a poverty in basic idioms tends to a necessary lengthening of discourse. But it is practical in another way: it greatly simplifies theoretical discourse *about* the language, through minimizing the terms and the forms of construction wherein the language consists.

Both sorts of economy, though prima facie incompatible, are valuable in their separate ways. The custom has consequently arisen of combining both sorts of economy by forging in effect two languages, the one a part of the other. The inclusive language, though redundant in grammar and vocabulary, is economical in message lengths, while the part, called primitive notation, is economical in grammar and vocabulary. Whole and part are correlated by rules of translation whereby each idiom not in primitive notation is equated to some complex built up of primitive notation. These rules of translation are the so-called *definitions* which appear in formalized systems. They are best viewed not as adjuncts to one language but as correlations between two languages, the one a part of the other.

But these correlations are not arbitrary. They are supposed to show how the primitive notations can accomplish all purposes, save brevity and convenience, of the redundant language. Hence the definiendum and its definiens may be expected, in each case, to be related in one or another of the three ways lately noted. The definiens may be a faithful paraphrase of the definiendum into the narrower notation, preserving a direct synonymy[5] as of antecedent usage; or the definiens may, in the spirit of explication, improve upon the antecedent usage of the definiendum; or finally, the definiendum may be a newly created notation, newly endowed with meaning here and now.

In formal and informal work alike, thus, we find that definition—except in the extreme case of the explicitly conventional introduction of new notations—hinges on prior relations of synonymy. Recognizing then that the notion of definition does not hold the key to synonymy and analyticity, let us look further into synonymy and say no more of definition.

---

[5] According to an important variant sense of 'definition', the relation preserved may be the weaker relation of mere agreement in reference; see Quine, op. cit., p. 132. But definition in this sense is better ignored in the present connection, being irrelevant to the question of synonymy.

3. INTERCHANGEABILITY

A natural suggestion, deserving close examination, is that the synonymy of two linguistic forms consists simply in their interchangeability in all contexts without change of truth value—interchangeability, in Leibniz's phrase, *salva veritate*.[6] Note that synonyms so conceived need not even be free from vagueness, as long as the vaguenesses match.

But it is not quite true that the synonyms 'bachelor' and 'unmarried man' are everywhere interchangeable *salva veritate*. Truths which become false under substitution of 'unmarried man' for 'bachelor' are easily constructed with the help of 'bachelor of arts' or 'bachelor's buttons'; also with the help of quotation, thus:

'Bachelor' has less than ten letters.

Such counterinstances can, however, perhaps be set aside by treating the phrases 'bachelor of arts' and 'bachelor's buttons' and the quotation "bachelor" each as a single indivisible word and then stipulating that the interchangeability *salva veritate* which is to be the touchstone of synonymy is not supposed to apply to fragmentary occurrences inside of a word. This account of synonymy, supposing it acceptable on other counts, has indeed the drawback of appealing to a prior conception of "word" which can be counted on to present difficulties of formulation in its turn. Nevertheless some progress might be claimed in having reduced the problem of synonymy to a problem of wordhood. Let us pursue this line a bit, taking "word" for granted.

The question remains whether interchangeability *salva veritate* (apart from occurrences within words) is a strong enough condition for synonymy, or whether, on the contrary, some heteronymous expressions might be thus interchangeable. Now let us be clear that we are not concerned here with synonymy in the sense of complete identity in psychological associations or poetic quality; indeed no two expressions are synonymous in such a sense. We are concerned only with what may be called *cognitive* synonymy. Just what this is cannot be said without successfully finishing the present study; but we know something about it from the need which arose for it in connection with analyticity in §1. The sort of synonymy needed there was merely such that any analytic statement could be turned into a logical truth by putting synonyms for synonyms. Turning the tables and assuming analyticity, indeed, we could explain cognitive synonymy of terms as follows (keeping to the familiar example): to say that 'bachelor' and 'unmarried man' are cognitively synonymous is to say no more nor less than that the statement:

(3) All and only bachelors are unmarried men

is analytic.[7]

---

[6] Cf. C.I. Lewis, *A Survey of Symbolic Logic* (Berkeley, 1918), p. 373.

[7] This is cognitive synonymy in a primary, broad sense. Rudolf Carnap, *Meaning and Necessity* (Chicago: University of Chicago Press, 1947), pp. 56ff; and C.I. Lewis, *An Analysis of Knowledge and Valuation* (LaSalle, Ill.: Open Court, 1946), pp. 83ff, have suggested how, once this notion is at hand, a narrower sense of cognitive synonymy which is preferable for some purposes can in turn be derived. But this special ramification of concept-building lies aside from the present purposes and must not be confused with the broad sort of cognitive synonymy here concerned.

What we need is an account of cognitive synonymy not presupposing analyticity—if we are to explain analyticity conversely with help of cognitive synonymy as undertaken in §1. And indeed such an independent account of cognitive synonymy is at present up for consideration, namely, interchangeability *salva veritate* everywhere except within words. The question before us, to resume the thread at last, is whether such interchangeability is a sufficient condition for cognitive synonymy. We can quickly assure ourselves that it is, by examples of the following sort. The statement:

(4) Necessarily all and only bachelors are bachelors

is evidently true, even supposing 'necessarily' so narrowly construed as to be truly applicable only to analytic statements. Then, if 'bachelor' and 'unmarried man' are interchangeable *salva veritate*, the result:

(5) Necessarily all and only bachelors are unmarried men

of putting 'unmarried man' for an occurrence of 'bachelor' in (4) must, like (4), be true. But to say that (5) is true is to say that (3) is analytic, and hence that 'bachelor' and 'unmarried man' are cognitively synonymous.

Let us see what there is about the above argument that gives it its air of hocuspocus. The condition of interchangeability *salva veritate* varies in its force with variations in the richness of the language at hand. The above argument supposes we are working with a language rich enough to contain the adverb 'necessarily', this adverb being so construed as to yield truth when and only when applied to an analytic statement. But can we condone a language which contains such an adverb? Does the adverb really make sense? To suppose that it does is to suppose that we have already made satisfactory sense of 'analytic'. Then what are we so hard at work on right now?

Our argument is not flatly circular, but something like it. It has the form, figuratively speaking, of a closed curve in space.

Interchangeability *salva veritate* is meaningless until relativized to a language whose extent is specified in relevant respects. Suppose now we consider a language containing just the following materials. There is an indefinitely large stock of one-place predicates (for example, 'F' where 'Fx' means that x is a man) and many-place predicates (for example, 'G' where 'Gxy' means that x loves y), mostly having to do with extralogical subject matter. The rest of the language is logical. The atomic sentences consist each of a predicate followed by one or more variables 'x', 'y', etc.; and the complex sentences are built up of the atomic ones by truth functions ('not', 'and', 'or', etc.) and quantification.[8] In effect such a language enjoys the benefits also of descriptions and indeed singular terms generally, these being contextually definable in known ways.[9] Even abstract singular terms naming classes, classes of classes, etc., are contextually definable in case the assumed stock of predicates includes the two-

---

[8] Quine, op. cit., pp. 81ff, below, contain a description of just such a language, except that there happens there to be just one predicate, the two-place predicate 'ϵ'.

[9] See Quine, op. cit., pp. 5–8; pp. 85f, 166f.

place predicate of class membership.[10] Such a language can be adequate to classical mathematics and indeed to scientific discourse generally, except in so far as the latter involves debatable devices such as contrary-to-fact conditionals or modal adverbs like 'necessarily'.[11] Now a language of this type is extensional, in this sense: any two predicates which agree extensionally (that is, are true of the same objects) are interchangeable *salva veritate*.[12]

In an extensional language, therefore, interchangeability *salva veritate* is no assurance of cognitive synonymy of the desired type. That 'bachelor' and 'unmarried man' are interchangeable *salva veritate* in an extensional language assures us of no more than that (3) is true. There is no assurance here that the extensional agreement of 'bachelor' and 'unmarried man' rests on meaning rather than merely on accidental matters of fact, as does the extensional agreement of 'creature with a heart' and 'creature with kidneys'.

For most purposes extensional agreement is the nearest approximation to synonymy we need care about. But the fact remains that extensional agreement falls far short of cognitive synonymy of the type required for explaining analyticity in the manner of §1. The type of cognitive synonymy required there is such as to equate the synonymy of 'bachelor' and 'unmarried man' with the analyticity of (3), not merely with the truth of (3).

So we must recognize that interchangeability *salva veritate*, if construed in relation to an extensional language, is not a sufficient condition of cognitive synonymy in the sense needed for deriving analyticity in the manner of §1. If a language contains an intensional adverb 'necessarily' in the sense lately noted, or other particles to the same effect, then interchangeability *salva veritate* in such a language does afford a sufficient condition of cognitive synonymy; but such a language is intelligible only in so far as the notion of analyticity is already understood in advance.

The effort to explain cognitive synonymy first, for the sake of deriving analyticity from it afterward as in §1, is perhaps the wrong approach. Instead we might try explaining analyticity somehow without appeal to cognitive synonymy. Afterward we could doubtless derive cognitive synonymy from analyticity satisfactorily enough if desired. We have seen that cognitive synonymy of 'bachelor' and 'unmarried man' can be explained as analyticity of (3). The same explanation works for any pair of one-place predicates, of course, and it can be extended in obvious fashion to many-place predicates. Other syntactical categories can also be accommodated in fairly parallel fashion. Singular terms may be said to be cognitively synonymous when the statement of identity formed by putting '=' between them is analytic. Statements may be said simply to be cognitively synonymous when their biconditional (the result of joining them by 'if and only if') is analytic.[13] If we care to lump all categories into a

---

[10] See Quine, op. cit., p. 87.

[11] On such devices see also Quine, op. cit., Essay VIII.

[12] This is the substance of W.V.O. Quine, *Mathematical Logic*, (Cambridge: Harvard University Press, 1951), *121.

[13] The 'if and only if' itself is intended in the truth functional sense. See Rudolf Carnap, *Meaning and Necessity*, op. cit., p. 14.

single formulation, at the expense of assuming again the notion of "word" which was appealed to early in this section, we can describe any two linguistic forms as cognitively synonymous when the two forms are interchangeable (apart from occurrences within "words") *salva* (no longer *veritate* but) *analyticitate*. Certain technical questions arise, indeed, over cases of ambiguity or homonymy; let us not pause for them, however, for we are already digressing. Let us rather turn our backs on the problem of synonymy and address ourselves anew to that of analyticity.

4. SEMANTICAL RULES

Analyticity at first seemed most naturally definable by appeal to a realm of meanings. On refinement, the appeal to meanings gave way to an appeal to synonymy or definition. But definition turned out to be a will-o'-the wisp, and synonymy turned out to be best understood only by dint of a prior appeal to analyticity itself. So we are back at the problem of analyticity.

I do not know whether the statement 'Everything green is extended' is analytic. Now does my indecision over this example really betray an incomplete understanding, an incomplete grasp of the "meanings", of 'green' and 'extended'? I think not. The trouble is not with 'green' or 'extended', but with 'analytic'.

It is often hinted that the difficulty in separating analytic statements from synthetic ones in ordinary language is due to the vagueness of ordinary language and that the distinction is clear when we have a precise artificial language with explicit "semantical rules." This, however, as I shall now attempt to show, is a confusion.

The notion of analyticity about which we are worrying is a purported relation between statements and languages: a statement S is said to be *analytic for* a language L, and the problem is to make sense of this relation generally, that is, for variable 'S' and 'L'. The gravity of this problem is not perceptibly less for artificial languages than for natural ones. The problem of making sense of the idiom 'S is analytic for L', with variable 'S' and 'L', retains its stubbornness even if we limit the range of the variable 'L' to artificial languages. Let me now try to make this point evident.

For artificial languages and semantical rules we look naturally to the writings of Carnap. His semantical rules take various forms, and to make my point I shall have to distinguish certain of the forms. Let us suppose, to begin with, an artificial language L_0 whose semantical rules have the form explicitly of a specification, by recursion or otherwise, of all the analytic statements of L_0. The rules tell us that such and such statements, and only those, are the analytic statements of L_0. Now here the difficulty is simply that the rules contain the word 'analytic', which we do not understand! We understand what expressions the rules attribute analyticity to, but we do not understand what the rules attribute to those expressions. In short, before we can understand a rule which begins 'A statement S is analytic for language L_0 if and only if … ', we must understand the general relative term 'analytic for'; we must understand 'S is analytic for L' where 'S' and 'L' are variables.

Alternatively we may, indeed, view the so-called rule as a conventional definition of a new simple symbol 'analytic-for-L_0', which might better be written untendentiously as 'K' so as not to seem to throw light on the interesting word 'analytic'.

Obviously any number of classes K, M, N, etc. of statements of L_0 can be specified for various purposes or for no purpose; what does it mean to say that K, as against M, N, etc., is the class of the "analytic" statements of L_0?

By saying what statements are analytic for L_0 we explain 'analytic-for-L_0' but not 'analytic', not 'analytic for'. We do not begin to explain the idiom 'S is analytic for L' with variable 'S' and 'L', even if we are content to limit the range of 'L' to the realm of artificial languages.

Actually we do know enough about the intended significance of 'analytic' to know that analytic statements are supposed to be true. Let us then turn to a second form of semantical rule, which says not that such and such statements are analytic but simply that such and such statements are included among the truths. Such a rule is not subject to the criticism of containing the un-understood word 'analytic'; and we may grant for the sake of argument that there is no difficulty over the broader term 'true'. A semantical rule of this second type, a rule of truth, is not supposed to specify all the truths of the language; it merely stipulates, recursively or otherwise, a certain multitude of statements which, along with others unspecified, are to count as true. Such a rule may be conceded to be quite clear. Derivatively, afterward, analyticity can be demarcated thus: a statement is analytic if it is (not merely true but) true according to the semantical rule.

Still there is really no progress. Instead of appealing to an unexplained word 'analytic', we are now appealing to an unexplained phrase 'semantical rule'. Not every true statement which says that the statements of some class are true can count as a semantical rule—otherwise *all* truths would be "analytic" in the sense of being true according to semantical rules. Semantical rules are distinguishable, apparently, only by the fact of appearing on a page under the heading 'Semantical Rules'; and this heading is itself then meaningless.

We can say indeed that a statement is *analytic-for-L_0* if and only if it is true according to such and such specifically appended "semantical rules," but then we find ourselves back at essentially the same case which was originally discussed: 'S is analytic-for-L_0 if and only if...' Once we seek to explain 'S is analytic for L' generally for variable 'L' (even allowing limitation of 'L' to artificial languages), the explanation 'true according to the semantical rules of L' is unavailing; for the relative term 'semantical rule of' is as much in need of clarification, at least, as 'analytic for'.

It may be instructive to compare the notion of semantical rule with that of postulate. Relative to a given set of postulates, it is easy to say what a postulate is: it is a member of the set. Relative to a given set of semantical rules, it is equally easy to say what a semantical rule is. But given simply a notation, mathematical or otherwise, and indeed as thoroughly understood a notation as you please in point of the translations or truth conditions of its statements, who can say which of its true statements rank as postulates? Obviously the question is meaningless—as meaningless as asking which points in Ohio are starting points. Any finite (or effectively specifiable infinite) selection of statements (preferably true ones, perhaps) is as much *a* set of postulates as any other. The word 'postulate' is significant only relative to an act of inquiry; we apply the word to a set of statements just in so far as we happen, for the year or the moment, to be thinking of those statements in relation to the statements which can be reached from them by some set of transformations to which we have seen fit to direct our attention. Now the notion of semantical rule is as sensible and meaningful as that of postulate, if conceived in a similarly relative spirit—relative, this time, to one or another particular enterprise of schooling unconversant persons in sufficient conditions for truth of statements of some natural or artificial language *L*. But from this point of view no one signalization of a subclass of the truths of *L* is intrinsically more a semantical rule than another; and, if 'analytic' means 'true by semantical rules', no one truth of *L* is analytic to the exclusion of another.[14]

It might conceivably be protested that an artificial language *L* (unlike a natural one) is a language in the ordinary sense *plus* a set of explicit semantical rules—the whole constituting, let us say, an ordered pair; and that the semantical rules of *L* then are specifiable simply as the second component of the pair *L*. But, by the same token and more simply, we might construe an artificial language *L* outright as an ordered pair whose second component is the class of its analytic statements; and then the analytic statements of *L* become specifiable simply as the statements in the second component of *L*. Or better still, we might just stop tugging at our bootstraps altogether.

Not all the explanations of analyticity known to Carnap and his readers have been covered explicitly in the above considerations, but the extension to other forms is not hard to see. Just one additional factor should be mentioned which sometimes enters: sometimes the semantical rules are in effect rules of translation into ordinary language, in which case the analytic statements of the artificial language are in effect recognized as such from the analyticity of their specified translations in ordinary language. Here certainly there can be no thought of an illumination of the problem of analyticity from the side of the artificial language.

From the point of view of the problem of analyticity the notion of an artificial language with semantical rules is a *feu follet par excellence*. Semantical rules determining the analytic statements of an artificial language are of interest only in so far as we already understand the notion of analyticity; they are of no help in gaining this understanding.

Appeal to hypothetical languages of an artificially simple kind could conceivably be useful in clarifying analyticity, if the mental or behavioral or cultural factors relevant to analyticity—whatever they may be—were somehow sketched into the simplified model. But a model which takes analyticity merely as an irreducible character is unlikely to throw light on the problem of explicating analyticity.

It is obvious that truth in general depends on both language and extralinguistic fact. The statement 'Brutus killed Caesar' would be false if the world had been different in certain ways, but it would also be false if the word 'killed' happened rather to have the sense of 'begat'. Thus one is tempted to suppose in general that the truth of a statement is somehow analyzable into a linguistic component and a factual component. Given this supposition, it next seems reasonable that in some statements the factual component should be null; and these are the analytic statements. But, for all its a priori reasonableness, a boundary between analytic and synthetic statements sim-

---

[14] The foregoing paragraph was not part of the present essay as originally published. It was prompted by R.M. Martin, "On 'analytic,'" *Philosophical Studies 3* (1952), pp. 42–47, as was the end of Essay VII, Quine, op. cit.

ply has not been drawn. That there is such a distinction to be drawn at all is an unempirical dogma of empiricists, a metaphysical article of faith.

5. THE VERIFICATION THEORY AND REDUCTIONISM

In the course of these somber reflections we have taken a dim view first of the notion of meaning, then of the notion of cognitive synonymy, and finally of the notion of analyticity. But what, it may be asked, of the verification theory of meaning? This phrase has established itself so firmly as a catchword of empiricism that we should be very unscientific indeed not to look beneath it for a possible key to the problem of meaning and the associated problems.

The verification theory of meaning, which has been conspicuous in the literature from Peirce onward, is that the meaning of a statement is the method of empirically confirming or infirming it. An analytic statement is that limiting case which is confirmed no matter what.

As urged in §1, we can as well pass over the question of meanings as entities and move straight to sameness of meaning, or synonymy. Then what the verification theory says is that statements are synonymous if and only if they are alike in point of method of empirical confirmation or infirmation.

This is an account of cognitive synonymy not of linguistic forms generally, but of statements.[15] However, from the concept of synonymy of statements we could derive the concept of synonymy for other linguistic forms, by considerations somewhat similar to those at the end of §3. Assuming the notion of "word," indeed, we could explain any two forms as synonymous when the putting of the one form for an occurrence of the other in any statement (apart from occurrences within "words") yields a synonymous statement. Finally, given the concept of synonymy thus for linguistic forms generally, we could define analyticity in terms of synonymy and logical truth as in §1. For that matter, we could define analyticity more simply in terms of just synonymy of statements together with logical truth; it is not necessary to appeal to synonymy of linguistic forms other than statements. For a statement may be described as analytic simply when it is synonymous with a logically true statement.

So, if the verification theory can be accepted as an adequate account of statement synonymy, the notion of analyticity is saved after all. However, let us reflect. Statement synonymy is said to be likeness of method of empirical confirmation or infirmation. Just what are these methods which are to be compared for likeness? What, in other words, is the nature of the relation between a statement and the experiences which contribute to or detract from its confirmation?

---

[15] The doctrine can indeed be formulated with terms rather than statements as the units. Thus Lewis describes the meaning of a term as "*a criterion in mind*, by reference to which one is able to apply or refuse to apply the expression in question in the case of presented, or imagined, things or situations" (*An Analysis of Knowledge and Valuation*, op. cit., p. 133).—For an instructive account of the vicissitudes of the verification theory of meaning, centered however on the question of meaning*fulness* rather than synonymy and analyticity, see Hempel.

The most naïve view of the relation is that it is one of direct report. This is *radical reductionism*. Every meaningful statement is held to be translatable into a statement (true or false) about immediate experience. Radical reductionism, in one form or another, well antedates the verification theory of meaning explicitly so called. Thus Locke and Hume held that every idea must either originate directly in sense experience or else be compounded of ideas thus originating; and taking a hint from Tooke we might rephrase this doctrine in semantical jargon by saying that a term, to be significant at all, must be either a name of a sense datum or a compound of such names or an abbreviation of such a compound. So stated, the doctrine remains ambiguous as between sense data as sensory events and sense data as sensory qualities; and it remains vague as to the admissible ways of compounding. Moreover, the doctrine is unnecessarily and intolerably restrictive in the term-by-term critique which it imposes. More reasonably, and without yet exceeding the limits of what I have called radical reductionism, we may take full statements as our significant units—thus demanding that our statements as wholes be translatable into sense-datum language, but not that they be translatable term by term.

This emendation would unquestionably have been welcome to Locke and Hume and Tooke, but historically it had to await an important reorientation in semantics—the reorientation whereby the primary vehicle of meaning came to be seen no longer in the term but in the statement. This reorientation, seen in Bentham and Frege, underlies Russell's concept of incomplete symbols defined in use;[16] also it is implicit in the verification theory of meaning, since the objects of verification are statements.

Radical reductionism, conceived now with statements as units, set itself the task of specifying a sense-datum language and showing how to translate the rest of significant discourse, statement by statement, into it. Carnap embarked on this project in the *Aufbau*.

The language which Carnap adopted as his starting point was not a sense-datum language in the narrowest conceivable sense, for it included also the notations of logic, up through higher set theory. In effect it included the whole language of pure mathematics. The ontology implicit in it (that is, the range of values of its variables) embraced not only sensory events but classes, classes of classes, and so on. Empiricists there are who would boggle at such prodigality. Carnap's starting point is very parsimonious, however, in its extralogical or sensory part. In a series of constructions in which he exploits the resources of modern logic with much ingenuity, Carnap succeeds in defining a wide array of important additional sensory concepts which, but for his constructions, one would not have dreamed were definable on so slender a basis. He was the first empiricist who, not content with asserting the reducibility of science to terms of immediate experience, took serious steps toward carrying out the reduction.

If Carnap's starting point is satisfactory, still his constructions were, as he himself stressed, only a fragment of the full program. The construction of even the simplest statements about the physical world was left in a sketchy state. Carnap's suggestions on this subject were, despite their sketchiness, very suggestive. He explained

---

[16] See Quine, op. cit., p. 6.

spatio-temporal point-instants as quadruples of real numbers and envisaged assignment of sense qualities to point-instants according to certain canons. Roughly summarized, the plan was that qualities should be assigned to point-instants in such a way as to achieve the laziest world compatible with our experience. The principle of least action was to be our guide in constructing a world from experience.

Carnap did not seem to recognize, however, that his treatment of physical objects fell short of reduction not merely through sketchiness, but in principle. Statements of the form 'Quality q is at point-instant $x;y;z;t$' were, according to his canons, to be apportioned truth values in such a way as to maximize and minimize certain over-all features, and with growth of experience the truth values were to be progressively revised in the same spirit. I think this is a good schematization (deliberately oversimplified, to be sure) of what science really does; but it provides no indication, not even the sketchiest, of how a statement of the form 'Quality q is at $x;y;z;t$' could ever be translated into Carnap's initial language of sense data and logic. The connective 'is at' remains an added undefined connective; the canons counsel us in its use but not in its elimination.

Carnap seems to have appreciated this point afterward; for in his later writings he abandoned all notion of the translatability of statements about the physical world into statements about immediate experience. Reductionism in its radical form has long since ceased to figure in Carnap's philosophy.

But the dogma of reductionism has, in a subtler and more tenuous form, continued to influence the thought of empiricists. The notion lingers that to each statement, or each synthetic statement, there is associated a unique range of possible sensory events such that the occurrence of any of them would add to the likelihood of truth of the statement, and that there is associated also another unique range of possible sensory events whose occurrence would detract from that likelihood. This notion is of course implicit in the verification theory of meaning.

The dogma of reductionism survives in the supposition that each statement, taken in isolation from its fellows, can admit of confirmation or infirmation at all. My countersuggestion, issuing essentially from Carnap's doctrine of the physical world in the *Aufbau*, is that our statements about the external world face the tribunal of sense experience not individually but only as a corporate body.[17]

The dogma of reductionism, even in its attenuated form, is intimately connected with the other dogma—that there is a cleavage between the analytic and the synthetic. We have found ourselves led, indeed, from the latter problem to the former through the verification theory of meaning. More directly, the one dogma clearly supports the other in this way: as long as it is taken to be significant in general to speak of the confirmation and infirmation of a statement, it seems significant to speak also of a limiting kind of statement which is vacuously confirmed, *ipso facto*, come what may; and such a statement is analytic.

The two dogmas are, indeed, at root identical. We lately reflected that in general the truth of statements does obviously depend both upon language and upon

---

[17] This doctrine was well argued by Pierre Duhem, *La Theorie physique: son objet et sa structure* (Paris, 1906), pp. 303–328. Or see Armand Lowinger, *The Methodology of Pierre Duhem* (New York: Columbia University Press, 1941), pp. 132–140.

extralinguistic fact; and we noted that this obvious circumstance carries in its train, not logically but all too naturally, a feeling that the truth of a statement is somehow analyzable into a linguistic component and a factual component. The factual component must, if we are empiricists, boil down to a range of confirmatory experiences. In the extreme case where the linguistic component is all that matters, a true statement is analytic. But I hope we are now impressed with how stubbornly the distinction between analytic and synthetic has resisted any straightforward drawing. I am impressed also, apart from prefabricated examples of black and white balls in an urn, with how baffling the problem has always been of arriving at any explicit theory of the empirical confirmation of a synthetic statement. My present suggestion is that it is nonsense, and the root of much nonsense, to speak of a linguistic component and a factual component in the truth of any individual statement. Taken collectively, science has its double dependence upon language and experience; but this duality is not significantly traceable into the statements of science taken one by one.

The idea of defining a symbol in use was, as remarked, an advance over the impossible term-by-term empiricism of Locke and Hume. The statement, rather than the term, came with Bentham to be recognized as the unit accountable to an empiricist critique. But what I am now urging is that even in taking the statement as unit we have drawn our grid too finely. The unit of empirical significance is the whole of science.

6. EMPIRICISM WITHOUT THE DOGMAS

The totality of our so-called knowledge or beliefs, from the most casual matters of geography and history to the profoundest laws of atomic physics or even of pure mathematics and logic, is a man-made fabric which impinges on experience only along the edges. Or, to change the figure, total science is like a field of force whose boundary conditions are experience. A conflict with experience at the periphery occasions readjustments in the interior of the field. Truth values have to be redistributed over some of our statements. Reëvaluation of some statements entails reëvaluation of others, because of their logical interconnections—the logical laws being in turn simply certain further statements of the system, certain further elements of the field. Having reëvaluated one statement we must reëvaluate some others, which may be statements logically connected with the first or may be the statements of logical connections themselves. But the total field is so underdetermined by its boundary conditions, experience, that there is much latitude of choice as to what statements to reëvaluate in the light of any single contrary experience. No particular experiences are linked with any particular statements in the interior of the field, except indirectly through considerations of equilibrium affecting the field as a whole.

If this view is right, it is misleading to speak of the empirical content of an individual statement—especially if it is a statement at all remote from the experiential periphery of the field. Furthermore it becomes folly to seek a boundary between synthetic statements, which hold contingently on experience, and analytic statements, which hold come what may. Any statement can be held true come what may, if we make drastic enough adjustments elsewhere in the system. Even a statement very close to the periphery can be held true in the face of recalcitrant experience by pleading hallucination or by amending certain statements of the kind called logical laws. Conversely, by the same token, no statement is immune to revision. Revision even of the logical law of the excluded middle has been proposed as a means of simplifying quantum mechanics; and what difference is there in principle between such a shift and the shift whereby Kepler superseded Ptolemy, or Einstein Newton, or Darwin Aristotle?

For vividness I have been speaking in terms of varying distances from a sensory periphery. Let me try now to clarify this notion without metaphor. Certain statements, though *about* physical objects and not sense experience, seem peculiarly germane to sense experience—and in a selective way: some statements to some experiences, others to others. Such statements, especially germane to particular experiences, I picture as near the periphery. But in this relation of "germaneness" I envisage nothing more than a loose association reflecting the relative likelihood, in practice, of our choosing one statement rather than another for revision in the event of recalcitrant experience. For example, we can imagine recalcitrant experiences to which we would surely be inclined to accommodate our system by reëvaluating just the statement that there are brick houses on Elm Street, together with related statements on the same topic. We can imagine other recalcitrant experiences to which we would be inclined to accommodate our system by reëvaluating just the statement that there are no centaurs, along with kindred statements. A recalcitrant experience can, I have urged, be accommodated by any of various alternative reëvaluations in various alternative quarters of the total system; but, in the cases which we are now imagining, our natural tendency to disturb the total system as little as possible would lead us to focus our revisions upon these specific statements concerning brick houses or centaurs. These statements are felt, therefore, to have a sharper empirical reference than highly theoretical statements of physics or logic or ontology. The latter statements may be thought of as relatively centrally located within the total network, meaning merely that little preferential connection with any particular sense data obtrudes itself.

As an empiricist I continue to think of the conceptual scheme of science as a tool, ultimately, for predicting future experience in the light of past experience. Physical objects are conceptually imported into the situation as convenient intermediaries—not by definition in terms of experience, but simply as irreducible posits[18] comparable, epistemologically, to the gods of Homer. For my part I do, qua lay physicist, believe in physical objects and not in Homer's gods; and I consider it a scientific error to believe otherwise. But in point of epistemological footing the physical objects and the gods differ only in degree and not in kind. Both sorts of entities enter our conception only as cultural posits. The myth of physical objects is epistemologically superior to most in that it has proved more efficacious than other myths as a device for working a manageable structure into the flux of experience.

Positing does not stop with macroscopic physical objects. Objects at the atomic level are posited to make the laws of macroscopic objects, and ultimately the laws of experience, simpler and more manageable; and we need not expect or demand full definition of atomic and subatomic entities in terms of macroscopic ones, any more

---

[18] Cf. Quine, op. cit., pp. 17f.

than definition of macroscopic things in terms of sense data. Science is a continuation of common sense, and it continues the common-sense expedient of swelling ontology to simplify theory.

Physical objects, small and large, are not the only posits. Forces are another example; and indeed we are told nowadays that the boundary between energy and matter is obsolete. Moreover, the abstract entities which are the substance of mathematics—ultimately classes and classes of classes and so on up—are another posit in the same spirit. Epistemologically these are myths on the same footing with physical objects and gods, neither better nor worse except for differences in the degree to which they expedite our dealings with sense experiences.

The over-all algebra of rational and irrational numbers is underdetermined by the algebra of rational numbers, but is smoother and more convenient; and it includes the algebra of rational numbers as a jagged or gerrymandered part.[19] Total science, mathematical and natural and human, is similarly but more extremely underdetermined by experience. The edge of the system must be kept squared with experience; the rest, with all its elaborate myths or fictions, has as its objective the simplicity of laws.

Ontological questions, under this view, are on a par with questions of natural science.[20] Consider the question whether to countenance classes as entities. This, as I have argued elsewhere,[21] is the question whether to quantify with respect to variables which take classes as values. Now Carnap [6] has maintained that this is a question not of matters of fact but of choosing a convenient language form, a convenient conceptual scheme or framework for science. With this I agree, but only on the proviso that the same be conceded regarding scientific hypotheses generally. Carnap ([6], p. 32n) has recognized that he is able to preserve a double standard for ontological questions and scientific hypotheses only by assuming an absolute distinction between the analytic and the synthetic; and I need not say again that this is a distinction which I reject.[22]

The issue over there being classes seems more a question of convenient conceptual scheme; the issue over there being centaurs, or brick houses on Elm Street, seems more a question of fact. But I have been urging that this difference is only one of degree, and that it turns upon our vaguely pragmatic inclination to adjust one strand of the fabric of science rather than another in accommodating some particular recalcitrant experience. Conservatism figures in such choices, and so does the quest for simplicity.

Carnap, Lewis, and others take a pragmatic stand on the question of choosing between language forms, scientific frameworks; but their pragmatism leaves off

---

[18] Cf. Quine, op. cit., pp. 17f.

[19] Cf. Quine, op. cit., p. 18.

[20] "L'ontologie fait corps avec la science elle-même et ne peut en être separée." Emile Meyerson, *Identite et realite* (Paris, 1908; 4th ed., 1932).

[21] Quine, op. cit., pp. 12f, pp. 102ff.

[22] For an effective expression of further misgivings over this distinction, see Morton White, "The analytic and the synthetic: an untenable dualism," in Sidney Hook (ed.), *John Dewey: Philosopher of Science and Freedom* (New York: Dial Press, 1950).

at the imagined boundary between the analytic and the synthetic. In repudiating such a boundary I espouse a more thorough pragmatism. Each man is given a scientific heritage plus a continuing barrage of sensory stimulation; and the considerations which guide him in warping his scientific heritage to fit his continuing sensory promptings are, where rational, pragmatic.

Introduction to W.V.O. Quine on Ontology

"Ontological Relativity" is a sophisticated distillation of ideas presented in Quine's earlier *Word and Object*, to the effect that there are no facts of the matter as to what one's words mean, or even what they refer to. This skepticism over meaning had, of course, been a Quinean theme at least since "Two Dogmas of Empiricism." However, in these later works he expands his thesis into a full-blown statement of ontological relativity; that is, that there is no fact of the matter as to what one's language ontologically commits one to. To set the scene for "Ontological Relativity," I will contrast it with an earlier piece, "On What There Is."

In the Positivist orthodoxy against which Quine was reacting, questions about one's most basic ontological commitments were regarded as devoid of factual content. Thus, Carnap distinguished "internal" and "external" questions. (See my "Introduction to Logical Positivism" for more details.) Once a certain foundational framework was given, certain questions could be asked "internally" from within it. So, given a framework of material objects, we could ask questions regarding the existence of certain sorts of objects. However, answers to "external" questions about the reality of objects *per se*, concerning the framework itself, could only be stipulated, but not discovered. Quine attempts to rehabilitate ontological discussion, and he argues that Carnap's distinction does not mark a difference in kind, but merely a difference in degree of generality of subject matter. Such a position is in line with his denial of any categorical difference between philosophy and the sciences, or between analytic and synthetic sentences.

Quine introduces two hypothetical opponents, McX and Wyman, with whom to enter into ontological dispute. These philosophers claim that the mythical creature Pegasus exists, taking a line reminiscent of Meinong and of Russell's *The Principles of Mathematics* that every linguistic term, in order to be part of an intelligible sentence, must stand for something. Thus, they say, unless "Pegasus" had a referent, any sentences including this term would be meaningless. However, since these clearly *are* intelligible, and "Pegasus" is therefore a referring expression, then any denial of Pegasus' existence is self-contradictory. However, they know that Pegasus does not exist in space-time and are forced to grant it some other form of existence. McX takes it to be an idea in the minds of those who understand "Pegasus," and Wyman as an "unactualized possible entity," where "actuality" is taken as a predicate expression, on a par with "red."

Quine opposes admitting such unactualized possibles into his ontology, on the grounds that any theoretically respectable concept must have clear conditions of identity and individuation. However, no rules have been given to let us establish whether something is *the same* unactualized possible as another, nor *how many* such supposed entities are present at any given place and time. In the words of one of Quine's most famous maxims, "no entity without identity."

McX and Wyman share the more fundamental error of taking all singular terms of ordinary language to be *names*, for which objects must be found. Quine supports Russell's Theory of Descriptions, which allows the elimination of such expressions by paraphrase into the language of the predicate calculus. He follows Russell in adopting Frege's "context principle" of considering the meaning of a word only in the context of a complete sentence. This, of course, frees him of the need to replace each single term with a synonym—all that matters is that you produce a sentence that expresses the content of the original in a more explicit way.

Quine takes Russell's techniques further, dispensing with the need to replace an ordinary name with an antecedently familiar definite description. Rather, new predicate-expressions can be introduced into the language, and the names be considered as derivative from them. Thus, "Pegasus" can be paraphrased as "the thing that pegasizes," or "the pegasizer." Thus names can be entirely eliminated from the language.

Quine then considers the ontological status of universals, for example, attributes, relations, functions, and the like. McX takes their existence to be trivially shown—given the existence of red books, red cars, red shirts, and so on, then "redness" must also exist. For Quine, this makes the elementary mistake indicated above, of taking every linguistic item as a name. However, suppose that McX were to grant Quine's point here but argue that universals still existed, with the ontological status of "meanings." That is, since expressions like "is red" *have* meanings, meanings is what they *are*. Quine replies that the distinction between meaningful and meaningless expressions, and sentences about "having a meaning" or "having the same meaning" do not require "special and irreducible intermediary entities called meanings." This is because any reference to such entities could be paraphrased away, as before.

Quine then comes to the crucial point of what our language does ontologically commit us to. His answer, famously, is "to be is to be the value of a variable." That is, we are committed to whatever are values of bound variables, as revealed when our assertions are translated into the language of the predicate calculus. Thus, we are ontologically committed to a certain type of thing if the truth of the sentences of our professed theory depends on the existence of such a class of things. We are not committed to anything that can be eliminated by this method of paraphrase. As Quine admits, such a method does not tell you what there *is*, but merely what someone *says there is*. That is, he has provided us with a criterion for ascertaining someone's ontological commitments, by logical analysis of their assertions. This is in opposition to the assumption that statements of logic are ontologically neutral.

As to the question of what there is, or of which ontology to adopt, Quine takes parsimony as a guide. That is, we should adopt the *simplest* framework with which we can explain and predict experience. In cases where different frameworks would function equally well, he recommends "tolerance and an experimental spirit." In taking this line, Quine rejects the Positivist assumption of a fundamental difference in kind between the issue of what ontological framework to adopt, and more "local" issues concerning the inhabitants of that scheme. Thus, "Are there objects?" and "Are there apples?" differ only in their degree of generality. Behind this pragmatic relativism over which ontology one should adopt, Quine still, at this stage, takes it for granted that there is a real fact of the matter over the ontological commitments of any given choice. He was soon to revise this assumption.

As I mentioned above, some of the themes of "Ontological Relativity" were given their first detailed presentation in Quine's masterpiece, *Word and Object*. My discussion of the article will employ various technical distinctions and examples introduced in that book.

Quine, like Wittgenstein, is opposed to the "myth of the museum," wherein it is assumed that words stand for ideas in the mind, and which function as "labels" for them or for objects associated with them. From Quine's behaviorist perspective, such a theory is not warranted by the facts. However, the price of dropping this myth is to give up on the belief that words have determinate meanings. And, if this goes, then the notions of meaning itself, and synonymy (sameness of meaning) are also gone.

As a pedagogical device to explicate these matters, Quine introduces the figure of the *radical translator*. This linguist is presented with the task of constructing a translation manual for some language N and English, with nothing to go on beyond the behavior (including verbal behavior) of N-speakers. He cannot rely on any historical or scientific data about these people; nor can he employ corollary information about N from neighboring languages. Quine claims that there are no "facts of the matter" to determine one uniquely correct translation, but rather that several manuals could be devised which would each be compatible with all the empirical evidence, yet be mutually incompatible: "Manuals for translating one language into another can be set up in divergent ways, all compatible with the totality of speech dispositions, yet incompatible with one another" (*Word and Object*, p. 27).

To argue for this radical conclusion, Quine introduces some technical distinctions. In "Two Dogmas of Empiricism," he had concluded that intensional concepts such as "meaning" and "synonymy" had no place in a science of language. He therefore had to replace these with some distinctions that were empirically warranted.

An *occasion sentence* can be assented to (or denied) only in the presence of certain stimuli. For example, a response to an utterance of "That man is very tall," would require the man to be visible at that moment. An important subclass of these are *observation sentences*, which are occasion sentences that would receive the same response from any person competent with the language, since the requirement of collateral information is minimized (although it can never be eliminated). For example, "This is an apple," or "It is raining" would count, in the presence of appropriate stimuli, since little extra background knowledge needs to be called upon. By contrast, responding to a sentence like "That woman is an accountant" would probably require one to have knowledge of this person's activities.

Quine's most important linguistic concept is that of *stimulus meaning*. The stimulus meaning of a sentence S must always be indexed to a particular speaker A and time t, and comprises the ordered pair of sets (X,Y), where X is the set of stimuli that would cause A to assent to S at t, and Y the stimuli that would likewise cause dissent. This notion of stimulus meaning applies most naturally to observation sentences, which can be learned ostensively, due to the minimization of collateral information. Suppose we then derive the notion of *stimulus analyticity*— that is, a sentence is stimulus analytic if one would assent to it after any stimulus. The set of stimulus analytic sentences would be larger than classical analytic sentences, since the former would also include items of common knowledge such as "Dogs are gluttons," "It has rained before," and "People have died."

The radical translator would be wise to begin by attempting to identify natives' observation sentences, dealing as they do with intersubjectively available sources of stimuli. So, for example, "A rabbit scurries by, the native says 'Gavagai' and the linguist notes down the sentence 'Rabbit' (or 'Lo, a rabbit') as a tentative translation, subject to testing in further cases" (*Word and Object*, p. 29). Now the linguist doesn't want to rely on N-speakers happening to make utterances in his presence. He wants to be able to elicit responses from them at will. Thus, were the rabbit to reappear, the linguist could utter "Gavagai" and check the N-speaker's response to his utterance. Of course, this assumes that the translator has already determined native words (or gestures) for assent and dissent. Granting this, the translator would be in a position to determine the stimulus meaning of "Gavagai," and whether it accords with "Lo, a rabbit."

At this stage in the translation process, the linguist is treating N-utterances as wholes, without any attempt to divide them into words. However, this move has to be made if his translation is to extend beyond observation sentences. He will have to employ *analytic hypotheses*: notice certain recurring sounds and hypothetically equate them with English words. "The linguist apprehends a parallelism in function between some component fragment of a translated whole native sentence and some component word of the translation of the sentence" (*Word and Object*, p. 70).

At this point, Quine asserts his infamous thesis of the *Indeterminacy of Translation*: "manuals for translating one language into another can be set up in divergent ways, all compatible with the totality of speech dispositions, yet incompatible with one another" (*Word and Object*, p. 27). This is not the merely *epistemological* claim that the correct translation cannot be discovered. Rather, it is the *ontological* point that there is no fact of the matter regarding a uniquely correct translation. There is no such thing to be discovered.

Quine goes even further, adding that the problem is not restricted to intensional concepts like meaning or synonymy, but extends to reference as well. The *Inscrutability of Reference* is the thesis that different mutually exclusive ontologies can be ascribed on the basis of the same evidence, where there are no restrictions on evidence available. The inscrutability of reference can be redescribed as the thesis of ontological relativity.

Take our example of "Gavagai." Suppose that our linguist translates this sentence as "Lo, a rabbit," and the term "gavagai" as equivalent to our concrete general term "rabbit." Quine does not deny that any other translation would be foolish, but does insist that the translation is a *choice*, not a *discovery*, and that its justification is ultimately pragmatic. The term "gavagai" could equally be taken as referring to rabbithood, or undetached rabbit parts, and so forth. Mere ostension is no help, because in pointing to a rabbit you are, ipso facto, pointing to an undetached rabbit part.

Progress would require translations of terms employed in the "apparatus of individuation" applied to terms which divide their reference; for example, number terms, "same," "other," pluralization devices, the "is" of identity, and the like. If this were achieved, he could then attempt translations of "Is this gavagai the same as that one?" (e.g., pointing to its head and tail, or to the same continuous object at different times). But, as Quine says, the indeterminacy thesis is general, and thus affects translations of all N-terms, this "apparatus" included. One set of analytic hypotheses might translate a certain N-term as "the same as," whereas another might offer "belongs with." It would follow that two different sentences, with the same stimulus meaning, could be produced as translations of an N-sentence, namely "Is this the same rabbit as that one?" and "Does this undetached rabbit part belong with that one?." Thus, two linguists could devise utterly different, mutually exclusive translation manuals, ascribing totally different ontologies to N-speakers, by making various synchronized adjustments to their analytical hypotheses. In fact, we cannot assume that "gavagai" be translated as a concrete general term at all. Quine gives the example of "green," which functions ambiguously, sometimes as a predicate applied to concrete things, sometimes as a name for the abstract entity "greenness." In a similar way, "gavagai" might stand, in some or all of its usages, for "rabbithood."

It must be kept in mind that Quine employs the radical translator as only an expository device, since "On deeper reflection, radical translation begins at home." Not only is the position of the linguist the same as that of an infant (except in already possessing a language), but it is our position every day when we communicate with others. This fact is obscured by the fact that we usually, unconsciously, translate our fellows' utterances homophonically. In fact, we are all familiar with cases in which we ascribe a different meaning to someone's words, to avoid ascribing inexplicable error, bizarre beliefs, or unintelligible desires to them. For example, every youth knows that "bad" sometimes means "good." It would be quite possible, although perverse, to systematically interpret someone's talk of rabbits as being about undetached rabbit stages, and make all the subsequent adjustment that would be necessary to explain and predict his behavior. In doing so, you would not be making any factual error, but merely making life unnecessarily difficult for yourself.

Quine then goes one stage further: Once the myth of the museum is given up, one can no longer claim that *one's own* words or thoughts have determinate content either. That is, what I say has no objective meaning or reference even for myself. My words have determinate meaning only relative to a language (i.e., a translation manual) and the facts do not uniquely determine one manual.

Whether translating a foreign language, trying to understand the utterances of a member of my own speech community, or even when considering my own words or thoughts, the idea of factually grounded *absolute* reference is nonsensical. It would be just as meaningless to ask for the absolute position of an object. Just as this can only be stated relative to a spatial coordinate system, so the ontological commitment of a sentence, or a theory, can be ascribed only relative to a far larger linguistic framework, and relative to its interpretation within this framework.

For the Bibliography, see my Introduction to W.V.O. Quine "Two Dogmas of Empiricism."

Ontological Relativity*

W.V.O. Quine

I

I listened to Dewey on Art as Experience when I was a graduate student in the spring of 1931. Dewey was then at Harvard as the first William James Lecturer. I am proud now to be at Columbia as the first John Dewey Lecturer.

Philosophically I am bound to Dewey by the naturalism that dominated his last three decades. With Dewey I hold that knowledge, mind, and meaning are part of the same world that they have to do with, and that they are to be studied in the same empirical spirit that animates natural science. There is no place for a prior philosophy.

When a naturalistic philosopher addresses himself to the philosophy of mind, he is apt to talk of language. Meanings are, first and foremost, meanings of language. Language is a social art which we all acquire on the evidence solely of other people's overt behavior under publicly recognizable circumstances. Meanings, therefore, those very models of mental entities, end up as grist for the behaviorist's mill. Dewey was explicit on the point: "Meaning ... is not a psychic existence; it is primarily a property of behavior."[1]

Once we appreciate the institution of language in these terms, we see that there cannot be, in any useful sense, a private language. This point was stressed by Dewey in the twenties. "Soliloquy," he wrote, "is the product and reflex of converse with others" (170). Farther along he expanded the point thus: "Language is specifically a mode of interaction of at least two beings, a speaker and a hearer; it presupposes an organized group to which these creatures belong, and from whom they have acquired their habits of speech. It is therefore a relationship" (185). Years later, Wittgenstein likewise rejected private language. When Dewey was writing in this naturalistic vein, Wittgenstein still held his copy theory of language.

The copy theory in its various forms stands closer to the main philosophical tradition, and to the attitude of common sense today. Uncritical semantics is the myth of a museum in which the exhibits are meanings and the words are labels. To switch languages is to change the labels. Now the naturalist's primary objection to this view is not an objection to meanings on account of their being mental entities, though that could be objection enough. The primary objection persists even if we take the labeled exhibits not as mental ideas but as Platonic ideas or even as the denoted concrete

By permission of *The Journal of Philosophy* and Professor Quine.

* Presented as a pair of lectures of the same title at Columbia University, March 26 and 28, 1968. The lectures are the first series of John Dewey Lectures, which will be delivered biennially and which have been established to honor the late John Dewey, from 1905 to 1930 a professor of philosophy at Columbia. The editors are pleased to have the opportunity to publish them.

[1] *Experience and Nature* (La Salle, Ill.: Open Court, 1925, 1958), p. 179.

objects. Semantics is vitiated by a pernicious mentalism as long as we regard a man's semantics as somehow determinate in his mind beyond what might be implicit in his dispositions to overt behavior. It is the very facts about meaning, not the entities meant, that must be construed in terms of behavior.

There are two parts to knowing a word. One part is being familiar with the sound of it and being able to reproduce it. This part, the phonetic part, is achieved by observing and imitating other people's behavior, and there are no important illusions about the process. The other part, the semantic part, is knowing how to use the word. This part, even in the paradigm case, is more complex than the phonetic part. The word refers, in the paradigm case, to some visible object. The learner has now not only to learn the word phonetically, by hearing it from another speaker; he also has to see the object; and in addition to this, in order to capture the relevance of the object to the word, he has to see that the speaker also sees the object. Dewey summed up the point thus: "The characteristic theory about B's understanding of A's sounds is that he responds to the thing from the standpoint of A" (178). Each of us, as he learns his language, is a student of his neighbor's behavior; and conversely, insofar as his tries are approved or corrected, he is a subject of his neighbor's behavioral study.

The semantic part of learning a word is more complex than the phonetic part, therefore, even in simple cases: we have to see what is stimulating the other speaker. In the case of words not directly ascribing observable traits to things, the learning process is increasingly complex and obscure; and obscurity is the breeding place of mentalistic semantics. What the naturalist insists on is that, even in the complex and obscure parts of language learning, the learner has no data to work with but the overt behavior of other speakers.

When with Dewey we turn thus toward a naturalistic view of language and a behavioral view of meaning, what we give up is not just the museum figure of speech. We give up an assurance of determinacy. Seen according to the museum myth, the words and sentences of a language have their determinate meanings. To discover the meanings of the native's words we may have to observe his behavior, but still the meanings of the words are supposed to be determinate in the native's *mind*, his mental museum, even in cases where behavioral criteria are powerless to discover them for us. When on the other hand we recognize with Dewey that "meaning ... is primarily a property of behavior," we recognize that there are no meanings, nor likenesses nor distinctions of meaning, beyond what are implicit in people's dispositions to overt behavior. For naturalism the question whether two expressions are alike or unlike in meaning has no determinate answer, known or unknown, except insofar as the answer is settled in principle by people's speech dispositions, known or unknown. If by these standards there are indeterminate cases, so much the worse for the terminology of meaning and likeness of meaning.

To see what such indeterminacy would be like, suppose there were an expression in a remote language that could be translated into English equally defensibly in either of two ways, unlike in meaning in English. I am not speaking of ambiguity within the native language. I am supposing that one and the same native use of the expression can be given either of the English translations, each being accommodated by compensating adjustments in the translation of other words. Suppose both translations, along with these accommodations in each case, accord equally well with all observable behavior on the part of speakers of the remote language and speakers of English. Suppose they accord perfectly not only with behavior actually observed, but with all dispositions to behavior on the part of all the speakers concerned. On these assumptions it would be forever impossible to know of one of these translations that it was the right one, and the other wrong. Still, if the museum myth were true, there would be a right and wrong of the matter; it is just that we would never know, not having access to the museum. See language naturalistically, on the other hand, and you have to see the notion of likeness of meaning in such a case simply as nonsense.

I have been keeping to the hypothetical. Turning now to examples, let me begin with a disappointing one and work up. In the French construction 'ne ... rien' you can translate 'rien' into English as 'anything' or as 'nothing' at will, and then accommodate your choice by translating 'ne' as 'not' or by construing it as pleonastic. This example is disappointing because you can object that I have merely cut the French units too small. You can believe the mentalistic myth of the meaning museum and still grant that 'rien' of itself has no meaning, being no whole label; it is part of 'ne ... rien', which has its meaning as a whole.

I began with this disappointing example because I think its conspicuous trait—its dependence on cutting language into segments too short to carry meanings—is the secret of the more serious cases as well. What makes other cases more serious is that the segments they involve are seriously long: long enough to be predicates and to be true of things and hence, you would think, to carry meanings.

An artificial example which I have used elsewhere[2] depends on the fact that a whole rabbit is present when and only when an undetached part of a rabbit is present; also when and only when a temporal stage of a rabbit is present. If we are wondering whether to translate a native expression 'gavagai' as 'rabbit' or as 'undetached rabbit part' or as 'rabbit stage', we can never settle the matter simply by ostension— that is, simply by repeatedly querying the expression 'gavagai' for the native's assent or dissent in the presence of assorted stimulations.

Before going on to urge that we cannot settle the matter by non-ostensive means either, let me belabor this ostensive predicament a bit. I am not worrying, as Wittgenstein did, about simple cases of ostension. The color word 'sepia', to take one of his examples,[3] can certainly be learned by an ordinary process of conditioning, or induction. One need not even be told that sepia is a color and not a shape or a material or an article. True, barring such hints, many lessons may be needed, so as to eliminate wrong generalizations based on shape, material, etc., rather than color, and so as to eliminate wrong notions as to the intended boundary of an indicated example, and so as to delimit the admissible variations of color itself. Like all conditioning, or induction, the process will depend ultimately also on one's own inborn propensity to find one stimulation qualitatively more akin to a second stimulation than to a third; otherwise there can never be any selective reinforcement and extinction of responses.[4] Still, in principle nothing more is needed in learning 'sepia' than in any conditioning or induction.

---

[2] *Word and Object* (Cambridge, Mass.: MIT Press, 1960), §12.

[3] *Philosophical Investigations* (New York: Macmillan, 1953), p. 14.

[4] Cf. *Word and Object*, §17.

But the big difference between 'rabbit' and 'sepia' is that whereas 'sepia' is a mass term like 'water', 'rabbit' is a term of divided reference. As such it cannot be mastered without mastering its principle of individuation: where one rabbit leaves off and another begins. And this cannot be mastered by pure ostension, however persistent.

Such is the quandary over 'gavagai': where one gavagai leaves off and another begins. The only difference between rabbits, undetached rabbit parts, and rabbit stages is in their individuation. If you take the total scattered portion of the spatiotemporal world that is made up of rabbits, and that which is made up undetached rabbit parts, and that which is made up of rabbit stages, you come out with the same scattered portion of the world each of the three times. The only difference is in how you slice it. And how to slice it is what ostension or simple conditioning, however persistently repeated, cannot teach.

Thus consider specifically the problem of deciding between 'rabbit' and 'undetached rabbit part' as translation of 'gavagai'. No word of the native language is known, except that we have settled on some working hypothesis as to what native words or gestures to construe as assent and dissent in response to our pointings and queryings. Now the trouble is that whenever we point to different parts of the rabbit, even sometimes screening the rest of the rabbit, we are pointing also each time to the rabbit. When, conversely, we indicate the whole rabbit with a sweeping gesture, we are still pointing to a multitude of rabbit parts. And note that we do not have even a native analogue of our plural ending to exploit, in asking 'gavagai?'. It seems clear that no even tentative decision between 'rabbit' and 'undetached rabbit part' is to be sought at this level.

How would we finally decide? My passing mention of plural endings is part of the answer. Our individuating of terms of divided reference, in English, is bound up with a cluster of interrelated grammatical particles and constructions: plural endings, pronouns, numerals, the 'is' of identity, and its adaptations 'same' and 'other'. It is the cluster of interrelated devices in which quantification becomes central when the regimentation of symbolic logic is imposed. If in his language we could ask the native 'Is this *gavagai* the same as that one?' while making appropriate multiple ostensions, then indeed we would be well on our way to deciding between 'rabbit', 'undetached rabbit part', and 'rabbit stage'. And of course the linguist does at length reach the point where he can ask what purports to be that question. He develops a system for translating our pluralizations, pronouns, numerals, identity, and related devices contextually into the native idiom. He develops such a system by abstraction and hypothesis. He abstracts native particles and constructions from observed native sentences, and tries associating these variously with English particles and constructions. Insofar as the native sentences and the thus associated English ones seem to match up in respect of appropriate occasions of use, the linguist feels confirmed in these hypotheses of translation—what I call *analytical hypotheses*.[5]

---

[5] *Word and Object*, §15. For a summary of the general point of view see also §I of my "Speaking of Objects," *Proceedings and Addresses of American Philosophical Association*, XXXI (1958): 5 ff; reprinted in Y. Krikorian and A. Edel, eds., *Contemporary Philosophical Problems* (New York: Macmillan, 1959), and in J. Fodor and J. Katz, eds., *The Structure of Language* (Englewood Cliffs, N.J.: Prentice-Hall, 1964), and in P. Kurtz, ed., *American Philosophy in the Twentieth Century* (New York: Macmillan, 1966).

But it seems that this method, though laudable in practice and the best we can hope for, does not in principle settle the indeterminacy between 'rabbit', 'undetached rabbit part', and 'rabbit stage'. For if one workable over-all system of analytical hypotheses provides for translating a given native expression into 'is the same as', perhaps another equally workable but systematically different system would translate that native expression rather into something like 'belongs with'. Then when in the native language we try to ask 'Is this *gavagai* the same as that?', we could as well be asking 'Does this *gavagai* belong with that?'. Insofar, the native's assent is no objective evidence for translating 'gavagai' as 'rabbit' rather than 'undetached rabbit part' or 'rabbit stage'.

This artificial example shares the structure of the trivial earlier example 'ne … rien'. We were able to translate 'rien' as 'anything' or as 'nothing', thanks to a compensatory adjustment in the handling of 'ne'. And I suggest that we can translate 'gavagai' as 'rabbit' or 'undetached rabbit part' or 'rabbit stage', thanks to compensatory adjustments in the translation of accompanying native locutions. Other adjustments still might accommodate translation of 'gavagai' as 'rabbithood', or in further ways. I find this plausible because of the broadly structural and contextual character of any considerations that could guide us to native translations of the English cluster of interrelated devices of individuation. There seem bound to be systematically very different choices, all of which do justice to all dispositions to verbal behavior on the part of all concerned.

An actual field linguist would of course be sensible enough to equate 'gavagai' with 'rabbit', dismissing such perverse alternatives as 'undetached rabbit part' and 'rabbit stage' out of hand. This sensible choice and others like it would help in turn to determine his subsequent hypotheses as to what native locutions should answer to the English apparatus of individuation, and thus everything would come out all right. The implicit maxim guiding his choice of 'rabbit', and similar choices for other native words, is that an enduring and relatively homogeneous object, moving as a whole against a contrasting background, is a likely reference for a short expression. If he were to become conscious of this maxim, he might celebrate it as one of the linguistic universals, or traits of all languages, and he would have no trouble pointing out its psychological plausibility. But he would be wrong; the maxim is his own imposition, toward settling what is objectively indeterminate. It is a very sensible imposition, and I would recommend no other. But I am making a philosophical point.

It is philosophically interesting, moreover, that what is indeterminate in this artificial example is not just meaning, but extension; reference. My remarks on indeterminacy began as a challenge to likeness of meaning. I had us imagining "an expression that could be translated into English equally defensibly in either of two ways, unlike in meaning in English." Certainly likeness of meaning is a dim notion, repeatedly challenged. Of two predicates which are alike in extension, it has never been clear when to say that they are alike in meaning and when not; it is the old matter of featherless bipeds and rational animals, or of equiangular and equilateral triangles. Reference, extension, has been the firm thing; meaning, intension, the infirm. The indeterminacy of translation now confronting us, however, cuts across extension and intension alike. The terms 'rabbit', 'undetached rabbit part', and 'rabbit stage' differ not only in meaning; they are true of different things. Reference itself proves behaviorally inscrutable.

Within the parochial limits of our own language, we can continue as always to find extensional talk clearer than intensional. For the indeterminacy between 'rabbit', 'rabbit stage', and the rest depended only on a correlative indeterminacy of translation of the English apparatus of individuation—the apparatus of pronouns, pluralization, identity, numerals, and so on. No such indeterminacy obtrudes so long as we think of this apparatus as given and fixed. Given this apparatus, there is no mystery about extension; terms have the same extension when true of the same things. At the level of radical translation, on the other hand, extension itself goes inscrutable.

My example of rabbits and their parts and stages is a contrived example and a perverse one, with which, as I said, the practicing linguist would have no patience. But there are also cases, less bizarre ones, that obtrude in practice. In Japanese there are certain particles, called "classifiers," which may be explained in either of two ways. Commonly they are explained as attaching to numerals, to form compound numerals of distinctive styles. Thus take the numeral for 5. If you attach one classifier to it you get a style of '5' suitable for counting animals; if you attach a different classifier, you get a style of '5' suitable for counting slim things like pencils and chopsticks; and so on. But another way of viewing classifiers is to view them not as constituting part of the numeral, but as constituting part of the term—the term for 'chopsticks' or 'oxen' or whatever. On this view the classifier does the individuative job that is done in English by 'sticks of' as applied to the mass term 'wood', or 'head of' as applied to the mass term 'cattle'.

What we have on either view is a Japanese phrase tantamount say to 'five oxen', but consisting of three words;[6] the first is in effect the neutral numeral '5', the second is a classifier of the animal kind, and the last corresponds in some fashion to 'ox'. On one view the neutral numeral and the classifier go together to constitute a declined numeral in the "animal gender," which then modifies 'ox' to give, in effect, 'five oxen'. On the other view the third Japanese word answers not to the individuative term 'ox' but to the mass term 'cattle'; the classifier applies to this mass term to produce a composite individuative term, in effect 'head of cattle'; and the neutral numeral applies directly to all this without benefit of gender, giving 'five head of cattle', hence again in effect 'five oxen'.

If so simple an example is to serve its expository purpose, it needs your connivance. You have to understand 'cattle' as a mass term covering only bovines, and 'ox' as applying to all bovines. That these usages are not the invariable usages is beside the point. The point is that the Japanese phrase comes out as 'five bovines', as desired, when parsed in either of two ways. The one way treats the third Japanese word as an individuative term true of each bovine, and the other way treats that word rather as a mass term covering the unindividuated totality of beef on the hoof. These are two very different ways of treating the third Japanese word; and the three-word phrase as a

---

[6] To keep my account graphic I am counting a certain postpositive particle as a suffix rather than a word.

whole turns out all right in both cases only because of compensatory differences in our account of the second word, the classifier.

This example is reminiscent in a way of our trivial initial example, 'ne … rien'. We were able to represent 'rien' as 'anything' or as 'nothing', by compensatorily taking 'ne' as negative or as vacuous. We are able now to represent a Japanese word either as an individuative term for bovines or as a mass term for live beef, by compensatorily taking the classifier as declining the numeral or as individuating the mass term. However, the triviality of the one example does not quite carry over to the other. The early example was dismissed on the ground that we had cut too small: 'rien' was too short for significant translation on its own, and 'ne … rien' was the significant unit. But you cannot dismiss the Japanese example by saying that the third word was too short for significant translation on its own and that only the whole three-word phrase, tantamount to 'five oxen', was the significant unit. You cannot take this line unless you are prepared to call a word too short for significant translation even when it is long enough to be a term and carry denotation. For the third Japanese word is, on either approach, a term; on one approach a term of divided reference, and on the other a mass term. If you are indeed prepared thus to call a word too short for significant translation even when it is a denoting term, then in a back-handed way you are granting what I wanted to prove: the inscrutability of reference.

Between the two accounts of Japanese classifiers there is no question of right and wrong. The one account makes for more efficient translation into idiomatic English; the other makes for more of a feeling for the Japanese idiom. Both fit all verbal behavior equally well. All whole sentences, and even component phrases like 'five oxen', admit of the same net over-all English translations on either account. This much is invariant. But what is philosophically interesting is that the reference or extension of shorter terms can fail to be invariant. Whether that third Japanese word is itself true of each ox, or whether on the other hand it is a mass term which needs to be adjoined to the classifier to make a term which is true of each ox—here is a question that remains undecided by the totality of human dispositions to verbal behavior. It is indeterminate in principle; there is no fact of the matter. Either answer can be accommodated by an account of the classifier. Here again, then, is the inscrutability of reference—illustrated this time by a humdrum point of practical translation.

The inscrutability of reference can be brought closer to home by considering the word 'alpha', or again the word 'green'. In our use of these words and others like them there is a systematic ambiguity. Sometimes we use such words as concrete general terms, as when we say the grass is green, or that some inscription begins with an alpha. Sometimes on the other hand we use them as abstract singular terms, as when we say that green is a color and alpha is a letter. Such ambiguity is encouraged by the fact that there is nothing in ostension to distinguish the two uses. The pointing that would be done in teaching the concrete general term 'green', or 'alpha', differs none from the pointing that would be done in teaching the abstract singular term 'green' or 'alpha'. Yet the objects referred to by the word are very different under the two uses; under the one use the word is true of many concrete objects, and under the other use it names a single abstract object.

We can of course tell the two uses apart by seeing how the word turns up in sentences: whether it takes an indefinite article, whether it takes a plural ending, whether it stands as singular subject, whether it stands as modifier, as predicate complement, and so on. But these criteria appeal to our special English grammatical constructions and particles, our special English apparatus of individuation, which, I already urged, is itself subject to indeterminacy of translation. So, from the point of view of translation into a remote language, the distinction between a concrete general and an abstract singular term is in the same predicament as the distinction between 'rabbit', 'rabbit part', and 'rabbit stage'. Here then is another example of the inscrutability of reference, since the the difference between the concrete general and the abstract singular is a difference in the objects referred to.

Incidentally we can concede this much indeterminacy also to the 'sepia' example, after all. But this move is not evidently what was worrying Wittgenstein.

The ostensive indistinguishability of the abstract singular from the concrete general turns upon what may be called "deferred ostension," as opposed to direct ostension. First let me define direct ostension. The *ostended point*, as I shall call it, is the point where the line of the pointing finger first meets an opaque surface. What characterizes *direct ostension*, then, is that the term which is being ostensively explained is true of something that contains the ostended point. Even such direct ostension has its uncertainties, of course, and these are familiar. There is the question how wide an environment of the ostended point is meant to be covered by the term that is being ostensively explained. There is the question how considerably an absent thing or substance might be allowed to differ from what is now ostended, and still be covered by the term that is now being ostensively explained. Both of these questions can in principle be settled as well as need be by induction from multiple ostensions. Also, if the term is a term of divided reference like 'apple', there is the question of individuation: the question where one of its objects leaves off and another begins. This can be settled by induction from multiple ostensions of a more elaborate kind, accompanied by expressions like 'same apple' and 'another', if an equivalent of this English apparatus of individuation has been settled on; otherwise the indeterminacy persists that was illustrated by 'rabbit', 'undetached rabbit part', and 'rabbit stage'.

Such, then, is the way of direct ostension. Other ostension I call *deferred*. It occurs when we point at the gauge, and not the gasoline, to show that there is gasoline. Also it occurs when we explain the abstract singular term 'green' or 'alpha' by pointing at grass or a Greek inscription. Such pointing is direct ostension when used to explain the concrete general term 'green' or 'alpha', but it is deferred ostension when used to explain the abstract singular terms; for the abstract object which is the color green or the letter alpha does not contain the ostended point, nor any point.

Deferred ostension occurs very naturally when, as in the case of the gasoline gauge, we have a correspondence in mind. Another such example is afforded by the Gödel numbering of expressions. Thus if 7 has been assigned as Gödel number of the letter alpha, a man conscious of the Gödel numbering would not hesitate to say 'Seven' on pointing to an inscription of the Greek letter in question. This is, on the face of it, a doubly deferred ostension: one step of deferment carries us from the inscription to the letter as abstract object, and a second step carries us thence to the number.

By appeal to our apparatus of individuation, if it is available, we can distinguish between the concrete general and the abstract singular use of the word 'alpha'; this we saw. By appeal again to that apparatus, and in particular to identity, we can evidently settle also whether the word 'alpha' in its abstract singular use is being used really to name the letter or whether, perversely, it is being used to name the Gödel number of the letter. At any rate we can distinguish these alternatives if also we have located the speaker's equivalent of the numeral '7' to our satisfaction; for we can ask him whether alpha *is* 7.

These considerations suggest that deferred ostension adds no essential problem to those presented by direct ostension. Once we have settled upon analytical hypotheses of translation covering identity and the other English particles relating to individuation, we can resolve not only the indecision between 'rabbit' and 'rabbit stage' and the rest, which came of direct ostension, but also any indecision between concrete general and abstract singular, and any indecision between expression and Gödel number, which come of deferred ostension.

However, this conclusion is too sanguine. The inscrutability of reference runs deep, and it persists in a subtle form even if we accept identity and the rest of the apparatus of individuation as fixed and settled; even, indeed, if we forsake radical translation and think only of English.

Consider the case of a thoughtful protosyntactician. He has a formalized system of first-order proof theory, or protosyntax, whose universe comprises just expressions, that is, strings of signs of a specified alphabet. Now just what sorts of things, more specifically, are these expressions? They are types, not tokens. So, one might suppose, each of them is the set of all its tokens. That is, each expression is a set of inscriptions which are variously situated in space-time but are classed together by virtue of a certain similarity in shape. The concatenate $x \frown y$ of two expressions x and y, in a given order, will be the set of all inscriptions each of which has two parts which are tokens respectively of x and y and follow one upon the other in that order. But $x \frown y$ may then be the null set, though x and y are not null; for it may be that inscriptions belonging to x and y happen to turn up head to tail nowhere, in the past, present, or future. This danger increases with the lengths of x and y. But it is easily seen to violate a law of protosyntax which says that $x = z$ whenever $x \frown y = z \frown y$.

Thus it is that our thoughtful protosyntactician will not construe the things in his universe as sets of inscriptions. He can still take his atoms, the single signs, as sets of inscriptions, for there is no risk of nullity in these cases. And then, instead of taking his strings of signs as sets of inscriptions, he can invoke the mathematical notion of sequence and take them as sequences of signs. A familiar way of taking sequences, in turn, is as a mapping of things on numbers. On this approach an expression or string of signs becomes a finite set of pairs each of which is the pair of a sign and a number.

This account of expressions is more artificial and more complex than one is apt to expect who simply says he is letting his variables range over the strings of such and such signs. Moreover, it is not the inevitable choice; the considerations that motivated it can be met also by alternative constructions. One of these constructions is Gödel numbering itself, and it is temptingly simple. It uses just natural numbers, whereas the foregoing construction used sets of one-letter inscriptions and also natural numbers and sets of pairs of these. How clear is it that at just *this* point we have dropped expressions in favor of numbers? What is clearer is merely that in both constructions we were artificially devising models to satisfy laws that expressions in an unexplicated sense had been meant to satisfy.

So much for expressions. Consider now the arithmetician himself, with his elementary number theory. His universe comprises the natural numbers outright. Is it clearer than the protosyntactician's? What, after all, is a natural number? There are Frege's version, Zermelo's, and von Neumann's, and countless further alternatives, all mutually incompatible and equally correct. What we are doing in any one of these explications of natural number is to devise set-theoretic models to satisfy laws which the natural numbers in an unexplicated sense had been meant to satisfy. The case is quite like that of protosyntax.

It will perhaps be felt that any set-theoretic explication of natural number is at best a case of *obscurum per obscurius*; that all explications must assume something, and the natural numbers themselves are an admirable assumption to start with. I must agree that a construction of sets and set theory from natural numbers and arithmetic would be far more desirable than the familiar opposite. On the other hand our impression of the clarity even of the notion of natural number itself has suffered somewhat from Gödel's proof of the impossibility of a complete proof procedure for elementary number theory, or, for that matter, from Skolem's and Henkin's observations that all laws of natural numbers admit nonstandard models.[7]

We are finding no clear difference between *specifying* a universe of discourse—the range of the variables of quantification—and *reducing* that universe to some other. We saw no significant difference between clarifying the notion of expression and supplanting it by that of number. And now to say more particularly what numbers themselves are is in no evident way different from just dropping numbers and assigning to arithmetic one or another new model, say in set theory.

Expressions are known only by their laws, the laws of concatenation theory, so that any constructs obeying those laws—Gödel numbers, for instance—are *ipso facto* eligible as explications of expression. Numbers in turn are known only by their laws, the laws of arithmetic, so that any constructs obeying those laws—certain sets, for instance—are eligible in turn as explications of number. Sets in turn are known only by their laws, the laws of set theory.

Russell pressed a contrary thesis, long ago. Writing of numbers, he argued that for an understanding of number the laws of arithmetic are not enough; we must know the applications, we must understand numerical discourse embedded in discourse of other matters. In applying number the key notion, he urged, is *Anzahl*: there are n so-and-sos. However, Russell can be answered. First take, specifically, *Anzahl*. We can define 'there are n so-and-sos' without ever deciding what numbers are, apart from their fulfillment of arithmetic. That there are n so-and-sos can be explained simply as meaning that the so-and-sos are in one-to-one correspondence with the numbers up to n.[8]

Russell's more general point about application can be answered too. Always, if the structure is there, the applications will fall into place. As paradigm it is perhaps sufficient to recall again this reflection on expressions and Gödel numbers: that even

---

[7] See Leon Henkin, "Completeness in the Theory of Types," *Journal of Symbolic Logic*, xv, 2 (June 1950): 81–91, and references therein.

[8] For more on this theme see my *Set Theory and Its Logic* (Cambridge, Mass.: Harvard, 1963, 1968), §11.

the pointing out of an inscription is no final evidence that our talk is of expressions and not of Gödel numbers. We can always plead deferred ostension.

It is in this sense true to say, as mathematicians often do, that arithmetic is all there is to number. But it would be a confusion to express this point by saying, as is sometimes said, that numbers are any things fulfilling arithmetic. This formulation is wrong because distinct domains of objects yield distinct models of arithmetic. Any progression can be made to serve; and to identify all progressions with one another, e.g., to identify the progression of odd numbers with the progression of evens, would contradict arithmetic after all.

So, though Russell was wrong in suggesting that numbers need more than their arithmetical properties, he was right in objecting to the definition of numbers as any things fulfilling arithmetic. The subtle point is that any progression will serve as a version of number so long and only so long as we stick to one and the same progression. Arithmetic is, in this sense, all there is to number: there is no saying absolutely what the numbers are; there is only arithmetic.[9]

II

I first urged the inscrutability of reference with the help of examples like the one about rabbits and rabbit parts. These used direct ostension, and the inscrutability of reference hinged on the indeterminacy of translation of identity and other individuative apparatus. The setting of these examples, accordingly, was radical translation: translation from a remote language on behavioral evidence, unaided by prior dictionaries. Moving then to deferred ostension and abstract objects, we found a certain dimness of reference pervading the home language itself.

Now it should be noted that even for the earlier examples the resort to a remote language was not really essential. On deeper reflection, radical translation begins at home. Must we equate our neighbor's English words with the same strings of phonemes in our own mouths? Certainly not; for sometimes we do not thus equate them. Sometimes we find it to be in the interests of communication to recognize that our neighbor's use of some word, such as 'cool' or 'square' or 'hopefully', differs from ours, and so we translate that word of his into a different string of phonemes in our idiolect. Our usual domestic rule of translation is indeed the homophonic one, which simply carries each string of phonemes into itself; but still we are always prepared to temper homophony with what Neil Wilson has called the "principle of charity."[10] We will construe a neighbor's word heterophonically now and again if thereby we see our way to making his message less absurd.

The homophonic rule is a handy one on the whole. That it works so well is no accident, since imitation and feedback are what propagate a language. We acquired a great fund of basic words and phrases in this way, imitating our elders and encour-

---

[9] Paul Benacerraf, "What Numbers Cannot Be," *Philosophical Review*, LXXIV, 1 (January 1965): 47–73, develops this point. His conclusions differ in some ways from those I shall come to.

[10] N. L. Wilson, "Substances without Substrata," *Review of Metaphysics*, XII, 4 (June 1959): 521–539, p. 532.

aged by our elders amid external circumstances to which the phrases suitably apply. Homophonic translation is implicit in this social method of learning. Departure from homophonic translation in this quarter would only hinder communication. Then there are the relatively rare instances of opposite kind, due to divergence in dialect or confusion in an individual, where homophonic translation incurs negative feedback. But what tends to escape notice is that there is also a vast mid-region where the homophonic method is indifferent. Here, gratuitously, we can systematically reconstrue our neighbor's apparent references to rabbits as really references to rabbit stages, and his apparent references to formulas as really references to Gödel numbers and vice versa. We can reconcile all this with our neighbor's verbal behavior, by cunningly readjusting our translations of his various connecting predicates so as to compensate for the switch of ontology. In short, we can reproduce the inscrutability of reference at home. It is of no avail to check on this fanciful version of our neighbor's meanings by asking him, say, whether he really means at a certain point to refer to formulas or to their Gödel numbers; for our question and his answer—"By all means, the numbers"—have lost their title to homophonic translation. The problem at home differs none from radical translation ordinarily so called except in the willfulness of this suspension of homophonic translation.

I have urged in defense of the behavioral philosophy of language, Dewey's, that the inscrutability of reference is not the inscrutability of a fact; there is no fact of the matter. But if there is really no fact of the matter, then the inscrutability of reference can be brought even closer to home than the neighbor's case; we can apply it to ourselves. If it is to make sense to say even of oneself that one is referring to rabbits and formulas and not to rabbit stages and Gödel numbers, then it should make sense equally to say it of someone else. After all, as Dewey stressed, there is no private language.

We seem to be maneuvering ourselves into the absurd position that there is no difference on any terms, interlinguistic or intralinguistic, objective or subjective, between referring to rabbits and referring to rabbit parts or stages; or between referring to formulas and referring to their Gödel numbers. Surely this is absurd, for it would imply that there is no difference between the rabbit and each of its parts or stages, and no difference between a formula and its Gödel number. Reference would seem now to become nonsense not just in radical translation, but at home.

Toward resolving this quandary, begin by picturing us at home in our language, with all its predicates and auxiliary devices. This vocabulary includes 'rabbit', 'rabbit part', 'rabbit stage', 'formula', 'number', 'ox', 'cattle'; also the two-place predicates of identity and difference, and other logical particles. In these terms we can say in so many words that this is a formula and that a number, this a rabbit and that a rabbit part, this and that the same rabbit, and this and that different parts. *In just those words*. This network of terms and predicates and auxiliary devices is, in relativity jargon, our frame of reference, or coordinate system. Relative to *it* we can and do talk meaningfully and distinctively of rabbits and parts, numbers and formulas. Next, as in recent paragraphs, we contemplate alternative denotations for our familiar terms. We begin to appreciate that a grand and ingenious permutation of these denotations, along with compensatory adjustments in the interpretations of the auxiliary particles, might still accommodate all existing speech dispositions. This was the inscrutability of reference, applied to ourselves; and it made nonsense of reference. Fair enough; reference *is* nonsense except relative to a coordinate system. In this principle of relativity lies the resolution of our quandary.

It is meaningless to ask whether, in general, our terms 'rabbit', 'rabbit part', 'number', etc., really refer respectively to rabbits, rabbit parts, numbers, etc., rather than to some ingeniously permuted denotations. It is meaningless to ask this absolutely; we can meaningfully ask it only relative to some background language. When we ask, "Does 'rabbit' really refer to rabbits?" someone can counter with the question: "Refer to rabbits in what sense of 'rabbits'?" thus launching a regress; and we need the background language to regress into. The background language gives the query sense, if only relative sense; sense relative in turn to it, this background language. Querying reference in any more absolute way would be like asking absolute position, or absolute velocity, rather than position or velocity relative to a given frame of reference. Also it is very much like asking whether our neighbor may not systematically see everything upside down, or in complementary color, forever undetectably.

We need a background language, I said, to regress into. Are we involved now in an infinite regress? If questions of reference of the sort we are considering make sense only relative to a background language, then evidently questions of reference for the background language make sense in turn only relative to a further background language. In these terms the situation sounds desperate, but in fact it is little different from questions of position and velocity. When we are given position and velocity relative to a given coordinate system, we can always ask in turn about the placing of origin and orientation of axes of that system of coordinates; and there is no end to the succession of further coordinate systems that could be adduced in answering the successive questions thus generated.

In practice of course we end the regress of coordinate systems by something like pointing. And in practice we end the regress of background languages, in discussions of reference, by acquiescing in our mother tongue and taking its words at face value.

Very well; in the case of position and velocity, in practice, pointing breaks the regress. But what of position and velocity apart from practice? what of the regress then? The answer, of course, is the relational doctrine of space; there is no absolute position or velocity; there are just the relations of coordinate systems to one another, and ultimately of things to one another. And I think that the parallel question regarding denotation calls for a parallel answer, a relational theory of what the objects of theories are. What makes sense is to say not what the objects of a theory are, absolutely speaking, but how one theory of objects is interpretable or reinterpretable in another.

The point is not that bare matter is inscrutable: that things are indistinguishable except by their properties. That point does not need making. The present point is reflected better in the riddle about seeing things upside down, or in complementary colors; for it is that things can be inscrutably switched even while carrying their properties with them. Rabbits differ from rabbit parts and rabbit stages not just as bare matter, after all, but in respect of properties; and formulas differ from numbers in respect of properties. What our present reflections are leading us to appreciate is that the riddle about seeing things upside down, or in complementary colors, should be taken seriously and its moral applied widely. The relativistic thesis to which we have come is this, to repeat: it makes no sense to say what the objects of a theory are, beyond saying how to interpret or reinterpret that theory in another. Suppose we are working within a theory and thus treating of its objects. We do so by using the variables of the theory, whose values those objects are, though there be no ultimate sense in which that universe can have been specified. In the language of the theory there are predicates by which to distinguish portions of this universe from other portions, and these predicates differ from one another purely in the roles they play in the laws of the theory. Within this background theory we can show how some subordinate theory, whose universe is some portion of the background universe, can by a reinterpretation be reduced to another subordinate theory whose universe is some lesser portion. Such talk of subordinate theories and their ontologies *is* meaningful, but only relative to the background theory with its own primitively adopted and ultimately inscrutable ontology.

To talk thus of theories raises a problem of formulation. A theory, it will be said, is a set of fully interpreted sentences. (More particularly, it is a deductively closed set: it includes all its own logical consequences, insofar as they are couched in the same notation.) But if the sentences of a theory are fully interpreted, then in particular the range of values of their variables is settled. How then can there be no sense in saying what the objects of a theory are?

My answer is simply that we cannot require theories to be fully interpreted, except in a relative sense, if anything is to count as a theory. In specifying a theory we must indeed fully specify, in our own words, what sentences are to comprise the theory and what things are to be taken as values of the variables and what things are to be taken as satisfying the predicate letters; insofar we do fully interpret the theory, *relative* to our own words and relative to our over-all home theory which lies behind them. But this fixes the objects of the described theory only relative to those of the home theory; and these can, at will, be questioned in turn.

One is tempted to conclude simply that meaninglessness sets in when we try to pronounce on everything in our universe; that universal predication takes on sense only when furnished with the background of a wider universe, where the predication is no longer universal. And this is even a familiar doctrine, the doctrine that no proper predicate is true of everything. We have all heard it claimed that a predicate is meaningful only by contrast with what it excludes, and hence that being true of everything would make a predicate meaningless. But surely this doctrine is wrong. Surely self-identity, for instance, is not to be rejected as meaningless. For that matter, any statement of fact at all, however brutally meaningful, can be put artificially into a form in which it pronounces on everything. To say merely of Jones that he sings, for instance, is to say of everything that it is other than Jones or sings. We had better beware of repudiating universal predication, lest we be tricked into repudiating everything there is to say.

Carnap took an intermediate line in his doctrine of universal words, or *Allwörter*, in *The Logical Syntax of Language*. He did treat the predicating of universal words as "quasi-syntactical"—as a predication only by courtesy, and without empirical content. But universal words were for him not just any universally true predicates, like 'is other than Jones or sings'. They were a special breed of universally true predicates, ones that are universally true by the sheer meanings of their words and no thanks to nature. In his later writing this doctrine of universal words takes the form of a distinction between "internal" questions, in which a theory comes to grips with facts about the world, and "external" questions, in which people come to grips with the relative merits of theories.

Should we look to these distinctions of Carnap's for light on ontological relativity? When we found there was no absolute sense in saying what a theory is about, were we sensing the infactuality of what Carnap calls "external questions"? When we found that saying what a theory is about did make sense against a background theory, were we sensing the factuality of internal questions of the background theory? I see no hope of illumination in this quarter. Carnap's universal words were not just any universally true predicates, but, as I said, a special breed; and what distinguishes this breed is not clear. What I said distinguished them was that they were universally true by sheer meanings and not by nature; but this is a very questionable distinction. Talking of "internal" and "external" is no better.

Ontological relativity is not to be clarified by any distinction between kinds of universal predication—unfactual and factual, external and internal. It is not a question of universal predication. When questions regarding the ontology of a theory are meaningless absolutely, and become meaningful relative to a background theory, this is not in general because the background theory has a wider universe. One is tempted, as I said a little while back, to suppose that it is; but one is then wrong.

What makes ontological questions meaningless when taken absolutely is not universality, but circularity. A question of the form 'What is an F?' can be answered only by recourse to a further term: 'An F is a G'. The answer makes only relative sense: sense relative to an uncritical acceptance of 'G'.

We may picture the vocabulary of a theory as comprising logical signs such as quantifiers and the signs for the truth functions and identity, and in addition descriptive or nonlogical signs, which, typically, are singular terms, or names, and general terms, or predicates. Suppose next that in the statements which comprise the theory, that is, are true according to the theory, we abstract from the meanings of the nonlogical vocabulary and from the range of the variables. We are left with the logical form of the theory, or, as I shall say, the *theory-form*. Now we may interpret this theory-form anew by picking a new universe for its variables of quantification to range over, and assigning objects from this universe to the names, and choosing subsets of this universe as extensions of the one-place predicates, and so on. Each such interpretation of the theory-form is called a model of it, if it makes it come out true. Which of these models is meant in a given actual theory cannot, of course, be guessed from the theory-form. The intended references of the names and predicates have to be learned rather by ostension, or else by paraphrase in some antecedently familiar vocabulary. But the first of these two ways has proved inconclusive, since, even apart from indeterminacies of translation affecting identity and other logical vocabulary, there is the problem of deferred ostension. Paraphrase in some antecedently familiar vocabulary, then, is our only recourse; and such is ontological relativity. To question the reference of all the terms of our all-inclusive theory becomes meaningless, simply for want of further terms relative to which to ask or answer the question.

It is thus meaningless within the theory to say which of the various possible models of our theory-form is our real or intended model. Yet even here we can make sense still of there being many models. For we might be able to show that for each of the models, however unspecifiable, there is bound to be another which is a permutation or perhaps a diminution of the first.

Suppose for example that our theory is purely numerical. Its objects are just the natural numbers. There is no sense in saying, from within that theory, just which of the various models of number theory is in force. But we can observe even from within the theory that, whatever 0, 1, 2, 3, etc. may be, the theory would still hold true if the 17 of this series were moved into the role of 0, and the 18 moved into the role of 1, and so on.

Ontology is indeed doubly relative. Specifying the universe of a theory makes sense only relative to some background theory, and only relative to some choice of a manual of translation of the one theory into the other. Commonly of course the background theory will simply be a containing theory, and in this case no question of a manual of translation arises. But this is after all just a degenerate case of translation still—the case where the rule of translation is the homophonic one.

A usual occasion for ontological talk is reduction, where it is shown how the universe of some theory can by a reinterpretation be dispensed with in favor of some other universe, perhaps a proper part of the first. I have treated elsewhere[11] of the reduction of one ontology to another with help of a *proxy function*: a function mapping the one universe into part or all of the other. For instance, the function "Gödel number of" is a proxy function. The universe of elementary proof theory or protosyntax, which consists of expressions or strings of signs, is mapped by this function into the universe of elementary number theory, which consists of numbers. The proxy function used in reducing one ontology to another is not necessarily one-to-one. This one is; and note that one ontology is *always* reducible to another when we are given a proxy function f that is one-to-one. The essential reasoning is as follows. Where P is any predicate of the old system, its work can be done in the new system by a new predicate which we interpret as true of just the correlates fx of the old objects x that P was true of. Thus suppose we take fx as the Gödel number of x, and as our old system we take a syntactical system in which one of the predicates is 'is a segment of'. The corresponding predicate of the new, or numerical system, then, would be one which amounts, so far as its extension is concerned, to the words 'is the Gödel number of a segment of that whose Gödel number is'. The numerical predicate would not be given this devious form, of course, but would be rendered as an appropriate purely arithmetical condition.

Our dependence upon a background theory becomes especially evident when we reduce our universe U to another V by appeal to a proxy function. For it is only in a theory with an inclusive universe, embracing U and V, that we can make sense of

---

[11] *The Ways of Paradox and Other Essays* (New York: Random House, 1966), pp. 204 ff, or "Ontological Reduction and the World of Numbers," *The Journal of Philosophy*, LXI, 7 (March 26, 1964): 209–215, pp. 214 ff.

the proxy function. The function maps U into V and, hence, needs all the old objects of U as well as their new proxies in V.

The proxy function need not exist as an object in the universe even of the background theory. It may do its work merely as what I have called a "virtual class,"[12] and Gödel has called a "notion."[13] That is to say, all that is required toward a function is an open sentence with two free variables, provided that it is fulfilled by exactly one value of the first variable for each object of the old universe as value of the second variable. But the point is that it is only in the background theory, with its inclusive universe, that we can hope to write such a sentence and have the right values at our disposal for its variables.

If the new objects happen to be among the old, so that V is a subclass of U, then the old theory with universe U can itself sometimes qualify as the background theory in which to describe its own ontological reduction. But we cannot do better than that; we cannot declare our new ontological economies without having recourse to the uneconomical old ontology.

This sounds, perhaps, like a predicament: as if no ontological economy is justifiable unless it is a false economy and the repudiated objects really exist after all. But actually this is wrong; there is no more cause for worry here than there is in *reductio ad absurdum*, where we assume a falsehood that we are out to disprove. If what we want to show is that the universe U is excessive and that only a part exists, or need exist, then we are quite within our rights to assume all of U for the space of the argument. We show thereby that if all of U were needed then not all of U would be needed; and so our ontological reduction is sealed by *reductio ad absurdum*.

Toward further appreciating the bearing of ontological relativity on programs of ontological reduction, it is worth while to reexamine the philosophical bearing of the Löwenheim-Skolem theorem. I shall use the strong early form of the theorem,[14] which depends on the axiom of choice. It says that if a theory is true and has an indenumerable universe, then all but a denumerable part of that universe is dead wood, in the sense that it can be dropped from the range of the variables without falsifying any sentences.

On the face of it, this theorem declares a reduction of all acceptable theories to denumerable ontologies. Moreover, a denumerable ontology is reducible in turn to an ontology specifically of natural numbers, simply by taking the enumeration as the proxy function, if the enumeration is explicitly at hand. And even if it is not at hand, it exists; thus we can still think of all our objects as natural numbers, and merely reconcile ourselves to not always knowing, numerically, which number an otherwise given object is. May we not thus settle for an all-purpose Pythagorean ontology outright?

---

[12] *Set Theory and Its Logic*, §§2 f.

[13] Kurt Gödel, *The Consistency of the Continuum Hypothesis* (Princeton, N.J.: The University Press, 1940), p. 11.

[14] Thoralf Skolem, "Logisch-kombinatorische Untersuchungen über die Erfüllbarkeit oder Beweisbarkeit mathematischer Sätze nebst einem Theorem über dichte Mengen," *Skrifter utgit av Videnskapsselskapet i Kristiania*, 1919. 37 pp. Translation in Jean van Heijenoort, ed., *From Frege to Gödel: Source Book in the History of Mathematical Logic* (Cambridge, Mass.: Harvard, 1967), pp. 252–263.

Suppose, afterward, someone were to offer us what would formerly have qualified as an ontological reduction—a way of dispensing in future theory with all things of a certain sort S, but still leaving an infinite universe. Now in the new Pythagorean setting his discovery would still retain its essential content, though relinquishing the form of an ontological reduction; it would take the form merely of a move whereby some numerically unspecified numbers were divested of some property of numbers that corresponded to S.

Blanket Pythagoreanism on these terms is unattractive, for it merely offers new and obscurer accounts of old moves and old problems. On this score again, then, the relativistic proposition seems reasonable: that there is no absolute sense in speaking of the ontology of a theory. It very creditably brands this Pythagoreanism itself as meaningless. For there is no absolute sense in saying that all the objects of a theory are numbers, or that they are sets, or bodies, or something else; this makes no sense unless relative to some background theory. The relevant predicates—'number', 'set', 'body', or whatever—would be distinguished from *one another* in the background theory by the roles they play in the laws of that theory.

Elsewhere I urged in answer to such Pythagoreanism that we have no ontological reduction in an interesting sense unless we can specify a proxy function. Now where does the strong Löwenheim-Skolem theorem leave us in this regard? If the background theory assumes the axiom of choice and even provides a notation for a general selector operator, can we in these terms perhaps specify an actual proxy function embodying the Löwenheim-Skolem argument?

The theorem is that all but a denumerable part of an ontology can be dropped and not be missed. One could imagine that the proof proceeds by partitioning the universe into denumerably many equivalence classes of indiscriminable objects, such that all but one member of each equivalence class can be dropped as superfluous; and one would then guess that where the axiom of choice enters the proof is in picking a survivor from each equivalence class. If this were so, then with help of Hilbert's selector notation we could indeed express a proxy function. But in fact the Löwenheim-Skolem proof has another structure. I see in the proof even of the strong Löwenheim-Skolem theorem no reason to suppose that a proxy function can be formulated anywhere that will map an indenumerable ontology into a denumerable one.

On the face of it, of course, such a function would have been a contradiction in terms to begin with: a mapping of an indenumerable domain into a denumerable one. We have to beware of loopholes, though, when reasoning about the Löwenheim-Skolem theorem. At any rate it is easy to show in the Zermelo-Fraenkel system of set theory that such a function would neither exist nor admit even of formulation as a virtual class in the notation of the system.

The discussion of the ontology of a theory can make variously stringent demands upon the background theory in which the discussion is couched. The stringency of these demands varies with what is being said about the ontology of the object theory. We are now in a position to distinguish three such grades of stringency.

The least stringent demand is made when, with no view to reduction, we merely explain what things a theory is about, or what things its terms denote. This amounts to showing how to translate part or all of the object theory into the background theory. It is a matter really of showing how we *propose*, with some arbitrariness, to relate terms of the object theory to terms of the background theory; for we have the inscrutability of reference to allow for. But there is here no requirement that the background theory have a wider universe or a stronger vocabulary than the object theory. The theories could even be identical; this is the case when some terms are clarified by definition on the basis of other terms of the same language.

A more stringent demand was observed in the case where a proxy function is used to reduce an ontology. In this case the background theory needed the unreduced universe. But we saw, by considerations akin to *reductio ad absurdum*, that there was little here to regret.

The third grade of stringency has emerged now in the kind of ontological reduction hinted at by the Löwenheim-Skolem theorem. If a theory has by its own account an indenumerable universe, then even by taking that whole unreduced theory as background theory we cannot hope to produce a proxy function that would be adequate to reducing the ontology to a denumerable one. To find such a proxy function, even just a virtual one, we would need a background theory essentially stronger than the theory we were trying to reduce. This demand cannot, like the second grade of stringency above, be accepted in the spirit of *reductio ad absurdum*. It is a demand that simply discourages any general argument for Pythagoreanism from the Löwenheim-Skolem theorem.

A place where we see a more trivial side of ontological relativity is in the case of a finite universe of named objects. Here there is no occasion for quantification, except as an inessential abbreviation; for we can expand quantifications into finite conjunctions and alternations. Variables thus disappear, and with them the question of a universe of values of variables. And the very distinction between names and other signs lapses in turn, since the mark of a name is its admissibility in positions of variables. Ontology thus is emphatically meaningless for a finite theory of named objects, considered in and of itself. Yet we are now talking meaningfully of such finite ontologies. We are able to do so precisely because we are talking, however vaguely and implicitly, within a broader containing theory. What the objects of the finite theory are, makes sense only as a statement of the background theory in its own referential idiom. The answer to the question depends on the background theory, the finite foreground theory, and, of course, the particular manner in which we choose to translate or imbed the one in the other.

Ontology is internally indifferent also, I think, to any theory that is complete and decidable. Where we can always settle truth values mechanically, there is no evident internal reason for interest in the theory of quantifiers nor, therefore, in values of variables. These matters take on significance only as we think of the decidable theory as imbedded in a richer background theory in which the variables and their values are serious business.

Ontology may also be said to be internally indifferent even to a theory that is not decidable and does not have a finite universe, if it happens still that each of the infinitely numerous objects of the theory has a name. We can no longer expand quantifications into conjunctions and alternations, barring infinitely long expressions. We can, however, revise our semantical account of the truth conditions of quantification, in such a way as to turn our backs on questions of reference. We can explain universal quantifications as true when true under all substitutions; and correspondingly for existential. Such is the course that has been favored by Leśniewski and by Ruth Marcus.[15] Its nonreferential orientation is seen in the fact that it makes no essential use of namehood. That is, additional quantifications could be explained whose variables are place-holders for words of any syntactical category. *Substitutional* quantification, as I call it, thus brings no way of distinguishing names from other vocabulary, nor any way of distinguishing between genuinely referential or value-taking variables and other place-holders. Ontology is thus meaningless for a theory whose only quantification is substitutionally construed; meaningless, that is, insofar as the theory is considered in and of itself. The question of its ontology makes sense only relative to some translation of the theory into a background theory in which we use referential quantification. The answer depends on both theories, and, again, on the chosen way of translating the one into the other.

A final touch of relativity can in some cases cap this, when we try to distinguish between substitutional and referential quantification. Suppose again a theory with an infinite lot of names, and suppose that, by Gödel numbering or otherwise, we are treating of the theory's notations and proofs within the terms of the theory. If we succeed in showing that every result of substituting a name for the variable in a certain open sentence is true in the theory, but at the same time we disprove the universal quantification of the sentence,[16] then certainly we have shown that the universe of the theory contained some nameless objects. This is a case where an absolute decision can be reached in favor of referential quantification and against substitutional quantification, without ever retreating to a background theory.

But consider now the opposite situation, where there is no such open sentence. Imagine on the contrary that, whenever an open sentence is such that each result of substituting a name in it can be proved, its universal quantification can be proved in the theory too. Under these circumstances we can construe the universe as devoid of nameless objects and, hence, reconstrue the quantifications as substitutional; but we need not. We could still construe the universe as containing nameless objects. It could just happen that the nameless ones are *inseparable* from the named ones, in this sense: it could happen that all properties of nameless objects that we can express in the notation of the theory are shared by named objects.

We could construe the universe of the theory as containing, e.g., all real numbers. Some of them are nameless, since the real numbers are indenumerable while the names are denumerable. But it could still happen that the nameless reals are inseparable from the named reals. This would leave us unable within the theory to prove a distinction between referential and substitutional quantification.[17] Every expressible

---

[15] Leśniewski, "Grundzüge eines neuen Systems der Grundlagen der Mathematik," §§1–11, *Fundamenta Mathematicae*, xiv (1929): 1–81; Marcus, "Modalities and Intensional Languages," *Synthese*, xiii, 4 (December 1961): 303–322. See further my "Existence and Quantification," in J. Margolis, ed., *Fact and Existence* (Oxford: Blackwell, 1968).

[16] Such is the typical way of a numerically insegregative system, misleadingly called "ω-inconsistent." See my *Selected Logic Papers* (New York: Random House, 1966), pp. 118 f, or *Journal of Symbolic Logic*, 1953, pp. 122 f.

[17] This possibility was suggested by Saul Kripke.

quantification that is true when referentially construed remains true when substitutionally construed, and vice versa.

We might still make the distinction from the vantage point of a background theory. In it we might specify some real number that was nameless in the object theory; for there are always ways of strengthening a theory so as to name more real numbers, though never all. Further, in the background theory, we might construe the universe of the object theory as exhausting the real numbers. In the background theory we could, in this way, clinch the quantifications in the object theory as referential. But this clinching is doubly relative: it is relative to the background theory and to the interpretation or translation imposed on the object theory from within the background theory.

One might hope that this recourse to a background theory could often be avoided, even when the nameless reals are inseparable from the named reals in the object theory. One might hope by indirect means to show within the object theory that there are nameless reals. For we might prove within the object theory that the reals are indenumerable and that the names are denumerable and hence that there is no function whose arguments are names and whose values exhaust the real numbers. Since the relation of real numbers to their names would be such a function if each real number had a name, we would seem to have proved within the object theory itself that there are nameless reals and hence that quantification must be taken referentially.

However, this is wrong; there is a loophole. This reasoning would prove only that a relation of all real numbers to their names cannot exist as an entity in the universe of the theory. This reasoning denies no number a name in the notation of the theory, as long as the name relation does not belong to the universe of the theory. And anyway we should know better than to expect such a relation, for it is what causes Berry's and Richard's and related paradoxes.

Some theories can attest to their own nameless objects and so claim referential quantification on their own; other theories have to look to background theories for this service. We saw how a theory might attest to its own nameless objects, namely, by showing that some open sentence became true under all constant substitutions but false under universal quantification. Perhaps this is the only way a theory can claim referential import for its own quantifications. Perhaps, when the nameless objects happen to be inseparable from the named, the quantification used in a theory cannot meaningfully be declared referential except through the medium of a background theory. Yet referential quantification is the key idiom of ontology.

Thus ontology can be multiply relative, multiply meaningless apart from a background theory. Besides being unable to say in absolute terms just what the objects are, we are sometimes unable even to distinguish objectively between referential quantification and a substitutional counterfeit. When we do relativize these matters to a background theory, moreover, the relativization itself has two components: relativity to the choice of background theory and relativity to the choice of how to translate the object theory into the background theory. As for the ontology in turn of the background theory, and even the referentiality of its quantification—these matters can call for a background theory in turn.

There is not always a genuine regress. We saw that, if we are merely clarifying the range of the variables of a theory or the denotations of its terms, and are taking the referentiality of quantification itself for granted, we can commonly use the object theory itself as background theory. We found that when we undertake an ontological reduction, we must accept at least the unreduced theory in order to cite the proxy function; but this we were able cheerfully to accept in the spirit of *reductio ad absurdum* arguments. And now in the end we have found further that if we care to question quantification itself, and settle whether it imports a universe of discourse or turns merely on substitution at the linguistic level, we in some cases have genuinely to regress to a background language endowed with additional resources. We seem to have to do this unless the nameless objects are separable from the named in the object theory.

Regress in ontology is reminiscent of the now familiar regress in the semantics of truth and kindred notions—satisfaction, naming. We know from Tarski's work how the semantics, in this sense, of a theory regularly demands an in some way more inclusive theory. This similarity should perhaps not surprise us, since both ontology and satisfaction are matters of reference. In their elusiveness, at any rate—in their emptiness now and again except relative to a broader background—both truth and ontology may in a suddenly rather clear and even tolerant sense be said to belong to transcendental metaphysics.[18]

---

[18] In developing these thoughts I have been helped by discussion with Saul Kripke, Thomas Nagel, and especially Burton Dreben.

CHAPTER 8

Truth and Meaning

<hr>

Introduction to Alfred Tarski

Alfred Tarski was born in Warsaw, Poland, in 1902. He received his Ph.D. in mathematics from the University of Warsaw in 1924, and taught there before emigrating to the United States in 1939. After research positions at Harvard and the Institute for Advanced Studies in Princeton, Tarski was a member of the Mathematics Department at Berkeley from 1944 until 1973. He died in 1983.

In this article, an informal exposition of his earlier monograph "The Concept of Truth in Formalized Languages," Tarski aims at a "satisfactory definition" of the concept of truth: that is, an account that is *materially adequate* and *formally correct*. In order to be materially adequate, the definition must accord with the basic facts of our usage of "true" and cognate expressions, as reflecting our pre-theoretical understanding of the concept as consisting in correspondence with reality. The formal correctness requirement establishes the extension of "true" by giving a complete specification of the formal properties of the languages for which, and in which, truth is to be defined.

Notice that the title refers to the Semantic *Conception* of Truth, not *Theory* of Truth. Tarski did not intend to give a novel theory of truth, but rather a precise articulation of an old theory, namely the correspondence theory. Semantics is the study of the relations between symbolic expressions and objects. Tarski calls his theory the *semantic* conception of truth, because truth is itself a semantic concept, being a property of sentences. The second part of the article's title refers to Tarski's aim of establishing semantics as a science. Since he accepted *Physicalism*, the doctrine that all legitimate concepts be definable in terms of the concepts of math, logic, or physical science, he endeavored to show that all semantic concepts were thus reducible. He did this first by taking truth as a penultimately basic concept into which all but one other semantic concept can be defined, then second by defining truth itself in terms of the one remaining semantic concept, namely satisfaction.

The concept of truth applies to *sentences*. The question of whether a sentence is true can apply only to a sentence as part of a particular language L. The same sentence S may be true in a language L_1, yet false in another, L_2. For example, take the sentence "Grass is green." Suppose L_1 to be English, and L_2 to be another language, exactly like English except that "green" designates blackness. In that case, "Grass is green" is true in L_1 but false in L_2. So, strictly speaking, Tarski is not attempting a definition of "true" *per se*, but of "*true-in-L*" for a given language. It is debatable whether this accords with our pre-theoretical sense of the concept of truth.

He offers a test to determine whether a definition of "true" is materially adequate: Any competent English speaker would say that "Snow is white" is true if snow is, in fact, white. Likewise, she would say that the sentence is false if snow is not white. Similar considerations obviously apply for every other indicative sentence. We would all affirm that "Grass is green" is true iff grass is green, that "Philosophy is hard" is true iff philosophy is hard, and so on. Consider one sentence of this structure:

"Snow is white" is true iff snow is white.

Compare the left and the right sides of the biconditional. I will call these "LH" and "RH" respectively. On RH we have the sentence "Snow is white." On LH, we have the sentence "'Snow is white' is true." The part of LH in quotes is a *name* for the sentence forming RH. In LH, the sentence is *mentioned*, and on RH it is *used*.

We can generalize this form as

X is true iff p,

and call such sentences "equivalences of form T," or "*T-sentences*." Despite initial appearances, these T-sentences are neither viciously circular nor empty. In RH, the expression "snow" is a syntactically distinct part of the sentence; whereas in LH it is not—rather, here "Snow is white" must be considered as a syntactically *simple* name for the sentence under consideration, rather than being a sentence itself. So, using the concatenation symbol, "^," the T-sentence could be expressed as

$s{\char`\^}n{\char`\^}o{\char`\^}w{\char`\^}$ $^i{\char`\^}s{\char`\^}$ $^w{\char`\^}h{\char`\^}i{\char`\^}t{\char`\^}e$ *is true iff snow is white.*

The test for material adequacy of a definition of truth is this: It must entail a T-sentence for every indicative sentence of the language under consideration. This test is called *Convention T*.

Each T-sentence is a *partial definition* of "true" for the language in question. A *complete* definition would therefore comprise a conjunction of all T-sentences. Consider a tiny artificial language with only two sentences, "Snow is white" and

"Grass is green." A complete definition of "true" for that language could be stated by a conjunction of its only two T-sentences:

(s)(s is true iff either (s = "Snow is white" and snow is white) or
(s = "Grass is green" and grass is green).

However, such a definition could be completed only for artificial languages comprising a finite number of sentences. This condition holds for no natural language. Such a definition is also of no use to Tarski, who wants to define truth for languages involving *logical constants* (whose introduction guarantees that the language will have an infinite number of sentences) and *quantifiers*.

Recall that to satisfy the requirement of formal correctness, the definition must state the formal properties of the language in which the concept of truth can be consistently applied. Tarski argues that a definition of "true" can be given only for an *exactly specified* language: This requires that the language allows

1. A clear and comprehensive specification of which words and other sub-sentential expressions are meaningful: a complete list of primitive terms and rules for introducing other terms from them;
2. A complete specification of axioms—that is, primitive sentences— and rules by which all other meaningful sentences—theorems—can be proved from them.

We have to be able to tell whether or not an expression is a sentence of that language, purely by an examination of its formal properties. This condition does not hold for natural languages. Take the English expression "Dark clouds mean rain." Is this a sentence? We cannot tell without more context. The word "mean" can be either (1) a verb, here equivalent to "are a reliable sign of," in which case the expression is a well-formed English sentence; or (2) an adjective, meaning "nasty." In this case, the expression does not make it as a sentence.

So Tarski holds that truth cannot be given a precise definition in natural languages because these are not exactly specifiable. One other reason for this negative conclusion is that in natural languages, the concept of truth leads to several notorious paradoxes, the most famous of which is the Liar paradox.

Notice these features of English:

1. It is semantically *closed*: It includes sentences and also names for these sentences; thus, complex sentences can be constructed involving both a sentence and a name for that sentence;
2. The concept of truth is part of the language: For any sentence S, we can construct another sentence S* which can assert (or deny) that S is true; we can even construct "self-referential" sentences which assert (or deny) their own truth. For example,

THE ONLY CAPITALIZED SENTENCE IN THIS ESSAY IS NOT TRUE.

Suppose we call this previous sentence "s." Let us apply our T-sentence:

1. *"s" is true iff THE ONLY CAPITALIZED SENTENCE IN THIS ESSAY IS NOT TRUE.*

We can establish the following sentence, since we have stipulated it:

> 2. *"s" is identical with THE ONLY CAPITALIZED SENTENCE IN THIS ESSAY.*

Given this identity, we can substitute the former for the latter in extensional contexts, deriving the following from line 1:

> 3. *"s" is true iff "s" is not true.*

If we assume the principle of bivalence, which says that every indicative sentence is either true or false, then any indicative sentence which is not true is false, and vice versa. Thus we have

> 4. *"s" is true iff "s" is false.*

Tarski claims that paradoxes will occur and therefore that the material adequacy test will fail for any semantically closed language, if the laws of classical logic are assumed. Truth can be defined only for "semantically open" languages, that is, those excluding (1) names for its own sentences, and (2) semantic terms, such as "true," applying to its sentences. That is, the definition of truth for any given language L cannot be given within L itself, but must be given in another language in which L can be discussed. We can call L, in this context, the *object-language* (i.e., the language under consideration) and the second language the *metalanguage* (i.e., the language in which the considerations take place). Thus recall

> *"Snow is white" is true iff snow is white.*

This T-sentence itself is part of the metalanguage. The sentence under discussion, "Snow is white," is within the object-language. Thus translations of object-language expressions must be included in the metalanguage. However, the metalanguage must exceed the object-language in expressiveness, since it must also have the capacity to construct a name for every object-language sentence, as well as to apply semantic concepts like "true" to them. In fact, the metalanguage can just be the object-language, plus these names for object-language sentences, and semantic concepts as applied to the object-language.

No language is *intrinsically* an object-language or a metalanguage: It has these functions only relative to some other language. There is a necessary asymmetry between an object-language and its metalanguage: If L_2 is L_1's metalanguage, then L_1 cannot in turn function as L_2's metalanguage, or paradoxes will result. So L_2 might function as a metalanguage for L_1; but any claims regarding the truth or falsity of L_2's sentences would have to occur in a third language L_3, where it would be a metalanguage for L_2's object-language. Tarski is thus committed to a hierarchical structure of languages, each one more expressive than all previous ones.

As I have said above, Tarski defines truth in terms of satisfaction. He therefore has to define satisfaction without reference to truth or to any other semantic concept. Satisfaction is a relation between objects and sentential functions. A sentential function is an expression with at least one unbound variable, which can be transformed into a sentence when the unbound variables are replaced by objects. The sentential function "x is a city" expresses no state of affairs, and is neither true nor false. However, when "x" is replaced by "London," we get the true sentence "London is a city." Thus, we say that "London" *satisfies* "x is a city."

Informally, we could say that a sequence (i.e., an ordered set) of objects satisfies a sentential function if a *true* sentence is produced when that sequence replaces the unbound variables. However, this account is clearly no use to Tarski, since he wants to define truth in terms of satisfaction, and a definition of satisfaction which relies on truth would be obviously circular.

Tarski begins by giving a *recursive* (or inductive) definition of a sentential function. A recursive definition of a concept aims to give its extension, by the following method: First, the simplest instances of the concept are enumerated, and then rules are stated that enable complex examples to be constructed from these basic cases. So for example, if "x is white" is a simple function, and so is "y is round," then "x is white or y is round" is a function. A *sentence* can then be defined in terms of sentential functions, namely as a sentential function with no free variables.

The same procedure is applied to the notion of satisfaction: We state which objects satisfy the most basic functions, then indicate rules to establish how, and by what, more complex functions can be satisfied. For example, a sequence satisfies "x is blue or x is red" if it satisfies "x is blue" or "x is red." Notice that this definition does not *reduce* satisfaction to any other concepts, semantic or physicalistic. It merely gives conditions in which any given sequence satisfies any given function. Notice also that Tarski's definition is going to apply only to languages with a finite number of basic sentential functions (e.g., for languages with a finite number of predicates).

We can now see why Tarski had to define truth in terms of satisfaction. While a *directly* recursive definition of truth can show that, say, the truth of *"p or q"* is a function of the truth-values of *"p"* and *"q,"* Tarski wanted to define truth for languages rich enough to contain the predicate calculus. But while a quantified sentence has a truth-value, it is constructed from components which themselves lack truth-values, that is, quantifiers and sentential functions. He therefore had to resort to some semantic concept that could be applied both to sentences and sentential functions. Satisfaction is such a concept.

Tarski defines satisfaction in terms of *infinite* sequences. This allows a single definition, rather than an unlimited number of separate definitions for sequences and functions of various different places. For example,

> one-place cases like *<snow> satisfies "x is white"*;
>
> two-place cases like *<Paris, France> satisfies "x is the capital city of y"*;
>
> three-place cases like *<Portland, Seattle, San Francisco> satisfies "x is located between y and z."*

The employment of infinite sequences forces us to replace our variables x, y, z, and the like, with numbered variables x_1, x_2, x_3, and so on. For example, we would say that "x_2 is white" is satisfied by a sequence S if its second member is white.

Take the two-place sequence above, *<Paris, France>*. We have seen that Tarski admits sequences of any length, without limit. So there are an enormous number of other sequences, sharing the first two members, for example *<Paris, France, Chicago, 4, Alfred Tarski, my desk, Sting>*. In fact, there is an infinite sequence corresponding to each possible ordering of objects. So take any sequence of which *Paris, France, Chicago, 4, Alfred Tarski, my desk,* and *Sting* are the first seven members. For any object O, there is some sequence exactly like it, except that O replaces *France* in the second place, and another sequence just like it except that O replaces *Sting* in the seventh place.

This seven-place sequence above satisfies "x_1 is the capital of x_2" just as well as does *<Paris, France>*. This is a two-place sentential function, and the first two members of the sequence satisfy that function, so all other members are irrelevant. The sequence satisfies the function, whatever values are assigned to these other members. In general, for any sentential function, members of a sequence that are not correlated with unbound variables are irrelevant to whether the sequence satisfies the function.

Now recall that we can define a sentence as a sentential function with no unbound variables. That means that for such a "zero-place function," *all* members of a sequence are irrelevant to whether satisfaction takes place. It follows that there are only two options here:

A *true* sentence can be defined as a function satisfied by *all* sequences;

A *false* sentence can be defined as a function satisfied by *no* sequences.

Given that *<snow>*, and all sequences of which this is the first member, satisfies "x is white," then all sequences satisfy "snow is white."

Finally, let us turn to how Tarski treats satisfaction for quantified sentences. Take the sentence $(\forall x_1)(x_1 \text{ is white})$. Tarski demands two conditions for a sequence S to satisfy this sentence:

1. S must satisfy "x_1 is white," that is, the sentential function formed by removing the quantifier;

2. "x_1 is white" must be satisfied by every sequence exactly like S except with some other object in its first place.

But there is, as we have seen, such a sequence for *every* object. It follows that S satisfies $(\forall x_1)(x_1 \text{ is white})$ if everything is white. Tarski proved this same result for existentially quantified sentences. They accord with his definition of truth as "satisfaction by all sequences."

BIBLIOGRAPHY

Works by Tarski
Tarski's main philosophical writings, including "The Concept of Truth in Formalized Languages," can be found in his *Logic, Semantics, Metamathematics* , 2nd ed., ed. J. H. Woodger (Indianapolis: Hackett, 1983).

Further Reading

Hartry Field, "Tarski's Theory of Truth," *Journal of Philosophy*, Vol. 69, 1972, influentially argues that Tarski failed to completely reduce truth and satisfaction to nonsemantic concepts.

Richard Kirkham, *Theories of Truth* (Cambridge: MIT Press, 1992) contains a useful discussion of Tarski's theory in Chapters 5 and 6.

George Romanos, *Quine and Analytic Philosophy* (Cambridge: MIT Press, 1983) brings out the importance of Tarski's work for the Logical Positivists and Quine.

The Semantic Conception of Truth and the Foundations of Semantics

Alfred Tarski

This paper consists of two parts; the first has an expository character, and the second is rather polemical.

In the first part I want to summarize in an informed way the main results of my investigations concerning the definition of truth and the more general problem of the foundations of semantics. These results have been embodied in a work which appeared in print several years ago.[1] Although my investigations concern concepts dealt with in classical philosophy, they happen to be comparatively little known in philosophical circles, perhaps because of their strictly technical character. For this reason I hope I shall be excused for taking up the matter once again.[2]

Since my work was published, various objections, of unequal value, have been raised to my investigations; some of these appeared in print, and others were made in public and private discussions in which I took part.[3] In the second part of the paper I should like to express my views regarding these objections. I hope that the remarks which will be made in this context will not be considered as purely polemical in character, but will be found to contain some constructive contributions to the subject.

In the second part of the paper I have made extensive use of material graciously put at my disposal by Dr. Marja Kokoszyńska (University of Lwów). I am especially indebted and grateful to Professors Ernest Nagel (Columbia University) and David Rynin (University of California, Berkeley) for their help in preparing the final text and for various critical remarks.

Alfred Tarski, "The Semantic Concept of Truth and the Foundations of Semantics," *Philosophy and Phenomenological Research*, Vol. IV, 1944. Reprinted by permission of Jan Tarski. [Editor's note: Only the first part of this article is reprinted in this anthology.]

I. EXPOSITION

1. The Main Problem—A Satisfactory Definition of Truth

Our discussion will be centered around the notion[4] of *truth*. The main problem is that of giving a *satisfactory definition* of this notion, i.e., a definition which is *materially adequate* and *formally correct*. But such a formulation of the problem, because of its generality, cannot be considered unequivocal, and requires some further comments.

In order to avoid any ambiguity, we must first specify the conditions under which the definition of truth will be considered adequate from the material point of view. The desired definition does not aim to specify the meaning of a familiar word used to denote a novel notion; on the contrary, it aims to catch hold of the actual meaning of an old notion. We must then characterize this notion precisely enough to enable anyone to determine whether the definition actually fulfills its task.

Secondly, we must determine on what the formal correctness of the definition depends. Thus, we must specify the words or concepts which we wish to use in defining the notion of truth; and we must also give the formal rules to which the definition should conform. Speaking more generally, we must describe the formal structure of the language in which the definition will be given.

The discussion of these points will occupy a considerable portion of the first part of the paper.

2. The Extension of the Term 'true'

We begin with some remarks regarding the extension of the concept of truth which we have in mind here.

The predicate *'true'* is sometimes used to refer to psychological phenomena such as judgments or beliefs, sometimes to certain physical objects, namely, linguistic expressions and specifically sentences, and sometimes to certain ideal entities called 'propositions.' By 'sentence' we understand here what is usually meant in grammar by 'declarative sentence'; as regards the term 'proposition,' its meaning is notoriously a subject of lengthy disputations by various philosophers and logicians, and it seems never to have been made quite clear and unambiguous. For several reasons it appears most convenient to *apply the term 'true' to sentences*, and we shall follow this course.[5]

Consequently, we must always relate the notion of truth, like that of a sentence, to a specific language; for it is obvious that the same expression which is a true sentence in one language can be false or meaningless in another.

Of course, the fact that we are interested here primarily in the notion of truth for sentences does not exclude the possibility of a subsequent extension of this notion to other kinds of objects.

3. The Meaning of the Term 'true'

Much more serious difficulties are connected with the problem of the meaning (or the intension) of the concept of truth.

The word *'true,'* like other words from our everyday language, is certainly not unambiguous. And it does not seem to me that the philosophers who have discussed this concept have helped to diminish its ambiguity. In works and discussions of philosophers we meet many different conceptions of truth and falsity, and we must indicate which conception will be the basis of our discussion.

We should like our definition to do justice to the intuitions which adhere to the *classical Aristotelian conception of truth*—intuitions which find their expression in the well-known words of Aristotle's *Metaphysics*:

> To say of what is that it is not, or of what is not that it is, is false, while to say of what is that it is, or of what is not that it is not, is true.

If we wished to adapt ourselves to modern philosophical terminology, we could perhaps express this conception by means of the familiar formula:

> The truth of a sentence consists in its agreement with (or correspondence to) reality.

(For a theory of truth which is to be based upon the latter formulation the term 'correspondence theory' has been suggested.)

If, on the other hand, we should decide to extend the popular usage of the term *'designate'* by applying it not only to names, but also to sentences, and if we agreed to speak of the designata of sentences as 'states of affairs,' we could possibly use for the same purpose the following phrase:

> A sentence is true if it designates an existing state of affairs.[6]

However, all these formulations can lead to various misunderstandings, for none of them is sufficiently precise and clear (though this applies much less to the original Aristotelian formulation than to either of the others); at any rate, none of them can be considered a satisfactory definition of truth. It is up to us to look for a more precise expression of our intuitions.

4. A Criterion for the Material Adequacy of the Definition[7]

Let us start with a concrete example. Consider the sentence *'snow is white.'* We ask the question under what conditions this sentence is true or false. It seems clear that if we base ourselves on the classical conception of truth, we shall say that the sentence is true of snow is white, and that it is false if snow is not white. Thus, if the definition of truth is to conform to our conception, it must imply the following equivalence:

> The sentence 'snow is white' is true if, and only if, snow is white.

Let me point out that the phrase *'snow is white'* occurs on the left side of this equivalence in quotation marks, and on the right without quotation marks. On the right side we have the sentence itself, and on the left the name of the sentence. Employing the medieval logical terminology we could also say that on the right side the words *'snow is white'* occur in *suppositio formalis*, and on the left in *suppositio materialis*.

It is hardly necessary to explain why we must have the name of the sentence, and not the sentence itself, on the left side of the equivalence. For, in the first place, from the point of view of the grammar of our language, an expression of the form '*X is true*' will not become a meaningful sentence if we replace in it 'X' by a sentence or by anything other than a name—since the subject of a sentence may be only a noun or an expression functioning like a noun. And, in the second place, the fundamental conventions regarding the use of any language require that in any utterance we make about an object it is the name of the object which must be employed, and not the object itself. In consequence, if we wish to say something about a sentence, for example, that it is true, we must use the name of this sentence, and not the sentence itself.[8]

It may be added that enclosing a sentence in quotation marks is by no means the only way of forming its name. For instance, by assuming the usual order of letters in our alphabet, we can use the following expression as the name (the description) of the sentence '*snow is white*':

> the sentence constituted by three words, the first of which consists of the 19th, 14th, 15th, and 23rd letters, the second of the 9th and 19th letters, and the third of the 23rd, 8th, 9th, 20th, and 5th letters of the English alphabet.

We shall now generalize the procedure which we have applied above. Let us consider an arbitrary sentence; we shall replace it by the letter '*p.*' We form the name of this sentence and we replace it by another letter, say 'X.' We ask now what is the logical relation between the two sentences '*X is true*' and '*p.*' It is clear that from the point of view of our basic conception of truth these sentences are equivalent. In other words, the following equivalence holds:

(T) X is true if, and only if, p.

We shall call any such equivalence (with '*p*' replaced by any sentence of the language to which the word '*true*' refers, and 'X' replaced by a name of this sentence) an '*equivalence of the form* (T).'

Now at last we are able to put into a precise form the conditions under which we will consider the usage and the definition of the term '*true*' as adequate from the material point of view: we wish to use the term '*true*' in such a way that all equivalences of the form (T) can be asserted, and *we shall call a definition of truth 'adequate' if all these equivalences follow from it.*

It should be emphasized that neither the expression (T) itself (which is not a sentence, but only a schema of a sentence) nor any particular instance of the form (T) can be regarded as a definition of truth. We can only say that every equivalence of the form (T) obtained by replacing '*p*' by a particular sentence, and 'X' by a name of this sentence, may be considered a partial definition of truth, which explains wherein the truth of this one individual sentence consists. The general definition has to be, in a certain sense, a logical conjunction of all these partial definitions.

(The last remark calls for some comments. A language may admit the construction of infinitely many sentences; and thus the number of partial definitions of truth referring to sentences of such a language will also be infinite. Hence to give our remark a precise sense we should have to explain what is meant by a 'logical conjunction of infinitely many sentences'; but this would lead us too far into technical problems of modern logic.)

5. Truth as a Semantic Concept

I should like to propose the name '*the semantic conception of truth*' for the conception of truth which has just been discussed.

Semantics is a discipline which, speaking loosely, *deals with certain relations between expressions of a language and the objects* (or 'states of affairs') '*referred to' by those expressions*. As typical examples of semantic concepts we may mention the concepts of *designation, satisfaction*, and *definition* as these occur in the following examples:

> the expression 'the father of this country' designates (denotes) George Washington;
>
> snow satisfies the sentential function (the condition) 'x is white';
>
> the equation '2.x = 1' defines (uniquely determines) the number 1/2.

While the words '*designates,*' '*satisfies,*' and '*defines*' express relations (between certain expressions and the objects 'referred to' by these expressions), the word '*true*' is of a different logical nature: it expresses a property (or denotes a class) of certain expressions, viz., of sentences. However, it is easily seen that all the formulations which were given earlier and which aimed to explain the meaning of this word (cf. Sections 3 and 4) referred not only to sentences themselves, but also to objects 'talked about' by these sentences, or possibly to 'states of affairs' described by them. And, moreover, it turns out that the simplest and the most natural way of obtaining an exact definition of truth is one which involves the use of other semantic notions, e.g., the notion of satisfaction. It is for these reasons that we count the concept of truth which is discussed here among the concepts of semantics, and the problem of defining truth proves to be closely related to the more general problem of setting up the foundations of theoretical semantics.

It is perhaps worth while saying that semantics as it is conceived in this paper (and in former papers of the author) is a sober and modest discipline which has no pretentions of being a universal patent-medicine for all the ills and diseases of mankind, whether imaginary or real. You will not find in semantics any remedy for decayed teeth or illusions of grandeur or class conflicts. Nor is semantics a device for establishing that everyone except the speaker and his friends is speaking nonsense.

From antiquity to the present day the concepts of semantics have played an important rôle in the discussions of philosophers, logicians, and philologists. Nevertheless, these concepts have been treated for a long time with a certain amount of suspicion. From a historical standpoint, this suspicion is to be regarded as completely justified. For although the meaning of semantic concepts as they are used in everyday language seems to be rather clear and understandable, still all attempts to characterize this meaning in a general and exact way miscarried. And what is worse, various arguments in which these concepts were involved, and which seemed otherwise quite correct and based upon apparently obvious premises, led frequently to paradoxes and antinomies. It is sufficient to mention here the *antinomy of the liar*, Richard's *antinomy of definability* (by means of a finite number of words), and Grelling-Nelson's *antinomy of heterological terms*.[9]

I believe that the method which is outlined in this paper helps to overcome these difficulties and assures the possibility of a consistent use of semantic concepts.

6. Languages with a Specified Structure

Because of the possible occurrence of antinomies, the problem of specifying the formal structure and the vocabulary of a language in which definitions of semantic concepts are to be given becomes especially acute; and we turn now to this problem.

There are certain general conditions under which the structure of a language is regarded as *exactly specified*. Thus, to specify the structure of a language, we must characterize unambiguously the class of those words and expressions which are to be considered *meaningful*. In particular, we must indicate all words which we decide to use without defining them, and which are called '*undefined* (or *primitive*) *terms*'; and we must give the so-called *rules of definition* for introducing new or *defined terms*. Furthermore, we must set up criteria for distinguishing within the class of expressions those which we call '*sentences*.' Finally, we must formulate the conditions under which a sentence of the language can be *asserted*. In particular, we must indicate all *axioms* (or *primitive sentences*), i.e., those sentences which we decide to assert without proof; and we must give the so-called *rules of inference* (or *rules of proof*) by means of which we can deduce new asserted sentences from other sentences which have been previously asserted. Axioms, as well as sentences deduced from them by means of rules of inference, are referred to as '*theorems*' or '*provable sentences*.'

If in specifying the structure of a language we refer exclusively to the form of the expressions involved, the language is said to be *formalized*. In such a language theorems are the only sentences which can be asserted.

At the present time the only languages with a specified structure are the formalized languages of various systems of deductive logic, possibly enriched by the introduction of certain non-logical terms. However, the field of application of these languages is rather comprehensive; we are able, theoretically, to develop in them various branches of science, for instance, mathematics and theoretical physics.

(On the other hand, we can imagine the construction of languages which have an exactly specified structure without being formalized. In such a language the assertability of sentences, for instance, may depend not always on their form, but sometimes on other, non-linguistic factors. It would be interesting and important actually to construct a language of this type, and specifically one which would prove to be sufficient for the development of a comprehensive branch of empirical science; for this would justify the hope that languages with specified structure could finally replace everyday language in scientific discourse.)

The problem of the definition of truth obtains a precise meaning and can be solved in a rigorous way only for those languages whose structure has been exactly specified. For other languages—thus, for all natural, 'spoken' languages—the meaning of the problem is more or less vague, and its solution can have only an approximate character. Roughly speaking, the approximation consists in replacing a natural language (or a portion of it in which we are interested) by one whose structure is exactly specified, and which diverges from the given language 'as little as possible.'

7. The Antinomy of the Liar

In order to discover some of the more specific conditions which must be satisfied by languages in which (or for which) the definition of truth is to be given, it will be advisable to begin with a discussion of that antinomy which directly involves the notion of truth, namely, the antinomy of the liar.

To obtain this antinomy in a perspicuous form,[10] consider the following sentence:

The sentence printed in this paper on [p. 368, l.11] is not true.

For brevity we shall replace the sentence just stated by the letter '*s*.'

According to our convention concerning the adequate usage of the term '*true*,' we assert the following equivalence of the form (T):

(1) '*s*' is true if, and only if, the sentence printed in this paper on [p. 368, l.11], is not true.

On the other hand, keeping in mind the meaning of the symbol '*s*,' we establish empirically the following fact:

(2) '*s*' is identical with the sentence printed in this paper on [p. 368, l.11].

Now, by a familiar law from the theory of identity (Leibniz's law), it follows from (2) that we may replace in (1) the expression '*the sentence printed in this paper on [p. 368, l.11]*' by the symbol '"*s*."' We thus obtain what follows:

(3) '*s*' is true if, and only if, '*s*' is not true.

In this way we have arrived at an obvious contradiction.

In my judgment, it would be quite wrong and dangerous from the standpoint of scientific progress to depreciate the importance of this and other antinomies, and to treat them as jokes or sophistries. It is a fact that we are here in the presence of an absurdity, that we have been compelled to assert a false sentence (since (3), as an equivalence between two contradictory sentences, is necessarily false). If we take our work seriously, we cannot be reconciled with this fact. We must discover its cause, that is to say, we must analyze premises upon which the antinomy is based; we must then reject at least one of these premises, and we must investigate the consequences which this has for the whole domain of our research.

It should be emphasized that antinomies have played a preëminent rôle in establishing the foundations of modern deductive sciences. And just as class-theoretical antinomies, and in particular Russell's antinomy (of the class of all classes that are not members of themselves), were the starting point for the successful attempts at a consistent formalization of logic and mathematics, so the antinomy of the liar and other semantic antinomies give rise to the construction of theoretical semantics.

8. The Inconsistency of Semantically Closed Languages[7]

If we now analyze the assumptions which lead to the antinomy of the liar, we notice the following:

1. We have implicitly assumed that the language in which the antinomy is constructed contains, in addition to its expressions, also the names of these expressions, as well as semantic terms such as the term *'true'* referring to sentences of this language; we have also assumed that all sentences which determine the adequate usage of this term can be asserted in the language. A language with these properties will be called *'semantically closed.'*
2. We have assumed that in this language the ordinary laws of logic hold.
3. We have assumed that we can formulate and assert in our language an empirical premise such as the statement (2) which has occurred in our argument.

It turns out that the assumption (3) is not essential, for it is possible to reconstruct the antinomy of the liar without its help.[11] But the assumptions (1) and (2) prove essential. Since every language which satisfies both of these assumptions is inconsistent, we must reject at least one of them.

It would be superfluous to stress here the consequences of rejecting the assumption (2), that is, of changing our logic (supposing this were possible) even in its more elementary and fundamental parts. We thus consider only the possibility of rejecting the assumption (1). Accordingly, we decide *not to use any language which is semantically closed* in the sense given.

This restriction would of course be unacceptable for those who, for reasons which are not clear to me, believe that there is only one 'genuine' language (or, at least, that all 'genuine' languages are mutually translatable). However, this restriction does not affect the needs or interests of science in any essential way. The languages (either the formalized languages or—what is more frequently the case—the portions of everyday language) which are used in scientific discourse do not have to be semantically closed. This is obvious in case linguistic phenomena and, in particular, semantic notions do not enter in any way into the subject-matter of a science; for in such a case the language of this science does not have to be provided with any semantic terms at all. However, we shall see in the next section how semantically closed languages can be dispensed with even in those scientific discussions in which semantic notions are essentially involved.

The problem arises as to the position of everyday language with regard to this point. At first blush it would seem that this language satisfies both assumptions (1) and (2), and that therefore it must be inconsistent. But actually the case is not so simple. Our everyday language is certainly not one with an exactly specified structure. We do not know precisely which expressions are sentences, and we know even to a smaller degree which sentences are to be taken as assertible. Thus the problem of consistency has no exact meaning with respect to this language. We may at best only risk the guess that a language whose structure has been exactly specified and which resembles our everyday language as closely as possible would be inconsistent.

9. Object-language and Meta-language

Since we have agreed not to employ semantically closed languages, we have to use two different languages in discussing the problem of the definition of truth and, more generally, any problems in the field of semantics. The first of these languages is the language which is 'talked about' and which is the subject-matter of the whole discussion; the definition of truth which we are seeking applies to the sentences of this language. The second is the language in which we 'talk about' the first language, and in terms of which we wish, in particular, to construct the definition of truth for the first language. We shall refer to the first language as '*the object-language*,' and to the second as '*the meta-language*.'

It should be noticed that these terms 'object-language' and 'meta-language' have only a relative sense. If, for instance, we become interested in the notion of truth applying to sentences, not of our original object-language, but of its meta-language, the latter becomes automatically the object-language of our discussion; and in order to define truth for this language, we have to go to a new meta-language—so to speak, to a meta-language of a higher level. In this way we arrive at a whole hierarchy of languages.

The vocabulary of the meta-language is to a large extent determined by previously stated conditions under which a definition of truth will be considered materially adequate. This definition, as we recall, has to imply all equivalences of the form (T):

(T) X is true if, and only if, p.

The definition itself and all the equivalences implied by it are to be formulated in the meta-language. On the other hand, the symbol 'p' in (T) stands for an arbitrary sentence of our object-language. Hence it follows that every sentence which occurs in the object-language must also occur in the meta-language; in other words, the meta-language must contain the object-language as a part. This is at any rate necessary for the proof of the adequacy of the definition—even though the definition itself can sometimes be formulated in a less comprehensive meta-language which does not satisfy this requirement.

(The requirement in question can be somewhat modified, for it suffices to assume that the object-language can be translated into the meta-language; this necessitates a certain change in the interpretation of the symbol 'p' in (T). In all that follows we shall ignore the possibility of this modification.)

Furthermore, the symbol 'X' in (T) represents the name of the sentence which 'p' stands for. We see therefore that the meta-language must be rich enough to provide possibilities of constructing a name for every sentence of the object-language.

In addition, the meta-language must obviously contain terms of a general logical character, such as the expression 'if, and only if.'[12]

It is desirable for the meta-language not to contain any undefined terms except such as are involved explicitly or implicitly in the remarks above, i.e.: terms of the object-language; terms referring to the form of the expressions of the object-language, and used in building names for these expressions; and terms of logic. In particular, we desire *semantic terms* (referring to the object-language) *to be introduced into the meta-language only by definition*. For, if this postulate is satisfied, the definition of truth, or of any other semantic concept, will fulfill what we intuitively expect from every definition; that is, it will explain the meaning of the term being defined in terms whose meaning appears to be completely clear and unequivocal. And, moreover, we have then a kind of guarantee that the use of semantic concepts will not involve us in any contradictions.

We have no further requirements as to the formal structure of the object-language and the meta-language; we assume that it is similar to that of other formalized languages known at the present time. In particular, we assume that the usual formal rules of definition are observed in the meta-language.

10. Conditions for a Positive Solution of the Main Problem

Now, we have already a clear idea both of the conditions of material adequacy to which the definition of truth is subjected, and of the formal structure of the language in which this definition is to be constructed. Under these circumstances the problem of the definition of truth acquires the character of a definite problem of a purely deductive nature.

The solution of the problem, however, is by no means obvious, and I would not attempt to give it in detail without using the whole machinery of contemporary logic. Here I shall confine myself to a rough outline of the solution and to the discussion of certain points of a more general interest which are involved in it.

The solution turns out to be sometimes positive, sometimes negative. This depends upon some formal relations between the object-language and its meta-language; or, more specifically, upon the fact whether the meta-language in its logical part is '*essentially richer*' than the object-language or not. It is not easy to give a general and precise definition of this notion of 'essential richness.' If we restrict ourselves to languages based on the logical theory of types, the condition for the meta-language to be 'essentially richer' than the object-language is that it contain variables of a higher logical type than those of the object-language.

If the condition of 'essential richness' is not satisfied, it can usually be shown that an interpretation of the meta-language in the object-language is possible; that is to say, with any given term of the meta-language a well-determined term of the object-language can be correlated in such a way that the assertible sentences of the one language turn out to be correlated with assertible sentences of the other. As a result of this interpretation, the hypothesis that a satisfactory definition of truth has been formulated in the meta-language turns out to imply the possibility of reconstructing in that language the antinomy of the liar; and this in turn forces us to reject the hypothesis in question.

(The fact that the meta-language, in its non-logical part, is ordinarily more comprehensive than the object-language does not affect the possibility of interpreting the former in the latter. For example, the names of expressions of the object-language occur in the meta-language, though for the most part they do not occur in the object-language itself; but, nevertheless, it may be possible to interpret these names in terms of the object-language.)

Thus we see that the condition of 'essential richness' is necessary for the possibility of a satisfactory definition of truth in the meta-language. If we want to develop the theory of truth in a meta-language which does not satisfy this condition, we must give up the idea of defining truth with the exclusive help of those terms which were indicated above (in Section 8). We have then to include the term '*true*,' or some other semantic term, in the list of undefined terms of the meta-language, and to express fundamental properties of the notion of truth in a series of axioms. There is nothing essentially wrong in such an axiomatic procedure, and it may prove useful for various purposes.[13]

It turns out, however, that this procedure can be avoided. For *the condition of the 'essential richness' of the meta-language proves to be, not only necessary, but also sufficient for the construction of a satisfactory definition of truth*; i.e., if the meta-language satisfies this condition, the notion of truth can be defined in it. We shall now indicate in general terms how this construction can be carried through.

11. The Construction (in Outline) of the Definition.[14]

A definition of truth can be obtained in a very simple way from that of another semantic notion, namely, of the notion of *satisfaction*.

Satisfaction is a relation between arbitrary objects and certain expressions called '*sentential functions*.' These are expressions like '*x is white*,' '*x is greater than y*,' etc. Their formal structural is analogous to that of sentences; however, they may contain the so-called free variables (like '*x*' and '*y*' in '*x is greater than y*'), which cannot occur in sentences.

In defining the notion of a sentential function in formalized languages, we usually apply what is called a 'recursive procedure'; i.e., we first describe sentential functions of the simplest structure (which ordinarily presents no difficulty), and then we indicate the operations by means of which compound functions can be constructed from simpler ones. Such an operation may consist, for instance, in forming the logical disjunction or conjunction of two given functions, i.e. by combining them by the word '*or*' or '*and*.' A sentence can now be defined simply as a sentential function which contains no free variables.

As regards the notion of satisfaction, we might try to define it by saying that given objects satisfy a given function if the latter becomes a true sentence when we replace in it free variables by names of given objects. In this sense, for example, snow satisfies the sentential function '*x is white*' since the sentence '*snow is white*' is true. However, apart from other difficulties, this method is not available to us, for we want to use the notion of satisfaction in defining truth.

To obtain a definition of satisfaction we have rather to apply again a recursive procedure. We indicate which objects satisfy the simplest sentential functions; and then we state the conditions under which given objects satisfy a compound function—assuming that we know which objects satisfy the simpler functions from which the compound one has been constructed. Thus, for instance, we say that given numbers satisfy the logical disjunction '*x is greater than y or x is equal to y*' if they satisfy at least one of the functions '*x is greater than y*' or '*x is equal to y.*'

Once the general definition of satisfaction is obtained, we notice that it applies automatically also to those special sentential functions which contain no free variables, i.e., to sentences. It turns out that for a sentence only two cases are possible: a sentence is either satisfied by all objects, or by no objects. Hence we arrive at a definition of truth and falsehood simply by saying that a *sentence is true if it is satisfied by all objects, and false otherwise.*[15]

(It may seem strange that we have chosen a roundabout way of defining the truth of a sentence, instead of trying to apply, for instance, a direct recursive procedure. The reason is that compound sentences are constructed from simpler sentential functions, but not always from simpler sentences; hence no general recursive method is known which applies specifically to sentences.)

From this rough outline it is not clear where and how the assumption of the 'essential richness' of the meta-language is involved in the discussion; this becomes clear only when the construction is carried through in a detailed and formal way.[16]

12. Consequences of the Definition

The definition of truth which was outlined above has many interesting consequences.

In the first place, the definition proves to be not only formally correct, but also materially adequate (in the sense established in Section 4); in other words, it implies all equivalences of the form (T). In this connection it is important to notice that the conditions for the material adequacy of the definition determine uniquely the extension of the term '*true.*' Therefore, every definition of truth which is materially adequate would necessarily be equivalent to that actually constructed. The semantic conception of truth gives us, so to speak, no possibility of choice between various non-equivalent definitions of this notion.

Moreover, we can deduce from our definition various laws of a general nature. In particular, we can prove with its help the *laws of contradiction and of excluded middle*, which are so characteristic of the Aristotelian conception of truth; i.e., we can show that one and only one of any two contradictory sentences is true. These semantic laws should not be identified with the related logical laws of contradiction and excluded middle; the latter belong to the sentential calculus, i.e., to the most elementary part of logic, and do not involve the term '*true*' at all.

Further important results can be obtained by applying the theory of truth to formalized languages of a certain very comprehensive class of mathematical disciplines; only disciplines of an elementary character and a very elementary logical structure are excluded from this class. It turns out that for a discipline of this class *the notion of truth never coincides with that of provability*; for all provable sentences are true, but there are true sentences which are not provable.[17] Hence it follows further that every such discipline is consistent, but incomplete; that is to say, of any two contradictory sentences at most one is provable, and—what is more—there exists a pair of contradictory sentences neither of which is provable.[18]

13. Extension of the Results to Other Semantic Notions

Most of the results at which we arrived in the preceding sections in discussing the notion of truth can be extended with appropriate changes to other semantic notions, for instance, to the notion of satisfaction (involved in our previous discussion), and to those of *designation* and *definition*.

Each of these notions can be analyzed along the lines followed in the analysis of truth. Thus, criteria for an adequate usage of these notions can be established; it can be shown that each of these notions, when used in a semantically closed language according to those criteria, leads necessarily to a contradiction;[19] a distinction between the object-language and the meta-language becomes again indispensable; and the 'essential richness' of the meta-language proves in each case to be a necessary and sufficient condition for a satisfactory definition of the notion involved. Hence the results obtained in discussing one particular semantic notion apply to the general problem of the foundations of theoretical semantics.

Within theoretical semantics we can define and study some further notions, whose intuitive content is more involved and whose semantic origin is less obvious; we have in mind, for instance, the important notions of *consequence, synonymity*, and *meaning*.[20]

We have concerned ourselves here with the theory of semantic notions related to an individual object-language (although no specific properties of this language have been involved in our arguments). However, we could also consider the problem of developing *general semantics* which applies to a comprehensive class of object-languages. A considerable part of our previous remarks can be extended to this general problem; however, certain new difficulties arise in this connection, which will not be discussed here. I shall merely observe that the axiomatic method (mentioned in Section 10) may prove the most appropriate for the treatment of the problem.[21]

NOTES

1. Compare Tarski [2] (see bibliography at the end of the paper). This work may be consulted for a more detailed and formal presentation of the subject of the paper, especially of the material included in Sections 6 and 9–13. It contains also references to my earlier publications on the problems of semantics (a communication in Polish, 1930; the article Tarski [1] in French, 1931; a communication in German, 1932; and a book in Polish, 1933). The expository part of the present paper is related in its character to Tarski [3]. My investigations on the notion of truth and on theoretical semantics have been reviewed or discussed in Hofstadter [1], Juhos [1], Kokoszyńska [1] and [2], Kotarbiński [2], Scholz [1], Weinberg [1], *et al.*

2. It may be hoped that the interest in theoretical semantics will now increase, as a result of the recent publication of the important work Carnap [2].

3. This applies, in particular, to public discussions during the I. International Congress for the Unity of Science (Paris, 1935) and the Conference of International Congresses for the Unity of Science (Paris, 1937); cf., e.g., Neurath [1] and Gonseth [1].

4. The words 'notion' and 'concept' are used in this paper with all of the vagueness and ambiguity with which they occur in philosophical literature. Thus, sometimes they refer simply to a term, sometimes to what is meant by a term, and in other cases to what is denoted by a term. Sometimes it is irrelevant which of these interpretations is meant; and in certain cases perhaps none of them applies adequately. While on principle I share the tendency to avoid these words in any exact discussion, I did not consider it necessary to do so in this informal presentation.

5. For our present purposes it is somewhat more convenient to understand by 'expressions,' 'sentences,' etc., not individual inscriptions, but classes of inscriptions of similar form (thus, not individual physical things, but classes of such things).

6. For the Aristotelian formulation see Article [1], 1', 7, 27. The other two formulations are very common in the literature, but I do not know with whom they originate. A critical discussion of various conceptions of truth can be found, e.g., in Kotarbiński [1] (so far available only in Polish), pp. 123 ff., and Russell [1], pp. 362 ff.

7. For most of the remarks contained in Sections 4 and 8, I am indebted to the late S. Leśniewski who developed them in his unpublished lectures in the University of Warsaw (in 1919 and later). However, Leśniewski did not anticipate the possibility of a rigorous development of the theory of truth, and still less of a definition of this notion; hence, while indicating equivalences of the form (T) as premisses in the antinomy of the liar, he did not conceive them as any sufficient conditions for an adequate usage (or definition) of the notion of truth. Also the remarks in Section 8 regarding the occurrence of an empirical premiss in the antinomy of the liar, and the possibility of eliminating this premiss, do not originate with him.

8. In connection with various logical and methodological problems involved in this paper the reader may consult Tarski [6].

9. The antinomy of the liar (ascribed to Eubulides or Epimenides) is discussed here in Sections 7 and 8. For the antinomy of definability (due to J. Richard) see e.g., Hilbert-Bernays [1], Vol. 2, pp. 263 ff.; for the antinomy of heterological terms see Grelling-Nelson [1], p. 307.

10. Due to Professor J. Lukasiewicz (University of Warsaw).

11. This can roughly be done in the following way. Let S be any sentence beginning with the words '*Every sentence.*' We correlate with S a new sentence S^* by subjecting S to the following two modifications: we replace in S the first word, '*Every*,' by '*The*'; and we insert after the second word, '*sentence*,' the whole sentence S enclosed in quotation marks. Let us agree to call the sentence S '(self-)applicable' or 'non-(self-)applicable' dependent on whether the correlated sentence S^* is true or false. Now consider the following sentence:

Every sentence is non-applicable.

It can easily be shown that the sentence just stated must be both applicable and non-applicable; hence a contradiction. It may not be quite clear in what sense this formulation of the antinomy does not involve an empirical premiss; however, I shall not elaborate on this point.

12. The terms 'logic' and 'logical' are used in this paper in a broad sense, which has become almost traditional in the last decades; logic is assumed here to comprehend the whole theory of classes and relations (i.e., the mathematical theory of sets). For many different reasons I am personally inclined to use the term 'logic' in a much narrower sense, so as to apply it only to what is sometimes called 'elementary logic,' i.e., to the sentential calculus and the (restricted) predicate calculus.

13. Cf. here, however, Tarski [3], pp. 5 f.

14. The method of construction we are going to outline can be applied—with appropriate changes—to all formalized languages that are known at the present time; although it does not follow that a language could not be constructed to which this method would not apply.

15. In carrying through this idea a certain technical difficulty arises. A sentential function may contain an arbitrary number of free variables; and the logical nature of the notion of satisfaction varies with this number. Thus, the notion in question when applied to functions with one variable is a binary relation between these functions and single objects; when applied to functions with two variables it becomes a ternary relation between functions and couples of objects; and so on. Hence, strictly speaking, we are confronted, not with one notion of satisfaction, but with infinitely many notions; and it turns out that these notions cannot be defined independently of each other, but must all be introduced simultaneously.

To overcome this difficulty, we employ the mathematical notion of an infinite sequence (or, possibly, of a finite sequence with an arbitrary number of terms). We agree to regard satisfaction, not as a many-termed relation between sentential functions and an indefinite number of objects, but as a binary relation between functions and sequences of objects. Under this assumption the formulation of a general and precise definition of satisfaction no longer presents any difficulty; and a true sentence can now be defined as one which is satisfied by every sequence.

16. To define recursively the notion of satisfaction, we have to apply a certain form of recursive definition which is not admitted in the object-language. Hence the 'essential richness' of the meta-language may simply consist in admitting this type of definition. On the other hand, a general method is known which makes it possible to eliminate all recursive definitions and to replace them by normal, explicit ones. If we try to apply this method to the definition of satisfaction, we see that we have either to introduce into the meta-language variables of a higher logical type than those which occur in the object-language; or else to assume axiomatically in the meta-language the existence of classes that are more comprehensive than all those whose existence can be established in the object-language. See here Tarski [2], pp. 393 ff., and Tarski [5], p. 7.

17. Due to the development of modern logic, the notion of mathematical proof has undergone a far-reaching simplification. A sentence of a given formalized discipline is provable if it can be obtained from the axioms of this discipline by applying certain simple and purely formal rules of inference, such as those of detachment and substitution. Hence to show that all provable sentences are true, it suffices to prove that all the sentences accepted as axioms are true, and that the rules of inference when applied to true sentences yield new true sentences; and this usually presents no difficulty.

On the other hand, in view of the elementary nature of the notion of provability, a precise definition of this notion requires only rather simple logical devices. In most cases, those logical devices which are available in the formalized discipline itself (to which the notion of provability is related) are more than sufficient for this purpose. We know, however, that as regards the definition of truth just the opposite holds. Hence, as a rule, the notions of truth and provability cannot coincide; and since every provable sentence is true, there must be true sentences which are not provable.

18. Thus the theory of truth provides us with a general method for consistency proofs for formalized mathematical disciplines. It can be easily realized, however, that a consistency proof obtained by this method may possess some intuitive value—i.e., may convince us, or strengthen our belief, that the discipline under consideration is actually consistent—only in case we succeed in defining truth in terms of a meta-language which does not contain the object-language as a part (cf. here a

remark in Section 9). For only in this case the deductive assumptions of the meta-language may be intuitively simpler and more obvious than those of the object-language—even though the condition of 'essential richness' will be formally satisfied. Cf. here also Tarski [3], p. 7.

The incompleteness of a comprehensive class of formalized disciplines constitutes the essential content of a fundamental theorem of K. Gödel; cf. Gödel [1], pp. 187 ff. The explanation of the fact that the theory of truth leads so directly to Gödel's theorem is rather simple. In deriving Gödel's result from the theory of truth we make an essential use of the fact that the definition of truth cannot be given in a meta-language which is only as 'rich' as the object-language (cf. note 17); however, in establishing this fact, a method of reasoning has been applied which is very closely related to that used (for the first time) by Gödel. It may be added that Gödel was clearly guided in his proof by certain intuitive considerations regarding the notion of truth, although this notion does not occur in the proof explicitly; cf. Gödel [1], pp. 174 f.

19. The notions of designation and definition lead respectively to the antinomies of Grelling-Nelson and Richard (cf. note 9). To obtain an antinomy for the notion of satisfaction, we construct the following expression:

The sentential function X does not satisfy X.

A contradiction arises when we consider the question whether this expression, which is clearly a sentential function, satisfies itself or not.

20. All notions mentioned in this section can be defined in terms of satisfaction. We can say, e.g., that a given term designates a given object if this object satisfies the sentential function 'x is identical with T' where 'T' stands for the given term. Similarly, a sentential function is said to define a given object if the latter is the only object which satisfies this function. For a definition of consequence see Tarski [4], and for that of synonymity—Carnap [2].

21. General semantics is the subject of Carnap [2]. Cf. here also remarks in Tarski [2], pp. 388 f.

BIBLIOGRAPHY

Only the books and articles referred to in the paper will be listed here.

Aristotle [1].*Metaphysica* (*Works*, Vol. VIII). English translation by W. D. Ross, Oxford, 1908.

Carnap, R. [2]. *Introduction to Semantics*, Cambridge, 1942.

Gödel, K. [1]. 'Über formal unentscheidbare Sätze der *Principia Mathematica* und verwandter Systeme, I,' *Monatshefte für Mathematik und Physik*, Vol. XXXVIII, 1931 pp. 173–198.

Gonseth, F. [1], 'Le Congrès Descartes Questions de Philosophie scientifique,' *Revue thomiste*, Vol. XLIV, 1938, pp. 183–193.

Grelling, K., and Nelson, L. [1]. 'Bemerkungen zu den Paradoxien von Russell und Burali-Forti,' *Abhandlungen der Fries'schen Schule*, Vol. II (new series), 1908, pp. 301–334.

Hilbert, D., and Bernays, P. [1]. *Grundlagen der Mathematik*, 2 vols., Berlin, pp. 1934–1939.

Hofstadter, A. [1]. 'On Semantic Problems,' *The Journal of Philosophy*, Vol. XXXV, 1938, pp. 225–232.

Juhos, B. von. [1]. 'The Truth of Empirical Statements,' *Analysis*, Vol. IV, 1937, pp. 65–70.

Kokoszyńska, M. [1]. 'Über den absoluten Wahrheitsbegriff und einige andere semantische Begriffe,' *Erkenntnis*, 6, 1936, pp 143–165.

Kokoszyńska, M. [2]. 'Syntax, Semantik und Wissenschaftslogik,' *Actes du Congrès International de Philosophie Scientifique*, Vol. III, Paris, 1936, pp. 9–14.

Kotarbiński, T. [1]. *Elementy teorji poznania, logiki formalnej i metodologji nauk* (*Elements of Epistemology, Formal Logic, and the Methodology of Sciences*, in Polish), Lwów, 1929.

Kotarbiński, T. [2]. 'W sprawie pojęcia prawdy' ('Concerning the Concept of Truth,' in Polish), *Przegląd filozoficzny*, Vol. XXXVII, pp. 85–91.

Neurath, O. [1]. 'Erster Internationaler Kongress für Einheit der Wissenschaft in Paris 1935.' *Erkenntnis*, Vol. V, 1935, pp. 377–406.

Russell, B. [1]. *An Inquiry Into Meaning and Truth*. New York, 1940.

Scholz, H. [1]. Review of *Studia philosophica*, Vol. I. *Deutsche Literaturzeitung*, Vol. LVIII, 1937, pp. 1914–1917.

Tarski, A. [1]. 'Sur les ensembles définissables de nombres réels. I.' *Fundamenta mathematicae*, Vol. XVII, 1931, pp. 210–239.

Tarski, A. [2]. 'Der Wahrheitsbegriff in den formalisierten Sprachen.' (German translation of a book in Polish, 1933.) *Studia philosophica*, Vol. I, 1935, pp. 261–405.

Tarski, A. [3]. 'Grundlegung der wissenschaftlichen Semantik.' *Actes du Congrès International de Philosophie Scientifique*, Vol. III, Paris, 1936, pp. 1–8.

Tarski, A. [4]. 'Über den Begriff der logischen Folgerung.' *Actes du Congrès International de Philosophie Scientifique*, Vol. VII, Paris, 1937, pp. 1–11.

Tarski, A. [5]. 'On Undecidable Statements in Enlarged Systems of Logic and the Concept of Truth.' *The Journal of Symbolic Logic*, Vol. IV, 1939, pp. 105–112.

Tarski, A. [6]. *Introduction to Logic*. New York, 1941.

Weinberg, J. [1]. Review of *Studia philosophica*, Vol. I. *The Philosophical Review*, Vol. XLVII, pp. 70–77,

Introduction to Donald Davidson

Before reading this Introduction, I recommend that you read the introductions to Alfred Tarski and to W.V.O. Quine on Ontology.

Donald Davidson was born in Springfield, Massachusetts, in 1917. He studied at Harvard, where he was to meet his greatest intellectual mentor, W.V. Quine. After serving in the U.S. Navy during World War II he returned to Harvard to complete a Ph.D., offering a thesis on Plato's *Philebus*. During the 1950s, he engaged in psychological research involving decision theory. Davidson began publishing relatively late in his career, and over the past three decades has produced scores of papers forming a deeply interconnected pattern of ideas, covering semantics, the logical form of natural language, philosophical psychology, and more. He has taught at Queens' University College NY, Stanford University, Princeton University, Rockefeller University, University of Chicago, and presently teaches at the University of California, Berkeley.

Davidson's views on the relationship between truth and meaning are best approached via Alfred Tarski's work. Tarski showed how one could define truth for a formal or exactly specified language, but he did not believe his theory could be applied to natural languages, for several reasons. First, their semantic closure led to paradoxes, such as the antinomy of the liar; second, they employed intensional idioms, whereas his theory applied only to extensional languages; and third, natural languages were full of structural and semantic vagueness and ambiguity, and thus resisted formal specification.

By contrast, Donald Davidson attempts to apply Tarski's theory to natural languages, or at least to significant parts of them, and holds that a theory of truth for such a language could function as a theory of meaning for it. Davidson is not attempting to *equate* truth with meaning, nor to *reduce* the latter to the former—after all, meaning is an intensional concept, whereas truth is merely extensional. Thus (unlike Paul Grice, for example), he is not offering an *analysis* of the concept of meaning. Rather, he is suggesting that most of what we want from a theory of meaning can be derived from a theory of truth. Davidson has developed this project in a number of papers, most famously in "Truth and Meaning." I will give a brief summary of these results, to prepare the way for an understanding of "Radical Interpretation."

"Theory of meaning" is a term of art for Davidson, so I should define it without further ado. A theory of meaning for a language L must "give the meaning" of each sentence in L. The theory must also be such that anyone who knew the theory would thereby understand L. Finally, it must explain how L is learnable. This last requirement touches on the phenomenon of linguistic creativity. Suppose that L is English. The average L-user can both understand and correctly apply a seemingly unlimited number of sentences. On the other hand, the average L-user has a vocabulary of only several thousand words. Still, from this meager base, she can grasp a multitude of sentences, even in the absence of prior exposure to them. A theory of meaning for L must account for how this is achieved.

Davidson applies formal semantics to natural languages to answer this question. He believes that natural languages must have a compositional structure in order to be learnable. That is, we grasp this infinite number of sentences from a finite base because we can combine and recombine the finite number of words according to a finite set of rules, of which we have an implicit or practical grasp. So a theory of meaning for L will comprise a finite list of axioms giving the reference and satisfaction conditions of L's words, plus rules for how they can be combined to form sentences. As we shall see, these axioms will yield an infinite number of theorems which together will give the meaning of L sentences. This idea that the meaning of a sentence depends on the semantic properties of its constituent parts is compatible with Frege's principle that only within the context of a sentence can a word be a vehicle for communication. In fact, Davidson follows Quine in going further than Frege, and holding the holistic thesis that the *language*, not the sentence, is the primary unit of meaning.

As I said, the idea is that anyone who knew this theory would thereby understand L. That is, knowledge of L's theory of meaning is *sufficient* for an understanding of L. Davidson is careful not to demand that it also be necessary. That is, he is not committed to saying that L-users possess this theory in this particular form.

Davidson's hypothesis is that a theory of meaning for L can take the form of a Tarskian theory of truth for L. Tarski showed how truth-for-L can be defined (for formal languages) by showing how each sentence's truth-conditions are determined by the reference and satisfaction conditions of its parts. Davidson attempts to reverse the picture, and use the theory of truth to serve as a theory of meaning. So now we can say that a theory of meaning for L will comprise a set of axioms stating the referents or satisfaction conditions for L's words, plus syntactic rules for how these can be combined to form sentences. These together entail a set of T-sentences as theorems, which together give the meanings of the sentences of L by stating their truth-conditions in some metalanguage M.

Davidson is not explicit over the precise form of these axioms, but we can assume that it will include the following types (where L is English):

1. Reference conditions, for names and mass terms—for example, "Donald Davidson" refers to Donald Davidson; "snow" refers to snow;
2. Satisfaction conditions, for predicates and relations—for example, "red" is satisfied by red things; $<x,y>$ satisfies "is the father of" iff x is y's father;
3. Axioms telling you how to combine subsentential parts to give L-sentences, and thereby form T-sentences.

Let us now consider these T-sentences in more detail. Given what a theory of meaning is meant to achieve, one might at first think that the theorems should take the following form:

s means that p

where "s" is a description of an L-sentence, and "p" is a meta-language sentence giving its meaning. However, Davidson is committed to working with purely extensional languages, and so suggests replacing the intensional "means that" with the extensional "if." If we do this, and add the as-yet-uninterpreted predicate "T" to complete the theorem, we have

s *is T iff p*

But when we do so, we see that the only candidate for "T" is *truth*. Nothing else can guarantee the co-extensionality of s and p. So now we have

s *is true iff p*,

which, of course, is the form of Tarski's T-sentences.

However, there is one important change. When Tarski devised Convention T, he set it up so that every sentence of L yielded a T-sentence, from which he could define truth-in-L. But to do this for any sentence requires us to already know what s *means*, because to employ Convention T requires us to know that p is either identical to s, or is a translation of it. In other words, Tarski is using the concept of meaning (via the concepts of synonymy or translation) in order to define truth. Since Davidson is doing the opposite—using a theory of truth to explicate a theory of meaning—he must take the mechanisms of Tarski's theory and apply them differently than did Tarski himself. In particular, he cannot take T-sentences as saying that p means the same as, or is a translation of s, since this would be to presuppose the semantic concepts that he's trying to elucidate. It follows that he can't take T-sentences as constituting a definition or explication of the concept of truth. Rather, he must take truth as an explanatory primitive, from which to derive a theory of meaning. A Tarskian theory of truth merely gives the *structure* of a theory of meaning.

Davidson regards a theory of meaning as a testable, empirical theory. It is to be tested against evidence independent of any knowledge of the language under scrutiny. But at this point, one might question how promising Davidson's proposal is. After all, his theorems don't imply any real or causal connection between s and p. They require only that their truth-conditions coincide. But, the objection might continue, how can we then distinguish these two potential T-sentences for "Snow is white"?:

(A) *"Snow is white" is true iff snow is white.*

(B) *"Snow is white" is true iff the Pope is Catholic.*

Davidson is aware of this problem. He does not claim that each T-sentence, taken individually, gives the meaning of its object-language sentence. Nor, contrary to Tarski, does he take "s" as a syntactically simple name for an object-language sentence, but rather as a structured entity, made up of parts each of which will have its own axiom within the theory. Recall that he is offering an axiomatic theory, where theorems are derived from axioms which state the denotative and satisfaction conditions for individual L-words. The choice of T-sentences is thus constrained by the demand for consistent translations of these sub-sentential particles in every utterance in which they appear. To see how this works, consider how a bad theory would be identified. In this example, the object-language is German.

Take two proposed T-sentences:

(1) *"Schnee ist weiss" is true iff grass is green.*

(2) *"Gras ist grun" is true iff snow is white.*

In order to derive these theorems, we would have to assume axioms like the following:

> *"Schnee" refers to grass.*
>
> *"Gras" refers to snow.*
>
> *"Weiss" is satisfied by green things.*
>
> *"Grun" is satisfied by white things.*

But recall that it is not T-sentences, taken individually, that give the meaning of any sentence. It is the entire set of such theorems. That means that any theory offering theorems like 1 and 2 would also contain many other theorems derived from these axioms. We could *test* the theory in the following way: Suppose you had confirmed that "hase" referred to rabbits. You would then expect an L-user to affirm "grun hase" on being confronted with a white rabbit. On the assumption that this response would not be forthcoming, we now have evidence that our theory is wrong.

I will now turn to "Radical Interpretation." Here, Davidson introduces an important qualification: As we have seen, our theory of meaning is to comprise a set of theorems of the form

> *s is true iff p.*

The *evidence* for this theory is the language-users' utterances. To be precise, it consists in what particular persons *hold true* at the specific time and place of the utterance. That is

> *Franz holds "Schnee ist weiss" true at time t_1 and location l_1, and there is white snow at l_1 at t_1;*
>
> *Karl holds "Schnee ist weiss" true at time t_2 and location l_2, and there is white snow at l_2 at t_2.*

These sentences can yield the generalization

> *L-speakers hold "Schnee ist weiss" true in their vicinity iff there is white snow in their vicinity at the time of utterance.*

This, in turn, constitutes evidence for

> *"Schnee ist weiss" is true-in-L iff snow is white.*

However, suppose that Otto affirms "Schnee ist weiss" while indicating white snow. He will do so on two conditions:

1. "Schnee ist weiss" *means* that snow is white.
2. He *believes* that snow is white.

Yet, since all beliefs have to be expressed in language, an interpreter has no independent access to the speaker's beliefs, beyond what he says. This is particularly highlighted in cases of *radical interpretation* (i.e., cases of Quine's "radical translation") where a linguist confronts a culture and a language with no prior knowledge of either. But, given that a speaker's assertion will depend on both the meanings of his words and also his beliefs, how can individual utterances function as evidence for T-sentences?

Davidson's solution is to utilize the *Principle of Charity*. This principle, or family of principles, imposes restrictions on the practice of translation by demanding that we ascribe a set of beliefs to L-users that is largely true. Davidson has been widely misunderstood on this issue, being accused of demanding that they believe exactly what we believe. However, agreement is not an end in itself in translation. The main aim is to make L-users intelligible to us. This would be impossible if we were to attribute too many false, contradictory, or bizarre beliefs. In fact, in some cases, intelligibility will demand that we ascribe ignorance or error to them, if, for example, the alternative is to attribute complex technological beliefs to primitive peoples. Any translation that ruled out the possibility of a speaker being in error would be highly dubious. Davidson has been falsely accused of such a commitment. This is to misunderstand the Principle of Charity. The point is, you would be motivated to ascribe a false belief to a speaker or linguistic community only when you had established to your own satisfaction that the axioms from which the theorem were derived were largely correct. But in that case, you would already have a multitude of other *true* theorems. This is another way of saying that this background of truth is a precondition for the attribution of error.

So, with the Principle of Charity on board, we can test our theory. Our set of axioms and theorems will lead us to predict that an L-user will assent to a certain sentence under certain conditions. If he does, then you have added some confirmation to your theory; if he does not, then a comparable disconfirmation takes place. Davidson agrees with Quine that in such cases there will always be more than one possible way to adjust your theory, but he holds that the Principle of Charity is powerful enough to eliminate many rogue theories.

While Davidson regards a theory of meaning as an empirical, and therefore falsifiable hypothesis, whose determination rests on the Principle of Charity, this principle is not itself an empirical hypothesis. Rather, Davidson regards it as *constitutive* of the concept of belief that one's beliefs will be largely true and consistent.

BIBLIOGRAPHY

Works by Davidson

Davidson's papers from the 1960s to the early 1980s are in two collections:
Essays on Actions and Events (Oxford: Clarendon Press, 1980).

Inquiries into Truth and Interpretation,(Oxford: Clarendon Press, 1984).
Davidson continues to publish widely. One recent notable paper is "The Structure and Content of Truth," *Journal of Philosophy* Vol. 87, 1990.

Further Reading
Two volumes of papers on Davidson's work, including Davidson's replies and good introductions by the editors, are
Actions and Events, ed. Ernest Lepore and Brian McLaughlin (Oxford: Basil Blackwell, 1985).
Truth and Interpretation, ed. Ernest Lepore (Oxford: Basil Blackwell, 1986).
Simon Evnine, *Donald Davidson* (Stanford: Stanford University Press, 1991), is an excellent introduction to all aspects of Davidson's work.
More technical and specialized, but also recommended, is Bjorn T. Ramberg, *Donald Davidson's Philosophy of Language*, (Oxford: Basil Blackwell, 1989).

Radical Interpretation

Donald Davidson

Kurt utters the words 'Es regnet' and under the right conditions we know that he has said that it is raining. Having identified his utterance as intentional and linguistic, we are able to go on to interpret his words: we can say what his words, on that occasion, meant. What could we know that would enable us to do this? How could we come to know it? The first of these questions is not the same as the question what we *do* know that enables us to interpret the words of others. For there may easily be something we could know and don't, knowledge of which would suffice for interpretation, while on the other hand it is not altogether obvious that there is anything we actually know which plays an essential role in interpretation. The second question, how we could come to have knowledge that would serve to yield interpretations, does not, of course, concern the actual history of language acquisition. It is thus a doubly hypothetical question: given a theory that would make interpretation possible, what evidence plausibly available to a potential interpreter would support the theory to a reasonable degree? In what follows I shall try to sharpen these questions and suggest answers.

The problem of interpretation is domestic as well as foreign: it surfaces for speakers of the same language in the form of the question, how can it be determined that the language is the same? Speakers of the same language can go on the assumption that for them the same expressions are to be interpreted in the same way, but this does not indicate what justifies the assumption. All understanding of the speech of another involves radical interpretation. But it will help keep assumptions from going

Donald Davidson, "Radical Interpretation," from *Dialectica*, Vol. 27. Reprinted by permission of Professor Davidson.

unnoticed to focus on cases where interpretation is most clearly called for: interpretation in one idiom of talk in another.[1]

What knowledge would serve for interpretation? A short answer would be, knowledge of what each meaningful expression means. In German, those words Kurt spoke mean that it is raining and Kurt was speaking German. So in uttering the words 'Es regnet', Kurt said that it was raining. This reply does not, as might first be thought, merely restate the problem. For it suggests that in passing from a description that does not interpret (his uttering of the words 'Es regnet') to interpreting description (his saying that it is raining) we must introduce a machinery of words and expressions (which may or may not be exemplified in actual utterances), and this suggestion is important. But the reply is no further help, for it does not say what it is to know what an expression means.

There is indeed also the hint that corresponding to each meaningful expression that is an entity, its meaning. This idea, even if not wrong, has proven to be very little help: at best it hypostasizes the problem.

Disenchantment with meanings as implementing a viable account of communication or interpretation helps explain why some philosophers have tried to get along without, not only meanings, but any serious theory at all. It is tempting, when the concepts we summon up to try to explain interpretation turn out to be more baffling than the explanandum, to reflect that after all verbal communication consists in nothing more than elaborate disturbances in the air which form a causal link between the non-linguistic activities of human agents. But although interpretable speeches are nothing but (that is, identical with) actions performed with assorted non-linguistic intentions (to warn, control, amuse, distract, insult), and these actions are in turn nothing but (identical with) intentional movements of the lips and larynx, this observation takes us no distance towards an intelligible general account of what we might know that would allow us to redescribe uninterpreted utterances as the right interpreted ones.

Appeal to meanings leaves us stranded further than we started from the non-linguistic goings-on that must supply the evidential base for interpretation; the 'nothing but' attitude provides no clue as to how the evidence is related to what it surely is evident for.

Other proposals for bridging the gap fall short in various ways. The 'causal' theories of Ogden and Richards and of Charles Morris attempted to analyse the meaning of sentences, taken one at a time, on the basis of behaviouristic data. Even if these theories had worked for the simplest sentences (which they clearly did not), they did not touch the problem of extending the method to sentences of greater complexity and abstractness. Theories of another kind start by trying to connect words rather than sentences with non-linguistic facts. This is promising because words are finite in number while sentences are not, and yet each sentence is no more than a concatenation of words: this offers the chance of a theory that interprets each of an infinity of sentences using only finite resources. But such theories fail to reach the evidence, for it seems clear that the semantic features of words cannot be explained directly on the basis of

---

[1] The term 'radical interpretation' is meant to suggest strong kinship with Quine's 'radical translation'. Kinship is not identity, however, and 'interpretation' in place of 'translation' marks one of the differences: a greater emphasis on the explicitly semantical in the former.

non-linguistic phenomena. The reason is simple. The phenomena to which we must turn are the extra-linguistic interests and activities that language serves, and these are served by words only in so far as the words are incorporated in (or on occasion happen to be) sentences. But then there is no chance of giving a foundational account of words before giving one of sentences.

For quite different reasons, radical interpretation cannot hope to take as evidence for the meaning of a sentence an account of the complex and delicately discriminated intentions with which the sentence is typically uttered. It is not easy to see how such an approach can deal with the structural, recursive feature of language that is essential to explaining how new sentences can be understood. But the central difficulty is that we cannot hope to attach a sense to the attribution of finely discriminated intentions independently of interpreting speech. The reason is not that we cannot ask necessary questions, but that interpreting an agent's intentions, his beliefs and his words are parts of a single project, no part of which can be assumed to be complete before the rest is. If this is right, we cannot make the full panoply of intentions and beliefs the evidential base for a theory of radical interpretation.

We are now in a position to say something more about what would serve to make interpretation possible. The interpreter must be able to understand any of the infinity of sentences the speaker might utter. If we are to state explicitly what the interpreter might know that would enable him to do this, we must put it in finite form.[2] If this requirement is to be met, any hope of a universal method of interpretation must be abandoned. The most that can be expected is to explain how an interpreter could interpret the utterances of speakers of a single language (or a finite number of languages): it makes no sense to ask for a theory that would yield an explicit interpretation for any utterance in any (possible) language.

It is still not clear, of course, what it is for a theory to yield an explicit interpretation of an utterance. The formulation of the problem seems to invite us to think of the theory as the specification of a function taking utterances as arguments and having interpretations as values. But then interpretations would be no better than meanings and just as surely entities of some mysterious kind. So it seems wise to describe what is wanted of the theory without apparent reference to meanings or interpretations: someone who knows the theory can interpret the utterances to which the theory applies.

The second general requirement on a theory of interpretation is that it can be supported or verified by evidence plausibly available to an interpreter. Since the theory is general—it must apply to a potential infinity of utterances—it would be natural to think of evidence in its behalf as instances of particular interpretations recognized as correct. And this case does, of course, arise for the interpreter dealing with a language he already knows. The speaker of a language normally cannot produce an explicit finite theory for his own language, but he can test a proposed theory since he can tell whether it yields correct interpretations when applied to particular utterances.

---

[2] See Donald Davidson, "Theories of Meaning and Learnable Languages," in Davidson, *Inquiries into Truth and Interpretation*, (Oxford: Clarendon Press, 1984).

In radical interpretation, however, the theory is supposed to supply an understanding of particular utterances that is not given in advance, so the ultimate evidence for the theory cannot be correct sample interpretations. To deal with the general case, the evidence must be of a sort that would be available to someone who does not already know how to interpret utterances the theory is designed to cover: it must be evidence that can be stated without essential use of such linguistic concepts as meaning, interpretation, synonymy, and the like.

Before saying what kind of theory I think will do the trick, I want to discuss a last alternative suggestion, namely that a method of translation, from the language to be interpreted into the language of the interpreter, is all the theory that is needed. Such a theory would consist in the statement of an effective method for going from an arbitrary sentence of the alien tongue to a sentence of a familiar language; thus it would satisfy the demand for a finitely stated method applicable to any sentence. But I do not think a translation manual is the best form for a theory of interpretation to take.[3]

When interpretation is our aim, a method of translation deals with a wrong topic, a relation between two languages, where what is wanted is an interpretation of one (in another, of course, but that goes without saying since any theory is in some language). We cannot without confusion count the language used in stating the theory as part of the subject matter of the theory unless we explicitly make it so. In the general case, a theory of translation involves three languages: the object language, the subject language, and the metalanguage (the languages from and into which translation proceeds, and the language of the theory, which says what expressions of the subject language translate which expressions of the object language). And in this general case, we can know which sentences of the subject language translate which sentences of the object language without knowing what any of the sentences of either language mean (in any sense, anyway, that would let someone who understood the theory interpret sentences of the object language). If the subject language happens to be identical with the language of the theory, then someone who understands the theory can no doubt use the translation manual to interpret alien utterances; but this is because he brings to bear two things he knows and that the theory does not state: the fact that the subject language is his own, and his knowledge of how to interpret utterances in his own language.

It is awkward to try to make explicit the assumption that a mentioned sentence belongs to one's own language. We could try, for example, '"Es regnet" in Kurt's language is translated as "It is raining" in mine', but the indexical self-reference is out of place in a theory that ought to work for any interpreter. If we decide to accept this difficulty, there remains the fact that the method of translation leaves tacit and beyond the reach of theory what we need to know that allows us to interpret our own

---

[3] The idea of a translation manual with appropriate empirical constraints as a device for studying problems in the philosophy of language is, of course, Quine's. This idea inspired much of my thinking on the present subject, and my proposal is in important respects very close to Quine's. Since Quine did not intend to answer the questions I have set, the claim that the method of translation is not adequate as a solution to the problem of radical interpretation is not a criticism of any doctrine of Quine's.

language. A theory of translation must read some sort of structure into sentences, but there is no reason to expect that it will provide any insight into how the meanings of sentences depend on their structure.

A satisfactory theory for interpreting the utterances of a language, our own included, will reveal significant semantic structure: the interpretation of utterances of complex sentences will systematically depend on the interpretation of utterances of simpler sentences, for example. Suppose we were to add to a theory of translation a satisfactory theory of interpretation for our own language. Then we would have exactly what we want, but in an unnecessarily bulky form. The translation manual churns out, for each sentence of the language to be translated, a sentence of the translator's language; the theory of interpretation then gives the interpretation of these familiar sentences. Clearly the reference to the home language is superfluous; it is an unneeded intermediary between interpretation and alien idiom. The only expressions a theory of interpretation has to mention are those belonging to the language to be interpreted.

A theory of interpretation for an object language may then be viewed as the result of the merger of a structurally revealing theory of interpretation for a known language, and a system of translation from the unknown language into the known. The merger makes all reference to the known language otiose; when this reference is dropped, what is left is a structurally revealing theory of interpretation for the object language—couched, of course, in familiar words. We have such theories, I suggest, in theories of truth of the kind Tarski first showed how to give.[4]

What characterizes a theory of truth in Tarski's style is that it entails, for every sentence s of the object language, a sentence of the form:

s is true (in the object language) if and only if p.

Instances of the form (which we shall call T-sentences) are obtained by replacing 's' by a canonical description of s, and 'p' by a translation of s. The important undefined semantical notion in the theory is that of *satisfaction* which relates sentences, open or closed, to infinite sequences of objects, which may be taken to belong to the range of the variables of the object language. The axioms, which are finite in number, are of two kinds: some give the conditions under which a sequence satisfies a complex sentence on the basis of the conditions of satisfaction of simpler sentences, others give the conditions under which the simplest (open) sentences are satisfied. Truth is defined for closed sentences in terms of the notion of satisfaction. A recursive theory like this can be turned into an explicit definition along familiar lines, as Tarski shows, provided the language of the theory contains enough set theory; but we shall not be concerned with this extra step.

Further complexities enter if proper names and functional expressions are irreducible features of the object language. A trickier matter concerns indexical devices. Tarski was interested in formalized languages containing no indexical or demonstrative aspects. He could therefore treat sentences as vehicles of truth; the extension of the theory to utterances is in this case trivial. But natural languages are

---

[4] A. Tarski, 'The Concept of Truth in Formalized Languages' in his *Logic, Semantics, Metamathematics*, 2nd ed., ed. J.H. Woodger (Indianapolis: Hackett, 1983).

indispensably replete with indexical features, like tense, and so their sentences may vary in truth according to time and speaker. The remedy is to characterize truth for a language relative to a time and a speaker. The extension to utterances is again straightforward.[5]

What follows is a defence of the claim that a theory of truth, modified to apply to a natural language, can be used as a theory of interpretation. The defence will consist in attempts to answer three questions:

1. Is it reasonable to think that a theory of truth of the sort described can be given for a natural language?
2. Would it be possible to tell that such a theory was correct on the basis of evidence plausibly available to an interpreter with no prior knowledge of the language to be interpreted?
3. If the theory were known to be true, would it be possible to interpret utterances of speakers of the language?

The first question is addressed to the assumption that a theory of truth can be given for a natural language: the second and third questions ask whether such a theory would satisfy the further demands we have made on a theory of interpretation.

1. CAN A THEORY OF TRUTH BE GIVEN FOR A NATURAL LANGUAGE?

It will help us to appreciate the problem to consider briefly the case where a significant fragment of a language (plus one or two semantical predicates) is used to state its own theory of truth. According to Tarski's Convention T, it is a test of the adequacy of a theory that it entails all the T-sentences. This test apparently cannot be met without assigning something very much like a standard quantificational form to the sentences of the language, and appealing, in the theory, to a relational notion of satisfaction.[6] But the striking thing about T-sentences is that whatever machinery must operate to produce them, and whatever ontological wheels must turn, in the end a T-sentence states the truth conditions of a sentence using resources no richer than, because the same as, those of the sentence itself. Unless the original sentence mentions possible worlds, intensional entities, properties, or propositions, the statement of its truth conditions does not.

There is no equally simple way to make the analogous point about an alien language without appealing, as Tarski does, to an unanalysed notion of translation. But what we can do for our own language we ought to be able to do for another; the problem, it will turn out, will be to know that we are doing it.

The restriction imposed by demanding a theory that satisfies Convention T seems to be considerable: there is no generally accepted method now known for deal-

---

[5] For a discussion of how a theory of truth can handle demonstratives and how Convention T must be modified, see S. Weinstein, 'Truth and Demonstratives', *Nous*, 8 (1974).

[6] See J. Wallace, 'On the Frame of Reference,' *Synthese*, 22 (1970); and Donald Davidson, "True to the Facts," in Davidson op. cit.

ing, within the restriction, with a host of problems, for example, sentences that attribute attitudes, modalities, general causal statements, counterfactuals, attributive adjectives, quantifiers like 'most', and so on. On the other hand, there is what seems to me to be fairly impressive progress. To mention some examples, there is the work of Tyler Burge on proper names,[7] Gilbert Harman on 'ought',[8] John Wallace on mass terms and comparatives,[9] and there is my own work on attributions of attitudes and performatives,[10] on adverbs, events, and singular causal statements,[11] and on quotation.[12]

If we are inclined to be pessimistic about what remains to be done (or some of what has been done!), we should think of Frege's magnificent accomplishment in bringing what Dummett calls 'multiple generality' under control.[13] Frege did not have a theory of truth in Tarski's sense in mind, but it is obvious that he sought, and found, structures of a kind for which a theory of truth can be given.

The work of applying a theory of truth in detail to a natural language will in practice almost certainly divide into two stages. In the first stage, truth will be characterized, not for the whole language, but for a carefully gerrymandered part of the language. This part, though no doubt clumsy grammatically, will contain an infinity of sentences which exhaust the expressive power of the whole language. The second part will match each of the remaining sentences to one or (in the case of ambiguity) more than one of the sentences for which truth has been characterized. We may think of the sentences to which the first stage of the theory applies as giving the logical form, or deep structure, of all sentences.

2. CAN A THEORY OF TRUTH BE VERIFIED BY APPEAL TO EVIDENCE AVAILABLE BEFORE INTERPRETATION HAS BEGUN?

Convention T says that a theory of truth is satisfactory if it generates a T-sentence for each sentence of the object language. It is enough to demonstrate that a theory of truth is empirically correct, then, to verify that the T-sentences are true (in practice, an adequate sample will confirm the theory to a reasonable degree). T-sentences mention only the closed sentences of the language, so the relevant evidence can consist entirely of facts about the behaviour and attitudes of speakers in relation to sentences (no doubt by way of utterances). A workable theory must, of course, treat sentences as concatenations of expressions of less than sentential length, it must introduce semantical notions like satisfaction and reference, and it must appeal to an ontology of sequences and the objects ordered by the sequences. All this apparatus is properly viewed as theoretical construction, beyond the reach of direct verification. It has done

---

[7] T. Burge, 'Reference and Proper Names,' *Journal of Philosophy*, 70 (1973).

[8] G. Harman, 'Moral Relativism Defended,' *Philosophical Review*, 84 (1975).

[9] J. Wallace, 'Positive, Comparative, Superlative,' *Journal of Philosophy*, 69 (1972).

[10] D. Davidson, "On Saying That" and "Modes of Performances," in Davidson, op. cit.

[11] D. Davidson "The Logical Form of Action Sentences," "Causal Relations," "The Individuation of Events," "Events as Particulars," "Eternal *vs*. Ephemeral Events," in Davidson, *Essays on Actions* and *Events*, (Oxford: Clarendon Press, 1980).

[12] D. Davidson "Quotation," in Davidson, *Inquiries into Truth and Interpretation*, op. cit.

[13] M. Dummett, *Frege: Philosophy of Language*, (Cambridge: Harvard University Press, 1973).

its work provided only it entails testable results in the form of T-sentences, and these make no mention of the machinery. A theory of truth thus reconciles the demand for a theory that articulates grammatical structure with the demand for a theory that can be tested only by what it says about sentences.

In Tarski's work, T-sentences are taken to be true because the right branch of the biconditional is assumed to be a translation of the sentence truth conditions for which are being given. But we cannot assume in advance that correct translation can be recognized without pre-empting the point of radical interpretation; in empirical applications, we must abandon the assumption. What I propose is to reverse the direction of explanation: assuming translation, Tarski was able to define truth; the present idea is to take truth as basic and to extract an account of translation or interpretation. The advantages, from the point of view of radical interpretation, are obvious. Truth is a single property which attaches, or fails to attach, to utterances, while each utterance has its own interpretation; and truth is more apt to connect with fairly simple attitudes of speakers.

There is no difficulty in rephrasing Convention T without appeal to the concept of translation: an acceptable theory of truth must entail, for every sentence *s* of the object language, a sentence of the form: *s* is true if and only if *p*, where '*p*' is replaced by any sentence that is true if and only if *s* is. Given this formulation, the theory is tested by evidence that T-sentences are simply true; we have given up the idea that we must also tell whether what replaces '*p*' translates *s*. It might seem that there is no chance that if we demand so little of T-sentences, a theory of interpretation will emerge. And of course this would be so if we took the T-sentences in isolation. But the hope is that by putting appropriate formal and empirical restrictions on the theory as a whole, individual T-sentences will in fact serve to yield interpretations.[14]

We have still to say what evidence is available to an interpreter—evidence, we now see, that T-sentences are true. The evidence cannot consist in detailed descriptions of the speaker's beliefs and intentions, since attributions of attitudes, at least where subtlety is required, demand a theory that must rest on much the same evidence as interpretation. The interdependence of belief and meaning is evident in this way: a speaker holds a sentence to be true because of what the sentence (in his language) means, and because of what he believes. Knowing that he holds the sentence to be true, and knowing the meaning, we can infer his belief; given enough information about his beliefs, we could perhaps infer the meaning. But radical interpretation should rest on evidence that does not assume knowledge of meanings or detailed knowledge of beliefs.

A good place to begin is with the attitude of holding a sentence true, of accepting it as true. This is, of course, a belief, but it is a single attitude applicable to all sentences, and so does not ask us to be able to make finely discriminated distinctions among beliefs. It is an attitude an interpreter may plausibly be taken to be able to identify before he can interpret, since he may know that a person intends to express a truth in uttering a sentence without having any idea *what* truth. Not that sincere assertion is the only reason to suppose that a person holds a sentence to be true. Lies, com-

---

14 D. Davidson, "Truth and Meaning," in Davidson, op. cit., footnote 11.

mands, stories, irony, if they are detected as attitudes, can reveal whether a speaker holds his sentences to be true. There is no reason to rule out other attitudes towards sentences, such as wishing true, wanting to make true, believing one is going to make true, and so on, but I am inclined to think that all evidence of this kind may be summed up in terms of holding sentences to be true.

Suppose, then, that the evidence available is just that speakers of the language to be interpreted hold various sentences to be true at certain times and under specified circumstances. How can this evidence be used to support a theory of truth? On the one hand, we have T-sentences, in the form:

(T) 'Es regnet' is true-in-German when spoken by x at time t if and only if it is raining near x at t.

On the other hand, we have the evidence, in the form:

(E) Kurt belongs to the German speech community and Kurt holds true 'Es regnet' on Saturday at noon and it is raining near Kurt on Saturday at noon.

We should, I think, consider (E) as evidence that (T) is true. Since (T) is a universally quantified conditional, the first step would be to gather more evidence to support the claim that:

(GE) $(x)(t)$ (if x belongs to the German speech community then (x holds true 'Es regnet' at t if and only if it is raining near x at t)).

The appeal to a speech community cuts a corner but begs no question: speakers belong to the same speech community if the same theories of interpretation work for them.

The obvious objection is that Kurt, or anyone else, may be wrong about whether it is raining near him. And this is of course a reason for not taking (E) as conclusive evidence for (GE) or for (T); and a reason not to expect generalizations like (GE) to be more than generally true. The method is rather one of getting a best fit. We want a theory that satisfies the formal constraints on a theory of truth, and that maximizes agreement, in the sense of making Kurt (and others) right, as far as we can tell, as often as possible. The concept of maximization cannot be taken literally here, since sentences are infinite in number, and anyway once the theory begins to take shape it makes sense to accept intelligible error and to make allowance for the relative likelihood of various kinds of mistake.[15]

The process of devising a theory of truth for an unknown native tongue might in crude outline go as follows. First we look for the best way to fit our logic, to the extent required to get a theory satisfying Convention T, on to the new language; this may mean reading the logical structure of first-order quantification theory (plus identity) into the language, not taking the logical constants one by one, but treating this much of logic as a grid to be fitted on to the language in one fell swoop. The evidence

---

[15] D. Davidson, "Belief and the Basis of Meaning," "Thought and Talk," and "Reply to Foster" in Davidson, op. cit.

here is classes of sentences always held true or always held false by almost everyone almost all of the time (potential logical truths) and patterns of inference. The first step identifies predicates, singular terms, quantifiers, connectives, and identity; in theory, it settles matters of logical form. The second step concentrates on sentences with indexicals; those sentences sometimes held true and sometimes false according to discoverable changes in the world. This step in conjunction with the first limits the possibilities for interpreting individual predicates. The last step deals with the remaining sentences, those on which there is not uniform agreement, or whose held truth value does not depend systematically on changes in the environment.[16]

This method is intended to solve the problem of the interdependence of belief and meaning by holding belief constant as far as possible while solving for meaning. This is accomplished by assigning truth conditions to alien sentences that make native speakers right when plausibly possible, according, of course, to our own view of what is right. What justifies the procedure is the fact that disagreement and agreement alike are intelligible only against a background of massive agreement. Applied to language, this principle reads: the more sentences we conspire to accept or reject (whether or not through a medium of interpretation), the better we understand the rest, whether or not we agree about them.

The methodological advice to interpret in a way that optimizes agreement should not be conceived as resting on a charitable assumption about human intelligence that might turn out to be false. If we cannot find a way to interpret the utterances and other behaviour of a creature as revealing a set of beliefs largely consistent and true by our own standards, we have no reason to count that creature as rational, as having beliefs, or as saying anything.

Here I would like to insert a remark about the methodology of my proposal. In philosophy we are used to definitions, analyses, reductions. Typically these are intended to carry us from concepts better understood, or clear, or more basic epistemologically or ontologically, to others we want to understand. The method I have suggested fits none of these categories. I have proposed a looser relation between concepts to be illuminated and the relatively more basic. At the centre stands a formal theory, a theory of truth, which imposes a complex structure on sentences containing the primitive notions of truth and satisfaction. These notions are given application by the form of the theory and the nature of the evidence. The result is a partially interpreted theory. The advantage of the method lies not in its free-style appeal to the notion of evidential support but in the idea of a powerful theory interpreted at the most advantageous point. This allows us to reconcile the need for a semantically articulated structure with a theory testable only at the sentential level. The more subtle gain is that

---

[16] Readers who appreciate the extent to which this account parallels Quine's account of radical translation in Chapter 2 of *Word and Object* will also notice the differences: the semantic constraint in my method forces quantificational structure on the language to be interpreted, which probably does not leave room for indeterminacy of logical form; the notion of stimulus meaning plays no role in my method, but its place is taken by reference to the objective features of the world which alter in conjunction with changes in attitude towards the truth of sentences; the principle of charity, which Quine emphasizes only in connection with the identification of the (pure) sentential connectives, I apply across the board.

very thin evidence in support of each of a potential infinity of points can yield rich results, even with respect to the points. By knowing only the conditions under which speakers hold sentences true, we can come out, given a satisfactory theory, with an interpretation of each sentence. It remains to make good on this last claim. The theory itself at best gives truth conditions. What we need to show is that if such a theory satisfies the constraints we have specified, it may be used to yield interpretations.

3. IF WE KNOW THAT A THEORY OF TRUTH SATISFIES THE FORMAL AND EMPIRICAL CRITERIA DESCRIBED, CAN WE INTERPRET UTTERANCES OF THE LANGUAGE FOR WHICH IT IS A THEORY?

A theory of truth entails a T-sentence for each sentence of the object language, and a T-sentence gives truth conditions. It is tempting, therefore, simply to say that a T-sentence 'gives the meaning' of a sentence. Not, of course, by naming or describing an entity that is a meaning, but simply by saying under what conditions an utterance of the sentence is true.

But on reflection it is clear that a T-sentence does not give the meaning of the sentence it concerns: the T-sentences does fix the truth value relative to certain conditions, but it does not say the object language sentence is true *because* the conditions hold. Yet if truth values were all that mattered, the T-sentence for 'Snow is white' could as well say that it is true if and only if grass is green or $2 + 2 = 4$ as say that it is true if and only if snow is white. We may be confident, perhaps, that no satisfactory theory of truth will produce such anomalous T-sentences, but this confidence does not license us to make more of T-sentences.

A move that might seem helpful is to claim that it is not the T-sentence alone, but the canonical proof of a T-sentence, that permits us to interpret the alien sentence. A canonical proof, given a theory of truth, is easy to construct, moving as it does through a string of biconditionals, and requiring for uniqueness only occasional decisions to govern left and right precedence. The proof does reflect the logical form the theory assigns to the sentence, and so might be thought to reveal something about meaning. But in fact we would know no more than before about how to interpret if all we knew was that a certain sequence of sentences was the proof, from some true theory, of a particular T-sentence.

A final suggestion along these lines is that we can interpret a particular sentence provided we know a correct theory of truth that deals with the language of the sentence. For then we know not only the T-sentence for the sentence to be interpreted, but we also 'know' the T-sentences for all other sentences; and of course, all the proofs. Then we would see the place of the sentence in the language as a whole, we would know the role of each significant part of the sentence, and we would know about the logical connections between this sentence and others.

If we knew that a T-sentence satisfied Tarski's Convention T, we would know that it was true, and we could use it to interpret a sentence because we would know that the right branch of the biconditional translated the sentence to be interpreted. Our present trouble springs from the fact that in radical interpretation we cannot assume that a T-sentence satisfies the translation criterion. What we have been overlooking, however, is that we have supplied an alternative criterion: this criterion is that the totality of T-sentences should (in the sense described above) optimally fit evidence about sentences held true by native speakers. The present idea is that what Tarski assumed outright for each T-sentence can be indirectly elicited by a holistic constraint. If that constraint is adequate, each T-sentence will in fact yield an acceptable interpretation.

A T-sentence of an empirical theory of truth can be used to interpret a sentence, then, provided we also know the theory that entails it, and know that it is a theory that meets the formal and empirical criteria.[17] For if the constraints are adequate, the range of acceptable theories will be such that any of them yields some correct interpretation for each potential utterance. To see how it might work, accept for a moment the absurd hypothesis that the constraints narrow down the possible theories to one, and this one implies the T-sentence (T) discussed previously. Then we are justified in using this T-sentence to interpret Kurt's utterance of 'Es regnet' as his saying that it is raining. It is not likely, given the flexible nature of the constraints, that all acceptable theories will be identical. When all the evidence is in, there will remain, as Quine has emphasized, the trade-offs between the beliefs we attribute to a speaker and the interpretations we give his words. But the resulting indeterminacy cannot be so great but that any theory that passes the tests will serve to yield interpretations.

---

[17] Davidson, "Truth and Meaning," footnote 2 and "Reply to Foster," in Davidson, op. cit.

CHAPTER 9

Reference and Essence

Introduction to Saul Kripke

Saul Kripke was born in 1940 in New York, and raised in Omaha, Nebraska. His first publication, "A Completeness Theorem in Modal Logic," appeared when he was only eighteen. He first achieved fame as a logician by developing a semantics for modal logic, thereby rehabilitating that sub-discipline. He studied at Harvard and Oxford Universities. For the past two decades, he has been McCosh Professor of Philosophy at Princeton, prior to which he taught at Rockefeller University.

This article, and the longer *Naming and Necessity*, which deals with the same issues, is a transcription of lectures given without notes. As with much of Kripke's work, the ideas had occurred to him many years before (1963 in this case) and had attained a legendary reputation prior to their eventual publication.

Starting from what seems to be a relatively technical and local problem in philosophical logic, Kripke draws many far-reaching and revolutionary consequences in metaphysics, philosophy of mind, philosophy of science, and philosophy of language. The question Kripke begins with is "How are contingent identity statements possible?" This way of phrasing the question is to assume that there are such statements, and this is what Kripke will deny. His argument goes like this: Take any case in which x is identical to y. He follows Leibniz in saying that x and y will have all properties in common. Thus, if x has some property F, so does y. Now x possesses the property of *self-identity*—that is, x is necessarily identical with itself. But then, if y is identical to x, and thus shares all x's properties, then y also has the property of being necessarily identical with x. In other words, if x is identical with y, then it is necessarily identical with y. All identities are necessary identities, and so no true statement can express a contingent identity. As Kripke notes, this goes against the popular assumption of innumerable contingent identities. He considers three types of such statements:

1. Those involving different definite descriptions; for example *The First Postmaster General of the United States is identical with the inventor of bifocals.*

2. Those involving two different ordinary names (which he calls "proper names"), for example *Hesperus is Phosphorus.*

3. "Theoretical identifications," for example *Heat is molecular motion.*

Let us begin with the first type. Now it is a contingent fact that Franklin actually took that job, or that he invented those spectacles. That is, it is a contingent fact that the world turned out such that the same man answers to both descriptions. Second, the fact that both descriptions are true of the same man is an empirically discoverable fact. Kripke grants all this, yet he argues that it does not affect the crucial point that given that the person who actually was the first postmaster general (i.e., Benjamin Franklin) is identical with the person who actually invented bifocals (Franklin again), then this identification holds necessarily. To deny it would amount to the claim that Benjamin Franklin might not have been himself.

Let us turn now to the case of identity statements involving names. As with the previous case, one reason for thinking that "Hesperus is Phosphorus" is contingent is that it is an a posteriori discovery. Kripke denies that "a posteriori" and "contingent" are synonymous terms, or that they are even co-extensive. The a priori/a posteriori distinction concerns the acquisition of knowledge in the actual world; the necessary/contingent distinction concerns how the world might have been. They are two separate distinctions, with entirely different functions—one epistemological, the other metaphysical.

Kripke argues that "Hesperus is Phosphorus," if true, is necessarily true. To show this, he introduces the distinction between rigid and nonrigid designators. A *rigid designator* is an expression that designates the same thing in all possible worlds in which the expression refers at all. (For Kripke, "possible worlds" are just counterfactual situations, possible ways that this world might have been.) A nonrigid designator, by contrast, can refer to different things in different counterfactual cases. Kripke argues that ordinary names are rigid designators. Most descriptions are nonrigid (an exception would be "the square root of 25"). So, given that "Hesperus" and "Phosphorus" do, in fact, refer to the same thing, then they do so in all possible worlds.

Kripke appeals to the intuitions underlying linguistic usage to determine whether or not an expression is a rigid designator. The "test" is merely to employ the expression in a counterfactual context, then see whether we would say that it referred to what it actually refers to or to something else. For example, if I say "Nixon might have been a Democrat," it is clear that I am talking about the very same Nixon who was in fact a Republican. Without such an assumption, the sense and import of the statement is completely lost. On the other hand, consider a statement like "The thirty-seventh President might have been a Democrat." This can be interpreted in two ways. When taken as a *de re* claim about the person who was in fact elected to that office—that is, as a claim that *he* might have been a Democrat—then it is about Nixon. However, when interpreted as a *de dicto* claim, namely that the statement "The thirty-seventh President was a Democrat" could have turned out true, then the description can pick out any number of persons in different counterfactual situations; for example, Hubert Humphrey, had he defeated Nixon in the 1968 election, or Robert Kennedy, had he not been murdered.

Kripke takes such considerations to refute Russell's claim that ordinary names are definite descriptions in disguise. If Russell were right, then a name and the description synonymous with it would have identical logical properties. But, as we have just seen, while "Nixon" is a rigid designator, the description "thirty-seventh President" could designate a variety of persons, in distinct counterfactual situations. The point extends to virtually all descriptions associated with Nixon. (The exception would be those mentioning his essential properties, which I will discuss shortly.)

Another diagnosis of resistance to the claim that identity statements are necessary is a failure to recognize that the claim that a name is a rigid designator is restricted to the way in which the word functions in a particular language. Of course there could be possible worlds with different word-world relations, such that, say, "Phosphorus" was our name for Mars. Then, in the language of that world, "Hesperus is Phosphorus" is false, since Venus is not Mars. Likewise, it could have happened that the orbit of Venus had altered such that some other body be located at that particular set of spatio-temporal coordinates in fact occupied by Venus (i.e., Phosphorus), and that we would then call that particular body "Phosphorus." Again, in that possible world, the identity statement "Hesperus is Phosphorus" is false, but only because we are using the name "Phosphorus" to stand for something else. To use such considerations to derive the claim that "Hesperus is Phosphorus" (as *we* use the terms) is contingent is to make the mistake of identifying the meaning of "Phosphorus" with a contingent property; that is, of being in a certain point of the sky at a particular time. We may use a certain description—for example, "the body located at a certain place at a certain time" to "fix the reference" of a term—but once that is done, the name is not synonymous with that description, nor does it stand for whatever fits that description in any given counterfactual situation. It stands for what is actually picked out by it.

In *Naming and Necessity*, Kripke offers other arguments to show that names are not synonymous with definite descriptions. We can interpret description theories in two ways: First as saying that the *meaning* of a name is synonymous with some descriptive phrase, or set of such expressions. Second, we can take it as saying that such descriptions determine the reference of a name— that is, in any given situation, actual or counterfactual, the name stands for whoever satisfies the description *in that situation*. Kripke denies both claims. As regarding the latter, he grants that in some cases a description can "fix the reference" of a name, but says that the name stands for *that actual person or thing,* even in counterfactual cases in which it does not satisfy that description.

Suppose we take "the discoverer of the incompleteness theorem" as the description synonymous with the name "Gödel." It would follow that Gödel is whoever made that mathematical discovery. But suppose researchers were to uncover evidence that the discovery had been made by someone else, Schmidt, whose work Gödel had passed off as his own. In that case, we would have to say that "Gödel proved the incompleteness of arithmetic" was a *true statement about Schmidt.* But Kripke would say that it is intuitively obvious that we would say that it has been discovered to be a false statement, but one about Gödel.

Next, consider a case in which everything we commonly associate with the bearer of a name is false, and where nobody fits the description. Kripke gives the example of Jonah. The only candidate for a description corresponding to this name is "the guy who was swallowed by a whale." Now it is almost certainly false that anyone was swallowed by a whale, and who survived to tell the tale. But, by the description theory, it would follow that "Jonah" was a nonreferring expression. Likewise, it would mean that "Jonah wasn't swallowed by a whale" could not be true of Jonah. As Kripke convincingly argues, it is a perfectly coherent possibility that there was a real person called Jonah, leading a normal life, about whom this strange story grew.

One of the assumptions of the description theory, whether in Frege's or Russell's versions, is that someone understands and uses a name correctly by virtue of possessing certain identifying information about the bearer of that name. That is, first, the claim that the referent of a name is determined by some description or "mode of presentation," associated in the user's mind with that name and, second, that one cannot understand or correctly apply that name without this information. Kripke denies both claims.

First, Kripke argues that one can understand a name and use it correctly without any identifying descriptions. Take "Albert Einstein." The description that most of us would associate with this name is "discoverer of Relativity Theory." However, this description contains a name, "Relativity Theory." Unless we are extremely well informed, the only description we could apply to this name is "The theory that Einstein discovered." Since this is obviously circular, it would seem that most of us can neither understand nor correctly apply the name "Albert Einstein." Kripke takes this to be a reductio ad absurdum of the descriptive theory: Given that we clearly do understand this name, this fact shows that we do so when in ignorance of supposed "identifying knowledge." In a closely related point, he argues that we can still use the name to refer to Einstein when we associate that name with false descriptions. For example, if all you believed about Einstein was that he invented the atomic bomb, you would still be referring to Einstein, not Oppenheimer, by the use of that name.

In *Naming and Necessity,* Kripke points out that his criticism of classical description theories equally extends to John Searle's "cluster theory," whereby a name stands for whoever satisfies *most of* a set of identifying descriptions, but where no one particular description is necessary. Kripke convincingly argues that it is just as possible that *all* such descriptions be false as it is that *any* one be false. In such a case, the old problems for the descriptive theory reappear.

After separating the a priori/a posteriori and the necessary/contingent distinctions, Kripke briefly touches on one of his most controversial theses, namely that objects have essential properties—that is, properties that that thing could not but have. With regard to individual persons, Kripke argues for the *necessity of origin* — that each person has the essential property of having developed from the union of that sperm and that ovum, as produced from those particular parents. As regards material objects, such as tables, he argues that it is essential to that table that it be made of the particular matter it is constituted of. As with rigid designators, intuition is the final court of appeal in deciding whether or not some property is essential or accidental. Take our old friend Nixon again. Suppose that we wanted to know whether it was essential to Nixon that he was the son of his actual parents. Consider a counterfactual case in which Nixon's parents never met, but there arose someone qualitatively identical to the actual Nixon, who lived a life exactly similar to Nixon's—for example, he was named "Richard Nixon," became the thirty-seventh President, resigned after Watergate, and so forth. For Kripke, it is intuitively clear that we would say that this person was not Nixon—merely someone extremely like him. By contrast, consider a possible world in which the person who developed from the egg and the sperm which, in the actual world, became Nixon. Suppose that this man devoted his life to civil liberties and was active against the Vietnam War. In such a case, Kripke would say, we have Nixon, leading a very different life.

I will now briefly describe Kripke's own positive view of the semantics of names, again developed in *Naming and Necessity*. Kripke's theory is called the "Causal Theory of Reference." The basic idea is remarkably simple. A name is introduced into a language when someone decides to name a particular thing or object, either via a formal ceremony, such as a baptism or birth certificate, or informally, as when I buy a cat and start calling him "Bob." As a result of my practice, linguistically competent witnesses (i.e., who understand the conventions of naming) will come to use the name "Bob" to refer to the cat. All future use of the name will designate the same thing, since this use will be connected back to the original dubbing by "causal chains of designation." Thus, while I have never met Kripke, my use of "Saul Kripke" designates Saul Kripke because it ultimately traces back to him by a chain, running through our linguistic community, back to the time in which Rabbi and Mrs. Kripke chose to call their newborn son "Saul."

I will finally turn to theoretical identifications, such as "heat is molecular motion." As before, Kripke argues that these are necessary but a posteriori. We may falsely take this statement to be contingent by identifying heat with a nonessential property, (that is, of producing sensations of heat in us), then by generating hypothetical cases in which such sensations are produced in the absence of molecular motion, and concluding that their possible divergence proves that their identification cannot be necessary.

In *Naming and Necessity*, Kripke extends these considerations to discuss "natural kinds" in general, and put forward the thesis that their essential properties are not phenomenal, but microstructural. So fool's gold is not gold, despite looking like gold; conversely, anything with atomic number 79 would be gold, whatever it looks like. Likewise, what makes something a tiger is not that it resembles a large carnivorous striped feline, but that it possesses certain genes.

However, Kripke argues that the necessity of identity goes against the mind-brain identity theory. Type-identity theorists explicitly modeled their hypothesis on theoretical identifications such as "heat is molecular motion." To Kripke, they are disanalogous. In the latter cases, we can separate the "true nature" of heat (i.e., empirically discovered to be mean kinetic molecular energy) and heat as it appears to us, that is, as a sensation. However, such a distinction cannot be made in the case of a sensation like pain, because the essential properties of sensations are irreducibly subjective. There is no distinction between having a pain and seeming to have one. However, it seems quite possible that pains be present (as picked out by their feel) yet brain processes be absent. But this possibility is sufficient to preclude their identification. Take any sensation A, and any brain process B. Kripke takes A and B to be rigid designators, like all terms in theoretical identifications. It will be an essential property of A that it has a subjective feel; it will be an essential property of B that it be of some particular physical type. Kripke goes along with the "Cartesian intuition" that it be possible that A occur in the absence of B, or vice versa. It is incumbent on the identity theorist to either show that this intuition is false or unpersuasive. If Kripke's argument succeeds, it rules out any identification between the mental and the physical.

BIBLIOGRAPHY

Works by Kripke

Kripke's two books are
Naming and Necessity (Oxford: Basil Blackwell, 1980).
Wittgenstein on Rules and Private Language (Oxford: Basil Blackwell, 1982).

Important articles include
"Semantical Considerations on Modal Logic." *Acta Philosophica Fennica 16* (also in L. Linsky, *Reference and Modality* [Oxford: Oxford University Press, 1971]).
"Outline of a Theory of Truth," *Journal of Philosophy*, 1975
"Is There a Problem about Substitutional Quantification?" in G. Evans and J. McDowell, *Truth and Meaning*, (Oxford: Oxford University Press, 1976).
"Speaker's Reference and Semantic Reference," in P. French, T. Uehling, and H. Wettstein, *Contemporary Perspectives in the Philosophy of Language*, (Minneapolis: University of Minnesota Press, 1977).
"A Puzzle about Belief," in A. Margalit, *Meaning and Use*, (Dordrecht: D. Reidel, 1979).

Further Reading

A good introduction to the debates between causal and descriptive theories of reference can be found in M. Devitt and K. Sterelny, *Language and Reality* (Oxford: Basil Blackwell, 1987). See also the introductions to and selections by Frege and Russell in this book.
For the cluster theory, see John Searle, "Proper Names," *Mind*, Vol. 67.

Identity and Necessity[1]

Saul Kripke

A problem which has arisen frequently in contemporary philosophy is: 'How are *contingent* identity statements possible?' This question is phrased by analogy with the way Kant phrased his question 'How are synthetic *a priori* judgments possible?' In both cases, it has usually been taken for granted, in the one case by Kant that synthetic *a priori* judgements were possible, and in the other case in contemporary philosophical literature, that contingent statements of identity are possible. I do not intend to deal with the Kantian question except to mention this analogy: After a rather thick book was written trying to answer the question how synthetic *a priori* judgements were possible, others came along later who claimed that the solution to the problem was that synthetic *a priori* judgements were, of course, impossible and that a book trying to show otherwise was written in vain. I will not discuss who was right on the possibility of synthetic *a priori* judgements. But in the case of contingent statements of identity, most philosophers have felt that the notion of a contingent identity statement ran into something like the following paradox. An argument like the following can be given against the possibility of contingent identity statements:

First, the law of the substitutivity of identity says that, for any objects x and y, if x is identical to y, then if x has a certain property F, so does y:

(1) $(x)(y)[(x = y) \supset (Fx \supset Fy)]$

On the other hand, every object surely is necessarily self-identical:

(2) $(x) \, \Box \, (x = x)$

But

(3) $(x) \, (y) \, (x = y) \supset [\, \Box \, (x = x) \supset \Box \, (x = y)]$

is a substitution instance of (1), the substitutivity law. From (2) and (3), we can conclude that, for every x and y, if x equals y, then, it is necessary that x equals y:

(4) $(x) \, (y) \, ((x = y) \supset \Box \, (x = y))$

This is because the clause $\Box \, (x = x)$ of the conditional drops out because it is known to be true.

This is an argument which has been stated many times in recent philosophy. Its conclusion, however, has often been regarded as highly paradoxical. For example, David Wiggins, in his paper, 'Identity-Statements', says,

> Now there undoubtedly exist contingent identity-statements. Let $a = b$ be one of them. From its simple truth and (5) [= (4) above] we can derive '$\Box(a = b)$'. But how then can there be any contingent identity statements?[2]

He then says that five various reactions to this argument are possible, and rejects all of these reactions, and reacts himself. I do not want to discuss all the possible reactions to this statement, except to mention the second of those Wiggins rejects. This says,

> We might accept the result and plead that provided 'a' and 'b' are proper names nothing is amiss. The consequence of this is that no contingent identity-statements can be made by means of proper names.

And then he says that he is discontented with this solution and many other philosophers have been discontented with this solution, too, while still others have advocated it.

What makes the statement (4) seem surprising? It says, for any objects x and y, if x is y, then it is necessary that x is y. I have already mentioned that someone might object to this argument on the grounds that premise (2) is already false, that it is not the case that everything is necessarily self-identical. Well, for example, am I myself necessarily self-identical? Someone might argue that in some situations which we can imagine I would not even have existed and therefore the statement 'Saul Kripke is Saul Kripke' would have been false or it would not be the case that I was self-identical. Perhaps, it would have been neither true nor false, in such a world, to say that Saul Kripke is self-identical. Well, that may be so, but really it depends on one's philosophical view of a topic that I will not discuss, that is, what is to be said about truth values of statements mentioning objects that do not exist in the actual world or any given possible world or counterfactual situation. Let us interpret necessity here weakly. We can count statements as necessary if whenever the objects mentioned therein exist, the statement would be true. If we wished to be very careful about this, we would have to go into the question of existence as a predicate and ask if the statement can be reformulated in the form: For every x it is necessary that, if x exists, then x is self-identical. I will not go into this particular form of subtlety here because it is not going to be relevant to my main theme. Nor am I really going to consider formula (4). Anyone who believes formula (2) is, in my opinion, committed to formula (4). If x and y are the same things and we can talk about modal properties of an object at all, that is, in the usual parlance, we can speak of modality *de re* and an object *necessarily* having certain properties as such, then formula (1), I think, has to hold. Where x is any property at all, including a property involving modal operators, and if x and y are the same object and x had a certain property F, then y has to have the same property F. And this is so even if the property F is itself of the form of necessarily having some other property G, in particular that of necessarily being identical to a certain object. Well, I will not discuss the formula (4) itself because by itself it does not assert, of any particular true statement of identity, that it is necessary. It does not say anything about *statements* at all. It says for every *object x* and *object y*, if *x* and *y* are the same object, then it is necessary that *x* and *y* are the same object. And this, I think, if we think about it (anyway, if someone does not think so, I will not argue for it here), really amounts to something very little different from the statement (2). Since *x*, by definition of identity, is the only object identical with *x*, '$(y)(y = x \supset Fy)$' seems to me to be little more than a garrulous way of saying 'Fx', and thus $(x)(y)(y = x \supset Fx)$ says the same as $(x)Fx$ no matter what 'F' is—in particular, even if 'F' stands for the property of necessary identity with x. So if *x* has this property (of necessary identity with *x*), trivially everything identical with *x* has it, as (4) asserts. But, from statement (4) one may apparently be able to deduce various particular statements of identity must be necessary and this is then supposed to be a very paradoxical consequence.

Wiggins says, 'Now there undoubtedly exist contingent identity statements.' One example of a contingent identity statement is the statement that the first Postmaster General of the United States is identical with the inventor of bifocals, or that both of these are identical with the man claimed by the *Saturday Evening Post* as its founder (*falsely* claimed, I gather, by the way). Now some such statements are plainly contingent. It plainly is a contingent fact that one and the same man both invented bifocals and took on the job of Postmaster General of the United States. How can we reconcile this with the truth of statement (4)? Well, that, too, is an issue I do not want to go into in detail except to be very dogmatic about it. It was I think settled quite well by Bertrand Russell in his notion of the scope of a description. According to Russell, one can, for example, say with propriety that the author of *Hamlet* might not have written '*Hamlet*', or even that the author of *Hamlet* might not have been the author of '*Hamlet*'. Now here, of course, we do not deny the necessity of the identity of an object with itself; but we say it is true concerning a certain man that he in fact was the unique person to have written '*Hamlet*' and secondly that the man, who in fact was the man who wrote '*Hamlet*', might not have written '*Hamlet*'. In other words, if Shakespeare had decided not to write tragedies, he might not have written '*Hamlet*'. Under these circumstances, the man who in fact wrote '*Hamlet*' would not have written '*Hamlet*'. Russell brings this out by saying that in such a statement, the first occurrence of the description 'the author of "*Hamlet*"' has large scope.[3] That is, we say 'The author of "*Hamlet*" has the following property: that he might not have written "*Hamlet*"'. We *do not* assert that the following statement might have been the case, namely that the author of '*Hamlet*' did not write '*Hamlet*', for that is not true. That would be to say that it might have been the case that someone wrote '*Hamlet*' and yet did not write '*Hamlet*', which would be a contradiction. Now, aside from the details of Russell's particular formulation of it, which depends on his theory of descriptions, this seems to be the distinction that any theory of descriptions has to make. For example, if someone were to meet the President of Harvard and take him to be a Teaching Fellow, he might say: 'I took the President of Harvard for a Teaching Fellow'. By this he does not mean that he took the proposition 'The President of Harvard is a Teaching Fellow' to be true. He could have meant this, for example, had he believed that some sort of democratic system had gone so far at Harvard that the President of it decided to take on the task of being a Teaching Fellow. But that probably is not what he means.

What he means instead, as Russell points out, is 'Someone is President of Harvard and I took him to be a Teaching Fellow'. In one of Russell's examples someone says, 'I thought your yacht is much larger than it is'. And the other man replies, 'No, my yacht is not much larger than it is'.

Provided that the notion of modality *de re*, and thus of quantifying into modal contexts, makes any sense at all, we have quite an adequate solution to the problem of avoiding paradoxes if we substitute descriptions for the universal quantifiers in (4) because the only consequence we will draw,[4] for example, in the bifocals case, is that there is a man who both happened to have invented bifocals and happened to have been the first Postmaster General of the United States, and is necessarily self-identical. There is an object *x* such that *x* invented bifocals, and as a matter of contingent fact an object *y*, such that *y* is the first Postmaster General of the United States, and finally, it is necessary, that *x* is *y*. What are *x* and *y* here? Here, *x* and *y* are both Benjamin Franklin, and it can certainly be necessary that Benjamin Franklin is identical with himself. So, there is no problem in the case of descriptions if we accept Russell's notion of scope.[5] And I just dogmatically want to drop that question here and go on to the question about names which Wiggins raises. And Wiggins says he might accept the result and plead that, provided *a* and *b* are proper names, nothing is amiss. And then he rejects this.

Now what is the special problem about proper names? At least if one is not familiar with the philosophical literature about this matter, one naïvely feels something like the following about proper names. First, if someone says 'Cicero was an orator', then he uses the name 'Cicero' in that statement simply to pick out a certain object and then to ascribe a certain property to the object, namely, in this case, he ascribes to a certain man the property of having been an orator. If someone else uses another name, such as say 'Tully', he is still speaking about the same man. One ascribes the same property, if one says 'Tully is an orator', to the same man. So to speak, the fact, or state of affairs, represented by the statement is the same whether one says 'Cicero is an orator' or one says 'Tully is an orator'. It would, therefore, seem that the function of names is *simply* to refer, and not to describe the objects so named by such properties as 'being the inventor of bifocals' or 'being the first Postmaster General'. It would seem that Leibniz's law and the law (1) should not only hold in the universally quantified form, but also in the form 'if *a* = *b* and *Fa*, then *Fb*', wherever '*a*' and '*b*' stand in place of names and '*F*' stands in place of a predicate expressing a genuine property of the object:

$$(a = b \cdot Fa) \supset Fb$$

We can run the same argument through again to obtain the conclusion where '*a*' and '*b*' replace any names, 'if *a* = *b*, then necessarily *a* = *b*'. And so, we could venture this conclusion: that whenever '*a*' and '*b*' are proper names, if *a* is *b*, that it is necessary that *a* is *b*. Identity statements between proper names have to be necessary if they are going to be true at all. This view in fact has been advocated, for example, by Ruth Barcan Marcus in a paper of hers on the philosophical interpretation of modal logic.[6] According to this view, whenever, for example, someone makes a correct statement of identity between two names, such as, for example, that Cicero is Tully, his statement has to be necessary if it is true. But such a conclusion *seems* plainly to be false. (I, like other philosophers, have a habit of understatement in which 'it seems plainly false' means 'it is plainly false'. Actually, I think the view is true, though not quite in the form defended by Mrs Marcus.) At any rate, it seems plainly false. One example was given by Professor Quine in his reply to Professor Marcus at the symposium: 'I think I see trouble anyway in the contrast between proper names and descriptions as Professor Marcus draws it. The paradigm of the assigning of proper names is tagging. We may tag the planet Venus some fine evening with the proper name "Hesperus". We may tag the same planet again someday before sunrise with the proper name "Phosphorus".' (Quine thinks that something like that actually was done once.) 'When, at last, we discover that we have tagged the same planet twice, our discovery is empirical, and not because the proper names were descriptions.' According to what we are told, the planet Venus seen in the morning was originally thought to be a star and was called 'the Morning Star', or (to get rid of any question of using a description) was called 'Phosphorus'. One and the same planet, when seen in the evening, was thought to be another star, the Evening Star, and was called 'Hesperus'. Later on, astronomers discovered that Phosphorus and Hesperus were one and the same. Surely no amount of *a priori* ratiocination on their part could conceivably have made it possible for them to deduce that Phosphorus is Hesperus. In fact, given the information they had, it might have turned out the other way. Therefore, it is argued, the statement 'Hesperus is Phosphorus' has to be an ordinary contingent, empirical truth, one which might have come out otherwise, and so the view that true identity statements between names are necessary has to be false. Another example which Quine gives in *Word and Object* is taken from Professor Schrödinger, the famous pioneer of quantum mechanics: A certain mountain can be seen from both Tibet and Nepal. When seen from one direction it was called 'Gaurisanker'; when seen from another direction, it was called 'Everest'; and then, later on, the empirical discovery was made that Gaurisanker *is* Everest. (Quine further says that he gathers the example is actually geographically incorrect. I guess one should not rely on physicists for geographical information.)

Of course, one possible reaction to this argument is to deny that names like 'Cicero', 'Tully', 'Gaurisanker', and 'Everest' really are proper names. Look, someone might say (someone has said it: his name was 'Bertrand Russell'), just because statements like 'Hesperus is Phosphorus' and 'Gaurisanker is Everest' are contingent, we can see that the names in question are not really purely referential. You are not, in Mrs Marcus's phrase, just 'tagging' an object; you are actually describing it. What does the contingent fact that Hesperus is Phosphorus amount to? Well, it amounts to the fact that *the* star in a certain portion of the sky in the evening is *the* star in a certain portion of the sky in the morning. Similarly, the contingent fact that Gaurisanker is Everest amounts to the fact that the mountain viewed from such and such an angle in Nepal is the mountain viewed from such and such another angle in Tibet. Therefore, such names as 'Hesperus' and 'Phosphorus' can only be abbreviations for descriptions. The term 'Phosphorus' *has* to mean 'the star seen ... ', or (let us be cautious because it actually turned out not to be a star), 'the *heavenly body* seen from such and such a position at such and such a time in the morning', and the name 'Hesperus' has to mean 'the heavenly body seen in such and such a position at such and such a time in the evening'. So, Russell concludes, if we want to reserve the term 'name' for things which really just name an object without describing it, the only real proper names we can have are names of our own immediate sense data, objects of our own 'immediate acquaintance'. The only such names which occur in language are demonstratives like 'this' and 'that'. And it is easy to see that this requirement of necessity of identity, understood as exempting identities between names from all imaginable doubt, can indeed be guaranteed only for demonstrative names of immediate sense data; for only in such cases can an identity statement between two different names have a general immunity from Cartesian doubt. There are some other things Russell has sometimes allowed as objects of acquaintance, such as one's self; we need not go into details here. Other philosophers (for example, Mrs Marcus in her reply, at least in the verbal discussion as I remember it—I do not know if this got into print, so perhaps this should not be 'tagged' on her[7]) have said, 'If names are really just tags, genuine tags, then a good dictionary should be able to tell us that they are names of the same object.' You have an object *a* and an object *b* with names 'John' and 'Joe'. Then, according to Mrs Marcus, a dictionary should be able to tell you whether or not 'John' and 'Joe' are names of the same object. Of course, I do not know what ideal dictionaries should do, but ordinary proper names do not seem to satisfy this requirement. You certainly *can*, in the case of ordinary proper names, make quite empirical discoveries that, let's say, Hesperus is Phosphorus, though we thought otherwise. We can be in doubt as to whether Gaurisanker is Everest or Cicero is in fact Tully. Even now, we could conceivably discover that we were wrong in supposing that Hesperus was Phosphorus. Maybe the astronomers made an error. So it seems that this view is wrong and that if by a name we do not mean some artificial notion of names such as Russell's, but a proper name in the ordinary sense, then there can be contingent identity statements using proper names, and the view to the contrary seems plainly wrong.

In recent philosophy a large number of other identity statements have been emphasized as examples of contingent identity statements, different, perhaps, from either of the types I have mentioned before. One of them is, for example, the statement 'Heat is the motion of molecules'. First, science is supposed to have discovered this. Empirical scientists in their investigations have been supposed to discover (and, I suppose, they did) that the external phenomenon which we call 'heat' is, in fact, molecular agitation. Another example of such a discovery is that water is H_2O, and yet other examples are that gold is the element with such and such an atomic number, that light is a stream of photons, and so on. These are all in some sense of 'identity statement' identity statements. Second, it is thought, they are plainly contingent identity statements, just because they were scientific discoveries. After all, heat might have turned out not to have been the motion of molecules. There were other alternative theories of heat proposed, for example, the caloric theory of heat. If these theories of heat had been correct, then heat would not have been the motion of molecules, but instead, some substance suffusing the hot object, called 'caloric'. And it was a matter of course of science and not of any logical necessity that the one theory turned out to be correct and the other theory turned out to be incorrect.

So, here again, we have, apparently, another plain example of a contingent identity statement. This has been supposed to be a very important example because of its connection with the mind–body problem. There have been many philosophers who have wanted to be materialists, and to be materialists in a particular form, which is known today as 'the identity theory'. According to this theory, a certain mental state, such as a person's being in pain, is identical with a certain state of his brain (or, perhaps, of his entire body, according to some theorists), at any rate, a certain material or neural state of his brain or body. And so, according to this theory, my being in pain at this instant, if I were, would be identical with my body's being or my brain's being in a certain state. Others have objected that this cannot be, because, after all, we can imagine my pain existing even if the state of the body did not. We can perhaps imagine my not being embodied at all and still being in pain, or, conversely, we could imagine my body existing and being in the very same state even if there were no pain. In fact, conceivably, it could be in this state even though there were no mind 'back of it', so to speak, at all. The usual reply has been to concede that all of these things might have been the case, but to argue that these are irrelevant to the question of the identity of the mental state and the physical state. This identity, it is said, is just another contingent scientific identification, similar to the identification of heat with molecular motion, or water with H_2O. Just as we can imagine heat without any molecular motion, so we can imagine a mental state without any corresponding brain state. But, just as the first fact is not damaging to the identification of heat and the motion of molecules, so the second fact is not at all damaging to the identification of a mental state with the corresponding brain state. And so, many recent philosophers have held it to be very important for our theoretical understanding of the mind–body problem that there can be contingent identity statements of this form.

To state finally what *I* think, as opposed to what seems to be the case, or what others think, I think that in both cases, the case of names and the case of the theoretical identifications, the identity statements are necessary and not contingent. That is to say, they are necessary if *true*; of course, false identity statements are not necessary. How can one possibly defend such a view? Perhaps I lack a complete answer to this question, even though I am convinced that the view is true. But to begin an answer, let me make some distinctions that I want to use. The first is between a *rigid* and a *nonrigid designator*. What do these terms mean? As an example of a nonrigid designator, I can give an expression such as 'the inventor of bifocals'. Let us suppose it was Benjamin Franklin who invented bifocals, and so the expression, 'the inventor of bifocals', designates or refers to a certain man, namely, Benjamin Franklin. However, we can easily imagine that the world could have been different, that under different circumstances someone else would have come upon this invention before Benjamin Franklin did, and in that case, *he* would have been the inventor of bifocals. So, in this sense, the expression 'the inventor of bifocals' is nonrigid: Under certain circumstances one man would have been the inventor of bifocals; under other circumstances, another man would have. In contrast, consider the expression 'the square root of 25'. Independently of the empirical facts, we can give an arithmetical proof that the square root of 25 is in fact the number 5, and because we have proved this mathematically, what we have proved is necessary. If we think of numbers as entities at all, and let us suppose, at least for the purpose of this lecture, that we do, then the expression 'the square root of 25' necessarily designates a certain number, namely 5. Such an expression I call 'a *rigid* designator'. Some philosophers think that anyone who even uses the notions of rigid or nonrigid designator has already shown that he has fallen into a certain confusion or has not paid attention to certain facts. What do I mean by 'rigid designator'? I mean a term that designates the same object in all possible worlds. To get rid of one confusion which certainly is not mine, I do not use 'might have designated a different object' to refer to the fact that language might have been used differently. For example, the expression 'the inventor of bifocals' might have been used by inhabitants of this planet always to refer to the man who corrupted Hadleyburg. This would have been the case, if, first, the people on this planet had not spoken English, but some other language, which phonetically overlapped with English; and if, second, in that language the expression 'the inventor of bifocals' meant the 'man who corrupted Hadleyburg'. Then it would refer, of course, in their language, to whoever in fact corrupted Hadleyburg in this counterfactual situation. That is not what I mean. What I mean by saying that a description might have referred to something different, I mean that in *our* language as *we* use it in describing a counterfactual situation, there might have been a different object satisfying the descriptive conditions *we* give for reference. So, for example, we use the phrase 'the inventor of bifocals', when we are talking about another possible world or a counterfactual situation, to refer to whoever in that counterfactual situation would have invented bifocals, not to the person whom people *in* that counterfactual situation would have called 'the inventor of bifocals'. *They* might have spoken a different language which phonetically overlapped with English in which 'the inventor of bifocals' is used in some other way. I am *not* concerned with that question here. For that matter, they might have been deaf and dumb, or there might have been no people at all. (There still could have been an inventor of bifocals even if there were no people—God, or Satan, will do.)

Second, in talking about the notion of a rigid designator, I do not mean to imply that the object referred to has to exist in all possible worlds, that is, that it has to necessarily exist. Some things, perhaps mathematical entities such as the positive integers, if they exist at all, necessarily exist. Some people have held that God both exists and necessarily exists; others, that he contingently exists; others, that he contingently fails to exist; and others, that he necessarily fails to exist:[8] all four options have been tried. But at any rate, when I use the notion of rigid designator, I do not imply that the object referred to necessarily exists. All I mean is that in any possible world where the object in question *does* exist, in any situation where the object *would* exist, we use the designator in question to designate that object. In a situation where the object does not exist, then we should say that the designator has no referent and that the object in question so designated does not exist.

As I said, many philosophers would find the very notion of rigid designator objectionable *per se*. And the objection that people make may be stated as follows: Look, you're talking about situations which are counterfactual, that is to say, you're talking about other possible worlds. Now these worlds are completely disjoint, after all, from the actual world which is not just another possible world; it is the actual world. So, before you talk about, let us say, such an object as Richard Nixon in another possible world at all, you have to say which object in this other possible world would *be* Richard Nixon. Let us talk about a situation in which, as *you* would say, Richard Nixon would have been a member of SDS. Certainly the member of SDS you are talking about is someone very different in many of his properties from Nixon. Before we even can say whether this man would have been Richard Nixon or not, we have to set up criteria of identity across possible worlds. Here are these other possible worlds. There are all kinds of objects in them with different properties from those of any actual object. Some of them resemble Nixon in some ways, some of them resemble Nixon in other ways. Well, which of these objects is Nixon? One has to give a criterion of identity. And this shows how the very notion of rigid designator runs in a circle. Suppose we designate a certain number as the number of planets. Then, if that is our favourite way, so to speak, of designating this number, then in any other possible worlds we will have to identify whatever number is the number of planets with the number 9, which in the actual world is the number of planets. So, it is argued by various philosophers, for example, implicitly by Quine, and explicitly by many others in his wake, we cannot really ask whether a designator is rigid or nonrigid because we first need a criterion of identity across possible worlds. An extreme view has even been held that, since possible worlds are so disjoint from our own, we cannot really say that any object in them is the *same* as an object existing now but only that there are some objects which resemble things in the actual world, more or less. We, therefore, should not really speak of what would have been true of Nixon in another possible world but, only of what 'counterparts' (the term which David Lewis uses[9]) of Nixon there would have been. Some people in other possible worlds have dogs whom they call 'Checkers'. Others favour the A B M but do not have any dog called Checkers. There are various people who resemble Nixon more or less, but none of them can really be said to be Nixon; they are only *counterparts* of Nixon, and you choose which one is the best counterpart by noting which resembles Nixon the most closely, according to your favourite criteria. Such views are widespread, both among the defenders of quantified modal logic and among its detractors.

All of this talk seems to me to have taken the metaphor of possible worlds much too seriously in some way. It is as if a 'possible world' were like a foreign country, or distant planet way out there. It is as if we see dimly through a telescope various actors on this distant planet. Actually David Lewis's view seems the most reasonable if one takes this picture literally. No one far away on another planet can be strictly identical with someone here. But, even if we have some marvellous methods of transportation to take one and the same person from planet to planet, we really need some epistemological criteria of identity to be able to say whether someone on this distant planet is the same person as someone here.

All of this seems to me to be a totally misguided way of looking at things. What it amounts to is the view that counterfactual situations have to be described purely qualitatively. So, we cannot say, for example, 'If Nixon had only given a sufficient bribe to Senator X, he would have got Carswell through' because that refers to certain people, Nixon and Carswell, and talks about what things would be true of them in a counterfactual situation. We must say instead 'If a man who has a hairline like such and such, and holds such and such political opinions had given a bribe to a man who was a senator and had such and such other qualities, then a man who was a judge in the South and had many other qualities resembling Carswell would have been confirmed.' In other words, we must describe counterfactual situations purely qualitatively and then ask the question, 'Given that the situation contains people or things with such and such qualities, which of these people is (or is a counterpart of) Nixon, which is Carswell, and so on?' This seems to me to be wrong. Who is to prevent us from saying 'Nixon might have got Carswell through had he done certain things'? We are speaking of *Nixon* and asking what, in certain counterfactual situations, would have been true of *him*. We can say that if Nixon had done such and such, he would have lost the election to Humphrey. Those I am opposing would argue, 'Yes, but how do you find out if the man you are talking about is in fact Nixon?' It would indeed be very hard to find out, if you were looking at the whole situation through a telescope, but that is not what we are doing here. Possible worlds are not something to which an epistemological question like this applies. And if the phrase 'possible worlds' is what makes anyone think some such question applies, he should just *drop* this phrase and use some other expression, say 'counterfactual situation', which might be less misleading. If we say 'If Nixon had bribed such and such a Senator, Nixon would have got Carswell through', what is *given* in the very description of that situation is that it is a situation in which we are speaking of Nixon, and of Carswell, and of such and such a Senator. And there seems to be no less objection to *stipulating* that we are speaking of certain *people* than there can be objection to stipulating that we are speaking of certain *qualities*. Advocates of the other view take speaking of certain qualities as unobjectionable. They do not say, 'How do we know that this quality (in another possible world) is that of redness?' But they do find speaking of certain *people* objectionable. But I see no more reason to object in the one case than in the other. I think it really comes from the idea of possible worlds as existing out there, but very far off, viewable only through a special telescope. Even more objectionable is the view of David Lewis. According to Lewis, when we say 'Under certain circumstances Nixon would have gotten Carswell through', we really mean 'Some man, other than Nixon but closely resembling him, would have got some judge, other than Carswell but closely resembling him, through'. Maybe that is so, that some man closely resembling Nixon could have got some man closely resembling Carswell through. But *that* would not comfort either Nixon or Carswell, nor would it make Nixon kick himself and say '*I* should have done such and such to get Carswell through'. The question is whether under certain circumstances Nixon *himself* could have got *Carswell* through. And I think the objection is simply based on a misguided picture.

Instead, we can perfectly well talk about rigid and nonrigid designators. Moreover, we have a simple, intuitive test for them. We can say, for example, that the number of planets might have been a different number from the number it in fact is. For example, there might have been only seven planets. We can say that the inventor of bifocals might have been someone other than the man who *in fact* invented bifocals.[10] We cannot say, though, that the square root of 81 might have been a different number from the number it in fact is, for that number just has to be 9. If we apply this intuitive test to proper names, such as for example 'Richard Nixon', they would seem intuitively to come out to be rigid designators. First, when we talk even about the counterfactual situation in which we suppose Nixon to have done different things, we assume we are still talking about Nixon himself. We say, 'If Nixon had bribed a certain Senator, he would have got Carswell through' and we assume that by 'Nixon' and

'Carswell' we are still referring to the very same people as in the actual world. And it seems that we cannot say 'Nixon might have been a different man from the man he in fact was', unless, of course, we mean it metaphorically: He might have been a different *sort* of person (if you believe in free will and that people are not inherently corrupt). You might think the statement true in that sense, but Nixon could not have been in the other literal sense a different person from the person he, in fact, is, even though the thirty-seventh President of the United States might have been Humphrey. So the phrase 'the thirty-seventh President' is nonrigid, but 'Nixon', it would seem, is rigid.

Let me make another distinction before I go back to the question of identity statements. This distinction is very fundamental and also hard to see through. In recent discussion, many philosophers who have debated the meaningfulness of various categories of truths, have regarded them as identical. Some of those who identify them are vociferous defenders of them, and others, such as Quine, say they are all identically meaningless. But usually they're not distinguished. These are categories such as 'analytic', 'necessary', '*a priori*', and sometimes even 'certain'. I will not talk about all of these but only about the notions of *a prioricity* and necessity. Very often these are held to be synonyms. (Many philosophers probably should not be described as holding them to be synonyms; they simply *use* them interchangeably.) I wish to distinguish them. What do we mean by calling a statement *necessary*? We simply mean that the statement in question, first, is true, and, second, that it could not have been otherwise. When we say that something is *contingently* true, we mean that, though it is in fact the case, it could have been the case that things would have been otherwise. If we wish to assign this distinction to a branch of philosophy, we should assign it to metaphysics. To the contrary, there is the notion of an *a priori truth*. An *a priori* truth is supposed to be one which can be *known* to be true independently of all experience. Notice that this does not in and of itself say anything about all possible worlds, unless this is put into the definition. All that it says is that it can be known to be true of the actual world, independently of all experience. It may, by some philosophical argument, follow from our knowing, independently of experience, that something is true of the actual world, that it has to be known to be true also of all possible worlds. But if this is to be established, it requires some philosophical argument to establish it. Now, *this* notion, if we were to assign it to a branch of philosophy, belongs, not to metaphysics, but to epistemology. It has to do with the way we can know certain things to be in fact true. Now, it may be the case, of course, that anything which is necessary is something which *can* be known *a priori*. (Notice, by the way, the notion *a priori* truth as thus defined has in it *another* modality: it *can* be known independently of all experience. It is a little complicated because there is a double modality here.) It will not have time to explore these notions in full detail here, but one thing we can see from the outset is that these two notions are by no means trivially the same. If they are coextensive, it takes some philosophical argument to establish it. As stated, they belong to different domains of philosophy. One of them has something to do with *knowledge*, with what can be known in certain ways about the *actual* world. The other one has to do with *metaphysics*, how the world *could* have been; given that it is the way it is, could it have been otherwise, in certain ways? Now I hold, as a matter of fact, that neither class of statements is contained in the other. But, all we need to talk about here is this: Is everything that is necessarily knowable *a priori* or known *a priori*? Consider the following example: the Goldbach conjecture. This says that every even number is the sum of two primes. It is a mathematical statement and if it is true at all, it has to be necessary. Certainly, one could not say that though in fact every even number is the sum of two primes, there could have been some extra number which was even and not the sum of two primes. What would that mean? On the other hand, the answer to the question whether every even number *is* in fact the sum of two primes is unknown, and we have no method at present for deciding. So we certainly do not know, *a priori* or even *a posteriori*, that every even number is the sum of two primes. (Well, perhaps we have some evidence in that no counterexample has been found.) But we certainly do not know *a priori* anyway, that every even number is, in fact, the sum of two primes. But, of course, the definition just says '*can* be known independently of experience' and someone might say that if it is true, we *could* know it independently of experience. It is hard to see exactly what this claim means. It might be so. One thing it might mean is that if it were true we could *prove* it. This claim is certainly wrong if it is generally applied to mathematical statements and we have to work within some fixed system. This is what Gödel proved. And even if we mean an 'intuitive proof in general' it might just be the case (at least, this view is as clear and as probable as the contrary) that though the statement is true, there is just no way the human mind could ever prove it. Of course, one way an *infinite* mind might be able to prove it is by looking through each natural number one by one and checking. In this sense, of course, it can, perhaps, be known *a priori*, but only by an infinite mind, and then this gets into other complicated questions. I do not want to discuss questions about the conceivability of performing an infinite number of acts like looking through each number one by one. A vast philosophical literature has been written on this: Some have declared it is logically impossible; others that it is logically possible; and some do not know. The main point is that it is not trivial that just because such a statement is necessary it can be known *a priori*. Some considerable clarification is required before we decide that it can be so known. And so this shows that even if everything necessary is *a priori* in some sense, it should not be taken as a trivial matter of definition. It is a substantive philosophical thesis which requires some work.

Another example that one might give relates to the problem of essentialism. Here is a lectern. A question which has often been raised in philosophy is: What are its essential properties? What properties, aside from trivial ones like self-identity, are such that this object has to have them if it exists at all,[11] are such that if an object did not have it, it would not be this object?[12] For example, being made of wood, and not of ice, might be an essential property of this lectern. Let us just take the weaker statement that it is not made of ice. That will establish it as strongly as we need it, perhaps as dramatically. Supposing this lectern is in fact made of wood, could this very lectern have been made from the very beginning of its existence from ice, say frozen from water in the Thames? One has a considerable feeling that it could *not*, though in fact one certainly could have made a lectern of water from the Thames, frozen it into ice by some process, and put it right there in place of this thing. If one had done so, one would have made, of course, a *different* object. It would not have been *this very lectern*, and so one would not have a case in which this very lectern here was made of ice, or was made from water from the Thames. The question of whether it could afterward, say in a minute from now, turn into ice is something else. So, it would seem, if an example like this is correct—and this is what advocates of essentialism have held—that this lectern could not have been made of ice, that is in any counterfactual situation of which we would say that this lectern existed at all, we would have to say also that it was not made from water from the Thames frozen into ice. Some have rejected, of course, any such notion of essential property as meaningless. Usually, it is because (and I think this is what Quine, for example, would say) they have held that it depends on the notion of identity across possible worlds, and that this is itself meaningless. Since I have rejected this view already, I will not deal with it again. We can talk about *this very object*, and whether it could have had certain properties which it does not in fact have. For example, it could have been in another room from the room it in fact is in, even at this very time, but it could not have been made from the very beginning from water frozen into ice.

If the essentialist view is correct, it can only be correct if we sharply distinguish between the notions of *a posteriori* and *a priori* truth on the one hand, and contingent and necessary truth on the other hand, for although the statement that this table, if it exists at all, was not made of ice, is necessary, it certainly is not something that we know *a priori*. What we know is that first, lecterns usually are not made of ice, they are usually made of wood. This looks like wood. It does not feel cold and it probably would if it were made of ice. Therefore, I conclude, probably this is not made of ice. Here my entire judgement is *a posteriori*. I could find out that an ingenious trick has been played upon me and that, in fact, this lectern is made of ice; but what I am saying is, given that it is in fact not made of ice, in fact is made of wood, one cannot imagine that under certain circumstances it could have been made of ice. So we have to say that though we cannot know *a priori* whether this table was made of ice or not, given that it is not made of ice, it is *necessarily* not made of ice. In other words, if *P* is the statement that the lectern is not made of ice, one knows by *a priori* philosophical analysis, some conditional of the form 'if *P*, then necessarily *P*'. If the table is not made of ice, it is necessarily not made of ice. On the other hand, then, we know by empirical investigation that *P*, the antecedent of the conditional, is true—that this table is not made of ice. We can conclude by *modus ponens*:

$$P \supset \Box P$$

$$\frac{P}{\Box P}$$

The conclusion—' $\Box P$'—is that it is necessary that the table not be made of ice, and this conclusion is known *a posteriori*, since one of the premises on which it is based is *a posteriori*. So, the notion of essential properties can be maintained only by distinguishing between the notions of *a priori* and necessary truth, and I do maintain it.

Let us return to the question of identities. Concerning the statement 'Hesperus is Phosphorus' or the statement 'Cicero is Tully', one can find all of these out by empirical investigation, and we might turn out to be wrong in our empirical beliefs. So, it is usually argued, such statements must therefore be contingent. Some have embraced the other side of the coin and have held 'Because of this argument about necessity, identity statements between names have to be knowable *a priori*, so, only a very special category of names, possibly, really works as names; the other things are bogus names, disguised descriptions, or something of the sort. However, a certain very narrow class of statements of identity are known *a priori*, and these are the ones which contain the genuine names.' If one accepts the distinctions that I have made, one need not jump to either conclusion. One can hold that certain statements of identity between names, though often known *a posteriori*, and maybe not knowable *a priori*, are in fact necessary, if true. So, we have some room to hold this. But, of course, to have some room to hold it does not mean that we should hold it. So let us see what the evidence is. First, recall the remark that I made that proper names seem to be rigid designators, as when we use the name 'Nixon' to talk about a certain man, even in counterfactual situations. If we say, 'If Nixon had not written the letter to Saxbe, maybe he would have got Carswell through', we are in this statement talking about Nixon, Saxbe, and Carswell, the very same men as in the actual world, and what would have happened to them under certain counterfactual circumstances. If names are rigid designators, then there can be no question about identities being necessary, because '*a*' and '*b*' will be rigid designators of a certain man or thing *x*. Then even in every possible world, *a* and *b* will both refer to this same object *x*, and to no other, and so there will be no situation in which *a* might not have been *b*. That would have to be a situation in which the object which we are also now calling '*x*' would not have been identical with itself. Then one could not possibly have a situation in which Cicero would not have been Tully or Hesperus would not have been Phosphorus.[13]

Aside from the identification of necessity with *a priority*, what has made people feel the other way? There are two things which have made people feel the other way.[14] Some people tend to regard identity statements as metalinguistic statements, to identify the statement 'Hesperus is Phosphorus' with the metalinguistic statement, '"Hesperus" and "Phosphorus" are names of the same heavenly body'. And that, of course, might have been false. We might have used the terms 'Hesperus' and 'Phosphorus' as names of *two* different heavenly bodies. But, of course, this has nothing to do with the necessity of identity. In the same sense '2 + 2 = 4' might have been false. The phrases '2 + 2' and '4' might have been used to refer to two different numbers. One can imagine a language, for example, in which '+', '2', and '=' were used in the standard way, but '4' was used as the name of, say, the square root of minus 1, as we should call it, '*i*'. Then '2 + 2 = 4' would be false, for 2 plus 2 is not equal to the square root of minus 1. But this is not what we want. We do not want just to say that a certain statement which we in fact use to express something true could have expressed something false. We want to use the statement in *our* way and see if it could have been false. Let us do this. What is the idea people have? They say, 'Look, Hesperus might not have been Phosphorus. Here a certain planet was seen in the morning, and it was seen in the evening; and it just turned out later on as a matter of empirical fact that they were one and the same planet. If things had turned out otherwise, they would have been two different planets, or two different heavenly bodies, so how can you say that such a statement is necessary?'

Now there are two things that such people can mean. First, they can mean that we do not know *a priori* whether Hesperus is Phosphorus. This I have already conceded. Second, they may mean that they can actually imagine circumstances that they would call circumstances in which Hesperus would not have been Phosphorus. Let us think what would be such a circumstance, using these terms here as *names* of a planet. For example, it could have been the case that Venus did indeed rise in the morning in exactly the position in which we saw it, but that on the other hand, in the position which is in fact occupied by Venus in the evening, Venus was not there, and Mars took its place. This is all counterfactual because in fact Venus is there. Now one can also imagine that in this counterfactual other possible world, the earth would have been inhabited by people and that they should have used the names 'Phosphorus' for Venus in the morning and 'Hesperus' for Mars in the evening. Now, this is all very good, but would it be a situation in which Hesperus was not Phosphorus? Of course, it is a situation in which people would have been able to *say*, truly, 'Hesperus is not Phosphorus'; but we are supposed to describe things in our language, not in theirs. So let us describe it in our language. Well, how could it actually happen that Venus would not be in that position in the evening? For example, let us say that there is some comet that comes around every evening and yanks things over a little bit. (That would be a very simple scientific way of imagining it: not really too simple—that is very hard to imagine actually.) It just happens to come around every evening, and things get yanked over a little bit. Mars gets yanked over to the very position where Venus is, then the comet yanks things back to their normal position in the morning. Thinking of this planet which we now call 'Phosphorus', what should we say? Well, we can say that the comet passes it and yanks Phosphorus over so that it is not in the position normally occupied by Phosphorus in the evening. If we do say this, and really use 'Phosphorus' as the name of a planet, then we have to say that, under such circumstances, Phosphorus in the evening would not be in the position where we, in fact, saw it; or alternatively, Hesperus in the evening would not be in the position in which we, in fact, saw it. We might say that under such circumstances, we would not have called Hesperus 'Hesperus' because Hesperus would have been in a different position. But that still would not make Phosphorus different from Hesperus; but what would then be the case instead is that Hesperus would have been in a different position from the position it in fact is and, perhaps, not in such a position that people would have called it 'Hesperus'. But that would not be a situation in which Phosphorus would not have been Hesperus.

Let us take another example which may be clearer. Suppose someone uses 'Tully' to refer to the Roman orator who denounced Cataline and uses the name 'Cicero' to refer to the man whose works he had to study in third-year Latin in high school. Of course, he may not know in advance that the very same man who denounced Cataline wrote these works, and that is a contingent statement. But the fact that this statement is contingent should not make us think that the statement that Cicero is Tully, if it is true, and it is in fact true, is contingent. Suppose, for example, that Cicero actually did denounce Cataline, but thought that this political achievement was so great that he should not bother writing any literary works. Would we say that these would be circumstances under which he would not have been Cicero? It seems to me that the answer is no, that instead we would say that, under such circumstances, Cicero would not have written any literary works. It is not a necessary property of Cicero—the way the shadow follows the man—that he should have written certain works; we can easily imagine a situation in which Shakespeare would not have written the works of Shakespeare, or one in which Cicero would not have written the works of Cicero. What may be the case is that we *fix the reference* of the term 'Cicero' by use of some descriptive phrase, such as 'the author of these works'. But once we have this reference fixed, we then use the name 'Cicero' *rigidly* to designate the man who in fact we have identified by his authorship of these works. We do not use it to designate whoever would have written these works in place of Cicero, if someone else wrote them. It might have been the case that the man who wrote these works was not the man who denounced Cataline. Cassius might have written these works. But we would not then say that Cicero would have been Cassius, unless we were speaking in a very loose and metaphorical way. We would say that Cicero, whom we may have identified and come to know by his works, would not have written them, and that someone else, say Cassius, would have written them in his place.

Such examples are not grounds for thinking that identity statements are contingent. To take them as such grounds is to misconstrue the relation between a *name* and a *description used to fix its reference*, to take them to be *synonyms*. Even if we fix the reference of such a name as 'Cicero' as the man who wrote such and such works, in speaking of counterfactual situations, when we speak of Cicero, we do not then speak of whoever in such counterfactual situations *would* have written such and such works, but rather of Cicero, whom we have identified by the contingent property that he is the man who in fact, that is, in the actual world, wrote certain works.[15]

I hope this is reasonably clear in a brief compass. Now, actually I have been presupposing something I do not really believe to be, in general, true. Let us suppose that we do fix the reference of a name by a description. Even if we do so, we do not then make the name *synonymous* with the description, but instead we use the name *rigidly* to refer to the object so named, even in talking about counterfactual situations where the thing named would not satisfy the description in question. Now, this is what I think in fact is true for those cases of naming where the reference is fixed by description. But, in fact, I also think, contrary to most recent theorists, that the reference of names is rarely or almost never fixed by means of description. And by this I do not just mean what Searle says: 'It's not a single description, but rather a cluster, a family of properties which fixes the reference'. I mean that properties in this sense are not used *at all*. But I do not have the time to go into this here. So, let us suppose that at least one half of prevailing views about naming is true, that the reference is fixed by descriptions. Even were that true, the name would not be synonymous with the description, but would be used to *name* an object which we pick out by the contingent fact that it satisfies a certain description. And so, even though we can imagine a case where the man who wrote these works would not have been the man who denounced Cataline, we should not say that that would be a case in which Cicero would not have been Tully. We should say that it is a case in which Cicero did not write these works, but rather that Cassius did. And the identity of Cicero and Tully still holds.

Let me turn to the case of heat and the motion of molecules. Here surely is a case that is contingent identity! Recent philosophy has emphasized this again and again. So, if it is a case of contingent identity, then let us imagine under what circumstances it would be false. Now, concerning this statement I hold that the circumstances philosophers apparently have in mind as circumstances under which it would have been false are not in fact such circumstances. First, of course, it is argued that 'Heat is the motion of molecules' is an *a posteriori* judgement; scientific investigation might have turned out otherwise. As I said before, this shows nothing against the view that it is necessary—at least if I am right. But here, surely, people had very specific circumstances in mind under which, so they thought, the judgement that heat is the motion of molecules would have been false. What were these circumstances? One can distill them out of the fact that we found out empirically that heat is the motion of molecules. How was this? What did we find out first when we found out that heat is the motion of molecules? There is a certain external phenomenon which we can sense by the sense of touch, and it produces a sensation which we call 'the sensation of heat'. We then discover that the external phenomenon which produces this sensation, which we sense, by means of our sense of touch, is in fact that of molecular agitation in the thing that we touch, a very high degree of molecular agitation. So, it might be thought, to imagine a situation in which heat would not have been the motion of molecules, we need only imagine a situation in which we would have had the very same sensation and it would have been produced by something other than the motion of molecules. Similarly, if we wanted to imagine a situation in which light was not a stream of photons, we could imagine a situation in which we were sensitive to something else in exactly the same way, producing what we call visual experiences, though not through a stream of photons. To make the case stronger, or to look at another side of the coin, we could also consider a situation in which we *are* concerned with the motion of molecules but in which such motion does not give us the sensation of heat. And it might also have happened that we, or, at least, the creatures inhabiting this planet, might have been so constituted that, let us say, an increase in the motion of molecules did not give us this sensation but that, on the contrary, a slowing down of the molecules did give us the very same sensation. This would be a situation, so it might be thought, in which heat would not be the motion of molecules, or, more precisely, in which temperature would not be mean molecular kinetic energy.

But I think it would not be so. Let us think about the situation again. First, let us think about it in the actual world. Imagine right now the world invaded by a number of Martians, who do indeed get the very sensation that we call 'the sensation of heat' when they feel some ice which has slow molecular motion, and who do not get a sensation of heat—in fact, maybe just the reverse—when they put their hand near a fire which causes a lot of molecular agitation. Would we say, 'Ah, this casts some doubt on heat being the motion of molecules, because there are these other people who don't get the same sensation'? Obviously not, and no one would think so. We would say instead that the Martians somehow feel the very sensation we get when we feel heat when they feel cold and that they do not get a sensation of heat when they feel heat. But now let us think of a counterfactual situation.[16] Suppose the earth had from the very beginning been inhabited by such creatures. First, imagine it inhabited by no creatures at all: then there is no one to feel any sensations of heat. But we would not say that under such circumstances it would necessarily be the case that heat did not exist; we would say that heat might have existed, for example, if there were fires that heated up the air.

Let us suppose the laws of physics were not very different: Fires do heat up the air. Then there would have been heat even though there were no creatures around to feel it. Now let us suppose evolution takes place, and life is created, and there are some creatures around. But they are not like us, they are more like the Martians. Now would we say that heat has suddenly turned to cold, because of the way the creatures of this planet sense it? No, I think we should describe this situation as a situation in which, though the creatures on this planet got our sensation of heat, they did not get it when they were exposed to heat. They got it when they were exposed to cold. And that is something we can surely well imagine. We can imagine it just as we can imagine our planet being invaded by creatures of this sort. Think of it in two steps. First there is a stage where there are no creatures at all, and one can certainly imagine the planet still having both heat and cold, though no one is around to sense it. Then the planet comes through an evolutionary process to be peopled with beings of different neural structure from ourselves. Then these creatures could be such that they were insensitive to heat; they did not feel it in the way we do; but on the other hand, they felt cold in much the same way that we feel heat. But still, heat would be heat, and cold would be cold. And particularly, then, this goes in no way against saying that in this counterfactual situation heat would still *be* the molecular motion, *be* that which is produced by fires, and so on, just as it would have been if there had been no creatures on the planet at all. Similarly, we could imagine that the planet was inhabited by creatures who got visual sensations when there were sound waves in the air. We should not therefore say, 'Under such circumstances, sound would have been light.' Instead we should say, 'The planet was inhabited by creatures who were in some sense visually sensitive to sound, and maybe even visually sensitive to light.' If this is correct, it can still be and will still be a necessary truth that heat is the motion of molecules and that light is a stream of photons.

To state the view succinctly: we use both the terms 'heat' and 'the motion of molecules' as rigid designators for a certain external phenomenon. Since heat is in fact the motion of molecules, and the designators are rigid, by the argument I have given here, it is going to be *necessary* that heat is the motion of molecules. What gives us the illusion of contingency is the fact we have identified the heat by the contingent fact that there happen to be creatures on this planet—(namely, ourselves) who are sensitive to it in a certain way, that is, who are sensitive to the motion of molecules or to heat—these are one and the same thing. And this is contingent. So we use the description, 'that which causes such and such sensations, or that which we sense in such and such a way', to identify heat. But in using this fact we use a contingent property of heat, just as we use the contingent property of Cicero as having written such and such works to identify him. We then use the terms 'heat' in the one case and 'Cicero' in the other *rigidly* to designate the objects for which they stand. And of course the term 'the motion of molecules' is rigid; it always stands for the motion of molecules, never for any other phenomenon. So, as Bishop Butler said, 'everything is what it is and not another thing'. Therefore, 'Heat is the motion of molecules' will be necessary, not contingent, and one only has the *illusion* of contingency in the way one could have the illusion of contingency in thinking that this table might have been made of ice. We might think one could imagine it, but if we try, we can see on reflection that what we are really imagining is just there being another lectern in this very position here which was in fact made of ice. The fact that we may identify this lectern by being the object we see and touch in such and such a position is something else.

Now how does this relate to the problem of mind and body? It is usually held that this is a contingent identity statement just like 'Heat is the motion of molecules'. That cannot be. It cannot be a contingent identity statement just like 'Heat is the motion of molecules' because, if I am right, 'Heat is the motion of molecules' is not a contingent identity statement. Let us look at this statement. For example, 'My being in pain at such and such a time is my being in such and such a brain state at such and such a time' or, 'Pain in general is such and such a neural (brain) state'.

This is held to be contingent on the following grounds. First, we can imagine the brain state existing though there is no pain at all. It is only a scientific fact that whenever we are in a certain brain state we have a pain. Second, one might imagine a creature being in pain, but not being in any specified brain state at all, maybe not having a brain at all. People even think, at least prima facie, though they may be wrong, that they can imagine totally disembodied creatures, at any rate certainly not creatures with bodies anything like our own. So it seems that we can imagine definite circumstances under which this relationship would have been false. Now, if these circumstances are circumstances, notice that we cannot deal with them simply by saying that this is just an illusion, something we can apparently imagine, but in fact cannot in the way we thought erroneously that we could imagine a situation in which heat was not the motion of molecules. Because although we can say that we pick out heat contingently by the contingent property that it affects us in such and such a way, we cannot similarly say that we pick out pain contingently by the fact that it affects us in such and such a way. On such a picture there would be the brain state, and we pick it out by the contingent fact that it affects us as pain. Now that might be true of the brain state, but it cannot be true of the pain. The experience itself has to be *this experience*, and I cannot say that it is contingent property of the pain I now have that it is a pain.[17] In fact, it would seem that both the terms, 'my pain' and 'my being in such and such a brain state' are, first of all, both rigid designators. That is, whenever anything is such-and-such a pain, it is essentially that very object, namely, such-and-such a pain, and wherever anything is such-and-such a brain state, it is essentially that very object, namely, such-and-such a brain state. So both of these are rigid designators. One cannot say this pain might have been something else, some other state. These are both rigid designators.

Second, the way we would think of picking them out—namely, the pain by its being an experience of a certain sort, and the brain state by its being the state of a certain material object, being of such and such molecular configuration—both of these pick out their objects essentially and not accidentally, that is, they pick them out by essential properties. Whenever the molecules *are* in this configuration, we *do* have such and such a brain state. Whenever you feel *this*, you do have a pain. So it seems that the identity theorist is in some trouble, for, since we have two rigid designators, the identity statement in question is necessary. Because they pick out their objects essentially, we cannot say the case where you seem to imagine the identity statement false is really an illusion like the illusion one gets in the case of heat and molecular motion, because that illusion one gets in the case of heat and molecular motion, because that illusion depended on the fact that we pick out heat by a certain contingent property. So there is very little room to manoeuvre; perhaps none.[18] The identity theorist, who holds that pain is the brain state, also has to hold that it necessarily is the brain state. He therefore cannot concede, but has to deny, that there would have been situations under which one would have had pain but not the corresponding brain state. Now usually in arguments on the identity theory, this is very far from being denied. In fact, it is conceded from the outset by the materialist as well as by his opponent. He says, 'Of course, it *could* have been the case that we had pains without the brain states. It is a contingent identity.' But that cannot be. He has to hold that we are under some illusion in thinking that we can imagine that there could have been pains without brain states. And the only model I can think of for what the illusion might be, or at least the model given by the analogy the materialists themselves suggest, namely, heat and molecular motion, simply does not work in this case. So the materialist is up against a very stiff challenge. He has to show that these things we think we can see to be possible are in fact not possible. He has to show that these things which we can imagine are not in fact things we can imagine. And that requires some very different philosophical argument from the sort which has been given in the case of heat and molecular motion. And it would have to be a deeper and subtler argument than I can fathom and subtler than has ever appeared in any materialist literature that I have read. So the conclusion of this investigation would be that the analytical tools we are using go against the identity thesis and so go against the general thesis that mental states are just physical states.[19]

The next topic would be my own solution to the mind–body problem, but that I do not have.

NOTES

1. This paper was presented orally, without a written text, to the New York University lecture series on identity which makes up the volume in which it was first published. The lecture was taped, and the present paper represents a transcription of these tapes, edited only slightly with no attempt to change the style of the original. If the reader imagines the sentences of this paper as being delivered, extemporaneously, with proper pauses and emphases, this may facilitate his comprehension. Nevertheless, there may still be passages which are hard to follow, and the time allotted necessitated a condensed presentation of the argument. Occasionally, reservations, amplifications, and gratifications of my remarks had to be repressed, especially in the discussion of theoretical identification and the mind–body problem. The footnotes, which were added to the original, would have become even more unwieldy if this had not been done.
2. R.J. Butler (ed.), *Analytical Philosophy, Second Series* (Oxford: Blackwell, 1965), p. 41.
3. The second occurrence of the description has small scope.
4. In Russell's theory, $F(\iota xGx)$ follows from $(x)Fx$ and $(\exists!x)Gx$, provided that the description in $F(\iota xGx)$ has the entire context for its scope (in Russell's 1905 terminology, has a 'primary occurrence'). Only then is $F(\iota xGx)$ 'about' the denotation of 'ιxGx'. Applying this rule to (14), we get the results indicated in the text. Notice that, in the ambiguous form $\Box(\iota xGx = \iota xHx)$, if one or both of the descriptions have 'primary occurrences' the formula does not assert the necessity of $\iota xGx = \iota xHx$; if both have secondary occurrences, it does. Thus in a language without explicit scope indicators, descriptions must be construed with the smallest possible scope—only then will $\sim A$ be the negation of A, $\Box A$ the necessitation of A, and the like.

5. An earlier distinction with the same purpose was, of course, the medieval one of *de dicto–de re*. That Russell's distinction of scope eliminates modal paradoxes has been pointed out by many logicians, especially Smullyan.

So as to avoid misunderstanding, let me emphasize that I am of course not asserting that Russell's notion of scope solves Quine's problem of 'essentialism'; what it does show, especially in conjunction with modern and model–theoretic approaches to modal logic, is that quantified modal logic need not deny the truth of all instances of $(x)(y)(x = y \cdot \supset \cdot Fx \supset Fy)$, nor of all instances of '$(x)(Gx \supset Ga)$' (where 'a' is to be replaced by a nonvacuous definite description whose scope is all of 'Ga'), in order to avoid making it a necessary truth that one and the same man invented bifocals and headed the original Postal Department. Russell's contextual definition of descriptions need not be adopted in order to ensure these results; but other logical theories, Fregean or other, which take descriptions as primitive must somehow express the same logical facts. Frege showed that a simple, non-iterated context containing a definite description with small scope, which cannot be interpreted as being 'about' the denotation of the description, can be interpreted as about its 'sense'. Some logicians have been interested in the question of the conditions under which, in an intensified context, a description with small scope is equivalent to the same one with large scope. One of the virtues of a Russellian treatment of descriptions in modal logic is that the answer (roughly that the description be a 'rigid designator' in the sense of this lecture) then often follows from the other postulates for quantified modal logic; no special postulates are needed, as in Hintikka's treatment. Even if descriptions are taken as primitive, special postulation of when scope is irrelevant can often be deduced from more basic axioms.

6. 'Modalities and Intensional Languages', *Boston Studies in the Philosophy of Science*, Vol. 1 (New York: Humanities Press, 1963), pp. 71 ff. See also the 'Comments' by Quine and the ensuing discussion.

7. It should. See her remark on p. 115, op. cit., in the discussion following the papers.

8. If there is no deity, and especially if the nonexistence of a deity is *necessary*, it is dubious that we can use 'he' to refer to a deity. The use in the text must be taken to be non-literal.

9. David K. Lewis, 'Counterpart Theory and Quantified Modal Logic', *Journal of Philosophy* LXV (1968), pp. 113 ff.

10. Some philosophers think that definite descriptions, in English, are ambiguous, that sometimes 'the inventor of bifocals' rigidly designates the man who in fact invented bifocals. I am tentatively inclined to reject this view, construed as a thesis about English (as opposed to a possible hypothetical language), but I will not argue the question here.

What I do wish to note is that, contrary to some opinions, this alleged ambiguity cannot replace the Russellian notion of the scope of a description. Consider the sentence, 'The number of planets might have been necessarily even.' This sentence plainly can be read so as to express a truth; had there been eight planets, the number of planets would have been necessarily even. Yet without scope distinctions, both a 'referential' (rigid) and a non-rigid reading of the description will make the statement false. (Since the number of planets is nine, the rigid reading amounts to the falsity that nine might have been necessarily even.)

The 'rigid' reading is equivalent to the Russellian primary occurrence; the non-rigid, to innermost scope—some, following Donnellan, perhaps loosely, have called this reading the 'attributive' use. The possibility of intermediate scopes is then ignored. In the present instance, the intended reading of $\Diamond \Box$ (the number of planets is even) makes the scope of the description $\Box$ (the number of planets is even), neither the largest nor the smallest possible.

11. This definition is the usual formulation of the notion of essential property, but an exception must be made for existence itself; on the definition given, existence would be trivially essential. We should regard existence as essential to an object only if the object necessarily exists. Perhaps there are other recherché properties, involving existence, for which the definition is similarly objectionable. (I thank Michael Slote for this observation.)

12. The two clauses of the sentence noted give equivalent definitions of the notion of essential property, since $\Box((\exists x) (x = a) \supset Fa)$ is equivalent to $\Box(x) (\sim Fx \supset x \neq a)$. The second formulation, however, has served as a powerful seducer in favour of theories of 'identification across possible worlds'. For it suggests that we consider 'an object b in another possible world' and test

whether it is identifiable with *a* by asking whether it lacks any of the essential properties of *a*. Let me therefore emphasize that, although an essential property is (trivially) a property without which an object cannot be *a*, it by no means follows that the essential, purely qualitative proper-ties of *a* jointly form a sufficient condition for being *a*, nor that *any* purely qualitative condi-tions are sufficient for an object to be *a*. Further, even if necessary and sufficient qualitative con-ditions for an object to be Nixon may exist, there would still be little justification for the demand for a purely qualitative description of all counterfactual situations. We can ask whether Nixon might have been a Democrat without engaging in these subtleties.

13. I thus agree with Quine, that 'Hesperus is Phosphorus' is (or can be) an empirical discovery; with Marcus, that it is necessary. Both Quine and Marcus, according to the present standpoint, err in identifying the epistemological and the metaphysical issues.

14. The two confusions alleged, especially the second, are both related to the confusion of the meta-physical question of the necessity of Hesperus is Phosphorus with the epistemological question of its *a priori*city. For if Hesperus is identified by its position in the sky in the evening, and Phosphorus by its position in the morning, an investigator may well know, in advance of empir-ical research, that Hesperus is Phosphorus if and only if one and the same body occupies posi-tion *x* in the evening and position *y* in the morning. The *a priori* material equivalence of the two statements, however, does not imply their strict (necessary) equivalence. (The same remarks apply to the case of heat and molecular motion below.) Similar remarks apply to some extent to the relationship between 'Hesperus is Phosphorus' and '"Hesperus" and "Phosphorus" name the same thing'. A confusion that also operates is, of course, the confusion between what *we* would say of a counterfactual situation and how people *in* that situation would have described it; this confusion, too, is probably related to the confusion between *a priori*city and necessity.

15. If someone protests, regarding the lectern, that it *could* after all have *turned out* to have been made of ice, and therefore could have been made of ice, I would reply that what he really means is that *a lectern* could have looked just like this one, and have been placed in the same position as this one, and yet have been made of ice. In short, I could have been in the *same epistemologi-cal situation* in relation to *a lectern made of ice* as I actually am in relation to *this* lectern. In the main text, I have argued that the same reply should be given to protests that Hesperus could have turned out to be other than Phosphorus, or Cicero other than Tully. Here, then, the notion of 'counterpart' comes into its own. For it is not this table, but an epistemic 'counterpart', which was hewn from ice; not Hesperus–Phosphorus–Venus, but two distinct counterparts thereof, in two of the roles Venus actually plays (that of Evening Star and Morning Star), which are differ-ent. Precisely because of this fact, it is not *this table* which could have been made of ice. Statements about the modal properties of *this table* never refer to counterparts. However, if someone confuses the epistemological and the metaphysical problems, he will be well on the way to the counterpart theory Lewis and others have advocated.

16. Isn't the situation I just described also counterfactual? At least it may well be, if such Martians never in fact invade. Strictly speaking, the distinction I wish to draw compares how we *would* speak *in* a (possibly counterfactual) situation, *if* it obtained, and how we *do* speak of a counter-factual situation, knowing that it does not obtain—i.e., the distinction between the language we would have used in a situation and the language we *do* use to describe it. (Consider the descrip-tion: 'Suppose we all spoke German.' This description is in English.) The former case can be made vivid by imagining the counterfactual situation to be actual.

17. The most popular identity theories advocated today explicitly fail to satisfy this simple require-ment. For these theories usually hold that a mental state is a brain state, and that what makes the brain state into a mental state is its 'causal role', the fact that it tends to produce certain behaviour (as intentions produce actions, or pain, pain behaviour) and to be produced by certain stimuli (e.g. pain, by pinpricks). If the relations between the brain state and its causes and effects are regarded as contingent, then *being such-and-such-a-mental state* is a contingent property of the brain state. Let *X* be a pain. The causal-role identity theorist holds (1) that *X* is a brain state. Let *X* be a pain. The causal-role identity theorist holds (1) that *X* is a brain state, (2) that the fact that *X* is a pain is to be analysed (roughly) as the fact that *X* is produced by certain stimuli and produces certain behaviour. The fact mentioned in (2) is, of course, regarded as contingent; the

brain state X might well exist and not tend to produce the appropriate behaviour in the absence of other conditions. Thus (1) and (2) assert that a certain pain X might have existed, yet not have been a pain. This seems to me self-evidently absurd. Imagine any pain: is it possible that *it itself* could have existed, yet not have been a pain?

If $X = Y$, then X and Y share all properties, including modal properties. If X is a pain and Y the corresponding brain state, then *being a pain* is an essential property of X, and *being a brain state* is an essential property of Y. If the correspondence relation is, in fact, identity, then it must be *necessary* of Y that it corresponds to a pain, and *necessary* of X that it correspond to a brain state, indeed to this particular brain state, Y. Both assertions seem false; it *seems* clearly possible that X should have existed without the corresponding brain state; or that the brain state should have existed without being felt as pain. Identity theorists cannot, contrary to their almost universal present practice, accept these intuitions; they must deny them, and explain them away. This is none too easy a thing to do.

18. A brief restatement of the argument may be helpful here. If 'pain' and 'C-fibre stimulation' are rigid designators of phenomena, one who identifies them must regard the identity as necessary. How can this necessity be reconciled with the apparent fact that C-fibre stimulation might have turned out not to be correlated with pain at all? We might try to reply by analogy to the case of heat and molecular motion; the latter identity, too, is necessary, yet someone may believe that, before scientific investigation showed otherwise, molecular motion might have turned out not to be heat. The reply is, of course, that what really is possible is that people (or some rational sentient beings) could have been in the *same epistemic situation* as we actually are, and identify *a phenomenon* in the same way we identify heat, namely, by feeling it by the sensation we call 'the sensation of heat', without the phenomenon being molecular motion. Further, the beings might not have been sensitive to molecular motion (i.e., to heat) by any neural mechanism whatsoever. It is impossible to explain the apparent possibility of C-fibre stimulations not having been pain in the same way. Here, too, we would have to suppose that we could have been in the same epistemological situation, and identify something in the same way we identify pain, without its corresponding to C-fibre stimulation. But the way we identify pain is by feeling it, and if a C-fibre stimulation could have occurred without our feeling any pain, then the C-fibre stimulation would have occurred without there *being* any pain, contrary to the necessity of the identity. The trouble is that although 'heat' is a rigid designator, heat is picked out by the contingent property of its being felt in a certain way; pain, on the other hand, is picked out by an essential (indeed necessary and sufficient) property. For a sensation to be *felt* as pain is for it to *be* pain.

19. All arguments against the identity theory which rely on the necessity of identity, or on the notion of essential property, are, of course, inspired by Descartes' argument for his dualism. The earlier arguments which superficially were rebutted by the analogies of heat and molecular motion, and the bifocals inventor who was also Postmaster General, had such an inspiration; and so does my argument here. R. Albritton and M. Slote have informed me that they independently have attempted to give essentialist arguments against the identity theory, and probably others have done so as well.

The simplest Cartesian argument can perhaps be restated as follows: Let 'A' be a *name* (rigid designator) of Descartes' body. Then Descartes argues that since he could exist even if A did not, $\diamond$ (Descartes $\neq A$), hence Descartes $\neq A$. Those who have accused him of a modal fallacy have forgotten that 'A' is rigid. His argument is valid, and his conclusion is correct, provided its (perhaps dubitable) premise is accepted. On the other hand, provided that Descartes is regarded as having ceased to exist upon his death, 'Descartes $\neq A$' can be established without the use of a modal argument; for if so, no doubt A survived Descartes when A was a corpse. Thus A had a property (existing at a certain time) which Descartes did not. The same argument can establish that a statue is not the hunk of stone, or the congery of molecules, of which it is composed. Mere non-identity, then, may be a weak conclusion. (See D. Wiggins, *Philosophical Review*, Vol. 77 (1968), pp. 90 ff.) The Cartesian modal argument, however, surely can be deployed to maintain relevant stronger conclusions as well.

Introduction to Hilary Putnam

Hilary Putnam was born in Chicago in 1926 and educated at the University of Pennsylvania and UCLA. He is the Walter Beverly Pearson Professor of Mathematical Logic at Harvard University, where he has taught since 1965, having previously taught at Northwestern University, Princeton University, and MIT. In a time of specialists, Putnam is unusual in having produced highly important work in almost every area of philosophy. After early work in the philosophy of mathematics and of science, he invented functionalism, still the dominant position in philosophy of mind. Functionalism is the theory that the mind is a computer, that mental states are the "functional" states in terms of which the program would be described, and that these states are type-individuated by their functional role—that is, their causal relations to perceptual stimuli, behavioral responses, and to other mental states. Functionalism differs from type-identity theory in saying that mental states are *multiply realizable*. Take the case of pain. Whereas a type-identity theorist would say that what made a mental state a state of pain was in being some process of the brain or nervous system, such as C-fiber stimulation, functionalism says that it is pain due to (1) being caused in certain typical ways, such as tissue damage; (2) typically resulting in certain behavior, for example, groaning; and (3) typically causing other mental states, such as a desire that it stop, or a plan to make it stop. Anything that fulfills this functional role counts as a case of pain, whatever its physical embodiment.

Turning now to the present article, Putnam is credited as giving the first explicit statement of "semantic externalism," the theory that the content of our words is (at least in part) determined by factors external to an individual speaker. Recall the picture of the relation between sense and reference inherited from Frege. On this conception, when we understand a term, there is something in the mind, a conceptual "mode of representation" corresponding to the word, which determines its reference. That is, the term refers to whatever matches that internal representation, and whenever two people share such a representation, then their words refer to the same thing. So knowing what a word means is to be in a certain type of psychological state, which, in turn, determines the extension of the term. Putnam denies that anything can satisfy this pair of requirements.

His argument rests on the Causal Theory of Reference (see "Introduction to Saul Kripke"). Consider this theory as applied to natural kind terms (a natural kind is a property located within a current scientific theory). The Causal Theory provides a picture of reference fixing and reference borrowing—that is, of how a term is introduced into a language, and how others come to grasp it. A natural kind term is introduced into the language by direct contact with typical examples. The extension of the term is taken to be the set of things having the same internal structure as these examples. In other words, natural kind terms are defined indexically, for example, "*This* stuff, and everything with the same internal structure, is water." What water really consists in, and what it is to be of the same kind as a given sample, are only discoverable by scientific research. However, Putnam insists, someone can use these expressions correctly in the absence of this information. (Compare Kripke's insight that my use of the name "Albert

Einstein" still designates Einstein, even though I may be in radical error or ignorance concerning facts about the man.) The discovery that water was H_2O is only two centuries old, yet someone in 1750 meant the same by "water" as I do today, since he was trained in the use of that word in an environment in which H_2O was present.

Putnam employs the now famous "Twin Earth" thought experiment to illustrate his thesis. Imagine a Twin Earth, a planet phenomenally indistinguishable from Earth, and physically identical with a few exceptions, such as that in the place of H_2O it has another qualitatively identical but internally distinct substance called XYZ. XYZ has the same range of social functions on Twin Earth as H_2O has on Earth. That is, people sail in it, bathe in it, make tea with it, and so on. Twin Earth inhabitants call this substance "water." Their language is phonetically identical to English. Everything happens in a seemingly identical way on earth and Twin Earth. Every object and property has a phenomenally identical counterpart. Thus, you have a twin who is currently reading about Twin-Putnam, in a book edited by Twin-me.

Since Earth and Twin Earth are phenomenally identical, all utterances by someone on Earth will be phonetically indistinguishable from that of his counterpart on Twin Earth. So my utterance "This water is freezing!" will be, in all physical aspects, identical to that of Twin-JB. However, Putnam argues, our utterances will differ semantically—that is, they will mean different things, since the extensions of the term "water" will differ. My term "water" refers to H_2O, whereas Twin-JB's refers to XYZ. It follows from this that the truth-conditions of our utterances will correspondingly differ. My claim will be true if this particular sample of H_2O has a low temperature, whereas that of Twin-JB requires that some XYZ be cold. But, ex hypothesi, H_2O and XYZ are distinct kinds.

I will now introduce Putnam's thesis of the division of linguistic labor, a corollary of his externalism. Recall Kripke's theory of how I can use a name to stand for someone whom I have never met. When I say "Aristotle was Plato's greatest pupil," I am talking about Aristotle and Plato. At some point, these persons were assigned these names, and, as a result, future uses of those names designate those persons. Thus, my usage of "Aristotle" denotes Aristotle because my use of that name is connected to the original naming by "causal chains" tracing back through the linguistic community. The important point here is that what my use of the name designates is determined by the usage of other persons, ultimately those I do not know. Something analogous occurs with natural kind terms. Putnam remarks that he cannot distinguish beeches from elms. That is, any mental images, descriptions, or associations he might have of either will be the same. So nothing "in his head" can distinguish the two concepts. Still, if he were to say "There's an elm in my garden," then he would be referring to *elms* (even if the tree is actually a beech), since his usage of 'elm' is dependent on that of a class of *experts*, those who are informed of the natural facts that make something an elm, as distinct from a beech. Putnam calls this practice of reference-borrowing the "division of linguistic labor." In such cases, however, it is important to remember that the ultimate determinant of the reference of natural kind terms is the physical environment itself. Experts are only discovering what is actually there.

Putnam's ideas have been extended in an influential series of articles by Tyler Burge, who argues that the meaning of many terms depends on features not of the natural environment, but of the "social environment." That is, the contents of utterances are determined by our community's linguistic conventions. For example, take the term "Professor." In America, all university teachers are called professors, whereas in Britain, this term is reserved for what Americans would call *full* professors. Since I am currently an associate professor, if I utter "I am a professor" in the United States, I say something true, whereas if I were to say it as a British resident, I would speak falsely.

Burge's other important development of Putnam's externalism was to show that it is not merely a semantic theory, about the meaning of words, but that it also applied to the individuation of *mental states*. Let us return to the case of my Twin and I, exclaiming the coldness of our water. Putnam would say that my twin and I would be in the same psychological state. This is potentially misleading. We are only in type-identical psychological states in the sense of everything in our respective heads being qualitatively identical, for example, on any physical level of description, or in attaching the same sense to "water"-thoughts, or on the subjective level of how it seems from the inside. On the other hand, Burge would emphasize that what we *say* expresses our *beliefs* (assuming a general honesty). Thus, my twin and I can have *thoughts* about bathing, swimming, drinking, and so on. When I *think* "This water is freezing!" then this thought is clearly about H_2O just as much as my utterance was. Likewise, my twin's corresponding thought will be about XYZ. That is, our thoughts will have different contents and different truth-conditions.

If we follow this line, some important implications emerge. For one thing, mind-brain type-identity would seem to be refuted, since we have a possible case of two persons in type-identical brain states, yet different mental states. Likewise, the local supervenience of mental and brain properties is challenged, since the content of one's mental states is determined by extra-cranial factors concerning the natural kinds in one's environment.

It is hard to think of any subject in contemporary Anglo-American philosophy that has generated as much interest as externalism. One reason for this is that it overturns hundreds of years of philosophical orthodoxy. When Descartes formulated his "method of doubt," by which he intended to place all his beliefs under suspicion, he overlooked his beliefs about the relations between minds, language, and reality. For example, he still implicitly held to the "methodological solipsism" that his thought-contents were fixed purely by internal factors, independent of anything going on in the external world. Thus, if a malicious demon were deceiving me, then my beliefs would be *false*—that is, their truth-values would be affected—but their *meanings* were assumed to be unaffected, even if the world was an illusion.

Externalism led Putnam to some radically anti-skeptical conclusions. In a thought-experiment just as famous as Twin Earth, he considers a modern analogue of Descartes' "demon doubt," where the standard skeptical position is that nothing can ever establish whether or not I am a brain in a vat. That is, suppose that my existence is that of a disembodied brain in a vat of nutrients, and connected to a computer electrodes, allowing the illusion of perceptual experience of the external world. Putnam argues that the hypothesis that I might now be a brain in a vat is incoherent. Recall causal theory, which bars me from referring to things of which I have had contact. Ex hypothesi, I cannot refer to things in the external world, that is, computer-simulation. It follows that my term "vat" refers not to mater space and time, but a computer-produced "vat image." Likewise "brain" refers not to actual gray matter but to brain images. So if I, as a brain-in-a-vat, say "I am a brain in a vat," what I say is false, since I am not the mere effect of a computer program. Now suppose that I am not a brain in a vat, but exist in the public world. In that case my claim to be a brain in a vat is straightforwardly false. Either way, whatever my situation, I cannot truly state that I am a brain in a vat. Thus, Putnam concludes, global skepticism is incoherent.

However, as well as ruling out such a skeptical stance, Putnam has, since the mid-1970s, rejected the realism ("metaphysical realism") that underlay his causal theory of reference, in favor of a neo-Kantian "internal realism." This distinction is most explicitly made in *Reason, Truth, and History.* By the former theory, "The world consists of some fixed totality of mind-independent objects. There is exactly one true and complete description of 'the way the world is'. Truth involves some sort of correspondence relation between words or thought-signs and external things and sets of things" (p. 49); whereas by the latter theory, "'*What objects does the world consist of?'* is a question that it only makes sense to ask *within* a theory or description. ... 'Truth' in an internalist view, is some sort of (idealized) rational acceptability—some sort of ideal coherence of our beliefs with each other and with our experiences *as these experiences are themselves represented in our belief system*—and not correspondence with mind-independent or discourse-independent 'states of affairs'" (pp. 49–50).

Most recently, Putnam has devoted much of his time to an investigation of Pragmatism, and is also cited (along with Richard Rorty) as one of the major "bridge-builders" between the Anglo-American and continental schools. One constant feature of Putnam's career is that the scope of his work continues to enlarge, such that he can no longer be considered as *only* an "analytic" philosopher.

BIBLIOGRAPHY

Works by Putnam

Mathematics, Matter and Method: Philosophical papers, Vol. 1 (Cambridge: Cambridge University Press, 1975).

Mind, Language and Reality: Philosophical Papers, Vol. 2 (Cambridge: Cambridge University Press, 1975).

Realism and Reason: Philosophical Papers, Vol. 3 (Cambridge: Cambridge University Press, 1983).

Meaning and the Moral Sciences (London: Routledge, 1978).

Reason, Truth, and History (Cambridge: Cambridge University Press, 1981).

Representation and Reality (Cambridge: MIT Press, 1988).

~wing Philosophy (Cambridge: Harvard University Press, 1992)

'Oxford: Basil Blackwell, 1995).

study of Putnam is currently available, there are several good collections of

Meaning and Method: Essays in Honor of Hilary Putnam (Cambridge: ersity Press, 1990).

Peter Clark and Bob Hale, eds. *Reading Putnam* (Oxford: Basil Blackwell, 1994).
Philosophical Topics, Vol. 20, no. 1, *The Philosophy of Hilary Putnam* (Fayetteville, AR: University of Arkansas Press).
The first and best-known of Tyler Burge's articles on externalism is " Individualism and the Mental," *Midwest Studies in Philosophy*, Vol. 10, 1979.
A helpful book-length discussion of externalism is Colin McGinn, *Mental Content* (Oxford: Basil Blackwell 1989).

Meaning and Reference

Hilary Putnam

Unclear as it is, the traditional doctrine that the notion "meaning" possesses the extension/intension ambiguity has certain typical consequences. The doctrine that the meaning of a term is a concept carried the implication that meanings are mental entities. Frege, however, rebelled against this "psychologism". Feeling that meanings are *public property*—that the *same* meaning can be "grasped" by more than one person and by persons at different times—he identified concepts (and hence "intensions" or meanings) with abstract entities rather than mental entities. However, "grasping" these abstract entities was still an individual psychological act. None of these philosophers doubted that understanding a word (knowing its intension) was just a matter of being in a certain psychological state (somewhat in the way in which knowing how to factor numbers in one's head is just a matter of being in a certain very complex psychological state).

Secondly, the timeworn example of the two terms 'creature with a kidney' and 'creature with a heart' does show that two terms can have the same extension and yet differ in intension. But it was taken to be obvious that the reverse is impossible: two terms cannot differ in extension and have the same intension. Interestingly, no argument for this impossibility was ever offered. Probably it reflects the tradition of the ancient and medieval philosophers, who assumed that the concept corresponding to a term was just a conjunction of predicates, and hence that the concept corresponding to a term must *always* provide a necessary and sufficient condition for falling into the extension of the term. For philosophers like Carnap, who accepted the verifiability theory of meaning, the concept corresponding to a term provided (in the ideal case, where the term had "complete meaning") a *criterion* for belonging to the extension (not just in the sense of "necessary and sufficient condition", but in the strong sense

From *The Journal of Philosophy*, 70/19 (8 November 1973), 699–711. Reprinted by permission of the author and *The Journal of Philosophy*.

of *way of recognizing* whether a given thing falls into the extension or not). So theory of meaning came to rest on two unchallenged assumptions:

(1) That knowing the meaning of a term is just a matter of being in a certain psychological state (in the sense of "psychological state", in which states of memory and belief are "psychological states"; no one thought that knowing the meaning of a word was a continuous state of consciousness, of course).

(2) That the meaning of a term determines its extension (in the sense that sameness of intension entails sameness of extension).

I shall argue that these two assumptions are not jointly satisfied by *any* notion, let alone any notion of meaning. The traditional concept of meaning is a concept which rests on a false theory.

ARE MEANINGS IN THE HEAD?

For the purpose of the following science-fiction examples, we shall suppose that somewhere there is a planet we shall call Twin Earth. Twin Earth is very much like Earth: in fact, people on Twin Earth even speak *English*. In fact, apart from the differences we shall specify in our science-fiction examples, the reader may suppose that Twin Earth is *exactly* like Earth. He may even suppose that he has a *Doppelgänger*—an identical copy—on Twin Earth, if he wishes, although my stories will not depend on this.

Although some of the people on Twin Earth (say, those who call themselves "Americans" and those who call themselves "Canadians" and those who call themselves "Englishmen", etc.) speak English, there are, not surprisingly, a few tiny differences between the dialects of English spoken on Twin Earth and standard English.

One of the peculiarities of Twin Earth is that the liquid called "water" is not H_2O but a different liquid whose chemical formula is very long and complicated. I shall abbreviate this chemical formula simply as XYZ. I shall suppose that XYZ is indistinguishable from water at normal temperatures and pressures. Also, I shall suppose that the oceans and lakes and seas of Twin Earth contain XYZ and not water, that it rains XYZ on Twin Earth and not water, etc.

If a space ship from Earth ever visits Twin Earth, then the supposition at first will be that 'water' has the same meaning on Earth and on Twin Earth. This supposition will be corrected when it is discovered that "water" on Twin Earth is XYZ, and the Earthian space ship will report somewhat as follows.

"On Twin Earth the word 'water' means XYZ."

Symmetrically, if a space ship from Twin Earth ever visits Earth, then the supposition at first will be that the word 'water' has the same meaning on Twin Earth and on Earth. This supposition will be corrected when it is discovered that "water" on Earth is H_2O, and the Twin Earthian space ship will report:

"On Earth the word 'water' means H_2O."

Note that there is no problem about the extension of the term 'water': the word simply has two different meanings (as we say); in the sense in which it is used on Twin Earth, the sense of water$_{TE}$, what *we* call "water" simply isn't water, while in the sense in which it is used on Earth, the sense of water$_E$, what the Twin Earthians call "water" simply isn't water. The extension of 'water' in the sense of water$_E$ is the set of all wholes consisting of H_2O molecules, or something like that; the extension of water in the sense of water$_{TE}$ is the set of all wholes consisting of XYZ molecules, or something like that.

Now let us roll the time back to about 1750. The typical Earthian speaker of English did not know that water consisted of hydrogen and oxygen, and the typical Twin Earthian speaker of English did not know that "water" consisted of XYZ. Let Oscar$_1$ be such a typical Earthian English speaker, and let Oscar$_2$ be his counterpart on Twin Earth. You may suppose that there is no belief that Oscar$_1$ had about water that Oscar$_2$ did not have about "water". If you like, you may even suppose that Oscar$_1$ and Oscar$_2$ were exact duplicates in appearance, feelings, thoughts, interior mono-logue, etc. Yet the extension of the term 'water' was just as much H_2O on Earth in 1750 as in 1950; and the extension of the term 'water' was just as much XYZ on Twin Earth in 1750 as in 1950. Oscar$_1$ and Oscar$_2$ understood the term 'water' differently in 1750 *although they were in the same psychological state*, and although, given the state of science at the time, it would have taken their scientific communities about fifty years to discover that they understood the term 'water' differently. Thus the extension of the term 'water' (and, in fact, its "meaning" in the intuitive preanalytical usage of that term) is *not* a function of the psychological state of the speaker by itself.[1]

But, it might be objected, why should we accept it that the term 'water' had the same extension in 1750 and in 1950 (on both Earths)? Suppose I point to a glass of water and say "this liquid is called water." My "ostensive definition" of water has the following empirical presupposition: that the body of liquid I am pointing to bears a certain sameness relation (say, *x is the same liquid as y*, or *x is the same$_L$ as y*) to most of the stuff I and other speakers in my linguistic community have on other occasions called "water". If this presupposition is false because, say, I am—unknown to me—pointing to a glass of gin and not a glass of water, then I do not intend my osten-sive definition to be accepted. Thus the ostensive definition conveys what might be called a "defeasible" necessary and sufficient condition: the necessary and sufficient condition for being water is bearing the relation *same$_L$* to the stuff in the glass; but this is the necessary and sufficient condition only if the empirical presupposition is satisfied. If it is not satisfied, then one of a series of, so to speak, "fallback" condi-tions becomes activated.

The key point is that the relation *same$_L$* is a *theoretical* relation: whether something is or is not the same liquid as *this* may take an indeterminate amount of scientific investigation to determine. Thus, the fact that an English speaker in 1750 might have called XYZ "water", whereas he or his successors would not have called XYZ water in 1800 or 1850 does not mean that the "meaning" of 'water' changed for the average speaker in the interval. In 1750 or in 1850 or in 1950 one might have pointed to, say, the liquid in Lake Michigan as an example of "water". What changed was that in 1750 we would have mistakenly thought that XYZ bore the relation *same$_L$*

---

[1] See n. 2 below, and the corresponding text.

to the liquid in Lake Michigan, whereas in 1800 or 1850 we would have known that it did not.

Let us now modify our science-fiction story. I shall suppose that molybdenum pots and pans *can't* be distinguished from aluminium pots and pans save by an expert. (This could be true for all I know, and, a fortiori, it could be true for all I know by virtue of "knowing the meaning" of the words *aluminium* and *molybdenum*.) We will now suppose that molybdenum is as common on Twin Earth as aluminium is on Earth, and that aluminium is as rare on Twin Earth as molybdenum is on Earth. In particular, we shall assume that "aluminium" pots and pans are made of molybdenum on Twin Earth. Finally, we shall assume that the words 'aluminium' and 'molybdenum' are *switched* on Twin Earth: 'aluminium' is the name of *molybdenum*, and 'molybdenum' is the name of *aluminium*. If a space ship from Earth visited Twin Earth, the visitors from Earth probably would not suspect that the "aluminium" pots and pans on Twin Earth were not made of aluminium, especially when the Twin Earthians *said* they were. But there is one important difference between the two cases. An Earthian metallurgist could tell very easily that "aluminium" was molybdenum, and a Twin Earthian metallurgist could tell equally easily that aluminium was "molybdenum". (The shudder quotes in the preceding sentence indicate Twin Earthian usages.) Whereas in 1750 no one on either Earth or Twin Earth could have distinguished water from "water", the confusion of aluminium with "aluminium" involves only a part of the linguistic communities involved.

This example makes the same point as the preceding example. If Oscar$_1$ and Oscar$_2$ are standard speakers of Earthian English and Twin Earthian English, respectively, and neither is chemically or metallurgically sophisticated, then there may be no difference at all in their psychological states when they use the word 'aluminium'; nevertheless, we have to say that 'aluminium' has the extension *aluminium* in the idiolect of Oscar$_1$ and the extension *molybdenum* in the idiolect of Oscar$_2$. (Also we have to say that Oscar$_1$ and Oscar$_2$ mean different things by 'aluminium'; that 'aluminium' has a different meaning on Earth than it does on Twin Earth, etc.) Again we see that the psychological state of the speaker does *not* determine the extension (*or* the "meaning", speaking preanalytically) of the word.

Before discussing this example further, let me introduce a *non*-science-fiction example. Suppose you are like me and cannot tell an elm from a beech tree. We still say that the extension of 'elm' in my idiolect is the same as the extension of 'elm' in anyone else's, viz., the set of all elm trees, and that the set of all beech trees is the extension of 'beech' in *both* of our idiolects. Thus 'elm' in my idiolect has a different extension from 'beech' in your idiolect (as it should). Is it really credible that this difference in extension is brought about by some difference in our *concepts*? My *concept* of an elm tree is exactly the same as my concept of a beech tree (I blush to confess). If someone heroically attempts to maintain that the difference between the extension of 'elm' and the extension of 'beech' in *my* idiolect is explained by a difference in my psychological state, then we can always refute him by constructing a "Twin Earth" example—just let the words 'elm' and 'beech' be switched on Twin Earth (the way 'aluminium' and "molybdenum" were in the previous example). Moreover, suppose I have a *Doppelgänger* on Twin Earth who is molecule for molecule "identical" with me. If you are a dualist, then also suppose my *Doppelgänger* thinks the same verbalized thoughts I do, has the same sense data, the same dispositions, etc. It is absurd to think *his* psychological state is one bit different from mine: yet he "means" *beech* when he says "elm", and *I* "mean" *elm* when I say "elm". Cut the pie any way you like, "meanings" just ain't in the *head*!

A SOCIOLINGUISTIC HYPOTHESIS

The last two examples depend upon a fact about language that seems, surprisingly, never to have been pointed out: that there is *division of linguistic labor*. We could hardly use such words as 'elm' and 'aluminium' if no one possessed a way of recognizing elm trees and aluminium metal; but not everyone to whom the distinction is important has to be able to make the distinction. Let us shift the example; consider *gold*. Gold is important for many reasons: it is a precious metal; it is a monetary metal; it has symbolic value (it is important to most people that the "gold" wedding ring they wear *really* consist of gold and not just *look* gold); etc. Consider our community as a "factory": in this "factory" some people have the "job" of *wearing gold wedding rings*; other people have the "job" of selling gold wedding rings; still other people have the job of *telling whether or not something is really gold*. It is not at all necessary or efficient that everyone who wears a gold ring (or a gold cufflink, etc.), or discusses the "gold standard", etc., engage in buying and selling gold. Nor is it necessary or efficient that everyone who buys and sells gold be able to tell whether or not something is really gold in a society where this form of dishonesty is uncommon (selling fake gold) and in which one can easily consult an expert in case of doubt. And it is *certainly* not necessary or efficient that everyone who has occasion to buy or wear gold be able to tell with any reliability whether or not something is really gold.

The foregoing facts are just examples of mundane division of labor (in a wide sense). But they engender a division of linguistic labor: everyone to whom gold is important for any reason has to *acquire* the word 'gold'; but he does not have to acquire the *method of recognizing* whether something is or is not gold. He can rely on a special subclass of speakers. The features that are generally thought to be present in connection with a general name—necessary and sufficient conditions for membership in the extension, ways of recognizing whether something is in the extension, etc.—are all present in the linguistic community *considered as a collective body*; but that collective body divides the "labor" of knowing and employing these various parts of the "meaning" of 'gold'.

This division of linguistic labor rests upon and presupposes the division of *non*-linguistic labor, of course. If only the people who know how to tell whether some metal is really gold or not have any reason to have the word 'gold' in their vocabulary, then the word 'gold' will be as the word 'water' was in 1750 with respect to that subclass of speakers, and the other speakers just won't acquire it at all. And some words do not exhibit any division of linguistic labor: 'chair', for example. But with the increase of division of labor in the society and the rise of science, more and more words begin to exhibit this kind of division of labor. 'Water', for example, did not exhibit it at all before the rise of chemistry. Today it is obviously necessary for every speaker to be able to recognize water (reliably under normal conditions), and probably most adult speakers even know the necessary and sufficient condition "water is

H_2O", but only a few adult speakers could distinguish water from liquids that superficially resembled water. In case of doubt, other speakers would rely on the judgement of these "expert" speakers. Thus the way of recognizing possessed by these "expert" speakers is also, through them, possessed by the collective linguistic body, even though it is not possessed by each individual member of the body, and in this way the most *recherché* fact about water may become part of the *social* meaning of the word although unknown to almost all speakers who acquire the word.

It seems to me that this phenomenon of division of linguistic labor is one that it will be very important for sociolinguistics to investigate. In connection with it, I should like to propose the following hypothesis:

> HYPOTHESIS OF THE UNIVERSALITY OF THE DIVISION OF LINGUISTIC LABOR: Every linguistic community exemplifies the sort of division of linguistic labor just described; that is, it possesses at least some terms whose associated "criteria" are known only to a subset of the speakers who acquire the terms, and whose use by the other speakers depends upon a structured co-operation between them and the speakers in the relevant subsets.

It is easy to see how this phenomenon accounts for some of the examples given above of the failure of the assumptions (1 and 2). When a term is subject to the division of linguistic labor, the "average" speaker who acquires it does not acquire anything that fixes its extension. In particular, his individual psychological state *certainly* does not fix its extension; it is only the sociolinguistic state of the collective linguistic body to which the speaker belongs that fixes the extension.

We may summarize this discussion by pointing out that there are two sorts of tools in the world: there are tools like a hammer or a screwdriver which can be used by one person; and there are tools like a steamship which require the co-operative activity of a number of persons to use. Words have been thought of too much on the model of the first sort of tool.

INDEXICALITY AND RIGIDITY

The first of our science-fiction examples—'water' on Earth and on Twin Earth in 1750—does not involve division of linguistic labor, or at least does not involve it in the same way the examples of 'aluminium' and 'elm' do. There were not (in our story, anyway) any "experts" on water on Earth in 1750, nor any experts on "water" on Twin Earth. The example *does* involve things which are of fundamental importance to the theory of reference and also to the theory of necessary truth, which we shall now discuss.

Let W_1 and W_2 be two possible worlds in which I exist and in which this glass exists and in which I am giving a meaning explanation by pointing to this glass and saying "This is water." Let us suppose that in W_1 the glass is full of H_2O and in W_2 the glass is full of XYZ. We shall also suppose that W_1 is the *actual* world, and that XYZ is the stuff typically called "water" in the world W_2 (so that the relation between

English speakers in W_1 and English speakers in W_2 exactly the same as the relation between English speakers on Earth and English speakers on Twin Earth). Then there are two theories one might have concerning the meaning of 'water':

(1) One might hold that 'water' was *world-relative* but *constant* in meaning (i.e., the word has a constant relative meaning). On this theory, 'water' means the same in W_1 and W_2; it's just that water is H_2O in W_1, and water is XYZ in W_2.

(2) One might hold that water is H_2O in all worlds (the stuff called "water" in W_2 isn't water), but 'water' doesn't have the same meaning in W_1 and W_2.

If what was said before about the Twin Earth case was correct, then (2) is clearly the correct theory. When I say "*this* (liquid) is water", the "this" is, so to speak, a *de re* "this"—i.e., the force of my explanation is that "water" is whatever bears a certain equivalence relation (the relation we called "*same*$_L$" above) to the piece of liquid referred to as "this" *in the actual world*.

We might symbolize the difference between the two theories as a "scope" difference in the following way. On theory (1), the following is true:

(1') (For every world W) (For every x in W) (x is water $\equiv x$ bears *same*$_L$ to the entity referred to as "this" in W)

while on theory (2):

(2') (For every world W) (For every x in W) (x is water $\equiv x$ bears *same*$_L$ to the entity referred to as "this" *in the actual world W_1*)

I call this a "scope" difference because in (1') 'the entity referred to as "this"' is within the scope of 'For every world W'—as the qualifying phrase 'in W' makes explicit—whereas in (2') 'the entity referred to as "this"' means "the entity referred to as 'this' *in the actual world*", and has thus a reference *independent* of the bound variable 'W'.

Kripke calls a designator "rigid" (in a given sentence) if (in that sentence) it refers to the same individual in every possible world in which the designator designates. If we extend this notion of rigidity to substance names, then we may express Kripke's theory and mine by saying that the term 'water' is *rigid*.

The rigidity of the term 'water' follows from the fact that when I give the "ostensive definition": "*this* (liquid) is water", I intend (2') and not (1').

We may also say, following Kripke, that when I give the ostensive definition "*this* (liquid) is water", the demonstrative 'this' is *rigid*.

What Kripke was the first to observe is that this theory of the meaning (or "use", or whatever) of the word 'water' (and other natural kind terms as well) has startling consequences for the theory of necessary truth.

To explain this, let me introduce the notion of a *cross-world relation*. A two-term relation R will be called *cross-world* when it is understood in such a way that its extension is a set of ordered pairs of individuals *not all in the same possible world*. For example, it is easy to understand the relation *same height as* as a cross-world relation: just understand it so that, e.g., if x is an individual in a world W_1 who is 5 feet tall (in W_1) and y is an individual in W_2 who is 5 feet tall (in W_2), then the ordered pair x,y belongs to the extension of *same height as*. (Since an individual may have different heights in different possible worlds in which that same individual exists, strictly speaking, it is not the ordered pair x,y that constitutes an element of the extension of *same height as*, but rather the ordered pair *x-in-world-W_1*, *y-in-world-W_2*.)

Similarly, we can understand the relation *same*$_L$ (same liquid as) as a cross-world relation by understanding it so that a liquid in world W_1 which has the same important physical properties (in W_1) that a liquid in W_2 possesses (in W_2) bears *same*$_L$ to the latter liquid.

Then the theory we have been presenting may be summarized by saying that an entity x, in an arbitrary possible world, is *water* if and only if it bears the relation *same*$_L$ (construed as a cross-world relation) to the stuff *we* call "water" in the actual world.

Suppose, now, that I have not yet discovered what the important physical properties of water are (in the actual world)—i.e., I don't yet know that water is H_2O. I may have ways of *recognizing* water that are successful (of course, I may make a small number of mistakes that I won't be able to detect until a later stage in our scientific development), but not know the microstructure of water. If I agree that a liquid with the superficial properties of "water" but a different microstructure *isn't really water*, then my ways of recognizing water cannot be regarded as an analytical specification of what *it is to be* water. Rather, the operational definition, like the ostensive one, is simply a way of pointing out a standard—pointing out the stuff *in the actual world* such that, for x to be water, in *any* world, is for x to bear the relation *same*$_L$ to the *normal* members of the class of *local* entities that satisfy the operational definition. "Water" on Twin Earth is not water, even if it satisfies the operational definition, because it doesn't bear *same*$_L$ to the *local* stuff that satisfies the operational definition, and local stuff that satisfies the operational definition but has a microstructure different from the rest of the local stuff that satisfies the operational definition isn't water either, because it doesn't bear *same*$_L$ to the *normal* examples of the local "water".

Suppose, now, that I discover the microstructure of water—that water is H_2O. At this point I will be able to say that the stuff on Twin Earth that I earlier *mistook* for water isn't really water. In the same way, if you describe, not another planet in the actual universe, but another possible universe in which there is stuff with the chemical formula XYZ which passes the "operational test" for *water*, we shall have to say that that stuff isn't water but merely XYZ. You will not have described a possible world in which "water is XYZ", but merely a possible world in which there are lakes of XYZ, people drink XYZ (and not water), or whatever. In fact, once we have discovered the nature of water, nothing counts as a possible world in which water doesn't have that nature. Once we have discovered that water (in the actual world) is H_2O, *nothing counts as a possible world in which water isn't H_2O.*

On the other hand, we can perfectly well imagine having experiences that would convince us (and that would make it rational to believe that) water *isn't* H_2O. In that sense, it is conceivable that water isn't H_2O. It is conceivable but it isn't possible! Conceivability is no proof of possibility.

Kripke refers to statements that are rationally unrevisable (assuming there are such) as *epistemically necessary*. Statements that are true in all possible worlds he refers to simply as necessary (or sometimes as "metaphysically necessary"). In this terminology, the point just made can be restated as: a statement can be (metaphysically) necessary and epistemically contingent. Human intuition has no privileged access to metaphysical necessity.

In this essay, our interest is in theory of meaning, however, and not in theory of necessary truth. Words like 'now', 'this', 'here' have long been recognized to be *indexical*, or *token-reflexive*—i.e., to have an extension which varies from context to context or token to token. For these words, no one has ever suggested the traditional theory that "intension determines extension". To take our Twin Earth example: if I have a *Doppelgänger* on Twin Earth, then when I think "I have a headache," *he* thinks "I have a headache." But the extension of the particular token of 'I' in his verbalized thought is himself (or his unit class, to be precise), while the extension of the token of 'I' in *my* verbalized thought is *me* (or my unit class, to be precise). So the same word, 'I', has two different extensions in two different idiolects; but it does not follow that the concept I have of myself is in any way different from the concept my *Doppelgänger* has of himself.

Now then, we have maintained that indexicality extends beyond the *obviously* indexical words and morphemes (e.g., the tenses of verbs). Our theory can be summarized as saying that words like 'water' have an unnoticed indexical component: "water" is stuff that bears a certain similarity relation to the water *around* here. Water at another time or in another place or even in another possible world has to bear the relation $same_L$ to *our* "water" *in order to be water*. Thus the theory that (1) words have "intensions", which are something like concepts associated with the words by speakers; and (2) intension determines extension—cannot be true of natural kind words like 'water' for the same reason it cannot be true of obviously indexical words like 'I'.

The theory that natural kind words like 'water' are indexical leaves it open, however, whether to say that 'water' in the Twin Earth dialect of English has the same *meaning* as 'water' in the Earth dialect and a different extension—which is what we normally say about 'I' in different idiolects—thereby giving up the doctrine that "meaning (intension) determines extension", or to say, as we have chosen to do, that difference in extension is *ipso facto* a difference in meaning for natural kind words, thereby giving up the doctrine that meanings are concepts, or, indeed, mental entities of *any* kind.[2]

---

[2] Our reasons for rejecting the first option—to say that 'water' has the same meaning on Earth and on Twin Earth, while giving up the doctrine that meaning determines references—are presented in "The Meaning of 'Meaning'". They may be illustrated thus: Suppose 'water' has the same meaning on Earth and on Twin Earth. Now, let the word 'water' become phonemically different on Twin Earth—say, it becomes 'quaxel'. Presumably, this is not a change in meaning *per se*, on any view. So 'water' and 'quaxel' have the same meaning (although they refer to different liquids). But this is highly counterintuitive. Why not say, then, that 'elm' in my idiolect has the same meaning as 'beech' in your idiolect, although they refer to different trees?

It should be clear, however, that Kripke's doctrine that natural kind words are rigid designators and our doctrine that they are indexical are but two ways of making the same point.

We have now seen that the extension of a term is not fixed by a concept that the individual speaker has in his head, and this is true both because extension is, in general, determined *socially*—there is division of linguistic labor as much as of "real" labor—and because extension is, in part, determined *indexically*. The extension of our terms depends upon the actual nature of the particular things that serve as paradigms, and this actual nature is not, in general, fully known to the speaker. Traditional semantic theory leaves out two contributions to the determination of reference—the contribution of society and the contribution of the real world; a better semantic theory must encompass both.